**The
Random
House**
Basic Dictionary

French-English
English-French

The
Random
House
Basic Dictionary

French-English
English-French

Edited by
Francesca L.V. Langbaum
University of Virginia

Under the General Editorship of
Professor Robert A. Hall, Jr.
Cornell University

The Ballantine Reference Library
Ballantine Books · New York

Library of Congress Catalog Card Number: 54-5962
ISBN 0-345-33712-3
This edition published by arrangement with Random House, Inc.
Previously published as *The French Vest Pocket Dictionary* and *The
Random House French Dictionary*.

Manufactured in the United States of America
First Ballantine Books Edition: August 1981
Fifth Printing: July 1984

Concise Pronunciation Guide

The following concise guide describes the approximate pronunciation of the letters and frequent combinations of letters occurring in the French language. A study of it will enable the reader to pronounce French adequately most of the time. While the guide cannot list all the exceptions to the established pronunciations, or cover the manner in which adjacent words affect each other in speech, such exceptions and variations will readily be learned as one develops facility in the language.

French Letter	Description of Pronunciation
a, à	Between *a* in *calm* and *a* in *hat*.
â	Like *a* in *calm*.
ai	Like *e* in *bed*.
au	Like *oa* in *coat*.
b	As in English. At end of words, usually silent.
c	Before *e, i, y,* like *s.* Elsewhere, like *k.* When *c* occurs at the end of a word and is preceded by a consonant, it is usually silent.
ç	Like *s.*
cc	Before *e, i,* like *x.* Elsewhere, like *k.*
ch	Usually like *sh* in *short.* *ch* is pronounced like *k* in words of Greek origin; before *a, o,* and *u;* and before consonants.
d	At beginning and in middle of words, as in English. At end of words, usually silent.
e	At end of words, normally silent; indicates that preceding consonant letter is pronounced. Between two single consonant sounds, usually silent. Elsewhere, like English *a* in *sofa.*
é	Approximately like *a* in *hate.*

French Letter	Description of Pronunciation
è, ê, ei	Like *e* in *bed.*
eau	Like *au.*
ent	Silent when it is the third person plural ending.
er (end of words)	At end of words of more than one syllable, usually like *a* in *hate,* the *r* being silent; otherwise like *air* in *chair.*
es	Silent at end of words.
eu	A vowel sound not found in English; like French *e,* but pronounced with the lips rounded as for *o.*
ez	At end of words, almost always like English *a* in *hate,* the *z* being silent.
f	As in English; silent at the end of a few words.
g	Before *e, i, y,* like *z* in *azure.* Elsewhere, like *g* in *get.* At end of words, usually silent.
gn	Like *ni* in *onion.*
gu	Before *e, i, y,* like *g* in *get.* Elsewhere, like *g* in *get* plus French *u* (see below).
h	In some words, represents a slight tightening of the throat muscles (in French, called "aspiration"). In most words, silent.
i, î	Like *i* in *machine.*
ill	(-il at end of words) like *y*

French Letter	Description of Pronunciation
	in *yes*, in many but not all words.
j	Like *z* in *azure*.
k	As in English.
l	As in English, but always pronounced "bright," with tongue in front of mouth.
m, n	When double, and when single between two vowel letters or at beginning of word, like English *m* and *n* respectively. When single at end of syllable (at end of word or before another consonant), indicates nasalization of preceding vowel.
o	Usually like *u* in English *mud*, but rounder. When final sound in word, and often before *s* and *z*, like *ô*.
ô	Approximately like *oa* in *coat*.
oe, oeu	Like *eu*.
oi	Approximately like a combination of the consonant *w* and the *a* of *calm*.
ou, oû, où	Like *ou* in *tour*.
p	At end of words, usually silent. Between *m* and *t*, *m* and *s*, *r* and *s*, usually silent. Elsewhere, as in English.
pn, ps	Unlike English, when *pn* and *ps* occur at the beginning of words the *p* is usually sounded.
ph	Like *f*.
qu	Usually like *k*.
r	A vibration either of the uvula, or of the tip of the tongue, against the upper front teeth.

French Letter	Description of Pronunciation
	See above under *er*.
s	Generally, like *s* in *sea*. Single *s* between vowels, like *z* in *zone*. At end of words, normally silent.
sc	Before *e* or *i*, like *s*. Elsewhere, like *sk*.
t	Approximately like English *t*, but pronounced with tongue tip against teeth. At end of words, normally silent. When followed by *ie*, *ion*, *ium*, *ius*, and other diphthongs beginning with a vowel, *t* generally is like English *s* in *sea* (unless the *t* itself is preceded by an *s* or an *x*).
th	Like *t*.
u, û	A vowel sound not found in English; like the *i* in *machine* but with lips rounded as for *ou*.
ue	After *c* or *g* and before *il*, like *eu*.
v	As in English.
w	Usually like *v*; in some people's pronunciation, like English *w*.
x	Generally sounds like *ks*; but when the syllable *ex* begins a word and is followed by a vowel, *x* sounds like *gz*. At end of words, usually silent.
y	Generally like *i* in *machine*; but when between two vowels, like *y* in *yes*.
z	Like *z* in *zone*. At end of words, often silent (see above under *ez*).

Note on Pronunciation

A few minutes' study of the *Concise Pronunciation Guide* will enable you to pronounce most French words without having to look each word up in the dictionary. For the relatively few cases in which the pronunciation does not follow the usual pattern, this dictionary provides a transcription in simple and familiar symbols.

ă   bat

ā   cape

â   dare

ä   calm

à   [a vowel intermediate in quality between the *a* of *cat* and the *a* of *calm*, but closer to the former]

ĕ   set

ē   bee

ĭ   big

ī   bite

N   [a symbol used to indicate nasalized vowels. There are four such vowels in French, found in *un bon vin blanc* (œN bōN vāN bläN)]

ŏ   hot

ō   no

ô   order

œ   [a vowel made with the lips rounded in position for *o* as in *over,* while trying to say *a* as in *able*]

oi   oil

ŏŏ   book

ōō   ooze

ou   loud

ŭ   up

ū   cute

û   burn

Y   [a vowel made with the lips rounded in position for *ōō* as in *ooze,* while trying to say *e* as in *easy*]

ə   [indicates the sound of *a* in *alone,* *e* in *system,* *i* in *easily,* *o* in *gallop,* *u* in *circus*]

Irregular Verbs

Infinitive	Pres. Part.	Past Part.	Pres. Indic.	Future
aller	allant	allé	vais	irai
asseoir	asseyant	assis	assieds	assiérai
atteindre	atteignant	atteint	atteins	atteindrai
avoir	ayant	eu	ai	aurai
battre	battant	battu	bats	battrai
boire	buvant	bu	bois	boirai
conduire	conduisant	conduit	conduis	conduirai
connaître	connaissant	connu	connais	connaîtrai
courir	courant	couru	cours	courrai
craindre	craignant	craint	crains	craindrai
croire	croyant	cru	crois	croirai
devoir	devant	dû	dois	devrai
dire	disant	dit	dis	dirai
dormir	dormant	dormi	dors	dormirai
écrire	écrivant	écrit	écris	écrirai
envoyer	envoyant	envoyé	envoie	enverrai
être	étant	été	suis	serai
faire	faisant	fait	fais	ferai
falloir	———	fallu	(il) faut	(il) faudra
joindre	joignant	joint	joins	joindrai
lire	lisant	lu	lis	lirai
mettre	mettant	mis	mets	mettrai
mourir	mourant	mort	meurs	mourrai
naître	naissant	né	nais	naîtrai
ouvrir	ouvrant	ouvert	ouvre	ouvrirai
plaire	plaisant	plu	plais	plairai
pleuvoir	pleuvant	plu	(il) pleut	(il) pleuvra
pouvoir	pouvant	pu	peux	pourrai
prendre	prenant	pris	prends	prendrai
recevoir	recevant	reçu	reçois	recevrai
rire	riant	ri	ris	rirai
savoir	sachant	su	sais	saurai
suffire	suffisant	suffi	suffis	suffirai
suivre	suivant	suivi	suis	suivrai
tenir	tenant	tenu	tiens	tiendrai
valoir	valant	valu	vaux	vaudrai
venir	venant	venu	viens	veindrai
vivre	vivant	vécu	vis	vivrai
voir	voyant	vu	vois	verrai
vouloir	voulant	voulu	veux	voudrai

Abbreviations

abbr.	abbreviation	*med.*	medical
adj.	adjective	*mil.*	military
adv.	adverb	*n.*	noun
art.	article	*naut.*	nautical
comm.	commercial	*pl.*	plural
conj.	conjunction	*pred.*	predicate
eccles.	ecclesiastical	*prep.*	preposition
f.	feminine	*pron.*	pronoun
fig.	figurative	*sg.*	singular
geom.	geometry	*tr.*	transitive (used only with
gramm.	grammar, grammatical		verbs which also have
interj.	interjection		reflexive use to indicate
intr.	intransitive		intransitive meaning)
lit.	literal, literally	*vb.*	verb
m.	masculine		

Useful Phrases

Good day. Bonjour.
Good evening. Bonsoir.
Good night. Bonne nuit.
Good bye. Au revoir.
How are you? Comment allez-vous?
Fine, thank you. Très bien, merci.
Glad to meet you. Enchanté de faire votre connaissance.
Thank you very much. Merci beaucoup.
You're welcome. Pas de quoi.
Please. S'il vous plaît.
Good luck. Bonne chance.
To your health. A votre santé.

Please help me. Aidez-moi, s'il vous plaît.
Do you understand? Comprenez-vous?
I don't understand. Je ne comprends pas.
Speak slowly, please. Parlez lentement, s'il vous plaît.
Please repeat. Répétez, s'il vous plaît.
I don't speak French. Je ne parle pas français.
Do you speak English? Parlez-vous anglais?
Does anyone here speak English? Y a-t-il quelqu'un qui parle anglais?
How do you say...in French? Comment dit-on...en français?

What is your name? Comment vous appelez-vous?
My name is... Je m'appelle...
I am an American. Je suis américain.

How is the weather?   Quel temps fait-il?
What time is it?   Quelle heure est-il?
What is it?   Qu'est-ce que c'est?

How much does this cost?   Combien est ceci?
It is too expensive.   C'est trop cher.
I want to buy…   Je voudrais acheter…

I want to eat.   Je voudrais manger.
Can you recommend a restaurant?   Pouvez-vous recommander un restaurant?
I am hungry.   J'ai faim.
Check, please.   L'addition, s'il vous plaît.
Is there a hotel here?   Y a-t-il un hôtel ici?

Where is…?   Où est…?
What is the way to…?   Quelle est la route de…?
Take me to…   Conduisez-moi à…
I need…   J'ai besoin de…
I am ill.   Je suis malade.
Please call a doctor.   Appelez un docteur, s'il vous plaît.
I want to send a telegram.   Je voudrais envoyer un télégramme.
Where can I change money?   Où puis-je changer de l'argent?
Will you accept checks?   Acceptez-vous des chèques?
What is the postage?   Quel est l'affranchissement?

Right away.   Tout de suite.
Help!   Au secours!
Come in.   Entrez.
Stop.   Arrêtez.
Hurry.   Dépêchez-vous.
Go on.   Continuez.
Right.   A droite.
Left.   A gauche.
Straight ahead.   Tout droit.

Signs

Attention	Caution	Ralentir	Go Slow
Danger	Danger	Défense de fumer	No smoking
Sortie	Exit	Défense d'entrer	No admittance
Entrée	Entrance	Dames	Women
Halte, Arrêtez	Stop	Hommes	Men
Fermé	Closed	Lavabos, toilettes	Lavatory
Ouvert	Open		

Weights and Measures

The French use the *Metric System* of weights and measures, a decimal system in which multiples are shown by the prefixes **déci-** (one-tenth); **centi-** (one hundredth); **milli-** (one thousandth); **hecto-** (hundred); and **kilo-** (thousand).

1 centimètre	=	.3937 inch
1 mètre	=	39.37 inches
1 kilomètre	=	.621 mile
1 centigramme	=	.1543 grain
1 gramme	=	15.432 grains
100 grammes	=	3.527 ounces
1 kilogramme	=	2.2046 pounds
1 tonne	=	2,204 pounds
1 centilitre	=	.338 ounce
1 litre	=	1.0567 quart (liquid);
	=	.908 quart (dry)
1 kilolitre	=	264.18 gallons

Numerals

Cardinal

1 un, une	22 vingt-deux	77 soixante-dix-sept
2 deux	23 vingt-trois	78 soixante-dix-huit
3 trois	24 vingt-quatre	79 soixante-dix-neuf
4 quatre	25 vingt-cinq	80 quatre-vingts
5 cinq	26 vingt-six	81 quatre-vingt-un
6 six	27 vingt-sept	82 quatre-vingt-deux
7 sept	28 vingt-huit	90 quatre-vingt-dix
8 huit	29 vingt-neuf	91 quatre-vingt-onze
9 neuf	30 trente	92 quatre-vingt-douze
10 dix	31 trente et un	
11 onze	32 trente-deux	100 cent
12 douze	40 quarante	101 cent un
13 treize	50 cinquante	102 cent deux
14 quatorze	60 soixante	200 deux cents
15 quinze	70 soixante-dix	300 trois cents
16 seize	71 soixante et onze	301 trois cent un
17 dix-sept	72 soixante-douze	1,000 mille
18 dix-huit	73 soixante-treize	5,000 cinq mille
19 dix-neuf	74 soixante-quartorze	1,000,000 un million
20 vingt	75 soixante-quinze	
21 vingt et un	76 soixante-seize	

Ordinal

1st premier, première	19th dix-neuvième
2nd deuxième, second	20th vingtième
3rd troisième	21th vingt-et-unième
4th quatrième	22nd vingt-deuxième
5th cinquième	30th trentième
6th sixième	40th quarantième
7th septième	50th cinquantième
8th huitième	60th soixantième
9th neuvième	70th soixante-dixième
10th dixième	80th quatre-vingtième
11th onzième	90th quatre-vingt-
12th douzième	dixième
13th treizième	100th centième
14th quatorzième	101st cent-unième
15th quinzième	102nd cent-deuxième
16th seizième	300th trois-centième
17th dix-septième	1,000th millième
18th dix-huitième	1,000,000th millionième

Days of the Week

Sunday	dimanche
Monday	lundi
Tuesday	mardi
Wednesday	mercredi
Thursday	jeudi
Friday	vendredi
Saturday	samedi

Months

January	janvier	July	juillet
February	février	August	août
March	mars	September	septembre
April	avril	October	octobre
May	mai	November	novembre
June	juin	December	décembre

French-English

A

à, *prep.* at, in, to.
abaisser, *vb.* depress, lower.
abandon, *n.m.* desertion, abandonment.
abandonné, *adj.* forlorn.
abandonner, *vb.* forsake, leave (desert). s'a., give up, resign oneself.
abasourdir, *vb.* astound.
abattage, *n.m.* slaughter.
abattement, *n.m.* depression, dejection.
abattre, *vb.* depress, reduce; slaughter. s'a., alight.
abbaye, *n.f.* abbey.
abbé, *n.m.* abbot.
abbesse, *n.f.* abbess.
abcès, *n.m.* abscess.
abdiquer, *vb.* abdicate.
abdomen, *n.m.* abdomen.
abeille, *n.f.* bee.
aberration, *n.f.* aberration.
abîme, *n.m.* abyss.
abîmer, *vb.* injure, spoil.
abject, *adj.* abject, low.
aboiement, *n.m.* barking.
abolir, *vb.* abolish.
abolition, *n.f.* abolition.
abominable, *adj.* vile, objectionable.
abondamment, *adv.* fully.
abondance, *n.f.* plenty.
abondant, *adj.* plentiful. peu a., scanty.
abonder de, *vb.* abound in.
abonnement, *n.m.* subscription.
abonner, *vb.* s'a., subscribe.
abord, 1. *n.m.* approach. 2. *adv.* d'a., at first.
aborder, *vb.* accost.
aboutir, *vb.* end (in).
aboyer, *vb.* bark.
abréger, *vb.* abridge, shorten, abbreviate.
abreuver, *vb.* water (animals).
abréviation, *n.f.* abbreviation.
abri, *n.m.* shelter. à l'a. de, safe from.
abricot, *n.m.* apricot.
abriter, *vb.* shelter.
abrupt (-pt), *adj.* steep.
absence, *n.f.* absence.
absent, *adj.* absent. rester a., stay away.
absenter, *vb.* s'a., go away.
abside, *n.f.* apse.
absinthe, *n.f.* absinthe.
absolu, *adj.* utter, absolute.
absolution, *n.f.* absolution.
absorbant, *adj. and n.m.* absorbent.
absorbé dans, *adj.* intent on.
absorber, *vb.* engross, absorb. s'a. dans, pore over.
absorption, *n.f.* absorption.
absoudre, *vb.* absolve.
abstenir, *vb.* forbear. s'a. de, abstain from.

abstinence, *n.f.* abstinence.
abstraction, *n.f.* abstraction.
abstrait, *adj.* abstract.
absurde, *adj.* absurd, preposterous.
absurdité, *n.f.* nonsense, absurdity.
abus, *n.m.* abuse.
abuser de, *vb.* abuse.
académie, *n.f.* academy.
académique, *adj.* academic.
acajou, *n.m.* mahogany.
accablant, *adj.* oppressive.
accabler, *vb.* overwhelm, burden.
accaparer, *vb.* get a corner on.
accélération, *n.f.* acceleration.
accélérer, *vb.* quicken, hurry.
accent, *n.m.* stress, emphasis, accent.
accentuer, *vb.* accentuate, accent, emphasize.
acceptable, *adj.* acceptable.
acceptation, *n.f.* acceptance.
accepter, *vb.* accept, admit.
accepteur, *n.m.* accepter.
accès, *n.m.* access, approach; fit (of anger); bout (of fever).
accessible, *adj.* accessible.
accessoire, *n.m. and adj.* accessory, adjunct.
accident, *n.m.* crash, accident.
accidentel, *adj.* accidental.
acclamation, *n.f.* acclamation.
acclamer, *vb.* acclaim, cheer.
accommoder, *vb.* accommodate.
accompagnement, *n.m.* accompaniment.
accompagner, *vb.* accompany, go with.
accompli, *adj.* accomplished, complete, perfect.
accomplir, *vb.* accomplish, achieve, fulfill, carry out, perform.
accomplissement, *n.m.* performance, fulfillment, achievement, accomplishment.
accord, *n.m.* agreement, harmony; settlement; chord, tune. être d'a., agree, concur.
accorder, *vb.* grant, bestow; allow; tune. s'a., agree.
accouchement, *n.m.* delivery.
accoucher, *vb.* deliver.
accoucheur, *n.m.* médecin-a., obstetrician.
accouder, *vb.* s'a., lean.
accourir, *vb.* flock, run up.
accoutumer, *vb.* accustom.
accréditer, *vb.* accredit.
accrocher, *vb.* hook, hitch.
accroissement, *n.m.* growth, addition.
accroître, *vb.* increase.
accroupir, *vb.* s'a., squat, crouch.
accueil, *n.m.* reception, greeting.
accueillir, *vb.* receive, greet.
accumuler, *vb.* heap up.

accusateur, *n.m.* accuser.
accusatif, *n.m.* accusative.
accusation, *n.f.* accusation.
accusatrice, *n.f.* accuser.
accusé, *n.m.* defendant.
accuser, *vb.* arraign, accuse.
acharné, *adj.* eager, fanatical.
achat, *n.m.* purchase.
acheminer, *vb.* start (toward).
acheter, *vb.* buy.
acheteur, *n.m.* buyer.
achèvement, *n.m.* completion.
achever, *vb.* complete, finish, achieve.
acide, *adj. and n.m.* acid.
acidité, *n.f.* acidity.
acier, *n.m.* steel.
acoustique, *n.f.* acoustics.
acquérir, *vb.* acquire, get, obtain.
acquiescement, *n.m.* acquiescence, compliance.
acquiescer à, *vb.* acquiesce, consent.
acquisition, *n.f.* acquisition, purchase.
acquittement, *n.m.* acquittal.
acquitter, *vb.* acquit.
âcre, *adj.* sharp.
acrobate, *n.m.f.* acrobat.
acte, *n.m.* act. a. notarié, deed. a. de naissance, birth certificate.
acteur, *n.m.* actor.
actif, 1. *n.m.* assets *(comm.).* 2. *adj.* active.
action, *n.f.* action, deed, act; *(comm.)* share.
action de contrôle en retour, *n.f.* feedback.
actionnaire, *n.m.* shareholder.
actionner, *vb.* operate.
activement, *adv.* busily.
activer, *vb.* activate, fan, hurry.
activité, *n.f.* activity.
actrice, *n.f.* actress.
actualités, *n.f.pl.* newsreel.
actuel, *adj.* present.
actuellement, *adv.* now, at present.
acuponcture, *n.f.* acupuncture.
adaptation, *n.f.* adaptation.
adapter, *vb.* adapt, fit, adjust, suit.
addition, *n.f.* addition, bill.
additionnel, *adj.* additional.
additionner, *vb.* add.
adhérent, *n.m.* follower.
adhérer, *vb.* cleave, adhere.
adhésif, *adj.* adhesive.
adieu, *n.m. and interj.* goodbye, farewell. faire ses adieux, take one's leave.
adjacent, *adj.* adjacent.
adjectif, *adj.* adjective.
adjoint, *n.m.* fellow-worker, associate.
adjuger, *vb.* grant.
admettre, *vb.* allow, admit, grant.
administrateur, *n.m.* administrator, director, manager.

administratif, *adj.* administrative.

administration, *n.f.* administration, direction.

administrer, *vb.* administer, manage.

admirable, *adj.* admirable.

admirateur, *n.m.* admirer.

admiration, *n.f.* admiration.

admirer, *vb.* admire.

admission, *n.f.* confession, admission.

adolescence, *n.f.* adolescence.

adolescent, *adj. and n.m.f.* adolescent.

adonner, *vb.* s'a. à, indulge in, become addicted to.

adopter, *vb.* adopt.

adoption, *n.f.* adoption.

adoration, *n.f.* adoration.

adorer, *vb.* worship, adore.

adosser, *vb.* s'a. à, lean on.

adoucir, *vb.* soothe.

adresse, *n.f.* address; skill, ability.

adresser, *vb.* address (a letter); direct. s'a. à, apply to.

adroit, *adj.* skillful, clever, handy.

adulte, *adj. and n.m.f.* adult.

adultère, *n.m.* adultery.

adultérer, *vb.* adulterate.

adverbe, *n.m.* adverb.

adversaire, *n.m.f.* opponent.

adverse, *adj.* adverse.

adversité, *n.f.* adversity.

aéré, *adj.* airy.

aérer, *vb.* air (a room).

aérien, *adj.* aerial.

aérogare, *n.f.* airline (city) station.

aéroglisseur, *n.m.* hovercraft.

aéroport, *n.m.* airport.

affable, *adj.* affable.

affaiblir, *vb.* weaken.

affaire, *n.f.* affair, matter; deal; *(pl.)* business. se tirer d'a., manage (somehow). homme d'a.s, businessman.

affairé, *adj.* busy.

affaissement, *n.m.* collapse.

affaisser, *vb.* s'a., collapse.

affamé, *adj.* hungry, famished.

affamer, *vb.* starve.

affectation, *n.f.* affectation.

affecter, *vb.* affect.

affection, *n.f.* affection.

affectueux, *adj.* affectionate.

affermir, *vb.* strengthen.

affété, *adj.* finicky.

affiche, *n.f.* poster.

afficher, *vb.* post.

affilier, *vb.* affiliate.

affinité, *n.f.* affinity.

affirmatif, *adj.* affirmative.

affirmation, *n.f.* statement.

affirmer, *vb.* assert, state, maintain, testify, affirm.

affliction, *n.f.* affliction.

affligé, *adj.* sorrowful.

affliger, *vb.* distress, afflict, grieve.

affluent, *n.m.* tributary.

affluer, *vb.* flow into.

affoler, *vb.* drive mad.

affranchir, *vb.* free.

affranchissement, *n.m.* postage.

affréter, *vb.* charter (boat).

affreusement, *adv.* terribly.

affreux, *adj.* dreadful, terrible, horrid, dire.

affront, *n.m.* affront, insult.

affronter, *vb.* confront, face.

afin, I. a. de, *prep.* in order to. 2. *conj.* a. que, so that.

Africain, *n.m.* African.

africain, *adj.* African.

Afrique, *n.f.* Africa.

agacer, *vb.* vex, irritate.

âge, *n.m.* age. d'un certain â., elderly. le moyen â., the Middle Ages.

âgé, *adj.* aged.

agence, *n.f. (comm.)* agency.

agenouiller, *vb.* s'a., kneel.

agent, *n.m.* agent. a. de police, policeman. a. de change, stockbroker.

aggraver, *vb.* aggravate.

agile, *adj.* nimble.

agir, *vb.* act. s'a. de, be a question of.

agitateur, *n.m.* agitator.

agitation, *n.f.* excitement, disturbance, commotion, flutter.

agité, *adj.* upset, excited.

agiter, *vb.* agitate, wave, wag, shake, stir. s'a., toss, flutter.

agneau, *n.m.* lamb.

agonie, *n.f.* agony.

agrafe, *n.f.* clasp.

agrafer, *vb.* clasp.

agrandir, *vb.* enlarge.

agréable, *adj.* likable, pleasant, enjoyable, agreeable.

agréer, *vb.* accept, consent.

agrégation, *n.f.* aggregation, fellowship.

agrément, *n.m.* pleasure.

agresseur, *n.m.* aggressor.

agressif, *adj.* aggressive.

agression, *n.f.* aggression.

agricole, *adj.* agricultural.

agriculture, *n.f.* agriculture.

ahurir, *vb.* bewilder, fluster.

aide, *n.f.* help, aid.

aider, *vb.* help, aid.

aïeul (à yœl), *n.m.* grandfather.

aïeule (à yœl), *n.f.* grandmother.

aïeux, *n.m.pl.* ancestors.

aigle, *n.m.f.* eagle.

aiglefin, *n.m.* haddock.

aigre, *adj.* sour.

aigu, *adj.* shrill, keen, pointed.

aiguille, *n.f.* needle.

aiguisé, *adj.* keen.

aiguiser, *vb.* sharpen.

ail (à ë) *n.m.* garlic.

aile, *n.f.* wing.

ailleurs, *adv.* elsewhere. d'a., in addition, anyhow.

aimable, *adj.* kind, pleasant, amiable.

aimant, *n.m.* magnet.

aimer, *vb.* love, like.

aine, *n.f.* groin.

aîné (è nä), 1. *adj. and n.m.* elder. 2. *adj.* eldest, senior.

ainsi, *adv.* thus, so.

air, *n.m.* air, looks. en plein air, in the open air.

aire, *n.f.* area.

aise, *n.f.* ease, comfort. à l'a., comfortable.

aisé, *adj.* substantial, well-to-do; easy.

aisselle, *n.f.* armpit.

ajourner, *vb.* put off. s'a., adjourn.

ajouter, *vb.* add.

ajustage, *n.m.* fitting.

ajuster, *vb.* fit, fix, adjust.

alarme, *n.f.* alarm.

alarmer, *vb.* alarm.

album, *n.m.* album.

alcool (-kòl), *n.m.* alcohol.

alcoolique (-kòl-), *adj.* alcoholic.

alcôve, *n.f.* alcove.

alentours, *n.m.pl.* neighborhood, surroundings.

alerte, *adj.* spry, active, alert.

algèbre, *n.f.* algebra.

aliéné, *n.m.* lunatic.

aliéner, *vb.* alienate.

aligner, *vb.* line up.

aliment, *n.m.* food.

alimentation, *n.f.* feeding.

alimenter, *vb.* feed.

alinéa, *n.m.* paragraph.

allaiter, *vb.* nurse.

allée, *n.f.* path, avenue, aisle.

allégation, *n.f.* allegation.

alléger, *vb.* lighten, soothe.

allégresse, *n.f.* glee, delight, mirth.

alléguer, *vb.* plead, allege.

Allemagne, *n.f.* Germany.

Allemand, *n.m.* German (person).

allemand, 1. *n.m.* German (language). 2. *adj.* German.

aller, *vb.* go. s'en a., go away. a. à, fit. se laisser a., drift. a. bien, fare well. a. mal, fare ill. a. et retour, round trip.

alliage, *n.m.* alloy.

alliance, *n.f.* alliance, union.

allié, 1. *n.m.* ally, relation. 2. *adj.* allied.

allier, *vb.* ally. s'a. à, join with.

allô, *interj.* hello.

allocation, *n.f.* allowance.

allonger, *vb.* lengthen, prolong.

allons, *interj.* well, come now.

allouer, *vb.* grant.

allumer, *vb.* light.

allumette, *n.f.* match.

allure, *n.f.* pace, gait.

allusion, *n.f.* hint, allusion. faire a. à, allude to.

almanach (-nä), *n.m.* almanac.

alors, 1. *adv.* then. 2. *conj.* a. que, when.

alouette, *n.f.* lark.

alphabet, *n.m.* alphabet.

altérer, *vb.* change.

alternatif, *adj.* alternate.

alternative, *n.f.* alternative.

alterner, *vb.* alternate.

Altesse, *n.f.* Highness (title).

altitude, *n.f.* altitude.

aluminium, *n.m.* aluminum.

amabilité, *n.f.* kindness.

amalgamer, *vb.* amalgamate.

amande, *n.f.* kernel; almond.

amant, *n.m.* lover.

amas, *n.m.* hoard, mass.

amasser, *vb.* hoard, gather, amass.

amateur, *n.m.* amateur.

ambassade, *n.f.* embassy.

ambassadeur, *n.m.* ambassador.

ambassadrice, *n.f.* ambassadress.

ambigu *m.*, **ambiguë** *f. adj.* ambiguous.

ambiguïté, *n.f.* ambiguity.

ambitieux, *adj.* ambitious.

ambition, *n.f.* ambition.

ambre, *n.m.* amber.

ambulance, *n.f.* ambulance.

âme, *n.f.* soul.

amélioration, *n.f.* improvement.

améliorer, *vb.* improve.

aménager, *vb.* fit up.

amende, *n.f.* fine. **mettre à l'a.,** fine.

amendement, *n.m.* amendment.

amender, *vb.* amend.

amener, *vb.* bring, lead.

amer (-r), *adj.* bitter.

Américain, *n.m.* American.

américain, *adj.* American.

Amérique *n.f.* America.

A. du Nord, North America.

A. du Sud, South America.

amertume, *n.f.* bitterness.

ameublement, *n.m.* furniture.

ami *m.*, **amie** *f. n.* friend.

amical, *adj.* friendly, amicable.

amidon, *n.m.* starch.

amiral, *n.m.* admiral.

amitié, *n.f.* friendship.

ammoniaque, *n.f.* ammonia.

amniocentèse, *n.f.* amniocentesis.

amoindrir, *vb.* lessen, reduce.

amollir, *vb.* soften.

amortir, *vb.* deaden, soften.

amour, *n.m.* love.

amoureux, 1. *n.m.* lover. **2.** *adj.* in love, amorous.

amour-propre, *n.m.* vanity, pride, conceit.

ample, *adj.* ample, spacious.

ampleur, *n.f.* plenty, compass.

amplifier, *vb.* increase, enlarge, develop.

ampoule, *n.f.* blister; (electric) bulb.

amputer, *vb.* amputate.

amusement, *n.m.* fun, pastime, entertainment.

amuser, *vb.* entertain. **s'a.,** have a good time.

amygdale, *n.f.* tonsil.

an, *n.m.* year.

analogie, *n.f.* analogy.

analogue, *adj.* similar, analogous.

analyse, *n.f.* analysis.

analyser, *vb.* analyze.

anarchie, *n.f.* anarchy.

anatomie, *n.f.* anatomy.

ancêtre, *n.m.* forefather, ancestor.

anche, *n.f.* reed.

anchois, *n.m.* anchovy.

ancien *m.*, **ancienne** *f. adj.* ancient, old, former.

ancre, *n.f.* anchor.

ancrer, *vb.* anchor.

âne *m.*, **ânesse** *f. n.* ass, donkey.

anéantir, *vb.* annihilate, destroy.

anecdote, *n.f.* anecdote.

anesthésique, *adj. and n.m.* anesthetic.

ange, *n.m.* angel.

Anglais, *n.m.* Englishman.

anglais, *adj. and n.m.* English.

Anglaise, *n.f.* Englishwoman.

angle, *n.m.* angle, corner.

Angleterre, *n.f.* England.

angoissant, *adj.* in anguish.

angoisse, *n.f.* agony, pang, anguish.

anguille, *n.f.* eel.

anguleux, *adj.* angular.

anicroche, *n.f.* hitch.

animal, *n.m. and adj.* animal.

animation, *n.f.* animation.

animer, *vb.* enliven, animate.

animosité, *n.f.* animosity.

anneau, *n.m.* ring, circle.

année, *n.f.* year; vintage.

annexe, *n.m.* annex.

annexer, *vb.* annex.

annexion, *n.f.* annexation.

anniversaire, *n.m.* anniversary, birthday.

annonce, *n.f.* advertisement, announcement.

annoncer, *vb.* advertise, announce.

annotation, *n.f.* annotation.

annoter, *vb.* annotate.

annuaire, *n.m.* directory.

annuel, *adj.* yearly, annual.

annulation, *n.f.* cancellation.

annuler, *vb.* cancel, void, annul.

ânonner, *vb.* stammer.

anonyme, *adj.* anonymous.

anormal, *adj.* irregular, abnormal.

anse, *n.f.* handle; bay.

antagonisme, *n.m.* antagonism.

antarctique, *adj.* antarctic.

antécédent, *adj. and n.m.* antecedent.

antécédents, *n.m.pl.* record.

antenne, *n.f.* antenna.

antérieur, *adj.* previous; fore, front.

anthracite, *n.m.* anthracite.

antichambre, *n.f.* entrance hall.

anticipation, *n.f.* anticipation.

anticiper, *vb.* anticipate.

antidote, *n.m.* antidote.

antilope, *n.f.* antelope.

antinucléaire, *adj.* antinuclear.

antipathie, *n.f.* antipathy.

antiquaire, *n.m.* antique dealer.

antique, *adj.* ancient, antiquated, antique.

antiquité, *n.f.* antiquity.

antiseptique, *adj. and n.m.* antiseptic.

antre, *n.m.* den.

anxiété, *n.f.* anxiety, worry.

anxieux, *adj.* anxious.

août (oo), *n.m.* August.

apaiser, *vb.* allay, quiet, appease.

apathie, *n.f.* apathy.

apercevoir, *vb.* perceive. **s'a. de**, realize.

aperçu, *n.m.* outline.

apéritif, *n.m.* appetizer.

apitoyer, *vb.* move (emotionally).

aplanir, *vb.* even off.

aplatir, *vb.* flatten.

aplomb, *n.m.* poise, boldness.

apoplexie, *n.f.* apoplexy.

apostolique, *adj.* apostolic.

apôtre, *n.m.* apostle.

apparaître, *vb.* appear.

appareil, *n.m.* gear, appliance, device. **a. photographique,** camera.

apparence, *n.f.* appearance, looks.

apparent, *adj.* noticeable, apparent.

apparition, *n.f.* appearance, ghost.

appartement, *n.m.* apartment.

appartenir, *vb.* belong, pertain.

appât, *n.m.* bait.

appel, *n.m.* call, appeal.

appeler, *vb.* call, summon, appeal. **s'a.**, be named.

appendice, *n.m.* appendix.

appétit, *n.m.* appetite.

applaudir, *vb.* applaud.

applaudissements, *n.m.pl.* applause.

applicable, *adj.* applicable.

application, *n.f.* application, industry.

appliqué, *adj.* industrious.

appliquer, *vb.* apply (put on), stick. **s'a.**, work hard.

appointements, *n.m.pl.* salary.

apporter, *vb.* bring, fetch.

apposer, *vb.* affix.

appréciable, *adj.* appreciable.

appréciation, *n.f.* appreciation.

apprécier, *vb.* appreciate, value.

appréhension, *n.f.* apprehension.

apprendre, *vb.* learn. **a. à**, teach (to). **a. par cœur**, memorize.

apprenti, *n.m.* apprentice.

apprentissage, *n.m.* apprenticeship.

apprêt, *n.m.* preparation.

apprêter, *vb.* **s'a.**, prepare, get ready.

apprivoiser, *vb.* tame.

approbation, *n.f.* endorsement, approval, approbation.

approche, *n.f.* approach.

approcher, *vb.* **s'a. de**, approach, go toward.

approfondir, *vb.* deepen.

appropriation, *n.f.* appropriation.

approprier, *vb.* **s'a.**, take over, appropriate.

approuver, *vb.* approve.

approvisionnement, *n.m.* supply.

approximatif, *adj.* approximate.

appui, *n.m.* support.

appuyer (-pwě-), *vb.* support, endorse, advocate. **a. sur**, emphasize.

après, **1.** *adv.*, *prep.* after. **2.** *conj.* **a. que**, after. **d'a.**, according to.

après-demain, *n.m.* day after tomorrow.

après-midi, *n.m.f.* afternoon.

âpreté, *n.f.* harshness, bitterness.

à-propos, *n.m.* fitness.

apte à, *adj.* apt, suitable for.

aptitude, *n.f.* fitness, ability, aptitude.

aqualit, *n.m.* waterbed.

aquarelle (-kwá-), *n.f.* water color.

aquarium (-kwà-), *n.m.* aquarium.

aquatique (-kwá-), *adj.* aquatic.

aqueux, *adj.* watery.

Arabe, *n.m.f.* Arab, Arabian.

arabe, **1.** *n.m.* Arabic. **2.** *adj.* Arab, Arabian, Arabic.

arachide, *n.f.* peanut.

araignée, *n.f.* spider. **toile d'a.**, cobweb.

arbitrage, *n.m.* arbitration.

arbitraire, *adj.* arbitrary.

arbitre, *n.m.* umpire, arbitrator.

arbitrer, *vb.* arbitrate.

arbre, *n.m.* tree.

arbrisseau, *n.m.* shrub.

arc (-k), *n.m.* arc, arch, bow.

arcade, *n.f.* arcade.

arc-boutant, *n.m.* flying buttress.

arc-en-ciel, *n.m.* rainbow.

archaïque (árk-), *adj.* archaic.

arche, *n.f.* arch (of bridge); ark.

archet, *n.m.* bow.

archevêque, *n.m.* archbishop.

archipel, *n.m.* archipelago.

architecte, *n.m.* architect.

architectural, *adj.* architectural.

architecture, *n.f.* architecture.

archives, *n.f.pl.* files, archives.

arctique, *adj.* arctic.

ardemment, *adv.* eagerly.

ardent, *adj.* eager, fiery, ardent.

ardeur, *n.f.* ardor.

ardoise, *n.f.* slate.

arène, *n.f.* arena, ring.

argent, *n.m.* silver, money.

argenterie, *n.f.* silverware.

Argentin, *n.m.* Argentine.

argentin, *adj.* Argentine.

argile, *n.f.* clay.

argot, *n.m.* slang.

argument, *n.m.* argument (reasoning).

argumenter, *vb.* argue (reason).

aride, *adj.* arid.

aristocrate, *n.m.f.* aristocrat.

aristocratie, *n.f.* aristocracy.

aristocratique, *adj.* aristocratic.

arithmétique, *n.f.* arithmetic.

arme, *n.f.* weapon; arm.

armée, *n.f.* army.

armement, *n.m.* armament.

arme nucléaire, *n.f.* nuclear weapon.

armer, *vb.* arm.

armistice, *n.m.* armistice.

armoire, *n.f.* cupboard, closet, wardrobe.

armure, *n.f.* armor.

aromatique, *adj.* aromatic.

arome, *n.m.* flavor, aroma.

arpenter, *vb.* pace.

arracher, *vb.* snatch.

arrangement, *n.m.* arrangement, settlement.

arranger, *vb.* settle, trim, fix, arrange.

arrestation, *n.f.* arrest, apprehension. **en état d'a.**, under arrest.

arrêt, *n.m.* stop.

arrêté, *n.m.* decree.

arrêter, *vb.* stop, check, halt, arrest.

arrière, *adv.* behind, back. **en a.**, backward. **marche a.**, reverse (gear).

arriéré, **1.** *n.m.* arrear. **2.** *adj.* backward.

arrière-garde, *n.f.* rear guard.

arrivée, *n.f.* arrival.

arriver, *vb.* happen, reach, arrive.

arrogance, *n.f.* arrogance.

arrogant, *adj.* arrogant.

arroger, *vb.* arrogate, assume.

arrondir, *vb.* round off.

arrondissement, *n.m.* district.

arroser, *vb.* water, sprinkle; baste (meat).

arsenal, *n.m.* arsenal.

arsenic, *n.m.* arsenic.

art, *n.m.* art. **beaux-arts**, fine arts.

artère, *n.f.* artery.

artichaut, *n.m.* artichoke.

article, *n.m.* article, item, entry. **a. de fond**, editorial.

articulation, *n.f.* joint, articulation.

articuler, *vb.* articulate.

artifice, *n.m.* artifice.

artificiel, *adj.* artificial.

artificieux, *adj.* artful.

artillerie, *n.f.* artillery.

artisan, *n.m.* craftsman, artisan.

artiste, *n.m.* artist.

artistique, *adj.* artistic.

as (ãs), *n.m.* ace.

ascenseur, *n.m.* elevator.

ascension, *n.f.* ascent (of a mountain).

Asiatique, *n.m.f.* Asian.

asiatique, *adj.* Asian.

Asie, *n.f.* Asia.

asile, *n.m.* haven, refuge, asylum.

aspect (-pě), *n.m.* looks, appearance, aspect.

asperger, *vb.* sprinkle.

asperges, *n.f.pl.* asparagus.

asphalte, *n.m.*, asphalt.

aspirateur, *n.m.* vacuum cleaner.

aspiration, *n.f.* aspiration, longing.

aspirer, *vb.* aspire, breathe.

assaillant, *n.m.* assailant.

assaillir, *vb.* assail, attack.

assaisonner, *vb.* season.

assassin, *n.m.* assassin, murderer.

assassinat, *n.m.* assassination, murder.

assassiner, *vb.* assassinate, murder.

assaut, *n.m.* assault, attack.

assemblage, *n.m.* collection.

assemblée, *n.f.* congregation, assembly.

assembler, *vb.* convene, gather. **s'a.**, assemble.

assentiment, *n.m.* assent.

asseoir, *vb.* seat. **s'a.**, sit down.

assertion, *n.f.* assertion.

asservir, *vb.* enslave.

assez (de), *n.* and *adv.* enough (of); pretty much.

assidu, *adj.* assiduous, industrious.

assiduité, *n.f.* industry.

assiéger, *vb.* besiege.

assiette, *n.f.* plate.

assigner, *vb.* assign.

assimiler, *vb.* assimilate.

assis, *adj.* seated.

assistance, *n.f.* those present.

assister à, *vb.* attend, be present at.

association, *n.f.* soccer; association, company; connection.

associé, **1.** *n.m.* partner, associate. **2.** *adj.* associated.

associer, *vb.* associate.

assombrir, *vb.* **s'a.**, grow dark.

assommer, *vb.* murder, slaughter.

Assomption, *n.f.* Assumption (*eccles.*).

assortiment, *n.m.* assortment.

assortir, *vb.* match; tune.

assoupir, *vb.* **s'a.**, get drowsy.

assourdir, *vb.* deafen.

assujetti, *adj.* subject.

assujettir, *vb.* subject.

assumer, *vb.* assume.

assurance, *n.f.* assurance, insurance.

assuré, *adj.* sure.

assurer, *vb.* insure; assure. **s'a. de**, make certain.

assureur, *n.m.* insurer.

astérisque, *n.m.* asterisk.

astre, *n.m.* star.

astronaute, *n.m.* astronaut.

astronome, *n.m.* astronomer.

astronomie, *n.f.* astronomy.

astucieux, *adj.* tricky.

atelier, *n.m.* studio, (work)shop.

athée, n.m.f. atheist.
athlète, n.m.f. athlete.
athlétique, adj. athletic.
atlantique, adj. Atlantic.
atlas (-s), n.m. atlas.
atmosphère, n.f. atmosphere.
atmosphérique, adj. atmospheric.
atome, n.m. atom.
atomique, adj. atomic.
atroce, adj. atrocious, outrageous.
atrocité, n.f. atrocity.
attachement, n.m. attachment, affection.
attacher, vb. tie, fasten, join, attach.
attaque, n.f. attack.
attaquer, vb. attack.
attardé, adj. belated.
attarder, vb. s'a., linger, delay.
atteindre, vb. reach, attain; strike.
atteint, adj. stricken.
atteinte, n.f. reach. **hors d'a.,** out of reach.
attelage, n.m. team.
atteler, vb. hitch up, harness.
attendre, vb. wait (for), await. **s'a. à,** expect.
attendrir, vb. soften, move. **se laisser a.,** relent.
attendrissement, n.m. feeling, emotion.
attentat, n.m. criminal attack, outrage.
attente, n.f. expectation, wait.
attentif, adj. thoughtful, attentive.
attention, n.f. notice, heed, attention. **faire a.,** heed, pay attention.
atténuer, vb. extenuate.
atterrir, vb. land.
attester, vb. attest.
attirer, vb. attract, entice, lure.
attitude, n.f. attitude.
attouchement, n.m. touch.
attraction, n.f. attraction.
attrait, n.m. charm.
attraper, vb. catch.
attrayant, adj. attractive.
attribuer, vb. ascribe, attribute.
attribut, n.m. attribute, characteristic.
attrister, vb. grieve.
au m., à la f., aux pl. prep. to the, in the.
aube, n.f. dawn.
auberge, n.f. inn.
aubergine, n.f. eggplant.
aubergiste, n.m. innkeeper.
aucun, pron. none.
aucunement, adv. not at all.
audace, n.f. audacity.
audacieux, adj. daring, bold.
au-dessous, 1. adv. below. **2.** prep. **au-d. de,** beneath, under.
au-dessus, 1. adv. above. **2.** prep. **au-d. de,** over, above.
audience, n.f. audience.
audiovisuel, adj. audiovisual.
auditoire, n.m. audience, assembly.

auge, n.f. trough.
augmentation, n.f. increase, raise, rise.
augmenter, vb. increase.
augure, n.m. omen, augury. **de bon a.,** auspicious. **de mauvais a.,** ominous.
augurer, vb. augur.
aujourd'hui, adv. today.
aumône, n.f. alms.
aumônier, n.m. chaplain.
auparavant, adv. before (time).
auprès de, prep. next, near, beside.
auréole, n.f. halo.
aurore, n.f. dawn.
auspice, n.m. auspice.
aussi, adv. too, also; so, as; therefore.
austère, adj. austere, severe.
austérité, n.f. austerity.
Australie, n.f. Australia.
Australien, n.m. Australian.
australien, adj. Australian.
autant, adv. so much, as much. **a. que,** as (so) much as. **d'a. que,** since. **a. plus,** so much the more.
autel, n.m. altar.
auteur, n.m. author, originator.
authentique, adj. true, genuine, authentic.
auto, n.f. auto.
autobus (-s), n.m. bus.
automatique, adj. automatic.
automne (-tôn), n.m. fall.
automobile, n.f. automobile.
autonomie, n.f. autonomy.
autorisation, n.f. license, authorization.
autoriser, vb. authorize.
autoritaire, adj. authoritative.
autorité, n.f. authority.
autour, 1. adv. around. **2.** prep. **a. de,** around.
autre, 1. adj. other. **2.** pron. other, else. **l'un l'a.,** one another. **quelqu'un d'a.,** someone else.
autrefois, adv. formerly.
autrement, adv. otherwise.
Autriche, n.f. Austria.
Autrichien, n.m. Austrian.
autrichien, adj. Austrian.
autruche, n.f. ostrich.
autrui, pron. someone else, others.
auxiliaire, adj. auxiliary.
avalanche, n.f. avalanche.
avaler, vb. swallow.
avance, n.f. advance. **d'a.,** beforehand. **en a.,** fast (clock).
avancé, adj. forward, advanced.
avancement, n.m. advance; advancement; promotion.
avancer, vb. proceed; come or go forward or onward.
avances, n.f.pl. advance. **faire des a. à,** make approaches to.
avant, 1. n.m. fore, bow. **2.** adv., prep. before. **3.** conj. **a. que,** before. **en a.,** forward, onward. **en a. de,** ahead of.
avantage, n.m. advantage.

avantageux, adj. advantageous; favorable; profitable.
avant-bras, n.m. forearm.
avant-garde, n.f. vanguard.
avant-hier (-yâr), n.m. day before yesterday.
avant-toit, n.m. eaves.
avare, 1. n.m.f. miser. **2.** adj. miserly, stingy.
avarice, n.f. avarice.
avec, prep. with.
avenant, adj. comely. **à l'a.,** accordingly.
avenir, n.m. future.
Avent, n.m. (eccles.) Advent.
aventure, n.f. adventure.
aventurer, vb. **s'a.,** take a chance.
aventureux, adj. adventurous.
aventurier, n.m. adventurer.
avenue, n.f. avenue.
averse, n.f. shower.
aversion, n.f. aversion, dislike.
avertir, vb. notify, warn.
avertissement, n.m. warning.
avertisseur d'incendie, n.m. fire alarm.
aveu, n.m. admission, confession.
aveugle, adj. blind.
aveuglement, n.m. blindness.
aveuglément, adv. blindly.
aveugler, vb. blind.
aviateur, n.m. flier, aviator.
aviation, n.f. air force, aviation.
avide, adj. eager, greedy, avid.
avidité, n.f. greediness.
avilir, vb. debase, disgrace.
avion, n.m. airplane. **a. de bombardement,** bomber. **par a.,** via air mail.
avis, n.m. notice, opinion, advice (comm.).
aviser, vb. inform, notify. **s'a. (de),** decide.
avocat, n.m. lawyer; advocate.
avoine, n.f. oat.
avoir, vb. have. **il y a,** ago.
avortement, n.m. abortion.
avoué, n.m. attorney, lawyer.
avouer, vb. confess, admit, avow.
avril (-l), n.m. April.
axe, n.m. axis.
ayatollah, n.m. ayatollah.
azur, n.m. azure, blue.
azuré, adj. azure.

B

babeurre, n.m. buttermilk.
babil, n.m. babble.
babiller, vb. babble.
bâbord, n.m. (naut.) port.
babouin, n.m. baboon.
bac, n.m. ferryboat. **passage en b.,** ferry.
bachelier, n.m. graduate.
bacille (-l), n.m. bacillus.
bactérie, n.f. bacterium.
bactériologie, n.f. bacteriology.
badaud, adj. silly.

bagages, *n.m.pl.* luggage.

bagatelle, *n.f.* trifle.

bague, *n.f.* ring.

baguette, *n.f.* wand, stick; long, thin loaf of bread.

baie, *n.f.* bay, creek; berry.

baigner, *vb.* bathe.

baigneur, *n.m.* bather.

baignoire, *n.f.* bathtub.

bail, *n.m.* lease.

bâillement, *n.m.* yawn.

bâiller, *vb.* yawn.

bâillon, *n.m.* gag.

bain, *n.m.* bath.

baïonnette, *n.f.* bayonet.

baiser, *n.m. and vb.* kiss.

baissé, *adj.* downcast.

baisser, *vb.* lower, sink.

bal, *n.m.* ball.

balai, *n.m.* broom. **b. à laver,** mop.

balance, *n.f.* scales, balance.

balancement, *n.m.* rocking, swinging.

balancer, *vb.* rock, swing, sway. **se b.,** roll, hover.

balayer, *vb.* sweep.

balbutier, *vb.* stammer.

balcon, *n.m.* balcony.

baldaquin, *n.m.* canopy.

baleine, *n.f.* whale.

ballade, *n.f.* ballad.

balle, *n.f.* bullet, ball; bale.

ballet, *n.m.* ballet.

ballon, *n.m.* balloon.

ballot, *n.m.* bundle.

ballotter, *vb.* shake.

balsamique, *adj.* balmy.

bambou, *n.m.* bamboo.

ban, *n.m.* ban. **mettre au b.,** ban.

banal, *adj.* trite.

banane, *n.f.* banana.

banc, *n.m.* bench.

bandage, *n.m.* bandage.

bande, *n.f.* strip, stripe; pack, gang, band.

bande vidéo, *n.f.* videotape.

bandit, *n.m.* bandit, robber, knave.

banlieue, *n.f.* suburbs.

bannière, *n.f.* banner.

bannir, *vb.* banish.

bannissement, *n.m.* banishment.

banque, *n.f.* bank. **billet de b.,** banknote.

banqueroute, *n.f.* bankruptcy.

banqueroutier, *n.* bankrupt.

banquet, *n.m.* banquet, feast.

banquier, *n.m.* banker.

baptême (bä têm), *n.m.* christening, baptism.

baptiser (bä tē-), *vb.* christen, baptize.

Baptiste (bä tēst), *n.m.* Baptist.

baptistère (bä tēs-), *n.m.* baptistery.

bar, *n.m.* bar; bass (fish).

baraque, *n.f.* booth, stall.

baratter, *vb.* churn.

barbare, 1. *n.m.f.* barbarian. **2.** *adj.* barbarian, barbarous, wild.

barbarie, *n.f.* cruelty.

barbe, *n.f.* beard.

barbouiller, *vb.* daub, blur.

baromètre, *n.m.* barometer.

baron, *n.m.* baron.

barque, *n.f.* boat.

barrage, *n.m.* dam.

barre, *n.f.* bar, rail(ing). **b. du gouvernail,** helm.

barreau, *n.m.* bar.

barrer, *vb.* shut out.

barricade, *n.f.* barricade.

barrière, *n.f.* gate; bar, barrier; fence.

barrique, *n.f.* barrel, cask.

bas, *n.m.* stocking.

bas *m.,* **basse** *f. adj.* base, low, soft. **en b.,** down(ward), downstairs. **b. côté,** aisle.

bascule, *n.f.* seesaw. **chaise à b.,** rocking-chair.

base, *n.f.* base, basis.

basse, *n.f.* bass (voice).

basse-cour, *n.f.* barnyard.

bassesse, *n.f.* baseness.

bassin, *n.m.* basin, dock.

bataille, *n.f.* battle.

bataillon, *n.m.* battalion.

bâtard, *adj. and n.m.* bastard.

bateau, *n.m.* boat.

bâtiment, *n.m.* building.

bâtir, *vb.* build.

bâton, *n.m.* stick, staff.

battant, *n.m.* flap, door.

batte, *n.f.* bat.

battement, *n.m.* beat.

batterie, *n.f.* battery.

battre, *vb.* beat, strike; flap, pulsate. **se b.,** fight.

baume, *n.m.* balm.

bavard, *adj.* talkative, gossipy.

bavardage, *n.m.* gossip, chatter.

bavarder, *vb.* gossip, chat(ter).

bavette, *n.f.* bib.

bazar, *n.m.* bazaar.

béatitude, *n.f.* bliss.

beau, bel *m.,* **belle** *f. adj.* beautiful, handsome, fair, lovely, fine. **avoir beau,** (to do something) in vain. **faire beau,** be fine (weather).

beaucoup (de), *adj.* a lot, a great deal; much, many. **de b.,** by far.

beau-frère, *n.m.* brother-in-law.

beau-père, *n.m.* father-in-law.

beauté, *n.f.* beauty. **grain de b.,** mole.

bébé, *n.m.* baby.

bec, *n.m.* beak, bill; spot; burner.

bêche, *n.f.* spade.

bêcher, *vb.* dig.

becqueter, *vb.* peck.

bée, *adj.* **rester bouche b.,** stand gaping.

bégayer, *vb.* stammer.

Belge, *n.m.f.* Belgian.

belge, *adj.* Belgian.

Belgique, *n.f.* Belgium.

bélier, *n.m.* ram.

belle-fille, *n.f.* daughter-in-law.

belle-mère, *n.f.* mother-in-law; stepmother.

belligérant, *adj. and n.m.* belligerent.

bénédiction, *n.f.* blsessing, benediction.

bénéfice, *n.m.* benefit, advantage, profit.

bénéficier, *vb.* benefit, profit.

bénin *m.,* **bénigne** *f. adj.* benign.

bénir, *vb.* bless.

béquille, *n.f.* crutch.

berceau, *n.m.* cradle, bower.

bercer, *vb.* rock.

berge, *n.f.* bank.

berger, *n.m.* shepherd.

besogne, *n.f.* (piece of) work.

besoin, *n.m.* need, want. **avoir b.,** need.

bestiaux, *n.m.pl.* cattle.

bétail, *n.m.* cattle, animals.

bête, 1. *n.f.* beast, animal. **2.** *adj.* stupid, dumb.

bêtise, *n.f.* nonsense.

béton, *n.m.* concrete.

betterave, *n.f.* beet.

beurre, *n.m.* butter.

bévue, *n.f.* blunder, boner.

biais, *n.m.* slant; bias. **en b.,** at an angle.

bibelot, *n.m.* trinket.

biberon, *n.m.* baby's bottle.

Bible, *n.f.* Bible.

bibliothèque, *n.f.* library; bookcase.

biblique, *adj.* biblical.

bicyclette, *n.f.* bicycle. **faire de la b.,** cycle.

bidon, *n.m.* can.

bien, *n.m.* good; *(pl.)* goods, property, estate. **faire du b. à,** benefit.

bien, *adv.* well. **b. entendu,** of course. **aller b.,** be well. **vouloir b.,** be willing. **b. que,** although.

bien-aimé, *n.m.f. and adj.* darling.

bien-être, *n.m.* welfare.

bienfaisant, *adj.* beneficent, kind, humane.

bienfait, *n.m.* benefit.

bienfaiteur, *n.m.* benefactor.

bienheureux, *adj.* blessed.

bientôt, *adv.* soon.

bienveillance, *n.f.* benevolence, kindness.

bienveillant, *adj.* benevolent, kindly.

bienvenu, *adj.* welcome.

bière, *n.f.* beer, ale.

biffer, *vb.* cancel, erase.

bifteck, *n.m.* beefsteak.

bigamie, *n.f.* bigamy.

bigot, *n.m.* bigot.

bigoterie, *n.f.* bigotry.

bijou, *n.m.* jewel.

bijouterie, *n.f.* jewelry.

bile, *n.f.* bile. **se faire de la b.,** worry.

billard, *n.m.* billiards.

bille, *n.f.* marble (toy).

billet, *n.m.* ticket, note. **b. de banque,** banknote.

billion (-l-), *n.m.* billion.
biographie, *n.f.* biography.
biologie, *n.f.* biology.
biscuit, *n.m.* biscuit.
bizarre, *adj.* queer, odd, strange, quaint.
blâme, *n.m.* blame.
blâmer, *vb.* blame.
blanc *m.,* **blanche** *f. adj.* white, blank. **en b.,** blank.
blancheur, *n.f.* whiteness.
blanchir, *vb.* whiten.
blanchisserie, *n.f.* laundry.
blasé, *adj.* sophisticated.
blasphème, *n.m.* blasphemy.
blasphémer, *vb.* curse, blaspheme.
blatte, *n.f.* cockroach.
blé, *n.m.* wheat.
blême, *adj.* pale.
blesser, *vb.* wound, hurt, injure.
blessure, *n.f.* wound, hurt, injury.
bleu, *adj.* blue.
bloc, *n.m.* pad, block.
blocus (-s), *n.m.* blockade.
blond, *adj.* fair, blond(e).
bloquer, *vb.* block.
blottir, *vb.* se b., cower.
blouse, *n.f.* blouse.
blue jeans, *n.m.pl.* blue jeans.
bluff, *n.m.* bluff.
bluffeur, *n.m.* bluffer.
bobine, *n.f.* spool, reel.
bœuf (bœf), *n.m.* ox, beef. **jeune b.,** steer.
Bohème, *n.f.* Bohemia.
bohème, 1. *n.m.f.* bohemian, happy-go-lucky person. **2.** *n.f.* artistic underworld. **3.** *adj.* bohemian.
Bohémien, *n.m.* Bohemian; gypsy.
bohémien, *adj.* Bohemian.
boire, *vb.* drink. **b. à petits coups,** sip.
bois, *n.m.* wood, forest, lumber.
boiserie, *n.f.* woodwork.
boisseau, *n.m.* bushel.
boisson, *n.f.* beverage, drink.
boîte, *n.f.* box; can (food). **b. aux lettres,** mail-box.
boiter, *vb.* limp.
boiteux, *adj.* lame.
bol, *n.m.* bowl.
bombardement, *n.m.* bombardment.
bombarder, *vb.* bomb, bombard.
bombe, *n.f.* bomb, shell.
bombe à neutrons, *n.f.* neutron bomb.
bon *m.,* **bonne** *f. adj.* good, kind. **de b. heure,** early. **b. marché,** cheap.
bon, *n.m.* bond.
bonbon, *n.m.* candy, bonbon.
bond, *n.m.* bound, leap.
bonder, *vb.* overcrowd, jam.
bondir, *vb.* bound, leap, spring.
bonheur, *n.m.* happiness.
bonhomme, *n.m.* fellow.

bonjour, *interj. and n.m.* good morning.
bonne, *n.f.* maid.
bonnement, *adv.* simply.
bonnet, *n.m.* cap, hood.
bonsoir, *interj. and n.m.* good evening.
bonté, *n.f.* kindness, goodness.
bord, *n.m.* edge, rim, brim **b. du toit,** eaves.
border, *vb.* bound, edge, border, hem.
borne, *n.f.* bound, limit.
borner, *vb.* bound, limit.
bosquet, *n.m.* clump (trees).
bosse, *n.f.* bump.
bosselure, *n.f.* dent.
bossu, *adj.* hunchbacked.
botanique, *n.f.* botany.
botte, *n.f.* boot; bunch.
bottine, *n.f.* boot.
bouche, *n.f.* mouth.
boucher, *vb.* stop up.
boucher, *n.m.* butcher.
boucherie, *n.f.* butcher shop.
bouchon, *n.m.* cork.
boucle, *n.f.* curl, loop, buckle. **b. d'oreille,** earring.
boucler, *vb.* curl.
bouclier, *n.m.* shield.
bouder, *vb.* sulk.
boue, *n.f.* mud.
bouée, *n.f.* buoy.
boueur, *n.m.* scavenger.
boueux, *adj.* muddy.
bouffée, *n.f.* puff.
bouffon, *n.m.* clown, fool.
bouffonnerie, *n.f.* antic(s).
bouger, *vb.* stir, move, budge.
bougie, *n.f.* candle.
bouillir, *vb.* boil.
bouilloire, *n.f.* kettle.
bouillon, *n.m.* broth.
bouillonner, *vb.* bubble.
bouillotte, *n.f.* kettle.
boulanger, *n.m.* baker.
boulangerie, *n.f.* bakery.
boule, *n.f.* ball.
bouleau, *n.m.* birch.
bouledogue, *n.m.* bulldog.
boulevard, *n.m.* boulevard.
bouleversement, *n.m.* upset.
bouleverser, *vb.* upset, overturn.
bouquet, *n.m.* cluster, bunch, bouquet.
bouquiniste, *n.m.* (secondhand) bookseller.
bourbeux, *adj.* sloppy.
bourdon, *n.m.* bumblebee.
bourdonnement, *n.m.* buzz.
bourdonner, *vb.* hum, buzz.
bourg, *n.m.* borough, village.
bourgeois, *adj.* middle-class, bourgeois.
bourgeoisie, *n.f.* middle class.
bourgeon, *n.m.* bud.
bourgeonner, *vb.* bud.
bourre, *n.f.* stuffing.
bourreau, *n.m.* executioner, hangman; brute.
bourrelet, *n.m.* pad.
bourrer, *vb.* stuff, pad.
bourru, *adj.* gruff.
bourse, *n.f.* purse, bag; stock

exchange; scholarship, fellowship.
boursoufler, *vb.* bloat.
bousculer, *vb.* jostle.
bousiller, *vb.* bungle.
boussole, *n.f.* compass.
bout, *n.m.* end, tip, butt, stub.
bouteille, *n.f.* bottle.
boutique, *n.f.* shop.
bouton, *n.m.* button, bud; pimple.
boutonnière, *n.f.* buttonhole.
boxe, *n.f.* boxing.
boxeur, *n.m.* boxer.
boycotter, *vb.* boycott.
bracelet, *n.m.* bracelet.
braconnier, *n.m.* poacher.
brailler, *vb.* bawl.
braise, *n.f.* coals, embers.
brancard, *n.m.* stretcher.
branche, *n.f.* branch, bough, limb.
brandir, *vb.* brandish.
branler, *vb.* waver.
braquer, *vb.* aim, point.
bras, *n.m.* arm.
brasse, *n.f.* fathom.
brasser, *vb.* brew.
brasserie, *n.f.* brewery, beerjoint.
bravade, *n.f.* bravado.
brave, *adj.* fine, good, brave.
braver, *vb.* brave, face, defy.
bravoure, *n.f.* courage.
brebis, *n.f.* lamb.
brèche, *n.f.* breach, gap.
bref, 1. *adj.m.,* **brève** *f.* brief, short. **2.** *adv.* in short.
Brésil, *n.m.* Brazil.
brevet, *n.m.* commission. **b. d'invention,** patent.
bribe, *n.f.* scrap, bit.
bride, *n.f.* bridle.
brider, *vb.* curb.
bridge, *n.m.* bridge (game).
brièveté, *n.f.* brevity.
brigade, *n.f.* brigade.
brigadier, *n.m.* corporal.
brigant, *n.m.* robber, knave.
brillant, *adj.* brilliant, bright, glowing.
briller, *vb.* shine, glisten, glare.
brin, *n.m.* blade (grass).
brindille, *n.f.* twig.
brioche, *n.f.* bun.
brique, *n.f.* brick.
briquet, *n.m.* pierre à b., flint.
brise, *n.f.* breeze.
briser, *vb.* break, shatter, smash.
britannique, *adj.* British.
brocart, *n.m.* brocade.
broche, *n.f.* spit, spindle; brooch.
brochure, *n.f.* pamphlet.
broder, *vb.* embroider.
broderie, *n.f.* embroidery.
bronchite, *n.f.* bronchitis.
bronze, *n.m.* bronze.
broquette, *n.f.* tack.
brosse, *n.f.* brush.
brouhaha, *n.m.* uproar.
brouillard, *n.m.* fog, mist.
brouiller, *vb.* jumble, embroil;

scramble (eggs). **se b.,** quarrel.
brouillon, *n.m.* (rough) draft.
broussailles, *n.f./pl.* brushwood.
brouter, *vb.* browse.
broyer, *vb.* crush.
bruine, *n.f.* drizzle.
bruiner, *vb.* drizzle.
bruissement, *n.m.* rustle.
bruit, *n.m.* noise, clatter; report, rumor.
brûler, *vb.* burn.
brume, *n.f.* mist. **b. légère,** haze.
brumeux, *adj.* foggy, misty.
brun, *adj.* brown.
brune, *adj. and n.f.* brunette.
brusque, *adj.* abrupt, curt, blunt, gruff, brusque.
brut, *adj.* crude, gross.
brutal, *adj.* brutal, savage.
brutalité, *n.f.* brutality.
brute, *n.f.* brute.
bruyant, *adj.* noisy, loud.
bruyère, *n.f.* heath, heather.
bûche, *n.f.* log.
bûcheron, *n.m.* wood-cutter.
budget, *n.m.* budget.
buffet, *n.m.* buffet.
buffle, *n.m.* buffalo.
buis, *n.m.* box (tree).
buisson, *n.m.* bush, shrub, thicket.
buissonneux, *adj.* bushy.
bulbe, *n.m.* bulb.
bulle, *n.f.* bubble; (papal) bull.
bulletin, *n.m.* bulletin, ticket.
bureau, *n.m.* office, bureau; desk. **b. de location,** box-office.
burin, *n.m.* chisel.
burlesque, *adj.* ludicrous.
buste, *n.m.* bust.
but, *n.m.* aim, goal, purpose.
butin, *n.m.* spoils, booty.
butte, *n.f.* hill, knoll.
buvard, *n.m.* blotter.

C

ça, *pron.* that.
cabane, *n.f.* cabin, hut.
cabaret, *n.m.* cabaret, tavern.
cabine, *n.f.* cabin, booth.
cabinet, *n.m.* closet; office. **c. de toilette,** lavatory. **c. de travail,** study.
câble, *n.m.* cable, rope.
câbler, *vb.* cable.
câblogramme, *n.m.* cablegram.
cacao, *n.m.* cocoa.
cacher, *vb.* hide, conceal. **se c.,** lurk.
cachet, *n.m.* seal.
cadavre, *n.m.* corpse.
cadeau, *n.m.* gift, present.
cadence, *n.f.* cadence.
cadet, 1. *n.m.* cadet. **2.** *adj.* junior.
cadran, *n.m.* dial.
cadre, *n.m.* frame.
café, *n.m.* coffee; café.
cage, *n.f.* cage.

cahier, *n.m.* notebook.
caille, *n.f.* quail.
caillot, *n.m.* clot.
caillou, *n.m.* pebble.
caisse, *n.f.* crate, case, box.
caissier, *n.m.* cashier, teller.
cajoler, *vb.* coax.
calamité, *n.f.* calamity.
calcium, *n.m.* calcium.
calcul, *n.m.* calculation.
calculer, *vb.* figure, reckon, calculate.
cale, *n.f.* hold.
calembour, *n.m.* pun.
calendrier, *n.m.* calendar.
calibre, *n.m.* caliber.
calicot, *n.m.* calico.
callosité, *n.f.* callus.
calme, *n.m. and adj.* quiet, calm.
calmer, *vb.* soothe, quiet, calm.
calomnie, *n.f.* slander.
calomnier, *vb.* slander.
calorie, *n.f.* calorie.
calotte, *n.f.* crown (of hat).
Calvaire, *n.m.* Calvary.
camarade, *n.m.f.* comrade, companion, mate.
camaraderie, *n.f.* companionship, fellowship.
cambrioleur, *n.m.* burglar.
camion, *n.m.* truck.
camoufler, *vb.* camouflage.
camp, *n.m.* camp.
campagnard, 1. *n.m.* countryman, peasant. **2.** *adj.* peasant.
campagne, *n.f.* country; campaign.
camper, *vb.* camp.
camphre, *n.m.* camphor.
Canada, *n.m.* Canada.
Canadien, *n.m.* Canadian.
canadien, *adj.* Canadian.
canaille, *n.f.* rabble; scoundrel.
canal, *n.m.* channel, canal.
canapé, *n.m.* sofa, couch; canapé.
canard, *n.m.* duck.
canari, *n.m.* canary.
cancer (-r), *n.m.* cancer.
cancérogène, *adj.* carcinogenic.
candeur, *n.f.* purity; candor.
candidat, *n.m.* candidate, applicant.
candidature, *n.f.* candidacy.
candide, *adj.* frank, open, candid.
canevas, *n.m.* canvas. **gros c.,** burlap.
canin, *adj.* canine.
canne, *n.f.* cane, stick.
canneberge, *n.f.* cranberry.
cannelle, *n.f.* cinnamon.
cannibale, *adj. and n.m.f.* cannibal.
canoë (-ô à), *n.m.* canoe.
canon, *n.m.* cannon.
canot, *n.m.* boat, canoe. **c. automobile,** motorboat.
cantaloup, *n.m.* cantaloupe.
cantique, *n.m.* hymn.
canton, *n.m.* district, canton.
caoutchouc (-choo), *n.m.* rubber.

cap (-p), *n.m.* cape (headland).
capable, *adj.* efficient, fit, capable, competent.
capacité, *n.f.* capability, capacity.
cape, *n.f.* cape (clothing).
capitaine, *n.m.* captain.
capital, *n.m. and adj.* capital.
capitale, *n.f.* capital (city).
capitaliser, *vb.* capitalize.
capitalisme, *n.m.* capitalism.
capitaliste, *n.m.f.* capitalist.
caporal, *n.m.* corporal.
capote, *n.f.* hood.
câpre, *n.f.* caper.
caprice, *n.m.* whim, fancy.
capricieux, *adj.* fickle, capricious.
capsule, *n.f.* capsule.
captif, *adj. and n.m.* captive.
captiver, *vb.* captivate, charm.
captivité, *n.f.* captivity.
capture, *n.f.* capture.
capturer, *vb.* capture.
capuchon, *n.m.* hood.
car, *conj.* for.
caractère, *n.m.* character, nature, disposition; type.
caractériser, *vb.* characterize; distinguish; mark.
caractéristique, *adj.* characteristic.
carafe, *n.f.* decanter, water-bottle.
caramel, *n.m.* caramel.
carat, *n.m.* carat.
caravane, *n.f.* caravan.
carbone, *n.m.* carbon.
carboniser, *vb.* char.
carburateur, *n.m.* carburetor.
carcasse, *n.f.* shell; carcass.
cardinal, *n.m.* cardinal.
carême, *n.m.* Lent.
caresse, *n.f.* caress.
caresser, *vb.* fondle, stroke, caress.
cargaison, *n.f.* cargo.
caricature, *n.f.* caricature.
carie, *n.f.* decay.
carillon, *n.m.* chime.
carillonner, *vb.* chime.
carnaval, *n.m.* carnival.
carnet, *n.m.* notebook.
carnivore, *adj.* carnivorous.
carotte, *n.f.* carrot.
carré, *n.m. and adj.* square.
carreau, *n.m.* diamond (cards); pane; tile.
carrefour, *n.m.* crossroads.
carrière, *n.f.* career; scope; quarry.
carriole, *n.f.* (light) cart.
carrosse, *n.m.* coach.
carte, *n.f.* chart, map, card. **c. de crédit,** *n.f.* credit card. **c. du jour,** bill of fare.
carton, *n.m.* cardboard; box, carton.
cartouche, *n.f.* cartridge.
cas, *n.m.* case; event.
case, *n.f.* pigeonhole; hut, shed.
caserne, *n.f.* barracks.
casque, *n.m.* helmet.
casquette, *n.f.* cap.

cassable, *adj.* breakable.
casse-croûte, *n.m.* snack.
casser, *vb.* break, crack.
casserole, *n.f.* pan.
cassette, *n.f.* 1. casket. 2. cassette.
cassis, *n.m.* black currant.
caste, *n.f.* caste.
castor, *n.m.* beaver.
casuel, *adj.* casual.
catalogue, *n.m.* catalogue.
cataracte, *n.f.* cataract.
catarrhe, *n.m.* catarrh.
catastrophe, *n.f.* disaster, catastrophe.
catéchisme, *n.m.* catechism.
catégorie, *n.f.* category.
cathédrale, *n.f.* cathedral.
catholicisme, *n.m.* Catholicism.
catholique, *adj.* Catholic.
cauchemar, *n.m.* nightmare.
cause, *n.f.* case; cause.
causer, *vb.* chat; cause.
causerie, *n.f.* chat, talk.
causette, *n.f.* chat.
caution, *n.f.* bail, security.
cavalerie, *n.f.* cavalry.
cavalier, *n.m.* rider, horseman; escort.
cave, *n.f.* cellar, cavern.
cavité, *n.f.* cavity.
ce (se), cet (sèt) *m.*, cette (sèt) *f.*, ces (sā) *pl. adj.* that, this.
ceci, *pron.* this.
cécité, *n.f.* blindness.
céder, *vb.* yield, give in, cede.
cèdre, *n.m.* cedar.
ceindre, *vb.* gird.
ceinture, *n.f.* belt, sash.
cela, *pron.* that.
célébration, *n.f.* celebration.
célèbre, *adj.* famous, noted.
célébrer, *vb.* celebrate.
célébrité, *n.f.* celebrity.
céleri, *n.m.* celery.
céleste, *adj.* heavenly, celestial.
célibataire, 1. *n.m.* bachelor. 2. *adj.* single.
celle, *pron. f.* See celui.
cellule, *n.f.* cell.
celluloïd (-lô ēd), *n.m.* celluloid.
celtique, *adj.* Celtic.
celui *m.*, celle *f.*, ceux *m.pl.*, celles *f.pl. pron.* the one. celui-ci, this one; the latter. celui-là, that one; the former.
cendre, *n.f.* ashes, cinders.
cendrier, *n.m.* ash-tray.
censeur, *n.m.* censor.
censure, *n.f.* censure.
censurer, *vb.* censor.
cent, *adj. and n.m.* hundred. pour c., percent.
centaine, *n.f.* hundred.
centenaire, *adj. and n.m.* centenary, centennial.
centième, *adj.* hundredth.
centigrade, *adj.* centigrade.
centimètre, *n.m.* centimeter.
central, *adj.* central.
centraliser, *vb.* centralize.
centre, *n.m.* center.

cependant, *adv.* however, still, yet.
cercle, *n.m.* circle, ring, hoop; club.
cercueil, *n.m.* coffin.
céréale, *adj. and n.f.* cereal.
cérémonial, *adj. and n.m.* ceremonial.
cérémonie, *n.f.* ceremony. sans c., informal.
cérémonieux, *adj.* formal, ceremonious.
cerf (sèr), *n.m.* deer.
cerf-volant, *n.m.* kite.
cerise, *n.f.* cherry.
certain, *adj.* certain, sure; *(pl.)* some.
certes, *adv.* indeed.
certificat, *n.m.* credentials; certificate.
certifier, *vb.* certify.
certitude, *n.f.* certainty, assurance.
cerveau, *n.m.* brain.
cervelle, *n.f.* brains.
cessation, *n.f.* stopping, cessation.
cesser, *vb.* stop, desist, cease.
cession, *n.f.* assignment (law).
cet, cette, *pron.* See ce.
chacun, *pron.* everybody, everyone; each; apiece.
chagrin, 1. *n.m.* grief, vexation. 2. *adj.* fretful.
chagriner, *vb.* grieve.
chaîne, *n.f.* chain; range.
chaînon, *n.m.* link.
chair, *n.f.* flesh.
chaire, *n.f.* pulpit; chair (university).
chaise, *n.f.* chair.
chaland, *n.m.* barge.
châle, *n.m.* shawl.
chaleur, *n.f.* warmth, heat, glow.
chaloupe, *n.f.* launch.
chambre, *n.f.* room, chamber; House (parliament). c. à coucher, bedroom.
chameau, *n.m.* camel.
chamois, *n.m.* chamois.
champ, *n.m.* field.
champignon, *n.m.* mushroom.
champion, *n.m.* champion.
championnat, *n.m.* championship.
chance, *n.f.* luck, risk, chance.
chanceler, *vb.* stagger, reel.
chancelier, *n.m.* chancellor.
chandail, *n.m.* sweater.
chandelier, *n.m.* candlestick.
chandelle, *n.f.* candle.
change, *n.m.* exchange.
changeant, *adj.* changeable.
changement, *n.m.* change, shift.
changer, *vb.* alter, shift, change.
chanson, *n.f.* song.
chant, *n.m.* song, chant. c. du coq, cock-crow.
chantage, *n.m.* blackmail.
chanter, *vb.* sing, chant.
chanteur, *n.m.* singer.
chantier, *n.m.* (work)yard.

chaos (k-), *n.m.* chaos.
chaotique (k-), *adj.* chaotic.
chapeau, *n.m.* hat, bonnet.
chapelle, *n.f.* chapel.
chaperon, *n.m.* chaperon.
chapiteau, *n.m.* capital.
chapitre, *n.m.* chapter.
chapon, *n.m.* capon.
chaque, *adj.* every, each.
char, *n.m.* chariot. c. d'assaut, (military) tank.
charbon, *n.m.* coal. c. de bois, charcoal.
charge, *n.f.* load, charge.
charger, *vb.* load, burden, charge.
chariot, *n.m.* wagon; baggage cart.
charisme, *n.m.* charisma.
charitable, *adj.* charitable.
charité, *n.f.* charity.
charlatan, *n.m.* charlatan.
charmant, *adj.* delightful, lovely, charming.
charme, *n.m.* spell, charm.
charmer, *vb.* charm.
charnel, *adj.* carnal.
charnu, *adj.* fleshy.
charpente, *n.f.* framework.
charpentier, *n.m.* carpenter.
charretier, *n.m.* carter.
charrette, *n.f.* cart.
charrue, *n.f.* plow.
charte, *n.f.* charter.
chasse, *n.f.* hunt(ing), chase.
châsse, *n.f.* shrine.
chasser, *vb.* hunt, chase; drive away.
chasseur, *n.m.* hunter; bellboy.
châssis, *n.m.* (window) sash.
chaste, *adj.* chaste.
chasteté, *n.f.* chastity.
chat *m.*, chatte *f. n.* cat.
châtaigne, *n.f.* chestnut.
château, *n.m.* mansion, castle.
châtier, *vb.* punish, chastise.
chatouiller, *vb.* tickle.
chatouilleux, *adj.* ticklish.
chaud, *adj.* hot, warm.
chaudière, *n.f.* boiler.
chauffage, *n.m.* heating.
chauffer, *vb.* heat, warm.
chauffeur, *n.m.* driver, chauffeur.
chaumière, *n.f.* cottage.
chaussée, *n.f.* road.
chausser, *vb.* wear shoes. se c., put on shoes.
chaussette, *n.f.* sock.
chaussure, *n.f.* footgear.
chauve, *adj.* bald.
chauve-souris, *n.f.* bat.
chaux, *n.f.* lime.
chavirer, *vb.* capsize.
chef, *n.m.* leader, chief.
chef-d'œuvre (shě-), *n.m.* masterpiece.
chemin, *n.m.* road. c. de fer, railway. à mi-c., halfway. c. de table, table-runner.
chemineau, *n.m.* tramp.
cheminée, *n.f.* fireplace, chimney; funnel.
chemise, *n.f.* shirt. c. de nuit, nightgown.

chêne, n.m. oak.

chenille, n.f. caterpillar.

chèque, n.m. check.

chèque de voyage, n.m. traveler's check.

cher (-r), adj. dear, expensive.

chercher, vb. seek, look for, search. aller c., fetch.

chère, n.f. fare.

chéri, adj. and n.m. beloved, darling.

chérir, vb. cherish.

cheval, n.m. horse. à c., on horseback. monter à c., ride (horseback). fer à c., horseshoe.

chevaleresque, adj. chivalrous.

chevalerie, n.f. chivalry.

chevalet, n.m. easel; knight.

chevalier, n.m. knight.

cheveu, n.m., pl. cheveux, hair.

cheville, n.f. ankle; peg.

chèvre, n.f. goat.

chevreau, n.m. kid.

chevreuil, n.m. roe.

chevron, n.m. rafter.

chevroter, vb. quaver.

chevrotine, n.f. buckshot.

chez, prep. at . . .'s (house, office, shop, etc.).

chic, adj. stylish.

chien, n.m. dog.

chienne, n.f. bitch.

chiffon, n.m. rag.

chiffonner, vb. crumple.

chiffre, n.m. figure.

chiffrer, vb. figure.

Chili, n.m. Chile.

Chilien, n.m.Chilean.

chilien, adj. Chilean.

chimie, n.f. chemistry.

chimiothérapie, n.f. chemotherapy.

chimique, adj. chemical.

chimiste, n.m.f. chemist.

Chine, n.f. China.

Chinois, n.m. Chinese (person).

chinois, n. 1. n.m. Chinese (language). 2. adj. Chinese.

chiquenaude, n.f. flip.

chirurgie, n.f. surgery.

chirurgien, n.m. surgeon.

chloroforme (k-), n.m. chloroform.

choc, n.m. shock, clash, brunt.

chocolat, n.m. chocolate.

chœur (k-), n.m. choir, chorus.

choisir, vb. choose, select, pick.

choix, n.m. choice.

chômage, n.m. stoppage (of work).

choquer, vb. shock, clash.

choral (k-), adj. choral.

chose, n.f. thing, matter. quelque c., anything.

chou, n.m. cabbage.

chou-fleur, n.m. cauliflower.

choyer, vb. pamper.

chrétien (k-), adj. and n.m. Christian.

chrétienté (k-), n.f. Christendom.

christianisme (k-), n.m. Christianity.

chronique (k-), 1. n.f. chronicle. 2. adj. chronic.

chronologique (k-), adj. chronological.

chrysanthème (k-), n.m. chrysanthemum.

chuchoter, vb. whisper.

chute, n.f. fall, drop, downfall.

cible, n.f. target.

cicatrice, n.f. scar.

cidre, n.m. cider.

ciel, n.m., pl. cieux, heaven, sky.

cierge, n.m. (church) candle.

cigale, n.m. locust.

cigare, n.m. cigar.

cigarette, n.f. cigarette.

cigogne, n.f. stork.

ci-joint, adj. enclosed.

cil (-l), n.m. eyelash.

cime, n.f. top, summit.

ciment, n.m. cement.

cimenter, vb. cement.

cimetière, n.m. churchyard, cemetery.

cinéma, n.m. cinema.

cinglant, adj. scathing.

cinq (-k), adj. and n.m. five.

cinquante, adj. and n.m. fifty.

cinquième, adj. and n.m. fifth.

cintre, n.m. semicircle; arch.

circonférence, n.f. circumference.

circonscription, n.f. c. électorale, borough.

circonscrire, vb. circumscribe.

circonstance, n.f. event, circumstance. c. critique, emergency.

circuit, n.m. circuit. hors c., disconnected.

circulaire, adj. circular.

circulation, n.f. traffic, circulation.

circuler, vb. circulate, turn, revolve.

cire, n.f. wax.

cirer, vb. polish, shine.

cireur, n.m. bootblack.

cirque, n.m. circus.

cisailles, n.f.pl. shears.

ciseau, n.m. chisel; (pl.) scissors.

ciseler, vb. chisel.

citadelle, n.f. citadel.

citation, n.f. quotation, citation.

cité, n.f. city. droit de c., citizenship.

citer, vb. quote, cite.

citoyen, n.m. citizen.

citron, n.m. lemon. c. pressé, lemonade.

citrouille, n.f. pumpkin.

civil (-l), 1. n.m. civilian. 2. adj. civil.

civilisation, n.f. civilization.

civilisé, adj. civilized.

civiliser, vb. civilize.

civique, adj. civic.

clair, adj. clear, bright. c. de lune, moonlight.

clairière, n.f. glade, clearing.

clairon, n.m. bugle.

clameur, n.f. clamor, outcry.

clandestin, adj. clandestine.

clapoteux, adj. choppy (sea).

claque, n.f. slap.

claquement, n.m. smack.

claquer, vb. slap, smack, chatter (teeth), bang.

clarifier, vb. clarify.

clarinette, n.f. clarinet.

clarté, n.f. clarity; light.

classe, n.f. class.

classement, n.m. classification.

classer, vb. classify, order, file, grade.

classeur, n.m. file.

classification, n.f. classification.

classifier, vb. classify.

classique, adj. classic, classical.

clause, n.f. clause.

clavicule, n.f. collarbone.

clef (klä), clé, n.f. key.

clémence, n.f. clemency.

clément, adj. merciful.

clerc, n.m. clerk.

clergé, n.m. clergy.

clérical, adj. clerical.

cliché, n.m. cliché; snapshot.

client, n.m. customer, patron, client.

clientèle, n.f. customers, practice.

cligner (de l'œil), vb. wink.

clignoter, vb. blink, wink.

climat, n.m. climate.

climatisation, n.f. air-conditioning.

climatiser, vb. air-condition.

clin, n.m. c. d'œil, wink.

clinique, 1. n.f. clinic. 2. adj. clinical.

cloche, n.f. bell.

clocher, n.m. belfry. de c., parochial.

cloison, n.f. partition.

cloître, n.m. cloister, convent.

clôture, n.f. fence.

clou, n.m. nail.

clouer, vb. nail, tack.

club (-b), n.m. club.

coaguler, vb. coagulate.

coalition, n.f. coalition.

coasser, vb. croak (frogs).

cocaïne, n.f. cocaine.

cochon, n.m. pig.

coco, n.m. noix de c., coconut.

cocon, n.m. cocoon.

code, n.m. code; laws.

code postal, n.m. zip code.

cœur, n.m. heart.

coffre, n.m. bin; coffer.

cogner, vb. bump, strike, run into, knock (down).

cohérent, adj. coherent.

cohésion, n.f. cohesion.

coiffer, vb. dress (hair).

coiffeur, n.m. hairdresser, barber.

coiffure, n.f. hair-do.

coin, n.m. corner, wedge.

coïncidence (kō ăn-), n.f. coincidence.

coïncider (kō ăn-), vb. coincide.

col, n.m. collar; pass.

colère, n.f. anger, temper. en c., angry.

colimaçon, n.m. snail.

colis, n.m. parcel.

collaborateur, n.m. fellow-worker.

collaboration, n.f. assistance, collaboration.

collaborer, vb. work together, collaborate.

collant, n.m. panty hose.

collatéral, adj. and n.m. collateral.

colle, n.f. glue, paste.

collecte, n.f. collection.

collectif, adj. collective.

collection, n.f. collection.

collectionneur, n.m. collector.

collège, n.m. college.

collègue, n.m.f. colleague.

coller, vb. glue, paste, stick.

collier, n.m. necklace; collar (dog).

colline, n.f. hill.

collision, n.f. collision.

colombe, n.f. dove.

colon, n.m. settler, colonist.

colonel, n.m. colonel.

colonial, adj. colonial.

colonie, n.f. settlement, colony.

coloniser, vb. colonize.

colonne, n.f. column.

coloré, adj. colorful.

colorer, vb. color.

colossal, adj. huge, colossal.

colosse, n.m. giant, colossus.

colporter, n.m. peddle.

colporteur, n.m. peddler.

combat, n.m. fight, battle. hors de c., disabled.

combattant, adj. and n.m. combatant.

combattre, vb. fight.

combien (de), adv. how much, how many.

combinaison, n.f. combination, slip, B.V.D.'s.

combiner, vb. devise, combine.

comble, n.m. climax, top.

combler, vb. heap up, fill.

combustible, 1. n.m. fuel. 2. adj. combustible.

combustion, n.f. combustion.

comédie, n.f. comedy.

comédien, n.m. actor, comedian.

comestible, adj. edible.

comète, n.f. comet.

comique, adj. funny, comic(al).

comité, n.m. committee.

commandant, n.m. major, commander.

commande, n.f. order; commission.

commandement, n.m. command, commandment.

commander, vb. order, command.

commanditer, vb. finance.

comme, 1. adv. as, how. 2. prep. as, like. c. il faut, proper, decent.

commémoratif, adj. memorial.

commémorer, vb. commemorate.

commençant, n.m. beginner.

commencement, n.m. beginning, start.

commencer, vb. begin, start.

comment, adv. how.

commentaire, n.m. comment, commentary.

commentateur, n.m. commentator.

commenter, vb. comment on.

commerçant, n.m. trader.

commerce, n.m. trade, commerce.

commercer, vb. trade.

commercial, adj. commercial.

commettre, vb. commit.

commis, n.m. clerk.

commissaire, n.m. commissary, commissioner.

commission, n.f. errand, commission.

commode, 1. n.f. dresser, bureau. 2. adj. handy, convenient, comfortable.

commodité, n.f. convenience.

commun, adj. joint, common.

communauté, n.f. community.

commune, n.f. commune, town(ship).

communicatif, adj. communicative.

communication, n.f. communication.

communion, n.f. communion.

communiquer, vb. communicate.

communisme, n.m. communism.

communiste, adj. and n.m.f. communist.

compacité, n.f. compactness.

compact (-kt), adj. compact.

compagne, n.f. mate, companion.

compagnie, n.f. company.

compagnon, n.m. mate, fellow, companion.

comparable, adj. comparable.

comparaison, n.f. comparison.

comparaître, vb. appear.

comparatif, adj. and n.m. comparative.

comparer, vb. compare.

compartiment, n.m. compartment.

compas, n.m. compass.

compassion, n.f. sympathy, compassion.

compatible, adj. compatible.

compatissant, adj. sympathetic, compassionate.

compatriote, n.m.f. compatriot.

compensation, n.f. amends; compensation.

compenser, vb. compensate.

compétence, n.f. qualification, efficiency, competence.

compiler, vb. compile.

complaire, vb. please.

complaisance, n.f. kindness, compliance.

complaisant, adj. obliging, kind.

complément, n.m. object; complement.

complet, 1. n.m. suit. 2. adj. full, thorough, complete.

compléter, vb. complete.

complexe, adj. and n.m. complex.

complexité, n.f. complexity.

complication, n.f. complication.

complice, n.m.f. party to, accomplice.

compliqué, adj. intricate, involved, complicated.

compliquer, vb. complicate.

complot, n.m. plot.

comporter, vb. se c., act, behave.

composant, adj. and n.m. component.

composé, adj. and n.m. compound.

composer, vb. compound, compose.

compositeur, n.m. composer.

composition, n.f. essay, theme, composition.

compote, n.f. stewed fruit.

compréhensif, adj. comprehensive.

compréhension, n.f. comprehension.

comprendre, vb. understand, realize, comprise, include. c. mal, misunderstand.

compresse, n.f. compress.

compression, n.f. compression.

comprimer, vb. compress.

compromettre, vb. compromise.

compromis, n.m. compromise.

comptabilité, n.f. accounting, bookkeeping.

comptable, n.m. accountant.

compte, n.m. account, count. rendre c. de, account for. tenir c. de, allow for.

compter, vb. count, reckon, c. sur, rely on.

compteur, n.m. meter.

comptoir, n.m. counter.

comte, n.m. count.

comtesse, n.f. countess.

concave, adj. concave.

concéder, vb. grant, concede.

concentration, n.f. concentration.

concentrer, vb. condense, concentrate.

concept (-pt), n.m. concept.

conception, n.f. conception.

concernant, prep. concerning.

concerner, vb. concern.

concert, n.m. concert.

concession, n.f. grant, license, admission, concession.

concevable, adj. conceivable.

concevoir, vb. conceive, imagine.

concierge, n.m.f. janitor, doorkeeper, porter.

concile, n.m. council.

conciliation, n.f. conciliation.

concilier, *vb.* reconcile, conciliate.

concis, *adj.* concise.

concision, *n.f.* conciseness.

concluant, *adj.* conclusive.

conclure, *vb.* complete, conclude, infer.

conclusion, *n.f.* conclusion.

concombre, *n.m.* cucumber.

concourir, *vb.* concur, contribute, contend.

concours, *n.m.* contest.

concret, *adj.* concrete.

concurrence, *n.f.* competition.

concurrent, *n.m.* rival, competitor.

condamnation (-dä nä-), *n.f.* conviction, condemnation, sentence.

condamner (-dä nä), *vb.* convict, doom, condemn, sentence.

condensation, *n.f.* condensation.

condenser, *vb.* condense.

condescendance, *n.f.* condescension.

condescendre, *vb.* condescend.

condition, *n.f.* condition.

conditionnel, *adj.* and *n.m.* conditional.

conditionner, *vb.* condition.

condoléance, *n.f.* condolence. **faire ses c.s à**, condole with.

condominium, *n.m.* condominium.

conducteur, *n.m.* conductor.

conduire, *vb.* lead, take, drive, conduct. **se c.**, behave, act.

conduite, *n.f.* behavior, conduct.

cône, *n.m.* cone.

cône de charge *n.m.* warhead.

confection, *n.f.* making (e.g. clothes); ready-made garment.

confédération, *n.f.* confederacy, confederation.

confédéré, *adj.* and *n.m.* confederate.

conférence, *n.f.* lecture, talk, conference.

conférer, *vb.* confer, grant.

confesser, *vb.* confess, admit.

confesseur, *n.m.* confessor.

confession, *n.f.* denomination, confession.

confiance, *n.f.* trust, belief, confidence. **digne de c.**, dependable.

confiant, *adj.* confident.

confidence, *n.f.* confidence.

confident, *n.m.* confidant.

confidentiel, *adj.* confidential.

confier, *vb.* confide, entrust. **se c. à**, trust.

confiner, *vb.* confine, limit.

confirmation, *n.f.* confirmation.

confirmer, *vb.* confirm.

confiserie, *n.f.* confectionery.

confisquer, *vb.* confiscate.

confiture, *n.f.* jam, jelly.

conflit, *n.m.* conflict.

confondre, *vb.* confuse, confound.

conforme, *adj.* similar.

conformer, *vb.* conform. **se c. à**, comply with.

conformité, *n.f.* accordance.

confort, *n.m.* comfort.

confortable, *adj.* cozy, snug, comfortable.

confronter, *vb.* confront.

confus, *adj.* confused.

confusion, *n.f.* confusion.

congé, *n.m.* discharge; leave of absence.

congédier, *vb.* discharge, dismiss.

congélateur, *n.m.* freezer.

congeler, *vb.* congeal.

congestion, *n.f.* congestion.

conglomération, *n.f.* conglomeration.

congrès, *n.m.* congress, assembly, conference.

conjecture, *n.f.* guess, conjecture.

conjonction, *n.f.* conjunction.

conjugaison, *n.f.* conjugation.

conjuguer, *vb.* conjugate.

conjuration, *n.f.* conspiracy.

conjurer, *vb.* conspire, plot.

connaissance, *n.f.* knowledge, acquaintance. **sans c.**, unconscious. **faire la c. de**, meet.

connaisseur, *n.m.* connoisseur.

connaître, *vb.* be acquainted with, know.

connexion, *n.f.* connection.

conquérir, *vb.* conquer.

conquête, *n.f.* conquest.

consacrer, *vb.* consecrate, devote, dedicate, hallow.

conscience, *n.f.* conscience, consciousness.

consciencieux, *adj.* conscientious.

conscient, *adj.* conscious.

conscription, *n.f.* draft.

conscrit, *adj.* and *n.m.* conscript.

consécration, *n.f.* consecration.

consécutif, *adj.* consecutive.

conseil, *n.m.* advice, counsel; council, board; staff.

conseiller, **1.** *vb.* advise, counsel. **2.** *n.m.* advisor.

consentement, *n.m.* consent.

consentir, *vb.* consent, assent, accede.

conséquence, *n.f.* outgrowth, result, consequence.

conséquent, *adj.* consequent, consistent. **par c.**, consequently.

conservateur, *adj.* and *n.m.* conservative.

conservation, *n.f.* conservation.

conserve, *n.f.* conserve, pickle.

conserver, *vb.* conserve, keep; preserve, can.

considérable, *adj.* considerable.

considération, *n.f.* consideration.

considérer, *vb.* consider.

consigne, *n.m.* check-room; (*mil.*) orders.

consigne automatique, *n.f.* (luggage) locker.

consigner, *vb.* consign.

consistance, *n.f.* consistency.

consistant, *adj.* consistent.

consister, *vb.* consist.

consolateur, *n.m.* comforter.

consolation, *n.f.* comfort, solace.

console, *n.f.* bracket.

consoler, *vb.* comfort, console.

consolider, *vb.* consolidate, strengthen.

consommateur, *n.m.* consumer.

consommation, *n.f.* consumption; end, consummation.

consommé, *adj.* consummate.

consommer, *vb.* consummate, complete, consume.

consomption, *n.f.* consumption.

consonne, *n.f.* consonant.

conspirateur, *n.m.* conspirator.

conspiration, *n.f.* conspiration.

conspirer, *vb.* conspire.

constamment, *adv.* continually, constantly.

constance, *n.f.* constancy, firmness.

constant, *adj.* constant, firm.

constater, *vb.* observe, state as a fact.

constellation, *n.f.* constellation.

consternation, *n.f.* dismay.

consterné, *adj.* aghast.

consterner, *vb.* dismay.

constipation, *n.f.* constipation.

constituant, *adj.* constituent.

constituer, *vb.* constitute.

constitution, *n.f.* constitution.

constitutionnel, *adj.* constitutional.

constructeur, *n.m.* builder.

constructif, *adj.* constructive.

construction, *n.f.* construction.

construire, *vb.* construct, build.

consul, *n.m.* consul.

consulat, *n.m.* consulate.

consultation, *n.f.* consultation.

consulter, *vb.* consult.

consumer, *vb.* consume.

contact (-kt), *n.m.* touch, contact.

contagieux, *adj.* contagious.

contagion, *n.f.* contagion.

contaminer, *vb.* contaminate.

conte, *n.m.* tale, story.

contemplation, *n.f.* contemplation.

contempler, *vb.* survey, observe, contemplate.

contemporain, *adj.* contemporary.

contenance, *n.f.* compass, capacity.

contenir, *vb.* hold, restrain, contain.

content de, *adj.* glad of, contented with. **c. de soi-même**, complacent.

contentement, *n.m.* content-

(ment), satisfaction. **c. de soi-même,** complacency.

contenter, vb. please, satisfy.

contenu, n.m. contents.

conter, vb. tell.

contester, vb. challenge (dispute), object to, contest.

contexte, n.m. context.

contigu, adj. adjoining.

continent, n.m. continent.

continental, adj. continental.

contingent, n.m. quota.

continu, adj. continuous.

continuation, n.f. continuation, continuance.

continuel, adj. continual.

continuer, vb. carry on, keep on, go on, continue.

continuité, n.f. continuity.

contour, n.m. outline.

contourner, vb. go round.

contracter, vb. contract.

contraction, n.f. contraction.

contradiction, n.f. discrepancy, contradiction.

contradictoire, adj. contradictory.

contraindre, vb. coerce, force.

contrainte, n.f. compulsion.

contraire, 1. n.m. reverse. 2. adj. contrary. **au c.,** on the contrary.

contrarier, vb. thwart, vex, annoy, oppose, keep (from).

contrariété, n.f. annoyance.

contraste, n.m. contrast.

contraster, vb. contrast.

contrat, n.m. contract.

contre, prep. against.

contre-balancer, vb. counterbalance.

contrebande, n.f. smuggling; contraband.

contre-cœur, adv. à c., unwillingly.

contredire, vb. contradict.

contrée, n.f. district, province.

contrefaire, vb. forge, counterfeit.

contrefort, n.m. buttress.

contremaître, n.m. foreman.

contre-partie, n.f. counterpart.

contrepoids (-pwä), n.m. counterbalance.

contribuer, vb. contribute.

contribution, n.f. share, contribution; tax.

contrôle, n.m. check.

contrôle des naissances, n.m. birth control, contraception.

contrôler, vb. control, check.

contrôleur, n.m. checker, collector.

controverse, n.f. controversy.

convaincre, vb. convince.

convaincu, adj. positive.

convalescence, n.f. convalescence.

convenable, adj. becoming, appropriate, suitable, congenial.

convenance, n.f. convenience.

convenir à, vb. suit, fit, befit, agree.

convention, n.f. convention; contract.

conventionnel, adj. conventional.

converger, vb. converge.

conversation, n.f. talk, conversation.

converser, vb. talk, converse.

conversion, n.f. conversion, change.

convertir, vb. convert, transform.

convexe, adj. convex.

conviction, n.f. conviction.

convive, n.m. guest, companion.

convoi, n.m. convoy, funeral procession.

convoiter, vb. covet.

convoitise, n.f. covetousness.

convoquer, vb. summon, call.

convulsion, n.f. convulsion.

coopératif (kŏ ŏ-), adj. coöperative.

coopération (kŏ ŏ-), n.f. coöperation.

coopérative (kŏ ŏ-), n.f. coöperative.

coopérer (kŏ ŏ-), vb. coöperate.

coordonner (kŏ ŏr-), vb. coördinate.

copie, n.f. copy.

copier, vb. copy.

copieux, adj. copious.

coq (-k), n.m. rooster.

coque, n.f. œuf à la c., boiled egg.

coquille, n.f. shell.

coquin, adj. and n.m. rogue, rascal.

cor, n.m. horn; corn.

corail, n.m., pl. **coraux,** coral.

corbeau, n.m. raven, crow.

corbeille, n.f. basket.

corde, n.f. rope, string, cord.

cordial, adj. hearty, cordial.

cordon, n.m. rope.

cordonnier, n.m. shoemaker.

Corée, n.f. Korea.

corne, n.f. horn.

corneille, n.f. crow.

cornemuse, n.f. bagpipe.

cornichon, n.m. gherkin.

corporation, n.f. corporation.

corporel, adj. bodily.

corps, n.m. body.

corpulent, adj. burly.

corpuscule (-sk-), n.m. corpuscle.

correct (-kt), adj. right, correct.

correction, n.f. correction, correctness.

corrélation, n.f. correlation.

correspondance, n.f. (train) connection: similarity; correspondence.

correspondant, 1. n.m. correspondent. 2. adj. similar, corresponding.

correspondre, vb. correspond.

corriger, vb. mend, reclaim, correct.

corroborer, vb. corroborate.

corroder, vb. corrode.

corrompre, vb. bribe, corrupt.

corrompu, adj. corrupt.

corruption, n.f. bribery, graft, corruption.

corsage, n.m. bodice.

corset, n.m. corset.

cortège, n.m. procession.

cosmétique, adj. and n.m. cosmetic.

cosmopolite, adj. and n.m.f. cosmopolitan.

costume, n.m. attire, dress.

cote, n.f. quotation.

côte, n.f. rib; coast.

côté, n.f. side, way. **mettre de c.,** put to one side (save; discard). **à c. de,** beside.

côtelette, n.f. chop, cutlet.

coton, n.m. cotton.

cou, n.m. neck.

couche, n.f. layer, bed; stratum; diaper.

coucher, vb. put to bed. **se c.,** lie down; set.

couchette, n.f. bunk, berth.

coucou, n.m. cuckoo.

coude, n.m. elbow.

coudoyer, vb. jostle.

coudre, vb. sew, stitch.

couler, vb. flow, sink, run; cast (metal).

couleur, n.f. hue, color; suit (cards).

couloir, n.m. corridor.

coup, n.m. blow, stroke, hit, bump, knock, cast. **c. de feu,** discharge (gun). **c. d'œil,** glance, look. **c. de pied,** kick. **c. de poing,** punch.

coupable, adj. guilty, to blame.

coupe, n.f. cut; goblet. **c. de cheveux,** haircut.

couper, vb. cut.

couple, n.f. couple, pair.

coupler, vb. couple.

coupon, n.m. remnant; coupon.

coupure, n.f. cut, clipping.

cour, n.f. court(yard).

courage, n.m. bravery, pluck, courage.

courageux, adj. brave.

couramment, adv. fluently.

courant, 1. adj. current. **peu c.,** unusual. **au c.,** well informed. 2. n.m. stream, current. **c. d'air,** draft.

courbe, n.f. curve, sweep.

courber, vb. bend, curve.

courbure, n.f. curvature.

coureur, n.m. runner.

courir, vb. run.

couronne, n.f. crown, wreath.

couronnement, n.m. coronation.

couronner, vb. crown.

courrier, n.m. mail.

courroie, n.f. strap.

courroux, n.m. wrath.

cours, n.m. course.

course, n.f. race, errand.

court, adj. short.

courtepointe, n.f. quilt.

courtier, n.m. broker.

courtisan, *n.m.* courtier.
courtois, *adj.* courteous.
courtoisie, *n.f.* courtesy.
cousin, *n.m.* cousin.
coussin, *n.m.* cushion.
coussinet, *n.m.* bearing.
coût, *n.m.* cost.
couteau, *n.m.* knife.
coutellerie, *n.f.* cutlery.
coûter, *vb.* cost.
coûteux, *adj.* expensive, costly.
coutume, *n.f.* custom.
couture, *n.f.* seam. **haute couture,** high fashion.
couturière, *n.f.* dressmaker.
couvée, *n.f.* brood.
couvent, *n.m.* convent.
couver, *vb.* brood, hatch; smolder.
couvercle, *n.m.* lid, cover.
couvert, 1. *n.m.* cover. **2.** *adj.* covered, cloudy.
couverture, *n.f.* blanket, cover; *(pl.)* bedclothes.
couvrir, *vb.* cover.
crabe, *n.m.* crab.
crachat, *n.m.* spit.
cracher, *vb.* spit.
craie, *n.f.* chalk.
craindre, *vb.* fear.
crainte, *n.f.* fear, dread, awe.
craintif, *adj.* fearful, apprehensive.
cramoisi, *adj. and n.m.* crimson.
crampe, *n.f.* cramp.
crampon, *n.m.* cramp, cramp-iron.
cramponner, *vb.* **se c.,** cling.
crâne, *n.m.* skull.
crapaud, *n.m.* toad.
craquement, *n.m.* crack.
craquer, *vb.* crack.
cratère, *n.m.* crater.
cravate, *n.f.* necktie.
crayon, *n.m.* pencil.
créance, *n.f.* belief. **lettres de c.,** credentials.
créancier, *n.m.* creditor.
créateur *m.,* **créatrice** *f.* **1.** *adj.* creative. **2.** *n.* creator.
création, *n.f.* creation.
créature, *n.f.* creature.
crédit, *n.m.* credit.
credo, *n.m.* creed.
crédule, *adj.* credulous.
créer, *vb.* create.
crème, *n.f.* cream, custard.
crêpe, *n.f.* pancake; crepe.
crépuscule (-sk-), *n.m.* dusk.
crête, *n.f.* ridge, crest.
crétin, *n.m.* dunce.
cretonne, *n.f.* cretonne.
creuser, *vb.* dig.
creuset, *n.m.* crucible.
creux, *adj. and n.m.* hollow.
crevasse, *n.f.* crevice.
crever, *vb.* burst; die.
crevette, *n.f.* shrimp.
cri, *n.m.* cry, call.
crible, *n.m.* sieve.
crier, *vb.* yell, shout.
crime, *n.m.* crime.
criminel, *adj.* criminal.
crinière, *n.f.* mane.

crise, *n.f.* crisis.
cristal, *n.m.* crystal.
cristallin, *adj.* crystalline.
cristalliser, *vb.* crystallize.
critérium, *n.m.* criterion.
critique, 1. *n.m.* critic. **2.** *n.f.* criticism. **3.** *adj.* critical.
critiquer, *vb.* criticize.
croasser, *vb.* croak.
croc (-ò), *n.m.* hook.
croche, *n.f.* quaver (music).
crochet, *n.m.* bracket, hook.
crochu, *adj.* hooked.
crocodile, *n.m.* crocodile.
croire, *vb.* believe.
croisade, *n.f.* crusade.
croisé, *n.m.* crusader.
croiser, *vb.* cross.
croiseur, *n.m.* cruiser.
croisière, *n.f.* cruise.
croissance, *n.f.* growth.
croissant, *n.m.* crescent.
croître, *vb.* grow.
croix, *n.f.* cross.
croquant, *adj.* crisp.
croquet, *n.m.* croquet.
croquis, *n.m.* sketch.
crosse, *n.f.* (golf) club.
crotale, *n.m.* rattlesnake.
crouler, *vb.* fall apart.
croup, *n.m.* croup.
croupir, *vb.* wallow.
croûte, *n.f.* crust.
croûton, *n.m.* crouton.
croyable, *adj.* believable.
croyance, *n.f.* belief.
croyant, *n.m.* believer.
cru, *adj.* raw.
cruauté, *n.f.* cruelty.
cruche, *n.f.* pitcher.
crucifier, *vb.* crucify.
crucifix, *n.m.* crucifix.
cruel, *adj.* cruel.
cryochirurgie, *n.f.* cryosurgery.
Cuba, *n.m.* Cuba.
Cubain, *n.m.* Cuban.
cubain, *adj.* Cuban.
cube, *n.m.* cube.
cubique, *adj.* cubic.
cueillir, *vb.* pick.
cuiller, *n.f.* spoon. **c. à thé,** teaspoon. **c. à bouche,** tablespoon.
cuillerée, *n.f.* spoonful.
cuir, *n.m.* leather.
cuirassé, *n.m.* battleship.
cuire, *vb.* cook; sting, smart.
cuisine, *n.f.* kitchen, cooking.
cuisinier, *n.m.* cook.
cuisse, *n.f.* thigh.
cuivre, *n.m.* copper **c. jaune,** brass.
cul-de-sac, *n.m.* blind alley.
culotte, *n.f.* breeches.
culpabilité, *n.f.* guilt.
eulte, *n.m.* worship; cult.
cultiver, *vb.* cultivate; grow, raise.
culture, *n.f.* culture, cultivation; farming.
cure, *n.f.* cure.
curé, *n.m.* (parish) priest.
curieux, *adj.* curious.
curiosité, *n.f.* curiosity, curio.
cursif, *adj.* cursive.

cuticule, *n.f.* cuticle.
cuve, *n.f.* vat.
cuver, *vb.* ferment.
cuvette, *n.f.* (wash) basin.
cuvier, *n.m.* washtub.
cycle, *n.m.* cycle.
cycliste, *n.m.f.* cyclist.
cyclomoteur, *n.m.* moped.
cyclone, *n.m.* cyclone.
cygne, *n.m.* swan.
cylindre, *n.m.* cylinder.
cylindrique, *adj.* cylindrical.
cymbale, *n.f.* cymbal.
cynique, 1. *n.m.* cynic. **2.** *adj.* cynical.
cynisme, *n.m.* cynicism.
cyprès, *n.m.* cypress.
czar, *n.m.* czar.

D

dactylographe, *n.m.f.* typist.
daigner, *vb.* deign.
daim, *n.m.* buck.
daine, *n.f.* doe.
dais, *n.m.* canopy.
dalle, *n.f.* slab, flag(stone).
dame, *n.f.* lady.
damner (dä nä), *vb.* damn.
Danemark, *n.m.* Denmark.
danger, *n.m.* danger.
dangereux, *adj.* dangerous.
Danois, *n.m.* Dane.
danois, *adj. and n.m.* Danish.
dans, *prep.* in, into.
danse, *n.f.* dance.
danser, *vb.* dance.
danseur, *n.m.* dancer.
dard, *n.m.* dart.
date, *n.f.* date.
dater, *vb.* date.
datte, *n.f.* date.
davantage, *adv.* more, further.
de, *prep.* of, from, by, about; some.
dé, *n.m.* die; thimble.
débarquer, *vb.* land.
débarrasser, *vb.* rid.
débat, *n.m.* debate.
débattre, *vb.* canvass; debate.
débit, *n.m.* delivery (speech); sale; debit.
débiter, *vb.* sell (retail).
débiteur, *n.m.* debtor.
déblayer, *vb.* clear.
déborder, *vb.* overflow.
débourser, *vb.* disburse.
debout, *adv.* up. **être d.,** stand.
débris, *n.m.pl.* wreck, debris.
début, *n.m.* beginning, first appearance, debut.
débuter, *vb.* make one's first appearance; begin.
décadence, *n.f.* decay, decadence.
décafféiné, *adj.* decaffeinated.
décapiter, *vb.* behead.
décéder, *vb.* die.
décembre, *n.m.* December.
décence, *n.f.* decency.
décent, *adj.* decent.

déception, n.f. disappointment.

décerner, vb. award.

décès, n.m. death.

décevoir, vb. disappoint.

décharge, n.f. discharge.

décharger. vb. unload, discharge.

décharné, adj. gaunt.

déchausser, vb. take off shoes.

déchets (-à), n.m.pl. waste.

déchets nucléaires, n.m.pl. nuclear waste.

déchiffrer, vb. decipher.

déchirer, vb. tear, rend.

déchirure, n.f. tear, rent.

décibel, n.m. decibel.

décider, vb. prevail upon, decide.

décimal, adj. decimal.

décisif, adj. decisive.

décision, n.f. decision.

déclamer, vb. recite.

déclaration, n.f. statement, declaration.

déclarer, vb. state, declare.

déclin, n.m. ebb.

décliner, vb. decline.

décolorer, vb. bleach, fade.

décomposer, vb. spoil, decompose.

déconcerter, vb. baffle, disconcert, embarrass.

décongestionnant, adj. decongestant.

décontracté, adj. relaxed.

décoratif, adj. decorative.

décoration, n.f. decoration, trimming.

décorer, vb. decorate.

décors, n.m.pl. scenery.

découper, vb. carve (meat).

découragé, adj. despondent.

découragement, n.m. discouragement.

décourager, vb. dishearten, discourage.

découverte, n.f. discovery.

découvreur, n.m. discoverer.

découvrir, vb. uncover detect, discover.

décrépit, adj. decrepit.

décret, n.m. decree.

décréter, vb. enact.

décrire, vb. describe.

dédaigneux, adj. scornful.

dédain, n.m. scorn, disdain.

dedans, n.m. inside, within.

dédicace, n.f. dedication.

dédier, vb. dedicate.

déduction, n.f. deduction.

déduire, vb. infer, deduce, deduct.

défaire, vb. undo.

défaite, n.f. defeat.

défaut, n.m. flaw, fault, failure, lack. **à d. de,** for want of.

défectueux, adj. faulty, defective.

défendeur, n.m. defendant.

défendre, vb. forbid, defend.

défense, n.f. prohibition, plea, defense.

défenseur, n.m. advocate, defender.

défensif, adj. defensive.

déférer, vb. defer.

défi, n.m. challenge, defiance.

défiance, n.f. mistrust.

déficit (-t), n.m. deficit.

défier, vb. challenge, defy. **se d. de,** mistrust.

défigurer, vb. deface.

défiler, vb. march off.

défini, adj. definite.

définir, vb. define.

définitif, adj. final, definitive.

définition, n.f. definition.

déformer, vb. distort, deform.

défraîchi, adj. dingy.

défricher, vb. reclaim.

défunt, n.m. and adj. deceased.

dégagé, adj. breezy.

dégât, n.m. damage.

dégénérer, vb. degenerate.

dégoût, n.m. distaste, disgust.

dégoûtant, adj. foul, disgusting.

dégoûter, vb. disgust.

dégoutter, vb. drip.

dégradation, n.f. degradation.

dégrader, vb. degrade.

degré, n.m. degree, step.

déguisement, n.m. disguise.

déguiser, vb. disguise.

dehors, adv. (out)doors, outside. **en d. de,** apart from.

déifier, vb. deify.

déité, n.f. deity.

déjà, adv. already.

déjeter, vb. make unsymmetrical.

déjeuner, n.m. and vb. lunch, breakfast. **petit d.,** breakfast.

déjouer, vb. foil, thwart.

delà, adv. beyond. **au d. de,** over, past, beyond.

délabrement, n.m. decay.

délabrer, vb. ruin, wreck.

délacer, vb. unlace.

délai, n.m. delay.

délaissement, n.m. desertion.

délaisser, vb. desert.

délassement, n.m. relaxation.

délasser, vb. refresh.

délateur, n.m. informer.

délavé, adj. faded, pallid.

délayer, vb. dilute with water.

délectable, adj. delicious.

délectation, n.f. enjoyment.

délecter, vb. delight.

délégation, n.f. delegation.

délégué, n.m. delegate.

déléguer, vb. delegate.

délester, vb. relieve of ballast.

délétère, adj. harmful; offensive.

délibératif, adj. deliberative.

délibération, n.f. deliberation.

délibéré, adj. deliberate.

délibérer, vb. deliberate.

délicat, adj. dainty, delicate.

délicatesse, n.f. delicacy.

délices, n.f.pl. delight.

délicieux, adj. delicious.

délié, adj. slender; keen.

délier, vb. untie.

délimiter, vb. mark the limits of.

délinéer, vb. delineate.

délinquant, 1. n.m. delinquent, offender. **2.** adj. delinquent.

délirant, adj. delirious.

délire, n.m. frenzy.

délirer, vb. rave.

délit, n.m. offense, crime.

délivrance, n.f. rescue, deliverance.

délivrer, vb. rescue, set free, deliver.

déloger, vb. dislodge.

déloyal, adj. disloyal.

déloyauté, n.f. disloyalty.

déluge, n.m. deluge.

déluré, adj. clever, cute.

démagogue, n.m. demagogue.

demain, adv. tomorrow.

demande, n.f. application, request, inquiry, claim. **d. en mariage,** proposal.

demander, vb. ask, request. **se d.,** wonder.

demandeur, n.m. plaintiff.

démangeaison, n.f. itch.

démanger, vb. itch.

démanteler, vb. dismantle.

démarcation, n.f. demarcation.

démarche, n.f. walk, bearing; step.

démarrage, n.m. start.

démarrer, vb. unmoor; start off.

démarreur, n.m. (self-)starter.

démasquer, vb. unmask; expose, reveal.

démêler, vb. disentangle.

démembrement, n.m. dismemberment.

démembrer, vb. dismember.

déménagement, n.m. moving.

déménager, vb. move.

déménageur, n.m. furniture mover.

démence, n.f. insanity.

démener, vb. struggle.

dément, adj. insane.

démenti, n.m. denial.

démentir, vb. give the lie to.

démesuré, adj. measureless, immense.

démettre, vb. **se d. (de),** resign.

demeure, n.f. abode.

demeurer, vb. dwell.

demi, n.m. and adj. half.

demi-cercle, n.m. semicircle.

demi-dieu, n.m. demigod.

demi-frère, n.m. stepbrother.

demi-heure, n.f. half an hour.

démilitariser, vb. demilitarize.

demi-place, n.f. half price; half fare.

demi-saison, adj. between-season.

demi-sœur, n.f. stepsister.

demi-solde, n.f. half-pay.

démission, n.f. resignation.

démobilisation, n.f. demobilization.

démobiliser, vb. demobilize.

démocrate, n.m.f. democrat.

démocratie, n.f. democracy.

démocratique, adj. democratic.

démodé, adj. old-fashioned.

demoiselle, n.f. young lady. **d. d'honneur,** bridesmaid.

démolir, vb. demolish.
démolition, n.f. demolition.
démon, n.m. demon.
démonétiser, vb. demonetize.
démoniaque, adj. demonic.
démonstratif, adj. effusive, demonstrative.
démonstration, n.f. demonstration.
démonter, vb. unhorse; dismantle.
démontrable, adj. demonstrable.
démontrer, vb. demonstrate.
démoralisation, n.f. demoralization.
démoraliser, vb. demoralize.
démouler, vb. remove from a mold.
démuni, adj. short of, lacking.
dénationaliser, vb. denationalize.
dénaturer, vb. denature.
dénégation, n.f. denial.
dénigrer, vb. disparage.
dénivelé, adj. not level.
dénombrement, n.m. enumeration; census.
dénombrer, vb. count.
dénomination, n.f. denomination.
dénommer, vb. name.
dénoncer, vb. report, denounce.
dénonciation, n.f. denunciation.
dénoter, vb. denote.
dénouement, n.m. result, outcome.
dénouer, vb. untie.
denrée, n.f. ware, produce.
dense, adj. dense.
densité, n.f. density.
dent, n.f. tooth. **mal de d.s,** toothache. **brosse à d.s,** toothbrush.
dental, adj. dental.
denté, adj. cogged.
dentelle, n.f. lace.
dentifrice, n.m. tooth paste or powder.
dentiste, n.m. dentist.
dentition, n.f. dentition.
denture, n.f. set of natural teeth.
dénuder, vb. denude.
dénué, adj. destitute, bare.
dénuement, n.m. destitution.
dénuer, vb. divest.
dépannage, n.m. emergency repairs.
dépareillé, adj. odd (unmatched).
départ, n.m. departure.
département, n.m. department.
départir, vb. divide in shares.
dépasser, vb. outrun, pass.
dépayser, vb. bewilder, confuse.
dépêche, n.f. dispatch.
dépêcher, vb. **se d.,** hurry.
dépeindre, vb. portray.
dépendance, n.f. annex (to a building).
dépendant, adj. dependent.

dépendre, vb. depend.
dépens, n.m.pl. expenses.
dépense, n.f. expenditure, expense.
dépenser, vb. spend, expend.
dépérir, vb. waste away; decline.
dépiécer, vb. dismember.
dépit, n.m. spite. **en d. de,** despite.
déplacement, n.m. displacement.
déplacer, vb. displace, move, shift.
déplaire à, vb. displease.
déplaisant, adj. displeasing.
déplanter, vb. transplant.
déplantoir, n.m. trowel.
déplier, vb. unfold.
déploiement, n.m. deployment.
déplorable, adj. wretched, deplorable.
déplorer, vb. deplore.
déployer, vb. deploy.
déplumer, vb. pluck.
déportation, n.f. deportation.
déportements, n.m.pl. misconduct.
déporter, vb. deport.
déposant, n.m. depositor.
déposer, vb. deposit, set down, depose.
dépositaire, n.m.f. trustee.
déposséder, vb. oust; dispossess.
dépôt, n.m. deposit, depot. **d. de vivres,** commissary.
dépouille, n.f. hide, skin, pelt.
dépouiller, vb. strip. **se d. de,** shed.
dépourvu, adj. devoid; needy.
dépoussiéreur, n.m. vacuum cleaner.
dépravation, n.f. depravity.
dépraver, vb. deprave.
dépréciation, n.f. depreciation.
déprécier, vb. depreciate, cheapen.
déprédation, n.f. depredation.
dépression, n.f. depression.
déprimer, vb. depress.
depuis, adv. and prep. since. **d. que,** conj. since.
députation, n.f. delegation.
député, n.m. representative, deputy.
déraciner, vb. uproot, eradicate.
déraison, n.f. unreason.
déraisonnable, adj. unreasonable.
dérangement, n.m. disturbance.
déranger, vb. disturb, trouble.
derechef, adv. once again.
dérégler, vb. upset, disorder.
dérider, vb. smooth; cheer up.
dérision, n.f. derision. **tourner en d.,** deride.
dérivation, n.f. derivation, etymology.
dérive, n.f. drift. **à la d.,** adrift.
dériver, vb. derive; drift.
dernier, adj. last, latter.
dernièrement, adv. lately.

dérober, vb. rob. **se d.,** steal away.
dérouiller, vb. remove the rust from.
dérouler, vb. unroll, unfold.
déroute, n.f. rout.
dérouter, vb. mislead; confuse.
derrière, n.m., adv. and prep. behind.
derviche, n.m. dervish.
dès, prep. since. **d. que,** conj. as soon as.
désabuser, vb. disillusion.
désaccord, n.m. disagreement.
désaccoutumer, vb. break of a habit.
désaffecter, vb. put (church) to secular use.
désagréable, adj. nasty, distasteful.
désagrégation, n.f. disintegration.
désaligné, adj. out of alignment.
désaltérer, vb. quench (one's) thirst.
désappointement, n.m. disappointment.
désappointer, vb. disappoint.
désapprobation, n.f. disapproval.
désapprouver, vb. disapprove.
désarmement, n.m. disarmament.
désarmer, vb. disarm.
désarroi, n.m. disorder.
désastre, n.m. disaster.
désastreux, adj. disastrous.
désavantage, n.m. disadvantage.
désaveu, n.m. denial.
désavouer, vb. disown.
descendance, n.f. descent.
descendant, 1. n.m. offspring, descendant. **2.** adj. downward, descending.
descendre, vb. go down, come down, alight, descend.
descente, n.f. raid; descent.
descriptif, adj. descriptive.
description, n.f. description.
désembarquer, vb. disembark, unload.
désenchanter, vb. disenchant.
désenivrer, vb. sober up.
désert, n.m. wilderness, desert.
déserter, vb. desert.
déserteur, n.m. deserter.
désertion, n.f. desertion.
désespéré, adj. hopeless, forlorn, desperate.
désespérer, vb. despair.
désespoir, n.m. desperation, despair.
déshabiller, vb. undress.
déshériter, vb. disinherit.
déshonnête, adj. improper, indecent.
déshonneur, n.m. disgrace, dishonor.
déshonorant, adj. dishonorable.
déshonorer, vb. disgrace, dishonor.
déshydrater, vb. dehydrate.

désignation, n.f. nomination.
désigner, vb. appoint, nominate; point out; designate.
désillusion, n.f. disillusion.
désinfectant, n.m. disinfectant.
désinfecter, vb. disinfect, fumigate.
désinfection, n.f. disinfection.
désintégration, n.f. disintegration.
désintegrer, vb. disintegrate.
désintéressé, adj. unselfish.
désintéressement, n.m. unselfishness.
désir, n.m. desire, wish.
désirable, adj. desirable.
désirer, vb. desire, wish.
désireux, adj. desirous.
désistement, n.m. withdrawal.
désobéir à, vb. disobey.
désobéissance, n.f. disobedience.
désobéissant, adj. disobedient.
désœuvré, adj. idle.
désolation, n.f. desolation.
désolé, adj. disconsolate; desolate.
désoler, vb. desolate.
désordonné, adj. disorderly.
désordonner, vb. upset, confuse.
désordre, n.m. disorder.
désorganisation, n.f. disorganization.
désorganiser, vb. disorganize.
désormais, adv. henceforth.
despote, n.m. despot.
despotique, adj. despotic.
despotisme, n.m. despotism.
dessécher, vb. dry out, parch; drain.
dessein, n.m. plan, intent.
desserrer, vb. loosen.
dessert, n.m. dessert.
dessin, n.m. drawing, design, sketch.
dessinateur, n.m. designer.
dessiner, vb. draw, design. se d., loom.
dessous, n.m. underside. en d., au-d. de, beneath, underneath.
dessus, n.m. top. en d., au-d. de, above. d. de lit, bedspread.
destin, n.m. fate, destiny.
destinataire, n.m./f. addressee.
destination, n.f. destination. à d. de, bound for.
destinée, n.f. destiny.
destiner, vb. destine, intend.
destituer, vb. dismiss.
destructif, adj. destructive.
destruction, n.f. destruction.
désuet, adj. obsolete.
désuétude, n.f. disuse.
désunion, n.f. disunion.
désunir, vb. disconnect.
détaché, adj. loose.
détachement, n.m. detachment.
détacher, vb. detach. se d., stand out.
détail, n.m. item, particular, detail. au d., at retail.

détective, n.m. detective.
déteindre, vb. run (of colors).
détenir, vb. detain.
détente, n.f. 1. trigger. 2. (politics) détente.
détention, n.f. custody, detention.
détérioration, n.f. deterioration.
détériorer, vb. deteriorate.
détermination, n.f. determination.
déterminer, vb. determine, fix.
détestable, adj. detestable, hateful.
détester, vb. abhor, loathe, detest.
détonation, n.f. detonation.
détoner, vb. detonate.
détour, n.m. turn; detour.
détourné, adj. devious.
détourner, vb. turn away; divert; avert; embezzle.
détresse, n.f. trouble, distress.
détriment, n.m. detriment.
détroit, n.m. strait.
détruire, vb. destroy.
dette, n.f. debt.
deuil, n.m. mourning.
deux, adj. and n.m. two. tous les d., both.
deuxième, adj. second.
deux-points, n.m. colon.
dévaliser, vb. rob.
dévaliseur, n.m. robber.
devancer, vb. be ahead of.
devant, 1. n.m. front. 2. prep. before, in front of.
devanture, n.f. window, (shop) front.
dévastation, n. devastation.
dévaster, vb. devastate.
déveine, n.f. bad luck.
développement, n.m. development.
développer, vb. develop.
devenir, vb. become.
déverser, vb. divert.
dévêtir, vb. undress, disrobe.
déviation, n.f. deviation.
dévider, vb. unwind.
dévier, vb. turn away.
deviner, vb. guess.
devinette, n.f. puzzle, riddle.
devis, n.m. estimate.
devise, n.f. motto.
dévisser, vb. unscrew.
dévoiler, vb. unveil, disclose, reveal.
devoir, n.m. duty.
devoir, vb. owe; be supposed to; have to; (conditional) ought.
dévorer, vb. devour.
dévot, adj. devout.
dévotion, n.f. devotion.
dévoué, adj. devoted.
dévouement, n.m. devotion.
dévouer, vb. dedicate, devote.
dextérité, n.f. dexterity.
diabétique, adj. and n. diabetic.
diable, n.m. devil.
diablerie, n.f. mischief.
diabolique, adj. diabolic.
diacre, n.m. deacon.

diacritique, adj. diacritic.
diadème, n.m. diadem.
diagnostic, n.m. diagnosis.
diagnostiquer, vb. diagnose.
diagonal, adj. diagonal.
diagramme, n.m. diagram.
dialectal, adj. dialect.
dialecte, n.m. dialect.
dialogue, n.m. dialogue.
dialoguer, vb. converse, talk together.
diamant, n.m. diamond.
diamétral, adj. diametric.
diamètre, n.m. diameter.
diaphane, adj. diaphanous.
diaphragme, n.m. diaphragm.
diarrhée, n.f. diarrhea.
diathermie, n.f. diathermy.
diatribe, n.f. diatribe.
dictateur, n.m. dictator.
dictature, n.f. dictatorship.
dictée, n.f. dictation.
dicter, vb. dictate.
diction, n.f. diction.
dictionnaire, n.m. dictionary.
dicton, n.m. maxim, proverb.
didactique, adj. didactic.
dièse, n.f. and n.m. sharp.
diète, n.f. diet.
diététique, adj. dietetic.
Dieu, n.m. God.
diffamant, adj. libelous.
diffamateur, n.m. libeier.
diffamation, n.f. libel.
diffamer, vb. defame.
différence, n.f. difference.
différenciation, n.f. differentiation.
différencier, vb. differentiate.
différend, n.m. difference, dispute.
différent, adj. different.
différer, vb. defer; differ.
difficile, adj. arduous, hard; difficult; fastidious.
difficilement, adv. with difficulty.
difficulté, n.f. trouble; difficulty.
difficulté psychologique, n.f. hangup.
difforme, adj. deformed.
difformité, n.f. deformity.
diffus, adj. diffuse.
diffusion, n.f. spread, diffusion.
digérer, vb. digest.
digestible, adj. digestible.
digestif, adj. and n.m. digestive.
digestion, n.f. digestion.
digital, adj. digital.
digitaline, n.f. digitalis.
digne, adj. worthy.
dignitaire, n.m. dignitary.
dignité, n.f. dignity.
digression, n.f. digression.
digue, n.f. dike, dam.
dilapidation, n.f. waste.
dilater, vb. expand, dilate.
dilemme, n.m. dilemma.
dilettante, n.m. amateur.
diligence, n.f. diligence.
diligent, adj. diligent.
diluer, vb. dilute.

dilution, *n.f.* dilution.
dimanche, *n.m.* Sunday.
dimension, *n.f.* dimension.
diminuer, *vb.* lessen, decrease, diminish.
diminutif, *adj. and n.m.* diminutive.
diminution, *n.f.* decrease.
dindon, *n.m.* turkey.
dîner, 1. *n.m.* dinner. **2.** *vb.* dine.
dîneur, *n.m.* diner.
diphtérie, *n.f.* diphtheria.
diphtongue, *n.f.* diphthong.
diplomate, *n.m.* diplomat.
diplomatie, *n.f.* diplomacy.
diplomatique, *adj.* diplomatic.
diplôme, *n.m.* diploma.
dipsomane, *n.* dipsomaniac.
dipsomanie, *n.f.* dipsomania.
dire, *vb.* say, tell. **vouloir d.,** mean. **c'est-à-d.,** namely; that is.
direct, *adj.* direct.
directement, *adv.* directly.
directeur, *n.m.* manager, director.
directif, *adj.* guiding.
direction, *n.f.* management, leadership, direction.
directorate, *n.m.* directorate.
dirigeable, *adj. and n.m.* dirigible.
dirigeant, *adj.* ruling.
diriger, *vb.* manage, boss, steer, direct.
discernable, *adj.* barely visible.
discernement, *n.m.* discernment, judgment.
discerner, *vb.* discern.
disciple, *n.m.* follower, disciple.
disciplinaire, *adj.* disciplinary.
discipline, *n.f.* discipline.
discipliner, *vb.* discipline.
disco, *n.m.* disco.
discontinuer, *vb.* discontinue.
disconvenance, *n.f.* unsuitability.
discordance, *n.f.* discord.
discorde, *n.f.* discord.
discothèque, *n.f.* discotheque.
discourir, *vb.* speak one's views.
discours, *n.m.* speech, oration, talk, discourse.
discourtois, *adj.* discourteous.
discrédit, *n.m.* disrepute.
discréditer, *vb.* disparage.
discret, *adj.* discreet.
discrétion, *n.f.* discretion.
disculper, *vb.* exonerate.
discursif, *adj.* discursive.
discussion, *n.f.* argument, discussion.
discutable, *adj.* debatable.
discuter, *vb.* argue, debate, discuss.
disette, *n.f.* famine.
diseur, *n.m.* talker.
disgrâce, *n.f.* disgrace.
disgracier, *vb.* put out of favor.
disjoindre, *vb.* sever, disjoint.
dislocation, *n.f.* dislocation.
disloquer, *vb.* dislocate.

disparaître, *vb.* disappear.
disparate, *adj.* unlike; badly matched.
disparition, *n.f.* disappearance.
dispendieux, *adj.* expensive.
dispensaire, *n.m.* dispensary.
dispensation, *n.f.* dispensation.
dispense, *n.f.* military exemption.
dispenser, *vb.* dispense.
disperser, *vb.* scatter, disperse.
dispersion, *n.f.* dispersal.
disponible, *adj.* available.
disposé, *adj.* disposed. **d. d'avance,** predisposed. **peu d.,** reluctant.
disposer, *vb.* dispose, settle.
dispositif, *n.m.* device.
disposition, *n.f.* arrangement, disposal, disposition.
disproportionné, *adj.* disproportionate.
dispute, *n.f.* row, fight, quarrel, dispute.
disputer, *vb.* dispute. **se d.,** quarrel.
disqualifier, *vb.* disqualify.
disque, *n.m.* disk, record.
dissemblable, *adj.* unlike.
dissemblance, *n.f.* dissimilarity.
dissension, *n.f.* dissension.
dissentiment, *n.m.* dissent.
disséquer, *vb.* dissect.
dissertation, *n.f.* essay.
dissimulation, *n.f.* pretense.
dissimuler, *vb.* dissemble, pretend.
dissipation, *n.f.* dissipation.
dissiper, *vb.* dispel, waste, dissipate.
dissolu, *adj.* dissolute.
dissolution, *n.f.* dissolution.
dissoudre, *vb.* dissolve.
dissuader, *vb.* dissuade.
distance, *n.f.* distance.
distancer, *vb.* outdistance.
distant, *adj.* distant.
distillation (-l-), *n.f.* distillation.
distiller (-l-), *vb.* distill.
distillerie (-l-), *n.f.* distillery.
distinct (-kt), *adj.* distinct.
distinctif, *adj.* distinctive.
distinction, *n.f.* distinction.
distingué, *adj.* distinguished.
distinguer, *vb.* discriminate; make out; distinguish.
distraction, *n.f.* distraction, pastime.
distraire, *vb.* distract, amuse. **se d.,** have fun.
distrait, *adj.* absent-minded.
distribuer, *vb.* give out, deal out, distribute.
distributeur, *n.m.* distributor.
distribution, *n.f.* distribution; delivery; cast.
district (-trèk), *n.m.* district.
dit, *adj.* called.
divaguer, *vb.* ramble.
divan, *n.m.* davenport, couch.
divergence, *n.f.* divergence.
diverger, *vb.* diverge.
divers, *adj.* various.

diversion, *n.f.* diversion.
diversité, *n.f.* diversity.
divertir, *vb.* divert, entertain. **se d.,** enjoy oneself.
divertissement, *n.m.* diversion.
dividende, *n.m.* dividend.
divin, *adj.* divine.
divinateur, *n.m.* soothsayer.
divinité, *n.f.* divinity.
diviser, *vb.* part, divide.
divisible, *adj.* divisible.
division, *n.f.* division.
divorce, *n.m.* divorce.
divorcer, *vb.* divorce.
divulger, *vb.* divulge.
dix (-s), *adj. and n.m.* ten.
dix-huit (-z-), *adj. and n.m.* eighteen.
dix-huitième (-z-), *adj. and n.m.f.* eighteenth.
dixième (-z-), *adj. and n.m.* tenth.
dix-neuf (-z-), *adj. and n.m.* nineteen.
dix-sept (-s-), *adj. and n.m.* seventeen.
dizaine, *n.f.* (group of) ten.
docile, *adj.* docile.
docilité, *n.f.* docility.
docte, *adj.* learned, wise.
docteur, *n.m.* doctor.
doctorat, *n.m.* doctorate.
doctrine, *n.f.* doctrine.
document, *n.m.* document.
documenter, *vb.* document.
dodu, *adj.* plump.
dogmatique, *adj.* dogmatic.
dogma, *n.m.* dogma.
dogue, *n.m.* watchdog.
doigt (dwä), *n.m.* finger. **d. de pied,** toe.
doit, *n.m.* debit.
dollar, *n.m.* dollar.
domaine, *n.m.* domain, property.
dôme, *n.m.* dome.
domestique, 1. *n.m.f.* servant. **2.** *adj.* domestic.
domicile, *n.m.* residence.
dominant, *adj.* dominant.
domination, *n.f.* sway, domination, dominion.
dominer, *vb.* rule, dominate.
domino, *n.m.* domino.
dommage, *n.m.* injury, damage. **c'est d.,** that's too bad. **quel d.!,** what a pity!
dompter, *vb.* tame, subdue.
don, *n.m.* gift.
donateur, *n.m.* donor.
donation, *n.f.* donation.
donc (-k), *adv.* therefore.
donjon, *n.m.* dungeon.
donne, *n.f.* deal (cards).
donner, *vb.* give.
donneur, *n.m.* giver.
dont, *pron.* whose.
dorénavant, *adv.* hereafter.
dorer, *vb.* gild.
dorloter, *vb.* coddle.
dormant, *adj.* dormant; asleep.
dormir, *vb.* sleep.
dos, *n.m.* back.
dose, *n.f.* dose.

doser, vb. decide the amount.

dossier, n.m. record.

dot (-t), n.f. dowry.

doter, vb. endow.

douaire, n.m. dowry.

douane, n.f. customs, custom house.

douanier, n.m. customs officer.

double, adj. and n.m. double. **faire le d. de,** duplicate.

doubler, vb. double.

doublure, n.f. lining.

doucement, adv. gently.

doucereux, adj. sugary; oversweet.

douceur, n.f. sweetness, gentleness, meekness.

douche, n.f. shower bath; douche.

douer, vb. endow.

douille, n.f. socket.

douleur, n.f. pain, ache, sorrow, grief.

douloureux, adj. painful.

doute, n.m. doubt.

douter, vb. doubt. **se d. de,** suspect.

douteux, adj. dubious, doubtful, questionable.

douve, n.f. ditch.

doux, m., **douce** f. adj. soft, sweet, gentle, mild, meek.

douzaine, n.f. dozen.

douze, adj. and n.m. twelve.

douzième, adj. and n.m. twelfth.

doyen, n.m. dean.

dragon, n.m. dragon; dragoon.

draguer, vb. dredge.

drainage, n.m. drainage.

drainer, vb. drain.

dramatique, adj. dramatic.

dramatiser, vb. dramatize.

dramaturge, n.m. playwright.

drame, n.m. drama.

drap, n.m. sheet.

drapeau, n.m. flag.

draper, vb. drape.

draperie, n.f. drapery.

drapier, n.m. clothier.

dresser, vb. draw up.

dressoir, n.m. dresser.

drogue, n.f. drug.

droguer, vb. drug.

droit, 1. n.m. right; law; claim. **2.** adj. and adv. (up)right, straight, fair. **d. d'auteur,** copyright.

droite, n.f. right. **à d.,** (to the) right.

drôle, adj. funny.

du, m., **de la,** f., **des,** pl. prep. some, any.

dû m., **due** f. adj. due.

duc, n.m. duke.

duché, n.m. dukedom.

duchesse, n.f. duchess.

ductile, adj. ductile.

duel, n.m. duel.

duelliste, n.m. duellist.

dûment, adv. duly.

dune, n.f. dune.

duo, n.m. duet.

dupe, n.f. dupe.

duper, vb. trick.

duperie, n.f. trickery.

duplicité, n.f. duplicity.

dur, adj. hard, tough.

durabilité, n.f. durability.

durable, adj. lasting, durable.

durant, prep. during.

durcir, vb. harden.

durcissement, n.m. hardening.

durée, n.f. duration.

durement, adv. hard, harshly, strongly.

durer, vb. last.

dureté, n.f. hardness.

duvet, n.m. down.

duveté, adj. downy.

dynamique, adj. dynamic.

dynamite, n.f. dynamite.

dynamo, n.f. dynamo.

dynastie, n.f. dynasty.

dynastique, adj. dynastic.

dysenterie, n.f. dysentery.

dyslexie, n.f. dyslexia.

dyspepsie, n.f. dyspepsia.

E

eau, n.f. water. **faire e.,** leak.

eau-de-vie, n.f. brandy.

eau-forte, n.f. nitric acid.

ébahir, vb. amaze.

ébahissement, n.m. amazement.

ébarber, vb. trim, clip.

ébauche, n.f. outline.

ébaucher, vb. outline.

ébène, n.m. ebony.

ébénisterie, n.f. cabinet work.

éblouir, vb. dazzle.

éboulement, n.m. cave-in.

ébouriffer, vb. ruffle.

ébranler, vb. shake.

ébriété, n.f. drunkenness.

écaille, n.f. scale.

écarlate, adj. and n.f. scarlet.

écart, n.m. separation. **à l'é.,** aloof.

écarté, adj. isolated; lonely.

écartement, n.m. gap, separation.

écarter, vb. set aside.

ecclésiastique, adj. and n.m. ecclesiastic.

écervelé, adj. scatterbrained.

échafaud, n.m. scaffold.

échafaudage, n.m. scaffolding.

échancrer, vb. scallop, notch.

échange, n.m. exchange.

échangeable, adj. exchangeable.

échanger, vb. exchange.

échantillon, n.m. sample.

échappatoire, n.f. loophole.

échappement, n.m. exhaust.

échapper, vb. escape.

écharde, n.f. splinter.

écharpe, n.f. scarf, sling.

échasse, n.f. stilt.

échauder, vb. scald.

échauffer, vb. heat up.

échéance, n.f. maturity.

échecs (-shè), n.m.pl. chess.

échelle, n.f. ladder, scale.

échelon, n.m. step; echelon.

échevelé, adj. dishevelled.

échine, n.f. spine.

échiner, vb. work like a slave.

écho (-kō), n.m. echo.

échoir, vb. fall due.

échoppe, n.f. booth, stall.

échouer, vb. fail. **faire é.,** frustrate.

éclabousser, vb. splash.

éclair, n.m. flash.

éclairage, n.m. lighting.

éclaircie, n.f. clearing.

éclaircir, vb. clear up.

éclairer, vb. (en)lighten, light, clear up, clarify.

éclaireur, n.m. scout.

éclat, n.m. chip, splinter; burst; brilliance, radiance, glamour.

éclatant, adj. bursting; loud; brilliant.

éclatement (de pneu), n.m. blowout.

éclater, vb. burst out.

éclectique, adj. eclectic.

éclipse, n.f. eclipse.

éclipser, vb. eclipse.

éclore, vb. hatch, open, blossom.

écluse, n.f. lock.

écœurer, vb. disgust.

école, n.f. school.

écolier, n.m. schoolboy.

écologie, n.f. ecology.

écologique, adj. ecological.

écologiste, n.m. ecologist; environmentalist.

économe, adj. economical.

économie, n.f. economy. **é. politique,** economics.

économique, adj. economic(al).

économiser, vb. economize.

économiste, n.m. economist.

écope, n.f. ladle.

écoper, vb. ladle or bail out.

écorce, n.f. bark.

écorcher, vb. skin.

écorchure, n.f. gall.

Écossais, n.m. Scotchman, Scotsman.

écossais, adj. Scotch, Scottish.

Écosse, n.f. Scotland.

écot, n.m. share.

écouler, vb. drain. **s'é.,** flow, elapse.

écouter, vb. listen (to).

écouteur, n.m. listener.

écran, n.m. screen.

écraser, vb. crush.

écrémer, vb. skim.

écrevisse, n.f. crayfish.

écrier, vb. **s'é.,** exclaim.

écrin, n.m. case, box.

écrire, vb. write. **machine à é.,** typewriter.

écrit, adj. written.

écriteau, n.m. notice.

écritoire, n.f. inkstand.

écriture, n.f. writing, scripture.

écrivain, n.m. writer.

écrou, n.m. nut.

écrouler, vb. **s'é.,** fall to pieces.

écru, adj. natural.

écu, n.m. shield.

écuelle, *n.f.* bowl, dish.
écume, *n.f.* lather, foam.
écuménique, *adj.* ecumenical.
écureuil, *n.m.* squirrel.
écurie, *n.f.* stable.
écusson, *n.m.* escutcheon.
écuyer (-kwĕ-), *n.m.* squire.
édenté, *adj.* toothless.
édifice, *n.m.* building.
édifier, *vb.* build; edify.
édit, *n.m.* edict.
éditeur, *n.m.* publisher.
édition, *n.f.* edition.
éditorial, *adj.* editorial.
éducateur, *n.m.* educator.
éducation, *n.f.* breeding, education.
éduquer, *vb.* educate.
effacer, *vb.* erase, efface.
effectif, *adj.* effective, actual.
effectivement, *adv.* effectively.
effectuer, *vb.* effect.
efféminé, *adj.* effeminate.
effet, *n.m.* effect; (*pl.*) belongings. **en e.,** as a matter of fact, indeed.
efficace, *adj.* effective.
efficacité, *n.f.* efficacy.
effigie, *n.f.* effigy.
effleurer, *vb.* skim, graze.
effondrement, *n.m.* collapse.
effondrer, *vb.* s'e., collapse, sink.
efforcer, *vb.* s'e., endeavor, try hard.
effort, *n.m.* endeavor, strain, exertion, effort.
effrayant, *adj.* fearful.
effrayer, *vb.* frighten, scare, startle.
effréné, *adj.* unrestrained; frantic.
effroi, *n.m.* fright.
effronté, *adj.* brazen.
effronterie, *n.f.* effrontery.
effusion, *n.f.* shedding.
égal, *adj.* even, equal, same.
également, *adv.* equally.
égaler, *vb.* equal.
égaliser, *vb.* equalize.
égalité, *n.f.* equality, evenness.
égard, *n.m.* regard, consideration, esteem. **à l'é. de,** as for. **plein d'é.s,** considerate.
égaré, *adj.* astray.
égarement, *n.m.* aberration.
égarer, *vb.* mislay, bewilder. **s'é.,** go astray, get lost.
égayer, *vb.* cheer up.
église, *n.f.* church.
égoïsme, *n.m.* selfishness, egoism.
égoïste, *adj.* selfish.
égorger, *vb.* kill.
égotisme, *n.m.* egotism.
égout, *n.m.* sewer.
égoutter, *vb.* drain; drip.
égratignure, *n.f.* scratch.
Égypte, *n.m.* Egypt.
Égyptien, *n.m.* Egyptian.
égyptien, *adj.* Egyptian.
éhonté, *adj.* brazen, shameless.
élaboration, *n.f.* working out, elaboration; data processing.
élaborer, *vb.* draft, elaborate.

élan, *n.m.* elk; zest.
élancer, *vb.* s'é., dash.
élargir, *vb.* widen, increase, enlarge.
élasticité, *n.f.* elasticity.
élastique, *adj. and n.m.* elastic.
électeur, *n.m.* voter.
électif, *adj.* elective.
élection, *n.f.* election.
électoral, *adj.* electoral.
électricien, *n.m.* electrician.
électricité, *n.f.* electricity.
électrique, *adj.* electric, electrical.
électrocardiogramme, *n.m.* electrocardiogram.
électrocuter, *vb.* electrocute.
élégance, *n.f.* elegance.
élégant, *adj.* elegant, smart, stylish.
élégie, *n.f.* elegy.
élément, *n.m.* element.
élémentaire, *adj.* elementary.
éléphant, *n.m.* elephant.
élevage, *n.m.* breeding.
élévation, *n.f.* elevation.
élève, *n.m.f.* pupil.
élevé, *adj.* lofty.
élever, *vb.* raise. **s'é.,** arise, soar.
éleveur, *n.m.* breeder.
élider, *vb.* elide.
éligibilité, *n.f.* eligibility.
éligible, *adj.* eligible.
élimination, *n.f.* elimination.
éliminer, *vb.* eliminate.
élire, *vb.* elect.
élite, *n.f.* elite.
elle, *pron.f.* she, her; (*pl.*) they, them (*f.*).
elle-même, *pron.* herself.
éloge, *n.m.* praise.
éloigné, *adj.* remote.
éloignement, *n.m.* distance.
éloigner, *vb.* take away. **s'é.,** go away, recede.
éloquence, *n.f.* eloquence.
éloquent, *adj.* eloquent.
élu, *adj.* chosen.
éluder, *vb.* evade, elude.
émacié, *adj.* emaciated.
émail, *n.m.,* pl. **émaux,** enamel.
émancipation, *n.f.* emancipation.
émanciper, *vb.* emancipate.
émaner, *vb.* emanate.
emballer, *vb.* pack.
embarcation, *n.f.* craft.
embargo, *n.m.* embargo.
embarquer, *vb.* embark.
embarras, *n.m.* embarrassment, trouble, fix.
embarrassant, *adj.* embarassing, awkward.
embarrasser, *vb.* embarrass.
embaumé, *adj.* balmy.
embaumer, *vb.* perfume, embalm.
embellir, *vb.* beautify.
embêter, *vb.* bore, irritate.
emblème, *n.m.* emblem.
embolie, *n.f.* embolism.
embouchure, *n.f.* mouth.
embourber, *vb.* bog.

embranchement, *n.m.* junction.
embrasser, *vb.* embrace, kiss.
embrayage, *n.m.* clutch.
embrouillement, *n.m.* tangle, mix-up.
embrouiller, *vb.* perplex, entangle.
embrun, *n.m.* spray.
embuscade, *n.f.* ambush.
émeraude, *n.f.* emerald.
émerger, *vb.* emerge.
émerveiller, *vb.* astonish.
émettre, *vb.* emit, send forth, issue.
émeute, *n.f.* riot.
émietter, *vb.* crumble.
émigrant, *n.m.* emigrant.
émigration, *n.f.* emigration.
émigré, *n.m.* political exile.
émigrer, *vb.* (e)migrate.
éminemment, *adv.* eminently.
éminence, *n.f.* eminence.
éminent, *adj.* eminent.
émission, *n.f.* issue.
emmagasinage, *n.m.* storage.
emmagasiner, *vb.* store.
emmener, *vb.* take away.
émotif, *adj.* emotional.
émotion, *n.f.* emotion, feeling.
émotionnable, *adj.* emotional.
émotionner, *vb.* thrill.
émoussé, *adj.* blunt.
émouvant, *adj.* moving.
émouvoir, *vb.* move.
empaler, *vb.* impale.
empan, *n.m.* span.
emparer, *vb.* s'e. de, take possession of.
empêchement, *n.m.* prevention.
empêcher, *vb.* prevent, stop, hinder, inhibit.
empereur, *n.m.* emperor.
empêtrer, *vb.* entangle.
emphase, *n.f.* emphasis.
emphatique, *adj.* emphatic.
empiéter, *vb.* encroach, trespass.
empire, *n.m.* empire.
empirique, *adj.* empirical.
emplette, *n.f.* purchase. **faire des e.s,** shop.
emploi, *n.m.* employment, use; job.
employé, *n.m.* employee, clerk; (public) servant.
employer, *vb.* employ, use.
employeur, *n.m.* employer.
empois, *n.m.* starch.
empoisonné, *adj.* poisonous.
empoisonner, *vb.* poison.
emporter, *vb.* take away. **s'e.,** get angry.
empreinte, *n.f.* print, impression.
empressé, *adj.* solicitous.
empressement, *n.m.* eagerness.
empresser, *vb.* s'e., be eager.
emprise, *n.f.* expropriation.
emprisonnement, *n.m.* imprisonment.
emprisonner, *vb.* imprison.
emprunt, *n.m.* loan.
emprunter à, *vb.* borrow from.
emprunteur, *n.m.* borrower.

ému, *adj.* touched, stirred.

émule, *n.* rival, competitor.

en, 1. *prep.* in, into. **2.** *adv.* thence; of it; some, any.

encadrer, *vb.* frame.

en-cas, *n.m.* reserve.

enceinte, *adj.f.* pregnant.

encens, *n.m.* incense.

enchaîner, *vb.* chain.

enchantement, *n.m.* enchantment.

enchanter, *vb.* delight, charm, enchant.

enchère, *n.f.* bid. **vente aux e,s,** auction.

enclore, *vb.* fence in, enclose.

enclos, 1. *n.m.* enclosure, **2.** *adj.* shut in.

enclume, *n.f.* anvil.

encoche, *n.f.* notch.

encoller, *vb.* paste.

encombrant, *adj.* cumbersome.

encombré, *adj.* crowded.

encombrement, *n.m.* congestion.

encombrer, *vb.* crowd, clutter, block up.

encontre, *adv.* à l'e., toward, counter (to).

encore, *adv.* still, yet, again.

encourageant, *adj.* encouraging.

encouragement, *n.m.* encouragement.

encourager, *vb.* encourage, urge, promote.

encourir, *vb.* incur.

encre, *n.f.* ink.

encrier, *n.m.* inkwell.

encyclopédie, *n.f.* encyclopedia.

endetté, *adj.* indebted.

endiguer, *vb.* dam up.

endive, *n.f.* chicory.

endolori, *adj.* painful.

endommager, *vb.* damage.

endormi, *adj.* asleep.

endormir, *vb.* put to sleep. **s'e.,** go to sleep.

endossement, *n.m.* endorsement.

endosser, *vb.* endorse.

endroit, *n.m.* place.

enduire, *vb.* smear, daub.

endurance, *n.f.* endurance.

endurant, *adj.* patient.

endurcir, *vb.* harden.

endurcissement, *n.m.* hardening.

énergie, *n.f.* energy.

énergique, *adj.* energetic.

énervant, *adj.* enervating.

énervé, *adj.* nervous.

enfance, *n.f.* childhood. **première e.,** infancy.

enfant, *n.m.f.* child.

enfantement, *n.m.* childbirth.

enfanter, *vb.* bear (children).

enfantillage, *n.m.* childishness.

enfantin, *adj.* childish.

enfariner, *vb.* coat with flour.

enfer (-r), *n.m.* hell.

enfermer, *vb.* shut in.

enfiévrer, *vb.* excite, inspire.

enfin, *adv.* finally, at last.

enflammer, *vb.* inflame.

enfler, *vb.* swell.

enflure, *n.f.* swelling.

enfoncer, *vb.* sink.

enfouir, *vb.* bury.

enfourchure, *n.f.* bifurcation; crotch of a tree.

enfreindre, *vb.* violate.

enfuir, *vb.* s'e., run away, flee, elope.

enfumer, *vb.* fill or cover with smoke.

engageant, *adj.* personable, charming.

engagement, *n.m.* pledge, agreement, engagement.

engager, *vb.* hire, engage. **s'e.,** volunteer.

engelure, *n.f.* chilblain.

engendrer, *vb.* beget.

engin, *n.m.* machine; engine, motor.

englober, *vb.* include.

engloutir, *vb.* devour.

engorgement, *n.m.* choking.

engouement, *n.m.* infatuation.

engouffrer, *vb.* engulf.

engourdir, *vb.* dull.

engrais, *n.m.* fertilizer.

engraisser, *vb.* fatten.

engraver, *vb.* strand or ground (a ship).

engrenage, *n.m.* gear.

engrener, *vb.* engage (gears).

enhardir, *vb.* make bolder.

énigmatique, *adj.* enigmatic.

énigme, *n.f.* riddle, puzzle, enigma.

enivrant, *adj.* intoxicating.

enivrement, *n.m.* intoxication.

enivrer, *vb.* intoxicate. **s'e.,** get drunk.

enjambée, *n.f.* stride.

enjamber, *vb.* stride.

enjeu, *n.m.* stake.

enjoindre, *vb.* enjoin; call upon.

enjôlement, *n.m.* cajolery.

enjôler, *vb.* cajole.

enjoliver, *vb.* beautify.

enjoué, *adj.* playful.

enjouement, *n.m.* playfulness.

enlacer, *vb.* entwine; interlace; embrace.

enlaidir, *vb.* make or become ugly.

enlevable, *adj.* detachable.

enlèvement, *n.m.* removal, abduction.

enlever, *vb.* take away, remove, abduct.

enneigé, *adj.* snow-covered.

ennemi, *adj. and n.m.* enemy.

ennoblir, *vb.* exalt; ennoble.

ennui (-nwè), *n.m.* nuisance, bore, bother; boredom.

ennuyer, *vb.* bore, annoy, vex, bother, irk.

ennuyeux, *adj.* boring, tedious, dull.

énoncer, *vb.* enunciate.

énonciation, *n.f.* enunciation.

énorme, *adj.* enormous.

énormité, *n.f.* enormity.

enquérir, *vb.* inquire.

enquête, *n.f.* inquiry.

enraciner, *vb.* root. **s'e.,** take root.

enragé, *adj.* rabid.

enrageant, *adj.* infuriating.

enrager, *vb.* be, go mad. **s'e.,** get angry.

enregistrement, *n.m.* registration, recording; checking.

enregistrer, *vb.* record, register, list; check (luggage).

enrichir, *vb.* enrich.

enrober, *vb.* coat, envelop.

enrôlement, *n.m.* enlistment, enrollment.

enrôler, *vb.* enlist, enroll.

enroué, *adj.* hoarse.

enrouement, *n.m.* hoarseness.

enrouler, *vb.* s'e., roll up, twist, wind.

enseigne, *n.f.* sign, ensign.

enseignement, *n.m.* teaching, instruction.

enseigner, *vb.* teach.

ensemble, 1. *n.m.* set. **2.** *adv.* together.

ensevelir, *vb.* bury.

ensoleillé, *adj.* sunny.

ensommeillé, *adj.* sleepy.

ensuite, *adv.* then, next, afterwards.

ensuivre, *vb.* s'e., ensue.

entablement, *n.m.* entablature.

entacher, *vb.* taint, besmirch.

entailler, *vb.* hack (notch).

entamer, *vb.* begin.

entassement, *n.m.* accumulation.

entasser, *vb.* heap up.

ente, *n.f.* scion (horticulture).

entendement, *n.m.* understanding, sense.

entendre, *vb.* hear, understand. **s'e.,** get on together.

entendu, *adj.* understood, agreed. **bien e.,** of course.

enténébré, *adj.* gloomy.

entente, *n.f.* understanding, agreement.

enterrement, *n.m.* burial.

enterrer, *vb.* bury.

entêté, *adj.* perverse.

entêtement, *n.m.* stubbornness.

entêter, *vb.* s'e., be stubborn, insist.

enthousiasme, *n.m.* enthusiasm.

enthousiaste, 1. *n.m.f.* enthusiast. **2.** *adj.* enthusiastic. **e. de,** keen on.

entichement, *n.m.* infatuation.

entier, *adj.* whole, complete, entire.

entité, *n.f.* entity.

entonnoir, *n.m.* funnel.

entorse, *n.f.* sprain.

entourage, *n.m.* circle of friends; surroundings.

entourer, *vb.* surround, encircle.

entournure, *n.f.* armhole.

entr'acte, *n.m.* intermission.

entr'aide, *n.f.* mutual assistance.

entrailles, *n.f.pl.* bowels.
entrain, *n.m.* zest.
entraîner, *prep.* draw along; involve, entail; coach, train.
entraîneur, *n.m.* coach.
entrant, *adj.* incoming.
entraver, *vb.* clog.
entre, *prep.* among, between.
entre-clos, *adj.* ajar.
entre-deux, *n.m.* interval.
entrée, *n.f.* admission, entry; main course.
entreface, *n.f.* interface.
entregent, *n.m.* tact; spirit.
entrelacer, *vb.* interlace.
entremets (-mě), *n.m.* (side) dish.
entremetteur, *n.m.* intermediary.
entreposer, *vb.* store.
entreposeur, *n.m.* warehouse-man.
entrepôt, *n.m.* warehouse.
entreprenant, *adj.* enterprising.
entreprendre, *vb.* undertake.
entrepreneur, *n.m.* contractor. **e. de pompes funèbres**, undertaker.
entreprise, *n.f.* concern, undertaking.
entrer (dans), *vb.* enter, come in, go in. **laisser e.**, admit.
entretenir, *vb.* entertain. **s'e.**, converse.
entretien, *n.m.* maintenance; conference; talk, conversation.
entrevoir, *vb.* glimpse.
entrevue, *n.f.* interview.
entr'ouvert, *adj.* ajar.
entr'ouvrir, *vb.* open halfway.
énumération, *n.f.* enumeration.
énumérer, *vb.* enumerate.
envahir, *vb.* invade.
envahissement, *n.m.* invasion.
enveloppe, *n.f.* envelope, wrapping.
envelopper, *vb.* envelop, wrap, enfold.
envers, **1.** *n.m.* wrong side. **2.** *prep.* toward.
enviable, *adj.* enviable.
envie, *n.f.* envy, desire. **avoir e. de**, want to, feel like.
envier, *vb.* envy.
envieux, *adj.* envious.
environ, *prep. and adv.* around, about; approximately.
environnement, *n.m.* surroundings.
environnementaliste, *n.m.* environmentalist.
environner, *vb.* surround.
envisager, *vb.* consider.
envoi, *n.m.* shipment, sending.
envoler, *vb.* **s'e.**, fly away.
envoyé, *n.m.* envoy.
envoyer, *vb.* send.
enzyme, *n.f.* enzyme.
éon, *n.m.* eon.
épais, *adj.* thick.
épaisseur, *n.f.* thickness.
épaissir, *vb.* thicken.
épancher, *vb.* shed (blood).
épanouir, *vb.* **s'é.**, bloom.

épargne, *n.f.* savings.
épargner, *vb.* save, spare.
éparpiller, *vb.* scatter.
épars, *adj.* scattered, sparse.
éparvin, *n.m.* spavin.
épatant, *adj.* (colloq.) grand.
épate, *n.f.* swagger.
épatement, *n.m.* amazement.
épater, *vb.* amaze.
épaule, *n.f.* shoulder.
épaulette, *n.f.* epaulette.
épée, *n.f.* sword.
épeler, *vb.* spell.
épellation, *n.f.* spelling.
éperdu, *adj.* distracted.
éperlan, *n.m.* smelt.
éperon, *n.m.* spur.
éperonner, *vb.* spur.
épervier, *n.m.* hawk.
épeuré, *adj.* frightened.
éphémère, *adj.* ephemeral, fleeting.
épice, *n.f.* spice.
épicé, *adj.* spicy.
épicerie, *n.f.* grocery.
épicier, *n.m.* grocer.
épidémie, *n.f.* epidemic.
épiderme, *n.m.* epidermis.
épidermique, *adj.* epidermal.
épier, *vb.* spy.
épigramme, *n.f.* epigram.
épilatoire, *n.m. and adj.* depilatory.
épilepsie, *n.f.* epilepsy.
épileptique, *adj. and n.* epileptic.
épilogue, *n.m.* epilogue.
épinards (-nar), *n.m.pl.* spinach.
épine, *n.f.* spine, thorn. **é. dorsale**, spinal column.
épinet, *n.m.* spinet.
épineux, *adj.* thorny.
épingle, *n.f.* pin. **é. à cheveux**, hairpin. **é. anglaise**, safety pin.
épingler, *vb.* pin.
épique, *adj.* epic.
épiscopal, *adj.* Episcopal.
épisode, *n.m.* episode.
épisodique, *adj.* episodic.
épistolaire, *adj.* epistolary.
épitaphe, *n.f.* epitaph.
épithète, *n.f.* epithet.
épitomé, *n.m.* epitome.
épître, *n.f.* epistle.
éploré, *adj.* tearful.
épointé, *adj.* dull, blunted.
éponge, *n.f.* sponge.
éponger, *vb.* sponge up.
épopée, *n.f.* epic.
époque, *n.f.* epoch.
épouffé, *adj.* breathless, panting.
épouiller, *vb.* delouse.
épouse, *n.f.* wife.
épouser, *vb.* marry.
épouseur, *n.m.* suitor.
épousseter, *vb.* dust.
époussette, *n.f.* duster.
épouvantable, *adj.* terrible.
épouvante, *n.f.* fright.
épouvanter, *vb.* frighten.
époux, *n.m.* husband.
épreindre, *vb.* squeeze.

éprendre, *vb.* **s'é.**, fall in love.
épreuve, *n.f.* trial, test, ordeal, proof.
éprouver, *vb.* experience.
éprouvette, *n.f.* test tube.
épuisant, *adj.* exhausting.
épuisement, *n.m.* exhaustion.
épuiser, *vb.* exhaust.
épuration, *n.f.* purification.
épurer, *vb.* purify.
équanimité (-kwà-), *n.f.* equanimity.
équateur (-kwà-), *n.m.* equator.
équation (-kwà-), *n.f.* equation.
équatorial (-kwà-), *adj.* equatorial.
équestre, *adj.* equestrian.
équidistant, *adj.* equidistant.
équilibre, *n.m.* poise.
équilibrer, *vb.* balance.
équilibriste, *n.* tight-rope walker.
équinoxe, *n.m.* equinox.
équinoxial, *adj.* equinoctial.
équipage, *n.m.* crew.
équipe, *n.f.* team, crew, gang, shift.
équipement, *n.m.* equipment.
équiper, *vb.* equip.
équitable, *adj.* fair.
équité, *n.f.* equity.
équivalent, *adj. and n.m.* equivalent.
équivaloir, *vb.* equal in value.
équivoque, *adj.* equivocal.
érable, *n.m.* maple.
éradication, *n.f.* eradication.
éraflure, *n.m.* scratch; graze.
érailler, *vb.* unravel.
ère, *n.f.* era.
érection, *n.f.* erection; construction.
éreintant, *adj.* exhausting.
éreinter, *vb.* exhaust.
erg, *n.m.* erg.
ériger, *vb.* erect.
ermitage, *n.m.* hermitage.
ermite, *n.m.* hermit.
éroder, *vb.* erode.
érosif, *adj.* erosive.
érosion, *n.f.* erosion.
érotique, *adj.* erotic.
errant, *adj.* wandering.
erratique, *adj.* erratic.
errer, *vb.* wander; err.
erreur, *n.f.* mistake, error.
erroné, *adj.* erroneous.
éructation, *n.f.* belch.
éructer, *vb.* belch.
érudit, *adj.* learned, scholarly.
érudition, *n.f.* learning.
éruption, *n.f.* rash, eruption.
érysipèle, *n.m.* erysipelas.
escabeau, *n.m.* stool.
escadrille, *n.f.* (ships) flotilla; (airplanes) squadron.
escadron, *n.m.* squadron.
escalader, *vb.* scale; escalate.
escalier, *n.m.* stairs.
escalope, *n.f.* cutlet.
escamotage, *n.m.* legerdemain.
escamoteur, *n.m.* conjurer, magician.
escapade, *n.f.* escapade.
escarcelle, *n.f.* wallet.

escargot, n.m. snail.
escarole, n.f. endive.
escarpé, adj. abrupt.
escarpement, n.m. steepness.
eschare, n.f. scab; bedsore.
esclandre, n.m. slander.
esclavage, n.m. slavery.
esclave, n.m.f. slave.
escompte, n.m. discount.
escorte, n.f. escort.
escorter, vb. escort.
escouade, n.f. squad.
escrime, n.f. fencing.
escrimer, vb. fight.
escrimeur, n.m. swordsman.
escroc (-ô), n.m. swindler.
escroquer, vb. swindle.
escroquerie, n.f. swindle.
esculent, adj. esculent.
espace, n.m. space.
espacé, adj. at great intervals.
espacer, vb. space out.
espadon, n.m. swordfish.
Espagne, n.f. Spain.
Espagnol, n.m. Spaniard.
espagnol, adj. and n.m. Spanish.
espalier, n.m. espalier.
espèce, n.f. species, kind; (pl.)
cash.
espérance, n.f. hope.
espéranto, n.m. Esperanto.
espérer, vb. hope.
espiègle, adj. mischievous.
espièglerie, n.f. mischief.
espion, n.m. spy.
espionnage, n.m. espionage.
espionner, vb. spy on.
esplanade, n.f. esplanade.
espoir, n.m. hope.
esprit, n.m. spirit, mind, wit.
Saint-E., Holy Ghost.
esquif, n.m. skiff.
Esquimau n.m., Esquimaude
f.n. Eskimo.
esquimau, adj. Eskimo.
esquinancie, n.f. quinsy.
esquinter, vb. exhaust, tire out.
esquisse, n.f. sketch.
esquisser, vb. sketch.
esquiver, vb. shirk.
essai, n.m. essay, attempt; experiment; assay.
essaim, n.m. swarm.
essaimer, vb. swarm.
essayer, vb. try; assay.
essence, n.f. gasoline; essence.
essentiel, adj. essential.
esseulement, n.m. solitude.
essieu, n.m. axle.
essor, n.m. flight.
essorer, vb. dry.
essoufflé, adj. breathless.
essoufflement, n.m. breathless-
ness.
essuie-glace, n.m. windshield
wiper.
essuyer, vb. wipe.
est (-t), n.m. east.
estacade, n.f. stockade.
estafette, n.m. courier.
estafier, n.m. bodyguard.
estagnon, n.m. oil drum.
estaminet, n.m. bar, taproom.
estampe, n.f. engraving.

estampille, n.f. trademark.
esthète, n.m. esthete.
esthétique, adj. aesthetic.
estimable, adj. estimable.
estimateur, n.m. estimator; appraiser.
estimatif, adj. estimated.
estimation, n.f. estimate.
estime, n.f. esteem; estimation.
estimer, vb. esteem; estimate,
value, rate.
estival, adj. of summer.
estivant, n.m. summer tourist.
estiver, vb. spend the summer.
estoc, n.m. tree trunk.
estomac (mä), n.m. stomach.
estourbir, vb. kill.
estrade, n.f. platform; stage.
estropié, 1. n.m. cripple. 2. adj.
crippled.
estropier, vb. cripple.
estuaire, n.m. estuary.
esturgeon, n.m. sturgeon.
et, conj. and.
étable, n.f. barn.
établi, n.m. worktable.
établir, vb. settle, establish.
établissement, n.m. establishment.
étage, n.m. floor, story.
étagère, n.f. whatnot shelf.
étain, n.m. tin.
étal, n.m. butcher shop.
étalage, n.m. display.
étalager, vb. display.
étaler, vb. display, spread.
étalon, n.m. standard.
étameur, n.m. tinsmith.
étamine, n.f. coarse muslin;
stamen.
étampe, n.f. stamp.
étamper, vb. stamp.
étanche, adj. impervious.
étancher, vb. quench, stanch.
étang, n.m. pond.
étape, n.m. stage.
état, n.m. state.
état-major, n.m. staff.
États-Unis, n.m.pl. United
States.
été, n.m. summer.
éteindre, vb. extinguish, put
out.
éteint, adj. extinct.
étendage, n.m. clotheslines.
étendard, n.m. standard.
étendre, vb. extend, spread,
reach.
étendu, adj. extensive.
étendue, n.f. extent.
éternel, adj. everlasting.
éterniser, vb. perpetuate.
éternité, n.f. eternity.
éternuement, n.m. sneeze.
éternuer, vb. sneeze.
éther (-r), n.m. ether.
éthéré, adj. ethereal.
Éthiopie, n.f. Ethiopia.
éthique, n.f. ethics.
ethnique, adj. ethnic.
étinceler, vb. sparkle.
étincelle, n.f. spark, sparkle.
étincellement, n.m. sparkle,
glitter.
étiolement, n.m. atrophy.

étioler, vb. blanch.
étiqueter, vb. label.
étiquette, n.f. label, tag; etiquette.
étirer, vb. stretch out.
étoffe, n.f. stuff, material,
cloth.
étoffer, vb. stuff.
étoile, n.f. star.
étoiler, vb. bespangle.
étonnement, n.m. astonishment.
étonner, vb. astonish.
étouffé, adj. braised.
étouffer, vb. smother.
étourdi, adj. thoughtless.
étourdir, vb. daze.
étourdissant, adj. dazing.
étourdissement, n.m. dizziness.
étrange, adj. strange.
étranger, n. and adj. alien.
étranglement, n.m. strangula-
tion.
étrangler, vb. strangle.
étrave, n.f. stem, bow.
être, 1. n.m. being. 2. vb. be.
étrécir, vb. shrink.
étreindre, vb. clasp.
étreinte, n.f. clasp, hug, embrace.
étrier, n.m. stirrup.
étrille, n.f. currycomb.
étroit, adj. narrow.
Étrusque, n.m.f. Etruscan.
étrusque, adj. Etruscan.
étude, n.f. study.
étudiant, n.m. student.
étudier, vb. study.
étui, n.m. 1. case. 2. needle
case.
étuve, n.f. steam room.
étymologie, n.f. etymology.
étymologique, adj. etymologi-
cal.
eucalyptus, n.m. eucalyptus.
eucharistie, n.f. eucharist.
eunuque, n.m. eunuch.
euphémique, adj. euphemistic.
euphémisme, n.m. euphemism.
euphonie, n.f. euphony.
euphonique, adj. euphonic.
euphorie, n.f. euphoria.
Europe, n.f. Europe.
Européen, n.m. European.
européen, adj. European.
euthanasie, n.f. euthanasia.
eux, pron.m. them.
évacuable, adj. able to be
evacuated.
évacuation, n.f. evacuation.
évacuer, vb. evacuate.
évader, vb. s'é., escape.
évaluateur, n.m. appraiser.
évaluation, n.f. appraisal.
évaluer, vb. evaluate, rate, assess.
évangélique, adj. evangelic.
évangéliste, n.m. evangelist.
évangile, n.m. gospel.
évanouir, vb. s'é., fade away;
faint.
évaporation, n.f. evaporation.
évaporer, vb. evaporate.
évasif, adj. evasive.
évasion, n.f. escape.

évêché, n.m. bishopric.
éveil, n.m. alertness.
éveillé, adj. sprightly.
éveiller, vb. wake.
événement, n.m. event.
éventail, n.m. fan.
éventrer, vb. disembowel.
éventualité, n.f. eventuality.
éventuel, adj. possible.
éventuellement, adv. eventually.
évêque, n.m. bishop.
éviction, n.f. eviction.
évidemment, adv. evidently.
évidence, n.f. evidence. **en é.,** conspicuous.
évident, adj. obvious, evident.
évider, vb. scoop out.
évier, n.m. sink.
évincer, vb. oust.
éviscérer, vb. eviscerate, disembowel.
évitable, adj. avoidable.
éviter, vb. avoid.
évocation, n.f. evocation.
évolution, n.f. evolution.
évoquer, vb. evoke.
exact (-kt), adj. exact, precise.
exactement, adv. exactly.
exactitude, n.f. precision.
exagération, n.f. exaggeration.
exagérer, vb. exaggerate.
exaltant, adj. exciting.
exaltation, n.f. exaltation.
exalté, adj. impassioned.
exalter, vb. exalt, elate.
examen, n.m. examination.
examiner, vb. examine.
exaspération, n.f. exasperation.
exaspérer, vb. exasperate, aggravate.
excavateur, n.m. steam shovel.
excavation, n.f. excavation.
excaver, vb. excavate.
excédent, n.m. excess; overweight.
excéder, vb. exceed.
excellence, n.f. excellence, excellency, highness.
excellent, adj. excellent.
exceller, vb. excel.
excentrique, adj. eccentric.
excepté, prep. except.
excepter, vb. except.
exception, n.f. exception.
exceptionnel, adj. exceptional.
excès, n.m. excess.
excessif, adj. excessive, extreme.
exciser, vb. excise; cut out.
excitabilité, n.f. excitability.
excitable, adj. excitable.
excitant, adj. exciting.
exciter, vb. excite.
exclamatif, adj. exclamatory.
exclamation, n.f. exclamation.
exclamer, vb. exclaim.
exclure, vb. exclude.
exclusif, adj. exclusive.
exclusion, n.f. exclusion.
excommunication, n.f. excommunication.
excommunier, vb. excommunicate.

excorier, vb. excoriate.
excrément, n.m. excrement.
excréter, vb. excrete.
excrétion, n.f. excretion.
excursion, n.f. excursion.
excursionniste, n. excursionist.
excusable, adj. excusable.
excuse, n.f. plea, excuse.
excuser, vb. excuse. **s'e. de,** apologize for.
exécuter, vb. perform, enforce.
exécuteur, n.m. executor.
exécutif, adj. and n.m. executive.
exécution, n.f. performance, enforcement, execution.
exemplaire, 1. n.m. copy. **2.** adj. exemplary.
exemple, n.m. instance, example.
exempt, adj. exempt.
exempt de droits, adj. duty-free.
exempter, vb. exempt.
exemption, n.f. exemption.
exerçant, adj. practicing.
exercer, vb. exercise, drill, train. **s'e.,** practice.
exercice, n.m. exercise, drill, practice.
exhalation, n.f. exhalation.
exhaler, vb. exhale.
exhaustion, n.f. exhaust.
exhiber, vb. show, present; exhibit.
exhibition, n.f. exhibition.
exhortation, n.f. exhortation.
exhorter, vb. exhort.
exhumer, vb. exhume.
exigence, n.f. requirement.
exiger, vb. require, exact, demand.
exil (-l), n.m. exile.
exilé, n.m. exile.
exiler, vb. banish.
existant, adj. existent.
existence, n.f. existence.
exister, vb. exist.
exode, n.m. exodus.
exonération, n.f. exoneration.
exonérer, vb. exonerate.
exorbitant, adj. exorbitant.
exorciser, vb. exorcise.
exotique, adj. exotic.
expansible, adj. expansible.
expansif, adj. expansive.
expansion, n.f. expansion.
expatriation, n.f. expatriation.
expatrié, n. exile, expatriate.
expectorant, n.m. and adj. expectorant.
expectorer, vb. expectorate.
expédient, n.m. makeshift.
expédier, vb. dispatch.
expéditif, adj. expeditious.
expédition, n.f. dispatch; expedition, shipment.
expérience, n.f. experience, experiment.
expérimental, adj. experimental.
expérimentation, n.f. experimentation.
expérimenté, adj. practiced, experienced.

expert, adj. and n.m. expert.
expiable, adj. expiable.
expiation, n.f. atonement.
expier, vb. atone for.
expiration, n.f. expiration.
expirer, vb. expire.
explétif, n. and adj. expletive.
explicatif, adj. explanatory.
explication, n.f. explanation.
explicite, adj. explicit, clear.
expliquer, vb. explain.
exploit, n.m. feat, exploit.
exploitation, n.f. exploitation, working.
exploiter, vb. exploit.
explorateur, n.m. explorer.
exploratif, adj. exploratory.
exploration, n.f. exploration.
explorer, vb. explore.
explosible, adj. explosive.
explosif, adj. and n.m. explosive.
explosion, n.f. blast, explosion.
exportation, n.f. export, exportation.
exporter, vb. export.
exposé, n.m. account, statement.
exposer, vb. expound, expose, exhibit.
exposition, n.f. exposition, exposure, show, display.
exprès, 1. n.m. special delivery. **2.** adj. express. **3.** adv. on purpose.
expressif, adj. expressive.
expression, n.f. expression.
exprimable, adj. expressible.
exprimer, vb. express.
exproprier, vb. expropriate.
expulser, vb. expel.
expulsion, n.f. expulsion.
expurgation, n.f. expurgation.
expurger, vb. expurgate.
exquis, adj. exquisite.
exsuder, vb. exude.
extase, n.f. ecstasy.
extasier, vb. **s'e. sur,** rave about.
extatique, adj. ecstatic.
extensif, adj. extensive.
extension, n.f. extension.
exténuation, n.f. extenuation.
exténuer, vb. extenuate, exhaust.
extérieur, 1. n.m. exterior. **2.** adj. exterior, outer.
extérieurement, adv. externally.
extermination, n.f. extermination.
exterminer, vb. exterminate.
externat, n.m. day school.
externe, adj. external.
exterritorialité, n.f. extraterritoriality.
extincteur, n.m. fire extinguisher.
extinction, n.f. extinction.
extirper, vb. extirpate, root out.
extorquer, vb. extort.
extorsion, n.f. extortion.
extra-, prefix extra.

extraction, *n.m.* extraction; descent.

extrader, *vb.* extradite.

extradition, *n.f.* extradition.

extra-fin, *adj.* extremely fine.

extraire, *vb.* extract.

extrait, *n.m.* extract, abstract.

extraordinaire, *adj.* extraordinary, unusual.

extraordinairement, *adv.* extraordinarily.

extravagance, *n.f.* extravagance.

extravagant, *adj.* extravagant.

extrême, *adj. and n.m.* extreme.

extrémiste, *n.* extremist.

extrémité, *n.f.* extremity.

extrinsèque, *adj.* extrinsic.

extroverti, *n.m.* extrovert.

extrusion, *n.f.* extrusion.

exubérance, *n.f.* exuberance.

exubérant, *adj.* exuberant.

exultation, *n.f.* exultation.

exulter, *vb.* exult.

F

fable, *n.f.* fable.

fabliau, *n.m.* fabliau.

fabricant, *n.m.* maker, manufacturer.

fabricateur, *n.m.* forger.

fabrication, *n.f.* make.

fabrique, *n.f.* factory.

fabriquer, *vb.* manufacture.

fabuleux, *adj.* fabulous.

fabuliste, *n.m.* fabulist.

façade, *n.f.* front.

face, *n.f.* face. **en f. de,** opposite. **faire f. à,** confront.

facétie, *n.f.* joke, prank.

facétieux, *adj.* facetious.

facette, *n.f.* facet.

fâché, *j.* angry; sorry.

fâcher, *vb.* anger, offend, grieve. **se f.,** get angry.

fâcherie, *n.f.* quarrel, argument.

fâcheux, *adj.* upleasant.

facial, *adj.* facial.

facile, *adj.* easy.

facilité, *n.f.* fluency, ease.

faciliter, *vb.* facilitate, make easy.

façon, *n.f.* way, manner, fashion. **de f. à,** so as to.

faconde, *n.f.* glibness; fluency.

façonner, *vb.* shape, fashion.

facsimilé, *n.m.* facsimile.

facteur, *n.m.* factor, element; mailman.

factice, *adj.* artificial.

factieux, *adj.* factious; quarrelsome.

faction, *n.f.* faction, party.

factionnaire, *n.m.* sentry.

facture, *n.f.* invoice, bill.

facturer, *vb.* bill; send an invoice to.

facultatif, *adj.* optional.

faculté, *n.f.* faculty.

fadaise, *n.f.* nonsense.

fade, *adj.* insipid.

fadeur, *n.f.* insipidity.

fagot, *n.m.* bundle.

faible, *adj.* weak, faint, dim, feeble.

faiblement, *adv.* feebly, weakly.

faiblesse, *n.f.* weakness, frailty, dimness.

faiblir, *vb.* weaken.

failli, *adj. and n.m.* bankrupt.

faillibilité, *n.f.* fallibility.

faillible, *adj.* fallible.

faillir, *vb.* fail.

faillite, *n.f.* bankrupcy.

faim, *n.f.* hunger.

fainéant, *n.m.* loafer.

faire, *vb.* make, do. **f. part,** inform. **f. mal à,** hurt. **f. voir,** show.

faisable, *adj.* feasible.

faisan, *n.m.* pheasant.

fait, *n.m.* fact. **tout à f.,** wholly.

falaise, *n.f.* cliff.

fallacieux, *adj.* fallacious.

falloir, *vb.* be necessary. **comme il faut,** decent.

falot, *n.m.* lamp.

falsificateur, *n.m.* forger; falsifier.

falsification, *n.f.* falsification.

falsifier, *vb.* falsify.

fameux, *adj.* famous.

familiariser, *vb.* familiarize.

familiarité, *n.f.* familiarity.

familier, *adj.* familiar.

familièrement, *adv.* familiarly.

famille, *n.f.* family, household.

famine, *n.f.* famine.

fanatique, *adj. and n.m.* fanatic.

fanatisme, *n.m.* fanaticism.

faner, *vb.* fade.

fanfare, *n.f.* fanfare.

fanfaronnade, *n.f.* boast.

fange, *n.f.* filth; vice.

fantaisie, *n.f.* fancy, fantasy.

fantastique, *adj.* fantastic.

fantoche, *n.m.* puppet.

fantôme, *n.m.* phantom, ghost.

faon, *n.m.* fawn.

farce, *n.f.* stuffing; farce.

farceur, *n.m.* jokester.

farcir, *vb.* stuff.

fard, *n.m.* facial makeup.

fardeau, *n.m.* burden.

farinacé, *adj.* farinaceous.

farine, *n.f.* meal, flour.

farniente, *n.m.* idleness.

farouche, *adj.* fierce, sullen, shy.

fascinant, *adj.* fascinating.

fascination, *n.f.* fascination.

fascine, *n.f.* faggot (of wood).

fasciner, *vb.* fascinate.

fascisme, *n.m.* fascism.

fasciste, *n.m.* fascist.

faste, *n.m.* ostentation.

fastidieux, *adj.* dull.

fat, *adj.* foppish.

fatal, *adj.* mortal; fatal.

fatalisme, *n.m.* fatalism.

fataliste, *n.m.f.* fatalist.

fatalité, *n.f.* fatality; misfortune.

fatigant, *adj.* tiring.

fatigue, *n.f.* weariness.

fatiguer, *vb.* tire.

fatuité, *n.f.* smugness.

faubourg, *n.m.* suburb.

faubourien, *adj.* suburban.

faucher, *vb.* mow.

faucheur, *n.m.* reaper, mower.

faucille, *n.f.* sickle.

faucon, *n.m.* hawk.

fauconneau, *n.m.* young falcon.

fauconnerie, *n.f.* falconry.

faufil, *n.m.* basting thread.

faufiler, *vb.* baste.

faune, *n.f.* fauna; wildlife.

faussaire, *n.* forger; liar.

faussement, *adv.* falsely.

fausser, *vb.* pervert, warp, distort.

fausset, *n.m.* falsetto; spigot, faucet.

fausseté, *n.f.* falseness.

faute, *n.f.* fault, mistake. **f. de,** for want of.

fauteuil, *n.m.* armchair.

fautif, *adv.* faulty, wrong.

fauve, *adj.* wild.

faux, **1.** *n.m.* forgery. **2.** *f.* scythe.

faux *m.,* **fausse** *f.* *adj.* false, wrong, spurious, counterfeit.

faux-filet, *n.m.* sirloin.

faveur, *n.f.* favor. **en f. de,** on behalf of.

favorable, *adj.* conducive, favorable.

favorablement, *adv.* favorably.

favori, *n.m.* whisker.

favori *m.,* **favorite** *f.* *adj. and n.* favorite.

favoriser, *vb.* favor.

favoritisme, *n.m.* favoritism.

fayot, *n.m.* kidney bean.

féal, *adj.* faithful.

fébrile, *adj.* feverish.

fécal, *adj.* fecal.

fécond, *adj.* fertile.

féconder, *vb.* fertilize.

fécondité, *n.f.* fertility.

féculent, *adj.* starchy.

fédéral, *adj.* federal.

fédéraliser, *vb.* federalize.

fédéraliste, *n. and adj.* federalist.

fédération, *n.f.* confederacy, federation.

fédérer, *vb.* federate.

fée, *n.f.* fairy.

féerie, *n.f.* fairyland.

féerique, *adj.* fairylike.

feindre, *vb.* feign, pretend.

fêler, *vb.* crack.

félicitation, *n.f.* congratulation.

félicité, *n.f.* bliss.

féliciter (de), *vb.* congratulate (on).

félin, *adj.* feline.

félon, *adj.* disloyal.

femelle, *adj. and n.f.* female.

féminin, *adj.* female, feminine.

femme, *n.f.* woman, wife. **f. de chambre,** chambermaid.

fémoral, *adj.* femoral.

fendille, *n.f.* crack.
fendiller, *vb.* **se f.,** crack.
fendoir, *n.m.* cleaver.
fendre, *vb.* split, rip.
fenêtre, *n.f.* window.
fenil, *n.m.* hayloft.
fente, *n.f.* crack, rip, split.
féodal, *adj.* feudal.
féodalité, *n.f.* feudalism.
fer (-r), *n.m.* iron. **chemin de f.,** railway. **fil de f.,** wire. **f. à cheval,** horseshoe.
fermail, *n.m.* brooch, clasp.
ferme, *n.f.* farm. **maison de f.,** farmhouse.
ferme, *adj.* firm, steady, fast.
fermement, *adv.* firmly.
fermentation, *n.f.* fermentation.
fermenter, *vb.* ferment.
fermer, *vb.* close. **f. à clef,** lock.
fermeté, *n.f.* firmness.
fermier, *n.m.* farmer.
féroce, *adj.* fierce.
férocité, *n.f.* ferocity.
ferraille, *n.f.* old iron.
ferreux, *adj.* ferrous.
ferrique, *adj.* ferric.
fertile, *adj.* fertile.
fertilisant, *n.m.* fertilizer.
fertilisation, *n.f.* fertilization.
fertiliser, *vb.* fertilize.
fertilité, *n.f.* fertility.
férule, *n.f.* cane, rod.
fervemment, *adv.* fervently.
fervent, *adj.* fervent.
ferveur, *n.f.* fervor.
fesse, *n.f.* buttock.
fessée, *n.f.* spanking.
fesser, *vb.* spank.
festin, *n.m.* feast.
festiner, *vb.* feast.
feston, *n.m.* festoon.
fête, *n.f.* feast, party. **jour de f.,** holiday.
fêter, *vb.* fete.
fétiche, *n.m.* fetish.
fétide, *adj.* fetid.
feu, *n.m.* fire. **f. de joie,** bonfire. **f. d'artifice,** fireworks. **prendre f.,** catch fire. **coup de f.,** shot.
feu, *adj.* late (deceased).
feuillage, *n.m.* foliage.
feuille, *n.f.* leaf, sheet, foil.
feuilleter, *vb.* skim (book).
feutre, *n.m.* felt.
fève, *n.f.* bean.
février, *n.m.* February.
fez, *n.m.* fez.
fi, *interj.* fie!
fiacre, *n.m.* cab.
fiançailles, *n.f.pl.* engagement, betrothal.
fiancé, *n.m.* fiancé.
fiancer, *vb.* betroth.
fiasco, *n.m.* fiasco.
fibre, *n.f.* fiber.
fibreux, *adj.* fibrous.
ficelle, *n.f.* string, twine.
fiche, *n.f.* slip (of paper).
ficher, *vb.* **se f. de,** care nothing about.
fichier, *n.m.* card index.
fichu, *adv.* ruined.

fictif, *adj.* fictitious.
fiction, *n.f.* fiction.
fidèle, *adj.* faithful.
fidélité, *n.f.* fidelity, loyalty, allegiance.
fief, *n.m.* feud.
fiel, *n.m.* gall.
fiente, *n.f.* dung.
fier (-r), *adj.* proud.
fier, *vb.* **se f.,** trust.
fierté, *n.f.* trust.
fièvre, *n.f.* fever.
fiévreux, *adj.* feverish.
fifre, *n.m.* fife(r).
figer, *vb.* coagulate.
figue, *n.f.* fig.
figuratif, *adj.* figurative.
figure, *n.f.* face, figure.
figurer, *vb.* figure, imagine. **se f.,** fancy.
fil (-l), *n.m.* thread, string. **f. de fer,** wire.
filament, *n.m.* filament.
filature, *n.f.* spinning-mill.
file, *n.f.* file.
filer, *vb.* spin.
filet, *n.m.* net.
filial, *adj.* filial.
filin, *n.m.* rope.
fille, *n.f.* daughter. **jeune f.,** girl. **vieille f.,** old maid.
film, *n.m.* film.
filmer, *vb.* film.
filou, *n.m.* thief.
fils (fês), *n.m.* son.
filtrant, *adj.* filterable.
filtration, *n.f.* filtration.
filtre, *n.m.* filter.
filtrer, *vb.* filter.
fin, **1.** *n.f.* end. **2.** *adj.* fine; sharp; clever.
final, *adj.* final.
finaliste, *n.m.* finalist.
finalité, *n.f.* finality.
finance, *n.f.* finance.
financer, *vb.* finance.
financier, **1.** *n.m.* financier. **2.** *adj.* financial.
finasser, *vb.* finesse.
finir, *vb.* finish.
Finlande, *n.f.* Finland.
Finnois, *n.m.* Finn.
finnois, *adj.* and *n.m.* Finnish.
firmament, *n.m.* firmament.
firme, *n.f.* company.
fiscal, *adj.* fiscal.
fissure, *n.f.* fissure.
fixation, *n.f.* fixation.
fixe, *adj.* set, fixed.
fixer, *vb.* fix, secure, settle.
fixité, *n.f.* fixity.
flaccidité, *n.f.* flabbiness.
flacon, *n.m.* bottle.
flagellation, *n.f.* flagellation.
flageller, *vb.* flog.
flagrant, *adj.* flagrant.
flair, *n.m.* flair.
flairer, *vb.* smell.
flamand, *adj.* Flemish.
flambant, *adj.* flaming.
flambeau, *n.m.* torch.
flambée, *n.f.* blaze.
flamber, *vb.* blaze.
flamboyant, *adj.* flaming; flamboyant.

flamboyer, *vb.* flame, flare.
flamme, *n.f.* flame.
flanc, *n.m.* side, flank.
flanchet, *n.m.* flank (of beef).
flanelle, *n.f.* flannel.
flâner, *vb.* saunter, stroll, loiter, loaf.
flâneur, *n.m.* idler.
flanquer, *vb.* flank.
flaque, *n.f.* puddle.
flasque, *adj.* flabby.
flatter, *vb.* flatter.
flatterie, *n.f.* flattery.
flatteur, *n.m.* flatterer.
fléau, *n.m.* scourge, plague.
flèche, *n.f.* arrow.
fléchir, *vb.* bend.
flegmatique, *adj.* phlegmatic.
flegme, *n.m.* phlegm.
flet, *n.m.* flounder.
flétan, *n.m.* halibut.
flétrir, *vb.* wilt, wither.
fleur, *n.f.* flower, blossom, bloom.
fleuret, *n.m.* foil.
fleuri, *adj.* flowery.
fleurir, *vb.* flower, bloom, blossom.
fleuriste, *n.m.f.* florist.
fleuve, *n.m.* river.
flexibilité, *n.f.* flexibility.
flexible, *adj.* flexible.
flirt (-t), *n.m.* flirtation.
flirter, *vb.* flirt.
flocon, *n.m.* flake.
florissant, *adj.* prosperous, flourishing.
flot, *n.m.* wave. **à flot,** afloat.
flottant, *adj.* floating; irresolute.
flotte, *n.f.* fleet.
flottement, *n.m.* fluctuation; wavering.
flotter, *vb.* float.
flou, *adj.* hazy, indistinct.
fluctuation, *n.f.* fluctuation.
fluctuer, *vb.* fluctuate.
fluet *m.,* **fluette** *f.* *adj.* thin, delicate.
fluide, *adj.* and *n.m.* fluid, liquid.
fluidité, *n.f.* fluidity.
flûte, *n.f.* flute.
flûté, *adj.* soft; flute-like.
flux, *n.m.* flow, flux.
fluxion, *n.f.* inflammation.
foi, *n.f.* faith; trust.
foie, *n.m.* liver.
foin, *n.m.* hay.
foire, *n.f.* fair.
fois, *n.f.* time. **à la f.,** at once.
foison, *n.f.* abundance.
foisonner, *vb.* abound.
folâtre, *adj.* frisky.
folâtrer, *vb.* frolic.
folichon, *adj.* playful.
folie, *n.f.* mania, madness, folly.
folklore, *n.m.* folklore.
follement, *adv.* foolishly.
follet, *adj.* merry, playful.
fomenter, *vb.* foment.
foncé, *adj.* dark.
foncer, *vb.* deepen.
fonction, *n.f.* function.

fonctionnaire, *n.m.* official, civil servant.

fonctionnement, *n.m.* operation, working.

fonctionner, *vb.* function, work.

fonctions, *n.f.pl.* office.

fond, *n.m.* bottom, (back)ground. **à f.,** thorough(ly). **au f.,** fundamentally.

fondamental, *adj.* basic, fundamental.

fondateur, *n.m.* founder.

fondation, *n.f.* foundation, establishment.

fondé, *adj.* authentic; (*comm.*) funded.

fondement, *n.m.* foundation.

fonder, *vb.* found.

fonderie, *n.f.* foundry.

fondre, *vb.* melt, fuse.

fondrière, *n.f.* bog.

fonds, *n.m.* fund.

fongus (-s), *n.m.* fungus.

fontaine, *n.f.* fountain.

fonte, *n.f.* melting.

fonts, *n.m.pl.* font.

football, *n.m.* football.

footing, *n.m.* walking.

forain, *n.m.* peddler.

forçat, *n.m.* convict.

force, *n.f.* strength, force; emphasis.

forcé, *adj.* forced, far-fetched.

forcément, *adv.* of necessity.

forcené, *adj.* frantic.

forcer, *vb.* force, compel.

forcir, *vb.* thrive.

forer, *vb.* bore, drill.

forestier, *n.m.* forest ranger.

foret, *n.m.* drill.

forêt, *n.f.* forest.

foreuse, *n.f.* drill.

forfait, *n.m.* crime; forfeit; contract.

forfaiture, *n.f.* mishandling.

forfanterie, *n.f.* bragging.

forge, *n.f.* forge.

forger, *vb.* forge.

forgeron, *n.m.* blacksmith.

forgeur, *n.m.* forger; inventor.

formaliser, *vb.* offend.

formaliste, *adj.* formal; precise.

formalité, *n.f.* formality, ceremony.

formation, *n.f.* formation.

forme, *n.f.* shape, form.

formel, *adj.* formal.

former, *vb.* form, shape.

formidable, *adj.* terrible, formidable.

formule, *n.f.* formula, form.

formuler, *vb.* formulate, draw up.

fort, 1. *n.m.* fort. **2.** *adj.* strong, loud. **3.** *adv.* hard.

forteresse, *n.f.* fort(ress).

fortifiant, *adj.* strengthening.

fortification, *n.f.* fortification.

fortifier, *vb.* strengthen.

fortuit, *adj.* accidental.

fortuité, *n.f.* fortuitousness.

fortune, *n.f.* fortune.

fortuné, *adj.* lucky, fortunate.

fosse, *n.f.* pit.

fossé, *n.m.* ditch; dike.

fossette, *n.f.* dimple.

fossile, *n.m.* fossil.

fossoyer, *vb.* dig a trench.

fou *m.,* **folle** *f. adj.* mad, crazy, demented.

foudre, *n.m.* thunderbolt.

foudroyant, *adj.* terrifying, crushing.

foudroyer, *vb.* crush, blast.

fouet, *n.m.* whip, lash.

fouetter, *vb.* flog, whip.

fougère, *n.f.* fern.

fougue, *n.f.* dash.

fougueux, *adj.* fiery, impetuous.

fouille, *n.f.* excavation.

fouiller, *vb.* ransack.

fouillis, *n.m.* litter, mess.

fouir, *vb.* dig, burrow.

foulard, *n.m.* scarf.

foule, *n.f.* crowd, mob.

fouler, *vb.* trample.

foulure, *n.f.* sprain, wrench.

four, *n.m.* oven.

fourbe, 1. *n.m.* knave. **2.** *adj.* scheming.

fourberie, *n.f.* knavery.

fourbir, *vb.* polish.

fourche, *n.f.* fork.

fourchette, *n.f.* fork.

fourgon, *n.m.* wagon.

fourmi, *n.f.* ant.

fourmillement, *n.m.* swarming, tingling.

fourmiller, *vb.* mill; swarm.

fourneau, *n.m.* stove, furnace.

fournée, *n.f.* batch.

fourniment, *n.m.* equipment.

fournir de, *vb.* supply, furnish.

fournisseur, *n.m.* tradesman.

fournitures, *n.f.pl.* supplies.

fourrage, *n.m.* fodder, forage.

fourrager, *vb.* forage.

fourré, *adj.* lined (of clothing); thick; wooded.

fourreau, *n.m.* sheath.

fourrer, *vb.* thrust in. **se f.,** interfere, meddle.

fourreur, *n.m.* furrier.

fourrure, *n.f.* fur.

fourvoyer, *vb.* mislead.

foyer, *n.m.* focus, hearth. **f. domestique,** home.

frac, *n.m.* dress coat.

fracas, *n.m.* crash; rattle; noise; ado.

fracasser, *vb.* **se f.,** shatter.

fraction, *n.f.* fraction.

fracture, *n.f.* fracture.

fracturer, *vb.* break, fracture.

fragile, *adj.* brittle, delicate, frail, fragile.

fragilité, *n.f.* fragility.

fragment, *n.m.* fragment.

fragmenter, *vb.* divide up.

fraîcheur, *n.f.* freshness, coolness.

fraîchir, *vb.* freshen.

frais, *n.m.pl.* expense(s), cost, fee.

frais *m.* **fraîche** *f. adj.* fresh, cool.

fraise, *n.f.* strawberry; ruffle.

framboise, *n.f.* raspberry.

franc, 1. *n.m.* franc. **2.** *adj.m.,* **franche** *f.* frank, open.

Français, *n.m.* Frenchman.

français, *adj. and n.m.* French.

Française, *n.f.* Frenchwoman.

France, *n.f.* France.

franchement, *adv.* frankly.

franchir, *vb.* clear, cross.

franchise, *n.f.* frankness.

franciser, *vb.* make French.

franc-maçon, *n.m.* Freemason.

franc-parler, *n.m.* frankness.

franc-tireur, *n.m.* sniper; freelancer.

frange, *n.f.* fringe.

frangible, *adj.* breakable.

frapper, *vb.* strike, hit, rap, knock. **f. du pied,** stamp.

frasque, *n.f.* prank.

fraternel, *adj.* brotherly.

fraterniser, *vb.* fraternize.

fraternité, *n.f.* brotherhood.

fraude, *n.f.* fraud.

frauder, *vb.* defraud.

fraudeur, *n.m.* smuggler.

frauduleux, *adj.* fraudulent.

frayer, *vb.* open up; rub.

frayeur, *n.f.* fright.

fredaine, *n.f.* prank.

fredonner, *vb.* hum.

frégate, *n.f.* frigate.

frein, *n.m.* brake, check.

freiner, *vb.* brake; restrain.

frelater, *vb.* adulterate.

frêle, *adj.* frail.

frelon, *n.m.* hornet.

frémir, *vb.* tremble. **faire f.,** thrill.

frémissement, *n.m.* shiver, thrill.

frêne, *n.m.* ash (tree).

frénésie, *n.f.* frenzy.

frénétique, *adj.* frantic.

fréquemment, *adv.* often.

fréquence, *n.f.* frequency.

fréquent, *adj.* frequent.

fréquenter, *vb.* frequent, associate with.

frère, *n.m.* brother.

fresque, *n.f.* fresco.

fret, *n.m.* freight.

fréter, *vb.* charter (ship); freight.

frétillant, *adj.* lively.

frétiller, *vb.* wag; quiver.

fretin, *n.m.* young fish.

frette, *n.f.* hoop.

friand, *adj.* dainty; fond (of).

friandise, *n.f.* love of delicacies.

fricoter, *vb.* cook, stew.

friction, *n.f.* friction.

frictionner, *vb.* chafe.

frigo, *n.m.* frozen meat.

frigorifier, *vb.* freeze, refrigerate.

frileux, *adj.* chilly; susceptible to cold.

frime, *n.f.* pretense, sham.

fringant, *adj.* lively, frisky.

friper, *vb.* crush, rumple.

fripier, *n.m.* second-hand clothing dealer.

fripon, 1. *adj.* knavish. 2. *n.m.* rascal.
friponnerie, *n.f.* roguery.
fripouille, *n.f.* rascal.
frire, *vb.* fry.
frisé, *adj.* curly.
friser, *vb.* curl.
frisoir, *n.m.* (hair) curler.
frisson, *n.m.* shudder, shiver.
frissonnement, *n.m.* shudder; shivering.
frissonner, *vb.* shudder, shiver.
frites, *n.f.pl.* (potato) chips.
friture, *n.f.* frying.
frivole, *adj.* frivolous.
frivolité, *n.f.* frivolity.
froc, *n.m.* (monk's) frock.
froid, *n.m. and adj.* cold. **un peu f.,** chilly. **avoir f.,** be cold.
froideur, *n.f.* coldness.
froissé, *adj.* bruised. **être f. de,** resent.
froissement, *n.m.* crumpling, rustling, jostling.
froisser, *vb.* crease, wrinkle; bruise, hurt.
frôler, *vb.* graze.
fromage, *n.m.* cheese.
froment, *n.m.* wheat.
froncement, *n.m.* puckering, contraction.
froncer, *vb.* pucker. **f. les sourcils,** frown.
frondaison, *n.f.* foliage.
fronde, *n.f.* sling.
fronder, *vb.* sling; censure.
front, *n.m.* forehead.
frontière, *n.f.* boundary, border, frontier.
frottement, *n.m.* rubbing.
frotter, *vb.* rub.
frou-frou, *n.m.* rustle.
fructueux, *adj.* fruitful.
frugal, *adj.* frugal.
frugalité, *n.f.* frugality.
fruit, *n.m.* fruit.
fruiterie, *n.f.* fruit store.
fruitier, *n.m.* fruit seller.
fugace, *adj.* fleeting.
fugitif, *adj.* fugitive.
fuir, *vb.* flee; shun; leak.
fuite, *n.f.* escape, flight; leak.
fumée, *n.f.* smoke.
fumer, *vb.* smoke.
fumeur, *n.m.* one who smokes.
fumeux, *adj.* smoky.
fumier, *n.m.* dung.
funèbre, *adj.* funereal.
funérailles, *n.f.pl.* funeral.
funeste, *adj.* disastrous.
fureter, *vb.* pry.
fureur, *n.f.* fury.
furie, *n.f.* fury.
furieux, *adj.* furious.
furtif, *adj.* sly.
fuseau, *n.m.* spindle.
fusée, *n.f.* rocket.
fuser, *vb.* melt, spread.
fusil, *n.m.* rifle.
fusiller (-zēl yā), *vb.* shoot.
fusion, *n.f.* merger; meltdown.
fusionner, *vb.* merge.
futé, *adj.* cunning, crafty.
futile, *adj.* futile.
futur, *n.m. and adj.* future.

futurologie, *n.f.* futurology.
fuyant, *adj.* passing, transitory, fugitive.
fuyard, *n.* fugitive.

G

gâcher, *vb.* mess.
gâchette, *n.f.* trigger.
gage, *n.m.* pledge, wage.
gageure, *n.f.* bet.
gagnant, *n.m.* winner.
gagner, *vb.* earn, gain, win, beat (in a game).
gai, *adj.* cheerful, cheery, merry, gay.
gaieté, *n.f.* mirth, cheer, merriment, gaiety.
gaillard, *adj.* hearty, sound.
gain, *n.m.* gain, profit.
gaine, *n.f.* girdle.
galant, 1. *n.m.* beau. 2. *adj.* gallant, civil, courteous. **g. homme,** gentleman.
galanterie, *n.f.* courtesy, compliment.
galbe, *n.m.* outline, contour.
galère, *n.f.* galley, ship.
galerie, *n.f.* gallery, balcony (theater).
galet, *n.m.* boulder.
gallon, *n.m.* gallon.
galon, *n.m.* stripe, braid.
galop, *n.m.* gallop.
galoper, *vb.* gallop.
gambader, *vb.* frolic.
gamin, *n.m.* boy, urchin.
gamme, *n.f.* scale.
gangster (-r), *n.m.* gangster.
gant, *n.m.* glove.
ganterie, *n.f.* glove shop.
garage, *n.m.* garage.
garagiste, *n.m.* garage keeper.
garant, *n.m.* sponsor.
garantie, *n.f.* guarantee, pledge.
garantir, *vb.* guarantee, pledge, warrant.
garçon, *n.m.* boy; waiter; bachelor; flight attendant.
garçonnière, *n.f.* bachelor's apartment.
garde, *n.f.* watch, guard, custody. **prendre g. à,** beware of. **avant-g.,** vanguard. **g. du corps,** bodyguard.
garde-boue, *n.m.* fender.
garde-feu, *n.m.* fender (fireplace).
garde-manger, *n.m.* pantry.
garder, *vb.* guard, keep, mind.
gardeur, *n.m.* keeper.
gardien, *n.m.* keeper, guard, watchman, guardian.
gare, 1. *n.f.* station. 2. *interj.* look out!
garer, *vb.* garage, park.
gargariser, *vb.* **se g.,** gargle.
gargarisme, *n.m.* gargle.
garni, *adj.* furnished, garnished.
garnir, *vb.* trim, garnish.
garnison, *n.f.* garrison.

garniture, *n.f.* fittings.
gars, *n.m.* chap.
gaspillage, *n.m.* waste.
gaspiller, *vb.* waste, squander.
gâteau, *n.m.* cake. **g. de miel,** honeycomb. **g. sec,** cookie.
gâter, *vb.* spoil.
gâterie, *n.f.* excessive indulgence.
gâteux, *adj.* senile.
gauche, *adj. and n.f.* left. **à g.,** on or to the left. *adj.* awkward, clumsy.
gaucherie, *n.f.* clumsiness.
gaufre, *n.f.* waffle.
gaule, *n.f.* pole.
gausser, *vb.* **se g. de,** mock, banter.
gaz (-z), *n.m.* gas.
gaze, *n.f.* gauze.
gazeux, *adj.* gassy, gaseous.
gazon, *n.m.* turf, lawn.
gazouillement, *n.m.* warble, twitter.
géant, *n.m.* giant.
geindre, *vb.* moan, whine.
gelé, *adj.* frozen.
gelée, *n.f.* jelly, frost.
geler, *vb.* freeze.
gémir, *vb.* groan, wail, moan.
gémissement, *n.m.* groan, moan.
gênant, *adj.* troublesome, bothersome.
gencive, *n.f.* gum.
gendarme, *n.m.* policeman.
gendarmerie, *n.f.* police force.
gendre, *n.m.* son-in-law.
gêne, *n.f.* trouble, uneasiness. **être à la g.,** be uneasy.
gêné, *adj.* uneasy.
généalogie, *n.f.* pedigree.
général, *n.m. and adj.* general, overhead (comm.). **quartier g.,** headquarters.
généraliser, *vb.* generalize.
généralissime, *n.m.* commander-in-chief.
généralité, *n.f.* generality.
génération, *n.f.* generation.
généreusement, *adv.* generously.
généreux, *adj.* generous, liberal.
générosité, *n.f.* generosity.
génial, *adj.* of genius, highly original.
génie, *n.m.* genius; engineer corps. **soldat du g.,** engineer.
genièvre, *n.m.* gin.
génisse, *n.f.* heifer.
genou, *n.m.* knee; (pl.) lap.
genre, *n.m.* kind, gender.
gens, *n.m.f.pl.* people, persons, folk.
gentiane, *n.f.* gentian.
gentil *m.,* **gentille** *f.* *adj.* pleasant, nice.
gentilhomme, *n.m.* nobleman, peer.
gentillesse, *n.f.* prettiness, gracefulness.
géographie, *n.f.* geography.

géographique, adj. geographical.

géologie, n.f. geology.

géométrie, n.f. geometry.

géométrique, adj. geometric.

gérance, n.f. managership.

géranium, n.m. geranium.

gérant, n.m. manager, director, superintendent.

gerbe, n.f. sheaf.

gerçure, n.f. chap.

gérer, vb. manage.

germain, adj. first (of cousins).

germe, n.f. germ.

germer, vb. sprout.

gésir, vb. lie.

geste, n.m. gesture.

gesticuler, vb. gesticulate.

gestion, n.f. management.

gibier, n.m. game.

giboulée, n.f. sudden storm, hailstorm.

gicler, vb. spurt.

gifler, vb. slap.

gigantesque, adj. great, huge.

gigue, n.f. leg; jig.

gilet, n.m. vest. g. de dessous, undershirt.

gingembre, n.m. ginger.

girofle, n.m. clou de g., clove.

giron, n.m. lap.

gitane, n.m.f. gypsy.

gîte, n.m. lodging, bed.

givre, n.m. frost.

glabre, adj. smooth-shaven.

glaçage, n.m. frosting.

glace, n.f. ice, ice cream; mirror.

glacer, vb. freeze.

glacial, adj. icy.

glacier, n.m. glacier.

glacière, n.f. icebox.

glacis, n.m. slope.

glaçon, n.m. block of ice.

glaise, n.f. clay.

gland, n.m. acorn.

glande, n.f. gland.

glaner, vb. glean.

glapir, vb. yelp; screech.

glas, n.m. knell.

glissade, n.f. slide, slip.

glissant, adj. slippery.

glisser, vb. slide, slip. se g., creep, sneak.

global, adj. entire.

globe, n.m. globe. g. de l'œil, eyeball.

gloire, n.f. glory.

glorieux, adj. glorious.

glorifier, vb. glorify.

glose, n.f. criticism; gloss.

glossaire, n.m. glossary.

glousser, vb. cluck.

gluant, adj. sticky.

gobelet, n.m. goblet.

gober, vb. swallow.

goéland, n.m. seagull.

golfe, n.m. gulf.

gomme, n.f. gum; eraser.

gommeux, adj. gummy.

gond, n.m. hinge.

gonfler, vb. inflate; swell.

gonfleur, n.m. tire pump.

gorge, n.f. throat; gorge.

gorger, vb. cram.

gosier, n.m. throat.

gosse, n.m.f. kid (child).

gothique, adj. Gothic.

goudron, n.m. tar.

gouffre, n.m. gulf, abyss.

goulu, adj. gluttonous.

gourde, n.f. flask.

gourmand, 1. n.m. glutton. 2. adj. greedy.

gourmander, vb. scold.

gourmandise, n.f. greediness.

gourmer, vb. curb.

gourmet, n.m. epicure.

gourmette, n.f. curb (horse).

gourou, n.m. guru.

gousse, n.f. shell, pod.

goût, n.m. taste, relish.

goûter, 1. n.m. snack. 2. vb. taste, relish.

goutte, n.f. drop; gout.

goutteux, adj. gouty.

gouttière, n.f. gutter.

gouvernail, n.m. rudder, helm.

gouvernante, n.f. governess, housekeeper.

gouvernement, n.m. government.

gouverner, vb. govern, rule, steer.

gouverneur, n.m. governor.

grabuge, n.m. squabble.

grâce, n.f. grace. faire g. de, spare.

gracier, vb. pardon.

gracieux, adj. graceful, gracious.

grade, n.m. grade, rank.

gradin, n.m. step, tier.

graduel, adj. gradual.

graduer, vb. graduate.

grain, n.m. grain, seed, berry, kernel. g. de beauté, mole.

graine, n.f. seed, berry.

graissage, n.m. greasing.

graisse, n.f. grease, fat.

graisser, vb. grease.

grammaire, n.f. grammar.

gramme, n.m. gram.

grand, adj. big, great, tall. grand'chose, much.

grandement, adv. grandly, greatly.

grandeur, n.f. size, height, greatness.

grandiose, adj. grand.

grandir, vb. grow.

grand'mère, n.f. grandmother.

grand-père, n.m. grandfather.

grange, n.f. barn.

granit (-t), n.m. granite.

graphique, n.m. chart.

grappe, n.f. bunch, cluster.

gras m., grasse f. adj. fat, stout.

grassement, adj. plentifully.

grasset, adj. plump.

grassouillet, adj. plump.

gratification, n.f. bonus.

gratifier, vb. bestow.

gratin, n.m. burnt part.

gratitude, n.f. gratitude.

gratte-ciel, n.m. skyscraper.

gratter, vb. scrape, scratch.

gratuit, adj. free.

grave, adj. grave.

graveleux, adj. gritty.

graver, vb. engrave.

graveur, n.m. engraver.

gravier, n.m. gravel.

gravir, vb. climb.

gravité, n.f. gravity.

graviter, vb. gravitate.

gravure, n.f. engraving. g. à l'eau-forte, etching.

gré, n.m. pleasure.

Grec m., Grecque f. n. Greek (person).

grec, n.m. Greek (language).

grec m., grecque f. adj. Greek.

Grèce, n.f. Greece.

gréement, n.m. rig.

gréer, vb. rig.

greffier, n.m. clerk.

grêle, 1. n.f. hail. 2. adj. thin, slight.

grêler, vb. hail.

grêlon, n.m. hailstone.

grelotter, vb. shiver.

grenier, n.m. attic.

grenouille, n.f. frog.

grève, n.f. strike. se mettre en g., strike, vb.

gréviste, n.m.f. striker.

gribouiller, vb. scribble.

grief, n.m. grievance.

grièvement, adv. seriously.

griffe, n.f. claw, clutch.

griffer, vb. seize; scratch.

griffonner, vb. scribble.

grignoter, vb. nibble.

gril, n.m. grill.

grillade, n.f. broiling.

grille, n.f. grate, gate.

griller, vb. broil, roast, toast.

grillon, n.m. cricket.

grimace, n.f. grimace.

grimacer, vb. make faces.

grimer, vb. make up.

grimper, vb. climb.

grincer, vb. creak, grate, grind.

gris, adj. gray; drab; drunk.

griser, vb. get drunk.

grive, n.f. thrush.

grogner, vb. growl, snarl, grumble.

grommeler, vb. mutter.

gronder, vb. scold, nag; roar, rumble.

gros m., grosse f. adj. overly large; gross, stout, rough. en g., wholesale.

groseille, n.f. currant.

grosseur, n.f. size, thickness.

grossier, adj. coarse, crude, gross.

grossièreté, n.f. coarseness.

grossir, vb. magnify, grow.

grotesque, adj. grotesque.

grouiller, vb. stir, swarm.

groupe, n.m. group, party; cluster.

groupement, n.m. grouping.

grouper, vb. group.

grue, n.f. crane.

gué, n.m. ford. traverser à g., wade.

guêpe, n.f. wasp.

guère, adv. hardly.

guérir, vb. cure, heal.

guérison, n.f. cure.

guerre, n.f. war.

guerrier, *adj.* warlike.

guetter, *vb.* watch (for).

gueule, *n.f.* mouth.

gueux, *n.m.* beggar, tramp.

guichet, *n.m.* ticket-window.

guide, *n.m.* guide(book).

guider, *vb.* guide.

guillotine, *n.f.* guillotine.

guingan, *n.m.* gingham.

guirlande, *n.f.* garland.

guise, *n.f.* way, manner.

guitare, *n.f.* guitar.

gymnase, *n.m.* gymnasium.

H

habile, *adj.* clever, skillful, smart, able.

habileté, *n.f.* craft, ability.

habillement, *n.m.* apparel.

habillements masculins, *n.m.pl.* menswear.

habiller, *vb.* dress.

habilleur *m.,* **habilleuse** *f. n.* dresser.

habit, *n.m.* coat; attire; (*pl.*) clothes.

habitant, *n.m.* inhabitant, resident.

habitation, *n.f.* dwelling.

habiter, *vb.* inhabit, live.

habitude, *n.f.* habit, practice. **d'h.,** customarily. **avoir l'h. de,** be accustomed to.

habituel, *adj.* customary, usual.

habituer, *vb.* get used to.

hâbleur, *n.m.* boaster.

hache, *n.f.* ax.

hacher, *vb.* mince, chop, hack up.

hachette, *n.f.* hatchet.

hachis, *n.m.* hash.

hagard, *adj.* haggard.

haie, *n.f.* hedge.

haillon, *n.m.* rag.

haine, *n.f.* hatred.

haineux, *adj.* hating.

haïr, *vb.* hate.

haïssable, *adj.* hateful.

halage, *n.m.* towage.

hâle, *n.m.* tan, sunburn.

haleine, *n.f.* breath.

haler, *vb.* haul, tow.

hâler, *vb.* tan. **se h.,** become sunburned.

haleter, *vb.* pant, gasp.

halle, *n.f.* market.

halte, *n.f.* halt.

hamac, *n.m.* hammock.

hameau, *n.m.* hamlet.

hameçon, *n.m.* hook.

hampe, *n.f.* handle.

hanche, *n.f.* hip.

hangar, *n.m.* shed.

hanter, *vb.* haunt.

hantise, *n.f.* obsession.

happer, *vb.* snap.

harcèlement, *n.m.* hassle, harassment.

harceler, *vb.* worry, bother; hassle; harass.

hardes, *n.f.pl.* togs.

hardi, *adj.,* bold.

hardiesse, *n.f.* boldness.

hareng, *n.m.* herring.

hargneux, *adj.* cross, snarling.

haricot, *n.m.* bean.

harmonie, *n.f.* harmony.

harmonieux, *adj.* harmonious.

harmoniser, *vb.* put in tune, harmonize.

harnacher, *vb.* harness.

harnais, *n.m.* harness.

harpe, *n.f.* harp.

harpin, *n.m.* boat hook.

hasard, *n.m.* chance. **au h. or par h.,** at random.

hasarder, *vb.* venture.

hasardeux, *adj.* hazardous, unsafe.

hâte, *n.f.* haste, hurry. **à la h.,** hastily.

hâter, *vb.* hasten, hurry.

hâtif, *adj.* early, hasty.

haussement, *n.m.* raising; shrug.

hausser, *vb.* raise; shrug.

haussier, *n.m.* bull (stock exchange).

haut, 1. *n.m.* top. 2. *adj.* high, loud. **à haute voix,** aloud. **en haut,** up, above.

hautain, *adj.* haughty, lofty, proud.

hautbois, *n.m.* oboe.

haute fidélité, *n.f.* high fidelity.

hauteur, *n.f.* height; haughtiness. **être à la h. de,** be up to.

hauturier, *adj.* sea-going.

hâve, *adj.* wan, gaunt.

havre, *n.m.* haven.

havresac, *n.m.* knapsack.

hebdomadaire, *adj.* weekly.

héberger, *vb.* shelter.

hébété, *adj.* dull.

hébreu, 1. *n.m.* Hebrew (language). 2. *adj.* Hebrew.

hein, *interj.* huh?

hélas (-s), *interj.* alas!

héler, *vb.* call, hail.

hélice, *n.f.* propeller.

hélicoptère, *n.m.* helicopter.

helvétique, *adj.* Swiss.

hémisphère, *n.m.* hemisphere.

hémorragie, *n.f.* hemorrhage.

hennir, *vb.* neigh.

héraut, *n.m.* herald.

herbage, *n.m.* grass, pasture.

herbe, *n.f.* grass, herb; marijuana. **mauvaise h.,** weed.

herbeux, *adj.* grassy.

héréditaire, *adj.* hereditary.

hérésie, *n.f.* heresy.

hérétique, 1. *n.m.f.* heretic. 2. *adj.* heretic, heretical.

hérisser, *vb.* bristle.

hérisson, *n.m.* hedgehog.

héritage, *n.m.* inheritance.

hériter, *vb.* inherit.

héritier, *n.m.* heir.

hermétique, *adj.* (sealed) tight.

hermine, *n.f.* ermine.

hernie, *n.f.* hernia.

héroïne, *n.f.* heroine.

héroïque, *adj.* heroic.

héroïsme, *n.m.* heroism.

héros, *n.m.* hero.

hertz, *n.m.* hertz.

hésitation, *n.f.* hesitation.

hésiter, *vb.* hesitate, waver, falter.

hétérosexuel, *adj.* heterosexual.

hêtre, *n.m.* beech.

heure, *n.f.* hour; time. **de bonne h.,** early.

heureusement, *adv.* happily, luckily.

heureux, *adj.* glad, happy; lucky, fortunate; successful.

heurt, *n.m.* blow, shock.

heurter, *vb.* collide (with).

heurtoir, *n.m.* (door) knocker.

hibou, *n.m.* owl.

hideux, *adj.* hideous.

hier (-r), *adv.* yesterday.

hilare, *adj.* hilarious.

hilarité, *n.f.* hilarity.

Hindou, *n.m.* Hindu.

hindou, *adj.* Hindu.

hippodrome, *n.m.* race course.

hippopotame, *n.m.* hippopotamus.

hirondelle, *n.f.* swallow.

hispanique, *adj.* Hispanic.

hisser, *vb.* hoist.

histoire, *n.f.* history, story; to-do, fuss.

historien, *n.m.* historian.

historique, *adj.* historic.

hiver (-r), *n.m.* winter.

hiverner, *vb.* **s'h.,** hibernate.

hocher, *vb.* shake, nod.

hochet, *n.m.* rattle.

hoirie, *n.f.* inheritance.

Hollandais, *n.m.* Hollander, Dutchman.

hollandais, *adj. and n.m.* Dutch.

Hollande, *n.f.* Holland; the Netherlands.

hologramme, *n.m.* hologram.

holographie, *n.f.* holography.

homard, *n.m.* lobster.

hommage, *n.m.* homage.

hommasse, *adj.* mannish.

homme, *n.m.* man. **h. d'affaires,** businessman.

homogène, *adj.* of the same kind, homogeneous.

homosexuel, *adj.* homosexual.

Hongrie, *n.f.* Hungary.

Hongrois, *n.m.* Hungarian (person).

hongrois, 1. *n.m.* Hungarian (language). 2. *adj.* Hungarian.

honnête, *adj.* honest.

honnêteté, *n.f.* honesty, fairness.

honneur, *n.m.* honor, credit.

honorable, *adj.* honorable.

honoraires, *n.m.pl.* fee.

honorer, *vb.* honor.

honte, *n.f.* shame. **avoir h. de,** be ashamed of. **faire h. à.,** shame.

honteux, *adj.* ashamed; shameful.

hôpital, *n.m.* hospital.

hoquet, *n.m.* hiccup.

horaire, *n.m.* timetable.

horde, n.f. horde.

horizon, n.m. horizon.

horizontal, adj. horizontal.

horloge, n.f. clock.

horloger, n.m. watchmaker.

hormis, prep. except.

horreur, n.f. horror.

horrible, adj. horrible, ghastly.

horrifier, vb. horrify.

horrifique, adj. hair-raising.

horripiler, vb. annoy.

hors-bord, n.m. outboard boat.

hors de, prep. out of, outside.

horticole, adj. horticultural.

hospice, n.m. refuge.

hospitalier, adj. hospitable.

hospitaliser, vb. hospitalize; shelter.

hospitalité, n.f. hospitality.

hostie, n.f. (eccles.) host.

hostile, adj. hostile.

hostilité, n.f. hostility.

hôte, n.m. host; guest.

hôtel, n.m. hotel; mansion. h. de ville, city hall.

hôtelier, n.m. innkeeper.

hôtesse, n.f. hostess.

hôtesse de l'air, n.f. stewardess, flight attendant.

hotte, n.f. basket carried on back.

houblon, n.m. hop.

houe, n.f. hoe.

houer, vb. hoe.

houille, n.f. coal.

houillère, n.f. coal mine.

houle, n.f. surge.

houleux, adj. stormy, rough.

houppe, n.f. tuft; powder puff.

hourra, n.m. cheer.

housse, n.f. covering.

houx, n.m. holly.

hublot, n.m. porthole.

huer, vb. shout, hoot.

huile, n.f. oil.

huiler, vb. oil.

huileux, adj. oily.

huissier, n.m. usher.

huit, adj. and n.m. eight.

huitième, adj. and n.m.f. eighth.

huître, n.f. oyster.

humain, adj. human, humane.

humanitaire, adj. humanitarian.

humanité, n.f. humanity.

humble, adj. lowly, humble.

humecter, vb. moisten.

humer, vb. suck up, sniff up.

humeur, n.f. humor; mood, temper.

humide, adj. damp, humid.

humidité, n.f. moisture.

humiliation, n.f. humiliation.

humilier, vb. humiliate, humble.

humilité, n.f. humility.

humoristique, adj. humorous.

humour, n.m. humor.

hune, n.f. (naut.) top.

huppe, n.f. tuft, crest.

hurlement, n.m. noise, howling.

hurler, vb. howl, roar, yell.

hutte, n.f. hut, shed.

hybride, adj. and n.m. hybrid.

hydrogène, n.m. hydrogen.

hyène, n.f. hyena.

hygiène, n.f. sanitation, hygiene.

hygiénique, adj. hygienic.

hymne, n.m. hymn; n.f. church hymn.

hypnotiser, vb. hypnotize.

hypocondriaque, adj. and n. hypochondriac.

hypocrisie, n.f. hypocrisy.

hypocrite, 1. n.m.f. hypocrite. 2. adj. hypocritical.

hypothèque, n.f. mortgage.

hypothéquer, vb. mortgage.

hypothèse, n.f. hypothesis.

hystérectomie, n.f. hysterectomy.

hystérie, n.f. hysteria.

hystérique, adj. hysterical.

I

ici, adv. here. d'i., hence.

ictère, n.m. jaundice.

idéal, adj. and n.m. ideal.

idéaliser, vb. idealize.

idéalisme, n.m. idealism.

idéaliste, n.m.f. idealist.

idée, n.f. idea, notion.

identification, n.f. identification.

identifier, vb. identify.

identique (à), adj. identical (with).

identité, n.f. identity.

idéologie, n.f. ideology.

idiome, n.m. idiom.

idiot, adj. and n.m. idiot(ic).

idiotie, n.f. idiocy.

idiotisme, n.m. idiom.

idolâtrer, vb. idolize.

idole, n.f. idol.

idyllique, adj. idyllic.

if, n.m. yew.

ignare, adj. ignorant.

ignoble, adj. ignoble.

ignorance, n.f. ignorance.

ignorant, adj. ignorant.

ignorer, vb. not know.

il (ēl), pron. he, it; (pl.) they.

île, n.f. island.

illégal (-l-), adj. illegal.

illégitime (-l-), adj. illegitimate.

illettré (-l-), adj. illiterate.

illicite (-l-), adj. illicit.

illimité (-l-), adj. boundless.

illogique (-l-), adj. illogical.

illuminer (-l-), vb. light, illuminate.

illusion (-l-), n.f. illusion, delusion.

illustration (-l-), n.f. illustration.

illustre (-l-), adj. illustrious, famous.

illustrer (-l-), vb. illustrate.

image, n.f. picture.

imaginaire, adj. fancied, imaginary.

imaginatif, adj. imaginative.

imagination, n.f. imagination.

imaginer, vb. imagine.

imam, n.m. imam.

imbattable, adj. unbeatable.

imbécillité, n.f. imbecility; stupidity.

imberbe, adj. beardless.

imbiber, vb. soak, steep.

imbu, adj. imbued; steeped.

imitation, n.f. imitation, copy.

imiter, vb. imitate, copy; mimic.

immaculé, adj. immaculate.

immangeable, adj. uneatable.

immatériel, adj. incorporeal.

immatriculer, vb. matriculate.

immédiat, adj. immediate.

immense, adj. immense, great, huge.

immensité, n.f. immensity.

immeuble, n.m. real estate.

imminent, adj. imminent.

immiscer, vb. s'i., meddle, interfere.

immixtion, n.f. mixing; interference.

immobile, adj. motionless.

immoler, vb. sacrifice. s'i., sacrifice oneself.

immonde, adj. filthy.

immoral, adj. immoral.

immortaliser, vb. immortalize.

immortalité, n.f. immortality.

immortel, adj. and n.m. immortal.

immuable, adj. unchangeable.

immunité, n.f. immunity.

impair, adj. odd.

impalpable, adj. intangible.

imparfait, adj. and n.m. imperfect.

impartial, adj. impartial.

impasse, n.f. dead end.

impassible, adj. impassive.

impatience, n.f. impatience.

impatient, adj. impatient.

impatienter, vb. provoke.

impayable, adj. invaluable; very funny.

impeccable, adj. faultless.

impécunieux, adj. impecunious.

impénétrable, adj. impenetrable.

impératif, adj. and n.m. imperative.

impératrice, n.f. empress.

imperceptible, adj. imperceptible.

impérial, adj. imperial.

impérialisme, n.m. imperialism.

impérieux, adj. domineering.

impérissable, adj. imperishable.

imperméabiliser, vb. waterproof.

imperméable, 1. n.m. raincoat. 2. adj. waterproof.

impertinence, n.f. impertinence.

impertinent, adj. saucy.

impétueux, adj. headlong, impetuous.

impie, adj. impious.

impitoyable, adj. merciless, pitiless, ruthless.
impliquer, vb. involve, imply.
implorer, vb. implore, beg.
impoli, adj. rude, impolite, discourteous.
impolitesse, n.f. discourtesy.
impopulaire, adj. unpopular.
importance, n.f. significance, importance.
important, adj. momentous, important.
importateur, n.m. importer.
importation, n.f. import.
importer, vb. matter; import.
importun, adj. tiresome, bothersome, importunate.
importuner, vb. pester, keep bothering.
importunité, n.f. importunity.
imposable, adj. taxable.
imposer (à), vb. impose (on); tax; enforce.
imposition, n.f. imposition.
impossibilité, n.f. impossibility. **dans l'i. de,** unable to.
impossible, adj. impossible.
imposteur, n.m. fraud (person), faker, impostor.
imposture, n.f. imposture, deception.
impôt, n.m. tax, tariff.
impotent, adj. weak, infirm.
impôt sur les ventes, n.m. sales tax.
imprécis, adj. imprecise.
imprégner, vb. impregnate, imbue.
imprenable, adj. impregnable.
impression, n.f. print, impression.
impressionnable, adj. sensitive, impressionable.
impressionnant, adj. impressive.
impressionner, vb. affect.
imprévoyance, n.f. improvidence.
imprévoyant, adj. not foresighted.
imprévu, adj. unexpected, unforeseen.
imprimé, n.m. printed matter.
imprimer, vb. impress; print.
imprimerie, n.f. printery, printing.
imprimeur, n.m. printer.
improbable, adj. improbable.
improbité, n.f. dishonesty.
improductif, adj. unproductive.
impromptu, adv., adj and n.m. impromptu.
impropre, adv. improper, unfit.
improviste, adv. **à l'i.,** all of a sudden.
imprudence, n.f. indiscretion.
impudence, n.f. impudence.
impudicité, n.f. lewdness.
impuissance, n.f. impotence.
impuissant, adj. impotent, powerless, helpless.
impulsif, adj. impulsive.
impulsion, n.f. impulse, spur.
impunément, adv. with impunity.

impunité, n.f. impunity.
impur, adj. impure.
impureté, n.f. impurity.
imputer, vb. impute.
inabordable, adj. inaccessible.
inaccoutumé, adj. unusual.
inachevé, adj. unfinished.
inactif, adj. inactive, indolent.
inadvertance, n.f. oversight.
inanimé, adj. lifeless.
inanité, n.f. uselessness.
inaperçu, adj. unperceived.
inattaquable, adj. unassailable.
inattendu, adj. unexpected.
inaugurer, vb. inaugurate.
inavouable, adj. unavowable, shameful.
incalculable, adj. countless, incalculable.
incapable, adj. unable.
incarcérer, vb. imprison.
incarnat, adj. flesh-colored, rosy.
incarner, vb. embody.
incartade, n.f. insult, prank.
incendie, n.m. fire.
incendier, vb. set fire to.
incertain, adj. uncertain.
incertitude, n.f. suspense.
incessamment, adv. incessantly; immediately.
inceste, n.m. incest.
incident, n.m. incident.
incinérer, vb. cremate; incinerate.
incision, n.f. incision.
inciter, vb. incite.
inclinaison, n.f. slope.
inclination, n.f. bow, nod; propensity.
incliner, vb. slant, nod, bow. **s'i.,** lean.
inclure, vb. include, enclose.
inclus, adj. included. **ci-inclus,** enclosed, herewith.
inclusif, adj. inclusive.
incolore, adj. colorless.
incomber, vb. devolve upon.
incommode, adj. uncomfortable, inconvenient.
incommoder, vb. inconvenience.
incomparable, adj. incomparable.
incompatible, adj. incompatible.
incompétence, n.f. incompetence.
incomplet, adj. imperfect, unfinished.
incompris, adj. unappreciated, not understood.
inconduite, n.f. misconduct.
inconnu, adj. unknown.
inconscient, adj. and n.m. unconscious.
inconséquent, adj. inconsistent.
inconsidéré, adj. thoughtless.
inconsistant, adj. weak, inconsistent.
inconstant, adj. inconstant.
incontestable, adj. unquestionable.
incontesté, adj. unquestioned.

incontinent, 1. adj. incontinent. 2. adv. immediately.
incontrôlable, adj. not verifiable.
inconvenance, n.f. impropriety.
inconvénient, n.m. inconvenience.
incorporer, vb. embody.
incorrect, adj. incorrect.
incriminer, vb. accuse.
incroyable, adj. incredible.
incroyant, n.m. unbeliever.
inculper, vb. charge, accuse.
inculte, adj. uncultivated, unkempt.
incurable, adj. incurable.
incurie, n.f. carelessness, neglect.
Inde, n.f. India.
indécis, adj. doubtful, vague, dim.
indéfini, adj. indefinite.
indéfinissable, adj. nondescript.
indéfrisable, n.f. permanent wave.
indélicat, adj. indelicate.
indélicatesse, n.f. indelicacy; blunder.
indépendance, n.f. independence.
indépendant, adj. independent.
index (-ks), n.m. index; forefinger.
indicateur, n.m. timetable.
indicatif, adj. and n.m. indicative.
indicatif interurbain, n.m. area code.
indication, n.f. indication.
indice, n.m. sign, proof.
indicible, adj. unspeakable, inexpressible.
Indien, n.m. Indian.
indien, adj. Indian.
indifférence, n.f. indifference.
indifférent, adj. indifferent.
indigène, n.m./f. native.
indigent, adj. destitute.
indigeste, adj. indigestible.
indignation, n.f. indignation, anger.
indigne, adj. worthless, unworthy.
indigné, adj. indignant.
indigner, vb. anger.
indiquer, vb. indicate, point out.
indirect, adj. indirect.
indiscret, adj. indiscreet.
indiscutable, adj. indisputable.
indispensable, adj. indispensable, essential.
indisposer, vb. indispose; set against.
indisposition, n.f. ailment.
indistinct, adj. indistinct.
individu, n.m. individual, person.
individuel, adj. individual.
indomptable, adj. adamant, unconquerable.
indu, adj. undue; not ordinary.
induire, vb. induce; infer.

indulgence, *n.f.* indulgence.

indulgent, *adj.* lenient, indulgent.

indûment, *adv.* unduly.

industrie, *n.f.* industry.

industriel, *adj.* industrial.

inébranlable, *adj.* immovable, firm.

inédit, *adj.* unpublished.

inefficace, *adj.* ineffectual.

inégal, *adj.* uneven, unequal.

inégalité, *n.f.* inequality, irregularity.

inepte, *adj.* inept, stupid.

ineptie, *n.f.* inept action.

inépuisable, *n.f.* inexhaustible.

inertie, *n.f.* inertia.

inestimable, *adj.* priceless.

inévitable, *adj.* inevitable.

inexact, *adj.* inexact.

inexécutable, *adj.* impracticable.

inexplicable, *adj.* inexplicable.

inexprimable, *adj.* inexpressible.

infaillible, *adj.* infallible.

infâme, *adj.* infamous.

infamie, *n.f.* infamy.

infanterie, *n.f.* infantry.

infatigable, *adj.* untiring.

infécond, *adj.* barren, sterile.

infect, *adj.* infected, rotten.

infecter, *vb.* infect.

infection, *n.f.* infection.

inférieur, *adj. and n.m.* inferior, low(er).

infernal, *adj.* infernal.

infester, *vb.* infest.

infidèle, *adj.* disloyal, unfaithful, false.

infidélité, *n.f.* infidelity.

infime, *adj.* lowest; mean.

infini, *adj. and n.m.* infinite.

infinité, *n.f.* infinity.

infirme, *adj. and n.m.f.* invalid.

infirmer, *vb.* invalidate, weaken.

infirmière, *n.f.* nurse.

infirmité, *n.f.* infirmity.

inflammation, *n.f.* inflammation.

inflation, *n.f.* inflation.

infliger, *vb.* inflict.

influence, *n.f.* influence.

influent, *adj.* influential.

information, *n.f.* inquiry; (*pl.*) news.

informatique, *n.f.* computer science.

informatiser, *vb.* computerize.

informe, *adj.* shapeless.

informer, *vb.* inform. **i. de.** acquaint with.

infraction, *n.f.* breach.

infructueux, *adj.* fruitless.

infuser, *vb.* infuse. **faire i.,** brew.

ingambe, *adj.* nimble.

ingénieur, *n.m.* engineer.

ingénieux, *adj.* ingenious.

ingéniosité, *n.f.* ingenuity.

ingénu, *adj.* naïve, ingenuous.

ingrat, *adj.* ungrateful.

ingrédient, *n.m.* ingredient.

inguérissable, *adj.* incurable.

inhabile, *adj.* awkward, incapable.

inhiber, *vb.* inhibit.

inhospitalier, *adj.* inhospitable.

inhumain, *adj.* cruel, inhuman.

inimitié, *n.f.* enmity.

inique, *adj.* unfair.

initial, *adj.* initial.

initiale, *n.f.* initial.

initiative, *n.f.* initiative.

initier, *vb.* initiate.

injecté, *adj.* **i. de sang,** bloodshot.

injecter, *vb.* inject.

injection, *n.f.* injection.

injonction, *n.f.* injunction.

injures, *n.f.pl.* abuse.

injurier, *vb.* abuse, insult.

injurieux, *adj.* abusive, insulting, offensive.

injuste, *adj.* unfair.

injustice, *n.f.* injustice.

inlassable, *adj.* untiring.

inné, *adj.* innate.

innocence, *n.f.* innocence.

innocent, *adj.* innocent.

innocenter, *vb.* declare innocent.

innombrable, *adj.* countless.

innovation, *n.f.* innovation.

inoccupé, *adj.* idle; unoccupied.

inoculer, *vb.* inoculate.

inodore, *adj.* odorless.

inoffensif, *adj.* innocuous, harmless.

inondation, *n.f.* flood.

inonder, *vb.* flood.

inopiné, *adj.* unexpected.

inoubliable, *adj.* unforgettable.

inouï, *adj.* unheard-of.

inquiet, *adj.* restless, anxious, uneasy.

inquiéter, *vb.* trouble. **s'i.,** worry.

inquiétude, *n.f.* misgiving, worry.

insaisissable, *adj.* imperceptible.

insalubre, *adj.* unhealthy.

inscription, *n.f.* incription, entry.

inscrire, *vb.* inscribe; enter.

insecte, *n.m.* bug, insect.

insensé, *adj.* mad.

insensible, *adj.* insensible; unfeeling.

inséparable, *adj.* inseparable.

insérer, *vb.* insert.

insigne, *n.m.* badge, sign.

insignifiant, *adj.* petty, insignificant.

insinuer, *vb.* hint.

insipide, *adj.* tasteless, dull.

insistance, *n.f.* insistence.

insister, *vb.* insist.

insolation, *n.f.* susntroke.

insolence, *n.f.* insolence.

insolite, *adj.* unusual.

insomnie, *n.f.* insomnia.

insondable, *adj.* bottomless.

insouciant, *adj.* casual, careless.

insoumis, *adj.* unsubdued.

inspecter, *vb.* examine, survey.

inspecteur, *n.m.* inspector.

inspection, *n.f.* inspection.

inspiration, *n.f.* inspiration.

inspirer, *vb.* inspire.

instable, *adj.* temperamental, unsteady, unstable.

installer, *vb.* install.

instamment, *adv.* urgently.

instance, *n.f.* entreaty; instance.

instant, *n.m.* instant. **à l'i.,** at once.

instantané, *adj.* instantaneous.

instinct, *n.m.* instinct.

instinctif, *adj.* instinctive.

instituer, *vb.* institute.

instituteur, *n.m.* teacher.

institution, *n.f.* institution, institute.

institutrice, *n.f.* teacher.

instructeur, *n.m.* teacher.

instructif, *adj.* instructive.

instruction, *n.f.* education, instruction; (*pl.*) directions.

instruire, *vb.* educate, teach, intruct.

instrument, *n.m.* instrument.

instrumentation, *n.f.* orchestration.

insu, *n.m.* **à l'i. de,** unknown to.

insuccès, *n.m.* failure.

insuffisance, *n.f.* deficiency.

insuffisant, *adj.* deficient.

insulaire, 1. *n.m.* islander. **2.** *adj.* insular.

insulte, *n.f.* affront, insult.

insulter, *vb.* affront, insult.

insurgé, *adj. and n.m.* insurgent.

insurger, *vb.* **s'i.,** revolt.

insurmontable, *adj.* insuperable.

intact (-kt), *adj.* intact.

intarissable, *adj.* inexhaustible.

intègre, *adj.* upright.

intégrité, *n.f.* integrity.

intellect, *n.m.* intellect.

intellectuel, *adj. and n.m.* intellectual.

intelligence, *n.f.* intelligence.

intelligent, *adj.* intelligent.

intelligible, *adj.* intelligible; audible.

intempérie, *n.f.* inclemency (of weather).

intempestif, *adj.* untimely.

intendance, *n.f.* administration.

intendant, *n.m.* director.

intendante, *n.f.* matron.

intense, *adj.* intense.

intensif, *adj.* intensive.

intensité, *n.f.* intensity.

intention, *n.f.* intention.

intentionné, *adj.* intentioned.

intentionnel, *adj.* intentional.

intercéder, *vb.* intercede.

intercepter, *vb.* intercept.

interdire, *vb.* forbid.

intéressant, *adj.* interesting.

intéresser, *vb.* interest, concern, affect.

intérêt, *n.m.* interest.

intérieur, *adj. and n.m.* interior.

interjection, *n.f.* interjection.

interloquer, *vb.* embarrass.

intermède, *n.m.* interlude.

intermédiaire, *adj. and n.m.f.* intermediate.

interminable, *adj.* interminable.

internat, *n.m.* boarding school.

international, *adj.* international.

interne, 1. *adj.* internal. **2.** *n.m.* resident student.

interner, *vb.* intern.

interpellation, *n.f.* questioning.

interpeller, *vb.* ask.

interposer, *vb.* interpose.

interprétation, *n.f.* interpretation.

interprète, *n.m.f.* interpreter.

interpréter, *vb.* interpret.

interrogateur, 1. *n.m.* examiner. **2.** *adj.* questioning.

interrogation, *n.f.* interrogation.

interrogatoire, *n.m.* cross-examination.

interroger, *vb.* question.

interrompre, *vb.* interrupt.

interrupteur, *n.m.* switch.

interruption, *n.f.* break, intermission, interruption.

intervalle, *n.m.* interval.

intervenir, *vb.* interfere.

intervention, *n.f.* interference.

intervertir, *vb.* transpose.

interview, *n.m. or f.* interview.

interviewer, *vb.* interview.

intestin, *n.m.* bowels.

intimation, *n.f.* notification.

intime, *adj.* intimate.

intimer, *vb.* notify.

intimider, *vb.* daunt, intimidate.

intimité, *n.f.* intimacy.

intituler, *vb.* entitle.

intolérance, *n.f.* intolerance.

intonation, *n.f.* intonation.

intoxication, *n.f.* poisoning.

intoxiquer, *vb.* poison.

intraitable, *adj.* intractable, difficult to deal with.

intrépide, *adj.* fearless.

intrigant, 1. *adj.* intriguing. **2.** *n.m.* schemer.

intrigue, *n.f.* plot, intrigue.

intriguer, *vb.* intrigue; puzzle.

introduction, *n.f.* introduction.

introduire, *vb.* introduce, insert.

introuvable, *adj.* unfindable.

intrus, *n.m.* intruder.

intrusion, *n.f.* intrusion; trespass.

intuitif, *adj.* intuitive.

intuition, *n.f.* intuition.

inusité, *adj.* unusual.

inutile, *adj.* useless, needless.

invalide, 1. *n.m.f.* invalid. **2.** *adj.* disabled, invalid.

invalider, *vb.* invalidate.

invasion, *n.f.* invasion.

invectiver, *vb.* abuse, revile.

inventaire, *n.m.* inventory.

inventer, *vb.* invent.

inventeur, *n.m.* inventor.

invention, *n.f.* invention.

inventorier, *vb.* inventory, catalogue.

inverse, *adj.* inverted, inverse.

investigateur, 1. *adj.* searching. **2.** *n.m.* investigator.

investigation, *n.f.* investigation, inquiry.

investir, *vb.* invest.

invétéré, *adj.* inveterate.

invincible, *adj.* invincible.

invisible, *adj.* invisible.

invitation, *n.f.* invitation.

invité, *n.m.* guest.

inviter, *vb.* invite, ask.

involontaire, *adj.* involuntary.

invoquer, *vb.* call upon.

invraisemblable, *adj.* improbable.

iode, *n.m.* iodine.

Irak, *n.m.* Iraq.

Iran, *n.m.* Iran.

iris (-s), *n.m.* iris.

irisé, *adj.* iridescent.

Irlandais, *n.m.* Irishman.

irlandais, *adj.* Irish.

Irlande, *n.f.* Ireland.

ironie, *n.f.* irony.

ironique, *adj.* ironical.

irradier, *vb.* radiate.

irraisonnable, *adj.* irrational.

irréfléchi, *adj.* thoughtless, rash.

irrégulier, *adj.* irregular.

irréligieux, *adj.* irreligious.

irrésistible, *adj.* irresistible.

irrésolu, *adj.* irresolute.

irrespectueux, *adj.* disrespectful.

irrévérence, *n.f.* disrespect.

irrigation, *n.f.* irrigation.

irriguer, *vb.* irrigate.

irritation, *n.f.* irritation.

irriter, *vb.* irritate, anger, provoke.

Islam, *n.m.* Islam.

islamique, *adj.* Islamic.

isolateur, *n.m.* insulating.

isolement, *n.m.* isolation.

isoler, *vb.* isolate.

Israël, *n.m.* Israel.

Israëli, *n.m.* Israeli.

issue, *n.f.* issue, outlet, outcome.

isthme, *n.m.* isthmus.

Italie, *n.f.* Italy.

Italien, *n.m.* Italian (person).

italien, 1. *n.m.* Italian (language). **2.** *adj.* Italian.

italique, 1. *n.m.* italics. **2.** *adj.* italic.

itinéraire, *n.m.* route, itinerary.

ivoire, *n.m.* ivory.

ivre, *adj.* drunk, intoxicated.

ivresse, *n.f.* drunkenness, intoxication.

ivrogne, *n.m.* drunkard.

ivrognerie, *n.f.* drunkenness.

J

jaboter, *vb.* prattle.

jacasser, *vb.* chatter.

jachère, *n.f.* fallow.

jacinthe, *n.f.* hyacinth.

jadis (-s), *adv.* formerly.

jaillir, *vb.* gush, spurt.

jaillissement, *n.m.* gush, spurt.

jais, *n.m.* jet (mineral).

jalon, *n.m.* staff; landmark.

jalonner, *vb.* mark out.

jalouser, *vb.* envy.

jalousie, *n.f.* jealousy.

jaloux, *adj.* jealous.

jamais, *adv.* ever, never.

jambe, *n.f.* leg.

jambière, *n.f.* legging.

jambon, *n.m.* ham.

jante, *n.f.* rim.

janvier, *n.m.* January.

Japon, *n.m.* Japan.

Japonais, *n.m.* Japanese (person).

japonais, 1. *n.m.* Japanese (language). **2.** *adj.* Japanese.

japper, *vb.* yelp.

jaquette, *n.f.* jacket.

jardin, *n.m.* garden.

jardinage, *n.m.* gardening.

jardinier, *n.m.* gardener.

jarre, *n.f.* jar.

jarretière, *n.f.* garter.

jaser, *vb.* jabber.

jatte, *n.f.* bowl.

jaunâtre, *adj.* yellowish.

jaune, 1. *adj.* yellow. **2.** *n.m.* yolk (of egg).

jaunir, *vb.* turn yellow.

jaunisse, *n.f.* jaundice.

jazz, *n.m.* jazz.

je (jə), *pron.* I.

jeans, *n.m.pl.* jeans.

jésuite, *n.m.* Jesuit.

jet, *n.m.* jet (water, gas).

jetée, *n.f.* pier.

jeter, *vb.* throw.

jeton, *n.m.* token.

jeu, *n.m.* play, game. **mettre en j.,** stake.

jeudi, *n.m.* Thursday.

jeune, *adj.* young, youthful.

jeûne, *n.m.* fast.

jeûner, *vb.* fast.

jeunesse, *n.f.* youth.

joaillerie, *n.f.* jewelry.

joaillier, *n.m.* jeweler.

jobard, *n.m.* fool.

joie, *n.f.* joy.

joindre, *vb.* join.

joint, *n.m.* joint.

jointure, *n.f.* joint (esp. of the body).

joli, *adj.* pretty.

joliment, *adv.* prettily; awfully.

jonc, *n.m.* rush.

joncher, *vb.* scatter.

jonction, *n.f.* junction.

jongler, *vb.* juggle.

jongleur, *n.m.* juggler.

jonquille, *n.f.* jonquil.

joue, *n.f.* cheek.

jouer, *vb.* play.

jouet, *n.m.* toy.

joueur, *n.m.* player.

joufflu, *adj.* chubby.

joug (-g), *n.m.* yoke.

jouir de, *vb.* enjoy.

jouissance, *n.f.* enjoyment.

jouisseur, *n.m.* pleasure-seeker.

jour, *n.m.* day, daylight. **j. de fête,** holiday. **point du j.,** dawn.

journal, *n.m.* newspaper, journal, diary.

journalier, *adj.* daily.

journalisme, *n.m.* journalism.

journaliste, *n.f.* journalist.

journée, *n.f.* day.

journellement, *adv.* daily.

joute, *n.f.* joust.

jovialité, *n.f.* jollity.

joyau, *n.m.* jewel.

joyeux, *adj.* joyful.

jubilé, *n.m.* jubilee.

jubiler, *vb.* exult.

judaïsme, *n.m.* Judaism.

judiciaire, *adj.* judicial, legal.

judicieux, *adj.* wise, judicious.

juge, *n.m.* judge.

jugement, *n.m.* judgment, reason. **mettre en j.,** try.

juger, *vb.* judge.

jugulaire, *adj.* jugular.

Juif *m.,* **Juive** *f. n.* Jew.

juif *m.,* **juive** *f. adj.* Jewish.

juillet, *n.m.* July.

juin, *n.m.* June.

jumeau *m.,* **jumelle** *f. adj. and n.* twin.

jumeler, *vb.* couple, join.

jumelles, *n.f.pl.* opera glasses.

jument, *n.f.* mare.

jupe, *n.f.* skirt.

jupon, *n.m.* petticoat.

jurer, *vb.* swear.

juridiction, *n.f.* jurisdiction.

juridique, *adj.* judicial.

jurisconsulte, *n.m.* jurist, lawyer.

jurisprudence, *n.f.* jurisprudence.

juriste, *n.m.* jurist.

juron, *n.m.* oath.

jury, *n.m.* jury.

jus, *n.m.* juice, gravy.

jusque, *prep.* up to. **jusqu'à,** as far as, until. **jusqu'ici,** hitherto.

juste, 1. *adj.* just, fair, right. **2.** *adv.* just.

justement, *adv.* precisely, exactly.

justesse, *n.f.* accuracy, precision.

justice, *n.f.* justice, fairness.

justifiant, *adj.* justifying.

justification, *n.f.* justification.

justifier, *vb.* justify.

juteux, *adj.* juicy.

juvénile, *adj.* juvenile.

K

kangourou, *n.m.* kangaroo.

karaté, *n.m.* karate.

képi, *n.m.* cap.

kermesse, *n.f.* fair.

kif, *n.m.* marijuana.

kilogramme, *n.m.* kilogram.

kilohertz, *n.m.* kilohertz.

kilométrage, *n.m.* mileage.

kilomètre, *n.m.* kilometer.

kilométrique, *adj.* kilometric.

kiosque, *n.m.* kiosk; newsstand; bandstand.

klaxon, *n.m.* car horn.

kyrielle, *n.f.* litany.

L

la, *pron.* her.

là, *adv.* there.

là-bas, *adv.* yonder, out there.

labeur, *n.m.* labor.

laboratoire, *n.m.* laboratory.

laborieux, *adj.* industrious, laborious.

labour, *n.m.* plowing.

labourer, *vb.* plow.

labyrinthe, *n.m.* maze.

lac, *n.m.* lake.

lacérer, *vb.* lacerate; tear up.

lacet, *n.m.* shoelace; winding.

lâche, 1. *n.m.f.* coward. **2.** *adj.* cowardly, loose.

lâchement, *adv.* loosely, shamefully.

lâcher, *vb.* loosen, let go. **l. pied,** give ground, flee.

lâcheté, *n.f.* cowardice.

lacis, *n.m.* network.

laconique, *adj.* laconic.

lacrymogène, *adj.* gaz **l.,** tear gas.

lacté, *adj.* milky.

lacune, *n.f.* gap, blank.

ladre, *adj.* stingy, mean.

lagune, *n.f.* lagoon.

laid, *adj.* ugly.

laideron, *n.m.* ugly person.

laideur, *n.f.* ugliness.

lainage, *n.m.* woolen goods.

laine, *n.f.* wool.

laineux, *adj.* wooly; downy.

laïque (lä ěk), *n.m.* layman.

laisse, *n.f.* leash.

laisser, *vb.* let, leave.

laisser-aller, *n.m.* freedom, negligence.

laissez-passer, *n.m.* pass.

lait, *n.m.* milk.

laitage, *n.m.* dairy foods.

laiterie, *n.f.* dairy.

laiteux, *adj.* milky.

laitier, *n.m.* milkman.

laiton, *n.m.* brass.

laitue, *n.f.* lettuce.

lambeau, *n.m.* rag.

lambin, *adj.* slow, dawdling.

lame, *n.f.* blade.

lamé, *adj.* gold- or silver-trimmed.

lamelle, *n.f.* (microscope) slide.

lamentable, *adj.* sad, grievous.

lamentation, *n.f.* lamentation.

lamenter, *vb.* mourn, lament.

laminer, *vb.* laminate.

lampe, *n.f.* lamp. **l. de poche,** flashlight.

lamper, *vb.* drink, gulp.

lampion, *n.m.* Chinese lantern.

lampiste, *n.m.* lamplighter.

lance, *n.f.* lance.

lancer, *vb.* hurl; launch.

lanceur, *n.m.* pitcher.

lancinant, *adj.* throbbing (of pain).

lande, *n.f.* wasteland, moor.

langage, *n.m.* language.

langoureux, *adj.* languishing.

langue, *n.f.* tongue, language.

languette, *n.f.* tonguelike strip.

langueur, *n.f.* languor.

languir, *vb.* pine, languish.

languissant, *adj.* languid.

lanière, *n.f.* strap, thong.

lanterne, *n.f.* lantern.

lapider, *vb.* stone; abuse.

lapin, *n.m.* rabbit.

laps, *n.m.* lapse of time.

lapsus (-sys), *n.m.* slip.

laquais, *n.m.* footman, lackey.

laque, *n.f.* shellac; hairspray.

larcin, *n.m.* larceny, theft.

lard, *n.m.* bacon, fat.

larder, *vb.* lard; pierce.

large, *adj.* wide.

largeur, *n.f.* width.

larguer, *vb.* loosen, let go.

larme, *n.f.* tear.

larmoyer, *vb.* weep, whimper.

larron, *n.m.* thief.

las, *adj.* weary.

lascif, *adj.* lewd, wanton.

laser, *n.m.* laser.

lasser, *vb.* weary.

latéral, *adj.* lateral.

Latin, *n.m.* Latin (person).

latin, 1. *n.m.* Latin (language). **2.** *adj.* Latin.

latte, *n.f.* lath.

laurier, *n.m.* bay, laurel.

lavabo, *n.m.* lavatory.

lavande, *n.f.* lavender.

lavandière, *n.f.* laundress.

lavement, *n.m.* enema.

laver, *vb.* wash.

lavette, *n.f.* dishrag.

laxatif, *n.m.* laxative.

le (lə), *m.,* **la** *f.,* **les** *pl.* **1.** *art.* the. **2.** *pron.* him, her, it.

lécher, *vb.* lick.

leçon, *n.f.* lesson.

lecteur, *n.m.* reader.

lecture, *n.f.* reading.

légal, *adj.* lawful, legal.

légaliser, *vb.* legalize.

légalité, *n.f.* legality.

légataire, *n.m.* legatee.

légation, *n.f.* legation.

légendaire, *adj.* legendary.

légende, *n.f.* legend; inscription.

léger, *adj.* light.

légèreté, *n.f.* lightness.

légion, *n.f.* legion.

législateur, *n.m.* legislator.

législatif, *adj.* legislative.

législation, *n.f.* legislation.

législature, *n.f.* legislature.

légitime, *adj.* legitimate, lawful.

legs, *n.m.* bequest.

léguer, *vb.* bequeath.

légume, *n.m.* vegetable.

lendemain, *n.m.* the next day.

lent, *adj.* slow.

lenteur, *n.f.* slowness.

lentille, *n.f.* lentil; lens.

lèpre, *n.f.* leprosy.

lépreux, 1. *adj.* leprous. **2.** *n.* leper.

lequel, *pron.* which, who.

les, *pron.* them.

lesbien, *adj.* Lesbian.

lesbienne, *n.f.* Lesbian.

léser, *vb.* wrong, hurt.

lésine, *n.f.* stinginess.

lésion, *n.f.* wrong; lesion.

lessive, *n.f.* laundry.

lessiveuse, *n.f.* washing machine.

lest (-t), *n.m.* ballast.

leste, *adj.* nimble, clever.

lettre, *n.f.* letter.

lettré, *adj.* lettered, literate.

leur, 1. *pron.* to them; **le leur, la leur,** theirs. **2. leur** *m.f.,* **leurs** *pl.* *adj.* their.

leurre, *n.m.* lure, trap.

leurrer, *vb.* lure.

levain, *n.m.* yeast, leaven.

levée, *n.f.* embankment, levy.

lever, *vb.* raise. **se l.,** get up.

levier, *n.m.* lever.

lèvre, *n.f.* lip.

lévrier, *n.m.* greyhound.

lexique, *n.m.* lexicon.

lézard, *n.m.* lizard.

lézarde, *n.f.* crevice.

liaison, *n.f.* connection, linkage.

liant, *adj.* supple; affable.

liasse, *n.f.* file.

libelle, *n.f.* libel.

libeller, *vb.* draw up, word.

libéral, *adj.* liberal.

libérateur, *n.m.* rescuer.

libérer, *vb.* free.

liberté, *n.f.* freedom, liberty.

libertin, 1. *adj.* wanton. **2.** *n.* libertine.

libraire, *n.m.* bookseller.

librairie, *n.f.* bookstore.

libre, *adj.* free.

libre-échange, *n.m.* free trade.

licence, *n.f.* license.

licencié, *n.m.* licensee; holder of university degree.

licencieux, *adj.* licentious.

licite, *adj.* lawful.

licorne, *n.f.* unicorn.

licou, *n.m.* halter.

lie, *n.f.* dreg.

liège, *n.m.* cork.

lien, *n.m.* bond, link, tie.

lier, *vb.* bind, tie, link.

lierre, *n.m.* ivy.

lieu, *n.m.* place. **au l. de,** instead of.

lieu-commun, *n.m.* commonplace.

lieue, *n.f.* league.

lieutenant, *n.m.* lieutenant.

lièvre, *n.m.* hare.

ligne, *n.f.* line.

lignée, *n.f.* offspring.

ligoter, *vb.* bind up.

ligue, *n.f.* league.

liguer, *vb.* league.

lilas, *n.m.* lilac.

limaçon, *n.m.* snail.

lime, *n.f.* file; lime (fruit).

limer, *vb.* file.

limier, *n.m.* bloodhound.

limitation, *n.f.* limitation.

limitation des naissances, *n.f.* birth control, contraception.

limite, *n.f.* limit, border.

limiter, *vb.* limit, confine.

limon, *n.m.* mud, slime.

limonade, *n.f.* lemon soda.

limoneux, *adj.* muddy.

limpide, *adj.* clear, limpid.

lin, *n.m.* flax.

linceul, *n.m.* shroud.

linéaire, *adj.* lineal.

linge, *n.m.* linen, wash.

lingerie, *n.f.* linen goods, underwear.

linguistique, *adj.* linguistic.

linon, *n.m.* lawn (sheer linen).

linteau, *n.m.* lintel.

lion, *n.m.* lion.

lippu, *adj.* thick-lipped.

liqueur, *n.m.* liquid, liqueur.

liquidation, *n.f.* liquidation, settling.

liquide, *adj. and n.m.* liquid, fluid.

liquider, *vb.* liquidate.

liquoreux, *adj.* sweet.

lire, *vb.* read.

lis (-s), *n.m.* lily.

liséré, *n.m.* piping, border.

liseur, *n.m.* reader.

liseuse, *n.f.* bookmark.

lisible, *adj.* legible.

lisière, *n.f.* edge.

lisse, *adj.* smooth.

lisser, *vb.* smooth.

liste, *n.f.* list, roll.

lit, *n.m.* bed.

litanie, *n.f.* litany.

lit-cage, *n.m.* (folding) cot.

lit de la mer, *n.m.* seabed.

literie, *n.f.* bedding.

litière, *n.f.* litter.

litige, *n.m.* litigation.

litigieux, *adj.* litigious.

litre, *n.m.* liter.

littéraire, *adj.* literary.

littéral, *adj.* literal.

littérature, *n.f.* literature.

liturgie, *n.f.* liturgy.

livide, *adj.* livid.

livraison, *n.f.* delivery. **l. contre remboursement,** C.O.D.

livre, *n.f.* pound.

livre, *n.m.* book.

livre broché, *n.m.* paperback.

livrée, *n.f.* livery.

livrer, *vb.* deliver.

livresque, *adj.* bookish, from books.

livreur, *n.m.* delivery man.

local, *adj.* local.

localiser, *vb.* locate.

localité, *n.f.* locality.

locataire, *n.m.f.* tenant.

location, *n.f.* action or price of renting.

loch (-k), *n.m.* log.

locomotive, *n.f.* locomotive.

locuste, *n.f.* locust.

locution, *n.f.* locution, phrase.

loge, *n.f.* box.

logement, *n.m.* lodging.

loger, *vb.* lodge.

logique, 1. *n.f.* logic. **2.** *adj.* logical.

logis, *n.m.* dwelling.

loi, *n.f.* law.

loin, *adv.* far, away.

lointain, *adj.* distant.

loir, *n.m.* dormouse.

loisible, *adj.* optional, allowable.

loisir, *n.m.* leisure.

Londres, *n.m.* London.

long *m.,* **longue** *f.* *adj.* long.

longe, *n.f.* leash; loin (of veal).

longer, *vb.* go along.

longeron, *n.m.* beam, girder.

longitude, *n.f.* longitude.

longtemps, *adv.* long.

longueur, *n.f.* length.

lopin, *n.m.* small piece, plot.

loquace, *adj.* talkative.

loque, *n.f.* morsel, rag.

loquet, *n.m.* latch.

loqueteux, *adj.* tattered.

lorgner, *vb.* glance at; ogle.

lorgnon, *n.m.* glasses.

loriot, *n.m.* oriole.

lors, *adv.* then. **l. de,** at the time of.

lorsque, *conj.* when.

losange, *n.m.* diamond, lozenge.

lot, *n.m.* lot, prize.

loterie, *n.f.* raffle, lottery.

lotion, *n.f.* lotion.

lotir, *vb.* divide, apportion.

louable, *adj.* praiseworthy.

louage, *n.m.* hire.

louange, *n.f.* praise.

louche, *adj.* shady.

loucher, *vb.* squint.

louer, *vb.* praise; hire, rent.

loueur, *n.m.* one who rents.

loup, *n.m.* wolf.

loupe, *n.f.* magnifying glass.

louper, *vb.* spoil, botch.

loup-garou, *n.m.* werewolf.

lourd, *adj.* heavy.

lourdaud, *n.m.* clod.

lourdeur, *n.f.* heaviness, dullness.

loyal, *adj.* loyal.

loyauté, *n.f.* loyalty.

loyer, *n.m.* rent.

lubricité, *n.f.* lewdness.

lubrifier, *vb.* lubricate.

lucarne, *n.f.* attic window.

lucide, *adj.* lucid.

lucidité, *n.f.* clearness.

luciole, *n.f.* firefly.

lueur, *n.f.* gleam.

lugubre, *adj.* doleful, dismal, lugubrious.

lui, *pron.* he; to him, to her.

lui-même, *pron.* himself, itself.

luire, *vb.* gleam.

luisant, *adj.* shiny.

lumière, *n.f.* light.

lumineux, *adj.* luminous.

lunaire, *adj.* lunar.

lunatique, *adj.* whimsical.

lundi, *n.m.* Monday.

lune, *n.f.* moon. **l. de miel,** honeymoon. **clair de l.,** moonlight.

lunetier, n.m. optician.

lunettes, n.f.pl. glasses.

lustre, n.m. chandelier; luster; five-year period.

lustrer, vb. polish, gloss.

luth, n.m. lute.

lutiner, vb. tease.

lutte, n.f. strife, struggle, contest.

lutter, vb. struggle, contend.

luxe, n.m. luxury.

luxer, vb. dislocate.

luxueux, adj. luxurious.

luxure, n.f. lust.

luzerne, n.f. alfalfa.

lycée, n.m. high school.

lycéen, n.m. high-school student.

lymphatique, adj. lymphatic.

lynchage, n.m. lynching.

lyncher, vb. lynch.

lyre, n.f. lyre.

lyrique, adj. lyric.

M

M. (abbr. for Monsieur), n.m. Mr.

macabre, adj. macabre, ghastly.

macédoine, n.f. salad; mixture.

macérer, vb. macerate, soak.

mâcher, vb. chew.

machin, n.m. thing, gadget.

machinal, adj. mechanical.

machination, n.f. plot, scheme.

machine, n.f. machine. m. à copier, copier. m. à écrire, typewriter.

machiner, vb. plot.

machiniste, n.m. machinist.

mâchoire, n.f. jaw.

mâchonner, vb. mumble, munch.

maçon, n.m. mason.

maculer, vb. spot, blot.

madame, n.f. madam, Mrs.

madeleine, n.f. light cake.

mademoiselle, n.f. Miss.

madone, n.f. Madonna.

mafia, m.f. mafia.

magasin, n.m. store.

mages, n.m.pl. wise men.

magicien, n.m. magician.

magie, n.f. magic.

magique, adj. magic.

magistrat, n.m. magistrate.

magnanime, adj. magnanimous.

magnat, n.m. magnate.

magnétique, adj. magnetic.

magnétophone, n.m. tape recorder.

magnificence, n.f. magnificence.

magnifique, adj. magnificent.

mahométan, adj. Mohammedan.

mai, n.m. May.

maigre, adj. lean, thin, meager.

maigrir, vb. lose weight.

maille, n.f. stitch; mesh.

maillot, n.m. shorts; T-shirt.

main, n.f. hand. sous la m., handy.

main-d'œuvre, n.f. manpower.

maintenant, adv. now. dès m., henceforth.

maintenir, vb. maintain.

maintien, n.m. upkeep; behavior.

maire, n.m. mayor.

mairie, n.f. city hall.

mais, conj. but.

maïs (mä ēs), n.m. corn.

maison, n.f. house.

maisonnée, n.f. household.

maître, n.m. master, teacher.

maîtresse, n.f. mistress, teacher.

maîtrise, n.f. mastery.

maîtriser, vb. master, overcome.

majesté, n.f. majesty.

majestueux, adj. majestic.

majeur, adj. major.

majordome, n.m. majordomo.

majorer, vb. increase price, over-price.

majorité, n.f. majority.

majuscule, n.f. capital.

mal, 1. n.m. harm, ill, evil. 2. adv. badly. faire m. à, hurt. avoir m. à, have a pain in.

malade, 1. n.m.f. sick person, patient. 2. adj. sick.

maladie, n.f. disease, illness, sickness.

maladif, adj. sickly.

maladresse, n.f. awkwardness.

maladroit, adj. awkward.

malaise, n.m. discomfort.

malappris, adj. ill-bred.

malaria, n.f. malaria.

malavisé, adj. indiscreet, ill-advised.

malchance, n.f. bad luck, mishap.

maldonne, n.f. misdeal.

mâle, adj. and n.m. male.

malédiction, n.f. curse.

maléfice, n.m. witchery, evil spell.

malencontre, n.f. unlucky incident.

malencontreux, adj. unlucky.

malentendu, n.m. misunderstanding.

malfaiteur, n.m. malefactor.

malfamé, adj. ill-famed.

malgré, prep. despite.

malhabile, adj. awkward, dull.

malheur, n.m. misfortune, accident.

malheureux, adj. unfortunate, unhappy, miserable.

malhonnête, adj. dishonest.

malhonnêteté, n.f. dishonesty.

malice, n.f. mischief, malice.

malicieux, adj. malicious, roguish.

malin m., maligne f. adj. malignant; sharp, sly.

malingre, adj. sickly, puny.

malintentionné, adj. ill-disposed.

malle, n.f. trunk.

mallette, n.f. small suitcase.

malotru, n.m. boor, lout.

malpropre, adj. messy.

malpropreté, n.f. messiness.

malsain, adj. unhealthy.

malséant, adj. improper.

maltraiter, vb. misuse.

malveillant, adj. malevolent.

malvenu, adj. without any right.

malversation, n.f. embezzlement.

maman, n.f. mamma.

mamelle, n.f. udder.

mammifère, n.m. mammal.

manche, n.m. handle. f. sleeve. La M., the English Channel.

manchette, n.f. cuff.

manchon, n.m. muff.

mandarine, n.f. tangerine.

mandat, n.m. warrant, writ, mandate. m.-poste, money order.

mandataire, n.m. agent, proxy.

mander, vb. send for, inform.

manège, n.m. horsemanship.

manette, n.f. handle, lever.

mangeable, adj. eatable.

mangeoire, n.f. manger.

manger, vb. eat.

maniable, adj. manageable; easygoing.

maniaque, 1. n.m. maniac. 2. adj. maniac, maniacal.

manie, n.f. mania.

manier, vb. handle, wield.

manière, n.f. manner.

maniéré, adj. affected.

manière de vivre, n.f. life style.

manifestation, n.f. demonstration.

manifeste, adj. manifest, evident, overt.

manifester, vb. manifest, show.

manigance, n.f. trick, intrigue.

manipuler, adj. manipulate.

manivelle, n.f. crank; winch.

mannequin, n.m. dummy.

manœuvre, n.f. maneuver.

manoir, n.m. country house, estate.

manquant, 1. adj. missing. 2. n.m. absentee.

manque, n.m. lack.

manquer, vb. miss, lack, fail.

mansarde, n.f. attic.

mansuétude, n.f. mildness, kindness.

manteau, n.m. cloak, coat.

manucure, n.m.f. manicurist.

manuel, adj. and n.m. manual.

manufacture, n.f. manufacture.

manuscrit, adj. and n.m. manuscript.

manutention, n.f. management.

maquereau, n.m. mackerel.

maquette, n.f. preliminary sketch or model.

maquillage, n.m. make-up.

maquis, n.m. scrub land; guerrilla fighters.

maquisard, n.m. guerrilla fighter.

marais, n.m. marsh.

marâtre, n.f. stepmother.

maraude, *n.f.* marauding.

marbre, *n.m.* marble.

marchand, *n.m.* merchant.

marchander, *vb.* bargain, haggle.

marchandises, *n.f.pl.* goods.

marche, *n.f.* march, step.

marché, *n.m.* market, bargain. **bon m.,** cheap.

marchepied, *n.m.* running-board.

marcher, *vb.* walk, step, march, run (machine).

marcheur, *n.m.* pedestrian.

mardi, *n.m.* Tuesday.

mare, *n.f.* pool.

marécage, *n.m.* bog.

marécageux, *adj.* marshy.

maréchal, *n.m.* marshal.

marée, *n.f.* tide.

mareyeur, *n.m.* fish seller.

margarine, *n.f.* margarine.

marge, *n.f.* margin.

margelle, *n.f.* edge, brink.

marguerite, *n.f.* daisy.

mari, *n.m.* husband.

mariage, *n.m.* marriage.

marié, 1. *n.m.* bridegroom. 2. *adj.* married.

mariée, *n.f.* bride.

marie-jeanne, *n.f.* marijuana.

marier, *vb.* marry.

marijuana, *n.f.* marijuana.

marin, 1. *n.m.* sailor. 2. *adj.* marine. **fusilier m.,** marine.

marinade, *n.f.* mixture for pickling.

marine, *n.f.* navy.

mariner, *vb.* pickle.

marionnette, *n.f.* puppet.

maritime, *adj.* marine.

marmite, *n.f.* pot.

marmiter, *vb.* blast (with gunfire).

marmot, *n.m.* urchin, brat.

marmotter, *vb.* mumble.

marotte, *n.f.* fad.

marque, *n.f.* brand, mark.

marquer, *vb.* mark.

marqueur, *n.m.* marker, score-keeper.

marquis, *n.m.* marquis.

marraine, *n.f.* godmother; sponsor.

marron, *n.m.* chestnut; brown.

marronier, *n.m.* chestnut tree.

mars (-s), *n.m.* March.

marteau, *n.m.* hammer.

marteler, *vb.* hammer.

martial, *adj.* warlike.

martre, *n.f.* marten.

martyr, *n.m.* martyr.

martyre, *n.m.* martyrdom.

marxisme, *n.m.* marxism.

mascarade, *n.f.* masquerade.

mascotte, *n.f.* mascot.

masculin, *adj.* masculine.

masque, *n.m.* mask.

masquer, *vb.* mask.

massacre, *n.m.* slaughter.

massage, *n.m.* massage.

masse, *n.f.* mass.

masser, *vb.* mass; massage.

massif, *adj.* massive, solid.

massue, *n.f.* club.

mastiquer, *vb.* chew.

mat (-t), *adj.* dull.

mât (mä), *n.m.* mast.

matelas, *n.m.* mattress.

matelot, *n.m.* sailor.

matérialiser, *vb.* materialize.

matérialisme, *n.m.* materialism.

matérialiste, *adj. and n.m.f.* materialist, materialistic.

matériaux, *n.m.pl.* stuff, materials.

matériel, *adj.* material, real.

maternel, *adj.* native; maternal.

maternité, *n.f.* maternity.

mathématique, *adj.* mathematical.

mathématiques, *n.f.pl.* mathematics.

matière, *n.f.* matter. **table des m.s,** index.

matin, *n.m.* morning.

mâtin, *n.m.* big dog.

matinal, *adj.* early.

matinée, *n.f.* morning.

matineux, *adj.* rising early.

matois, *adj.* cunning, sly.

matou, *n.m.* tomcat.

matraque, *n.f.* heavy club.

matrice, *n.f.* womb.

matricule, *n.f.* roster, registration.

matriculer, *vb.* enroll, register.

matrimonial, *adj.* marital.

mâture, *n.f.* masts (of boats).

maturité, *n.f.* maturity.

maudire, *vb.* curse.

maudit, *adj.* cursed, miserable.

maugréer, *vb.* curse, grumble.

maussade, *adj.* glum, sullen, cross.

mauvais, *adj.* bad.

maxime, *n.f.* maxim.

maximum, *n.m.* maximum.

me (mə), *pron.* me, myself.

méandre, *n.m.* winding.

mécanicien, *n.m.* mechanic, engineer.

mécanique, *adj.* mechanical.

mécaniser, *vb.* mechanize.

mécanisme, *n.m.* mechanism, machinery.

mécano, *n.m.* mechanic.

méchamment, *adv.* maliciously.

méchanceté, *n.f.* wickedness, malice.

méchant, *adj.* wicked, malicious.

mèche, *n.f.* lock; wick, fuse.

mécompte, *n.m.* error, disappointment.

méconnaissable, *adj.* unrecognizable.

méconnaître, *vb.* fail to recognize.

mécontent, *adj.* discontented.

mécontentement, *n.m.* discontent.

mécontenter, *vb.* dissatisfy.

mécréant, *n.m.* unbeliever.

médaille, *n.f.* medal.

médaillon, *n.m.* locket.

médecin, *n.m.* physician.

médecine, *n.f.* medicine.

médiateur, *n.m.* mediator; ombudsman (in France).

médiation, *n.f.* mediation.

médical, *adj.* medical.

médicament, *n.m.* medicament.

médicinal, *adj.* medicinal.

médiéval, *adj.* medieval.

médiocre, *adj.* mediocre.

médiocrité, *n.f.* mediocrity.

médire, *vb.* slander, defame.

médisance, *n.f.* slander.

méditation, *n.f.* meditation.

méditer, *vb.* meditate, muse, brood.

méditerrané, *adj.* Mediterranean.

médium, *n.m.* medium.

méduse, *n.f.* jellyfish.

méduser, *vb.* stupefy.

méfait, *n.m.* crime, misdeed.

méfiance, *n.f.* distrust.

méfiant, *adj.* distrustful.

méfier, *vb.* **se m. de,** distrust.

mégarde, *n.f.* heedlessness.

mégère, *n.f.* vixen, shrew.

mégot, *n.m.* cigarette butt.

meilleur, *adj.* better, best.

mélancolie, *n.f.* melancholy.

mélancolique, *adj.* melancholy.

mélange, *n.m.* mixture.

mélasse, *n.f.* molasses.

mêlée, *n.f.* struggle.

mêler, *vb.* mix. **se m. de,** meddle in.

mélèze, *n.m.* larch.

mellifiu, *adj.* sweet, honeyed.

mélodie, *n.f.* melody.

mélodieux, *adj.* melodious.

mélodique, *adj.* melodic.

mélodrame, *n.m.* melodrama.

mélomane, *n.m.* lover of music.

melon, *n.m.* melon.

membrane, *n.f.* membrane.

membre, *n.m.* member, limb.

membrure, *n.f.* frame, limbs.

même, 1. *adj.* same, very, self. **moi-m.,** myself; **lui-m.,** himself, etc. 2. *adv.* even. **de m.,** likewise. **tout de m.,** notwithstanding. **mettre à m. de,** enable to.

mémento, *n.m.* memento, notebook.

mémoire, *n.f.* memory, memoir.

mémorable, *adj.* memorable.

mémorandum, *n.m.* memorandum.

mémorial, *n.m.* memorial; memoirs.

menaçant, *adj.* threatening.

menace, *n.f.* threat.

menacer, *vb.* threaten.

ménage, *n.m.* household.

ménagement, *n.m.* discretion.

ménager, 1. *n.m.* manager. 2. *vb.* manage.

ménagère, *n.f.* housewife, housekeeper.

ménagerie, *n.f.* menagerie.

mendiant, *n.m.* beggar.

mendicité, *n.f.* begging.

mendier, vb. beg.

menées, n.f.pl. schemes.

mener, vb. lead.

ménestrel, n.m. minstrel.

ménétrier, n.m. country fiddler.

meneur, n.m. leader, ringleader.

méningite, n.f. meningitis.

menottes, n.f.pl. handcuffs.

mensonge, n.m. falsehood, lie.

mensonger, adj. false, deceptive.

mensualité, n.f. remittance paid monthly.

mensuel, adj. monthly.

mensurable, adj. measurable.

mental, adj. mental.

mentalité, n.f. mentality.

menterie, n.f. lie.

menteur, n.m. liar.

menthe, n.f. mint.

mention, n.f. mention.

mentionner, vb. mention.

mentir, vb. lie.

menton, n.m. chin.

menu, 1. n.m. menu. 2. adj. little, minute.

menuet, n.m. minuet.

menuiserie, n.f. woodwork.

menuisier, n.m. carpenter.

méprendre, vb. se m., be mistaken.

mépris, n.m. contempt, scorn.

méprisable, adj. mean, contemptible.

méprisant, adj. contemptuous.

méprise, n.f. mistake, misunderstanding.

mépriser, vb. scorn, despise.

mer (-r), n.f. sea. mal de m., seasickness.

mercanti, n.m. profiteer.

mercantile, adj. mercantile.

mercenaire, adj. and n.m. mercenary.

mercerie, n.f. haberdashery.

merci, n.m. thanks, mercy.

mercredi, n.m. Wednesday.

mercure, n.m. mercury.

mère, n.f. mother.

méridien, n.m. meridian.

méridional, adj. southern.

meringue, n.f. meringue.

méritant, adj. meritorious.

mérite, n.m. merit, desert.

mériter, vb. merit, deserve.

méritoire, adj. meritorious.

merle, n.m. blackbird.

merveille, n.f. marvel.

merveilleux, adj. wonderful, marvelous.

mésalliance, n.f. misalliance.

mésallier, vb. marry badly.

mésaventure, n.f. accident, mishap.

mesdames, pl. of madame.

mesdemoiselles, pl. of mademoiselle.

mésestime, n.f. low opinion or repute.

mésintelligence, n.f. difficulty, discord.

mesquin, adj. shabby, mean, stingy.

mesquinerie, n.f. meanness.

message, n.m. message.

messager, n.m. messenger.

messe, n.f. Mass.

Messie, n.m. Messiah.

messieurs, pl. of monsieur.

mesurage, n.m. measurement.

mesure, n.f. measure. à m. que, as.

mesuré, adj. measured, cautious.

mesurer, vb. measure.

métairie, n.f. small farm.

métal, n.m. metal.

métallique, adj. metallic.

métallurgie, n.f. metallurgy.

métamorphose, n.f. transformation.

métaphore, n.f. metaphor.

métaphysique, 1. n.f. metaphysics. 2. adj. metaphysical.

métayer, n.m. small farmer.

météore, n.m. meteor.

météorologie, n.f. meteorology.

mètèque, n.m. alien.

méthode, n.f. method.

méthodique, adj. methodical, systematic.

méticuleux, adj. meticulous.

métier, n.m. loom; craft, trade.

métis, adj. hybrid, crossbred.

métrage, n.m. measurement.

mètre, n.m. meter.

métrique, adj. metric.

métro, n.m. subway.

métropole, n.f. metropolis; native land.

métropolitain, adj. metropolitan.

mets, n.m. food, dish.

mettable, adj. wearable.

metteur, n.m. m. en scène, play director.

mettre, vb. put, place, set. se m. à, begin.

meuble, n.m. piece of furniture; (pl.) furniture.

meubler, vb. furnish, outfit.

meule, n.f. stack.

meunier, n.m. miller.

meurtre, n.m. murder.

meurtrier, n.m. murderer.

meurtrière, n.f. murderess.

meurtrir, vb. bruise.

meurtrissure, n.f. bruise.

meute, n.f. dog pack; mob.

Mexicain, n.m. Mexican.

mexicain, adj. Mexican.

Mexique, n.m. Mexico.

mezzanine, n.f. mezzanine.

mi, adj. mid, half.

miaou, n.m. mew.

miauler, vb. mew.

mica, n.m. mica.

miche, n.f. loaf of bread.

micro, n.m. microphone.

microbe, n.m. microbe.

microfiche, n.f. microfiche.

microforme, n.f. microform.

microphone, n.m. microphone.

microscope, n.m. microscope.

microscopique, adj. microscopic.

midi, n.m. noon; south.

midinette, n.f. young saleswoman, business woman.

mie, n.f. crumb.

miel, n.m. honey.

mielleux, adj. honeyed, sweet.

mien, pron. le mien, la mienne, mine.

miette, n.f. crumb.

mieux, adv. better, best.

mièvre, adj. affected.

mignard, adj. dainty, mincing.

mignon, 1. adj. delicate, dainty. 2. n.m.f. darling.

migraine, n.f. headache.

migration, n.f. migration.

mijoter, vb. cook slowly, simmer.

mil (mēl), num. thousand.

milice, n.f. militia.

milieu, n.m. middle, center, environment.

militaire, adj. military.

militant, adj. militant.

militarisme, n.m. militarism.

militer, vb. militate.

mille (-l), 1. n.m. mile. 2. adj. and n.m. thousand.

millet, n.m. millet.

millier (-l-), n.m. thousand.

milligramme (-l-), n.m. milligram.

million (-l-), n.m. million.

millionnaire (-l-), adj. and n.m.f. millionaire.

mime, n.m. mime, mimic.

mimique, adj. mimic.

minable, adj. shabby, poor.

minauder, vb. simper.

mince, adj. slender, slight, thin.

minceur, n.f. slimness.

mine, n.f. mine; mien; lead.

miner, vb. mine; wear away; weaken.

minerai, n.m. ore.

minéral, adj. and n.m. mineral.

mineur, 1. n.m. miner. 2. adj. and n.m. minor.

miniature, n.f. miniature.

miniaturiser, vb. miniaturize.

minier, adj. of mines.

minime, adj. very small.

minimum, n.m. minimum.

ministère, n.m. ministry, department, board.

ministériel, adj. ministerial.

ministre, n.m. minister. premier m., premier.

minorité, n.f. minority.

minotier, n.m. miller.

minuit, n.m. midnight.

minuscule, adj. minute.

minute, n.f. minute.

minutie, n.f. trifle; care with details.

minutieux, adj. minute.

mioche, n.m.f. urchin.

miracle, n.m. miracle.

miraculeux, adj. miraculous.

mirage, n.m. mirage.

mirer, vb. aim at, look at.

mirifique, adj. wonderful.

miroir, n.m. mirror.

miroiter, vb. glisten.

misanthrope, 1. n.m. misanthrope. **2.** *adj.* misanthropic.

mise, *n.f.* putting; mode. **mise en scène,** setting.

miser, *vb.* bid.

misérable, *adj.* miserable, wretched, squalid.

misère, *n.f.* misery.

miséreux, *adj.* poor, miserable.

miséricorde, *n.f.* mercy.

miséricordieux, *adj.* merciful.

misogyne, 1. *n. m.* misogynist. **2.** woman-hating; misogynist.

missel, *n.m.* missal.

mission, *n.f.* mission.

missionnaire, *adj. and n.m.f.* missionary.

missive, *n.f.* missive.

mitaine, *n.f.* mitten.

mite, *n.f.* moth.

miteux, *adj.* shabby.

mitiger, *vb.* moderate.

mitoyen, *adj.* midway; jointly owned.

mitrailleuse, *n.f.* machine gun.

mixte, *adj.* mixed, joint.

Mlle. (abbr. for **Mademoiselle**), *n.f.* Miss.

Mme. (abbr. for **Madame**), *n.f.* Mrs.

mobile, *adj.* movable.

mobilier, *adj.* movable.

mobilisation, *n.f.* mobilization.

mobiliser, *vb.* mobilize.

mobilité, *n.f.* mobility; instability.

mode, *n.f.* fashion, mode, mood; (*pl.*) millinery. **à la m.,** fashionable.

modèle, *n.m.* model, pattern.

modeler, *vb.* model, shape.

modelliste, *n.m.f.* dress designer.

modérateur, *n.m.* moderator.

modération, *n.f.* moderation.

modéré, *adj.* moderate.

modérer, *vb.* check, moderate.

moderne, *adj.* modern.

moderniser, *vb.* modernize.

modernité, *n.f.* modernity.

modeste, *adj.* modest.

modestie, *n.f.* modesty.

modicité, *n.f.* small quantity.

modification, *n.f.* alteration.

modifier, *vb.* modify, qualify.

modique, *adj.* moderate, unimportant.

modiste, *n.f.* milliner.

modulation, *n.f.* modulation.

moduler, *vb.* modulate.

moelle, *n.f.* marrow.

moelleux (mwä ly), *adj.* mellow, soft.

mœurs (-s), *n.f.pl.* manner(s), custom.

moi, 1. *n.m.* ego. **2.** *pron.* me.

moignon, *n.m.* stump.

moindre, *adj.* less, lesser, least.

moine, *n.m.* monk.

moineau, *n.m.* sparrow.

moins, *adv.* less, least. **au m.,** at least. **à m. que,** unless.

moire, *n.f.* watered silk.

mois, *n.m.* month.

moisi, *adj.* moldy.

moisir, *vb.* mold.

moisissure, *n.f.* mold.

moisson, *n.f.* harvest, crop.

moissonner, *vb.* reap, harvest.

moissonneur, *n.m.* harvester.

moissonneuse, *n.f.* reaping machine.

moite, *adj.* moist.

moiteur, *n.f.* dampness.

moitié, *n.f.* half. **à m.,** half, *adv.*

molaire, *adj. and n.f.* molar.

môle, *n.m.* pier.

molécule, *n.f.* molecule.

molester, *vb.* molest.

mollah, *n.m.* mullah.

mollasse, *adj.* flabby, soft.

mollesse, *n.f.* softness, weakness.

mollet, 1. *adj.* soft. **œufs mollets,** soft-boiled eggs. **2.** *n.m.* calf of leg.

molletière, *n.f.* legging.

molleton, *n.m.* heavy flannel.

mollir, *vb.* soften, slacken.

mollusque, *n.m.* mollusc.

moment, *n.m.* moment.

momentané, *adj.* momentary.

mon m., ma f., mes pl. *adj.* my.

monacal, *adj.* pertaining to monks.

monarchie, *n.f.* monarchy.

monarchiste, *n.m.* monarchist.

monarque, *n.m.* monarch.

monastère, *n.m.* monastery.

monastique, *adj.* monastic.

monceau, *n.m.* pile.

mondain, *adj.* worldly.

monde, *n.m.* world, people. **tout le m.,** everybody, everyone. **mettre au m.,** bear.

mondial, *adj.* world-wide.

monétaire, *adj.* monetary.

moniteur, *n.m.* monitor.

monnaie, *n.f.* money, change, currency. **Hôtel de la M.,** mint.

monnayer, *vb.* mint.

monocle, *n.m.* monocle.

monogramme, *n.m.* monogram.

monologue, *n.m.* monologue.

monologuer, *vb.* soliloquize.

monoplan, *n.m.* monoplane.

monopole, *n.m.* monopoly.

monopoliser, *vb.* monopolize.

monosyllabe, *n.m.* monosyllable.

monosyllabique, *adj.* monosyllabic.

monotone, *adj.* monotonous.

monotonie, *n.f.* monotony, dullness.

monseigneur, *n.m.* title of honor; My Lord.

monsieur, *n.m.,* **messieurs,** *pl.* gentleman, sir; Mr.

monstre, *n.m.* monster.

monstrueux, *adj.* monstrous.

monstruosité, *n.f.* monstrosity.

mont, *n.m.* mountain, hill.

montage, *n.m.* carrying up.

montagnard, *n.m.* mountaineer.

montagne, *n.f.* mountain.

montagneux, *adj.* mountainous.

montant, *n.m.* amount.

mont-de-piété, *n.m.* pawnshop.

monté, *adj.* mounted, supplied.

montée, *n.f.* ascent, rise, climb.

monter, *vb.* go up, mount, climb, rise.

montre, *n.f.* watch; display. **m.-bracelet,** wrist watch.

montrer, *vb.* show.

montreur, *n.m.* showman.

montueux, *adj.* hilly.

monture, *n.f.* mount.

monument, *n.m.* monument.

monumental, *adj.* monumental.

moquer, *vb.* **se m. de,** make fun of, mock, laugh at.

moquerie, *n.f.* mockery, ridicule.

moqueur, *adj.* mocking.

moral, *adj.* ethical, moral.

morale, *n.f.* morals, morality, morale.

moraliser, *vb.* moralize.

moraliste, *n.m.f.* moralist.

moralité, *n.f.* morals, morality.

morbide, *adj.* morbid.

morceau, *n.m.* piece, bit, morsel. **gros m.,** lump, chunk.

morceler, *vb.* cut up.

mordant, *adj.* pointed.

mordiller, *vb.* nibble.

mordre, *vb.* bite.

morfondre, *vb.* chill.

morgue, *n.f.* morgue.

moribond, *adj.* dying.

morne, *adj.* bleak, dismal, dreary.

morose, *adj.* morose.

morosité, *n.f.* moroseness.

morphine, *n.f.* morphine.

morphinomane, *n.f.* drug addict.

morphologie, *n.f.* morphology.

mors, *n.m.* horse's bit.

morse, *n.m.* walrus.

morsure, *n.f.* bite.

mort, 1. *n.m.* dummy, dead man. **2.** *n.f.* death. **3.** *adj.* dead.

mortaise, *n.f.* mortise.

mortalité, *n.f.* mortality.

mortel, 1. *adj.* deadly, mortal. **morte-saison,** *n.f.* off season.

mortier, *n.m.* mortar.

mortifier, *vb.* mortify.

mort-né, *adj.* still-born.

mortuaire, *adj.* mortuary.

morue, *n.f.* cod.

mosaïque (-à ēk), *n.f.* mosaic.

Moscou, *n.m.* Moscow.

mosquée, *n.f.* mosque.

mot, *n.m.* word; cue.

moteur, *n.m.* motor.

motif, *n.m.* motive.

motion, *n.f.* motion.

motiver, *vb.* motivate, justify.

motocyclette, *n.f.* motorcycle.

motocycliste, *n.m.* motorcyclist.

motte, *n.f.* clod.

mou m., molle f. *adj.* soft.

mouchard, *n.m.* spy.

moucharder, vb. spy.
mouche, n.f. fly.
moucher, vb. blow the nose.
moucheron, n.m. gnat.
moucheté, adj. spotted.
moucheture, n.f. spot.
mouchoir, n.m. handkerchief.
moudre, vb. grind.
moue, n.f. pout, wry face.
mouette, n.f. gull.
moufette, n.f. skunk.
moufle, n.f. mitten.
mouillage, n.m. wetting.
mouillé, adj. wet.
mouiller, vb. soak.
moulage, n.m. cast (from mold).
moule, n.m. mold.
mouler, vb. mold.
mouleur, n.m. molder.
moulin, n.m. mill.
moulure, n.f. molding.
mourant, adj. dying.
mourir, vb. die.
mouron, n.m. pimpernel.
mousquetaire, n.m. musketeer.
mousse, n.f. moss; foam, lather.
mousseline, n.f. muslin.
mousser, vb. foam, froth.
mousseux, adj. foaming.
mousson, n.f. monsoon.
moustache, n.f. mustache, whisker.
moustiquaire, n.f. mosquito net.
moustique, n.m. mosquito.
moutarde, n.f. mustard.
mouton, n.m. sheep; mutton.
moutonner, vb. curl; make wooly.
mouture, n.f. grinding.
mouvant, adj. moving, shifting.
mouvement, n.m. movement, stir.
mouvoir, vb. move.
moyen, 1. n.m. means, medium. 2. adj. middle, average.
moyennant, prep. by means of.
moyenne, n.f. average.
Moyen Orient, n.m. Middle East.
muabilité, n.f. changeability.
mue, n.f. molting; changing (esp. of voice).
muer, vb. molt (animals); break, change (voice).
muet m., muette f. adj. dumb, mute.
mufle, n.m. cad.
mugir, vb. roar, bellow.
mugissement, n.m. roaring, bellowing.
muguet, n.m. lily of the valley.
mulâtre, n.m. and adj. mulatto.
mulet, n.m. mule.
muletier, n.m. muleteer.
mulot, n.m. field mouse.
multinational, adj. multinational.
multiple, adj. multiple, manifold.
multiplicande, n.m. multiplicand.

multiplication, n.f. multiplication.
multiplicité, n.f. multiplicity.
multiplier, vb. multiply.
multitude, n.f. multitude.
municipal, adj. municipal.
municipalité, n.f. municipality.
munificence, n.f. munificence, liberality.
munificent, adj. very generous.
munir, vb. provide, supply.
munitionner, vb. provision, supply.
munitions (de guerre), n.f.pl. ammunition.
muqueux, adj. mucous.
mur, n.m. wall.
mûr, adj. ripe, mature.
muraille, n.f. wall.
mural, adj. mural.
mûre (de ronce), n.f. blackberry.
mûrier, n.m. mulberry tree.
mûrir, vb. ripen, mature.
murmure, n.m. murmur.
murmurer, vb. murmur.
musarder, vb. waste time, dawdle.
muscade, n.f. nutmeg.
muscle, n.m. muscle.
musculaire, adj. muscular.
musculeux, adj. muscular.
muse, n.f. muse.
museau, n.m. muzzle.
musée, n.m. museum.
museler, vb. muzzle; gag.
muselière, n.f. muzzle.
muser, vb. trifle, dawdle.
musical, adj. musical.
musicien, adj. and n.m. musical, musician.
musique, n.f. music.
musulman, adj. and n.m. Mohammedan.
mutabilité, n.f. mutability.
mutation, n.f. change, replacement.
mutilation, n.f. mutilation.
mutiler, vb. mutilate, mangle, mar.
mutin, adj. refractory, mutinous.
mutiner, vb. se m., mutiny, revolt.
mutinerie, n.f. mutiny.
mutisme, n.m. muteness, lack of speech.
mutuel, adj. mutual.
myope, adj. near-sighted.
myopie, n.f. near-sightedness.
myosotis, n.m. forget-me-not.
myriade, n.f. myriad.
myrrhe, n.f. myrrh.
myrte, n.m. myrtle.
mystère, n.m. mystery.
mystérieux, adj. mysterious, weird.
mysticisme, n.m. mysticism.
mystification, n.f. hoax.
mystifier, vb. mystify.
mystique, adj. mystic.
mythe, n.m. myth.
mythique, adj. mythical.
mythologie, n.f. mythology.

N

nabot, n.m. dwarf.
nacre, n.f. mother-of-pearl.
nacré, adj. pearly.
nage, n.f. act of swimming.
nageoire, n.f. fin.
nager, vb. swim.
nageur, n.m. swimmer.
naguère, adv. a short time ago.
naïf (nä ēf) m., naïve f. adj. naïve.
nain, adj. and n.m. dwarf.
naissance, n.f. birth.
naissant, adj. beginning, newborn.
naître, vb. be born.
naïveté (nä ēv-), n.f. simplicity.
nantir, vb. give as security; furnish.
nantissement, n.m. pledge, guarantee.
naphte, n.m. naphtha.
nappe, n.f. tablecloth.
narcisse, n.m. daffodil.
narcotique, n.m. narcotic.
narguer, vb. defy, flout.
narine, n.f. nostril.
narrateur, n.m. narrator, storyteller.
narration, n.f. narrative, recital.
narrer, vb. narrate, relate.
nasal, adj. nasal.
naseau, n.m. nostril.
nasiller, vb. talk with a nasal voice.
nasse, n.f. fish trap.
natal, adj. native.
natalité, n.f. rate of birth.
natation, n.f. swimming.
natif, n.m. and adj. native.
nation, n.f. nation.
national, adj. national.
nationalisation, n.f. nationalization.
nationaliser, vb. nationalize.
nationalisme, n.m. nationalism.
nationalité, n.f. nationality.
nativité, n.f. nativity.
naturaliser, vb. naturalize; (of animals) stuff.
naturalisme, n.m. naturalism, naturalness.
naturaliste, n.m. naturalist.
nature, n.f. nature.
naturel, 1. n.m. nature. 2. adj. natural.
naufrage, n.m. shipwreck.
naufragé, adj. shipwrecked.
nauséabond, adj. nauseous, offensive.
nausée, n.f. nausea.
nautique, adj. nautical.
naval, adj. naval.
navet, n.m. turnip.
navette spatiale, n.f. space shuttle.
navigable, adj. navigable.
navigateur, n.m. navigator, seaman.
navigation, n.f. seafaring, navigation.

naviguer, *vb.* sail, navigate.

navire, *n.m.* ship.

navrant, *adj.* distressing, causing grief.

navrer, *vb.* wound, grieve.

né, *adj.* born.

néanmoins, *adv.* yet, nevertheless, however.

néant, *n.m.* nothing(ness).

nébuleux, *adj.* cloudy; worried.

nécessaire, *adj.* requisite, necessary.

nécessité, *n.f.* necessity. **n. préalable,** prerequisite.

nécessiter, *vb.* make necessary or imperative.

nécessiteux, *adj.* needy.

nécrologe, *n.m.* obituary.

nef, *n.f.* nave.

néfaste, *adj.* ill-omened, unlucky.

négatif, *adj.* negative.

négation, *n.f.* negation; negative word.

négative, *n.f.* negative argument or opinion.

négligé, 1. *adj.* neglected, sloppy. **2.** *n.m.* state of undress.

négligeable, *adj.* negligible.

négligence, *n.f.* neglect.

négligent, *adj.* negligent.

négliger, *vb.* overlook, neglect.

négoce, *n.m.* commerce, trade.

négociable, *adj.* negotiable.

négociant, *n.m.* merchant.

négociation, *n.f.* negotiation.

négocier, *vb.* negotiate.

nègre, *adj.* and *n.m.* Black.

négresse, *n.f.* Black.

neige, *n.f.* snow.

neiger, *vb.* snow.

neigeux, *adj.* snowy.

néon, *n.m.* neon.

néophyte, *n.m.* neophyte, convert.

néphrite, *n.f.* nephritis.

nerf (nĕr), *n.m.* nerve.

nerveux, *adj.* nervous.

nervosité, *n.f.* nervousness.

net (-t) *m.,* **nette** *f.* *adj.* net, clear, clean, neat.

netteté, *n.f.* clearness, neatness.

nettoyer, *vb.* clean, cleanse, scour.

nettoyeur, *n.m.* one who or that which cleans.

neuf, *adj.* and *n.m.* nine.

neuf *m.,* **neuve** *f.* *adj.* brand-new.

neutraliser, *vb.* counteract.

neutralité, *n.f.* neutrality.

neutre, *adj.* and *n.m.* neutral.

neutron, *n.m.* neutron.

neuvième, *adj.* and *n.m.* ninth.

neveu, *n.m.* nephew.

névralgie, *n.f.* neuralgia.

névrite, *n.f.* neuritis.

névrose, *n.f.* neurosis.

névrosé, *adj.* and *n.m.* neurotic.

nez, *n.m.* nose.

ni, *conj.* nor. **ni . . . ni . . .,** neither . . . nor . . . .

niais, *adj.* foolish.

niaiserie, *n.f.* silliness, trifle.

niche, *n.f.* alcove.

nichée, *n.f.* brood.

nicher, *vb.* **se n.,** nestle.

nickel, *n.m.* nickel.

nid, *n.m.* nest.

nièce, *n.f.* niece.

nielle, *n.f.* wheat blight.

nier, *vb.* deny.

nigaud, *n.m.* fool, simpleton.

nihilisme, *n.m.* nihilism.

nimbe, *n.m.* halo.

n'importe, *interj.* never mind.

nippes, *n.f.pl.* old clothes.

nitrate, *n.m.* nitrate.

niveau, *n.m.* level. **au n. de,** level with.

niveler, *vb.* make level; survey.

nivellement, *n.m.* leveling, surveying.

noble, 1. *n.m.* nobleman, peer. **2.** *adj.* noble.

noblesse, *n.f.* nobility.

noce, *n.f.* wedding. **faire la n.,** revel.

noceur, *n.m.* gay blade.

nocif, *adj.* harmful.

noctambule, *n.m.* sleep-walker, prowler.

nocturne, *adj.* nocturnal.

Noël (nō ĕl), *n.m.* Christmas; carol.

nœud (nœ), *n.m.* knot.

noir, *adj.* and *n.m.* black.

noircir, *vb.* blacken.

noisetier, *n.m.* hazel (tree).

noisette, 1. *n.f.* hazelnut. **2.** *adj.* light reddish brown.

noix, *n.f.* nut, walnut.

nolis, *n.m.* freight.

nom, *n.m.* name; noun.

nomade, *adj.* wandering, roaming.

nombre, *n.m.* number.

nombrer, *vb.* number.

nombreux, *adj.* numerous, manifold.

nombril, *n.m.* navel.

nominal, *adj.* nominal.

nominatif, *adj.* and *n.m.* nominative.

nomination, *n.f.* nomination, appointment.

nommément, *adv.* particularly, namely.

nommer, *vb.* name, nominate, appoint.

non, *adv.* no. **non plus,** neither.

non-aligné, *adj.,* non-aligned.

nonchalamment, *adv.* carelessly, nonchalantly.

nonchalant, *adj.* nonchalant.

non-combattant, *adj.* and *n.m.* non-combatant.

nonne, *n.f.* nun.

nonobstant, *prep.* in spite of, notwithstanding.

nonpareil, *adj.* unequaled.

non-sens, *n.m.* nonsense.

nord, *n.m.* north.

normal, *adj.* normal.

normand, *adj.* Norman; equivocal.

norme, *n.f.* norm.

Norvège, *n.f.* Norway.

Norvégien, *n.m.* Norwegian (person).

norvégien, 1. *n.m.* Norwegian (language). **2.** *adj.* Norwegian.

nostalgie, *n.f.* nostalgia.

notabilité, *n.f.* notability.

notable, 1. *n.m.* notable. **2.** remarkable, notable.

notaire, *n.m.* lawyer, notary.

notamment, *adv.* particularly.

notation, *n.f.* notation.

note, *n.f.* note, bill.

noter, *vb.* note.

notice, *n.f.* notice, review.

notification, *n.f.* notification.

notifier, *vb.* notify.

notion, *n.f.* notion.

notoire, *adj.* notorious.

notoriété, *n.f.* notoriety.

notre *sg.,* **nos** *pl.* *adj.* our.

nôtre, *pron.* **le n.,** ours.

nouer, *vb.* tie.

noueux, *adj.* knotty.

nouilles, *n.f.pl.* noodles.

nourrice, *n.f.* (wet-)nurse.

nourricier, *adj.* nourishing; of nursing.

nourrir, *vb.* feed, nourish, foster.

nourriture, *n.f.* food, nourishment.

nous, *pron.* we, us, ourselves.

nouveau *m.,* **nouvelle** *f.* *adj.* new, fresh. **de n.,** anew.

nouveauté, *n.f.* novelty.

nouvel an, *n.m.* new year.

nouvelle, *n.f.* news.

nouvellement, *adv.* recently, newly.

novembre, *n.m.* November.

novice, *n.m.f.* novice.

noviciat, *n.m.* novitiate.

noyade, *n.f.* drowning.

noyau, *n.m.* kernel, nucleus.

noyer, *vb.* drown.

noyer, *n.m.* walnut (tree).

nu, *adj.* naked, bare.

nuage, *n.m.* cloud; gloom.

nuageux, *adj.* cloudy.

nuance, *n.m.* shade, degree.

nucléaire, *adj.* nuclear.

nudité, *n.f.* bareness.

nuire à, *vb.* injure, harm.

nuisible, *adj.* injurious, hurtful.

nuit, *n.f.* night.

nul, *adj.* no, none; void. **nulle part,** nowhere.

nullement, *adv.* not at all.

nullité, *n.f.* nonentity.

numéral, *adj.* and *n.m.* numeral.

numérique, *adj.* numerical.

numéro, *n.m.* number.

nu-pieds, *adv.* barefoot.

nuptial, *adj.* bridal.

nuque, *n.f.* nape.

nutritif, *adj.* nutritious.

nutrition, *n.f.* nutrition.

nylon, *n.m.* nylon.

nymphe, *n.f.* nymph.

O

oasis (-s), *n.f.* oasis.
obéir à, *vb.* obey.
obéissance, *n.f.* obedience.
obéissant, *adj.* obedient.
obélisque, *n.m.* obelisk.
obérer, *vb.* burden with debt.
obèse, *adj.* obese.
obésité, *n.f.* obesity.
objecter, *vb.* object.
objectif, *adj. and n.m.* objective.
objection, *n.f.* objection.
objet, *n.m.* object.
obligation, *n.f.* obligation.
obligatoire, *adj.* compulsory, mandatory, binding.
obligeance, *n.f.* obligingness.
obliger, *vb.* oblige, accommodate.
oblique, *adj.* slanting; devious.
oblitération, *n.f.* obliteration.
oblitérer, *vb.* obliterate.
oblong, *adj.* oblong.
obscène, *adj.* filthy, obscene.
obscénité, *n.f.* obscenity.
obscur, *adj.* obscure, dark, dim.
obscurcir, *vb.* darken, obscure.
obscurcissement, *n.m.* darkening, state of being obscure.
obscurément, *adv.* obscurely.
obscurité, *n.f.* darkness, dimness, obscurity.
obséder, *vb.* harass, haunt.
obsèques, *n.f.pl.* funeral.
obséquieusement, *adv.* obsequiously.
obséquieux, *adj.* obsequious.
observance, *n.f.* observance.
observateur, *n.m.* observer.
observation, *n.f.* observation, remark.
observer, *vb.* observe, watch.
obsession, *n.f.* obsession.
obstacle, *n.m.* obstacle, bar.
obstétrical, *adj.* obstetrical.
obstination, *n.f.* stubbornness.
obstiné, *adj.* obstinate, stubborn.
obstiner, *vb.* s'o., persist.
obstruction, *n.f.* obstruction.
obstruer, *vb.* obstruct, stop up.
obtempérer, *vb.* obey.
obtenir, *vb.* obtain, get.
obtention, *n.f.* obtaining.
obtus, *adj.* obtuse, dull, stupid.
obus (-s), *n.m.* shell.
obusier, *n.m.* howitzer.
occasion, *n.f.* opportunity, chance; bargain.
occasionnel, *adj.* occasional.
occasionner, *vb.* cause, bring about.
occident, *n.m.* west.
occidental, *adj.* western.
occulte, *adj.* occult.
occupant, *n.m.* occupant, tenant.
occupation, *n.f.* pursuit, occupation.
occupé, *adj.* busy.

occuper, *vb.* occupy, busy. s'o. de, attend to.
occurrence, *n.f.* occurrence.
océan, *n.m.* ocean.
océanique, *adj.* oceanic.
ocre, *n.f.* ochre.
octave, *n.f.* octave.
octobre, *n.m.* October.
octroyer, *vb.* grant.
oculaire, *adj.* ocular.
oculiste, *n.m.* oculist.
ode, *n.f.* ode.
odeur, *n.f.* odor, scent, perfume.
odieux, *adj.* hateful, obnoxious, odious.
odorant, *adj.* having a fragrant odor.
odorat, *n.m.* (sense of) smell.
œil, *n.m.*, *pl.* yeux, eye. coup d'o., glance.
œillade, *n.f.* wink, quick look.
œillère, *n.f.* eyetooth.
œillet, *n.m.* carnation.
œuf, *n.m.* egg.
œuvre, *n.f.* work.
offensant, *adj.* offensive.
offense, *n.f.* offense.
offenser, *vb.* offend.
offenseur, *n.m* offender.
offensif, *adj.* offensive.
offensive, *n.f.* offensive.
offensivement, *adv.* offensively.
office, *n.m.* office, pantry; (church) service.
officiant, *n.m.* one who officiates.
officiel, *adj.* official.
officier, 1. *n.m.* officer; mate. 2. *vb.* officiate.
officieux, *adj.* officious.
offrande, *n.f.* offering.
offre, *n.f.* offer.
offrir, *vb.* offer, present.
offusquer, *vb.* obscure, shadow, irritate.
ogre, *n.m.* ogre.
oie, *n.f.* goose.
oignon (ô nyôN), *n.m.* onion, bulb.
oindre, *vb.* anoint.
oiseau, *n.m.* bird.
oiselet, *n.m.* small bird.
oiseux, *adj.* idle, empty, useless.
oisif, *adj.* idle.
oisillon, *n.m.* young bird.
oisiveté, *n.f.* idleness.
oléagineux, *adj.* oily.
olivâtre, *adj.* olive-colored.
olive, *n.f.* olive.
olivier, *n.m.* olive tree.
olympique, *adj.* Olympic.
ombilical, *adj.* umbilical.
ombrage, *n.m.* shade.
ombragé, *adj.* shady.
ombrager, *vb.* shade.
ombrageux, *adj.* suspicious, doubtful.
ombre, *n.f.* shade, shadow.
ombreux, *adj.* shady.
omelette, *n.f.* omelet.
omettre, *vb.* omit.
omission, *n.f.* omission.

omnibus (-s), *n.m.* bus.
omnipotent, *adj.* omnipotent.
omoplate, *n.f.* shoulder blade.
on, *pron.* one (indef. subj.).
once, *n.f.* ounce.
oncle, *n.m.* uncle.
onction, *n.f.* unction.
onctueux, *adj.* unctuous.
onde, *n.f.* wave.
ondé, *adj.* wavy.
ondoyer, *vb.* wave.
ondulation, *n.f.* wave. o. permanente, permanent wave.
onduler, *vb.* wave.
onéreux, *adj.* burdensome.
ongle, *n.m.* (finger)nail.
onglée, *n.f.* numb feeling.
onguent, *n.m.* salve, ointment.
onomatopée, *n.f.* onomatopœia.
onze, *adj. and n.m.* eleven.
onzième, *adj. and n.m.f.* eleventh.
opacité, *n.f.* opacity.
opale, *n.f.* opal.
opaque, *adj.* opaque.
opéra, *n.m.* opera.
opérateur, *n.m.* operator.
opération, *n.f.* operation, transaction.
opératoire, *adj.* operative.
opéré, *n.* patient undergoing surgery.
opérer, *vb.* operate.
opérette, *n.f.* operetta.
opiner, *vb.* hold or express an opinion.
opiniâtre, *adj.* stubborn.
opiniâtreté, *n.f.* stubbornness.
opinion, *n.f.* opinion.
opium, *n.m.* opium.
opportun, *adj.* timely.
opportunité, *n.f.* timeliness.
opposé, *adj.* opposite, averse.
opposer, *vb.* oppose. s'o. à, oppose, resist.
opposition, *n.f.* opposition.
oppresser, *vb.* weigh heavily on.
oppresseur, *n.m.* oppressor.
oppressif, *adj.* oppressive.
oppression, *n.f.* oppression.
opprimer, *vb.* oppress.
opprobre, *n.m.* disgrace, infamy.
opter, *vb.* select, decide.
opticien, *n.m.* optician.
optimisme, *n.m.* optimism.
optimiste, 1. *adj.* optimistic. 2. *n.m.f.* optimist.
option, *n.f.* option.
optique, *adj.* optic.
opulence, *n.f.* opulence, riches.
opuscule, *n.m.* small work.
or, 1. *n.m.* gold. 2. *conj.* now.
oracle, *n.m.* oracle.
orage, *n.m.* storm.
orageusement, *adv.* turbulently, stormily.
orageux, *adj.* stormy.
oraison, *n.f.* prayer, oration.
oral, *adj.* oral.
orange, *n.f.* orange.
oranger, *n.m.* orange tree.

orateur, n.m. speaker, orator.

oratoire, adj. oratorical. art o., oratory.

orbe, n.m. orb, sphere.

orbite, n.m. orbit, socket (as of eye).

orchestre (-k-), n.m. orchestra, band.

orchestrer (-k-), vb. orchestrate.

orchidée, n.f. orchid.

ordinaire, adj. and n.m. ordinary.

ordinal, adj. and n.m. ordinal.

ordinateur, n.m. computer.

ordonnance, n.f. prescription, ordinance, decree.

ordonné, adj. orderly, tidy.

ordonner, vb. order, ordain, bid, command.

ordre, n.m. order. de premier o., first-rate.

ordure, n.f. filth, garbage, refuse.

ordurier, adj. foul.

oreille, n.f. ear.

oreiller, n.m. pillow.

oreillons, n.m.pl. mumps.

orfèvrerie, n.f. gold or silver jewelry.

organdi, n.m. organdy.

organe, n.m. organ.

organique, adj. organic.

organisateur, 1. n.m. organizer. 2. adj. organizing.

organisation, n.f. organization, arrangement.

organiser, vb. organize.

organisme, n.m. organism.

organiste, n.m.f. organist.

orge, n.f. barley.

orgelet, n.m. sty (of eye).

orgie, n.f. orgy.

orgue, n.m. organ.

orgueil, n.m. pride.

orgueilleux, adj. proud, haughty.

Orient, n.m. Orient, East.

Oriental, n.m. Oriental.

oriental, adj. Oriental, eastern.

orienter, vb. orient.

orifice, n.m. orifice, hole.

originaire, adj. original, native.

originairement, adv. originally.

original, 1. n.m. queer person. 2. adj. original.

originalement, adv. originally; unusually.

originalité, n.f. originality.

origine, n.f. origin, source.

originel, adj. original.

oripeau, n.m. tinsel, showy clothes.

orme, n.m. elm.

orné, adj. ornate.

ornement, n.m. ornament, adornment, trimming.

ornemental, adj. ornamental.

ornementation, n.f. ornamentation.

orner, vb. adorn, trim.

ornière, n.f. rut, track.

ornithologie, n.f. ornithology.

orphelin, n.m. orphan.

orphelinat, n.m. orphanage.

orphéon, n.m. choral group.

orteil, n.m. toe.

orthodoxe, adj. orthodox.

orthodoxie, n.f. orthodoxy.

orthographe, n.f. spelling, orthography.

orthographier, vb. spell.

ortie, n.f. nettle.

os, n.m. bone.

oscillant, adj. oscillating.

oscillation, n.f. sway.

osciller, vb. fluctuate, oscillate.

osé, adj. attempted, bold.

oser, vb. dare.

osier, n.m. willow.

ossature, n.f. bony structure, skeleton.

ossements, n.m.pl. human remains.

osseux, adj. bony.

ossifier, vb. ossify.

ostensible, adj. ostensible.

ostentation, n.f. ostentation.

ostraciser, vb. ostracize.

otage, n.m. hostage.

ôter, vb. take off, take away.

ou, conj. or. ou . . . ou . . ., either . . . or . . . .

où, adv. where.

ouailles, n.f.pl. religious congregation.

ouater (wä-), vb. pad.

oubli, n.m. forgetfulness, oblivion.

oublier, vb. forget.

oublieux, adj. forgetful.

ouest (wèst), n.m. west.

oui (wè), adv. yes.

ouï-dire, n.m. gossip, hearsay.

ouïe, n.f. gill.

ouïr, vb. hear.

ouragan, n.m. hurricane.

ourler, vb. hem.

ourlet, n.m. hem.

ours (-s), n.m. bear. o. blanc, polar bear.

ourson, n.m. bear cub.

outil, n.m. tool, implement.

outillage, n.m. quantity of tools, plant.

outiller, vb. supply with tools.

outrage, n.m. outrage.

outrageant, adj. outrageous.

outrager, vb. outrage, affront.

outrance, n.f. extreme degree. à o. to the very end.

outre, adv. and prep. beyond. en o., besides, furthermore.

outré, adj. excessive, extreme.

outrecuidant, adj. excessively bold and forward.

outre-mer, adv. across the seas.

outrer, vb. overdo, irritate.

ouvert, adj. open.

ouverture, n.f. opening, gap; overture.

ouvrable, adj. work, workable.

ouvrage, n.m. work.

ouvrer, vb. work.

ouvreuse, n.f. usher or usherette.

ouvrier, n.m. workman; (pl.) labor.

ouvrir, vb. open.

ouvroir, n.m. work room or shop.

ovaire, n.m. ovary.

ovale, adj. and n.m. oval.

ovation, n.f. ovation.

oxygène, n.m. oxygen.

P

pacage, n.m. land used for pasture.

pacificateur, 1. adj. pacifying. 2. n.m. peacemaker.

pacification, n.f. peace-making.

pacifier, vb. pacify, appease, soothe.

pacifique, adj. pacific, peaceful, peaceable.

pacifisme, n.m. pacifism.

pacotille, n.f. small wares.

pacte, n.m. covenant, pact.

pactiser, vb. make a pact, compromise.

pagaie, n.f. paddle.

pagaie, n.f. disorder, rush.

paganisme, n.m. paganism.

pagayer, vb. paddle.

pagayeur, n.m. paddler.

page, 1. n.m. page (boy). 2. n.f. page (in book).

pages centrales, n.f.pl. centerfold.

pagination, n.f. pagination.

paginer, vb. number pages.

pagode, n.f. pagoda.

paiement, payement, n.m. payment.

païen, adj. and n.m. pagan, heathen.

paillard, adj. lewd, indecent.

paillasse, n.f. mattress of straw, ticking.

paillasson, n.m. (door-)mat.

paille, n.f. straw; defect (in gems).

paillette, n.f. spangle; defect.

pain, n.m. bread, loaf. petit p., roll.

pair, 1. n.m. peer. 2. adj. even, equal.

paire, n.f. pair.

pairesse, n.f. peeress.

pairie, n.f. peerage.

paisible, adj. peaceful.

paître, vb. graze.

paix, n.f. peace.

palabre, n.m. palaver.

palais, n.m. palace; palate.

palan, n.m. gear for hoisting.

palatal, adj. and n.f. and adj. palatal.

pale, n.f. blade, stake.

pâle, adj. pale.

palefrenier, n.m. groom.

palet, n.m. quoit.

paletot, n.m. overcoat.

pâleur, n.f. paleness.

palier, n.m. stair landing.

pâlir, vb. grow pale or dim.

palissade, n.f. paling, fence.

pâlissant, adj. becoming pale.

palme, n.f. palm.

palmier, n.m. palm (tree).

palpable, *adj.* palpable.
palper, *vb.* touch, feel.
palpitant, *adj.* fluttering, palpitating.
palpiter, *vb.* flutter, beat, palpitate.
paludéen, *adj.* marshy.
pâmer, *vb.* se p., faint.
pamphlet, *n.m.* pamphlet, satire.
pamphlétaire, *n.m.* pamphleteer.
pamplemousse, *n.m.* grapefruit.
pan, *n.m.* side, piece, flap.
panacée, *n.f.* panacea.
panache, *n.m.* plume.
panais, *n.m.* parsnip.
pandit, *n.m.* pundit.
pané, *adj.* dotted with bread crumbs.
panier, *n.m.* basket.
panique, *n.f. and adj.* panic.
panne, *n.f.* fat, lard; accident.
panneau, *n.m.* panel.
panse, *n.f.* paunch, cud.
pansement, *n.m.* dressing.
panser, *vb.* groom; dress.
pantalon, *n.m.* trousers.
panteler, *vb.* pant, gasp.
panthère, *n.f.* panther.
pantomime, *n.f.* pantomime.
pantoufle, *n.f.* slipper.
pantoufler, *vb.* act silly.
paon, (pän), *n.m.* peacock.
papal, *adj.* papal.
papauté, *n.f.* papacy.
pape, *n.m.* pope.
paperasse, *n.f.* waste paper; official documents.
paperassier, *adj.* scribbling, petty.
papeterie, *n.f.* stationery.
papetier, *n.m.* stationer.
papier, *n.m.* paper.
papier à notes, *n.m.* notepaper.
papier à tapisser, *n.m.* wallpaper.
papier peint, *n.m.* wallpaper.
papillon, *n.m.* butterfly.
papillonner, *vb.* flutter, trifle.
papoter, *vb.* prate, prattle.
pâque, *n.f.* Passover.
paquebot, *n.m.* small liner, packet.
pâquerette, *n.f.* daisy.
Pâques, *n.m.* Easter.
paquet, *n.m.* package, parcel, bundle; deck (cards).
par, *prep.* by; through.
parabole, *n.f.* parabola; parable.
parachute, *n.m.* parachute.
parade, *n.f.* parade, procession.
parader, *vb.* parade, show off.
paradis, *n.m.* paradise.
paradoxal, *adj.* paradoxical.
paradoxe, *n.m.* paradox.
paraffine, *n.f.* paraffin.
parage, *n.m.* ancestry, descent; locality.
paragraphe, *n.m.* paragraph.
paraître, *vb.* appear, seem.

parallèle, *adj. and n.m.f.* parallel.
paralyser, *vb.* paralyze.
paralysie, *n.f.* paralysis.
paralytique, *adj. and n.m.f.* paralytic.
paramètre, *n.m.* parameter.
parangon, *n.m.* model, paragon.
paraphraser, *vb.* paraphrase.
parapluie, *n.m.* umbrella.
parasite, *n.m.* parasite.
paratonnerre, *n.m.* lightning rod.
paravent, *n.m.* screen.
parc (-k), *n.m.* park.
parcelle, *n.f.* part, instalment.
parce que, *conj.* because.
parchemin, *n.m.* parchment.
parcimonie, *n.f.* parsimony.
parcourir, *vb.* run through.
parcours, *n.m.* course, journey.
pardessus, *n.m.* overcoat.
par-dessus, *adv. and prep.* above, over.
pardon, 1. *n.m.* pardon, forgiveness. 2. *interj.* sorry!
pardonner (à), *vb.* forgive, pardon.
pardonneur, *n.m.* pardoner.
pare-boue, *n.m.* mudguard.
pare-chocs, *n.m.* bumper.
pareil, *adj.* like.
parent, *n.m.* relative; (*pl.*) parents.
parenté, *n.f.* relationship.
parenthèse, *n.f.* parenthesis.
parer, *vb.* attire, deck out; parry.
paresse, *n.f.* sloth.
paresser, *vb.* laze, waste time.
paresseux, *adj.* lazy.
parfaire, *vb.* complete, finish up.
parfait, *adj.* perfect.
parfois, *adv.* sometimes.
parfum, *n.m.* perfume.
parfumé, *adj.* fragrant.
parfumer, *vb.* perfume.
parfumerie, *n.f.* perfumery.
pari, *n.m.* bet.
parier, *vb.* bet.
parieur, *n.m.* one who bets.
Parisien, *n.m.* Parisian.
parisien, *adj.* Parisian.
parité, *n.f.* equality, parity.
parjure, *n.m.* perjury.
parjurer, *vb.* se p., commit perjury.
parlant, *adj.* speaking, chatty.
parlement, *n.m.* parliament.
parlementaire, *adj.* parliamentary.
parlementer, *vb.* parley.
parler, *vb.* talk, speak.
parleur, *n.m.* one who speaks or talks.
parloir, *n.m.* parlor.
parmi, *prep.* among.
parodie, *n.f.* parody.
parodier, *vb.* parody, imitate.
parol, *n.f.* wall lining.
paroisse, *n.f.* parish.
paroissial, *adj.* parochial.
parole, *n.f.* speech, word.

prendre la p., take the floor.
paroxysme, *n.m.* fit of violence.
parquer, *vb.* park, enclose.
parquet, *n.m.* floor.
parqueterie, *n.f.* parquetry.
parrain, *n.m.* godfather.
parsemer, *vb.* spread, strew.
part, *n.f.* share, part. de la p. de, on behalf of. quelque p., somewhere. nulle p., nowhere. faire p. à, share; inform.
partage, *n.m.* partition, sharing, share.
partager, *vb.* share, divide.
partance, *n.f.* going, sailing.
partant, *n.m.* one who leaves.
partenaire, *n.m.f.* partner.
parti, *n.m.* party.
partial, *adj.* partial.
partialité, *n.f.* bias, partiality.
participant, *adj. and n.m.* participant.
participation, *n.f.* participation, share.
participe, *n.m.* participle.
participer à, *vb.* partake of, take part in.
particularité, *n.f.* peculiarity.
particule, *n.f.* particle.
particulier, *adj.* particular, private, peculiar, special.
partie, *n.f.* part, party.
partiel, *adj.* partial.
partir, *vb.* depart, leave, go (come) away, sail.
partisan, *n.m.* partisan, follower.
partitif, *adj.* partitive.
partition, *n.f.* score.
partout, *adv.* everywhere, throughout. p. où, wherever.
parure, *n.f.* ornament.
parvenir, *vb.* reach.
parvenu, *n.m.* upstart.
pas, 1. *n.m.* step, pace. faux p., slip. 2. *adv.* not. p. du tout, not at all.
passable, *adj.* fair.
passage, *n.m.* aisle, passage, alley.
passager, 1. *n.m.* passenger. 2. *adj.* passing, fugitive.
passant, *n.m.* passer-by.
passavant, *n.m.* permit.
passe, *n.f.* passing, permit.
passé, *adj. and n.m.* past.
passe-partout, *n.m.* skeleton key, passport.
passeport, *n.m.* passport.
passer, *vb.* pass; go by; spend; strain. se p. de, go without.
passereau, *n.m.* sparrow.
passerelle, *n.f.* bridge.
passe-temps, *n.m.* pastime.
passible, *adj.* capable of feeling.
passif, *adj. and n.m.* passive.
passion, *n.f.* passion.
passionné, *adj.* passionate.
passionnel, *adj.* concerning or due to passion.
passionner, *vb.* interest, excite.

se p., be eager or excited over.

passoire, n.f. device for straining.

pastel, n.m. crayon.

pastèque, n.f. watermelon.

pasteur, n.m. pastor.

pasteuriser, vb. pasteurize.

pastille, n.f. (Lord's) prayer.

pastoral, adj. pastoral.

pataud, adj. awkward.

patauger, vb. flounder.

pâte, n.f. paste, dough, batter.

pâté, n.m. block; pie.

patenôtre, n.f. (Lord's) prayer.

patent, adj. patent, evident.

patente, n.f. license.

patenter, vb. license.

paterne, adj. paternal.

paternel, adj. paternal.

paternité, n.f. fatherhood.

pâteux, adj. pasty, thick, muddy.

pathétique, adj. pathetic.

pathologie, n.f. pathology.

patience, n.f. patience.

patient, adj. and n.m. patient.

patin, n.m. skate.

patiner, vb. skate.

patineur, n.m. skater.

pâtir, n.f. suffer.

pâtisserie, n.f. pastry.

patois, n.m. dialect, gibberish.

pâtre, n.m. shepherd.

patriarche, n.m. patriarch.

patricien, adj. and n.m. patrician.

patrie, n.f. native country, homeland.

patrimoine, n.m. patrimony.

patriote, n.m.f. patriot.

patriotique, adj. patriotic.

patriotisme, n.m. patriotism.

patron, n.m. employer; boss; model, pattern; patron.

patronat, n.m. management, employers.

patronner, vb. patronize, provide for.

patrouille, n.f. patrol

patrouiller, vb. patrol

patte, n.f. paw, leg, flap.

pâturage, n.m. pasture.

pâture, n.f. fodder, pasture.

paume, n.f. palm.

paupière, n.f. eyelid.

pause, n.f. pause.

pauvre, adj. poor.

pauvreté, n.f. poverty.

pavaner, vb. se p., swagger, strut.

pavé, n.m. pavement.

paver, vb. pave.

pavillon, n.m. pavilion.

pavot, n.m. poppy.

paye, n.f. payment, salary.

payement, n.m. payment.

payer, vb. pay, settle.

payeur, n.m. payer.

pays, n.m. country.

paysage, n.m. landscape, scenery.

paysager, adj. of the country, rural.

paysan, n.m. peasant.

Pays-Bas, les, n.m.pl. Holland; the Netherlands.

péage, n.m. toll.

peau, n.f. skin, hide.

pêche, n.f. peach; fishing.

péché, n.m. sin.

pécher, vb. sin.

pêcher, 1. vb. fish. 2. n.m. peach tree.

pêcherie, n.f. fishing place.

pêcheur m., **pêcheresse** f. 1. n. sinner. 2. adj. sinful.

pêcheur, n.m. fisherman.

pécule, n.m. savings.

pécuniaire, adj. pecuniary.

pédagogie, n.f. pedagogy.

pédale, n.f. pedal.

pédant, adj. and n.m.f. pedant, pedantic.

pédanterie, n.f. pedantry.

pédestre, adj. pedestrian.

pédiatre, n.m. pediatrician.

pédicure, n.m. chiropodist.

peigne, n.m. comb.

peigner, vb. comb.

peignoir, n.m. dressing-gown.

peindre, vb. paint, portray, depict.

peine, n.f. pain, penalty. à p., hardly, barely; faire de la p. à, pain, vb.; valoir la p. de, be worth while to; se donner la p., take the trouble.

peiner, vb. labor; grieve.

peintre, n.m. painter.

peinture, n.f. paint, painting.

pelage, n.m. coat.

pelé, adj. bald, uncovered.

pêle-mêle, adv. pell-mell.

peler, vb. peel, pare.

pèlerin, n.m. pilgrim.

pèlerinage, n.m. pilgrimage.

pèlerine, n.f. cape.

pélican, n.m. pelican.

pelle, n.f. shovel.

pelletier, n.m. furrier.

pellicule, n.f. film.

pelote, n.f. ball, pellet.

peloton, n.m. ball; group of soldiers.

pelure, n.f. peel.

pénal, adj. penal.

pénalité, n.f. penalty.

penaud, adj. awkwardly bashful or embarrassed.

penchant, n.m. bent, liking, tendency.

pencher, vb. tilt, lean, droop. se p., bend.

pendaison, n.f. hanging (execution).

pendant, prep. during, pending. p. que, as, while.

pendiller, vb. dangle.

pendre, vb. hang.

pendule, n.f. clock; pendulum.

pénétrable, adj. penetrable.

pénétrant, adj. keen.

pénétration, n.f. penetration.

pénétrer, vb. penetrate, pervade.

pénible, adj. painful.

péninsule, n.f. peninsula.

pénitence, n.f. penance.

pénitencier, n.m. penitentiary.

pénitent, adj. and n.m. penitent.

penne, n.f. feather.

pénombre, n.f. gloom, shadow.

pensée, n.f. thought; pansy.

penser (à), vb. think (of).

penseur, n.m. thinker.

pensif, adj. thoughtful, pensive.

pension, n.f. board, pension.

pensionnaire, n.m.f. boarder.

pensionnat, n.m. boarding school.

pente, n.f. slope, slant.

pénurie, n.f. penury, scarcity.

pépier, vb. chirp.

pépin, n.m. pip, kernel.

pépinière, n.f. nursery.

pépite, n.f. nugget.

perçant, adj. sharp.

perce, n.f. boring tool.

perce-neige, n.f. snowdrop.

percepteur, n.m. tax collector.

perception, n.f. perception, collecting.

percer, vb. pierce, bore.

percevoir, vb. collect, amass, perceive.

perche, n.f. pole, perch.

percher, vb. se p., perch.

perchoir, n.m. perch.

perclus, adj. lame, crippled.

percussion, n.f. percussion.

percuter, vb. hit, strike.

perdition, n.f. perdition.

perdre, vb. lose; waste.

perdrix, n.f. partridge.

père, n.m. father.

péremptoire, adj. peremptory.

perfection, n.f. perfection.

perfectionnement, n.m. improvement, finishing.

perfectionner, vb. perfect, finish.

perfide, adj. treacherous.

perfidie, n.f. treachery.

perforation, n.f. perforation.

perforer, vb. perforate, drill.

péricliter, vb. be in danger, shake.

péril (-l), n.m. peril, danger.

périlleux, adj. perilous, dangerous.

périmètre, n.m. perimeter.

période, n.f. period, term, stage.

périodique, adj. periodic.

péripétie, n.f. shift of luck.

périr, vb. perish.

périscope, n.m. periscope.

périssable, adj. perishable.

perle, n.f. pearl, bead.

perlé, adj. pearly, perfect.

permanence, n.f. permanence.

permanent, adj. permanent.

perméable, adj. permeable.

permettre, vb. permit, allow.

permis, n.m. permit, license.

permission, n.f. permission, leave (of absence); furlough.

permissionnaire, n.m. one having a permit; one on leave.

permuter, vb. change, exchange.

pernicieux, adj. pernicious.

pérorer, vb. harangue, argue.

perpétrer, vb. commit.

perpétuel, adj. perpetual.

perpétuer, vb. perpetuate.

perplexe, adj. perplexed, undecided.

perplexité, n.f. perplexity.

perquisition, n.f. exploration, search.

perron, n.m. flight of steps.

perroquet, n.m. parrot.

perruque, n.f. wig.

perse, adj. Persian.

persécuter, vb. persecute.

persécution, n.f. persecution.

persévérance, n.f. perseverance.

persévérant, adj. persevering, resolute.

persévérer, vb. persevere.

persienne, n.f. blind, shutter.

persifler, vb. banter, ridicule.

persil, n.m. parsley.

persistance, n.f. persistence.

persistant, adj. persistent.

persister, vb. persist.

personnage, n.m. personage; character.

personnalité, n.f. personality.

personne, 1. n.f. person. **2.** pron. nobody.

personnel, 1. n.m. personnel, staff. **2.** adj. personal.

personnifier, vb. personify.

perspective, n.f. perspective, prospect.

perspicace, adj. discerning.

perspicacité, n.f. insight.

persuader, vb. persuade, convince, induce.

persuasif, adj. persuasive.

perte, n.f. loss, waste; (pl.) casualties.

pertinence, n.f. pertinence.

pertinent, adj. relevant, pertinent.

perturbateur, n.m. agitator, disturber.

pervers, adj. perverse, contrary.

pervertir, vb. pervert.

pesant, adj. heavy, ponderous.

pesanteur, n.f. weight, dullness.

peser, vb. weigh.

pessimisme, n.m. pessimism.

pessimiste, n.m. pessimist.

peste, n.f. pestilence; nuisance.

pestilence, n.f. pestilence, plague, nuisance.

pétale, n.m. petal.

pétiller, vb. twinkle, crackle.

petit, 1. adj. little, small, petty. **2.** n.m. cub.

petite-fille, n.f. granddaughter.

petitesse, n.f. smallness, pettiness.

petit-fils (-fēs), n.m. grandson.

petit-gris, n.m. fur of the squirrel.

pétition, n.f. petition.

pétitionner, vb. request, ask.

petits-enfants, n.m.pl. grandchildren.

pétrifiant, adj. petrifying.

pétrifier, vb. petrify or (se p.) become petrified.

pétrir, vb. knead, mold.

pétrole, n.m. petroleum, kerosene.

pétulance, n.f. petulance.

peu, 1. n.m. little; few. **2.** adv. not. **p. à p.,** gradually.

peuplade, n.f. tribe, clan.

peuple, n.m. people.

peupler, vb. people.

peuplier, n.m. poplar.

peur, n.f. fear. **avoir p.,** be afraid. **de p. que . . . ne,** lest.

peureux, adj. shy, timid.

peut-être, adv. perhaps, maybe.

phallocratie, n.f. machismo.

phallocrate, adj. macho.

phare, n.m. beacon, lighthouse; headlight.

pharmacie, n.f. drug store, pharmacy.

pharmacien, n.m. druggist.

phase, n.f. phase.

phénix, n.m. phoenix; superior person.

phénoménal, adj. phenomenal.

phénomène, n.m. phenomenon; freak.

philanthrope, n.m. philanthropist.

philanthropie, n.f. philanthropy.

philatélie, n.f. stamp-collecting.

philosophe, n.m. philosopher.

philosophie, n.f. philosophy.

philosophique, adj. philosophical.

phobie, n.f. phobia.

phonéticien, n.m. phonetician.

phonétique, adj. and n.f. phonetic, phonetics.

phonographe, n.m. phonograph.

phoque, n.m. seal.

photocopie, n.f. photocopy.

photocopieur, n.m. photocopier.

photographe, n.m. photographer.

photographie, n.f. photograph, photography.

phrase, n.f. sentence.

phtisie, n.f. consumption.

phtisique, adj. and n.m. consumptive.

physicien, n.m. physical scientist.

physionomie, n.f. looks, expression.

physique, 1. n.f. physics. **2.** adj. physical.

piailler, vb. peep, squeal.

pianiste, n.m.f. pianist.

piano, n.m. piano.

pic, n.m. peak.

picoter, vb. prick, peck.

pièce, n.f. piece, coin, patch, room. **p. de théâtre,** play.

pied, n.m. foot. **aller à p.,** walk. **coup de p.,** kick.

pied-à-terre, n.m. temporary quarters.

piédestal, n.m. pedestal.

piège, n.m. snare, trap.

pierre, n.f. stone.

pierreries, n.f.pl. jewelry, gems.

pierreux, adj. full of stone or grit.

pierrot, n.m. clown in pantomime.

piété, n.f. piety.

piétiner, vb. trample.

piéton, n.m. pedestrian.

piètre, adj. pitiful, mean, wretched.

pieu, n.m. stake, pile.

pieuvre, n.f. octopus.

pieux, adj. pious.

pigeon, n.m. pigeon, dove.

pile, n.f. stack; battery.

piler, vb. crush, blast.

pilier, n.m. pillar, column.

pillage, n.m. plundering.

piller, vb. plunder.

pilotage, n.m. piloting; driving piles.

pilote, n.m. pilot.

piloter, vb. pilot, lead.

pilule, n.f. pill.

piment, n.m. chili.

pimenter, vb. flavor, season.

pimpant, adj. stylish, smart.

pin, n.m. pine.

pinacle, n.m. pinnacle.

pince, n.f. clip; (pl.) pliers.

pinceau, n.m. paint-brush.

pince-nez, n.m. eyeglasses.

pincer, vb. pinch, nip.

pinte, n.f. pint.

pioche, n.f. pickax.

piocher, vb. dig.

piocheur, n.m. digger.

pion, n.m. pawn, peon.

pioncer, vb. nap, sleep.

pionnier, n.m. pioneer.

pipe, n.f. pipe.

piper, vb. catch, decoy, trick.

piquant, adj. sharp. **mot p.,** quip.

pique, n.m. spade.

pique-nique, n.m. picnic.

piquer, vb. prick, sting.

piquet, n.m. picket, peg, stake.

piqûre, n.f. prick, sting, puncture.

pirate, n.m. pirate.

pirate de l'air, n.m. hijacker.

piraterie, n.f. piracy.

pire, adj. worse, worst.

pirouette, n.f. pirouette, shift.

pis, adv. worse, worst.

piscine, n.f. pool.

pissenlit, n.m. dandelion.

pistache, n.f. pistachio.

piste, n.f. track.

pistolet, n.m. pistol.

piston, n.m. piston.

pistonner, vb. help, push.

pitance, n.f. meager amount, as of food.

piteux, adj. pitiful.

pitié, n.f. pity, mercy.

pitoyable, *adj.* pitiful, miserable.

pitre, *n.m.* clown.

pittoresque, *adj.* picturesque, colorful.

pivoine, *n.f.* peony.

pivot, *n.m.* pivot.

pivoter, *vb.* turn, pivot, revolve.

pizza, *n.f.* pizza.

placard, *n.m.* closet; poster.

placarder, *vb.* post, display.

place, *n.f.* place, room.

placement, *n.m.* investment, placing.

placer, *vb.* invest, place.

placet, *n.m.* petition, demand.

placide, *adj.* placid.

placidité, *n.f.* placidness.

plafond, *n.m.* ceiling.

plage, *n.f.* beach.

plagiaire, *n.m.* one who plagiarizes.

plagiat, *n.m.* plagiarism.

plagier, *vb.* plagiarize.

plaid, *n.m.* plaid.

plaider, *vb.* plead.

plaideur, *n.m.* pleader.

plaidoirie, *n.f.* lawyer's speech.

plaie, *n.f.* wound, sore.

plaignant, *n.m.* plaintiff.

plaindre, *vb.* pity. **se p.**, complain.

plaine, *n.f.* plain.

plainte, *n.f.* complaint.

plaintif, *adj.* mournful.

plaire à, *vb.* please. **s'il vous plaît**, if you please.

plaisance, *n.f.* pleasure, ease.

plaisant, *adj.* joking.

plaisanter, *vb.* joke.

plaisanterie, *n.f.* joke.

plaisir, *n.m.* pleasure.

plan, *n.m.* plan; plane; schedule, scheme. **premier p.**, foreground.

planche, *n.f.* board, shelf, plank.

planche à roulettes, *n.f.* skateboard.

plancher, *n.m.* floor.

planer, *vb.* glide; hover.

planétaire, 1. *adj.* planetary. 2. *n.m.* planetarium.

planète, *n.f.* planet.

planeur, *n.m.* glider (plane).

plantation, *n.f.* plantation.

plante, *n.f.* plant; sole.

planter, *vb.* plant.

planteur, *n.m.* planter.

planton, *n.m.* military orderly.

plantureux, *adj.* fertile, rich.

plaque, *n.f.* plate, slab. **p. de projection**, lantern-slide.

plaquer, *vb.* plate; abandon.

plaquette, *n.f.* booklet, medal.

plastique, *adj.* plastic.

plastronner, *vb.* pose, strut jauntily.

plat, 1. *n.m.* dish, platter. 2. *adj.* flat. **œuf sur le p.**, fried egg.

platane, *n.m.* plane-tree.

plat-bord, *n.m.* gunwale.

plateau, *n.m.* plateau, tray.

plate-bande, *n.f.* flower bed.

plate-forme, *n.f.* platform.

platine, 1. *n.f.* platen, plate. 2. *n.m.* platinum.

platitude, *n.f.* flatness.

plâtras, *n.m.* rubbish, rubble.

plâtre, *n.m.* plaster.

plausible, *adj.* plausible.

plébéien, *adj.* ignoble.

plébiscite, *n.m.* plebiscite.

plein, *adj.* full, crowded.

plénier, *adj.* complete, plenary.

plénitude, *n.f.* fullness.

pleurer, *vb.* cry, weep, lament, mourn.

pleurésie, *n.f.* pleurisy.

pleurnicher, *vb.* complain, whine.

pleurs, *n.m.pl.* tears, weeping.

pleutre, *n.m.* cad, coward.

pleuvoir, *vb.* rain.

pli, *n.m.* fold, envelope, pleat, crease.

pliable, *adj.* pliable.

pliant, *n.m.* folding chair.

plier, *vb.* fold, bend.

plissement, *n.m.* fold, folding.

plisser, *vb.* pleat.

plomb, *n.m.* lead.

plomberie, *n.f.* plumbing.

plombier, *n.m.* plumber.

plongeon, *n.m.* plunge.

plonger, *vb.* plunge, dive, dip.

plongeur, *n.m.* diver; dishwasher.

plouf, *interj. and n.m.* splash, plop.

ploutocrate, *n.m.* plutocrat.

ployer, *vb.* incline, bend.

pluie, *n.f.* rain.

pluie radioactive, *n.f.* fallout.

plumage, *n.m.* feathers.

plume, *n.f.* pen, feather.

plumeau, *n.m.* feather duster.

plumer, *vb.* pluck.

plumet, *n.m.* plume.

plumeux, *adj.* feathery.

plumier, *n.m.* pen or pencil case.

plupart, *n.f.* greater part, majority. **pour la p.**, mostly.

pluralité, *n.f.* plurality.

pluriel, *adj. and n.m.* plural.

plus, *adv.* more, most. **ne . . . p.**, no more. **non p.**, neither. **en p.**, extra.

plusieurs, *adj. and pron.* several.

plus-que-parfait, *n.m. (gramm.)* pluperfect.

plutôt, *adv.* rather.

pluvieux, *adj.* rainy, wet.

pneumatique, *abbr.* pneu, *n.m.* tire.

pneumonie, *n.f.* pneumonia.

pochade, *n.f.* hasty sketch.

poche, *n.f.* pocket.

pocher, *vb.* poach.

pocheter, *vb.* pocket.

pochette, *n.f.* little pocket, handkerchief.

pochoir, *n.m.* stencil.

poêle, *n.m.* stove.

poème, *n.m.* poem.

poésie, *n.f.* poem, poetry.

poète, *n.f.* poet.

poétique, *adj.* poetic.

poids (pwä), *n.m.* weight.

poignant, *adj.* poignant, keen.

poignard, *n.m.* dagger.

poignarder, *vb.* stab.

poigne, *n.f.* grip, power.

poignée, *n.f.* handful; handle.

poignet, *n.m.* wrist; cuff.

poil (pwäl), *n.m.* hair.

poilu, 1. *adj.* hairy, strong. 2. *n.m.* French soldier.

poinçon, *n.m.* punch.

poing, *n.m.* fist.

point, *n.m.* point, dot, period, stitch. **p. de vue**, point of view. **p. du jour**, dawn. **ne . . . p.**, none. **être sur le p. de**, be about to. **au p.**, in focus. **deux p.s**, colon. **p. d'interrogation**, question mark.

pointage, *n.m.* pointing; (*mil.*) sighting.

pointe, *n.f.* point, tip, touch (small amount).

pointer, *vb.* point, aim.

pointeur, *n.m.* pointer, checker.

pointillage, *n.m.* dotting.

pointiller, *vb.* dot; tease.

pointilleux, *adj.* fussy, precise.

pointu, *adj.* pointed.

pointure, *n.f.* size.

poire, *n.f.* pear.

poireau, *n.m.* leek.

poirier, *n.m.* pear tree.

pois, *n.m.* pea.

poison, *n.m.* poison.

poisser, *vb.* make gluey or sticky.

poisson, *n.m.* fish.

poissonnerie, *n.f.* fish store.

poissonneux, *adj.* filled with fish.

poissonnier, *n.m.* fish dealer.

poitrinaire, *adj. and n.m.* consumptive.

poitrine, *n.f.* chest.

poivre, *n.m.* pepper.

poivrer, *vb.* spice with pepper.

poivrier, *n.m.* pepper plant.

poix, *n.f.* pitch.

polaire, *adj.* polar.

pôle, *n.m.* pole.

polémique, *n.f.* argument.

poli, 1. *adj.* civil, polite. 2. *n.m.* polish.

police, *n.f.* police; (insurance) policy.

policer, *vb.* refine.

polichinelle, *n.m.* Punch (puppet).

policier, *n.m.* policeman. **roman p.**, detective story.

polir, *vb.* polish.

polisseur, *n.m.* polisher.

polisson, 1. *n.m.* gamin, scamp. 2. *adj.* running wild.

polissonnerie, *n.f.* naughty action or remark.

politesse, *n.f.* good manners.

politicien, *n.m.* politician.

politique, 1. *n.f.* policy, politics. 2. *adj.* politic, political.

polka, *n.f.* polka.

pollen, *n.m.* pollen.
polluer, *vb.* pollute.
pollution, *n.f.* pollution.
Pologne, *n.f.* Poland.
Polonais, *n.m.* Pole.
polonais, *adj. and n.m.* Polish.
poltron, 1. *adj.* craven, cowardly. **2.** *n.m.f.* coward.
poltronnerie, *n.f.* cowardly behavior.
polygame, 1. *n.m.* polygamist. **2.** *adj.* polygamous.
polygamie, *n.f.* polygamy.
polygone, *n.m.* polygon.
pommade, *n.f.* pomade, salve.
pomme, *n.f.* apple. **p. de terre,** potato.
pommeau, *n.m.* pommel.
pommette, *n.f.* cheekbone.
pommier, *n.m.* apple tree.
pompe, *n.f.* pump; pomp.
pomper, *vb.* pump.
pompeux, *adj.* pompous.
pompier, *n.m.* fireman.
pompon, *n.m.* pompon, tuft.
ponce, *n.f.* pumice.
ponctualité, *n.f.* punctuality.
ponctuation, *n.f.* punctuation.
ponctuel, *adj.* punctual.
ponctuer, *vb.* punctuate.
poney, *n.m.* pony.
pont, *n.m.* bridge; deck.
pontife, *n.m.* pontiff.
pont-levis, *n.m.* drawbridge.
ponton, *n.m.* pontoon.
popeline, *n.f.* poplin.
popote, *n.f.* mess (military).
populace, *n.f.* mob.
populaire, *adj.* popular.
populariser, *vb.* popularize.
popularité, *n.f.* popularity.
population, *n.f.* population.
populeux, *adj.* populous.
porc, *n.m.* pig, pork.
porcelaine, *n.f.* china.
porc-épic, *n.m.* porcupine.
porche, *n.m.* porch.
porcherie, *n.f.* pigpen.
pore, *n.m.* pore.
poreux, *adj.* porous.
pornographie, *n.f.* pornography.
port, *n.m.* port, harbor; carrying; postage.
portable, *adj.* wearable.
portail, *n.m.* portal.
portatif, *adj.* portable.
porte, *n.f.* door, gate.
porte-affiches, *n.m.* billboard.
porte-avions, *n.m.* aircraft carrier.
portée, *n.f.* range, import, scope, reach; litter. **hors de p.,** out of reach.
portefaix, *n.m.* porter.
portefeuille, *n.m.* wallet, case, portfolio.
portemanteau, *n.m.* cloak rack.
portement, *n.m.* carrying.
porte-monnaie, *n.m.* purse.
porter, *vb.* carry, bear; wear. **se p.,** be (in health).
porte-rame, *n.m.* oarlock.
porteur, *n.m.* porter, bearer.

portier, *n.m.* doorman, porter.
portière, *n.f.* door-curtain.
portion, *n.f.* portion, share.
portique, *n.m.* portico, porch.
porto, *n.m.* port wine.
portrait, *n.m.* portrait.
portraitiste, *n.m.* painter of portraits.
Portugais, *n.m.* Portuguese (person).
portugais, 1. *n.m.* Portuguese (language). **2.** *adj.* Portuguese.
Portugal, *n.m.* Portugal.
pose, *n.f.* pose, attitude.
posé, *n.f.* poised, set.
poser, *vb.* place, stand, set, lay. **se p.,** settle, alight.
poseur, *n.m.* person or thing that places or applies; affected person.
positif, *adj. and n.m.* positive.
position, *n.f.* stand, place, position.
positiviste, *n.m.f.* positivist.
posséder, *vb.* own, possess.
possesseur, *n.m.* possessor.
possessif, *adj. and n.m.* possessive.
possession, *n.f.* possession.
possibilité, *n.f.* possibility.
possible, *adj.* possible. **tout son p.,** one's utmost.
postal, *adj.* postal.
poste, *n.f.* mail. **mettre à la p.,** mail. **p. restante,** general delivery.
poste, *n.m.* post. **p. d'essence,** gas station. **p. de secours,** first-aid station.
poster, *vb.* post (letter); place.
postérieur, *adj.* rear, posterior.
postérité, *n.f.* posterity.
posthume, *adj.* posthumous.
postiche, *adj.* false, unnecessary.
post-scriptum, *n.m.* postscript.
postulant, *n.m.* applicant.
postuler, *vb.* apply for.
posture, *n.f.* posture.
pot, *n.m.* pot, pitcher, jar.
potable, *adj.* drinkable.
potage, *n.m.* soup.
potager, *adj.* vegetable.
potasse, *n.f.* potash.
pot-de-vin, *n.m.* tip, bribe.
poteau, *n.m.* post.
potée, *n.f.* potful.
potence, *n.f.* gallows.
potentat, *n.m.* potentate.
potentiel, *adj. and n.m.* potential.
poterie, *n.f.* pottery.
poterne, *n.f.* postern.
potier, *n.m.* potter.
potion, *n.f.* potion.
potiron, *n.m.* pumpkin.
pou, *n.m.* louse.
pouce, *n.m.* thumb; inch.
pouding, *n.m.* pudding.
poudre, *n.f.* powder.
poudrer, *vb.* powder.
poudreux, *adj.* full of powder or dust.

poudrier, *n.m.* compact (cosmetic).
poudroyer, *vb.* be dusty.
pouilleux, *adj.* infected with lice.
poulailler, *n.m.* hen-house.
poulain, *n.m.* colt.
poule, *n.f.* hen, chicken.
poulet, *n.m.* chicken.
poulette, *n.f.* pullet.
poulie, *n.f.* pulley.
poulpe, *n.m.* octopus.
pouls, *n.m.* pulse.
poumon, *n.m.* lung.
poupe, *n.f.* poop (of ship).
poupée, *n.f.* doll.
poupin, *adj.* smart, chic.
pour, *prep.* for; in order to. **p. que,** so that.
pourboire, *n.m.* tip, gratuity.
pourceau, *n.m.* hog.
pour-cent, *n.m.* percent.
pourcentage, *n.m.* percentage.
pourchasser, *vb.* pursue.
pourfendeur, *n.m.* killer, bully.
pourparler, *n.m.* discussion, parley.
pourpoint, *n.m.* doublet.
pourpre, *adj.* purple.
pourquoi, *adv.* why.
pourri, *adj.* rotten.
pourrir, *vb.* rot, spoil.
pourriture, *n.f.* rot.
poursuite, *n.f.* pursuit.
poursuivant, *n.m.* one who sues or prosecutes.
poursuivre, *vb.* pursue, sue, prosecute.
pourtant, *adv.* however.
pourvoi, *n.m.* appeal (at court).
pourvoir (de), *vb.* provide (with), supply. **p. à,** cater to.
pourvoyeur, *n.m.* caterer, purveyor.
pourvu que, *conj.* provided that.
pousse, *n.f.* shoot, sprouting.
poussée, *n.f.* push.
pousser, *vb.* push, urge, drive; grow.
poussier, *n.m.* coal dust.
poussière, *n.f.* dust.
poussiéreux, *adj.* dusty.
poussin, *n.m.* newly-hatched chick.
poussoir, *n.m.* push-button.
poutre, *n.f.* beam.
pouvoir, 1. *vb.* be able, can, may. **2.** *n.m.* power.
prairie, *n.f.* meadow.
praline, *n.f.* burnt almond.
praticable, *adj.* practicable.
praticien, *n.m.* practitioner.
pratique, 1. *n.f.* practice, exercise. **2.** *adj.* practical.
pratiquer, *vb.* practice, exercise.
pré, *n.m.* meadow.
préalable, *adj.* preliminary.
préambule, *n.m.* preamble.
préau, *n.m.* yard, as of a prison.
préavis, *n.m.* advance notice.
précaire, *adj.* precarious.

précaution, *n.f.* precaution, discretion.
précédent, *n.m.* precedent.
précéder, *vb.* precede; come (go) before.
précepte, *n.m.* precept.
précepteur, *n.m.* tutor.
prêche, *n.m.* sermon; the Protestant religion.
prêcher, *vb.* preach.
précieux, *adj.* precious, valuable.
préciosité, *n.f.* preciosity.
précipice, *n.m.* precipice.
précipitamment, *adv.* headlong.
précipitation, *n.f.* hurry.
précipité, *adj.* hasty.
précipiter, *vb.* precipitate. se p., rush, hasten.
précis, *adj.* precise, exact, accurate.
précisément, *adv.* precisely, definitely, just so.
préciser, *vb.* state.
précision, *n.f.* accuracy, precision.
précité, *adj.* previously cited.
précoce, *adj.* precocious.
précocité, *n.f.* precociousness.
précompter, *vb.* deduct in advance.
préconçu, *adj.* preconceived.
préconiser, *vb.* extol, praise.
préconnaissance, *n.f.* foreknowledge.
précurseur, *n.m.* precursor.
prédécesseur, *n.m.* predecessor.
prédestination, *n.f.* predestination.
prédicateur, *n.m.* preacher.
prédiction, *n.f.* prediction.
prédilection, *n.f.* preference, predilection.
prédire, *vb.* foretell, predict.
prédisposer, *vb.* predispose.
prédisposition, *n.f.* predisposition.
prédominant, *adj.* predominant.
prééminence, *n.f.* preëminence.
préface, *n.f.* preface.
préfecture, *n.f.* prefecture, district.
préférable, *adj.* preferable.
préférence, *n.f.* preference.
préférer, *vb.* prefer.
préfet, *n.m.* prefect.
préfixe, *n.m.* prefix.
préfixer, *vb.* fix in advance.
prégnant, *adj.* pregnant.
préhistorique, *adj.* prehistoric.
préjudice, *n.m.* injury.
préjudiciel, *adj.* interlocutory (as in law).
préjugé, *n.m.* prejudice.
préjuger, *vb.* prejudge.
prélasser, *vb.* se p., bask, lounge.
prélat, *n.m.* prelate.
prélèvement, *n.m.* deduction in advance.

prélever, *vb.* deduct previously.
préliminaire, *adj.* preliminary.
prélude, *n.m.* prelude.
prématuré, *adj.* premature.
préméditation, *n.f.* premeditation.
préméditer, *vb.* premeditate.
prémices, *n.f.pl.* first fruits, first works.
premier, *adj.* first, foremost; early; former.
prémisse, *n.f.* premise.
prémunir, *vb.* warn, take precautions.
prendre, *vb.* take.
prénom, *n.m.* given name.
prénommé, *adj.* previously named.
préoccupation, *n.f.* care, worry.
préoccuper, *vb.* worry.
prépaiement, *n.m.* prepayment.
préparatifs, *n.m.pl.* preparation.
préparation, *n.f.* preparation.
préparatoire, *adj.* preparatory.
préparer, *vb.* prepare.
prépondérance, *n.f.* preponderance.
prépondérant, *adj.* preponderant.
préposé, *n.m.* one in charge.
préposition, *n.f.* preposition.
prérogative, *n.f.* prerogative.
près, 1. *adv.* near. 2. *prep.* p. de, near. de p., nearby.
présage, *n.m.* omen.
présager, *vb.* (fore)bode.
presbyte, *adj.* far-sighted.
presbytère, *n.m.* parsonage, presbytery.
prescription, *n.f.* prescription.
prescrire, *vb.* prescribe.
préséance, *n.f.* precedence.
présélection, *n.f.* triage.
présence, *n.f.* presence, attendance.
présent, *adj. and n.m.* present.
présentable, *adj.* presentable.
présentation, *n.f.* presentation, introduction.
présentement, *adv.* now, at present.
présenter, *vb.* present, introduce. se p. à l'esprit, come to mind.
préservatif, *adj. and n.m.* preservative.
préservation, *n.f.* preservation.
préserver, *vb.* preserve.
présidence, *n.f.* presidency.
président, *n.m.* president, chairman.
présidente, *n.f.* chairwoman.
présidentiel, *adj.* presidential.
présider, *vb.* preside.
présomptif, *adj.* apparent, presumed.
présomptueux, *adj.* presumptuous.
presque, *adv.* almost, nearly.
presqu'île, *n.f.* peninsula.
pressage, *n.m.* pressing.
pressant, *adj.* urgent.

presse, *n.f.* press, crowd.
pressentiment, *n.m.* foreboding, misgiving.
pressentir, *vb.* foresee.
presse-papiers, *n.m.* paperweight.
presser, *vb.* press; urge; hurry.
pression, *n.f.* pressure.
pressoir, *n.m.* machine or device for squeezing.
pressurer, *vb.* squeeze, put pressure on.
prestance, *n.f.* imposing appearance.
preste, *adj.* dexterous, nimble.
prestesse, *n.f.* vivacity, nimbleness.
prestige, *n.m.* prestige, illusion.
prestigieux, *adj.* enchanting.
présumer, *vb.* presume.
présupposer, *vb.* presuppose.
prêt, 1. *n.m.* loan. 2. *adj.* ready.
prêtable, *adj.* lendable.
prétendant, *n.m.* claimant.
prétendre, *vb.* claim.
prétendu, *adj.* supposed, so-called.
prétentieux, *adj.* pretentious.
prétention, *n.f.* claim.
prêter, *vb.* lend.
prêteur, *n.m.* lender.
prétexte, *n.m.* pretext.
prétexter, *vb.* pretend, feign.
prêtre, *n.m.* priest.
prêtresse, *n.f.* priestess.
preuve, *n.f.* proof.
preux, *adj. and n.m.* gallant, brave.
prévaloir, *vb.* prevail.
prévenance, *n.f.* attentiveness, obligingness.
prévenant, *adj.* prepossessing, obliging.
prévenir, *vb.* prevent; warn.
préventif, 1. *adj.* preventive. 2. *n.m.* deterrent.
prévention, *n.f.* bias; prevention.
prévenu, *adj.* partial, biased.
prévision, *n.f.* forecast, expectation.
prévoir, *vb.* foresee.
prévôt, *n.m.* provost.
prévoyance, *n.f.* foresight.
prévoyant, *adj.* farseeing, prudent.
prier, *vb.* beg; pray.
prière, *n.f.* prayer.
prieur, *n.m.* prior.
prieuré, *n.m.* priory.
primaire, *adj.* primary.
primauté, *n.f.* preëminence, primacy.
prime, 1. *n.f.* premium, subsidy, 2. *adj.* first; accented.
primer, *vb.* outdo, excel.
primeur, *n.f.* freshness, earliness.
primitif, *adj.* primitive; original.
primordial, *adj.* primordial.
prince, *n.m.* prince.
princesse, *n.f.* princess.
princier, *adj.* princely.

principal, adj. chief, main. principal.

principauté, n.f. principality.

principe, n.m. principle.

printanier, adj. of spring.

printemps, n.m. spring.

priorité, n.f. priority.

prisable, adj. estimable.

prise, n.f. grasp, hold, grip. **p. de courant,** (electric) plug.

prisée, n.f. appraisal.

priser, vb. appraise.

priseur, n.m. auctioneer, appraiser.

prisme, n.m. prism.

prison, n.f. jail, prison.

prisonnier, n.m. prisoner.

privation, n.f. privation, want, hardship.

privé, adj. private.

priver, vb. deprive.

privilège, n.m. privilege, license.

privilégier, vb. license.

prix, n.m. price, charge, fare; prize, award.

prix-courant, n.m. list of prices.

probabilité, n.f. probability, chances.

probable, adj. likely, probable.

probité, n.f. probity.

problématique, adj. problematical.

problème, n.m. problem.

procédé, n.m. procedure, process.

procéder, vb. proceed.

procédure, n.f. proceeding.

procès, n.m. trial; (law)suit.

procession, n.f. procession.

processionnel, adj. processional.

procès-verbal, n.m. minutes (of meeting).

prochain, 1. n.m. neighbor. **2.** adj. next.

prochainement, adv. soon.

proche, adj. near, close.

proclamation, n.f. proclamation.

proclamer, vb. proclaim.

procréation, n.f. procreation.

procurer, vb. procure, get.

procureur, n.m. attorney.

prodigalement, adv. prodigally.

prodigalité, n.f. extravagance.

prodige, n.m. prodigy.

prodigieux, adj. wondrous.

prodigue, adj. extravagant, lavish, profuse.

prodiguer, vb. lavish.

producteur, n.m. producer.

productif, adj. productive.

production, n.f. production.

productivité, n.f. productivity.

produire, vb. produce, yield, breed.

produit, n.m. product, commodity.

proéminence, n.f. prominence.

proéminent, adj. prominent, standing out.

profane, adj. profane.

profaner, vb. misuse, debase, profane.

proférer, vb. say, utter.

professer, vb. profess.

professeur, n.m. professor, teacher.

profession, n.f. profession.

professionnel, adj. professional.

professoral, adj. professorial.

professorat, n.m. professorship.

profil (-1), n.m. profile.

profiler, vb. show a profile of.

profit, n.m. profit.

profitable, adj. profitable.

profiter, vb. profit.

profiteur, n.m. profiteer.

profond, adj. deep, profound; in-depth.

profondeur, n.f. depth.

profus, adj. profuse.

profusion, n.f. profusion, excess.

progéniture, n.f. offspring.

programme, n.m. program.

progrès, n.m. progress, advance.

progresser, vb. progress.

progressif, adj. progressive.

progressiste, n.m. progressive.

prohiber, vb. prohibit.

prohibitif, adj. prohibitive.

prohibition, n.f. prohibition.

proie, n.f. prey.

projecteur, n.m. projector.

projectile, n.m. missile.

projection, n.f. projection.

projet, n.m. project. **p. de loi,** bill.

projeter, vb. project, plan.

prolétaire, adj. and n.m. proletarian.

prolétariat, n.m. proletariat.

prolifération, n.f. proliferation.

prolifique, adj. prolific.

prolixe, adj. prolix, wordy.

prologue, n.m. prologue.

prolongation, n.f. extension, prolongation.

prolonger, vb. extend, prolong.

promenade, n.f. excursion; walk; ride.

promener, vb. take out. **se p.,** take a walk (ride).

promeneur, n.m. walker.

promesse, n.f. promise.

promettre, vb. promise.

promontoire, n.m. promontory.

promoteur, n.m. promoter.

promotion, n.f. promotion.

promouvoir, vb. promote.

prompt, adj. prompt.

promptitude, n.f. quickness.

promulguer, vb. promulgate.

prôner, vb. lecture to, praise.

pronom, n.m. pronoun.

prononcer, vb. pronounce, utter; deliver.

prononciation, n.f. pronunciation.

pronostic, n.m. prognosis, prediction.

propagande, n.f. propaganda.

propagandiste, n.m. propagandist.

propagateur, n.m. propagator.

propagation, n.f. propagation.

propager, vb. propagate.

propension, n.f. inclination, propensity.

prophète, n.m. prophet.

prophétie, n.f. prophecy.

prophétique, adj. prophetic.

prophétiser, vb. prophesy, predict.

propice, adj. favorable. **peu p.,** unfavorable.

propitiation, n.f. propitiation, conciliation.

proportion, n.f. proportion.

proportionné, adj. proportionate.

proportionnel, adj. proportional.

proportionner, vb. keep in proportion.

propos, n.m. subject; discourse. **à p.,** relevant. **à p. de,** with regard to.

proposable, adj. sutable, appropriate.

proposer, vb. propose; move. **se p. de,** intend, mean.

proposition, n.f. proposal, proposition.

propre, adj. proper; clean, neat: own. **peu p.,** unfit.

propreté, n.f. cleanliness, neatness.

propriétaire, n.m.f. proprietor.

propriété, n.f. property (landed), estate.

propulser, vb. push, propel.

propulseur, n.m. propeller.

propulsion, n.f. propulsion.

proroger, vb. postpone, extend time limit.

prosaïque (-zä ēk), adj. prosaic.

prosaïsme, n.m. prosaicness, dullness.

prosateur, n.m. writer of prose.

proscription, n.f. proscription.

proscrire, vb. outlaw, proscribe.

proscrit, adj. and n.m. exile(d); forbidden.

prose, n.f. prose.

prosodie, n.f. prosody.

prospecter, vb. search, as for gold.

prospecteur, n.m. prospector.

prospère, adj. prosperous.

prospérer, vb. flourish, thrive, prosper.

prospérité, n.f. prosperity.

prosterner, vb. prostrate.

prostituée, n.f. prostitute.

prostitution, n.f. prostitution.

protecteur, 1. n.m. protector; patron. **2.** adj. protective.

protecteur du citoyen, n.m. ombudsman (in Quebec).

protection, n.f. protection.

protectorat, n.m. protectorate.

protéger, vb. protect, patronize, foster.

protéine, n.f. protein.

protestant, adj. and n.m. Protestant.

protestantisme, *n.m.* Protestantism.

protestation, *n.f.* protest.

protester. *vb.* protest.

protêt, *n.m.* protest.

prothèse, *n.f.* artificial aid, as a denture.

protocole, *n.m.* protocol.

protubérance, *n.f.* protuberance.

proue, *n.f.* prow, front.

prouesse, *n.f.* prowess.

prouver, *vb.* prove.

provenance, *n.f.* place of origin; product.

provençal, 1. *adj.* of Provence. 2. *n.m.* language of Provence.

provende, *n.f.* provender, foodstuffs.

provenir, *vb.* come from.

proverbe, *n.m.* proverb, saying.

proverbial, *adj.* proverbial.

providence, *n.f.* providence.

providentiel, *adj.* providential.

province, *n.f.* province.

provincial, *adj. and n.m.* provincial.

provincialisme, *n.m.* provincialism.

provision, *n.f.* supply, store, provision.

provisoire, *adj.* temporary.

provocateur, *n.m.* one who provokes action.

provocation, *n.f.* provocation.

provoquer, *vb.* provoke.

proximité, *n.f.* closeness, proximity.

prude, 1. *n.f.* prude. 2. *adj.* like a prude.

prudence, *n.f.* caution, prudence.

prudent, *adj.* cautious, prudent.

pruderie, *n.f.* prudishness.

prune, *n.f.* plum.

pruneau, *n.m.* prune.

prunelle, *n.f.* pupil (of eye).

prunier, *n.m.* plum tree.

Prusse, *n.f.* Prussia.

Prussien, *n.m.* Prussian.

prussien, *adj.* Prussian.

psalmiste, *n.m.* psalmist.

psaume, *n.m.* psalm.

psautier, *n.m.* psalm book.

pseudonyme, *n.m.* pseudonym.

psychanalyse (-k-), *n.f.* psychoanalysis.

psychédélique (-k), *adj.* psychedelic.

psychiatre (-k-), *n.m.* psychiatrist.

psychiatrie (-k-), *n.f.* psychiatry.

psychique (-k), *adj.* psychic.

psychologie (-k-), *n.f.* psychology.

psychologique (-k-), *adj.* psychological.

psychologue (-k-), *n.m.* psychologist.

psychose (-k-), *n.f.* psychosis.

puant, *adj.* foul, shameful.

puberté, *n.f.* puberty.

public, 1. *adj. m.*, **publique** *f.* public. 2. *n.m.* public.

publication, *n.f.* publication.

publiciste, *n.m.* publicist.

publicité, *n.f.* publicity, advertisement(s).

publier, *vb.* publish, issue.

puce, *n.f.* flea.

pucelle, *n.f.* young girl, virgin.

pudeur, *n.f.* modesty.

pudique, *adj.* modest.

puer, *vb.* smell, have an offensive odor.

puéril (-l), *adj.* childish.

pugiliste, *m.* boxer.

puîné, *adj.* younger (of a brother or sister).

puis, *adv.* then.

puisard, *n.m.* cesspool.

puisatier, *n.m.* well-digger.

puiser, *vb.* draw up, derive.

puisque, *conj.* since, as.

puissamment, *adv.* very, powerfully.

puissance, *n.f.* power.

puissant, *adj.* potent, powerful, mighty.

puits (pwē), *n.m.* well; shaft.

pulluler, *vb.* breed abundantly, multiply.

pulmonaire, *adj.* pulmonary.

pulpe, *n.f.* pulp.

pulpeux, *adj.* pulpy.

pulsar, *n.m.* pulsar.

pulsation, *n.f.* pulsation, beating.

pulvérisateur, *n.m.* vaporizer, spray.

pulvériser, *vb.* spray, pulverize.

punaise, *n.f.* bedbug.

punir, *vb.* punish.

punitif, *adj.* punitive.

punition, *n.f.* punishment.

pupille (-l), *n.m.f.* ward: pupil (of the eye).

pupitre, *n.m.* desk.

pur, *adj.* pure.

purée, *n.f.* mash.

purement, *adv.* purely, solely.

pureté, *n.f.* purity.

purgatoire, *n.m.* purgatory.

purge, *n.f.* purge.

purger, *vb.* purge.

purification, *n.f.* purification.

purifier, *vb.* purify, cleanse.

puritain, *adj. and n.m.* Puritan.

purulent, *adj.* purulent.

pustule, *n.f.* pimple.

putois, *n.m.* skunk, polecat.

putréfier, *vb.* corrupt, rot, spoil.

putride, *adj.* putrid.

pygmée, *n.m.* Pygmy.

pyjama, *n.m.* pajamas.

pyramidal, *adj.* pyramidal, overwhelming.

pyramide, *n.f.* pyramid.

Q

quadrangle (kw-), *n.m.* quadrangle.

quadrillé, *adj.* checked, ruled off.

quadriphonique (kw-), *adj.* quadraphonic.

quadrupède (kw-), *n.m. and adj.* quadruped.

quadruple (kw-), *adj.* quadruple.

quai, *n.m.* pier, dock; (station) platform.

qualification, *n.f.* qualification.

qualifier, *vb.* qualify.

qualité, *n.f.* quality, nature, grade.

quand, *adv.* when.

quant à, *prep.* as to, as for.

quantité, *n.f.* amount, quantity.

quarantaine, *n.f.* quarantine.

quarante, *adj. and n.m.* forty.

quart, *n.m.* fourth, quarter.

quartier, *n.m.* district, quarter. **q. général**, headquarters.

quartz (kw-), *n.m.* quartz.

quasar, (kw-), *n.m.* quasar.

quasi, *adv.* nearly, quasi.

quatorze, *adj.* and *n.m.* fourteen.

quatrain, *n.m.* quatrain.

quatre, *adj. and n.m.* four.

quatre-vingt-dix, *adj. and n.m.* ninety.

quatre-vingts, *adj. and n.m.* eighty.

quatrième, *adj.* and *n.m.* fourth.

quatuor (kw-), *n.m.* quartet.

que, 1. *pron.* whom, which, that. 2. *conj.* that, than.

quel, *adj.* which, what; of what kind.

quelconque, *adj.* of any kind.

quelque, *adj.* some, any. **q. chose**, something. **q. part**, somewhere.

quelquefois, *adv.* sometimes.

quelques, *adj.* a few.

quelques-uns, *pron.* a few.

quelqu'un, *pron.* somebody.

querelle, *n.f.* quarrel.

quereller, *vb.* quarrel (with); scold.

querelleur, 1. *n.m.* quarreler. 2. *adj.* inclined to quarrel.

question, *n.f.* question, issue, matter.

questionner, *vb.* question.

quête, *n.f.* quest, seeking.

quêter, *vb.* seek, look for.

queue (kœ), *n.f.* tail; line. **faire la q.**, stand in line.

qui, 1. *interr. pron.* who, whom. 2. *rel. pron.* who, which. **q. que**, whoever.

quiconque, *pron.* whoever.

quignon, *n.m.* large piece of bread.

quincaillerie, *n.f.* hardware.

quinine, *n.f.* quinine.

quintal, *n.m.* unit of weight (100 kilograms).

quinze, *adj. and n.m.* fifteen.

quinzième, *adj. and n.m.* fifteenth.

quittance, *n.f.* receipt.

quitte, *adj.* free, quit, released.
quitter, *vb.* quit, leave.
quoi, *pron. and interj.* what.
quoique, *conj.* though.
quote-part, *n.f.* quota.
quotidien, *adj.* daily.

R

rabais, *n.m.* reduction.
rabaisser, *vb.* diminish, lower.
rabattre, *vb.* put down, suppress, quell.
rabbin, *n.m.* rabbi.
rabbinique, *adj.* rabbinical.
rabot, *n.m.* plane.
raboter, *vb.* plane, perfect.
roboteux, *adj.* rugged.
rabougri, *adj.* puny, stunted.
raccommodage, *n.m.* fixing, mending.
raccommoder, *vb.* mend.
raccorder, *vb.* join, bring together.
raccourcir, *vb.* shorten, curtail.
raccourcissement, *n.m.* shortening, curtailing.
raccrocher, *vb.* hook up; recover.
race, *n.f.* race.
rachat, *n.m.* redemption.
racheter, *vb.* redeem.
rachitique, *adj.* rickety, affected with rickets.
rachitisme, *n.m.* rickets.
racine, *n.f.* root.
raclage, *n.m.* action of scraping.
racler, *vb.* scrape.
racoler, *vb.* recruit, esp. by fraud.
raconter, *vb.* tell, narrate, recount.
raconteur, *n.m.* story-teller.
radar, *n.m.* radar.
radeau, *n.m.* raft.
radiant, *adj.* radiant.
radiateur, *n.m.* radiator.
radical, *adj. and n.m.* radical.
radier, *vb.* radiate; erase.
radieux, *adj.* radiant, beaming, glorious.
radio, *n.f.* radio; wireless.
radio-actif, *adj.* radioactive.
radiodiffuser, *vb.* broadcast.
radio-émission, *n.f.* broadcast.
radiogramme, *n.m.* radiogram.
radiographie, *n.f.* radiography.
radis, *n.m.* radish.
radium, *n.m.* radium.
radoter, *vb.* babble, drivel.
radoub, *n.m.* refitting (of ship).
radoucir, *vb.* quiet, soften, appease.
rafale, *n.f.* blast, gust, squall.
raffermir, *vb.* make stronger or more secure.
raffinement, *n.m.* refinement.
raffiner, *vb.* refine.
raffinerie, *n.f.* refinery.
raffoler, *vb.* dote on, be mad about.
rafistoler, *vb.* mend, patch.

rafler, *vb.* carry off.
rafraîchir, *vb.* refresh.
rafraîchissement, *n.m.* refreshment.
rage, *n.f.* rage, fury.
rager, *vb.* be angry, rage.
rageur, *n.f.* irritable person.
ragoût, *n.m.* stew.
ragoûtant, *adj.* tasty, pleasing.
ragréer, *vb.* refinish, renovate.
raid, *n.m.* raid.
raide, *adj.* stiff; taut; steep.
raideur, *n.f.* stiffness.
raidir, *vb.* stiffen.
raie, *n.f.* streak; part (in hair).
raifort, *n.m.* horseradish.
rail, *n.m.* rail.
railler, *vb.* make fun of.
raillerie, *n.f.* jesting.
railleur, *n.m.* scoffer, jester.
rainure, *n.f.* groove.
rais, *n.m.* ray, spoke.
raisin, *n.m.* grape(s). **r. sec,** raisin.
raison, *n.f.* reason, judgment. **avoir r.,** be right.
raisonnable, *adj.* reasonable, rational.
raisonnement, *n.m.* reason, argument.
raisonner, *vb.* reason.
rajeunir, *vb.* rejuvenate.
rajuster, *vb.* readjust.
râle, *n.m.* rail (bird); rattle in throat.
ralentir, *vb.* slacken, slow down.
râler, *vb.* rattle (in dying).
rallier, *vb.* rally.
rallonger, *vb.* make an addition to, lengthen.
ramage, *n.m.* flower pattern; chirping; babble.
ramassé, *adj.* thick-set, dumpy.
ramasser, *vb.* pick up.
ramasseur, *n.m.* collector.
rame, *n.f.* oar.
rameau, *n.m.* branch.
ramener, *vb.* bring (take) back.
rameneur, *vb.* restorer.
ramer, *vb.* row.
rameur, *n.m.* rower.
ramifier, *vb.* divide into branches, ramify.
ramille, *n.f.* twig.
ramollir, *vb.* soften, weaken.
rampe, *n.f.* banister; ramp.
ramper, *vb.* crawl, creep.
rance, *adj. and n.m.* rancid, rancidness.
rancœur, *n.f.* rancor.
rançon, *n.f.* ransom.
rancune, *n.f.* grudge, spite, rancor. **garder de la r.,** bear a grudge.
rancunier, *adj.* rancorous, bitter.
rang, *n.m.* row; rank.
rangée, *n.f.* file, row.
ranger, *vb.* rank, array, (ar)range.
rapace, *adj.* predatory, greedy.
râpe, *n.f.* file, rasp.
râper, *vb.* grate.

rapide, 1. *n.m.* rapid. **2.** *adj.* rapid, fast, quick.
rapidité, *n.f.* rapidity.
rapiécer, *vb.* patch.
rapière, *n.f.* rapier.
rapin, *n.m.* art student, pupil
rapiner, *vb.* plunder, rob.
rappel, *n.m.* recall, repeal, reminder.
rappeler, *vb.* recall, remind. **se r.,** remember.
rapport, *n.m.* report; relation.
rapporter, *vb.* bring back; report. **se r. à,** relate to, refer to.
rapporteur, *n.m.* reporter, tattle-tale.
rapprochement, *n.m.* bringing close, junction.
rapprocher, *vb.* bring together. **se r. de,** approximate.
rapt, *n.m.* rape, kidnapping.
raquette, *n.f.* racket.
rare, *adj.* scarce, rare.
raréfier, *vb.* rarefy.
rarement, *adv.* seldom.
rareté, *n.f.* rarity, uniqueness, scarcity.
ras, *adj.* smooth-shaven, open.
raser, *vb.* shave.
rasoir, *n.m.* razor.
rassasier, *vb.* cloy, sate.
rassemblement, *n.m.* rally.
rassembler, *vb.* gather, congregate, muster.
rasseoir, *vb.* reseat. **se r.,** be seated again.
rasséréner, *vb.* clear up (weather).
rassis, *adj.* stale.
rassurer, *vb.* reassure, comfort.
rat, *n.m.* rat.
ratatiner, *vb.* shrivel, shrink.
rate, *n.f.* spleen.
râteau, *n.m.* rake.
râteler, *vb.* rake.
râtelier, *n.m.* rack.
rater, *vb.* miss.
ratière, *n.f.* rat trap.
ratifier, *vb.* ratify.
ration, *n.f.* ration.
rationnel, *adj.* rational.
rationnement, *n.m.* rationing.
rationner, *vb.* ration.
ratissoire, *n.f.* scraper, rake.
rattacher, *vb.* fasten.
rattraper, *vb.* overtake.
rature, *n.f.* erasure.
raturer, *vb.* erase, blot out.
rauque, *adj.* hoarse, raucous.
ravage, *n.m.* havoc.
ravager, *vb.* lay waste.
ravauder, *vb.* mend, patch.
ravigoter, *vb.* enliven, refresh.
ravin, *n.m.* ravine.
ravir, *vb.* ravish; delight.
ravissant, *adj.* ravishing, charming; ravenous.
ravissement, *n.m.* rapture.
ravisseur, *n.m.* ravisher, robber.
raviver, *vb.* revive.
rayer, *vb.* streak; cross out.
rayon, *n.m.* ray, beam; shelf. **r. X,** X-ray.

rayonnant, *adj.* beaming.
rayonne, *n.f.* rayon.
rayonnement, *n.m.* radiation; radiance.
rayonner, *vb.* radiate, beam.
rayure, *n.f.* streak, blemish.
re-, ré-, *prefix.* re-, again.
réabonnement, *n.m.* renewal of subscription.
réabonner, *vb.* renew, resubscribe.
réaction, *n.f.* reaction. avion à r., jet-plane.
reactionnaire, *adj. and n.* reactionary.
réagir, *vb.* react.
réalisable, *adj.* realizable.
réalisation, *n.f.* attainment, carrying out.
réaliser, *vb.* realize. se r., materialize.
réaliste, 1. *n.m.f.* realist. 2. *adj.* realist, realistic.
réalité, *n.f.* reality.
réassurer, *vb.* reinsure.
rébarbatif, *adj.* forbidding.
rebattre, *vb.* repeat, beat again.
rebattu, *adj.* trite.
rebelle, 1. *n.m.f.* rebel. 2. *adj.* rebel, rebellious.
rebeller, *vb.* se r., rebel.
rébellion, *n.f.* rebellion.
rebondi, *adj.* plump.
rebondir, *vb.* bounce.
rebord, *n.m.* border, edge.
rebuffade, *n.f.* rebuff, rebuke.
rebut, *n.m.* trash, refuse, junk, rubbish.
rebuter, *vb.* rebuke, discard.
recéler, *vb.* accept stolen goods, hide.
récemment, *adv.* recently.
recensement, *n.m.* census.
recenser, *vb.* make a census.
récent, *adj.* recent.
réceptacle, *n.m.* receptacle.
récepteur, *n.m.* receiver.
réceptif, *adj.* receptive.
réception, *n.f.* reception, receipt.
recette, *n.f.* recipe, receipt; (*pl.*) returns.
receveur, *n.m.* conductor; receiver.
recevoir, *vb.* receive, get; entertain.
réchapper, *vb.* escape, get out.
réchaud, *n.m.* food warmer, chafing dish.
réchauffer, *vb.* warm again, excite.
recherche, *n.f.* inquiry, (re)-search; quest.
rechercher, *vb.* seek again, investigate.
rechute, *n.f.* relapse.
récif, *n.m.* reef.
récipient, *n.m.* container.
réciproque, *adj.* mutual.
récit, *n.m.* account.
réciter, *vb.* recite, tell.
réclamation, *n.f.* complaint.
réclame, *n.f.* advertisement.
réclamer, *vb.* claim, demand.

reclus, 1. *adj.* withdrawn, secluded. 2. *n.m.* recluse.
réclusion, *n.f.* (solitary) confinement.
recoin, *n.m.* recess, corner.
récolte, *n.f.* crop, harvest.
récolter, *vb.* harvest, gather.
recommandable, *adj.* advisable.
recommandation, *n.f.* recommendation.
recommander, *vb.* recommend; register (letter).
recommencer, *vb.* start again.
récompense, *n.f.* reward.
récompenser, *vb.* reward.
réconcilier, *vb.* reconcile.
reconduire, *vb.* accompany, show out, dismiss.
reconnaissance, *n.f.* recognition; gratitude.
reconnaissant, *adj.* grateful.
reconnaître, *vb.* recognize; admit, acknowledge.
reconstituer, *vb.* rebuild, restore.
recourir, *vb.* resort (to).
recours, *n.m.* resort, recourse. avoir r. à, resort to; appeal to.
recouvrement, *n.m.* recovery.
recouvrer, *vb.* recover, retrieve.
recouvrir, *vb.* re-cover, cover completely.
récréation, *n.f.* amusement.
récréer, *vb.* entertain. se r., amuse oneself.
recrue, *n.f.* recruit.
recruter, *vb.* recruit.
rectangle, *n.m.* rectangle.
recteur, *n.m.* rector.
rectifier, *vb.* rectify, correct.
reçu, *n.m.* receipt.
recueil, *n.m.* collection, compilation.
recueillir, *vb.* gather, collect, glean.
recul, *n.m.* kick, recoil.
reculade, *n.f.* backing, retreat.
reculer, *vb.* recoil, draw back, go back.
récuser, *vb.* challenge, reject.
recycler, *vb.* recycle.
rédacteur, *n.m.* editor.
rédaction, *n.f.* editorial staff.
reddition, *n.f.* surrendering.
rédemption, *n.f.* redemption.
rédiger, *vb.* draw up.
redingote, *n.f.* frock-coat.
redire, *vb.* repeat, echo, reveal.
redoutable, *adj.* redoubtable, alarming.
redouter, *vb.* dread.
redresser, *vb.* straighten.
réduction, *n.f.* reduction, decrease, cut.
réduire, *vb.* reduce. se r. à, amount to.
réduit, *n.m.* retreat, hovel.
réel, *adj.* real, actual.
réfection, *n.f.* reconstruction; refreshments.
réfectoire, *n.m.* dining-room.
référence, *n.f.* reference.
référer, *vb.* refer.
refermer, *vb.* close up or again.

réfléchir, *vb.* reflect, consider, ponder.
reflet, *n.m.* reflection.
refléter, *vb.* reflect.
réflexe, *adj. and n.m.* reflex.
réflexion, *n.f.* reflection, consideration, thought.
refluer, *vb.* return to source, ebb.
reflux, *n.m.* ebb.
refondre, *vb.* cast gain; remodel, improve.
réformateur, 1. *adj.* reforming. 2. *n.m.* reformer, crusader.
réforme, *n.f.* reform, reformation.
réformer, *vb.* reform.
refoulement, *n.m.* forcing back, retreat.
refouler, *vb.* drive back, repel.
réfractaire, *adj.* refractory.
rafraîchir, *vb.* freshen.
réfrigérant, *n.m.* refrigerator.
réfrigérer, *vb.* put under refrigeration.
refroidir, *vb.* chill, cool.
refroidissement, *n.m.* cooling, refrigeration, chill.
refuge, *n.m.* refuge.
réfugié, *n.m.* refugee.
réfugier, *vb.* se r., take refuge.
refus, *n.m.* refusal, denial.
refuser, *vb.* refuse, withhold, deny.
réfutation, *n.f.* rebuttal.
réfuter, *vb.* disprove, refute.
regagner, *vb.* regain, recover.
regain, *n.m.* regrowth, renewal.
régal, *n.m.* feast, repast.
régaler, *vb.* entertain, treat.
regard, *n.m.* look.
regarder, *vb.* look (at); concern.
régence, *n.f.* regency.
régénérer, *vb.* regenerate.
régent, *adj. and n.m.* regent.
régenter, *vb.* direct, dominate.
régime, *n.m.* diet; government; direction.
régiment, *n.m.* regiment.
région, *n.f.* area, region.
régional, *adj.* regional.
régir, *vb.* rule.
régisseur, *n.m.* manager.
registre, *n.m.* register, record.
règle, *n.f.* rule; ruler.
règlement, *n.m.* regulation; settlement.
réglementaire, *adj.* according to regulations.
régler, *vb.* regulate; rule; settle.
règne, *n.m.* reign.
régner, *vb.* reign.
régression, *n.f.* regression.
regret, *n.m.* regret.
regrettable, *adj.* regrettable.
regretter, *vb.* regret, be sorry for.
régulariser, *vb.* regularize.
régularité, *n.f.* regularity.
régulateur, *n.m.* regulator.
régulier, *adj.* regular.
réhabiliter, *vb.* rehabilitate.
rehausser, *vb.* enhance.

rein, *n.m.* kidney; (*pl.*) loins, back.

reine, *n.f.* queen.

réitérer, *vb.* reiterate.

rejet, *n.m.* rejection.

rejeter, *vb.* reject.

rejeton, *n.m.* plant shoot; scion.

rejoindre, *vb.* rejoin; catch up with, overtake.

réjouir, *vb.* rejoice, delight, cheer up.

réjouissance, *n.f.* festivity.

relâché, *adj.* loose.

relâcher, *vb.* relax, slacken.

relais, *n.m.* relay.

relater, *vb.* relate.

relatif, *adj.* relative.

relation, *n.f.* relation, connection.

relaxation, *n.f.* relaxation, release.

relayer, *vb.* relay.

reléguer, *vb.* relegate, banish.

relève, *n.f.* (*mil.*) relief, replacement.

relèvement, *n.m.* bearing.

relever, *vb.* lift; relieve; point out.

relief, *n.m.* relief. **mettre en r.,** emphasize.

relier, *vb.* bind; link.

relieur, *n.m.* binder, esp. of books.

religieuse, *n.f.* nun.

religieux, *adj.* religious.

religion, *n.f.* religion.

reliquaire, *n.m.* receptacle for relic.

relique, *n.f.* relic.

reliure, *n.f.* binding.

reluire, *vb.* shine, glisten.

remanier, *vb.* redo, modify.

remarquable, *adj.* remarkable; noticeable.

remarque, *n.f.* remark.

remarquer, *vb.* remark; notice.

rembarrer, *vb.* drive back; put in one's place.

remblai, *n.m.* embankment.

remboursement, *n.m.* refund.

rembourser, *vb.* repay, refund.

remède, *n.m.* remedy, cure.

remédiable, *adj.* remediable.

remédier à, *vb.* remedy.

remerciement, *n.m.* thanks.

remercier, *vb.* thank.

remettre, *vb.* put back; restore; remit; pardon; deliver. **se r.,** recover.

remise, *n.f.* discount; delivery.

rémission, *n.f.* remission.

remontrance, *n.f.* remonstrance.

remontrer, *vb.* show anew, point out error.

remords (-môr), *n.m.* remorse.

remorquer, *vb.* tow.

remorqueur, *n.m.* tug(boat).

rémouleur, *n.m.* sharpener, grinder.

remous, *n.m.* eddy.

rempart, *n.m.* bulwark, rampart.

remplaçant, *n.m.* substitute.

remplacer, *vb.* replace, substitute.

rempli, *n.m.* tuck, hitch.

remplier, *vb.* take a tuck in.

remplir, *vb.* fill; carry out; crowd.

remporter, *vb.* take away, bring back.

remuer, *vb.* stir. **se r.,** bustle.

renaissance, *n.f.* rebirth, revival.

renaître, *vb.* be reborn, get new life.

renard, *n.m.* fox; sly person.

rencontre, *n.f.* meeting. **aller à la r. de,** go to meet.

rencontrer, *vb.* meet; come across.

rendement, *n.m.* output.

rendez-vous, *n.m.* date, appointment.

rendre, *vb.* give back; repay; surrender. **se r. compte de,** realize.

rendu, *adj.* tired out, all in.

rêne, *n.f.* rein.

rené, *adj.* born-again.

renégat, *adj. and n.m.* renegade.

renfermer, *vb.* enclose.

renfler, *vb.* swell, inflate.

renforcer, *vb.* reinforce.

renfort, *n.m.* reinforcement, aid.

renfrogner, *vb.* **se r.** scowl, frown.

rengaine, *n.f.* often-told story.

renne, *n.m.* reindeer.

renom, *n.m.* renown, repute.

renommée, *n.f.* fame, renown.

renoncer à, *vb.* renounce, give up, forego.

renonciation, *n.f.* renunciation.

renouement, *n.m.* renewing, retying.

renouveau, *n.m.* springtime.

renouveler, *vb.* renew, renovate.

renouvellement, *n.m.* renewal.

renseignements, *n.m.pl.* information.

renseigner, *vb.* inform. **se r.,** inquire.

rente, *n.f.* income; interest; annuity.

rentier, *n.m.* one who lives off interest on investments.

rentrée, *n.f.* return.

rentrer, *vb.* go back, go home.

renversant, *adj.* amazing, overwhelming.

renverser, *vb.* overthrow, overturn; reverse.

renvoi, *n.m.* dismissal; return.

renvoyer, *vb.* send back, return; dismiss.

repaire, *n.m.* den, animal's lair.

repaître, *vb.* feed, feast.

répandre, *vb.* diffuse, scatter, spill.

répandu, *adj.* prevalent, widespread.

reparaître, *vb.* reappear.

réparateur, *n.m.* restorer, repairer.

réparation, *n.f.* repair; amends.

réparer, *vb.* repair, make up for, make amends for.

repartie, *n.f.* reply, quick retort.

repartir, *vb.* leave again; retort.

répartir, *vb.* apportion, allot, distribute.

repas, *n.m.* meal.

repasser, *vb.* press; pass; look over.

repentir, 1. *n.m.* repentance. **2.** *vb.* **se r.,** repent.

répercussion, *n.f.* repercussion.

répercuter, *vb.* reverberate, echo.

repère, *n.m.* guiding mark.

repertoire, *n.m.* list, repertory.

répéter, *vb.* repeat; rehearse.

répétition, *n.f.* repetition.

répit, *n.m.* respite.

replacer, *vb.* replace.

replier, *vb.* fold again or up.

réplique, *n.f.* rejoinder; cue.

répliquer, *vb.* rejoin.

répondant, *n.m.* respondent, bail.

répondre, *vb.* answer, reply. **r. de,** vouch for.

réponse, *n.f.* answer, reply.

report, *n.m.* (in bookkeeping) amount brought forward.

reportage, *n.m.* reporting.

reporter, 1. *n.m.* reporter. **2.** *vb.* carry or take back.

repos, *n.m.* rest.

reposer, *vb.* rest, repose.

repousser, *vb.* push back, repel; spurn.

repoussoir, *n.m.* foil.

répréhensible, *adj.* objectionable.

répréhension, *n.f.* reprehension, censure.

reprendre, *vb.* take back, resume.

représailles, *n.f.pl.* retaliation.

représentant, *n.m.* representative.

représentatif, *adj.* representative.

représentation, *n.f.* representation, performance.

représenter, *adj.* represent.

répressif, *adj.* repressive.

répression, *n.f.* repression.

réprimande, *n.f.* reproof, rebuke, reprimand.

réprimander, *vb.* chide, reprove, reprimand.

réprimer, *vb.* quell.

reprise, *n.f.* recovery; turn; darn. **à plusieurs r.s,** repeatedly.

repriser, *vb.* darn.

réprobation, *n.f.* reprobation.

reproche, *n.m.* reproach.

reprocher, *vb.* reproach.

reproduction, *n.f.* reproduction.

reproduction exacte, *n.f.* clone.

reproduire, *vb.* reproduce.

réprouver, *vb.* censure.

reptile, *n.m.* reptile.

républicain, *adj. and n.m.* republican.
république, *n.f.* republic.
répudier, *vb.* repudiate.
répugnance, *n.f.* repugnance.
répulsion, *n.f.* repulsion.
réputation, *n.f.* reputation.
réputer, *vb.* consider, esteem.
requête, *n.f.* request, plea.
requin, *n.m.* shark.
requis, *adj.* required, necessary.
réquisition, *n.f.* requisition.
rescousse, *n.f.* rescue.
réseau, *n.m.* network.
réserve, *n.f.* reserve, reservation; qualification. **de r.,** spare, extra.
réservé, *adj.* aloof, reticent.
réserver, *vb.* reserve.
réserviste, *n.f.* reservist *(mil.).*
réservoir, *n.m.* tank, reservoir.
résidant, *adj.* resident.
résidence, *n.f.* residence, dwelling.
résider, *vb.* reside.
résidu, *n.m.* residue.
résignation, *n.f.* resignation.
résigner, *vb.* resign.
résiliation, *n.f.* cancelling.
résine, *n.f.* resin.
résistance, *n.f.* endurance, resistance.
résister (à), *vb.* resist.
résolu, *adj.* resolute.
résolument, *adv.* resolutely.
résolution, *n.f.* resolution.
résonnance, *n.f.* resonnance.
résonnant, *adj.* resonant.
résonner, *vb.* resound.
résoudre, *vb.* resolve, solve.
respect (-spè), *n.m.* respect.
respectable, *adj.* decent, respectable.
respecter, *vb.* respect.
respectif, *adj.* respective.
respectueux, *adj.* respectful.
respiration, *n.f.* respiration, breathing.
respirer, *vb.* breathe.
resplendir, *vb.* gleam resplendently.
responsabilité, *n.f.* responsibility.
responsable, *adj.* responsible; accountable, liable.
ressaisir, *vb.* regain possession.
ressemblance, *n.f.* likeness.
ressembler (à), *vb.* resemble. **se r.,** look alike.
ressentiment, *n.m.* resentment.
ressentir, *vb.* feel, resent, show.
resserrer, *vb.* tighten, compress.
ressort, *n.m.* spring, elasticity.
ressortir, *vb.* stand out.
ressource, *n.f.* resort, resource.
ressusciter, *vb.* revive, resuscitate.
restaurant, *n.m.* restaurant.
restaurateur, *n.m.* restorer; restaurant man.
restauration, *n.f.* restoration.
restaurer, *vb.* restore.

reste, *n.m.* remainder, rest, remnant.
rester, *vb.* remain, stay.
restituer, *vb.* give back, restore.
restreindre, *vb.* restrict.
restrictif, *adj.* restrictive.
restriction, *n.f.* restriction.
résultat, *n.m.* outcome, upshot, result.
résulter, *vb.* result.
résumé, *n.m.* summing up.
résumer, *vb.* sum up.
rétablir, *vb.* restore, reëstablish. **se r.,** recover.
rétablissement, *n.m.* recovery.
retard, *n.m.* delay. **en r.,** late; slow.
retarder, *vb.* delay, retard; be slow.
retenir, *vb.* retain; keep; hold (back); detain. **se r. de,** refrain from.
rétentif, *adj.* retentive.
retentir, *vb.* resound.
retentissant, *adj.* reëchoing.
réticence, *n.f.* silence, reticence.
retirer, *vb.* withdraw. **se r.,** retire, retreat.
retoucher, *vb.* retouch, alter.
retour, *n.m.* return. **de r.,** back.
retourner, *vb.* go back, invert, return. **se r.,** turn around.
retrait, *n.m.* contraction, retraction.
retraite, *n.f.* retreat; privacy.
retrancher, *vb.* cut off, curtail.
rétrécir, *vb.* shrink, contract.
rétribution, *n.f.* salary, recompense.
retrousser, *vb.* turn up.
retrouver, *vb.* find; recover.
réunion, *n.f.* meeting, convention, reunion.
réunir, *vb.* unite. **se r.,** assemble.
réussir, *vb.* succeed.
réussite, *n.f.* successful outcome.
revanche, *n.f.* revenge. **en r.,** in return.
rêve, *n.m.* dream.
réveil, *n.m.* awaking; revival.
réveiller, *vb.* wake (up), rouse, arouse.
révélateur, 1. *adj.* revealing. **2.** *n.m.* revealer.
révélation, *n.f.* revelation.
révéler, *vb.* disclose, reveal.
revenant, *n.m.* ghost, specter.
revendeur, *n.m.* retailer, old-clothes dealer.
revendiquer, *vb.* claim.
revenir, *vb.* come back, return, recur; amount to.
revenu, *n.m.* income, revenue.
rêver, *vb.* dream.
réverbérer, *vb.* reverberate.
révéremment, *adv.* reverently.
révérence, *n.f.* reverence; bow, curtsy.
révérend, *adj.* reverend.
révérer, *vb.* revere.
rêverie, *n.f.* dreaming, reverie.

revers, *n.m.* reverse, wrong side; lapel.
revêtir, *vb.* clothe; assume.
rêveur, 1. *n.m.* dreamer. **2.** *adj.* pensive.
réviser, *vb.* revise.
réviseur, *n.m.* reviser, inspector.
révision, *n.f.* revision, review.
revivre, *vb.* revive.
révocation, *n.f.* revocation, annulment.
revoir, *vb.* see again. **au r.,** good-bye.
révolte, *n.f.* revolt.
révolter, *vb.* **se r.,** revolt.
révolution, *n.f.* revolution, turn.
révolutionnaire, *adj. and n.m.* revolutionary.
revolver, *n.m.* revolver.
révoquer, *vb.* revoke.
revue, *n.f.* review, magazine.
rez-de-chaussée, *n.m.* ground floor.
rhétorique, *n.f.* rhetoric.
rhinocéros, *n.m.* rhinoceros.
rhubarbe, *n.f.* rhubarb.
rhum, *n.m.* rum.
rhumatisme, *n.m.* rheumatism.
rhume, *n.m.* cold.
ricaner, *vb.* laugh objectionably.
riche, *adj.* rich, wealthy.
richesse, *n.f.* wealth.
ricocher, *vb.* ricochet, spring back.
rictus, *n.m.* grin.
ride, *n.f.* wrinkle, ripple.
rideau, *n.m.* curtain.
rider, *vb.* ripple, wrinkle.
ridicule, 1. *n.m.* ridicule. **2.** *adj.* ridiculous.
ridiculiser, *vb.* ridicule.
rien, *pron.* nothing.
rieur, *n.m.* laugher.
rigide, *adj.* rigid.
rigidité, *n.f.* rigidity.
rigole, *n.f.* ditch, gutter.
rigoureux, *adj.* rigorous.
rigueur, *n.f.* rigor.
rime, *n.f.* rhyme.
rimer, *vb.* rhyme.
rince-doigts, *n.m.* finger bowl.
rincer, *vb.* rinse.
ripaille, *n.f.* feasting, revelry.
riposte, *n.f.* retort.
rire, 1. *n.m.* laugh, laughter. **2.** *vb.* laugh.
ris, *n.m.* laugh; reef in a sail; sweetbread.
risée, *n.f.* laugh, mocking.
risible, *adj.* laughable.
risque, *n.m.* risk.
risquer, *vb.* risk.
risque-tout, *n.m.* daredevil.
rissoler, *vb.* brown, as in cooking.
rite, *n.m.* rite.
rituel, *adj.* ritual.
rivage, *n.m.* shore, bank.
rival, *adj. and n.m.* rival.
rivaliser, *vb.* compete, rival.
rivalité, *n.f.* rivalry.
rive, *n.f.* bank.

river, *vb.* clinch.
rivet, *n.m.* rivet.
rivière, *n.f.* river.
rixe, *n.f.* brawl.
riz, *n.m.* rice.
rizière, *n.f.* rice field.
robe, *n.f.* dress, gown, frock, robe.
robinet, *n.m.* faucet, tap.
robuste, *adj.* hardy, strong, robust.
roc, *n.m.* rock.
rocailleux, *adj.* rocky, rough.
rocher, *n.m.* rock.
rocheux, *adj.* rocky.
rock, *adj.* rock (music).
rôder, *vb.* prowl.
rôdeur, *n.m.* prowler.
rogner, *vb.* pare, trim down.
rognon, *n.m.* kidney.
rogue, *adj.* proud, arrogant.
roi, *n.m.* king.
rôle, *n.m.* role, part.
Romain, *n.m.* Roman.
romain, *adj.* Roman.
roman, *n.m.* novel.
romance, *n.f.* ballad.
romancier, *n.m.* novelist.
romanesque, *adj.* romantic.
roman-feuilleton, *n.m.* serial.
romanichel, *n.m.* gypsy.
romantique, *adj.* romantic.
romarin, *n.m.* rosemary.
rompre, *vb.* break.
ronce, *n.f.* bramble.
rond, 1. *n.m.* round; circle. 2. *adj.* round.
ronde, *n.f.* round, patrol.
rondeur, *n.f.* roundness.
ronflement, *n.m.* snoring, roar.
ronfler, *vb.* snore.
ronger, *vb.* gnaw; fret.
rongeur, *adj. and n.m.* rodent.
ronronner, *vb.* purr, murmur.
rosaire, *n.m.* rosary.
rosbif, *n.m.* roast beef.
rose, 1. *n.f.* rose. 2. *adj.* pink.
roseau, *n.m.* reed.
rosée, *n.f.* dew.
rosier, *n.m.* rosebush.
rossignol, *n.m.* nightingale.
rôt, *n.m.* roast (meat).
rotation, *n.f.* rotation.
rotatoire, *adj.* rotary.
roter, *vb.* belch.
rôti, *n.m.* roast.
rôtir, *vb.* roast.
rotondité, *n.f.* rotundity.
rotule, *n.f.* kneecap.
roturier, *adj.* commonplace, vulgar.
roublardise, *n.f.* cunningness.
roue, *n.f.* wheel.
roué, 1. *n.m.* rake, debauchee. 2. *adj.* crafty.
rouge, 1. *n.m.* rouge. 2. *adj.* red. r. foncé, maroon.
rouge-gorge, *n.m.* robin.
rougeole, *n.f.* measles.
rougeur, *n.f.* flush, blush.
rougir, *vb.* blush.
rouille, *n.f.* rust.
rouiller, *vb.* rust.
rouir, *vb.* soak.

rouleau, *n.m.* roll, roller, scroll, coil.
roulement, *n.m.* rolling, winding; rotation.
rouler, *vb.* roll, wind.
roulette, *n.f.* little wheel, caster.
roulis, *n.m.* roll.
Roumain, *n.m.* Rumanian (person).
roumain, 1. *n.m.* Rumanian (language). 2. *adj.* Rumanian.
Roumanie, *n.f.* Rumania.
rousseur, *n.f.* redness. tache de r., freckle.
roussir, *vb.* scorch.
route, *n.f.* road, way, course, route. en r., under way. en r. de, on the way to.
routine, *n.f.* routine.
routinier, *adj.* routine.
roux, *adj. and n.m.* red, reddish-brown.
royal, *adj.* royal, regal.
royaliste, *adj. and n.m.f.* royalist.
royaume, *n.m.* kingdom.
royauté, *n.f.* royalty.
ruban, *n.m.* ribbon, tape.
rubis, *n.m.* ruby.
rubrique, *n.f.* red ocher; heading.
ruche, *n.f.* hive.
rude, *adj.* rough, gruff, harsh; rugged.
rudesse, *n.f.* harshness.
rudiment, *n.m.* rudiment, element.
rudimentaire, *adj.* rudimentary.
rudoyer, *vb.* bully.
rue, *n.f.* street, road.
ruée, *n.f.* rush.
ruelle, *n.f.* lane, alley.
ruer, *vb.* se r., rush.
rugir, *vb.* roar.
rugissement, *n.m.* roar.
rugueux, *adj.* rugged, harsh.
ruine, *n.f.* ruin.
ruiner, *vb.* ruin.
ruineux, *adj.* ruinous.
ruisseau, *n.m.* brook, creek, gutter.
ruisseler, *vb.* stream, flow.
rumeur, *n.f.* rumor, noise.
ruminant, *adj. and n.m.* ruminant.
ruminer, *vb.* chew the cud.
rupture, *n.f.* break, rupture.
rural, *adj.* rural.
ruse, *n.f.* trick; cunning.
rusé, *adj.* sly, cunning.
Russe, *n.m.f.* Russian (person).
russe, 1. *n.m.* Russian (language). 2. *adj.* Russian.
Russie, *n.f.* Russia.
rusticité, *n.f.* rusticity, uncouthness.
rustique, *adj.* rustic.
rustre, *adj. and n.m.* boor, boorish.
rythme, *n.m.* rhythm.
rythmique, *adj.* rhythmical.

S

sabbat, *n.m.* Sabbath.
sable, *n.m.* sand.
sabler, *vb.* sand; quaff.
sablier, *n.m.* sandbox, sandman; hourglass.
sablonneux, *adj.* sandy.
sablonnière, *n.f.* sand pit.
sabord, *n.m.* porthole.
sabot, *n.m.* hoof; wooden shoe.
sabotage, *n.m.* sabotage.
saboter, *vb.* sabotage.
saboteur, *n.m.* saboteur; awkward bungler.
sabre, *n.m.* saber.
sac, *n.m.* sack, bag. s. à main, pocketbook. s. à air, airbag.
saccade, *n.f.* jerk.
saccager, *vb.* ransack, sack, plunder.
sacerdoce, *n.m.* priesthood.
sachet, *n.m.* sachet.
sacre, *n.m.* consecration, coronation.
sacré, *adj.* sacred.
sacrement, *n.m.* sacrament.
sacrer, *vb.* crown, consecrate; curse.
sacrifice, *n.m.* sacrifice.
sacrifier, *vb.* sacrifice.
sacrilège, *n.m.* sacrilege.
sacristain, *n.m.* sexton.
sac tyrolien, *n.m.* backpack.
sadisme, *n.m.* sadism.
sagace, *adj.* shrewd.
sagacité, *n.f.* sagacity.
sage, 1. *n.m.* sage. 2. *adj.* wise, good.
sage-femme, *n.f.* midwife.
sagesse, *n.f.* wisdom.
saignée, *n.f.* bleeding.
saigner, *vb.* bleed.
saillant, *adj.* prominent, projecting.
saillie, *n.f.* projection.
saillir, *vb.* protrude.
sain, *adj.* healthy, sound, wholesome. s. d'esprit, sane.
saindoux, *n.m.* lard.
saint, 1. *n.m.* saint. 2. *adj.* holy.
Saint-Esprit, *n.m.* Holy Ghost.
sainteté, *n.f.* holiness.
saisie, *n.f.* seizure.
saisir, *vb.* seize, grasp, snatch, grab.
saisissement, *n.m.* chill, seizure.
saison, *n.f.* season.
salade, *n.f.* salad.
saladier, *n.m.* salad bowl or dish.
salaire, *n.m.* wages, earnings, pay.
salarié, 1. *adj.* salaried. 2. *n.m.f.* person earning a salary.
sale, *adj.* dirty.
saler, *vb.* salt.
saleté, *n.f.* dirt.
salière, *n.f.* saltcellar.
salin, *adj.* salt, salty.
salir, *vb.* get dirty.

salive, *n.f.* saliva.
salle, *n.f.* (large) room, hall, auditorium, (hospital) ward. **s. de. classe,** classroom. **s. de bain,** bathroom.
salon, *n.m.* parlor.
saltimbanque, *n.m.* charlatan, buffoon.
salubre, *adj.* healthful.
salubrité, *n.f.* healthfulness.
saluer, *vb.* bow, greet, salute.
salut, *n.m.* bow, salute; salvation.
salutaire, *adj.* wholesome, beneficial.
salutation, *n.f.* greeting.
salve, *n.f.* salvo, salute.
samedi, *n.m.* Saturday.
sanctifier, *vb.* halllow.
sanction, *n.f.* sanction.
sanctionner, *vb.* sanction, countenance.
sanctuaire, *n.m.* sanctuary.
sandale, *n.f.* sandal.
sang, *n.m.* blood.
sang-froid, *n.m.* calmness, composure.
sanglant, *adj.* bloody.
sangler, *vb.* strap, fasten.
sanglier, *n.m.* (wild) boar.
sanglot, *n.m.* sob.
sangloter, *vb.* sob.
sangsue, *n.f.* leech.
sanguin, *adj.* pertaining to blood.
sanguinaire, *adj.* bloodthirsty.
sanitaire, *adj.* sanitary.
sans, *prep.* without, out of. **s. doute,** without doubt. **s. plomb,** unleaded. **s. repos,** restless. **s. valeur,** worthless. **s. nom,** nameless.
sans-souci, *adj.* carefree, careless.
santé, *n.f.* health.
saper, *vb.* sap, weaken.
saphir, *n.m.* sapphire.
sapin, *n.m.* fir.
sarcasme, *n.m.* sarcasm.
sarcastique, *adj.* sarcastic.
sarcler, *vb.* weed, root out.
sardine, *n.f.* sardine.
sardonique, *adj.* sardonic.
satanique, *adj.* satanic.
satellite, *n.m.* satellite.
satin, *n.m.* satin.
satire, *n.f.* satire.
satiriser, *vb.* satirize.
satisfaction, *n.f.* satisfaction.
satisfaire, *vb.* satisfy.
satisfaisant, *adj.* satisfactory.
saturer, *vb.* saturate.
satyre, *n.m.* satyr.
sauce. *n.f.* sauce. **s. piquante,** catsup.
saucisse, *n.f.* sausage.
sauf, 1. *prep.* but. **2.** *adj.* safe. **sain et sauf,** safe and sound.
sauf-conduit, *n.m.* safe-conduct pass.
sauge, *n.f.* sage.
saugrenu, *adj.* absurd, preposterous.
saule, *n.f.* willow.
saumon, *n.m.* salmon.

saumure, *n.f.* brine.
saut, *n.m.* spring, jump.
saute, *n.f.* wind shift.
sauter, *vb.* spring, jump, leap, skip. **faire s.,** blow up.
sauterelle, *n.f.* grasshopper.
sautiller, *vb.* hop.
sauvage, 1. *n.m.f.* savage. **2.** *adj.* wild, savage.
sauvegarde, *n.f.* safeguard.
sauvegarder, *vb.* safeguard.
sauve-qui-peut, *n.m.* stampede, panic.
sauver, *vb.* save. **se s.,** run away.
sauvetage, *n.m.* salvage.
sauveteur, *n.m.* rescuer, saver.
sauveur, *n.m.* savior, Saviour.
savane, *n.f.* prairie.
savant, 1. *n.m.* scholar. **2.** *adj.* learned.
saveur, *n.f.* flavor, savor, zest.
savoir, 1. *vb.* know, be aware, have knowledge. **vouloir s.,** wonder. **2.** *n.m.* knowledge.
savoir-faire, *n.m.* poise, ability.
savoir-vivre, *n.m.* breeding, manners.
savon, *n.m.* soap.
savonner, *vb.* soap, lather.
savourer, *vb.* relish.
savoureux, *adj.* tasty.
scabreux, *adj.* rough, harsh, indelicate.
scalper, *vb.* scalp.
scandale, *n.m.* scandal.
scandaleux, *adj.* scandalous.
scandaliser, *vb.* shock.
scander, *vb.* scan.
Scandinave, *n.m.f.* Scandinavian.
scandinave, *adj.* Scandinavian.
Scandinavie, *n.f.* Scandinavia.
scarabée, *n.m.* beetle.
scarlatine, *n.f.* scarlet fever.
sceau, *n.m.* seal.
scélérat, *n.m.* villain, criminal, knave, ruffian.
sceller, *vb.* seal.
scénario, *n.m.* scenario.
scène, *n.f.* scene, stage.
scénique, *adj.* scenic.
scepticisme, *n.m.* skepticism.
sceptique, 1. *n.m.f.* skeptic. **2.** *adj.* skeptical.
sceptre, *n.m.* scepter.
schampooing, *n.m.* shampoo.
schisme, *n.m.* schism.
sciatique, *n.f.* sciatica.
scie, *n.f.* saw.
science, *n.f.* science.
science-fiction, *n.f.* science fiction.
scientifique, *adj.* scientific.
scier, *vb.* saw.
scinder, *vb.* divide.
scintiller, *vb.* twinkle.
scission, *n.f.* cutting, division.
sclérose, *n.f.* sclerosis.
scolaire, *adj.* scholastic. **système s.,** school system.
scolastique, *adj.* scholastic.
scrofule, *n.f.* scrofula.
scrupule, *n.m.* scruple.
scrupuleux, *adj.* scrupulous.

scruter, *vb.* scan, scrutinize.
scrutin, *n.m.* ballot, poll.
sculpter (-lt-), *vb.* carve.
sculpteur (-lt-), *n.f.* sculptor.
sculpture (-lt-), *n.f.* sculpture.
se (sə), *pron.* himself, herself, itself, oneself, themselves, each other.
séance, *n.f.* sitting; session; meeting.
séant, *adj.* sitting, proper.
seau, *n.m.* pail, bucket.
sec *m.,* **sèche** *f.* *adj.* dry.
sécession, *n.f.* secession.
sécher, *vb.* dry.
sécheresse, *n.f.* dryness, drought.
second (-g-), *adj.* second.
secondaire (-g-), *adj.* secondary.
seconde (-g-), *n.f.* second.
seconder (-g-), *vb.* second, help.
secouer, *vb.* shake, rouse.
secourir, *vb.* relieve, succor, help.
secours, *n.m.* help, relief. **premiers s.,** first aid. **poste de s.,** first aid station. **au s.!,** help!
secousse, *n.f.* jar, shock.
secret, *adj.* and *n.m.* secret.
secrétaire, *n.m.f.* secretary.
sécréter, *vb.* secrete.
sécrétion, *n.f.* secretion.
sectaire, *adj.* sectarian.
secte, *n.f.* sect.
secteur, *n.m.* district, sector.
section, *n.f.* section.
sectionner, *vb.* cut into sections.
séculaire, *adj.* secular.
séculier, *adj.* secular, lay.
sécurité, *n.f.* safety.
sédatif, *adj.* and *n.m.* sedative.
sédentaire, *adj.* sedentary, stationary.
séditieux, *adj.* seditious.
sédition, *n.f.* sedition.
séduction, *n.f.* seduction.
séduire, *vb.* seduce, attract, allure.
séduisant, *adj.* attractive.
segment, *n.m.* segment.
ségrégation, *n.f.* segregation.
seigle, *n.m.* rye.
seigneur, *n.m.* lord, peer.
seigneurie, *n.f.* lordship.
sein, *n.m.* bosom, breast.
seize, *adj.* and *n.m.* sixteen.
seizième, *adj.* and *n.m.* sixteenth.
séjour, *n.m.* stay. **lieu de s.,** resort.
séjourner, *vb.* sojourn.
sel, *n.m.* salt.
sélection, *n.f.* selection.
selle, *n.f.* saddle.
seller, *vb.* saddle.
sellette, *n.f.* little stool or saddle.
selon, *prep.* according to.
seltz, *n.m.* **eau de s.,** soda water.
semailles, *n.f.pl.* sowing.

semaine, *n.f.* week; weekly pay.

semblable, *adj.* similar, alike.

semblant, *n.m.* show; appearance. **faire s.**, make believe.

sembler, *vb.* seem, appear.

semelle, *n.f.* sole.

semence, *n.f.* seed.

semer, *vb.* sow.

semestre, *n.m.* semester.

semeur, *n.m.* sower.

sémillance, *n.f.* briskness, liveliness.

sémitique, *adj.* Semitic.

semoncer, *vb.* lecture, scold.

sénat, *n.m.* senate.

sénateur, *n.m.* senator.

sénile, *adj.* senile.

sénilité, *n.f.* senility.

sens (-s), *n.m.* meaning, sense; direction.

sensation, *n.f.* sensation, feeling.

sensationnel, *adj.* sensational.

sensé, *adj.* sensible.

sensibilité, *n.f.* sensitivity.

sensible, *adj.* sensible, sensitive; conscious (of).

sensitif, *adj.* sensitive.

sensualisme, *n.m.* sensualism.

sensualité, *n.f.* sensuality.

sensuel, *adj.* sensual.

sentence, *n.f.* sentence.

sentencieux, *adj.* sententious.

senteur, *n.m.* smell.

sentier, *n.m.* path.

sentiment, *n.m.* feeling.

sentimental, *adj.* sentimental.

sentimentalité, *n.f.* sentimentality.

sentinelle, *n.f.* sentry.

sentir, *vb.* feel; smell.

séparable, *adj.* separable.

séparation, *n.f.* separation, parting.

séparé, *adj.* separate.

séparer, *vb.* separate, segregate. **se s.**, part.

sept (sèt), *adj.* and *n.m.* seven.

septembre, *n.m.* September.

septième (sèt-), *adj.* and *n.m.* seventh.

septique, *adj.* septic.

sépulcre, *n.m.* sepulcher.

séquestrer, *vb.* withdraw, remove.

serein, *adj.* serene, placid.

sérénade, *n.f.* serenade.

sérénité, *n.f.* serenity.

serf, 1. *adj.* in serf-dom or the like.

sergent, *n.m.* sergeant.

série, *n.f.* series.

sérieux, 1. *adj.* serious, sober, grave. **2.** *n.m.* gravity.

serin, *n.m.* canary.

seringue, *n.f.* syringe.

serment, *n.m.* oath.

sermon, *n.m.* sermon.

sermonner, *vb.* lecture, preach.

serpent, *n.m.* snake, serpent.

serpenter, *vb.* wind, wander.

serre, *n.f.* green-house; claw.

serré, *adj.* tight.

serre-joint, *n.m.* clamp.

serrer, *vb.* tighten, squeeze, press, crowd, shake (hands). **s. dans ses bras**, hug.

serrure, *n.f.* lock.

sérum, *n.m.* serum.

servage, *n.m.* servitude.

servant, 1. *adj.* serving. **2.** *n.m.* server, gunner.

servante, *n.f.* maid.

serviable, *adj.* helpful.

service, *n.m.* service, favor. **être de s.**, be on duty.

serviette, *n.f.* napkin; towel; brief case.

servile, *adj.* menial

servilité, *n.f.* servility.

servir, *vb.* serve. **se s. de**, use. **ne s. à rien**, be of no use.

serviteur, *n.m.* attendant, servant.

servitude, *n.f.* slavery.

session, *n.f.* session.

seuil, *n.m.* threshold.

seul, *adj.* alone, only, single.

seulement, *adv.* only, solely.

sève, *n.f.* sap.

sévère, *adj.* severe, stern.

sévérité, *n.f.* severity, rigor.

sévir, *vb.* punish, rage.

sevrer, *vb.* wean, withhold.

sexe, *n.m.* sex.

sexisme, *n.m.* sexism.

sexiste, *adj.* sexist.

sexuel, *adj.* sexual.

seyant, *adj.* becoming.

shrapnel, *n.m.* shrapnel.

si, 1. *adv.* so, so much, yes. **si . . . que**, however (+*adj.*). **2.** *conj.* if, whether.

siècle, *n.m.* century.

siège, *n.m.* seat; siege.

siéger, *vb.* sit, convene, reside.

sien, *pron.* **le sien, la sienne,** his, hers, its.

sieste, *n.f.* siesta.

siffler, *vb.* whistle, hiss.

sifflerie, *n.f.* hissing, whistling.

sifflet, *n.m.* whistle.

signal, *n.m.* signal.

signalement, *n.m.* description, details.

signaler, *vb.* point out.

signature, *n.f.* signature.

signe, *n.m.* sign. **s. de la tête**, nod. **faire s. à**, beckon.

signer, *vb.* sign. **se s.**, cross oneself.

significatif, *adj.* significant, meaningful.

signification, *n.f.* significance, meaning.

signifier, *vb.* signify, mean.

silence, *n.m.* silence.

silencieux, *adj.* noiseless, silent.

silex, *n.m.* flint.

sillage, *n.m.* wake, course.

sillon, *n.m.* furrow.

sillonner, *vb.* plow.

similaire, *adj.* similar.

simple, *adj.* plain, simple, mere; no-frills.

simplicité, *n.f.* simplicity.

simplifier, *vb.* simplify.

simulation, *n.f.* simulation.

simuler, *vb.* pretend.

simultané, *adj.* simultaneous.

sincère, *adj.* candid, sincere.

sincérité, *n.f.* candor, sincerity.

singe, *n.m.* monkey; imitator.

singularité, *n.f.* singularity; peculiar trait.

singulier, *adj.* and *n.m.* singular; peculiar, strange.

sinistre, 1. *n.m.* disaster. **2.** *adj.* sinister.

sinon, *conj.* otherwise.

sinueux, *adj.* winding, sinuous.

sirène, *n.f.* siren.

sirop, *n.m.* syrup.

siroter, *vb.* sip.

site, *n.m.* site.

sitôt, *adv.* as soon (as).

situation, *n.f.* situation, position, location, office.

situer, *vb.* situate, locate.

six (sès), *adj.* and *n.m.* six.

sixième (-z-), *adj.* and *n.m.* sixth.

ski, *n.m.* ski. **faire du s.**, ski, *vb.*

skieur, *n.m.* skier.

smoking, *n.m.* dinner-jacket, tuxedo.

sobre, *adj.* temperate, sober.

sobriété, *n.f.* moderation, temperance.

sobriquet, *n.m.* nickname.

soc, *n.m.* plowshare.

sociable, *adj.* sociable.

social, *adj.* social.

socialisme, *n.m.* socialism.

socialiste, *adj.* and *n.m.f.* socialist.

société, *n.f.* society; company.

sociologie, *n.f.* sociology.

sociologiste, *n.m.* sociologist.

sœur, *n.f.* sister.

soi-disant, *adj.* so-called.

soie, *n.f.* silk; bristle.

soierie, *n.f.* silk goods.

soif, *n.f.* thirst. **avoir s.**, be thirsty.

soigné, *adj.* trim. **mal s.**, sloppy.

soigner, *vb.* tend, look after, take care of.

soigneux, *adj.* careful.

soi-même, *pron.* oneself.

soin, *n.m.* care. **prendre s. de**, take care of.

soir, *n.m.* evening. **hier s.**, last night. **ce s.**, tonight. **le s.**, at night.

soirée, *n.f.* evening.

soit, *vb.* so be it. **s. . . . s.**, whether . . . or. **s. que**, whether.

soixante (-s-), *adj.* and *n.m.* sixty.

soixante-dix, *adj.* and *n.m.* seventy.

sol, *n.m.* earth, soil, ground.

solaire, *adj.* solar.

soldat, *n.m.* soldier.

solde, *n.m.* balance.

sole, *n.f.* sole.

solécisme, *n.m.* solecism.

soleil, *n.m.* sun, sunshine. **coucher du s.**, sunset. **lever du s.**, sunrise.

solennel, *adj.* solemn.

solenniser, *vb.* solemnize.

solennité, *n.f.* solemnity.

solidaire, *adj.* jointly binding.

solidariser, *vb.* se s., unite, join together.

solidarité, *n.f.* joint responsibility.

solide, *adj.* and *n.m.* solid.

solidifier, *vb.* solidify.

solidité, *n.f.* solidity.

soliloque, *n.m.* soliloquy.

soliste, *n.m.* soloist.

solitaire, *adj.* lonely, lonesome.

solitude, *n.f.* solitude.

solliciter, *vb.* solicit, ask, apply.

sollicitude, *n.f.* solicitude.

soluble, *adj.* soluble.

solution, *n.f.* solution.

solvable, *adj.* solvent.

sombre, *adj.* dark, dim, gloomy, somber.

sombrer, *vb.* sink.

sommaire, *n.m.* summary.

sommation, *n.f.* appeal, summons.

somme, 1. *n.f.* amount, sum. 2. *n.m.* nap.

sommeil, *n.m.* sleep. avoir s., be sleepy.

sommeiller, *vb.* doze, slumber.

sommer, *vb.* summon.

sommet, *n.m.* top, peak, summit.

somnolence, *n.f.* drowsiness.

somnolent, *adj.* drowsy, sleepy.

somptueux, *adj.* lavish, sumptuous.

son *m.*, **sa** *f.*, **ses** *pl. adj.* his, her, its.

son, *n.m.* sound, ring; bran.

sonate, *n.f.* sonata.

sonder, *vb.* fathom; probe.

songe, *n.m.* dream.

songer à, *vb.* think of, dream.

songeur, 1. *adj.* dreamy, thoughtful. 2. *n.m.* dreamer.

sonner, *vb.* sound, ring, strike.

sonnerie, *n.f.* ringing.

sonnette, *n.f.* bell.

sonore, *adj.* sonorous.

sophiste, *n.m.* sophist.

soprano, *n.m.* soprano.

sorcellerie, *n.f.* sorcery.

sorcier, *n.m.* wizard.

sorcière, *n.f.* witch.

sordide, *adj.* sordid.

sort, *n.m.* lot.

sorte, *n.f.* sort, kind. de s. que, so that.

sortie, *n.f.* exit, way out.

sortilège, *n.m.* sorcery.

sortir, *vb.* go (come, get) out.

sot *m.*, **sotte** *f. adj.* silly, stupid, foolish, dumb.

sottise, *n.f.* foolishness.

sou, *n.m.* cent. sans le s., penniless.

soubassement, *n.m.* basement.

soubresaut, *n.m.* bound, jerk.

souche, *n.f.* stub, stump.

souci, *n.m.* care, worry, concern.

soucier, *vb.* se s. (de), care, worry (about).

soucieux, *adj.* anxious.

soucoupe, *n.f.* saucer.

soudain, *adj.* sudden.

soudaineté, *n.f.* suddenness.

soude, *n.f.* soda.

souder, *vb.* solder, fuse.

souffle, *n.m.* breath.

souffler, *vb.* blow.

soufflet, *n.m.* bellows; blow, slap.

souffleter, *vb.* slap one's face.

souffrance(s), *n.f. (pl.)* misery, pain, suffering.

souffrir, *vb.* suffer, bear.

soufre, *n.m.* sulphur.

souhait, *n.m.* wish.

souhaiter, *vb.* wish for.

souiller, *vb.* soil, defile.

souillure, *n.f.* stain, dirt.

soulager, *vb.* relieve, alleviate.

soûler, *vb.* fill with food and drink, inebriate.

soulever, *vb.* lift, raise, arouse.

soulier, *n.m.* shoe.

souligner, *vb.* underline.

soumettre, *vb.* submit, subdue.

soumis, *adj.* obedient, submissive.

soumission, *n.f.* submission.

soupape, *n.f.* valve.

soupçon, *n.m.* suspicion.

soupçonner, *vb.* suspect.

soupçonneux, *adj.* suspicious.

soupe, *n.f.* soup.

souper, *n.m.* supper.

soupir, *n.m.* sigh.

soupirer, *vb.* sigh. s. après, yearn for.

souple, *adj.* flexible.

souplesse, *n.f.* suppleness, pliability.

source, *n.f.* source; spring.

sourcil, *n.m.* eyebrow.

sourciller, *vb.* frown.

sourcilleux, *adj.* haughty, disdainful.

sourd, *adj.* deaf.

sourd-muet, *n.m.* deaf mute.

souricière, *n.f.* (mouse)trap.

sourire, *n.m. and vb.* smile.

souris, *n.f.* mouse.

sournois, *adj.* sly.

sous, *prep.* under.

souscription, *n.f.* subscription.

souscrire, *vb.* subscribe.

sous-estimer, *vb.* underestimate.

sous-louer, *vb.* sublet.

sous-marin, *n.m.* submarine.

sous-produit, *n.m.* by-product.

soussigné, *adj.* undersigned.

sous-sol, *n.m.* basement.

sous-titre, *n.m.* subtitle.

soustraction, *n.f.* subtraction.

soustraire, *vb.* subtract.

soutane, *n.f.* cassock.

soute, *n.f.* storeroom.

soutenir, *vb.* support, uphold, maintain; claim; back up.

soutenu, *adj.* steady.

souterrain, *adj.* underground.

soutien, *n.m.* support.

soutien-gorge, *n.m.* brassière.

souvenance, *n.f.* recall, recollection.

souvenir, 1. *n.m.* remembrance, memory. 2. *vb.* se s. de, remember.

souvent, *adv.* often.

souverain, *n.m.* ruler, sovereign.

souveraineté, *n.f.* sovereignty.

soyeux, *adj.* silky.

spacieux, *adj.* spacious.

spasme, *n.m.* spasm.

spatule, *n.f.* spatula.

spécial, *adj.* special.

spécialiser, *vb.* specialize.

spécialiste, *n.m.f.* specialist.

spécialité, *n.f.* specialty.

spécifier, *vb.* specify.

spécifique, *adj.* specific.

spécimen, *n.m.* specimen.

spectacle, *n.m.* sight, show.

spectaculaire, *adj.* spectacular.

spectateur, *n.m.* spectator.

spectre, *n.m.* ghost; spectrum.

spéculation, *n.f.* speculation.

spéculer, *vb.* speculate.

sphère, *n.f.* sphere.

spinal, *adj.* spinal.

spiral, *adj.* spiral.

spirale, *n.f.* spiral.

spirite, *n.m.f.* spiritualist.

spiritisme, *n.m.* spiritualism.

spirituel, *adj.* spiritual; witty.

spiritueux, *adj.* pertaining to alcohol.

splendeur, *n.f.* splendor.

splendide, *adj.* splendid.

spolier, *vb.* plunder, pillage.

spontané, *adj.* spontaneous.

spontanéité, *n.f.* spontaneity.

sporadique, *adj.* sporadic.

sport, *n.m.* sport.

sportif, *adj.* of sport.

squelette, *n.m.* skeleton.

stabiliser, *vb.* stabilize.

stabilité, *n.f.* stability.

stable, *adj.* stable, steady.

stage, *n.m.* period of probation.

stagflation, *n.f.* stagflation.

stagnant, *adj.* stagnant.

stalle, *n.f.* stall.

stance, *n.f.* stanza.

station, *n.f.* stand, stop, station (subway).

stationnaire, *adj.* stationary.

stationner, *vb.* park.

statique, *adj.* static.

statistique, *n.f.* statistics.

statue, *n.f.* statue.

statuer, *vb.* decree, decide.

stature, *n.f.* stature.

statut, *n.m.* statute.

sténographe, *n.m.f.* stenographer.

sténographie, *n.f.* stenography.

stéréophonique, *adj.* stereophonic.

stérile, *adj.* barren.

stériliser, *vb.* sterilize.

stéthoscope, *n.m.* stethoscope.

stigmatiser, *vb.* mark, stigmatize.

stimulant, *n.m.* stimulus.

stimuler, *vb.* stimulate.

stipuler, vb. stipulate.

stoïque, adj. and n.m.f. stoic.

store, n.m. (window) shade, blind.

stratagème, n.m. stratagem.

stratégie, n.f. strategy.

stratégique, adj. strategic.

strict (-kt), adj. severe, strict.

strier, vb. mark, streak, make grooves.

structure, n.f. structure.

stuc, n.m. stucco.

studieux, adj. studious.

stupéfait, adj. astounded.

stupéfiant, n.m. narcotic, dope.

stupéfier, vb. astound.

stupeur, n.f. amazement.

stupide, adj. stupid.

stupidité, n.f. stupidity.

style, n.m. style.

styler, vb. train, teach.

stylet, n.m. stiletto.

stylographe, stylo, n.m. fountain pen.

suavité, n.f. suavity.

subalterne, adj. and n.m.f. junior (rank).

subdiviser, vb. subdivide.

subir, vb. undergo, bear.

subit, adj. sudden.

subjectif, adj. subjective.

subjonctif, adj. and n.m. subjunctive.

subjuguer, vb. subdue, overcome.

sublime, adj. sublime, exalted.

submerger, vb. submerge, flood.

subordonné, adj. and n.m. subordinate.

subordonner, vb. subordinate.

subreptice, adj. surreptitious.

subséquent, adj. subsequent.

subside, n.m. subsidy.

subsister, vb. subsist, live.

substance, n.f. substance.

substantiel, adj. substantial.

substantif, n.m. noun.

substituer, vb. substitute.

substitution, n.f. substitution.

subtil (-l), adj. subtle.

subtilité, n.f. subtlety.

subvention, n.f. grant, subsidy.

subventionner, vb. subsidize.

subversif, adj. subversive.

suc, n.m. juice.

succéder à, vb. succeed, follow.

succès, n.m. success; hit.

successeur, n.m. successor.

successif, adj. successive.

succession, n.f. succession.

succion, n.f. suction.

succomber, vb. succumb.

succursale, n.f. branch office.

sucer, vb. suck.

sucre, n.m. sugar.

sucrer, vb. add sugar.

sud (-d), n.m. south.

sudation, n.f. sweating.

sud-est, n.m. southeast.

sud-ouest, n.m. southwest.

Suède, n.f. Sweden.

Suédois, n.m. Swede.

suédois, adj. and n.m. Swedish.

suer, vb. sweat.

sueur, n.m. sweat.

suffire, vb. suffice.

suffisance, n.f. adequacy, conceit.

suffisant, adj. sufficient, adequate; conceited.

suffixe, n.m. suffix.

suffoquer, vb. suffocate.

suffrage, n.m. suffrage.

suggérer, vb. suggest.

suggestion, n.f. suggestion.

suicide, n.m. suicide.

suicider, vb. se s., kill oneself.

suie, n.f. soot.

suif, n.m. tallow.

suinter, vb. seep.

Suisse, 1. n.m. Swiss. 2. n.f. Switzerland.

suisse, adj. Swiss.

suite, n.f. sequence; retinue; (pl.) results, aftermath. et ainsi de s., and so on. tout de s., at once.

suivant, 1. n.m. follower. 2. adj. next, following, subsequent. 3. prep. by, according to.

suivi, adj. followed, coherent.

suivre, vb. follow; attend. faire s., forward.

sujet, 1. n.m. subject; topic. 2. adj. subject. s. à, liable to.

sujétion, n.f. subjection, slavery.

superbe, adj. superb, magnificent.

superficie, n.f. surface.

superficiel, adj. superficial, shallow.

superflu, adj. superfluous.

supérieur, adj. and n.m. superior, higher, upper; senior.

supériorité, n.f. superiority.

superlatif, adj. and n.m. superlative.

superstar, n.m. superstar.

superstitieux, adj. superstitious.

superstition, n.f. superstition.

suppléant, n.m. and adj. assistant, substitute.

suppléer, vb. substitute.

supplément, n.m. supplement.

supplémentaire, adj. extra. heures s.s, overtime.

supplice, n.m. punishment, torture.

supplier, vb. beseech, entreat, beg, supplicate.

support, n.m. support, stand.

supporter, vb. support, bear, stand, endure.

supposer, vb. suppose, assume.

supposition, n.f. assumption, conjecture, supposition.

suppôt, n.m. implement, tool, agent.

suppression, n.f. suppression.

supprimer, vb. suppress, put down, take out.

supputation, n.f. computation.

supputer, vb. compute.

suprématie, n.f. supremacy.

suprême, adj. supreme.

sur, prep. on, upon, over.

sûr, adj. safe, sure, secure.

surabonder, vb. be very abundant.

suranné, adj. out-of-date.

surcroît, n.m. addition.

surdité, n.f. deafness.

suret, adj. sour.

sûreté, n.f. safety, security, reliability.

surface, n.f. surface, area.

surgélateur, n.m. deep freeze.

surgir, vb. spring up, arise.

surhumain, adj. superhuman.

surintendant, n.m. superintendent.

sur-le-champ, adv. at once, immediately.

surmener, vb. overwork.

surmonter, vb. overcome, surmount.

surnaturel, adj. and n.m. supernatural.

surnom, n.m. nickname.

surpasser, vb. surpass.

surplis, n.m. surplice.

surplomber, vb. overhang.

surplus, n.m. surplus, excess.

surprendre, vb. surprise.

surprise, n.f. surprise.

sursaut, n.m. start.

sursauter, vb. give a start.

sursis, n.m. delay, putting off.

surtaxe, n.f. surtax.

surtout, 1. n.m. overcoat. 2. adv. above all.

surveillance, n.f. supervision, watch.

surveillant, n.m. superintendent.

surveiller, vb. supervise, watch over.

survenir, vb. happen.

survie, n.f. survival.

survivance, n.f. survival.

survivre, vb. survive.

susceptible, adj. susceptible; liable.

suspect (-kt), adj. suspicious.

suspecter, vb. suspect.

suspendre, vb. suspend, hang, sling.

suspension, n.f. suspension.

suspicion, n.f. suspicion.

sustenter, vb. sustain, bulwark.

svelte, adj. slender, slim.

syllabe, n.f. syllable.

sylphe, n.m. sylph.

sylphide, n.f. sylph.

sylvestre, adj. sylvan, woody.

sylviculture, n.f. forestry.

symbole, n.m. symbol.

symboliser, vb. symbolize.

symétrie, n.f. symmetry.

sympathie, n.f. sympathy. avoir de la s. pour, like.

sympathique, adj. congenial, likeable.

sympathiser, vb. sympathize.

symphonie, n.f. symphony.

symptôme, n.m. symptom.

synchroniser, vb. synchronize.

syndical, adj. of a trade-union.

syndicat, n.m. syndicate s. ouvrier, trade-union.

syndrome, n.m. syndrome.

synonyme, n.m. synonym.

syntaxe, n.f. syntax.

synthèse, *n.f.* synthesis.
synthétique, *adj.* synthetic.
systématique, *adj.* systematic.
système, *n.m.* system.

T

tabac (-bâ), *n.m.* tobacco.
tabernacle, *n.m.* tabernacle.
table, *n.f.* table. **t. des matières,** index.
tableau, *n.m.* picture. **t. noir,** blackboard.
tabler, *vb.* count on, depend.
tablette, *n.f.* tablet.
tablier, *n.m.* apron.
tabou, *n.m.* taboo.
tabouret, *n.m.* stool.
tache, *n.f.* spot, stain, blot, smear.
tâche, *n.f.* task; assignment.
tacher, *vb.* spot, stain, blot.
tâcher, *vb.* try.
tacite, *adj.* tacit, silent.
taciturne, *adj.* unspeaking.
tact (-kt), *n.m.* tact.
tacticien, *n.m.* tactician.
tactique, 1. *adj.* of tactics, tactical. **2.** *n.f.* tactics.
taffetas, *n.m.* taffeta.
taie, *n.f.* pillowcase.
taillade, *n.f.* slash.
taille, *n.f.* waist, figure, size.
tailler, *vb.* trim, cut.
tailleur, *n.m.* tailor.
taire, *vb.* keep quiet. **se t.,** be silent.
talent, *n.m.* ability, talent.
talon, *n.m.* heel.
talus, *n.m.* slope.
tambour, *n.m.* drum.
tambourin, *n.m.* tambourine.
tamis, *n.m.* sieve.
tampon, *n.m.* plug, pad.
tamponner, *vb.* plug; run together.
tan, *n.m.* tan (leather).
tandis que, *conj.* while, whereas.
tangible, *adj.* tangible.
tanguer, *vb.* cover with pitch.
tant, *adv.* so much, so many. **t. que,** as long as.
tante, *n.f.* aunt.
tantième, *n.m.* part, percentage.
tantôt, *adv.* presently, soon.
tapage, *n.m.* din.
tapageur, *adj.* rowdy.
taper, *vb.* pat, knock, tap; type.
tapir, *vb.* **se t.,** squat, cower, lurk.
tapis, *n.m.* carpet, rug.
tapisserie, *n.f.* tapestry.
tapissier, *n.m.* upholsterer.
taquiner, *vb.* tease.
taquinerie, *n.f.* teasing.
tard, *adv.* late.
tarder, *vb.* delay.
tardif, *adj.* slow, tardy, late.
tarière, *n.f.* auger.
tarif, *n.m.* scale of charges;

rate; fare. **t. douanier,** tariff.
tartan, *n.m.* plaid.
tarte, *n.f.* pie.
tartre, *n.m.* tartar.
tas, *n.m.* heap, pile.
tasse, *n.f.* cup.
tasser, *vb.* pack, fill up.
tâter, *vb.* feel.
tâtonner, *vb.* grope.
taudis, *n.m.* hovel.
taupe, *n.f.* mole.
taureau, *n.m.* bull.
taux, *n.m.* rate.
taverne, *n.f.* tavern.
taxe, *n.f.* tax. **t. (à la) valeur ajoutée,** value-added tax.
taxer, *vb.* tax, assess.
taxi, *n.m.* cab, taxi.
te (tə), *pron.* you, yourself.
technicien, *n.m.* technician.
technique, 1. *n.f.* technique. **2.** *adj.* technical.
technologie, *n.f.* technology.
teindre, *vb.* dye.
teint, *n.m.* complexion.
teinte, *n.f.* tint, shade.
teinter, *vb.* tint, stain.
teinture, *n.f.* dye.
teinturier, *n.m.* dry-cleaner, dyer.
tel, *adj.* such.
télégramme, *n.m.* telegram.
télégraphe, *n.m.* telegraph.
télégraphie, *n.f.* telegraphy. **t. sans fil,** *abbrev.* T.S.F., radio, wireless.
télégraphier, *vb.* telegraph.
téléphone, *n.m.* telephone. **coup de t.,** ring.
téléphoner, *vb.* telephone.
télescope, *n.m.* telescope.
télescoper, *vb.* crash, run together.
télévision, *n.f.* television.
tellement, *adv.* so much.
téméraire, *adj.* rash.
témoignage, *n.m.* testimony, token.
témoigner, *vb.* testify.
témoin, *n.m.* witness.
tempe, *n.f.* temple.
tempérament, *n.m.* temper, temperament.
tempérance, *n.f.* temperance.
tempérant, *adj.* temperate.
température, *n.f.* temperature.
tempéré, *adj.* temperate.
tempérer, *vb.* moderate, calm, lessen.
tempête, *n.f.* storm, tempest.
tempétueux, *adj.* tempestuous.
temple, *n.m.* temple.
temporaire, *adj.* temporary.
temporiser, *vb.* temporize, evade.
temps (tän), *n.m.* time; weather.
tenace, *adj.* tenacious.
ténacité, *n.f.* tenacity.
tenailles, *n.f.pl.* tongs.
tendance, *n.f.* tendency, trend, leaning.
tendre, 1. *adj.* tender, fond, loving. **2.** *vb.* tend, extend.

tendresse, *n.f.* tenderness, fondness.
tendu, *adj.* tense; uptight.
ténèbres, *n.f.pl.* gloom, darkness.
ténébreux, *adj.* dismal.
teneur, *n.m.* **t. de livres,** bookkeeper.
tenir, *vb.* hold.
tennis (-s), *n.m.* tennis.
ténor, *n.m.* tenor.
tension, *n.f.* strain; stress.
tentacule, *n.m.* tentacle.
tentatif, *adj.* tentative.
tentation, *n.f.* temptation.
tentative, *n.f.* attempt.
tente, *n.f.* tent; awning.
tenter, *vb.* tempt, try, attract.
tenture, *n.f.* wallcovering.
tenue, *n.f.* rig; conduct, manners.
ténuité, *n.f.* tenuity, unimportance.
térébenthine, *n.f.* turpentine.
terme, *n.m.* term, period; end.
terminaison, *n.f.* ending.
terminer, *vb.* end.
terminologie, *n.f.* terminology.
terminus, *n.m.* terminus.
terne, *adj.* drab, dull, dim, dingy.
ternir, *vb.* tarnish, dull.
terrain, *n.m.* ground(s).
terrasse, *n.f.* terrace.
terrasser, *vb.* heap up, embank; knock down, conquer.
terre, *n.f.* earth, ground, land. **pomme de t.,** potato. **à t.,** ashore.
terrestre, *adj.* earthly.
terreur, *n.f.* terror, fright, fear.
terrible, *adj.* terrible, awful, tremendous.
terrifier, *vb.* terrify.
territoire, *n.m.* territory.
terroir, *n.m.* soil.
terroriser, *vb.* terrorize.
tertre, *n.m.* mound.
tesson, *n.m.* broken piece, fragment.
testament, *n.m.* testament, will.
testateur, *n.m.* testator.
tête, *n.f.* head. **tenir t. à,** cope with.
téter, *vb.* suck.
téton, *n.m.* breast.
texte, *n.m.* text.
textile, *adj.* textile.
textuel, *adj.* textual.
texture, *n.f.* texture.
thé, *n.m.* tea.
théâtral, *adj.* theatrical.
théâtre, *n.m.* theater.
théière, *n.f.* teapot.
thème, *n.m.* theme.
théologie, *n.f.* theology.
théorie, *n.f.* theory.
théorique, *adj.* theoretical.
thermomètre, *n.m.* thermometer.
thésauriser, *vb.* hoard.
thèse, *n.f.* thesis.
thym, *n.m.* thyme.

ticket, *n.m.* check, ticket, coupon.

tiède, *adj.* lukewarm.

tiédir, *vb.* make or become cool.

tien, *pron.* **le tien, la tienne,** yours.

tiers, *n.m.* third.

Tiers Monde, *n.m.* Third World.

tige, *n.f.* stem, stalk.

tigre, *n.m.* tiger.

tilleul, *n.m.* linden, limetree.

timbre, *n.m.* stamp. **t.-poste,** postage stamp.

timbrer, *vb.* stamp.

timide, *adj.* timid, shy, coy, bashful.

timidité, *n.f.* timidity.

timoré, *adj.* timorous.

tintamarre, *n.m.* racket.

tinter, *vb.* ring, knell, tinkle.

tirailleur, *n.m.* sharpshooter.

tire, *n.f.* pull, yank.

tire-bouchon, *n.m.* corkscrew.

tirer, *vb.* draw, pull; shoot.

tiret, *n.m.* blank.

tiroir, *n.m.* drawer.

tisane, *n.f.* drink, broth.

tisser, *vb.* weave.

tisserand, *n.m.* weaver.

tissu, *n.m.* web; cloth, fabric.

titre, *n.m.* title, right.

titrer, *vb.* invest with a title.

toast (-t), *n.m.* toast.

toaster, *n.m.* toast.

toile, *n.f.* web; canvas; linen.

toilette, *n.f.* toilet; dressing, dress.

toison, *n.f.* fleece.

toit, *n.m.* roof.

toiture, *n.f.* roofing.

tolérance, *n.f.* tolerance.

tolérer, *vb.* tolerate, bear.

tomate, *n.f.* tomato.

tombe, *n.f.* grave.

tombeau, *n.m.* tomb.

tombée, *n.f.* fall, decline.

tomber, *vb.* fall. **laisser t.,** drop.

ton, *n.m.* tone, pitch.

ton *m.,* **ta** *f.,* **tes** *pl. adj.* your.

tondeuse, *n.f.* (lawn) mower.

tondre, *vb.* shear; mow.

tonique, *adj. and n.m.* tonic.

tonne, *n.f.* ton; barrel.

tonneau, *n.m.* cask, barrel.

tonner, *vb.* thunder.

tonnerre, *n.m.* thunder.

topaze, *n.f.* topaz.

topographie, *n.f.* topography.

torche, *n.f.* torch.

tordre, *vb.* twist, wrench, wring. **se t.,** writhe.

torpeur, *n.f.* torpor.

torpille, *n.f.* torpedo.

torrent, *n.m.* torrent.

torride, *adj.* torrid.

torse, *n.m.* torso.

tort, *n.m.* wrong. **avoir t.,** be wrong.

tortiller, *vb.* twist, wiggle.

tortu, *adj.* crooked.

tortue, *n.f.* turtle, tortoise.

torture, *n.f.* torture.

torturer, *vb.* torture.

tôt, *adv.* soon, early.

total, *adj. and n.m.* total.

totalisateur, *n.m.* adding machine.

totaliser, *vb.* total, add up.

totalitaire, *adj.* totalitarian.

totalité, *n.f.* entirety.

touchant, *prep.* concerning.

touche, *n.f.* key.

toucher, 1. *n.m.* touch. 2. *vb.* touch; collect; affect; border on.

touffe, *n.f.* tuft, bunch.

touffu, *adj.* bushy.

toujours, *adv.* always, still, ever, yet.

toupie, *n.f.* top (child's toy).

tour, 1. *n.m.* turn; trick; stroll. **faire le t. de,** go around. 2. *n.f.* tower.

tourbe, *n.f.* rabble.

tourbillon, *n.m.* whirl. **t. d'eau,** whirlpool. **t. de vent,** whirlwind.

tourbillonner, *vb.* whirl.

tourelle, *n.f.* turret.

touriste, *n.m.f.* tourist.

tourment, *n.m.* torment.

tourmenter, *vb.* torment.

tourne-disques, *n.m.* record player.

tournedos, *n.f.* beefsteak.

tournée, *n.f.* round.

tourner, *vb.* turn, revolve, spin.

tournesol, *n.m.* sunflower.

tournevis, *n.m.* screwdriver.

tournoi, *n.m.* tournament.

tournure, *n.f.* figure.

tousser, *vb.* cough.

tout, 1. *adj.m.* **toute** *f.,* **tous** *m.pl.,* **toutes** *f.pl.* all, each, every. 2. *pron.* everything. **t. les deux,** both. **t. d'un coup,** all at once. **t. de même,** all the same. **pas du t.,** not at all.

toutefois, *adv.* however.

tout-puissant, *adj.* almighty.

toux, *n.f.* cough.

toxique, *adj.* toxic.

tracasser, *vb.* worry.

trace, *n.f.* trace, step, track, footprint.

tracer, *vb.* outline, trace.

tracteur, *n.m.* tractor.

traction, *n.f.* traction.

tradition, *n.f.* tradition.

traditionnel, *adj.* traditional.

traducteur, *n.m.* translator.

traduction, *n.f.* translation.

traduire, *vb.* translate.

trafic, *n.m.* traffic.

trafiquer, *vb.* traffic, carry on dealings.

tragédie, *n.f.* tragedy.

tragique, *adj.* tragic.

trahir, *vb.* betray.

trahison, *n.f.* treason.

train, *n.m.* train.

traînard, *n.m.* loiterer, dawdler.

traîne, *n.f.* train of dress.

traîneau, *n.m.* sled, sleigh.

traîner, *vb.* drag, haul.

traire, *vb.* milk.

trait, *n.m.* feature; draft; shot. **t. d'union,** hyphen.

traité, *n.m.* treaty.

traitement, *n.m.* treatment.

traiter, *vb.* treat, deal.

traître, *n.m.* traitor.

traîtrise, *n.f.* treachery.

trajet, *n.m.* crossing.

trame, *n.f.* web (woof); plan, plot.

tramer, *vb.* devise.

tramway, *n.m.* streetcar.

tranchant, *adj.* sharp, crisp.

tranche, *n.f.* slice.

tranchée, *n.f.* trench.

trancher, *vb.* cut.

tranquille (-l-), *adj.* quiet. **laisser t.,** leave alone.

tranquilliser (-l-), *vb.* soothe, make tranquil.

tranquillité (-l-), *n.f.* quiet, stillness.

transaction, *n.f.* transaction.

transe, *n.f.* fright, fear.

transférer, *vb.* transfer.

transformer, *vb.* transform.

transfuser, *vb.* transfuse.

transfusion, *n.f.* transfusion.

transition (-z-), *n.f.* transition.

transitoire (-z-), *adj.* transitory.

transmettre, *vb.* transmit, convey, send.

transparent, *adj.* transparent.

transpiration, *n.f.* perspiration.

transpirer, *vb.* perspire.

transplanter, *vb.* transplant.

transport, *n.m.* transfer, transport, transportation; bliss, ecstasy.

transporter, *vb.* transport, transfer, convey.

transposer, *vb.* transpose.

transsexuel, *adj.* transsexual.

travail, *n.m.* work, job, labor.

travailler, *vb.* work.

travailleur, 1. *n.m.* worker, laborer. 2. *adj.* industrious.

travée, *n.f.* span.

travers, *n.m.* breadth. **à t.,** across, through. **de t.,** askance, awry.

traversée, *n.f.* crossing.

traverser, *vb.* cross.

traversin, *n.m.* bolster.

travesti, *n.m.* transvestite.

travestir, *vb.* disguise.

trébucher, *vb.* stumble, trip.

trèfle, *n.m.* clover; club (cards).

treillis, *n.m.* denim.

treize, *adj. and n.m.* thirteen.

tréma, *n.m.* dieresis.

tremblement, *n.m.* trembling. **t. de terre,** earthquake.

trembler, *vb.* tremble, shake, quake.

trembloter, *vb.* quiver.

trémousser, *vb.* flutter.

trempe, *n.f.* temper, cast.

tremper, *vb.* soak, drench, temper.

trente, *adj. and n.m.* thirty.

trépasser, *vb.* die.

trépied, *n.m.* tripod, trivet.

très, *adv.* very.
trésor, *n.m.* treasure, treasury; darling.
trésorier, *n.m.* treasurer.
tressaillement, *n.m.* thrill; start.
tressaillir, *vb.* thrill; start.
tresse, *n.f.* braid.
tresser, *vb.* braid.
tréteau, *n.m.* trestle.
trêve, *n.f.* truce.
triangle, *n.m.* triangle.
tribade, *n.f.* Lesbian.
tribu, *n.f.* tribe.
tribulation, *n.f.* tribulation.
tribut, *n.m.* tribute.
tributaire, *adj.* tributary.
tricher, *vb.* cheat.
tricherie, *n.f.* cheating.
tricoter, *vb.* knit.
trier, *vb.* sort.
trimestre, *n.m.* term.
trimestriel, *adj.* quarterly.
trinquer, *vb.* touch glasses in making a toast.
triomphant, *adj.* triumphant.
triomphe, *n.m.* triumph.
triompher, *vb.* triumph.
triple, *adj.* and *n.m.* triple.
tripoter, *vb.* fiddle with, dabble in; bother.
triste, *adj.* sad.
tristesse, *n.f.* sadness.
trivial, *adj.* trivial.
trivialité, *n.f.* triviality.
troc, *n.m.* barter.
trois, *adj.* and *n.m.* three.
troisième, *adj.* third.
trompe, *n.f.* horn, trumpet, elephant's trunk.
trompe l'œil, *n.m.* make-believe, sham.
tromper, *vb.* deceive, cheat. se t., be wrong, make a mistake.
tromperie, *n.f.* deceit.
trompette, *n.f.* trumpet.
trompeur, *adj.* deceitful.
tronc, *n.m.* trunk.
trône, *n.m.* throne.
trop, *adv.* too; too much, too many.
trophée, *n.m.* trophy.
tropical, *adj.* tropical.
tropique, *n.m.* tropic.
troquer, *vb.* barter, dicker, trade.
trot, *n.m.* trot.
trotter, *vb.* trot.
trottiner, *vb.* trot, jog.
trottoir, *n.m.* sidewalk.
trou, *n.m.* hole.
trouble, *n.m.* disturbance, riot.
troublé, *adj.* anxious, worried.
troubler, *vb.* perturb.
trouer, *vb.* pierce, bore.
troupe, *n.f.* troop.
troupeau, *n.m.* herd, flock, drove.
troupier, *n.m.* soldier, trooper.
trousseau, *n.m.* bunch; outfit.
trousser, *vb.* truss up, turn up.
trouvaille, *n.f.* discovery.
trouver, *vb.* find. se t., be located.
truc, *n.m.* trick; thing.

truelle, *n.f.* trowel.
truite, *n.f.* trout.
truquer, *vb.* fake.
trust, *n.m.* trust.
T.S.F., *n.f.* radio.
tu, *pron.* you.
tube, *n.m.* tube, pipe.
tuberculeux, *adj.* tuberculous.
tuberculose, *n.f.* tuberculosis.
tuer, *vb.* kill.
tuerie, *n.f.* slaughter, massacre.
tuile, *n.f.* tile.
tulipe, *n.f.* tulip.
tuméfier, *vb.* make swollen.
tumulte, *n.m.* tumult, turmoil, uproar.
tunique, *n.f.* tunic.
tunnel, *n.f.* tunnel.
Turc *m.*, Turque *f.n.* Turk.
turc, *n.m.* Turkish (language).
turc *m.*, turque *f. adj.* Turkish.
Turquie, *n.f.* Turkey.
tutelle, *n.f.* tutelage, protection.
tuteur, *n.m.* guardian.
tutoyer, *vb.* use "tu" (familiar form) to.
tuyau, *n.f.* pipe; hose.
tympan, *n.m.* eardrum.
type, *n.m.* type; fellow, guy.
typique, *adj.* typical.
tyran, *n.m.* tyrant.
tyrannie, *n.f.* tyranny.
tyranniser, *vb.* tyrannize.
tzigane, *n.* gypsy.

U

ubiquité, *n.f.* ubiquity.
ulcère, *n.m.* ulcer.
ultérieur, *adj.* ulterior, further.
ultime, *adj.* ultimate, last.
un *m.*, une *f.* 1. *art. a.* 2. *adj. and n.m.* one.
unanime, *adj.* unanimous.
unanimité, *n.f.* unanimity.
unifier, *vb.* unify.
uniforme, *adj.* and *n.m.* uniform.
union, *n.f.* union.
unique, *adj.* unique; only.
unir, *vb.* unite.
unisexuel, *adj.* unisex.
unisson, *n.m.* unison.
unité, *n.f.* unit, unity.
univers, *n.m.* universe.
universel, *adj.* universal.
université, *n.f.* university, college.
urbain, *adj.* urban.
urgence, *n.f.* urgency.
urgent, *adj.* urgent, pressing.
urne, *n.f.* urn; ballot box.
urticaire, *n.f.* hives.
usage, *n.m.* use; custom.
usager, *adj.* for daily use.
usé, *adj.* shabby, worn-out.
user, *vb.* wear out.
usine, *n.f.* factory.
ustensile, *n.f.* utensil.
usuel, *adj.* usual.
usure, *n.f.* wear and tear; usury; interest.

usurper, *vb.* usurp.
utile, *adj.* helpful, useful.
utilisation, *n.f.* use.
utiliser, *vb.* use.
utilité, *n.f.* utility.
utopie, *n.f.* utopia.

V

vacance, *n.* vacancy; *(pl.)* vacation.
vacarme, *n.m.* uproar.
vaccin, *n.m.* vaccine.
vacciner, *vb.* vaccinate.
vache, *n.f.* cow.
vaciller (-l-), *vb.* waver.
vacuité, *n.f.* emptiness, vacuity.
vagabond, *adj.* vagrant.
vagabonder, *vb.* roam, tramp.
vague, 1. *n.f.* wave. 2. *adj.* vague.
vaguer, *vb.* wander.
vaillant, *adj.* valiant, brave, gallant.
vain, *adj.* idle, vain, futile.
vaincre, *vb.* defeat.
vainqueur, *n.m.* victor.
vaisseau, *n.m.* ship.
vaisselle, *n.f.* dishes.
valeur, *n.f.* valor; value, worth; *(pl.)* securities.
valeureux, *adj.* brave, valorous.
valide, *adj.* valid.
valise, *n.f.* suitcase.
vallée, *n.f.* valley.
vallon, *n.m.* valley, vale.
valoir, *vb.* be worth. v. mieux, be better.
valse, *n.f.* waltz.
vandale, *n.m.f.* vandal.
vanille, *n.f.* vanilla.
vanité, *n.f.* conceit, vanity.
vaniteux, *adj.* vain.
vantard, *adj.* boastful.
vanter, *vb.* extol. se v., boast, brag.
vapeur, 1. *n.m.* steamship. 2. *n.f.* vapor, steam.
vaporisateur, *n.f.* vaporizer, spray.
variation, *n.f.* variation, change.
varicelle, *n.f.* chicken-pox.
varier, *vb.* vary.
variété, *n.f.* variety.
variole, *n.f.* smallpox.
vase, *n.m.* vase, jar, pot.
vasectomie, *n.f.* vasectomy.
vaseux, *adj.* slimy.
vassal, *n.f.* vassal.
vaste, *adj.* vast, spacious.
vaurien, *n.m.* worthless person, idler.
veau, *n.m.* calf.
végéter, *vb.* vegetate.
véhicule, *n.m.* vehicle.
veille, *n.f.* eve, day before.
veiller, *vb.* watch over, sit up.
veine, *n.f.* vein; luck.
velours, *n.m.* velvet. v. côtelé, corduroy.

velouté, *adj.* like velvet.
velu, *adj.* hairy.
vendange, *n.f.* vintage.
vendeur, *n.m.* seller; clerk; salesman.
vendre, *vb.* sell.
vendredi, *n.m.* Friday.
vénéneux, *adj.* poisonous.
vénérer, *vb.* venerate.
vengeance, *n.f.* revenge.
venger, *vb.* avenge. se v., get revenge.
venimeux, *adj.* poisonous.
venin, *n.m.* poison.
venir, *vb.* come. v. de, have just. . . . à v., forthcoming.
vent, *n.m.* wind.
vente, *n.f.* sale.
venteux, *adj.* windy.
ventilateur, *n.m.* fan.
ventiler, *vb.* ventilate.
ventre, *n.m.* belly.
venue, *n.f.* advent, arrival.
vêpres, *n.f.pl.* vespers.
ver (-r), *n.m.* worm.
veracité, *n.f.* veracity.
véranda, *n.f.* porch.
verbe, *n.m.* verb.
verbeux, *adj.* wordy, verbose.
verdeur, *n.f.* greenness, sharpness, vigor.
verdict (-kt), *n.m.* verdict.
verdir, *vb.* make or become green.
verge, *n.f.* rod.
verger, *n.m.* orchard.
vérification, *n.f.* check.
vérifier, *vb.* check, confirm.
véritable, *adj.* genuine, real.
verité, *n.f.* truth.
vermine, *n.f.* vermin.
vernir, *vb.* varnish.
vernis, *n.m.* varnish.
vérole, *n.f.* petite v., smallpox.
verre, *n.m.* glass.
verrou, *n.m.* bolt.
verrouiller, *vb.* bolt.
vers, 1. *n.m.* verse. 2. *prep.* toward.
verse, *adj.* tomber à v., pour.
verser, *vb.* pour, shed.
versifier, *vb.* versify.
version, *n.f.* version, translation.
vert, *adj.* green.
vertical, *adj.* upright, vertical.
vertige, *n.m.* dizziness.
vertigineux, *adj.* dizzy.
vertu, *n.f.* virtue.
vertueux, *adj.* virtuous.
verveux, *adj.* lively, animated.
vessie, *n.f.* bladder.
veste, *n.f.* jacket.
vestiaire, *n.m.* cloak-room.
vestibule, *n.m.* hall, lobby.
vestige, *n.m.* vestige, remains.
veston, *n.m.* jacket, coat.
vêtement, *n.m.* garment; *(pl.)* clothes.
vétéran, *n.m.* veteran.
vétérinaire, *n.m.* veterinary.
vêtir, *vb.* clothe.
véto, *n.m.* veto.
veuf, *n.m.* widower.
veuve, *n.f.* widow.

vexation, *n.f.* vexation.
vexer, *vb.* vex.
viaduc, *n.m.* viaduct.
viande, *n.f.* meat.
vibrant, *adj.* vibrant, vibrating.
vibration, *n.f.* vibration.
vibrer, *vb.* vibrate.
vicaire, *n.m.* vicar.
vice, *n.m.* vice.
vice-roi, *n.m.* viceroy.
vicieux, *adj.* vicious.
vicomte, *n.m.* viscount.
victime, *n.f.* victim.
victoire, *n.f.* victory.
victorieux, *adj.* victorious.
vidange, *n.f.* emptying, cleaning.
vide, 1. *n.m.* emptiness, vacuum, blank, gap. 2. *adj.* empty, void, vacant, blank.
vidéodisque, *n.m.* videodisc.
vider, *vb.* empty, drain.
vie, *n.f.* life.
vieil, *adj.* old.
vieillard, *n.m.* old man.
vieille, 1. *n.f.* old woman. 2. *adj.* (*f.*) old.
vieillesse, *n.f.* old age.
vieillir, *vb.* age.
vierge, *n.f.* virgin.
vieux, *adj.m.* old.
vif *m.*, vive *f. adj.* lively, quick, brisk, bright, vivacious.
vif-argent, *n.m.* quicksilver.
vigie, *n.f.* lookout man or station.
vigilance, *n.f.* vigilance.
vigilant, *adj.* watchful.
vigne, *n.f.* vine; vineyard.
vigoureux, *adj.* lusty, hardy, vigorous.
vigueur, *n.f.* vigor, force.
vil (-l), *adj.* vile.
vilain, *adj.* ugly, mean, wicked.
village (-l-), *n.m.* village.
ville (-l), *n.f.* city, town.
villégiature (-l-), *n.f.* country holiday.
vin, *n.m.* wine.
vinaigre, *n.m.* vinegar.
vindicatif, *adj.* vindictive.
vingt (văN), *adj. and n.m.* twenty.
vingtaine (văN-), *n.f.* score.
vingtième (văN-), *adj. and n.m.* twentieth.
violateur, *n.m.* violator.
violation, *n.f.* violation.
violemment, *adj.* violently.
violence, *n.f.* violence.
violent, *adj.* violent.
violer, *vb.* violate.
violet, *adj.* purple, violet.
violette, *n.f.* violet.
violon, *n.m.* violin.
vipère, *n.f.* viper.
virgule, *n.f.* comma.
viril (-l), *adj.* manly.
virilité, *n.f.* manhood.
virtuel, *adj.* virtual.
virtuose, *n.m.f.* virtuoso.
virus (-s), *n.m.* virus.
vis (-s), *n.f.* screw.
visa, *n.m.* visa.
visage, *n.m.* face.

vis-à-vis, *adv.* opposite, across from.
viser, *vb.* aim.
visibilité, *n.f.* visibility.
visible, *adj.* visible.
visière, *n.f.* visor; keenness.
vision, *n.f.* vision.
visionnaire, *adj. and n.m.f.* visionary.
visite, *n.f.* call, visit.
visiter, *vb.* visit.
visiteur, *n.m.* visitor.
visqueux, *adj.* viscous, sticky.
visser, *vb.* screw.
visuel, *adj.* visual.
vital, *adj.* vital.
vitalité, *n.f.* vitality.
vitamine, *n.f.* vitamin.
vite, *adv.* quick, fast.
vitesse, *n.f.* speed, rate; gear. changer de v., shift gears.
vitrail, *n.m.* (church) window.
vitre, *n.f.* pane.
vitrine, *n.f.* display case, shop-window.
vitupération, *n.f.* vituperation.
vivace, *adj.* long-lived; perennial (of plant).
vivacité, *n.f.* vivacity.
vivant, *adj.* alive.
vivement, *adv.* quickly, smartly, vividly.
vivre, *vb.* live.
vocabulaire, *n.m.* vocabulary.
vocal, *adj.* vocal.
vocation, *n.f.* vocation.
vœu (vœ), *n.m.* vow.
vogue, *n.f.* vogue.
voici, *vb.* here is, behold.
voie, *n.f.* track, road. v. d'eau, leak.
voilà, *vb.* there is; behold.
voile, *n.m.* veil; sail.
voiler, *vb.* veil, hide.
voilure, *n.f.* sails.
voir, *vb.* see. faire v., show.
voirie, *n.f.* dump.
voisin, 1. *n.m.* neighbor. 2. *adj.* nearby, adjoining.
voisinage, *n.m.* neighborhood.
voisiner, *vb.* act like a neighbor.
voiture, *n.f.* car, carriage. en v.!, all aboard!
voix, *n.f.* voice.
vol, *n.m.* flight; theft, robbery; ripoff.
volage, *adj.* fickle.
volaille, *n.f.* fowl, poultry.
volatil, *adj.* volatile.
volcan, *n.m.* volcano.
volcanique, *adj.* volcanic.
volée, *n.f.* flight, covey; herd.
voler, *vb.* fly; steal, rob; rip off.
volet, *n.m.* shutter, blind.
voleur, *n.m.* thief, robber.
vol frété, *n.m.* charter flight.
volontaire, 1. *n.m.* volunteer. 2. *adj.* voluntary, volunteer.
volonté, *n.f.* will.
volontiers, *adv.* gladly, willingly.
voltigement, *n.m.* flutter.
voltiger, *vb.* flutter; hover.

volubilité, *n.f.* volubility, glibness.
volume, *n.m.* volume.
volumineux, *adj.* bulky.
volupté, *n.f.* pleasure, voluptuousness.
vomir, *vb.* vomit.
vorace, *adj.* voracious.
votant, *n.m.* voter.
vote, *n.m.* vote.
voter, *vb.* vote.
votre *sg.,* **vos** *pl. adj.* your.
vôtre, *pron.* **le v.,** yours.
vouer, *vb.* vow.
vouloir, *vb.* want, wish, will. **v. dire,** mean. **v. savoir,** wonder. **v. bien,** be willing. **en v. à,** bear a grudge against.
vous, *pron.* you, yourself.
voûte, *n.f.* vault.
voûter, *vb.* arch.
voyage, *n.m.* journey, trip.
voyager, *vb.* travel.

voyageur, *n.m.* traveler, passenger.
voyageur de banlieue, *n.m.* commuter.
voyant, 1. *n.m.* clairvoyant. **2.** *adj.* gaudy, flashy.
voyelle, *n.f.* vowel.
vrai, *adj.* true, real.
vraisemblable, *adj.* probable, likely.
vraisemblance, *n.f.* probability.
vue, *n.f.* view, sight.
vue d'ensemble, *n.f.* overview.
vulcaniser, *vb.* vulcanize.
vulgaire, *adj.* vulgar, coarse, rude.
vulgarité, *n.f.* vulgarity.
vulnérable, *adj.* vulnerable.

W, X, Y, Z

wagon, *n.m.* coach, car.

wagon-lits, *n.m.* sleeping car.
wagon-restaurant, *n.m.* diner, dining-car.
watt, *n.m.* watt.
xérès (k-), *n.m.* sherry.
xylophone (ks-), *n.m.* xylophone.
y, *adv.* there, in it, to it.
yacht, *n.m.* yacht.
zèbre, *n.m.* zebra.
zèle, *n.m.* zeal.
zélé, *adj.* zealous.
zénith, *n.m.* zenith.
zéro, *n.m.* zero.
zézayer, *vb.* lisp.
zibeline, *n.f.* sable.
zigzaguer, *vb.* zigzag.
zodiaque, *n.m.* zodiac.
zone, *n.f.* zone, district.
zoologie, *n.f.* zoology.
zoologique, *adj.* zoological. **jardin z.,** zoo.

English-French

A

a, *art.* un *m.,* une *f.*

aardvark, *n.* aardvark *m.*

abacus, *n.* abaque *m.*

abandon, *vb.* abandonner.

abandon, *n.* abandon *m.*

abandoned, *adj.* abandonné.

abandonment, *n.* abandon *m.*

abase, *vb.* abaisser; avilir.

abasement, *n.* abaissement *m.;* avilissement *m.*

abash, *vb.* déconcerter.

abate, *vb.* diminuer.

abatement, *n.* diminution *f.*

abbess, *n.* abbesse *f.*

abbey, *n.* abbaye *f.*

abbot, *n.* abbé *m.*

abbreviate, *vb.* abréger.

abbreviation, *n.* abréviation *f.*

abdicate, *vb.* abdiquer.

abdication, *n.* abdication *f.*

abdomen, *n.* abdomen *m.*

abdominal, *adj.* abdominal.

abduct, *vb.* enlever.

abduction, *n.* enlèvement *m.*

abductor, *n.* ravisseur *m.*

aberrant, *adj.* aberrant, égaré.

aberration, *n.* égarement *m.*

abet, *vb.* aider, encourager, appuyer.

abetment, *n.* encouragement *m.,* appui *m.*

abettor, *n.* aide *m.,* complice *m.*

abeyance, *n.* suspension *f.*

abhor, *vb.* détester.

abhorrence, *n.* aversion extrême *f.,* horreur *f.*

abhorrent, *adj.* odieux, répugnant (à).

abide, *vb.* (tolerate) supporter; (remain) demeurer; **(a. by the law)** respecter la loi.

abiding, *adj.* constant, durable.

ability, *n.* talent *m.*

abject, *adj.* abject.

abjuration, *n.* abjuration *f.*

abjure, *vb.* abjurer, renoncer à.

abjurer, *n.* personne *f.* qui abjure.

ablative, *adj. and n.* ablatif *m.*

ablaze, *adj.* en feu, en flammes.

able, *adj.* capable; **(to be a.)** pouvoir.

able-bodied, *adj.* fort, robuste.

able-bodied seaman, *n.* marin de première classe *m.*

ablution, *n.* ablution *f.*

ably, *adv.* capablement.

abnegate, *vb.* nier.

abnegation, *n.* abnégation *f.*

abnormal, *adj.* anormal.

abnormality, *n.* irrégularité *f.*

abnormally, *adv.* anormalement.

aboard, **1.** *adv. (naut.)* à bord; **(all a.)** en voiture. **2.** *prep.* à bord de.

abode, *n.* demeure *f.*

abolish, *vb.* abolir.

abolishment, *n.* abolissement *m.*

abolition, *n.* abolition *f.*

abominable, *adj.* abominable.

abominate, *vb.* abominer.

abomination, *n.* abomination *f.*

aboriginal, *adj.* aborigène, primitif.

abortion, *n.* avortement *m.*

abortive, *adj.* abortif, manqué.

abound, *vb.* abonder (en).

about, **1.** *adv.* (approximately) à peu près; (around) autour; **(to be a. to)** être sur le point de. **2.** *prep.* (concerning) au sujet de; (near) auprès de; (around) autour de.

about-face, *n.* volte-face *f.*

above, **1.** *adv.* au-dessus. **2.** *prep.* (higher than) au-dessus de; (more than) plus de.

aboveboard, *adj. and adv.* ouvertement, franchement.

abrasion, *n.* abrasion *f.*

abrasive, *adj.* abrasif.

abreast, *adv.* de front.

abridge, *vb.* abréger.

abridgment, *n.* abrégé *m.,* réduction *f.*

abroad, *adv.* à l'étranger.

abrogate, *vb.* abroger.

abrogation, *n.* abrogation *f.*

abrupt, *adj.* brusque; (steep) escarpé.

abruptly, *adv.* brusquement, subitement.

abruptness, *n.* brusquerie *f.,* précipitation *f.*

abscess, *n.* abcès *m.*

abscond, *vb.* disparaître, se dérober.

absence, *n.* absence *f.*

absent, *adj.* absent.

absentee, *n.* absent *m.,* manquant *m.*

absinthe, *n.* absinthe *f.*

absolute, *adj.* absolu.

absolutely, *adv.* absolument.

absoluteness, *n.* pouvoir absolu *m.;* arbitraire *m.*

absolution, *n.* absolution *f.*

absolutism, *n.* absolutisme *m.*

absolve, *vb.* absoudre.

absorb, *vb.* absorber.

absorbed, *adj.* absorbé, préoccupé.

absorbent, *n. and adj.* absorbant *m.*

absorbing, *adj.* absorbant, préoccupant.

absorption, *n.* absorption *f.*

abstain from, *vb.* s'abstenir de.

abstemious, *adj.* abstème.

abstinence, *n.* abstinence *f.*

abstract, **1.** *n.* (book) extrait *m.* **2.** *adj.* abstrait.

abstracted, *adj.* détaché, pensif.

abstraction, *n.* abstraction *f.*

abstruse, *adj.* caché, abstrus.

abundance, *n.* abondance *f.*

abundant, *adj.* abondant.

abundantly, *adv.* abondamment.

absurd, *adj.* absurde.

absurdity, *n.* absurdité *f.*

absurdly, *adv.* absurdement.

abuse, **1.** *n.* (misuse) abus *m.;* (insult) injures *f.pl.* **2.** *vb.* abuser de, injurier.

abusive, *adj.* (insulting) injurieux.

abusively, *adv.* abusivement, injurieusement.

abut, *vb.* s'embrancher (sur), aboutir (à).

abutment, *n.* contrefort *m.;* (of a bridge) culée *f.*

abyss, *n.* abîme *m.*

academic, *adj.* académique.

academic freedom, *n.* liberté de l'enseignement *f.*

academy, *n.* académie *f.*

acanthus, *n.* acanthe *f.*

accede, *vb.* consentir.

accelerate, *vb.* accélérer.

acceleration, *n.* accélération *f.*

accelerator, *n.* accélérateur *m.*

accent, *n.* accent *m.*

accentuate, *vb.* accentuer.

accept, *vb.* accepter.

acceptability, *n.* acceptabilité *f.*

acceptable, *adj.* acceptable.

acceptably, *adv.* agréablement.

acceptance, *n.* acceptation *f.*

access, *n.* accès *m.*

accessible, *adj.* accessible.

accessory, *n. and adj.* accessoire *m.*

accident, *n.* accident *m.*

accidental, *adj.* accidentel.

accidentally, *adv.* accidentellement, par hasard.

acclaim, *vb.* acclamer.

acclamation, *n.* acclamation *f.*

acclimate, *vb.* acclimater.

acclivity, *n.* montée *f.,* rampe *f.*

accolade, *n.* accolade *f.*

accommodate, *vb.* (lodge) loger; (oblige) obliger.

accommodating, *adj.* accommodant, obligeant.

accommodation, *n.* (lodging) logement *m.*

accompaniment, *n.* accompagnement *m.*

accompanist, *n.* accompagnateur *m.,* accompagnatrice *f.*

accompany, *vb.* accompagner.

accomplice, *n.* complice *m.f.*

accomplish, *vb.* accomplir.

accomplished, *adj.* accompli, achevé.

accord, *n.* accord *m.*

accordance, *n.* conformité *f.*

accordingly, *adv.* (correspondingly) à l'avenant; (therefore) donc.

according to, *prep.* selon.

accordion, *n.* accordéon *m.*

accost, *vb.* aborder.

account, *n.* (comm.) compte *m.;* (narrative) récit *m.*

accountable for, *adj.* responsable de.

accountant, n. comptable m.

account for, vb. rendre compte de.

accounting, n. comptabilité f.

accouter, vb. habiller, équiper.

accouterments, n. équipements m.pl., accoutrements m.pl.

accredit, vb. accréditer.

accretion, n. accroissement m.

accrual, n. accroissement m.

accrue, vb. provenir.

accumulate, vb. entasser.

accumulation, n. entassement m.

accumulative, adj. (thing) qui s'accumule, (person) qui accumule.

accumulator, n. accumulateur m., accumulatrice f.

accuracy, n. précision f.

accurate, adj. précis.

accursed, adj. maudit, exécrable.

accusation, n. accusation f.

accusative, n. and adj. accusatif m.

accuse, vb. accuser.

accused, n. and adj. accusé m., accusée f.

accuser, n. accusateur m., accusatrice f.

accustom, vb. accoutumer.

accustomed, adj. accoutumé, habituel.

ace, n. as m.

acerbity, n. acerbité f., âpreté f.

acetate, n. acétate m.

acetic acid, n. acide acétique m.

acetylene, n. acétylène m.

ache, 1. n. douleur f. 2. vb. faire mal à.

achieve, vb. accomplir.

achievement, n. accomplissement m.

acid, adj. and n. acide m.

acidify, vb. acidifier.

acidity, n. acidité f.

acidosis, n. acidose f.

acid test, n. épreuve concluante f.

acidulous, adj. acidulé.

acknowledge, vb. reconnaître; (a. receipt of) accuser réception de.

acme, n. comble m., apogée m.

acne, n. acné f.

acolyte, n. acolyte m.

acorn, n. gland m.

acoustics, n. acoustique f.

acquaint, vb. informer (de); (be a.d with) connaître.

acquaintance, n. connaissance f.

acquainted, adj. connu, familier (avec).

acquiesce in, vb. acquiescer à.

acquiescence, n. acquiescement m.

acquire, vb. acquérir.

acquirement, n. acquis m., acquisition f.

acquisition, n. acquisition f.

acquisitive, adj. porté à acquérir.

acquit, vb. acquitter.

acquittal, n. acquittement m.

acre, n. arpent m., acre f.

acreage, n. superficie f.

acrid, adj. âcre.

acrimonious, adj. acrimonieux.

acrimony, n. acrimonie f., aigreur f.

acrobat, n. acrobate m.f.

across, 1. prep. à travers; (on the other side of) de l'autre côté de. 2. adv. en travers.

acrostic, n. acrostiche m.

act, 1. n. acte m. 2. vb. (do) agir; (play) jouer; (behave) se conduire.

acting, 1. n. (theater) jeu m.; feinte f. 2. adj. (taking the place of) suppléant; (comm.) gérant.

actinism, n. actinisme m.

actinium, n. actinium m.

action, n. action f.

activate, vb. activer.

activation, n. activation f.

activator, n. activateur m.

active, adj. actif.

activity, n. activité f.

actor, n. acteur m.

actress, n. actrice f.

actual, adj. réel.

actuality, n. réalité f., actualité f.

actually, adv. réellement, véritablement, en effet.

actuary, n. actuaire m.

actuate, vb. mettre en action, animer.

acumen, n. finesse f., pénétration f.

acupuncture, n. acuponcture f.

acute, adj. (geom.) aigu m., aiguë f.; (mind) fin.

acutely, adv. vivement, d'une manière poignante.

acuteness, n. finesse f., vivacité f.

adage, n. adage m., proverbe m.

adamant, adj. indomptable.

Adam's apple, n. pomme d'Adam f.

adapt, vb. adapter.

adaptable, adj. adaptable.

adaptability, n. faculté d'adaptation f.

adaptation, n. adaptation f.

adapter, n. qui adapte.

adaptive, adj. adaptable.

add, vb. (join) ajouter; (arith.) additionner.

adder, n. vipère f.

addict, n. personne adonnée à f.

addict oneself to, vb. s'adonner à.

addition, n. addition f.

additional, adj. additionnel.

addle, 1. vb. corrompre, rendre couvi (of eggs). 2. adj. couvi, pourri.

address, 1. n. (on letters, etc.) adresse f.; (speech) discours

m. 2. vb. (a letter) adresser; (a person) adresser la parole à.

addressee, n. destinataire m.f.

adduce, vb. alléguer, avancer.

adenoid, adj. and n. adénoïde f.

adeptly, adv. habilement, adeptement.

adeptness, n. habileté f.

adequacy, n. suffisance f.

adequate, adj. suffisant.

adequately, adv. suffisamment, convenablement.

adhere, vb. adhérer.

adherence, n. adhérence f., attachement m.

adherent, n. adhérent m.

adhesion, n. adhésion f.

adhesive, adj. adhésif.

adhesiveness, n. propriété d'adhérer f.

adieu, n. and adv. adieu m.

adjacent, adj. adjacent.

adjective, n. adjectif m.

adjoin, vb. adjoindre, être contigu (à).

adjourn, vb. ajourner, tr. s'ajourner, intr.

adjournment, n. ajournement m.

adjunct, n. and adj. adjoint m., accessoire m.

adjust, vb. ajuster, arranger, régler.

adjuster, n. ajusteur m.

adjustment, n. ajustement m., accommodement m.

adjutant, n. capitaine adjudant major m.

administer, vb. administrer.

administration, n. administration f.

administrative, adj. administratif.

administrator, n. administrateur m.

admirable, adj. admirable.

admirably, adv. admirablement.

admiral, n. amiral m.

admiralty, n. amirauté f.

admiration, n. admiration f.

admire, vb. admirer.

admirer, n. admirateur m.

admiringly, adv. avec admiration.

admissible, adj. admissible.

admission, n. (entrance) entrée f.; (confession) aveu m.

admit, vb. (let in) laisser entrer; (confess) avouer.

admittance, n. entrée f.

admittedly, adv. de l'aveu de tout le monde.

admixture, n. mélange m.

admonish, vb. réprimander.

admonition, n. admonition f., avertissement m.

ado, n. fracas m.

adolescence, n. adolescence f.

adolescent, adj. and n. adolescent m.f.

adopt, vb. adopter.

adoption, n. adoption f.

adorable, adj. adorable.

adoration, n. adoration f.

adore, vb. adorer.

adorn, vb. orner.

adornment, n. ornement m.

adrenal glands, n.pl. capsules surrénales f.pl.

adrenalin, n. adrénaline f.

adrift, adv. (naut.) à la dérive.

adroit, adj. adroit.

adulate, vb. aduler.

adulation, n. adulation f.

adult, adj. and n. adulte m.f.

adulterant, n. adultérant m.

adulterate, vb. adultérer; (of wines, milk, etc.) frelater.

adulterer, n. adultère m.

adulteress, n. femme adultère f.

adultery, n. adultère m.

advance, 1. n. (motion forward) avancement m.; (progress) progrès m.; (pay) avances f.pl.; (in a.) d'avance. 2. vb. avancer.

advanced, adj. avancé.

advancement, n. avancement m., progrès m.

advantage, n. avantage m.

advantageous, adj. avantageux.

advantageously, adv. avantageusement.

advent, n. venue f.; (eccles.) Avent m.

adventitious, adj. adventice, fortuit.

adventure, n. aventure f.

adventurer, n. aventurier m.

adventurous, adj. aventureux.

adventurously, adv. aventureusement.

adverb, n. adverbe m.

adverbial, adj. adverbial.

adversary, n. adversaire m.

adverse, adj. adverse.

adversely, adv. défavorablement, d'une manière hostile.

adversity, n. adversité f.

advert, vb. faire allusion (à).

advertise, vb. annoncer; (a. a product) faire de la réclame pour un produit.

advertisement, n. publicité f.; (in a paper) annonce f.; (on a wall) affiche f.

advertiser, n. personne qui fait de réclame f.

advertising, n. publicité f., annonce (newspaper) f.

advice, n. conseil m.; (comm.) avis m.

advisability, n. convenance f., utilité f.

advisable, adj. recommandable.

advisably, adv. convenablement.

advise, vb. conseiller.

advisedly, adv. de propos délibéré.

advisement, n. délibération.

advocacy, n. défense f., plaidoyer m.

advocate, 1. n. (law) avocat m.; (supporter) défenseur m. 2. vb. appuyer.

aegis, n. égide f.

aerate, vb. aérer.

aeration, n. aération f.

aerial, adj. aérien.

aerially, adv. d'une manière aérienne.

aerie, n. aire f.

aeronautics, n. aéronautique f.

aesthetic, adj. esthétique.

afar, adv. loin, de loin.

affability, n. affabilité f.

affable, adj. affable.

affably, adv. affablement.

affair, n. affair f.

affect, vb. (move) toucher; (concern) intéresser; (pretend) affecter.

affectation, n. affectation f.

affected, adj. maniéré.

affecting, adj. touchant, émouvant.

affection, n. affection f.

affectionate, adj. affectueux.

affectionately, adv. affectueusement.

afferent, adj. afférent.

affiance, vb. fiancer.

affidavit, n. attestation (sous serment) f.

affiliate, vb. affilier.

affiliation, n. affiliation f.

affinity, n. affinité f.

affirm, vb. affirmer.

affirmation, n. affirmation f.

affirmative, adj. affirmatif.

affirmatively, adv. affirmativement.

affix, vb. apposer.

afflict, vb. affliger (de).

affliction, n. affliction f.

affluence, n. affluence f., opulence f.

affluent, adj. affluent, opulent.

afford, vb. (have the means to) avoir les moyens de.

affray, n. bagarre m., tumulte m.

affront, 1. n. affront m. 2. vb. insulter.

afield, adv. aux champs, en campagne.

afire, adv. en feu.

afloat, adv. à flot, en train.

aforementioned, adj. mentionné plus haut, susdit.

aforesaid, adj. susdit, ledit.

afraid, pred. adj. (be afraid) avoir peur.

Africa, n. Afrique f.

African, 1. n. Africain m. 2. adj. africain.

aft, adv. à l'arrière.

after, 1. adv. and prep. après. 2. conj. après que.

aftereffect, n. effet m.

aftermath, n. suites f. pl.

afternoon, n. après-midi m. or f.

afterthought, n. réflexion tardive f.

afterward, adv. ensuite.

again, adv. de nouveau, encore; (again and again) maintes et maintes fois.

against, prep. contre.

agape, adv. bouche bée.

agate, n. agate f.

age, 1. n. âge m. 2. vb. vieillir.

aged, adj. vieux, âgé.

ageism, n. attitude discriminative basée sur l'âge f.

ageless, adj. qui ne vieillit jamais.

agency, n. (comm.) agence f.

agenda, n. ordre du jour m., agenda m.

agent, n. agent m.

agglutinate, vb. agglutiner.

agglutination, n. agglutination f.

aggrandize, vb. agrandir.

aggrandizement, n. agrandissement m.

aggravate, vb. (intensify) aggraver; (exasperate) exaspérer.

aggravation, n. aggravation f., agacement m.

aggregate, n. masse f.

aggregation, n. agrégation f., assemblage m.

aggression, n. agression f.

aggressive, adj. agressif.

aggressively, adv. agressivement.

aggressiveness, n. caractère agressif m.

aggressor, n. agresseur m.

aghast, adj. consterné.

agile, adj. agile.

agility, n. agilité f.

agitate, vb. agiter.

agitation, n. agitation f.

agitator, n. agitateur m.

agnostic, n. and adj. agnostique m.

ago, adv. il y a (always precedes).

agonized, adj. torturé, déchirant.

agony, n. (anguish) angoisse f.; (death agony) agonie f.

agrarian, adj. agraire, agrarien.

agree, vb. être d'accord.

agreeable, adj. agréable.

agreeably, adv. agréablement.

agreement, n. accord m.

agriculture, n. agriculture f.

ahead, 1. adv. and interj. en avant. 2. prep. (ahead of) en avant de.

aid, 1. n. aide f.; (first aid) premiers secours; (first-aid station) poste de secours. 2. vb. aider.

aide, n. aide m., assistant m.

ail, vb. intr. être souffrant.

ailment, n. indisposition f.

aim, 1. n. (fig.) but m. 2. vb. viser.

aimless, adj. sans but.

aimlessly, adv. sans but, à la dérive.

air, 1. n. air m.; (a. force) aviation f.; (by a. mail) par avion; (in the open a.) en plein air. 2. vb. aérer.

airbag, n. (in automobiles) sac à air m.

air base, n. champs d'aviation m.

airborne, *adj.* par voie de l'air.

air-condition, *vb.* climatiser.

air-conditioning, *n.* climatisation *f.*

aircraft, *n.* avions *m.pl.;* (aircraft carrier) porte-avions *m.*

air fleet, *n.* aéroflotte *f.*

air gun, *n.* fusil à vent.

airing, *n.* aérage *m.,* tour *m.*

air line, *n.* ligne aérienne *f.*

air liner, *n.* avion *m.*

air mail, *n.* poste aérienne *f.*

airplane, *n.* avion *m.*

air pollution, *n.* pollution de l'air *f.*

airport, *n.* aéroport *m.*

air pressure, *n.* pression d'air *f.*

air raid, *n.* raid aérien *m.*

airsick, *adj.* (to be a.) avoir le mal d'air.

airtight, *adj.* imperméable à l'air, étanche.

airy, *adj.* (well aired) aéré; (light) léger.

aisle, *n.* (passageway) passage *m.;* (arch.) bas côté *m.*

ajar, *adv.* entr'ouvert.

akin, *adj.* allié (à), parent (de).

alacrity, *n.* empressement *m.*

alarm, *n.* alarme *f.*

alarmist, *n.* alarmiste *m.*

albino, *n.* albinos *m.*

album, *n.* album *m.*

alcohol, *n.* alcool *m.*

alcoholic, *adj.* alcoolique.

alcove, *n.* (recess) niche *f.;* (sleeping alcove) alcôve *f.*

ale, *n.* bière *f.*

alert, *adj.* alerte.

alfalfa, *n.* luzerne *f.*

algebra, *n.* algèbre *f.*

alias, **1.** *n.* nom d'emprunt *m.* **2.** *adv.* autrement nommé, dit.

alibi, *n.* alibi *m.*

alien, *adj.* étranger.

alienate, *vb.* aliéner.

alight, *vb.* (descend) descendre; (stop after descent) s'abattre.

align, *vb.* aligner.

alike, **1.** *adj.* semblable; (be alike) se ressembler. **2.** *adv.* également.

alimentary canal, *n.* canal alimentaire *m.*

alive, *adj.* vivant.

alkali, *n.* alcali *m.*

alkaline, *adj.* alcalin.

all, **1.** *adj.* tout *m.sg.,* toute *f.sg.,* tous *m.pl.,* toutes *f.pl.* **2.** *adv. and pron.* (everything) tout; (above all) surtout; (all at once) tout d'un coup; (all the same) tout de même; (that's all) c'est tout; (not at all) pas du tout; (everybody) tous; (all of you) vous tous.

allay, *vb.* apaiser.

allegation, *n.* allégation *f.*

allege, *vb.* alléguer.

allegiance, *n.* fidélité *f.*

allegory, *n.* allégorie *f.*

allergy, *n.* allergie *f.*

alleviate, *vb.* soulager.

alley, *n.* (in town) ruelle *f.;* (blind alley) cul-de-sac *m.*

alliance, *n.* alliance *f.*

allied, *adj.* allié.

alligator, *n.* alligator *m.*

allocate, *vb.* assigner.

allot, *vb.* (grant) accorder; (distribute) répartir.

allotment, *n.* partage *m.,* lot *m.*

allow, *vb.* (permit) permettre; (admit) admettre; (grant) accorder; (allow for) tenir compte de.

allowance, *n.* (money granted) allocation *f.;* (food) ration *f.;* (tolerance) tolérance *f.;* (pension) rente *f.;* (weekly allowance) semaine *f.*

alloy, *n.* alliage *m.*

all right, *adv.* très bien.

allude to, *vb.* faire allusion à.

allure, *vb.* séduire.

allusion, *n.* allusion *f.*

ally, **1.** *n.* allié *m.* **2.** *vb.* allier.

almanac, *n.* almanach *m.*

almighty, *adj.* tout-puissant.

almond, *n.* amande *f.*

almost, *adv.* presque.

alms, *n.* aumône *f.*

aloft, *adv.* en haut.

alone, *adj.* seul; (let alone) laisser tranquille.

along, **1.** *prep.* le long de. **2.** *adv.* (come along!) venez donc!

alongside, *prep.* le long de.

aloof, **1.** *adv.* à l'écart. **2.** *adj.* réservé.

aloud, *adv.* à haute voix.

alpaca, *n.* alpaga (fabric) *m.;* alpaca (animal) *m.*

alphabet, *n.* alphabet *m.*

alphabetical, *adj.* alphabétique.

alphabetize, *vb.* alphabétiser.

Alps, *n.pl.* Alpes *f.pl.*

already, *adv.* déjà.

also, *adv.* aussi.

altar, *n.* autel *m.*

alter, *vb.* changer.

alteration, *n.* modification *f.*

alternate, **1.** *n.* remplaçant *m.* **2.** *adj.* alternatif. **3.** *vb.* alterner.

alternative, *n.* alternative *f.*

although, *conj.* bien que.

altitude, *n.* altitude *f.*

altogether, *adv.* tout à fait.

altruism, *n.* altruisme *m.*

alum, *n.* alun *m.*

aluminum, *n.* aluminium *m.*

always, *adv.* toujours.

amalgam, *n.* amalgame *n.*

amalgamate, *vb.* amalgamer.

amass, *vb.* amasser.

amateur, *n.* amateur *m.*

amaze, *vb.* étonner.

amazement, *n.* stupeur *f.*

amazing, *adj.* étonnant.

ambassador, *n.* ambassadeur *m.,* ambassadrice *f.*

amber, *n.* ambre *m.*

ambidextrous, *adj.* ambidextre.

ambiguity, *n.* ambiguïté *f.*

ambiguous, *adj.* ambigu *m.,* ambiguë *f.*

ambition, *n.* ambition *f.*

ambitious, *adj.* ambitieux.

ambulance, *n.* ambulance *f.*

ambulatory, *adj.* ambulatoire.

ambush, *n.* embuscade *f.*

ameliorate, *vb.* améliorer.

amenable, *adj.* responsable, soumis (à), sujet (à).

amend, *vb.* amender.

amendment, *n.* amendement *m.*

amenity, *n.* aménité *f.,* agrément *m.*

America, *n.* Amérique *f.;* (North A.) A. du Nord; (South A.) A. du Sud.

American, **1.** *n.* Américain *m.* **2.** *adj.* américain.

amethyst, *n.* améthyste *f.*

amiable, *adj.* aimable.

amicable, *adj.* amical.

amid, *prep.* au milieu de.

amidships, *adv.* par le travers.

amiss, *adv.* de travers.

amity, *n.* amitié *f.*

ammonia, *n.* ammoniaque *f.*

ammunition, *n.* munitions (*f.pl.*) de guerre.

amnesia, *n.* amnésie *f.*

amnesty, *n.* amnistie *f.*

amniocentesis, *n.* amniocentèse *f.*

amoeba, *n.* amibe *f.*

among, *prep.* parmi, entre.

amoral, *adj.* amoral.

amorous, *adj.* amoureux.

amorphous, *adj.* amorphe.

amortize, *vb.* amortir.

amount, **1.** *n.* (sum) somme *f.;* (quantity) quantité *f.* **2.** *vb.* (amount to) se réduire à.

ampere, *n.* ampère *m.*

amphibian, *n.* amphibie *m.*

amphibious, *adj.* amphibie.

amphitheater, *n.* amphithéâtre *m.*

ample, *adj.* ample.

amplify, *vb.* amplifier.

amputate, *vb.* amputer.

amputee, *n.* amputé *m.*

amuse, *vb.* amuser.

amusement, *n.* amusement *m.*

an, *art.* un *m.,* une *f.*

anachronism, *n.* anachronisme *m.*

analogous, *adj.* analogue.

analogy, *n.* analogie *f.*

analysis, *n.* analyse *f.*

analyst, *n.* analyste *m.*

analytic, *adj.* analytique.

analyze, *vb.* analyser.

anarchy, *n.* anarchie *f.*

anatomy, *n.* anatomie *f.*

ancestor, *n.* ancêtre *m.*

ancestral, *adj.* d'ancêtres, héréditaire.

ancestry, *n.* aïeux, *m.pl.*

anchor, **1.** *vb.* ancrer. **2.** *n.* ancre *f.*

anchorage, *n.* mouillage *m.,* ancrage *m.*

anchovy, *n.* anchois *m.*

ancient, *adj.* ancien *m.,* ancienne *f.*

and, *conj.* et.

anecdote, n. anecdote f.
anemia, n. anémie f.
anesthetic, adj. and n. anesthésique m.
anesthetist, n. anesthésiste m.
anew, adv. de nouveau.
angel, n. ange m.
anger, n. colère f.
angle, 1. n. angle m.; **(at an angle)** en biais. 2. vb. (fish) pêcher à la ligne.
angry, adj. fâché; **(to get angry)** se fâcher.
anguish, n. angoisse f.
angular, adj. anguleux.
aniline, n. aniline f.
animal, n. and adj. animal m.
animate, vb. animer.
animated, adj. animé.
animated cartoon, n. dessin animé m.
animation, n. animation f.
animosity, n. animosité f.
anise, n. anis m.
ankle, n. cheville f.
annals, n.pl. annales f.pl.
annex, n. (to a building) dépendance f.
annexation, n. annexion f.
annihilate, vb. anéantir.
anniversary, n. anniversaire m.
annotate, vb. annoter.
annotation, n. annotation f.
announce, vb. annoncer.
announcement, n. annonce f.
announcer, n. speaker m.
annoy, vb. (vex) contrarier; (bore) ennuyer.
annoyance, n. contrariété f.
annual, adj. annuel.
annuity, n. annuité f., rente annuelle f.
annul, vb. annuler.
anode, n. anode f.
anoint, vb. oindre.
anomalous, adj. anomal, irrégulier.
anonymous, adj. anonyme.
another, adj. and pron. un autre m., une autre f.; **(one another)** l'un l'autre.
answer, vb. répondre.
answer, n. réponse f.
answerable, adj. responsable (de), susceptible de réponse.
ant, n. fourmi f.
antacid, adj. antiacide.
antagonism, n. antagonisme m.
antagonist, n. antagoniste m.
antagonistic, adj. en opposition (à), hostile (à), opposé (à).
antagonize, vb. s'opposer à.
antarctic, adj. antarctique.
antecedent, adj. and n. antécédent m.
antedate, vb. antidater.
antelope, n. antilope f.
antenna, n. antenne f.
anterior, adj. antérieur.
anteroom, n. antichambre m. or f.
anthem, n. (national) hymne national m.
anthology, n. anthologie f.

anthracite, n. anthracite m.
anthrax, n. anthrax m.
anthropology, n. anthropologie f.
antiaircraft, adj. contre-avion.
antibody, n. anticorps m.
antic, n. bouffonerie f.
anticipate, vb. (advance) anticiper; (expect) s'attendre à; (foresee) prévoir.
anticipation, n. anticipation f.
anticlerical, adj. anticlérical.
anticlimax, n. anticlimax m.
antidote, n. antidote m.
antimony, n. antimoine f.
antinuclear, adj. antinucléaire.
antipathy, n. antipathie f.
antiquated, adj. antique.
antique, 1. n. antique m.; **(antique dealer)** antiquaire f.
antiquity, n. antiquité f.
antiseptic, adj. and n. antiseptique m.
antisocial, adj. antisocial.
antitoxin, n. antitoxine f.
antler, n. andouiller m.
anvil, n. enclume f.
anxiety, n. anxiété f.
anxious, adj. inquiet m., inquiète f.
any, 1. adj. (in questions, for "some") du m.sg., de la f.sg., des pl.; (not . . . any) ne . . . pas de; (no matter which) n'importe quel; (every) tout. 2. pron. **(any of it or them,** with verb) en.
anybody, pron. (somebody) quelqu'un; (somebody, implying negation) personne; (not . . . anybody) ne . . . personne; (no matter who) n'importe qui.
anyhow, adv. en tout cas; d'une manière quelconque.
anyone, pron. see anybody.
anything, pron. (something) quelque chose; (something, implying negation) rien; (not . . . anything) ne . . . rien; (no matter what) n'importe quoi.
anyway, adv. see anyhow.
anywhere, adv. n'importe où.
apart, 1. adv. à part. 2. prep. **(apart from)** en dehors de.
apartheid, n. ségrégation des populations noire et blanche, f.
apartment, n. appartement m.
apathetic, adj. apathique.
apathy, n. apathie f.
ape, 1. n. singe m. 2. vb. singer.
aperture, n. ouverture f.
apex, n. sommet m.
aphorism, n. aphorisme m.
apiary, n. rucher m.
apiece, adv. chacun.
apologetic, adj. use verb s'excuser.
apologist, n. apologiste m.
apologize for, vb. s'excuser de.
apology, n. excuses f. pl.
apoplectic, adj. apoplectique.
apoplexy, n. apoplexie f.
apostate, n. apostat m.

apostle, n. apôtre m.
apostolic, adj. apostolique.
appall, vb. épouvanter.
apparatus, n. appareil m.
apparel, n. habillement m.
apparent, adj. apparent.
apparition, n. apparition f.
appeal, 1. n. appel m. 2. vb. **(a. to)** en appeler à.
appear, vb. (become visible) apparaître; (seem) sembler.
appearance, n. (apparition) apparition f.; (semblance) apparence f.; (aspect) aspect m.
appease, vb. apaiser.
appeaser, n. personne qui apaise.
appellant, n. appelant m.
appellate, adj. d'appel.
appendage, n. accessoire m., apanage m.
appendectomy, n. appendéctomie f.
appendicitis, n. appendicite f.
appendix, n. appendice m.
appetite, n. appétit m.
appetizer, n. (drink) apéritif m.
appetizing, adj. appétissant.
applaud, vb. applaudir.
applause, n. applaudissements m.pl.
apple, n. pomme f.
applesauce, n. compote (f.) de pommes.
appliance, n. appareil m.
applicable, adj. applicable.
applicant, n. postulant m.
application, n. (request) demande f.
applied, adj. appliqué.
apply, vb. (a. to somebody) s'adresser à; (a. for a job) solliciter; (put on) appliquer; **(a. oneself)** s'appliquer.
appoint, vb. (a person) nommer; (time, place) désigner.
appointment, n. (meeting) rendez-vous m.; **(make an a. with)** donner un rendez-vous à; (nomination) nomination f.
apportion, vb. répartir.
apposition, n. apposition f.
appraisal, n. évaluation f.
appraise, vb. priser.
appreciable, adj. appréciable.
appreciate, vb. apprécier.
appreciation, n. appréciation f.
apprehend, vb. saisir.
apprehension, n. (seizure) arrestation f.; (understanding) compréhension f.; (fear) appréhension f.
apprehensive, adj. craintif.
apprentice, n. apprenti m.
apprise, vb. prévenir, informer.
approach, 1. n. approche f.; **(make approaches to)** faire des avances à. 2. vb. s'approcher de.
approachable, adj. abordable, accessible.
approbation, n. approbation f.
appropriate, 1. adj. convenable. 2. vb. s'approprier.

appropriation, *n.* appropriation *f.*
approval, *n.* approbation *f.*
approve, *vb.* approuver.
approximate, 1. *adj.* approximatif. **2.** *vb.* se rapprocher
(de).
approximately, *adv.* approxi-
mativement, à peu près.
approximation, *n.* approximation *f.*
appurtenance, *n.* appartenance
f., dépendance *f.*
apricot, *n.* abricot *m.*
April, *n.* avril *m.*
apron, *n.* tablier *m.*
apropos, *adj.* à propos.
apse, *n.* abside *f.*
apt, *adj.* (likely to) sujet à;
(suitable for) apte à; (appropriate) à propos; (clever) habile.
aptitude, *n.* aptitude *f.*
aquarium, *n.* aquarium *m.*
aquatic, *adj.* aquatique.
aqueduct, *n.* aqueduc *m.*
aqueous, *adj.* aqueux.
aquiline, *adj.* aquilin.
Arab, 1. *n.* Arabe *m.f.* **2.** *adj.*
arabe.
Arabic, *adj. and n.* arabe *m.*
arable, *adj.* arable, labourable.
arbiter, *n.* arbitre *m.*
arbitrary, *adj.* arbitraire.
arbitrate, *vb.* arbitrer.
arbitration, *n.* arbitrage *m.*
arbitrator, *n.* arbitre *m.*
arbor, *n.* (bower) berceau *m.*
arboreal, *adj.* arboricole.
arc, *n.* arc *m.*
arcade, *n.* arcade *f.*
arch, 1. *n.* arc *m.;* (of bridge)
arche *f.* **2.** *adj.* espiègle.
archaeology, *n.* archéologie *f.*
archaic, *adj.* archaïque.
archbishop, *n.* archevêque *m.*
archdiocese, *n.* archidiocèse *m.*
archduke, *n.* archiduc *m.*
archer, *n.* archer *m.*
archery, *n.* tir à l'arc *m.*
archipelago, *n.* archipel *m.*
architect, *n.* architecte *m.*
architectural, *adj.* architectural.
architecture, *n.* architecture *f.*
archives, *n.* archives *f.pl.*
archway, *n.* voûte *f.,* passage
(sous une voûte) *m.*
arctic, *adj.* arctique.
ardent, *adj.* ardent.
ardor, *n.* ardeur *f.*
arduous, *adj.* difficile.
area, *n.* (geom.) aire *f.;* (locality) région *f.;* (surface) surface *f.*
area code, *n.* indicatif interurbain *m.*
arena, *n.* arène *f.*
argentine, *adj.* argentin.
argue, *vb.* (reason) argumenter; (indicate) prouver; (discuss) discuter.
argument, *n.* (reasoning) argument *m.;* (dispute) discussion
f.

argumentative, *adj.* disposé à
argumenter, raisonneur.
aria, *n.* air *m.,* chanson *f.*
arid, *adj.* aride.
arise, *vb.* (move upward) s'élever; (originate from) provenir
de.
aristocracy, *n.* aristocratie *f.*
aristocrat, *n.* aristocrate *m.f.*
aristocratic, *adj.* aristocratique.
arithmetic, *n.* arithmétique *f.*
ark, *n.* arche *f.*
arm, 1. *n.* (limb) bras *m.;*
(weapon) arme *f.* **2.** *vb.*
armer.
armament, *n.* armement *m.*
armchair, *n.* fauteuil *m.*
armed forces, *n.* forces armées
f.pl.
armful, *n.* brassée *f.*
armhole, *n.* emmanchure *f.,*
entournure *f.*
armistice, *n.* armistice *m.*
armor, *n.* armure *f.*
armory, *n.* (drill hall) salle (*f.*)
d'exercice.
armpit, *n.* aisselle *f.*
arms, *n.* armes *f.pl.*
army, *n.* armée *f.*
arnica, *n.* arnica *f.*
aroma, *n.* arome *m.*
aromatic, *adj.* aromatique.
around, 1. *adv.* autour. **2.** *prep.*
autour de.
arouse, *vb.* (stir) soulever;
(awake) réveiller.
arraign, *vb.* accuser, poursuivre en justice.
arrange, *vb.* arranger.
arrangement, *n.* arrangement
m.
array, *n.* (military) rangs *m.pl.;*
(display) étalage *m.*
array, *vb.* ranger.
arrear, *n.* arriéré *m.*
arrest, 1. *n.* (capture) arrestation *f.;* (military) arrêts *m.pl.;*
(halt) arrêt *m.* **2.** *vb.* arrêter.
arrival, *n.* arrivée *f.*
arrive, *vb.* arriver.
arrogance, *n.* arrogance *f.*
arrogant, *adj.* arrogant.
arrogate, *vb.* usurper, (to oneself) s'arroger.
arrow, *n.* flèche *f.*
arrowhead, *n.* pointe de flèche
f.; (plant) sagittaire *f.*
arsenal, *n.* arsenal *m.*
arsenic, *n.* arsenic *m.*
arson, *n.* crime d'incendie *m.*
art, *n.* art *m.;* (fine arts) beaux-
arts.
arterial, *adj.* artériel.
arteriosclerosis, *n.* artériosclé-
rose *f.*
artery, *n.* artère *f.*
artesian well, *n.* puits artésien
m.
artful, *adj.* (crafty) artificieux;
(skillful) adroit.
arthritis, *n.* arthrite *f.*
artichoke, *n.* artichaut *m.*
article, *n.* article *m.*
articulate, *vb.* articuler.

articulation, *n.* articulation *f.*
artifice, *n.* artifice *m.*
artificial, *adj.* artificiel.
artificiality, *n.* nature artifici-
elle *f.*
artillery, *n.* artillerie *f.*
artisan, *n.* artisan *m.*
artist, *n.* artiste *m.*
artistic, *adj.* artistique.
artistry, *n.* habileté *f.*
artless, *adj.* ingénu, naïf.
as, 1. *adv.* comme; (as . . . as)
aussi . . . que; (as much as)
autant que; (such as) tel que.
2. *conj.* (so . . . as) de façon à;
(while) pendant que; (since)
puisque; (progress) à mesure
que. **3.** *prep.* (as to) quant à.
asbestos, *n.* asbeste *m.*
ascend, *vb.* monter.
ascendancy, *n.* ascendant *m.*
ascendant, *adj.* ascendant, supérieur.
ascent, *n.* montée *f.;* (of a
mountain) ascension *f.*
ascertain, *vb.* s'assurer (de).
ascetic, *n.* ascétique *m.*
ascribe, *vb.* attribuer.
ash, *n.* cendre *f.;* (tree) frêne
m.
ashamed, *adj.* honteux; (be a.
of) avoir honte de.
ashen, *adj.* cendré, gris pâle.
ashes, *n.* cendres *f.pl.*
ashore, *adv.* à terre; (go a.)
débarquer.
ash-tray, *n.* cendrier *m.*
Asia, *n.* Asie *f.*
Asian, 1. *n.* Asiatique *m.f.* **2.**
adj. asiatique.
aside, *adv.* de côté.
ask, *vb.* demander à; (invite)
inviter.
askance, *adv.* de travers, obli-
quement.
asleep, *adj.* endormi.
asparagus, *n.* asperges *f.pl.*
aspect, *n.* aspect *m.*
asperity, *n.* aspérité *f.,* rudesse
f.
aspersion, *n.* aspersion *f.*
asphalt, *n.* asphalte *m.*
asphyxia, *n.* asphyxie *f.*
asphyxiate, *vb.* asphyxier.
aspirant, *n.* aspirant *m.,* candidat *m.*
aspirate, *vb.* aspirer.
aspiration, *n.* aspiration *f.*
aspirator, *n.* aspirateur *m.*
aspire, *vb.* aspirer.
ass, *n.* âne *m.,* ânesse *f.*
assail, *vb.* assaillir.
assailable, *adj.* attaquable.
assailant, *n.* assaillant *m.*
assassin, *n.* assassin *m.*
assassinate, *vb.* assassiner.
assassination, *n.* assassinat *m.*
assault, *n.* assaut *m.*
assay, 1. *n.* essai *m.,* vérification *f.,* épreuve *f.* **2.** *vb.* essayer.
assemblage, *n.* assemblage *m.*
assemble, *vb.* assembler, *tr.;*
s'assembler, *intr.*
assembly, *n.* assemblée *f.*

assent, 1. n. assentiment m. **2.** vb. consentir.

assert, vb. affirmer.

assertion, n. assertion f.

assertive, adj. assertif.

assertiveness, n. qualité d'être assertif.

assess, vb. (tax) taxer; (evaluate) évaluer.

assessor, n. assesseur m.

assets, n.pl. (comm.) actif m.; (property) biens m.pl.

asseverate, vb. affirmer solennellement.

asseveration, n. affirmation f.

assiduous, adj. assidu.

assiduously, adv. assidûment.

assign, vb. assigner.

assignable, adj. assignable, transférable.

assignation, n. assignation f., rendez-vous m.

assignment, n. (law) cession f.; (school) tâche f.

assimilate, vb. assimiler, tr.; s'assimiler, intr.

assimilation, n. assimilation f.

assimilative, adj. assimilatif, assimilateur.

assistance, n. aide f.

assistant, n. aide m.f.

assist in, vb. aider à.

associate, vb. associer, tr.; s'associer, intr.

association, n. association f.

assonance, n. assonance f.

assort, vb. assortir.

assorted, adj. assorti.

assortment, n. assortiment m.

assuage, vb. adoucir, appaiser.

assume, vb. (take) prendre; (appropriate) s'arroger; (feign) simuler; (suppose) supposer.

assuming, adj. prétentieux, arrogant.

assumption, n. supposition f.; (eccles.) Assomption f.

assurance, n. assurance f.

assure, vb. assurer.

assured, adj. assuré.

assuredly, adv. assurément.

aster, n. aster m.

asterisk, n. astérisque m.

astern, adv. à l'arrière, de l'arrière.

asteroid, n. astéroïde m.

asthma, n. asthme m.

astigmatism, n. astigmatisme m.

astir, adj. agité, debout.

astonish, vb. étonner.

astonishment, n. étonnement m.

astound, vb. stupéfier.

astral, adj. astral.

astray, adj. égaré; (go a.) s'égarer.

astride, adv. à califourchon.

astringent, n. and adj. astringent m.

astrology, n. astrologie f.

astronaut, n. astronaute m.

astronomy, n. astronomie f.

astute, adj. fin.

asunder, adv. (apart) écartés; (to pieces) en morceaux.

asylum, n. asile m.

asymmetry, n. asymétrie f.

at, prep. (time, place, price) à; (someone's house, shop, etc.) chez.

ataxia, n. ataxie f.

atheist, n. athée m.f.

athlete, n. athlète m.f.

athletic, adj. athlétique.

athletics, n. sports m.pl.

athwart, adv. de travers.

Atlantic, adj. atlantique.

Atlantic Ocean, n. océan Atlantique m.

atlas, n. atlas m.

atmosphere, n. atmosphère f.

atmospheric, adj. atmosphérique.

atoll, n. atoll m.

atom, n. atome m.

atomic, adj. atomique.

atomic bomb, n. bombe atomique f.

atomic energy, n. énergie atomique f.

atomic theory, n. théorie atomique f.

atomic warfare, n. guerre atomique f.

atomic weight, n. poids atomique m.

atonal, adj. atonal.

atone for, vb. expier.

atonement, n. expiation f.

atrocious, adj. atroce.

atrocity, n. atrocité f.

atrophy, n. atrophie f.

atropine, n. atropine f.

attach, vb. attcher.

attaché, n. attaché m.

attachment, n. attachement m.; (device) accessoire m.

attack, 1. n. attaque f. **2.** vb. attaquer.

attacker, n. agresseur m.

attain, vb. atteindre.

attainable, adj. qu'on peut atteindre.

attainment, n. (realization) réalisation f.; (knowledge) connaissance f.

attempt, n. tentative f.

attend, vb. (give heed to) faire attention à; (medical) soigner; (serve) servir; (meeting) assister à; (lectures) suivre; (see to) s'occuper de.

attendance, n. service m.; présence f.

attendant, n. serviteur m.; (retinue) suite f.

attention, n. attention f.; (pay attention to) faire attention à.

attentive, adj. attentif.

attentively, adv. attentivement.

attenuate, vb. atténuer.

attest, vb. attester.

attic, n. grenier m.

attire, 1. n. costume m. **2.** vb. parer, tr.; se parer, intr.

attitude, n. attitude f.

attorney, n. avoué m.

attract, vb. attirer.

attraction, n. attraction f.

attractive, adj. attrayant.

attributable, adj. attributable, imputable.

attribute, n. attribut m.

attrition, n. attrition f.

attune, vb. accorder, mettre à l'unisson.

auction, n. vente (f.) aux enchères.

auctioneer, n. commissaire-priseur m.

audacious, adj. audacieux.

audacity, n. audace f.

audible, adj. intelligible.

audience, n. (listeners) auditoire m.; (interview) audience f.

audiovisual, adj. audiovisuel.

audit, 1. vb. vérifier (des comptes). **2.** n. vérification (des comptes) f.

audition, n. audition f.

auditor, n. vérificateur m., censeur m.

auditorium, n. salle f.

auditory, adj. auditif.

auger, n. tarière f.

augment, vb. augmenter.

augur, vb. augurer.

August, n. août m.

aunt, n. tante f.

auspice, n. auspice m.

auspicious, adj. de bon augure.

austere, adj. austère.

austerity, n. austérité f.

Australia, n. Australie f.

Australian, 1. n. Australien m. **2.** adj. australien.

Austria, n. Autriche f.

Austrian, 1. n. Autrichien m. **2.** adj. autrichien.

authentic, adj. authentique.

authenticate, vb. authentiquer, valider.

authenticity, n. authenticité f.

author, n. auteur m.

authoritarian, adj. autoritaire.

authoritative, adj. autoritaire.

authoritatively, adv. avec autorité, en maître.

authority, n. autorité f.

authorization, n. autorisation f.

authorize, vb. autoriser.

auto, n. auto f.

autobiography, n. autobiographie f.

autocracy, n. autocratie f.

autocrat, n. autocrate m.

autograph, 1. n. autographe m. **2.** vb. autographier.

automatic, adj. automatique.

automatically, adv. automatiquement.

automobile, n. automobile f.

automotive, adj. automoteur.

autonomously, adv. d'une manière autonome.

autonomy, n. autonomie f.

autopsy, n. autopsie f.

autumn, n. automne m.

auxiliary, adj. auxiliaire.

avail, vb. servir; (be of no a.) ne servir à rien.

available, *adj.* disponible.

avalanche, *n.* avalanche *f.*

avarice, *n.* avarice *f.*

avariciously, *adv.* avec avarice.

avenge, *vb.* venger.

avenger, *n.* vengeur *m.*, vengeresse *f.*

avenue, *n.* avenue *f.*

average, 1. *n.* moyenne *f.* **2.** *adj.* moyen.

averse, *adj.* opposé.

aversion, *n.* aversion *f.*

avert, *vb.* détourner.

aviary, *n.* volière *f.*

aviation, *n.* aviation *f.*

aviator, *n.* aviateur *m.*

aviatrix, *n.* aviatrice *f.*

avid, *adj.* avide.

avocation, *n.* distraction *f.*, profession *f.*, métier *m.*

avoid, *vb.* éviter.

avoidable, *adj.* évitable.

avoidance, *n.* action d'éviter *f.*

avow, *vb.* avouer.

avowal, *n.* aveu *m.*

avowed, *adj.* avoué, confessé.

avowedly, *adj.* de son propre aveu, ouvertement.

await, *vb.* attendre.

awake, *vb.* éveiller, *tr.*; s'éveiller, *intr.*

awaken, *vb. see* awake.

award, 1. *n.* (prize) prix *m.*; (law) sentence *f.* **2.** *vb.* décerner.

aware, *adj.* (be a.) savoir; (not to be a.) ignorer.

awash, *adv.* dans l'eau.

away, *adv.* loin; (go a.) s'en aller; (a. from) absent de.

awe, *n.* crainte *f.*

awesome, *adj.* inspirant du respect.

awful, *adj.* terrible.

awhile, *adv.* pendant quelque temps.

awkward, *adj.* (clumsy) gauche; (embarrassing) embarrassant.

awning, *n.* tente *f.*

awry, *adj.* de travers.

ax, *n.* hache *f.*

axiom, *n.* axiome *m.*

axis, *n.* axe *m.*

axle, *n.* essieu *m.*

ayatollah, *n.* ayatollah *m.*

azure, *n.* azur *m.*

azure, *adj.* azuré.

B

babble, *vb.* babiller.

babbler, *n.* babillard *m.*

babe, *n.* enfant *m.* or *f.*

baboon, *n.* babouin *m.*

baby, *n.* bébé *m.*

babyish, *adj.* enfantin.

bachelor, *n.* célibataire *m.*

bacillus, *n.* bacille *m.*

back, 1. *n.* dos *m.* **2.** *vb.* (b. up, go b.) reculer; (uphold) soutenir. **3.** *adv.* en arrière.

backbone, *n.* épine dorsale *f.*

backer, *n.* partisan *m.*

backfire, *vb.* donner des retours de flamme, retomber (sur).

background, *n.* fond *m.*

backhand, *adj.* donné avec le revers de la main.

backing, *n.* soutien *m.*

backlash, *n.* réaction conservatrice *f.*

backlog, *n.* réserve *f.*

back out, *vb.* se retirer.

backpack, *n.* sac tyrolien *m.*

backstage, *adv.* dans les coulisses.

backward, *adj.* en arrière.

backwardness, *n.* rétard *m.*

backwards, *adv.* en arrière.

backwater, 1. *n.* eau stagnante *f.* **2.** *vb.* aller en arrière (dans l'eau).

backwoods, *n.* forêts vierges *f.pl.*

bacon, *n.* porc *(m.)* salé et fumé.

bacteriologist, *n.* bactériologue *m.*

bacteriology, *n.* bactériologie *f.*

bacterium, *n.* bactérie *f.*

bad, *adj.* mauvais; (wicked) méchant.

badge, *n.* insigne *m.*

badger, *vb.* ennuyer.

badness, *n.* mauvaise qualité *f.*; (wickedness) méchanceté *f.*

baffle, *vb.* déconcerter.

bafflement, *n.* confusion *f.*, frustration *f.*

bag, *n.* sac *m.*; (suitcase) valise *f.*

baggage, *n.* bagage *m.*

baggage cart, *n.* (airport) chariot *m.*

baggy, *adj.* bouffant.

bagpipe, *n.* cornemuse *f.*

bail, 1. *n.* (law) caution *f.* **2.** *vb.* (b. out water) vider (l'eau).

bailiff, *n.* huissier *m.*

bait, *n.* appât *m.*

bake, *vb.* faire cuire au four, *tr.*

baker, *n.* boulanger *m.*

bakery, *n.* boulangerie *f.*

baking, *n.* boulangerie *f.*

balance, 1. *n.* (equilibrium) équilibre *m.*; (bank) solde *m.*; account, scales) balance *f.* **2.** *vb.* balancer, *tr.*

balcony, *n.* balcon *m.*; (theater) galerie *f.*

bald, *adj.* chauve.

baldness, *n.* calvitie *f.*; (fig.) sécheresse *f.*

bale, *n.* balle *f.*

balk, *vb.* frustrer.

balky, *adj.* regimbé.

ball, *n.* (games, bullet) balle *f.*; (round object) boule *f.*; (dance) bal *m.*

ballad, *n.* (song) romance *f.*; (poem) ballade *f.*

ballast, *n.* lest *m.*

ball bearing, *n.* roulement à billes *m.*

ballerina, *n.* ballérina *f.*

ballet, *n.* ballet *m.*

balloon, *n.* ballon *m.*

ballot, *n.* scrutin *m.*

ballroom, *n.* salon de bal *m.*

balm, *n.* baume *m.*

balmy, *adj.* embaumé; doux *m.*, douce *f.*

balsa, *n.* balsa *f.*

balsam, *n.* baume *m.*

balustrade, *n.* balustrade *f.*

bamboo, *n.* bambou *m.*

ban, 1. *n.* ban *m.* **2.** *vb.* mettre au ban, *tr.*

banal, *adj.* banal.

banana, *n.* banane *f.*

band, *n.* bande *f.*; (music) orchestre *m.*

bandage, *n.* bandage *m.*

bandanna, *n.* foulard (de soie de couleur) *m.*

bandbox, *n.* carton (de modiste) *m.*

bandit, *n.* bandit *m.*

bandmaster, *n.* chef de musique *m.*

bandsman, *n.* musicien *m.*

bandstand, *n.* kiosque *m.*

baneful, *adj.* pernicieux.

bang, *vb.* frapper.

bang, *n.* coup *m.*

banish, *vb.* bannir.

banishment, *n.* bannissement *m.*

banister, *n.* rampe *f.*

bank, *n.* banque *f.*; (river) rive *f.*

bankbook, *n.* livret de banque *m.*

banker, *n.* banquier *m.*

banking, *n.* banque *f.*, affaires de banque *f.pl.*

bank note, *n.* billet de banque *m.*

bankrupt, *adj. and n.* failli *m.*

bankruptcy, *n.* faillite *f.*

banner, *n.* bannière *f.*

banquet, *n.* banquet *m.*

banter, 1. *n.* badinage *m.* **2.** *vb.* badiner, railler.

baptism, *n.* baptême *m.*

baptismal, *adj.* baptismal.

Baptist, *n.* Baptiste *m.*

baptistery, *n.* baptistère *f.*

baptize, *vb.* baptiser.

bar, *n.* (drinks) bar *m.*; (metal) barre *f.*; (law) barreau *m.*

barb, *n.* barbillon *m.*

barbarian, barbarous, *adj. and n.* barbare *m.f.*

barbarism, *n.* barbarie *f.*; (gramm.) barbarisme *m.*

barber, *n.* coiffeur *m.*

barbiturate, *n.* barbiturat *m.*

bare, 1. *adj.* nu. **2.** *vb.* découvrir.

bareback, *adv.* à dos nu.

barefoot, *adv.* nu-pieds.

barely, *adv.* à peine.

bareness, *n.* nudité *f.*

bargain, *n.* marché *m.*

bargain, *vb.* marchander.

barge, *n.* chaland *m.*

barium, *n.* barium *m.*

bark, 1. *n.* (tree) écorce *f.*;

(dog) aboiement *m.* 2. *vb.* (dog) aboyer.
barley, *n.* orge *f.*
barn, *n.* (grain) grange *f.;* (livestock) étable *f.*
barnacle, *n.* anatife (shellfish) *m.;* barnache (goose) *f.*
barnyard, *n.* basse-cour *f.*
barometer, *n.* baromètre *m.*
barometric, *adj.* barométrique.
baron, *n.* baron *m.*
baroness, *n.* baronne *f.*
baronial, *adj.* baronnial, seigneurial.
baroque, *adj.* baroque.
barracks, *n.* caserne *f.*
barrage, *n.* barrage *m.*
barred, *adj.* barré, empêché, exclus, défendu.
barrel, *n.* tonneau *m.*
barren, *adj.* stérile.
barrenness, *n.* stérilité *f.*
barricade, *n.* barricade *f.*
barrier, *n.* barrière *f.*
barroom, *n.* buvette *f.*, comptoir *m.*, bar *m.*
bartender, *n.* barman *m.*
barter, *n.* troc *m.*
base, 1. *n.* base *f.* 2. *adj.* bas *m.*, basse *f.*
baseball, *n.* baseball *m.*
baseboard, *n.* moulure de base *f.*
basement, *n.* sous-sol *m.*
baseness, *n.* bassesse *f.*
bashful, *adj.* timide.
bashfully, *adv.* timidement, modestement.
bashfulness, *n.* timidité *f.*, modestie *f.*
basic, *adj.* fondamental.
basin, *n.* (wash) cuvette *f.;* (river) bassin *m.*
basis, *n.* base *f.*
bask, se chauffer *intr.*
basket, *n.* (with handle) panier *m.;* (without handle) corbeille *f.*
bass, *n.* (music) basse *f.;* (fish) bar *m.*
bassinet, *n.* bercelonnette *f.*
bassoon, *n.* basson *m.*
bastard, *n.* bâtard *m.*, (law) enfant naturel *m.*
baste, *vb.* (cooking) arroser; (sewing) faufiler.
bat, *n.* (animal) chauve-souris *f.;* (baseball) batte *f.*
batch, *n.* fournée *f.*
bate, *vb.* rabattre, diminuer.
bath, *n.* bain *m.*
bathe, *vb.* se baigner.
bather, *n.* baigneur *m.*
bathrobe, *n.* peignoir (*m.*) de bain.
bathroom, *n.* salle (*f.*) de bain.
bathtub, *n.* baignoire *f.*
baton, *n.* bâton *m.*
battalion, *n.* bataillon *m.*
batter, *n.* (cooking) pâte *f.*
battery, *n.* (military) batterie *f.;* (electric) pile *f.*
battle, *n.* bataille *f.*
battle, *vb.* lutter.

battlefield, *n.* champ (*m.*) de bataille.
battleship, *n.* cuirassé *m.*
bauxite, *n.* bauxite *f.*
bawl, *vb.* brailler.
bay, *n.* (geography) baie *f.;* (plant) laurier *m.*
bayonet, *n.* baïonnette *f.*
bazaar, *n.* bazar *m.*
be, *vb.* être.
beach, *n.* plage *f.*
beachhead, *n.* (haut de) plage *f.*
beacon, *n.* phare *m.*
bead, *n.* perle *f.*
beading, *n.* ornement de grains *m.*
beady, *adj.* comme un grain, couvert de grains.
beak, *n.* bec *m.*
beaker, *n.* gobelet *m.*, coupe *f.*
beam, 1. *n.* (construction) poutre *f.;* (light) rayon *m.* 2. *vb.* rayonner.
beaming, *adj.* rayonnant.
bean, *n.* haricot *m.*
bear, 1. *n.* ours *m.* 2. *vb.* (carry) porter; (endure) supporter; (birth) enfanter.
bearable, *adj.* supportable.
beard, *n.* barbe *f.*
bearded, *adj.* barbu.
beardless, *adj.* imberbe.
bearer, *n.* porteur *m.*
bearing, *n.* (person) maintien *m.;* (machinery) coussinet *m.;* (naut.) relèvement *m.*
bearskin, *n.* peau d'ours *f.*
beast, *n.* bête *f.*
beat, 1. *vb.* battre. 2. *n.* battement *m.*
beaten, *adj.* battu.
beatify, *vb.* béatifier.
beating, *n.* battement *m.*, rossée *f.*
beau, *n.* galant *m.*
beautiful, *adj.* beau (bel) *m.*, belle *f.*
beautifully, *adv.* admirablement.
beautify, *vb.* embellir
beauty, *n.* beauté *f.*
beaver, *n.* castor *m.*
becalm, *vb.* calmer, apaiser; (naut.) abriter.
because, *conj.* parce que.
beckon, *vb.* faire signe (à).
become, *vb.* devenir.
becoming, *adj.* convenable; (dress) seyant.
bed, *n.* lit *m.*
bedbug, *n.* punaise *f.*
bedclothes, *n.* couvertures *f.pl.*
bedding, *n.* literie *f.*
bedfellow, *n.* camarade de lit *m.*
bedizen, *vb.* parer, attifer.
bedridden, *adj.* alité.
bedrock, *n.* roche solide *f.*
bedroom, *n.* chambre (*f.*) à coucher.
bedside, *n.* bord du lit *m.*
bedspread, *n.* dessus (*m.*) de lit.
bedstead, *n.* bois de lit *m.*, couchette *f.*

bedtime, *n.* heure (*f.*) de se coucher.
bee, *n.* abeille *f.*
beef, *n.* bœuf *m.*
beefsteak, *n.* bifteck *m.*, tournedos *m.*
beehive, *n.* ruche *f.*
beer, *n.* bière *f.*
beeswax, *n.* cire jaune *f.*
beet, *n.* betterave *f.*
beetle, *n.* scarabée *m.*
befall, *vb.* arriver (à).
befit, *vb.* convenir (à).
befitting, *adj.* convenable.
before, 1. *adv.* (place) en avant; (time) avant. 2. *prep.* (place) devant; (time) avant. 3. *conj.* avant que.
beforehand, *adv.* d'avance.
befriend, *vb.* aider; traiter en ami.
befuddle, *vb.* embrouiller, déconcerter.
beg, *vb.* (of beggar) mendier; (ask) prier.
beget, *vb.* engendrer, produire.
beggar, *n.* mendiant *m.*
beggarly, *adj.* chétif, misérable.
begin, *vb.* commencer.
beginner, *n.* commençant *m.*
beginning, *n.* commencement *m.*
beguile, *vb.* tromper, séduire.
behalf, *n.* (on b. of) de la part de; (in b. of) en faveur de.
behave, *vb.* se conduire.
behavior, *n.* conduite *f.*
behead, *vb.* décapiter.
behind, *adv. and prep.* derrière.
behind, *n.* derrière *m.*
behold, 1. *vb.* voir. 2. *interj.* voici.
beige, *adj.* beige.
being, *n.* être *m.*
bejewel, *vb.* orner de bijoux.
belated, *adj.* attardé.
belch, *vb.* éructer.
belfry, *n.* clocher *m.*, beffroi *m.*
Belgian, 1. *n.* Belge *m.f.* 2. *adj.* belge.
Belgium, *n.* Belgique *f.*
belie, *vb.* démentir.
belief, *n.* croyance *f.;* (confidence) confiance *f.*
believable, *adj.* croyable.
believe, *vb.* croire.
believer, *n.* croyant *m.*
belittle, *vb.* rabaisser.
bell, *n.* (house) sonnette *f.;* (church) cloche *f.*
bellboy, *n.* chasseur *m.*
bell buoy, *n.* bouée sonore *f.*
belligerence, *n.* belligérance *f.*
belligerent, *adj. and n.* belligérant *m.*
belligerently, *adv.* d'une manière belligérante.
bellow, *vb.* mugir.
bellows, *n.* soufflet *m.*
bell-tower, *n.* clocher *m.*
belly, *n.* ventre *m.*
belongings, *n.* effets, *m.pl.*
belong to, *vb.* appartenir (à).
beloved, *adj. and n.* chéri *m.*

below, 1. *adv.* en bas. 2. *prep.* au-dessous de.

belt, *n.* ceinture *f.*

bench, *n.* banc *m.*

bend, *vb.* plier; (curve) courber *tr.*

beneath, *see* below.

benediction, *n.* bénédiction *f.*

benefactor, *n.* bienfaiteur *m.*

benefactress, *n.* bienfaitrice *f.*

beneficent, *adj.* bienfaisant.

beneficial, *adj.* salutaire.

beneficiary, *n.* bénéficiaire *m.*

benefit, *n.* (favor) bienfait *m.;* (advantage) bénéfice *m.*

benevolence, *n.* bienveillance *f.*

benevolent, *adj.* bienveillant.

benevolently, *adv.* bénévolement.

benign, *adj.* bénin *m.* bénigne *f.*

benignity, *n.* bénignité *f.*

bent, *n.* penchant *m.*

benzene, *n.* benzène *m.*

benzine, *n.* benzine *f.*

bequeath, *vb.* léguer.

bequest, *n.* legs *m.*

berate, *vb.* gronder.

bereave, *vb.* priver (de).

bereavement, *n.* privation *f.,* perte *f.,* deuil *m.*

beriberi, *n.* béribéri *m.*

berry, *n.* baie *f.*

berth, *n.* couchette *f.*

beseech, *vb.* supplier.

beseechingly, *adv.* en suppliant.

beset, *vb.* attaquer, presser, assiéger.

beside, *prep.* à côté de.

besides, *adv.* en outre.

besiege, *vb.* assiéger.

besieged, *adj.* assiégé.

besieger, *n.* assiégeant *m.*

besmirch, *vb.* tacher, salir.

best, 1. *adj.* (le) meilleur. 2. *adv.* (le) mieux.

bestial, *adj.* bestial.

bestir, *vb.* remuer.

best man, *n.* garçon d'honneur (at weddings) *m.*

bestow, *vb.* accorder.

bestowal, *n.* dispensation *f.*

bet, 1. *n.* pari *m.* 2. *vb.* parier.

betake (oneself), *vb.* se rendre.

betray, *vb.* trahir.

betroth, *vb.* fiancer.

betrothal, *n.* fiançailles *f.pl.*

better, 1. *adj.* meilleur. 2. *adv.* mieux.

between, *prep.* entre.

bevel, 1. *n.* biseau *m.* 2. *vb.* biaiser.

beverage, *n.* boisson *f.*

bewail, *vb.* lamenter, pleurer.

beware of, *vb.* prendre garde à.

bewilder, *vb.* égarer.

bewildered, *adj.* égaré.

bewildering, *adj.* déconcertant.

bewilderment, *n.* égarement *m.*

bewitch, *vb.* ensorceler.

beyond, 1. *adv.* au delà. 2. *prep.* au delà de.

biannual, *adj.* semestriel.

bias, *n.* (slant) biais *m.;* (prejudice) prévention *f.*

bib, *n.* bavette *f.*

Bible, *n.* Bible *f.*

biblical, *adj.* biblique.

bibliography, *n.* bibliographie *f.*

bicarbonate, *n.* bicarbonat *m.*

bicentennial, *n.* and *adj.* bicentenaire *m.*

biceps, *n.* biceps *m.*

bicker, *vb.* se quereller, se chamailler.

bicycle, *n.* bicyclette *f.*

bicyclist, *n.* cycliste *m.*

bid, 1. *n.* (auction) enchère *f.;* (bridge) appel *m.* 2. *vb.* (order) ordonner; (invite) inviter.

bidder, *n.* enchérisseur *m.*

bide, *vb.* (live) demeurer; (wait) attendre.

bier, *n.* corbillard *m.,* civière *f.*

bifocal, *adj.* bifocal.

big, *adj.* grand.

bigamy, *n.* bigamie *f.*

bigot, *n.* bigot *m.*

bigotry, *n.* bigoterie *f.*

bilateral, *adj.* bilatéral.

bile, *n.* bile *f.*

bilingual, *adj.* bilingue.

bilious, *adj.* bilieux.

bill, *n.* (restaurant) addition *f.;* (hotel, profession) note *f.;* (money) billet *m.* de banque; (poster) affiche *f.;* (politics) projet *(m.)* de loi; (b. of fare) carte *(f.)* du jour; (bird) bec *m.*

billet, *n.* (mil.) billet de logement *m.*

billfold, *n.* portefeuille *m.*

billiard balls, *n.pl.* billes *n.pl.*

billiards, *n.* billard *m.*

billion, *n.* billion *m.*

bill of health, *n.* patente de santé *f.*

bill of lading, *n.* connaissement *m.*

bill of sale, *n.* lettre de vente *f.,* acte de propriété *f.*

billow, *n.* grande vague *f.,* lame *f.*

bimetallic, *adj.* bimétallique.

bimonthly, *adj. and adv.* bimensuel.

bin, *n.* coffre *m.*

bind, *vb.* lier; (books) relier.

bindery, *n.* atelier de reliure *m.*

binding, 1. *n.* (book) reliure *f.* 2. *adj.* obligatoire.

binocular, *adj.* binoculaire.

binoculars, *n.* binocle *m.*

biochemistry, *n.* biochimie *f.*

biodegradable, *adj.* sujet à la putréfaction.

biofeedback, *n.* biofeedback *m.,* information reçue par un organisme pendant un processus biologique *f.*

biographer, *n.* biographe *m.*

biographical, *adj.* biographique.

biography, *n.* biographie *f.*

biological, *adj.* biologique.

biologically, *adv.* biologiquement.

biology, *n.* biologie *f.*

bipartisan, *adj.* représentant les deux partis.

biped, *n.* bipède *m.*

bird, *n.* oiseau *m.*

birdlike, *adj.* comme un oiseau.

bird of prey, *n.* oiseau de proie *m.*

birth, *n.* naissance *f.*

birth control, *n.* contrôle des naissances *m.*

birthday, *n.* anniversaire *(m.)* de naissance.

birthmark, *n.* tache de naissance *f.*

birthplace, *n.* lieu *(m.)* de naissance.

birth rate, *n.* natalité *f.*

birthright, *n.* droit d'aînesse *f.*

biscuit, *n.* (hard) biscuit *m.;* (soft) petit pain *(m.)* au lait.

bisect, *vb.* couper en deux.

bishop, *n.* évêque *m.*

bishopric, *n.* évêché *m.*

bismuth, *n.* bismuth *m.*

bison, *n.* bison *m.*

bit, *n.* (piece) morceau *m.;* (a b. (of)) un peu (de); (harness) mors *m.;* unité unique d'information *f.*

bitch, *n.* chienne *f.*

bite, 1. *n.* morsure *f.* 2. *vb.* mordre.

biting, *adj.* mordant.

bitter, *adj.* amer.

bitterly, *adv.* amèrement, avec amertume.

bitterness, *n.* amertume *f.*

bivouac, *n.* bivouac *m.*

biweekly, *adj. and adv.* tous les quinze jours.

black, *adj.* noir.

Black, *n. and adj. (for person)* nègre *m.;* négresse *f.*

blackberry *n.* mûre *(f.)* de ronce.

blackbird, *n.* merle *m.*

blackboard, *n.* tableau *(m.)* noir.

blacken, *vb.* noircir.

black eye, *n.* oeil poché *m.*

blackguard, *n.* gredin *m.,* polisson *m.,* salaud *m.*

blackmail, *n.* chantage *m.*

black market, *n.* marché noir *m.*

blackout, *n.* blackout *m.*

blacksmith, *n.* forgeron *m.*

bladder, *n.* vessie *f.*

blade, *n.* (sword, knife) lame *f.;* (grass) brin *m.*

blame, 1. *n.* blâme *m.* 2. *vb.* blâmer.

blameless, *adj.* innocent, sans tache.

blanch, *vb.* blanchir, pâlir.

bland, *adj.* doux *m.,* douce *f.*

blank, 1. *adj.* (space) blanc *m.;* (void) vide *m.;* (printing) tiret *m.* 2. *adj.* (page) blanc *m.,* blanche *f.;* (empty) vide.

blanket, *n.* couverture *f.*

blare, n. son (de la trompette) m., rugissement m.

blare, vb. retentir, intr.

blaspheme, vb. blasphémer.

blasphemer, n. blasphémateur m.

blasphemous, adj. blasphématoire.

blasphemy, n. blasphème m.

blast, n. (wind) rafale f.; (mine) explosion f.

blatant, adj. criard, bruyant.

blaze, 1. n. flambée f. 2. vb. flamber.

blazing, adj. enflammé, flamboyant.

bleach, vb. décolorer, tr.

bleak, adj. morne.

bleakness, n. froideur f.

bleed, vb. saigner.

blemish, n. défaut m.

blend, 1. n. mélange m. 2. vb. mêler tr.

blended, adj. mélangé.

bless, vb. bénir.

blessed, adj. béni.

blessing, n. bénédiction f.

blight, 1. vb. flétrir, détruire, nieller, brouir. 2. n. brouissure f., flétrissure f.

blind, 1. n. store m. 2. adj. aveugle; (b. alley) cul-de-sac m.

blindfold, adj. and adv. les yeux bandés.

blinding, adj. aveuglant.

blindly, adv. aveuglément.

blindness, n. cécité f.

blink, vb. clignoter.

bliss, n. béatitude f.

blissful, adj. bienheureux.

blissfully, adv. heureusement.

blister, n. ampoule f.

blithe, adj. gai, joyeux.

blizzard, n. tempête (f.) de neige.

bloat, vb. boursoufler.

bloc, n. bloc m.

block, 1. n. bloc m.; (houses) pâté m. 2. vb. bloquer.

blockade, n. blocus m.

blond, adj. and n. blond m.

blood, n. sang m.

bloodhound, n. limier m.

bloodless, adj. exsangue, sans effusion de sang.

blood plasma, n. plasma du sang m.

blood poisoning, n. empoisonnement du sang m.

blood pressure, n. tension artérielle f.

bloodshed, n. effusion (f.) de sang.

bloodshot, adj. injecté de sang.

bloodthirsty, adj. sanguinaire.

bloody, adj. sanglant.

bloom, 1. n. fleur f. 2. vb. fleurir.

blooming, 1. n. floraison f. 2. adj. fleurissant.

blossom, see bloom.

blot, 1. n. tache f. 2. vb. (spot) tacher; (dry ink) sécher l'encre.

blotch, n. tache f.

blotchy, adj. couvert de taches.

blotter, n. buvard m.

blouse, n. blouse f.

blow, 1. n. coup m. 2. vb. souffler; (b. out) éteindre; (b. over) passer; (b. up) faire sauter, tr.

blowout, n. éclatement (m.) de pneu.

blubber, 1. vb. pleurer comme un veau. 2. n. graisse de baleine f.

bludgeon, 1. n. matraque f. 2. vb. donner des coups de matraque.

blue, adj. bleu.

blue jeans, n. blue jeans m.pl.

blueprint, n. dessin négatif m.

bluff, n. bluff m.

bluffer, n. bluffeur m.

blunder, n. bévue f.

blunderer, n. maladroit m.

blunt, adj. (blade) émoussé; (person) brusque.

bluntly, adv. brusquement.

bluntness, n. brusquerie f.

blur, vb. (smear) barbouiller.

blush, 1. n. rougeur f. 2. vb. rougir.

bluster, n. rodomontade f., fanfaronnade f.

boar, n. (wild) sanglier m.

board, n. (plank) planche f.; (daily meals) pension f.; (boat) bord m.; (politics) ministère m.; (administration) conseil m.

boarder, n. pensionnaire m.f.

boast (of), vb. se vanter (de).

boaster, n. vantard m.

boastful, adj. vantard.

boastfulness, n. vantardise f.

boat, n. bateau m.

boathouse, n. garage (à bateaux) m.

boatswain, n. maître d'équipage m.

bob, vb. (hair) couper court.

bobbin, n. bobine f.

bode, vb. présager.

bodice, n. corsage m.

bodily, adj. corporel.

body, n. corps m.

bodyguard, n. garde (f.) du corps.

bog, 1. n. marécage m. 2. vb. embourber.

Bohemia, n. (geographical) Bohême f.; (fig.) bohème f.

Bohemian, 1. n. (geographical) Bohémien m.; (fig.) bohème m.f. 2. adj. (geographical) bohémien; (fig.) bohème.

boil, 1. vb. bouillir, intr.; faire bouillir, tr. 2. n. (med.) furoncle m., (popular) clou m.

boiler, n. chaudière f.

boisterous, adj. (person) bruyant.

boisterously, adv. bruyamment.

bold, adj. hardi.

boldface, adj. (type) caractères gras m.pl.

boldly, adv. hardiment, avec audace.

boldness, n. hardiesse f.

bologna, n. saucisson (m.) de Bologne.

bolster, n. traversin m.

bolster up, vb. soutenir.

bolt, 1. n. verrou m. 2. vb. verrouiller.

bomb, n. bombe f.

bombard, vb. bombarder.

bombardier, n. bombardier m.

bombardment, n. bombardement m.

bomber, n. avion (m.) de bombardement.

bombproof, adj. à l'épreuve des bombes.

bombshell, n. bombe f.

bombsight, n. viseur de lancement m.

bonbon, n. bonbon m.

bond, n. lien m.; (law, finance) obligation f.

bondage, n. servitude f.

bonded, adj. entreposé.

bone, n. os m.

boneless, adj. sans os.

bonfire, n. feu (m.) de joie.

bonnet, n. chapeau m.

bonus, n. gratification f.

bony, adj. osseux.

book, n. livre m.

bookbindery, n. atelier de reliure m.

bookcase, n. bibliothèque f.

bookkeeper, n. teneur (m.) de livres.

bookkeeping, n. comptabilité f.

booklet, n. opuscule m.

bookseller, n. libraire m.; (second-hand) bouquiniste m.

bookstore, bookshop, n. librairie f.

boon, n. bienfait m., don m.

boor, n. rustre m.

boorish, adj. rustre.

boost, vb. (push) pousser; (praise) louer.

boot, n. bottine f.

bootblack, n. cireur m.

booth, n. (fair) baraque f.; (telephone) cabine f.

booty, n. butin m.

border, n. bord m.; (of country) frontière f.

borderline, adj. touchant (à), avoisinant.

bore, vb. (make a hole) forer; (annoy) ennuyer.

boredom, n. ennui m.

boric acid, n. acide borique m.

boring, adj. ennuyeux.

born, 1. adj. né. 2. vb. (be b.) naître.

born-again, adj. réné.

borough, n. (administration) circonscription électorale f.; (large village) bourg m.

borrower, n. emprunteur m.

borrow from, vb. emprunter à.

bosom, n. sein m.

boss, 1. n. patron m. 2. vb. diriger.

bossy, *adj.* comme un patron, impérieux.

botanical, *adj.* botanique.

botany, *n.* botanique *f.*

botch, 1. *n.* ravaudage *m.* **2.** *vb.* ravauder, faire une mauvaise besogne.

both, *adj. and pron.* tous (les) deux *m.,* toutes (les) deux *f.*

bother, 1. *n.* ennui *m.* **2.** *vb.* gêner.

bothersome, *adj.* gênant.

bottle, *n.* bouteille *f.*

bottom, *n.* fond *m.*

bottomless, *adj.* sans fond.

bough, *n.* branche *f.*

bouillon, *n.* bouillon *m.*

boulder, *n.* galet *m.*

boulevard, *n.* boulevard *m.*

bounce, *vb.* (ball) rebondir.

bound, 1. *n.* (limit) borne *f.;* (jump) bond *m.* **2.** *vb.* (limit) borner; (jump) bondir.

boundary, *n.* frontière *f.*

bound for, *adj.* en route pour.

boundless, *adj.* sans bornes, illimité.

boundlessly, *adv.* sans bornes.

bounteous, *adj.* généreux, bienfaisant.

bounty, *n.* largesse *f.;* (premium) prime *f.*

bouquet, *n.* bouquet *m.*

bourgeois, *adj.* bourgeois.

bout, *n.* (fever) accès *m.*

bovine, *n.* bovine *f.; adj.* bovin.

bow, *n.* (weapon) arc *m.;* (violin) archet *m.;* (curtsy) révérence *f.;* (ship) avant *m.*

bow, *vb.* incliner, *tr.*

bowels, *n.* entrailles *f.pl.*

bowl, 1. *n.* bol *m.* **2.** *vb.* jouer aux boules.

bowlegged, *adj.* à jambes arquées.

bowler, *n.* joueur de boule *m.*

box, *n.* boîte *f.;* (theater) loge *f.*

boxcar, *n.* wagon de marchandises *m.*

boxer, *n.* boxeur *m.*

boxing, *n.* boxe *f.*

box office, *n.* bureau *(m.)* de location.

boy, *n.* garçon *m.*

boycott, *vb.* boycotter.

boyhood, *n.* première jeunesse *f.*

boyish, *adj.* enfantin, puéril.

boyishly, *adv.* comme un gamin.

brace, 1. *vb.* fortifier. **2.** *n.* vilebrequin (tool) *m.,* paire *f.,* couple *m.*

bracelet, *n.* bracelet *m.*

bracket, *n.* (wall) console *f.;* (printing) crochet *m.*

brag, *vb.* se vanter.

braggart, *n.* fanfaron *m.*

braid, *n.* (hair) tresse *f.;* (sewing) galon *m.*

brain, *n.* cerveau *m.;* **(brains)** cervelle *f.*

brainy, *adj.* intelligent.

brake, *n.* frein *m.*

bran, *n.* son *m.*

branch, *n.* branche *f.*

brand, *n.* marque *f.*

brandish, *vb.* brandir.

brand-new, *adj.* tout neuf.

brandy, *n.* eau-de-vie *f.*

brash, *adj.* impertinent.

brass, *n.* cuivre *(m.)* jaune.

brassiere, *n.* soutien-gorge *m.*

brat, *n.* gosse *m.f.*

bravado, *n.* bravade *f.*

brave, *adj.* courageux.

bravery, *n.* courage *m.*

brawl, *n.* rixe *f.*

brawn, *n.* partie charnue *f.,* muscles *m.pl.*

bray, *vb.* braire.

brazen, *adj.* (person) effronté.

Brazil, *n.* Brésil *m.*

breach, *n.* infraction *f.;* *(mil.)* brèche *f.*

bread, *n.* pain *m.*

breadth, *n.* largeur *f.*

break, 1. *n.* rupture *f.;* (pause) interruption *f.* **2.** *vb.* rompre, briser, casser.

breakable, *adj.* cassable.

breakage, *n.* cassure *f.,* rupture *f.*

breakfast, *n.* (petit) déjeuner *m.*

breakwater, *n.* brise-lames *m.,* jetée *f.*

breast, *n.* poitrine *f.,* sein *m.*

breath, *n.* haleine *f.;* *(fig.,* wind) souffle *m.*

breathe, *vb.* respirer.

breathless, *adj.* (out of breath) essoufflé.

breathlessly, *adv.* hors d'haleine.

bred, *adj.* élevé.

breeches, *n.* pantalon *m.sg.*

breed, *vb.* produire; (livestock) élever.

breeder, *n.* (raiser) éleveur *m.*

breeding, *n.* (manners) éducation *f.;* (animals) élevage *m.*

breeze, *n.* brise *f.*

breezy, *adj.* (windy) venteux; (manner) dégagé.

brevity, *n.* brièveté *f.*

brew, *vb.* (beer) brasser; (tea) faire infuser, *tr.*

brewery, *n.* brasserie *f.*

briar, *n.* ronce *f.*

bribe, *vb.* corrompre.

briber, *n.* corrupteur *m.*

bribery, *n.* corruption *f.*

brick, *n.* brique *f.*

bricklaying, *n.* maçonnerie *f.*

bricklike, *adj.* comme une brique.

bridal, *adj.* nuptial.

bride, *n.* mariée *f.*

bridegroom, *n.* marié *m.*

bridesmaid, *n.* demoiselle *(f.)* d'honneur.

bridge, *n.* pont *m.;* (boat) passerelle *f.;* (cards) bridge *m.*

bridged, *adj.* lié.

bridgehead, *n.* tête de pont *f.*

bridle, *n.* bride *f.*

brief, *adj.* bref *m.,* brève *f.*

brief case, *n.* serviette *f.*

briefly, *adv.* brièvement.

briefness, *n.* brièveté *f.*

brier, *n.* bruyère *f.,* ronces *f.pl.*

brig, *n.* brick *m.*

brigade, *n.* brigade *f.*

bright, *adj.* vif *m.,* vive *f.;* intelligent.

brighten, *vb.* faire briller, *tr.*

brightness, *n.* éclat *m.*

brilliance, *n.* éclat *m.*

brilliant, *adj.* brillant.

brim, *n.* bord *m.*

brine, *n.* saumure *f.*

bring, *vb.* (thing) apporter; (person) amener; **(b. about)** amener, causer.

brink, *n.* bord *m.*

briny, *adj.* salé.

brisk, *adj.* vif *m.,* vive *f.*

brisket, *n.* poitrine (meat) *f.*

briskly, *adv.* vivement.

briskness, *n.* vivacité *f.*

bristle, *n.* soie *f.*

bristly, *adj.* hérissé (de), poilu.

British, *adj.* britannique.

British Empire, *n.* Empire Britannique *m.*

British Isles, *n.* Îles Britanniques *f.pl.*

brittle, *adj.* fragile.

broad, *adj.* large.

broadcast, *vb.* radiodiffuser.

broadcast, *n.* radio-émission *f.*

broadcaster, *n.* speaker *m.*

broadcloth, *n.* drap *(m.)* fin.

broaden, *vb.* élargir.

broadly, *adv.* largement.

broadminded, *adj.* large d'esprit.

broadside, *n.* côte *f.,* bordée *f.*

brocade, *n.* brocart *m.*

brocaded, *adj.* de brocart.

broil, *vb.* griller.

broiler, *n.* gril *m.*

broken-hearted, *adj.* qui a le coeur brisé.

broker, *n.* courtier *m.;* (stockb.) agent *(m.)* de change.

brokerage, *n.* courtage *m.*

bronchial, *adj.* bronchique.

bronchitis, *n.* bronchite *f.*

bronze, *n.* bronze *m.*

brooch, *n.* broche *f.*

brood, 1. *n.* couvée *f.* **2.** *vb.* couver.

brook, *n.* ruisseau *m.*

broom, *n.* balai *m.*

broomstick, *n.* manche à balai *m.*

broth, *n.* bouillon *m.*

brothel, *n.* bordel *m.,* maison mal famée *f.*

brother, *n.* frère *m.*

brotherhood, *n.* fraternité *f.*

brother-in-law, *n.* beau-frère *m.*

brotherly, *adj.* fraternel.

brow, *n.* front *m.*

brown, *adj.* brun.

browse, *vb.* (animals) brouter; (books) feuilleter (des livres).

bruise, 1. *n.* meurtrissure *f.* **2.** *vb.* meurtrir.

brunette, *adj. and n.* brune *f.*

brunt, *n.* choc *m.*

brush, n. brosse f.; **(paint-b.)** pinceau m.

brushwood, n. broussailles f.pl.

brusque, adj. brusque.

brusquely, adv. brusquement.

brutal, adj. brutal.

brutality, n. brutalité f.

brutalize, vb. abrutir.

brute, n. brute f.

bubble, 1. n. bulle f. 2. vb. bouillonner.

buck, n. daim m.; (male) mâle m.

bucket, n. seau m.

buckle, n. boucle f.

buckram, n. bougran m.

buckshot, n. chevrotine f.

buckwheat, n. sarrasin m., blé noir m.

bud, 1. n. bourgeon m. 2. vb. bourgeonner.

budding, adj. en herbe.

budge, vb. bouger.

budget, n. budget m.

buffalo, n. buffle m.

buffer, n. tampon m.

buffet, n. (sideboard) buffet m.

buffoon, n. bouffon m.

bug, n. insecte m.

bugle, n. clairon m.

build, vb. bâtir.

builder, n. (buildings) entrepreneur m.; (ships) constructeur m.

building, n. bâtiment m.

bulb, n. (electricity) ampoule f.; (botany) bulbe m.

bulge, n. bosse f.

bulk, n. masse f.

bulkhead, n. cloison étanche f.

bulky, adj. volumineux.

bull, n. taureau m.

bulldog, n. bouledogue m.

bulldozer, n. machine à refouler f.

bullet, n. balle f.

bulletin, n. bulletin m.

bulletproof, adj. à l'épreuve des balles.

bullfinch, n. bouvreuil m.

bullion, n. lingot m.

bully, vb. rudoyer.

bulwark, n. rempart m.

bum, n. fainéant m.

bumblebee, n. bourdon m.

bump, 1. n. (blow) coup m.; (protuberance) bosse f. 2. vb. cogner.

bumper, n. (auto) pare-chocs m.

bun, n. brioche f.

bunch, n. (flowers) bouquet m.; (grapes) grappe f.; (keys) trousseau m.

bundle, n. paquet m.

bungle, vb. bousiller.

bunion, n. cor m.

bunk, n. couchette f.

bunny, n. lapin m.

bunting, n. drapeaux m.pl.

buoy, n. bouée f.

buoyant, adj. qui a du ressort.

burden, n. fardeau m.

burdensome, adj. onéreux.

bureau, n. (office) bureau m.;

(chest of drawers) commode f.

burglar, n. cambrioleur m.

burglarize, vb. cambrioler.

burglary, n. vol (m.) avec effraction.

burial, n. enterrement m.

burlap, n. gros canevas m.

burly, adj. corpulent.

burn, vb. brûler.

burner, n. bec m.

burning, adj. brûlant.

burnish, vb. brunir, polir.

burrow, n. terrier m.

burst, vb. éclater.

bury, vb. enterrer.

bus, n. autobus m.

bush, n. buisson m.

bushel, n. boisseau m.

bushy, adj. buissonneux; (hair) touffu.

busily, adv. activement.

business, n. affaire f.; (comm.) affaires f.pl.

businesslike, adj. pratique.

businessman, n. homme (m.) d'affaires.

business-woman, n. femme (f.) d'affaires.

bust, n. buste m.

bustle, vb. se remuer.

busy, adj. occupé.

busybody, n. officieux m.

but, conj. mais; (only) ne . . . que; (except) sauf.

butcher, n. boucher m.

butchery, n. tuerie f., massacre m.

butler, n. maître (m.) d'hôtel.

butt, n. bout m., (of jokes) plastron m.

butter, n. beurre m.

buttercup, n. bouton d'or m.

butterfly, n. papillon m.

buttermilk, n. babeurre m.

butterscotch, n. caramel au beurre m.

buttock, n. fesse f.

button, n. bouton m.

buttonhole, n. boutonnière f.

buttress, n. contrefort m.; (flying b.) arc-boutant m.

buxom, adj. (of women) aux formes rebondies.

buy, vb. acheter.

buyer, n. acheteur m.

buzz, 1. n. bourdonnement m. 2. vb. bourdonner.

buzzard, n. buse f.

buzzer, n. trompe f., sirène f.

by, prep. (through) par; (near) près de.

by-and-by, adv. bientôt.

bygone, adj. passé, d'autrefois.

bylaw, n. règlement local m.

by-pass, 1. n. route d'évitement f. 2. vb. faire un détour.

by-product, n. sous-produit m.

bystander, n. spectateur m.

byte, n. unité fondamentale de données f.

byway, n. sentier détourné m.

C

cab, n. (taxi) taxi m.; (horse) fiacre m.

cabaret, n. cabaret m.

cabbage, n. chou m.

cabin, n. (hut) cabane f.; (boat) cabine f.

cabinet, n. cabinet m.

cabinetmaker, n. ébéniste m.

cable, 1. n. câble m. 2. vb. câbler.

cablegram, n. câblogramme m.

cachet, n. cachet m.

cackle, 1. n. caquet m. 2. vb. caqueter.

cacophony, n. cacophonie f.

cactus, n. cactus m.

cad, n. mufle m.

cadaver, n. cadavre m.

cadaverous, adj. cadavérique.

cadence, n. cadence f.

cadet, n. cadet m.

cadmium, n. cadmium m.

cadre, n. cadre m.

café, n. café, (-restaurant) m.

cafeteria, n. restaurant m.

caffeine, n. caféine f.

cage, n. cage f.

caged, adj. mis en cage.

caisson, n. caisson m.

cajole, vb. cajoler.

cake, n. gâteau m.

calamitous, adj. calamiteux, désastreux.

calamity, n. calamité f.

calcify, vb. calcifier.

calcium, n. calcium m.

calculable, adj. calculable.

calculate, vb. calculer.

calculating, adj. qui fait des calculs.

calculation, n. calcul m.

calculus, n. calcul m.

caldron, n. chaudron m.

calendar, n. calendrier m.

calender, n. calandre f.

calf, n. veau m.

calfskin, adj. en peau de veau.

caliber, n. calibre m.

calico, n. calicot m.

calisthenic, adj. callisthénique.

calisthenics, n. callisthénie f.

calk, vb. ferrer à glace.

call, 1. n. appel m.; (visit) visite f. 2. vb. appeler; (call on) faire visite à.

calligraphy, n. calligraphie f.

calling, n. vocation f., profession f.

calling card, n. carte de visite f.

callously, adv. d'une manière insensible.

callousness, n. insensibilité f.

callow, adj. blanc-bec.

callus, n. callosité f.

calm, 1. adj. calme. 2. vb. calmer.

calmly, adv. calmement.

calmness, n. calme m., tranquillité f.

caloric, adj. calorique.

calorie, n. calorie f.

calorimeter, n. calorimètre m.
calumniate, vb. calomnier.
calumny, n. calomnie f.
Calvary, n. Calvaire m.
calve, vb. vêler.
calyx, n. calice m.
camaraderie, n. camaraderie f.
cambric, n. batiste f.
camel, n. chameau m.
camellia, n. camélia m.
camel's hair, n. poil de chameau m.
cameo, n. camée m.
camera, n. appareil photographique m.
camouflage, vb. camoufler.
camouflaged, adj. camouflé.
camouflaging, adj. camouflant.
camp, 1. n. camp m.; (holiday camp) camping m. **2.** vb. camper.
campaign, n. campagne f.
camper, n. qui fait du camping.
camphor, n. camphre m.
camphor ball, n. balle de camphre f.
campus, n. terrains (m.pl.) de l'université.
can, 1. n. (food) boîte f.; (general) bidon m. **2.** vb. (be able) pouvoir; (put in a can) conserver.
Canada, n. Canada m.
Canadian, 1. n. Canadien m. **2.** adj. canadien.
canal, n. canal m.
canalize, vb. canaliser.
canapé, n. canapé m.
canard, n. canard m.
canary, n. serin m.
Canary Islands, n. Îles Canaries f.pl.
cancel, vb. annuler; (erase) biffer.
cancellation, n. annulation f.
cancer, n. cancer m.
candelabrum, n. candélabre m.
candid, adj. sincère.
candidacy, n. candidature f.
candidate, n. candidat m.
candidly, adv. franchement.
candidness, n. candeur f.
candied, adj. candi.
candle, n. bougie f.; (church) cierge m.
candler, n. fabricant de chandelles m.
candlestick, n. chandelier m.
candor, n. sincérité f.
candy, n. bonbon m.
cane, n. canne f.
canine, adj. canin.
canister, n. boîte à thé f.
canker, n. chancre m.
cankerworm, n. ver rongeur m.
canned, adj. conservé en boîtes (de fer blanc).
canner, n. travailleur dans une conserverie m.
cannery, n. conserverie f.
cannibal, adj. and n. cannibale m.f.
canning, n. mise en conserve, en boîtes (de fer blanc) f.

cannon, n. canon m.
cannonade, n. canonnade f.
cannoneer, n. canonier m.
cannot, vb. ne peut pas.
canny, adj. avisé, rusé.
canoe, n. canot m.
canon, n. chanoine m.; canon (rule) m.
canonical, adj. canonique.
canonize, vb. canoniser.
canopy, n. dais m.
cant, n. hypocrisie f.
can't, vb. ne peut pas.
cantaloupe, n. melon m., cantaloup m.
canteen, n. cantine f.; bidon m.
canter, 1. n. petit galop f. **2.** vb. aller au petit galop.
cantonment, n. cantonnement m.
canvas, n. toile f.
canvass, 1. n. sollicitation f. **2.** vb. solliciter; (discuss) débattre.
canyon, n. gorge f., défilé m.
cap, n. bonnet m.; (peaked) casquette f.
capability, n. capacité f.
capable, adj. capable.
capably, adv. capablement.
capacious, adj. ample, spacieux.
capacity, n. capacité f.
caparison, 1. n. caparaçon m. **2.** vb. caparaçonner.
cape, n. (geography) cap m.; (cloak) cape f.
caper, 1. n. bond m.; (plant) câpre f. **2.** vb. bondir.
capillary, adj. capillaire.
capital, adj. capital.
capital, n. (finance) capital m.; (city) capitale f.; (letter) majuscule f.; (architecture) chapiteau m.
capitalism, n. capitalisme m.
capitalist, n. capitaliste m.f.
capitalistic, adj. capitaliste.
capitalization, n. capitalisation f.
capitalize, vb. capitaliser.
capitulate, vb. capituler.
capon, n. chapon m.
caprice, n. caprice m.
capricious, adj. capricieux.
capriciously, adv. capricieusement.
capriciousness, n. caractère capricieux m., humeur fantasque f.
capsize, vb. chavirer, intr.; faire chavirer, tr.
capsule, n. capsule f.
captain, n. capitaine m.
caption, n. en-tête m.
captious, adj. chicaneur.
captivate, vb. captiver.
captivating, adj. séduisant.
captive, adj. and n. captif m.
captivity, n. captivité f.
captor, n. capteur m.
capture, 1. n. capture f. **2.** vb. capturer.
car, n. (auto) voiture f.; (train) wagon m.

caracul, n. caracul m.
carafe, n. carafe f.
caramel, n. caramel m.
carat, n. carat m.
caravan, n. caravane f.
caraway, n. carvi m., cumin (des prés) m.
carbide, n. carbure m.
carbine, n. carabine f.
carbohydrate, n. carbohydrate m.
carbon, n. carbone m.
carbon dioxide, n. acide carbonique m.
carbon monoxide, n. oxyde de carbone m.
carbon paper, n. papier carbone m.
carbuncle, n. escarboucle f., charbon (med.) m.
carburetor, n. carburateur m.
carcass, n. carcasse f.
carcinogenic, adj. cancérogène.
card, n. carte f.
cardboard, n. carton m.
cardiac, adj. cardiaque.
cardigan, n. gilet de tricot m.
cardinal, n. cardinal m.
care, 1. n. (worry) souci m.; (attention) attention f.; (take c.!) faites attention!; (charge) soin m.; (take c. of) prendre soin de. **2.** vb. (c. about) se soucier de; (c. for) aimer; (look after) soigner.
careen, vb. caréner.
career, n. carrière f.
carefree, adj. insouciant.
careful, adj. soigneux.
carefully, adv. soigneusement, attentivement.
carefulness, n. soin m., attention f.
careless, adj. insouciant.
carelessly, adv. nonchalamment, négligemment.
carelessness, n. insouciance f., négligence f.
caress, 1. n. caresse f. **2.** vb. caresser.
caretaker, n. concierge m.f.
cargo, n. cargaison f.
caricature, n. caricature f.
caries, n. carie f.
carillon, n. carillon m.
carload, n. voiturée f.
carnal, adj. charnel.
carnation, n. œillet m.
carnival, n. carnaval m.
carnivorous, adj. carnivore.
carol, n. (Xmas c.) noël m.
carouse, vb. faire la fête.
carpenter, n. charpentier m.
carpet, n. tapis m.
carpeting, n. pose de tapis f.
car pool, n. groupe de personnes qui voyagent régulièrement ensemble en auto m.
carriage, n. (vehicle) voiture f.; (bearing) maintien m.; (transport) transport m.
carrier, n. porteur m., messager m.
carrier pigeon, n. pigeon voyageur m.

carrot, n. carotte f.
carrousel, n. carrousel m.
carry, vb. porter; (c. on) continuer; (c. out) exécuter; (c. through) mener à bonne fin.
cart, n. charrette f.
cartage, n. charriage m., transport m.
cartel, n. cartel m.
carter, n. charretier m.
cartilage, n. cartilage m.
carton, n. carton m.
cartoon, n. dessin satirique m.
cartoonist, n. caricaturiste m.
cartridge, n. cartouche f.
carve, vb. (art) sculpter; (meat) découper.
carver, n. découpeur m., sculpteur m.
carving, n. découpage m., sculpture f.
cascade, n. cascade f.
case, n. (instance, state of things) cas m.; (law) cause f.; (packing) caisse f.; (holder) étui m.; (in any c.) en tout cas.
cash, 1. n. espèces f.pl.; (C.O.D.) livraison contre remboursement f. 2. vb. (c. a check) toucher.
cashier, n. caissier m.
cashmere, n. cachemire m.
casing, n. revêtement m., enveloppe f.
casino, n. casino m.
cask, n. tonneau m.
casket, n. cassette f.
casserole, n. casserole f.
cassette, n. cassette f.
cast, 1. n. (throw) coup m.; (characteristic) trempe f.; (theater) distribution f.; (c. from mold) moulage m.; (hue) nuance f. 2. vb. (throw) jeter; (metal) couler.
castaway, n. naufragé m., rejeté m.
caste, n. caste f.
caster, n. fondeur m.
castigate, vb. châtier, punir.
cast iron, n. fonte f.
castle, n. château m.
castoff, adj. abandonné.
casual, adj. (accidental) casuel; (person) insouciant.
casually, adv. fortuitement, en passant.
casualness, n. nonchalance f.
casualties, n. (mil.) pertes f.pl.
cat, n. chat m., chatte f.
cataclysm, n. cataclysme m.
catacomb, n. catacombe f.
catalogue, n. catalogue m.
catapult, n. catapulte f.
cataract, n. cataracte f.
catarrh, n. catarrhe m.
catastrophe, n. catastrophe f.
catch, vb. attraper; (seize, understand) saisir.
catcher, n. qui attrape.
catchword, n. mot d'ordre m.
catchy, adj. (musical air) facile à retenir; (question) insidieuse.

catechism, n. catéchisme m.
catechize, vb. catéchiser.
categorical, adj. catégorique.
category, n. catégorie f.
cater, vb. pourvoir à.
caterpillar, n. chenille f.
catgut, n. corde à boyau f.
catharsis, n. catharsis f., (med.) purgation f.
cathartic, adj. cathartique, purgatif.
cathedral, n. cathédrale f.
cathode, n. cathode f.
Catholic, adj. catholique.
Catholic Church, n. Église catholique f.
Catholicism, n. catholicisme m.
cat nap, n. somme m.
catsup, n. sauce piquante f.
cattle, n. bétail m., bestiaux m.pl.
cattleman, n. éleveur de bétail m.
catwalk, n. coursive f.
cauliflower, n. chou-fleur m.
causation, n. causation f.
cause, n. cause f.
causeway, n. chaussée f.
caustic, adj. caustique.
cauterize, vb. cautériser.
cautery, n. cautère m.
caution, n. prudence f.
caution, vb. avertir.
cautious, adj. prudent.
cavalcade, n. cavalcade f.
cavalier, adj. and n. cavalier m.
cavalry, n. cavalerie f.
cave, n. caverne f.
cave-in, n. effondrement m.
cavern, n. caverne f.
caviar, n. caviar m.
cavity, n. cavité f.
cease, vb. cesser (de).
ceaseless, adj. incessant, continuel.
cedar, n. cèdre m.
cede, vb. céder.
ceiling, n. plafond m.
celebrant, n. célébrant m.
celebrate, vb. célébrer.
celebration, n. célébration f.
celebrity, n. célébrité f.
celerity, n. célérité f., vitesse f.
celery, n. céleri m.
celestial, adj. céleste.
celibacy, n. célibat m.
celibate, adj. célibataire.
cell, n. cellule f.
cellar, n. cave f.
cellist, n. violoncelliste m.
cello, n. violoncelle m.
cellophane, n. cellophane f.
cellular, adj. cellulaire.
celluloid, n. celluloïd m.
cellulose, n. cellulose f.
Celtic, adj. celtique.
cement, 1. n. ciment m. 2. vb. cimenter.
cemetery, n. cimetière m.
censor, 1. n. censeur m. 2. vb. censurer.
censorious, adj. critique, hargneux.
censorship, n. censure f.

censure, n. censure f.
census, n. recensement m.
cent, n. cent m.; (per c.) pour cent.
centenary, centennial, adj. and n. centenaire m.
center, n. centre m.
centerfold, n. pages centrales f.pl.
centerpiece, n. pièce de milieu f.
centigrade, adj. centigrade.
centigrade thermometer, n. thermomètre centigrade m.
central, adj. central.
centralize, vb. centraliser.
century, n. siècle m.
century plant, n. agave d'Amérique m.
ceramic, adj. céramique.
ceramics, n. céramique f.
cereal, adj. and n. céréale f.
cerebral, adj. cérébral.
ceremonial, adj. and n. cérémonial m.
ceremonious, adj. cérémonieux.
ceremony, n. cérémonie f.
certain, adj. certain.
certainly, adv. certainement.
certainty, n. certitude f.
certificate, n. certificat m.; (birth c.) acte de naissance.
certification, n. certification f.
certified, adj. certifié, diplômé, breveté.
certifier, n. (personne) qui certifie.
certify, vb. certifier.
certitude, n. certitude f.
cervical, adj. cervical.
cervix, n. cervix m.
cessation, n. cessation f., suspension f.
cession, n. cession f.
cesspool, n. fosse d'aisances f.
chafe, vb. frictionner.
chaff, 1. n. menue paille f.; (colloq.) blague f. 2. vb. blaguer.
chafing dish, n. réchaud m.
chagrin, n. chagrin m.
chain, n. chaîne f.
chain reaction, n. réaction caténaire f.
chain store, n. succursale de grand magasin f.
chair, n. chaise f.; (arm-c.) fauteuil m.
chairman, n. président m.
chairmanship, n. présidence f.
chairperson, n. président m.; présidente f.
chairwoman, n. présidente f.
chalice, n. calice m.
chalk, n. craie f.
chalky, adj. de craie, calcaire.
challenge, n. défi m.
challenge, vb. défier; (dispute) contester.
challenger, n. qui fait un défi, prétendant m.
chamber, n. chambre f.
chamberlain, n. chambellan m.

chambermaid, n. femme de chambre f.

chamber music, n. musique de chambre f.

chameleon, n. caméléon m.

chamois, n. chamois m.

champ, vb. ronger, mâcher.

champion, n. champion m.

championship, n. championnat m.

chance, n. chance f.; (by c.) par hasard.

chancel, n. sanctuaire m., chœur m.

chancellery, n. chancellerie f.

chancellor, n. chancelier m.

chandelier, n. lustre m.

change, 1. n. changement m.; (money) monnaie f.; (exchange) change m. **2.** vb. changer.

changeable, adj. changeant.

changeability, n. variabilité f.

changer, n. changeur m.

channel, n. canal m.; (the English C.) la Manche f.

chant, 1. n. chant m. **2.** vb. chanter.

chaos, n. chaos m.

chaotic, adj. chaotique.

chap, n. (on skin) gerçure f.; (young man) gars m.

chapel, n. chapelle f.

chaperon, n. (person) duègne f.; chaperon m.

chaplain, n. aumônier m.

chapman, n. colporteur m.

chapped, adj. gercé.

chapter, n. chapitre m.

char, vb. carboniser.

character, n. caractère m.; (in fiction) personnage m.; (role) rôle m.

characteristic, 1. n. trait caractéristique m. **2.** adj. caractéristique.

characteristically, adv. d'une manière caractéristique.

characterization, n. action de caractériser f.

characterize, vb. caractériser.

charcoal, n. charbon (m.) de bois.

charge, 1. n. (guns, legal, office) charge f.; (price) prix m.; (care) soin m. **2.** vb. charger; (c. with) charger de; (price) demander.

charger, n. grand plat m.; cheval de bataille m.

chariot, n. char m., chariot m.

charioteer, n. conducteur de chariot m.

charisma, n. charisme m.

charitable, adj. charitable.

charitableness, n. bienveillance f.

charitably, adv. charitablement.

charity, n. charité f.

charlatan, n. charlatan m.

charlatanism, n. charlatanisme m.

charm, 1. n. charme m. **2.** vb. charmer.

charmer, n. charmeur m., enchanteur m.

charming, adj. charmant.

charred, adj. carbonisé.

chart, n. (map) carte f.; (graph) graphique m.

charter, 1. n. charte f. **2.** vb. (boat) affréter.

charter flight, n. vol frété m.; charter m.

charwoman, n. femme de journée f., femme de ménage f.

chase, 1. n. chasse f. **2.** vb. chasser.

chaser, n. chasseur m.; ciseleur m.

chasm, n. abîme m.

chassis, n. chassis m.

chaste, adj. chaste.

chasten, vb. châtier, corriger.

chasteness, n. pureté f.

chastise, vb. châtier.

chastisement, n. châtiment m.

chastity, n. chasteté f.

chat, 1. n. causette f. **2.** vb. causer.

chateau, n. château m.

chattel, n. bien m., meuble m.

chatter, 1. n. bavardage m. **2.** vb. bavarder.

chatterbox, n. bavard m.

chauffeur, n. chauffeur m.

cheap, adj. (inexpensive) bon marché, (mean) de peu de valeur.

cheapen, vb. déprécier.

cheaply, adv. à bon marché.

cheapness, n. bon marché m., bas prix m.; basse qualité f.

cheat, vb. tromper; (at games) tricher.

cheater, n. tricheur m., trompeur m.

check, 1. n. (restraint) frein m.; (verification) vérification f.; (stub) ticket m.; (bill) addition f.; (bank draft) chèque m. **2.** vb. (stop) arrêter; (restrain) modérer; (verify) vérifier; (luggage) enregistrer.

checker, n. enregistreur m., contrôleur m.

checkers, n. jeu de dames m.

checkmate, 1. n. échec et mat m. **2.** vb. mater.

cheek, n. joue f.

cheer, 1. n. (applause) hourra m. **2.** vb. (acclaim) acclamer; (c. up, tr.) réjouir.

cheerful, cheery, adj. gai.

cheerfully, adv. gaiement, de bon cœur.

cheerfulness, n. gaieté f., bonne humeur f.

cheerless, adj. triste, morne, sombre.

cheery, adj. gai, joyeux.

cheese, n. fromage m.

cheesecloth, n. gaze f.

cheesy, adj. fromageux.

chemical, adj. chimique.

chemically, adv. chimiquement.

chemist, n. chimiste m.f.

chemistry, n. chimie f.

chemotherapy, n. chimiothérapie f.

chenille, n. chenille f.

cherish, vb. chérir.

cherry, n. cerise f.

cherub, n. chérubin m.

chess, n. échecs m.pl.

chessman, n. pièce f.

chest, n. (box) coffre m.; (body) poitrine f.; (c. of drawers) commode f.

chestnut, n. châtaigne f.

chevron, n. chevron m.

chew, vb. mâcher.

chewer, n. mâcheur m.

chic, adj. chic.

chicanery, n. chicane f., chicanerie f.

chick, n. poussin m.

chicken, n. poulet m.

chicken-hearted, adj. peureux.

chicken-pox, n. varicelle f.

chicle, n. chiclé m.

chicory, n. chicorée f.

chide, vb. gronder, réprimander.

chief, 1. n. chef m. **2.** adj. principal.

chiefly, adv. surtout, principalement.

chieftain, n. chef de clan m.

chiffon, n. chiffon m.

chilblain, n. engelure f.

child, n. enfant m.f.

childbirth, n. enfantement m.

childhood, n. enfance f.

childish, adj. enfantin.

childishness, n. puérilité f., enfantillage m.

childless, adj. sans enfant.

childlessness, n, l'état d'être sans enfants.

childlike, adj. comme un enfant, en enfant.

Chile, n. Chili m.

Chilean, 1. n. Chilien m. **2.** adj. chilien.

chili, n. piment m.

chill, 1. n. froid m.; (shiver) frisson m. **2.** vb. refroidir.

chilliness, n. froid m., frisson m.

chilly, adj. un peu froid.

chime, 1. n. carillon m. **2.** vb. carillonner.

chimney, n. cheminée f.

chimney sweep, n. ramoneur m.

chimpanzee, n. chimpanzé m.

chin, n. menton m.

China, n. Chine f.

china, n. (ware) porcelaine f.

chinchilla, n. chinchilla m.

Chinese, 1. n. (person) Chinois m.; (language) chinois m. **2.** adj. chinois.

chink, n. fente f., crevasse f.

chintz, n. perse f.

chip, n. éclat m.; (potato c.s) frites f.pl.

chipmunk, n. tamias m.

chiropodist, n. pédicure m.

chiropractor, n. chiropracteur m.

chirp, vb. pépier, gazouiller.

chisel, 1. vb. ciseler. 2. n. ciseau m.
chivalrous, adj. chevaleresque.
chivalry, n. chevalerie f.
chive, n. ciboulette f.
chloride, n. chlorure m.
chlorine, n. chlore m.
chloroform, n. chloroforme m.
chlorophyll, n. chlorophylle m.
chockfull, adj. plein comme un œuf.
chocolate, n. chocolat m.
choice, n. choix m.
choir, n. chœur m.
choke, vb. étouffer.
choker, n. foulard m.
cholera, n. choléra m.
choleric, adj. colérique.
choose, vb. choisir.
chop, 1. n. (meat) côtelette f. 2. vb. couper.
chopper, n. couperet m.
choppy, adj. (sea) clapoteux.
chopstick, n. baguette f., bâtonnet m.
choral, adj. choral.
chord, n. (music) accord m.
chore, n. travail (m.) de ménage.
choreography, n. chorégraphie f.
chorister, n. choriste m. enfant de chœur m.
chortle, vb. glousser de joie.
chorus, n. chœur m.
chowder, n. (sorte de) bouillabaisse f.
christen, vb. baptiser.
Christendom, n. chrétienté f.
christening, n. baptême m.
Christian, adj. and n. chrétien m.
Christianity, n. christianisme m.
Christmas, n. Noël m.
chromatic, adj. chromatique.
chromium, n. chrome m.
chromosome, n. chromosome m.
chronic, adj. chronique.
chronically, adv. chroniquement.
chronicle, n. chronique f.
chronological, adj. chronologique.
chronology, n. chronologie f.
chrysalis, n. chrysalide f.
chrysanthemum, n. chrysanthème m.
chubby, adj. joufflu.
chuck, n. petite tape f., gloussement (de volaille) m.
chuckle, vb. rire tout bas.
chug, 1. n. souffle m. (d'une machine à vapeur). 2. vb. souffler.
chum, n. camarade m., copain m.
chummy, adj. familier, intime.
chunk, n. gros morceau m.
chunky, adj. en gros morceaux.
church, n. église f.
churchman, n. homme d'église m., ecclésiastique m.
churchyard, n. cimetière m.

churn, vb. baratter.
chute, n. glissière f.
chutney, n. chutney m.
cicada, n. cigale f.
cider, n. cidre m.
cigar, n. cigare m.
cigarette, n. cigarette f.
cilia, n. cils m.pl.
ciliary, adj. ciliaire.
cinch, n. (it's a c.) c'est facile.
cinchona, n. quinquina m.
cinder, n. cendre f.
cinema, n. cinéma m.
cinematic, adj. cinématographique.
cinnamon, n. cannelle f.
cipher, n. chiffre m.; (nought) zéro m.
circle, 1. n. cercle m. 2. vb. entourer (de).
circuit, n. circuit m.
circuitous, adj. détourné, sinueux.
circuitously, adv. d'une manière détournée, par des détours.
circular, adj. circulaire.
circularize, vb. envoyer des circulaires.
circulate, vb. circuler, tr.; faire circuler, intr.
circulation, n. circulation f.
circulator, n. circulateur m.
circulatory, adj. circulaire, circulatoire.
circumcise, vb. circoncire.
circumcision, n. circoncision f.
circumference, n. circonférence f.
circumlocution, n. circonlocution f.
circumscribe, vb. circonscrire.
circumspect, adj. circonspect.
circumstance, n. (condition) circonstance f.; (financial) moyens m.pl.
circumstantial, adj. circonstancié.
circumstantially, adv. en détail.
circumvent, vb. circonvenir.
circumvention, n. circonvention f.
circus, n. cirque m.
cirrhosis, n. cirrhose f.
cistern, n. citerne f.
citadel, n. citadelle f.
citation, n. citation f.
cite, vb. citer.
citizen, n. citoyen m.
citizenry, n. tous les citoyens m.pl.
citizenship, n. droit (m.) de cité.
citric acid, n. acide citrique m.
city, n. ville f.; cité f.
civic, adj. civique.
civics, n. instruction (f.) civique.
civil, adj. civil; (polite) poli; (c. servant) fonctionnaire m.
civilian, n. civil m.
civility, n. civilité f., politesse f.
civilization, n. civilisation f.
civilize, vb. civiliser.
civilized, adj. civilisé.

civil service, n. administration (civile) f.
civil war, n. guerre civile f.
clad, adj. habillé, vêtu.
claim, 1. n. (demand) demande f.; (right) droit m. 2. vb. (demand) réclamer, prétendre; (insist) soutenir.
claimant, n. réclamateur m., prétendant m.
clairvoyance, n. clairvoyance f.
clairvoyant, n. voyant m.
clam, n. palourde f., mollusque m.
clamber, vb. grimper.
clammy, adj. visqueux, moite.
clamor, n. clameur f.
clamorous, adj. bruyant.
clamp, 1. n. (metal) crampon m.; (carpentry) serre-joint m. 2. vb. cramponner, serrer.
clan, n. clan m., clique f., coterie f.
clandestine, adj. clandestin.
clandestinely, adv. clandestinement.
clang, 1. n. cliquetis m., son métallique m. 2. vb. résonner.
clangor, n. cliquetis m.
clannish, adj. de clan.
clap, vb. (applaud) applaudir.
clapboard, n. bardeau m.
clapper, n. claqueur m., battant (of a bell) m.
claque, n. claque f.
claret, n. vin rouge de Bordeaux m.
clarification, n. clarification f.
clarify, vb. (lit.) clarifier; (fig.) éclaircir.
clarinet, n. clarinette f.
clarinetist, n. clarinettiste m.
clarion, n. clairon m.
clarity, n. clarté f.
clash, 1. vb. choquer, tr.; s'entre-choquer, intr. 2. n. choc m.
clasp, 1. n. agrafe f.; (embrace) étreinte f. 2. vb. agrafer, étreindre.
class, n. classe f.
classic, classical, adj. classique.
classicism, n. classicisme m.
classifiable, adj. classifiable.
classification, n. classification f.
classify, vb. classifier, classer.
classmate, n. camarade (m.) de classe.
classroom, n. salle (f.) de classe.
clatter, n. bruit m.
clause, n. clause f.
claustrophobia, n. claustrophobie f.
claw, n. griffe f.
claw-hammer, n. marteau à dent m.
clay, n. argile f., glaise f.
clean, 1. adj. propre. 2. vb. nettoyer.
clean-cut, adj. net, fin.
cleaner, n. (dry-c.) teinturier m.

cleanliness, cleanness, *n.* propreté *f.*

cleanse, *vb.* nettoyer, curer.

cleanser, *n.* chose qui nettoie *f.*, détersif *m.*, cureur *m.*

clear, 1. *adj.* clair. **2.** *vb.* (c. up) déblayer; (profit) gagner; (get over) franchir; (weather, *intr.*) s'éclaircir.

clear-cut, *adj.* nettement dessiné.

clearing, *n.* (open place) clairière *f.*, éclaircissement *m.* (comm.) acquittement *m.*, (woods) éclaircie *f.*

clearing house, *n.* banque de virement *f.*, chambre de compensation *f.*

clearly, *adv.* clairement, nettement, évidemment.

clearness, *n.* clarté *f.*, netteté *f.*

cleat, *n.* fer *m.*, (naut.) taquet *m.*

cleavage, *n.* fendage *m.*, scission *f.*

cleave, *vb.* (split) fendre; (adhere) adhérer.

cleaver, *n.* fendeur (person) *m.*; fendoir *m.*, couperet (instrument) *m.*

cleft, *n.* fente *f.*

clemency, *n.* clémence *f.*

clench, *vb.* serrer.

clergy, *n.* clergé *m.*

clergyman, *n.* ecclésiastique *m.*

clerical, *adj.* (clergy) clérical; (business) de bureau.

clericalism, *n.* cléricalisme *m.*

clerk, *n.* (business) employé *m.*; (store) commis *m.*; (law, eccles.) clerc *m.*

clerkship, *n.* place de clerc *f.*, place de commis *f.*

clever, *adj.* habile.

cleverly, *adv.* habilement.

cleverness, *n.* adresse *f.*

clew, *n.* fil *m.*

cliché, *n.* cliché *m.*

click, 1. *n.* cliquetis *m.*, déclic *m.* **2.** *vb.* cliqueter.

client, *n.* client *m.*

clientele, *n.* clientèle *f.*

cliff, *n.* falaise *f.*

climactic, *adj.* arrivé à son apogée.

climate, *n.* climat *m.*

climatic, *adj.* climatique.

climax, *n.* comble *m.*

climb, 1. *n.* montée *f.* **2.** *vb.* monter, grimper.

climber, *n.* grimpeur *m.*, ascensioniste *m.*

clinch, *vb.* river; (settle) conclure.

cling, *vb.* s'accrocher.

clinging, *adj.* qui se cramponne, qui s'accroche (à).

clinic, *n.* clinique *f.*

clinical, *adj.* clinique.

clinically, *adv.* d'une manière clinique.

clip, 1. *vb.* couper. **2.** *n.* pince *f.*

clipper, *n.* rogneur *m.*, tondeuse (instrument) *f.*, (naut.) fin voilier *m.*

clipping, *n.* coupure *f.*

clique, *n.* clique *f.*

cloak, *n.* manteau *m.*; (cloak-room) vestiaire *m.*

clock, *n.* horloge *f.*; (two o'clock) deux heures.

clockwise, *adv.* dans le sens des aiguilles d'une montre.

clockwork, *n.* mouvement *(m.)* d'horlogerie.

clod, *n.* motte *(f.)* de terre; (person) lourdaud *m.*

clog, *vb.* entraver.

cloister, *n.* cloître *m.*

clone, *n.* reproduction exacte *f.*

close, 1. *adj.* (closed) fermé; (narrow) étroit; (near) proche; (secret) réservé. **2.** *vb.* fermer. **3.** *adv.* tout près. **4.** *prep.* (c. to) près de.

closely, *adv.* de près, étroitement.

closeness, *n.* proximité *f.*, lourdeur (of the weather) *f.*, réserve *f.*

closet, *n.* (room) cabinet *m.*; (clothes) placard *m.*

clot, *n.* (blood) caillot *m.*

cloth, *n.* étoffe *f.*

clothe, *vb.* vêtir (de); habiller.

clothes, *n.* habits *m.pl.*

clothespin, *n.* pince *f.*

clothier, *n.* drapier *m.*, tailleur *m.*

clothing, *n.* vêtements *m.pl.*

cloud, *n.* nuage *m.*

cloudburst, *n.* trombe *f.*, rafale de pluie *f.*

cloudiness, *n.* état nuageux *m.*, obscurité *f.*

cloudless, *adj.* sans nuage.

cloudy, *adj.* nuageux, couvert.

clout, 1. *n.* gifle *f.*, tape *f.* **2.** *vb.* gifler, taper.

clove, *n.* clou *(m.)* de girofle.

clover, *n.* trèfle *m.*

clown, *n.* bouffon *m.*

clownish, *adj.* rustre, grossier, de payan.

cloy, *vb.* rassasier.

club, *n.* (society) club *m.*, société *f.*, cercle *m.*; (stick) massue *f.*; (golf) crosse *f.*; (cards) trèfle *m.*

clubfoot, *n.* pied bot *m.*

clue, *n.* fil *m.*

clump, *n.* (trees) bosquet *m.*; massif *m.*

clumsiness, *n.* gaucherie *f.*, maladresse *f.*

clumsy, *adj.* gauche.

cluster, 1. *n.* (people) groupe *m.*; (fruit) grappe *f.*; (flowers, trees) bouquet *m.* **2.** *vb.* se grouper.

clutch, 1. *n.* (claw) griffe *f.*; (auto) embrayage *m.* **2.** *vb.* saisir.

clutter, *vb.* encombrer.

coach, *n.* (carriage) carrosse *m.*; (train) wagon *m.*; (sports) entraîneur *m.* **2.** *vb.* (sports) entraîner; (school) donner des leçons particulières à.

coachman, *n.* cocher *m.*

coagulate, *vb.* se coaguler.

coagulation, *n.* coagulation *f.*

coal, *n.* charbon *(m.)* de terre, houille *f.*

coalesce, *vb.* se fondre, se fusionner, s'unir.

coalition, *n.* coalition *f.*

coal tar, *n.* goudron de houille *m.*

coarse, *adj.* grossier.

coarsen, *vb.* rendre plus grossier.

coarseness, *n.* grossièreté *f.*

coast, *n.* côte *f.*

coastal, *adj.* de la côte, littoral.

coaster, *n.* caboteur *m.*, dessous de carafe *m.*

coast guard, *n.* garde-côtes *m.*

coat, 1. *n.* (man) pardessus *m.*; (woman) manteau *m.*; (paint) couche *f.* **2.** *vb.* (c. with) revêtir de.

coating, *n.* couche *f.*, enduit *m.*, étoffe pour habits *f.*

coat of arms, *n.* écusson *f.*, cotte d'armes *f.*

coax, *vb.* cajoler.

cobalt, *n.* cobalt *m.*

cobbler, *n.* savetier *m.*, cordonnier *m.*

cobblestone, *n.* pierre du pavé *f.*

cobra, *n.* cobra *m.*

cobweb, *n.* toile *(f.)* d'araignée.

cocaine, *n.* cocaïne *f.*

cock, 1. *n.* (fowl) coq *m.*; (male) mâle *m.* **2.** *vb.* faire de l'œil.

cocker spaniel, *n.* épagneul cocker *m.*

cockeyed, *adj.* louche.

cockhorse, *n.* dada *m.*

cockroach, *n.* blatte *f.*

cocksure, *adj.* sûr et certain.

cocktail, *n.* cocktail *m.*

cocky, *adj.* suffisant.

cocoa, *n.* cacao *m.*

coconut, *n.* noix *(f.)* de coco; coco *m.*

cocoon, *n.* cocon *m.*

cod, *n.* morue *f.*

coddle, *vb.* dorloter.

code, *n.* code *m.*

codeine, *n.* codéine *f.*

codfish, *n.* morue *f.*

codify, *vb.* codifier.

cod-liver oil, *n.* huile de foie de morue *f.*

coeducation, *n.* enseignement mixte *m.*

coequal, *adj.* égal.

coerce, *vb.* contraindre.

coercion, *n.* coercition *f.*, contrainte *f.*

coercive, *adj.* coercitif.

coexist, *vb.* coexister.

coffee, *n.* café *m.*

coffer, *n.* coffre *m.*

coffin, *n.* cercueil *m.*

cog, *n.* dent *f.*

cogent, *adj.* puissant, fort.

cogitate, *vb.* méditer, penser.

cognizance, *n.* connaissance *f.*

cognizant, *adj.* instruit, (law) compétent.

cogwheel, n. roue d'engrenage f.

coherent, adj. cohérent.

cohesion, n. cohésion f.

cohesive, adj. cohésif.

cohort, n. cohorte f.

coiffure, n. coiffure f.

coil, n. rouleau m.

coin, n. pièce (f.) de monnaie.

coinage, n. monnayage m., monnaie f.

coincide, vb. coïncider.

coincidence, n. coïncidence f.

coincident, adj. coïncident.

coincidental, adj. coïncident, d'accord (avec).

coincidentally, adv. par coïncidence.

colander, n. passoire f.

cold, 1. n. (temperature) froid m.; (medical) rhume m. 2. adj. froid; (it is cold) il fait froid; (feel cold) avoir froid.

cold-blooded, adj. de sang froid.

coldly, adv. froidement.

coldness, n. froideur f.

collaborate, vb. collaborer.

collaboration, n. collaboration f.

collaborator, n. collaborateur m.

collapse, 1. n. effrondrement m.; (med.) affaissement m. 2. vb. s'effrondrer; (med.) s'affaisser.

collar, n. col m.; (dog) collier m.

collarbone, n. clavicule f.

collate, vb. collationner, comparer.

collateral, adj. and n. collatéral m.

collation, n. collation f., comparaison f., repas froid m.

colleague, n. collègue m.f.

collect, vb. rassembler.

collection, n. collection f.; (money) collecte f.

collective, adj. collectif.

collectively, adv. collectivement.

collector, n. (art) collectionneur m.; (tickets) contrôleur m.

college, n. collège m.; (higher education) université f.

collegiate, adj. de collège, collégial.

collide, vb. se heurter (contre).

colliery, n. houillère f., mine de charbon f.

collision, n. collision f.

colloquial, adj. familier.

colloquialism, n. expression de style familier f.

colloquially, adv. en style familier.

colloquy, n. colloque m., entretien m.

collusion, n. collusion f., connivence f.

colon, n. (gramm.) deux points m.pl.

colonel, n. colonel m.

colonial, adj. colonial.

colonist, n. colon m.

colonization, n. colonisation f.

colonize, vb. coloniser.

colony, n. colonie f.

color, 1. n. couleur f. 2. vb. colorer, tr.

coloration, n. coloris m.

colored, adj. coloré, de couleur, colorié.

colorful, adj. coloré, pittoresque.

coloring, n. coloris m., couleur f.

colorless, adj. sans couleur, incolore, terne.

colossal, adj. colossal.

colt, n. poulain m.

colter, n. coutre m.

column, n. colonne f.

columnist, n. journaliste (qui a sa rubrique à lui) m.

coma, n. coma m.

comb, 1. n. peigne m. 2. vb. peigner.

combat, n. combat m.

combatant, adj. and n. combattant m.

combative, adj. combatif.

combination, n. combinaison f.

combination lock, n. serrure à combinaisons f.

combine, vb. combiner, tr.

combustible, adj. and n. combustible m.

combustion, n. combustion f.

come, vb. venir; (c. about) arriver; (c. across) rencontrer; (c. away) partir; (c. back) revenir; (c. down) descendre; (c. in) entrer; (c. out) sortir; (c. up) monter.

comedian, n. comédien m.

comedienne, n. comédienne f.

comedy, n. comédie f.

comely, adj. avenant.

comet, n. comète f.

comfort, 1. n. (mental) consolation f.; (material) confort m. 2. vb. consoler.

comfortable, adj. commode.

comfortably, adv. confortablement, commodément.

comforter, n. consolateur m.

comfortingly, adv. d'une manière réconfortante.

comfortless, adj. sans consolation, inconsolable, désolé.

comic, comical, adj. comique.

comic strip, n. dessein comique m.

coming, n. venue f., arrivée f., approche f.

comma, n. virgule f.

command, 1. n. commandement m. 2. vb. commander (à).

commandeer, vb. réquisitionner.

commander, n. commandant m.

commander in chief, n. généralissime m.

commandment, n. commandement m.

commemorate, vb. commémorer.

commemoration, n. célébration f., commémoration f.

commemorative, adj. commémoratif.

commence, vb. commencer.

commencement, n. (school) distribution (f.) des diplômes.

commend, vb. (entrust) recommander; (praise) louer.

commendable, adj. louable, recommandable.

commendably, adv. d'une manière louable.

commendation, n. louange f.

commensurate, adj. proportionné.

comment, 1. n. commentaire m. 2. vb. commenter.

commentator, n. commentateur m.

commerce, n. commerce m.

commercial, adj. commercial.

commercialism, n. commercialisme m.

commercialize, vb. commercialiser.

commercially, adv. commercialement.

commiserate, vb. plaindre, avoir pitié de.

commissary, n. (person) commissaire m.; (supply store) dépôt (m.) de vivres.

commission, n. (assignment) commande f.; (officer) brevet m.; (committee, percentage) commission f.

commissioner, n. commissaire m.

commit, vb. commettre.

commitment, n. engagement m.

committee, n. comité m.

commodious, adj. spacieux.

commodity, n. produit m., commodité f., denrée f.

common, adj. commun; (vulgar) vulgaire.

common law, n. droit coutumier m.

commonly, adv. communément, ordinairement.

commonness, n. vulgarité f.

commonplace, n. lieu-commun m.

commonwealth, n. état m.

commotion, n. agitation f.

communal, adj. communal.

commune, n. commune f.

communicable, adj. communicable.

communicant, n. communiant m.

communicate, vb. communiquer.

communication, n. communication f.

communicative, adj. communicatif.

communion, n. communion f.

communiqué, n. communiqué m.

communism, n. communisme m.

communist, adj. and n. communiste m.f.

communistic, adj. communiste.

community, n. communauté f.

commutation, n. commutation f.

commute, vb. changer, (law) commuer.

commuter, n. voyageur de banlieue m.

compact, 1. n. (agreement) accord m.; (cosmetic) poudrier m. 2. adj. compact.

compactness, n. compacité f.

companion, n. compagnon m., compagne f.

companionable, adj. sociable.

companionship, n. camaraderie f.

company, n. compagnie f.

comparable with, adj. comparable à.

comparative, adj. and n. comparatif m.

comparatively, adv. comparativement, relativement.

compare, vb. comparer.

comparison, n. comparaison f.

compartment, n. compartiment m.

compass, n. (naut.) boussole f.; (geom.) compas m.

compassion, n. compassion f.

compassionate, adj. compatissant.

compassionately, adv. avec compassion.

compatible, adj. compatible.

compatriot, n. compatriote m.f.

compel, vb. forcer.

compensate, vb. compenser.

compensation, n. compensation f.

compensatory, adj. compensateur.

compete, vb. rivaliser.

competence, n. compétence f.

competent, adj. capable.

competently, adv. convenablement, avec compétence.

competition, n. concurrence f.

competitor, n. concurrent m.

compile, vb. compiler.

complacency, n. contentement (m.) de soi-même.

complacent, adj. content de soi-même.

complacently, adv. avec un air (un ton) suffisant.

complain, vb. se plaindre.

complainer, n. plaignant m., réclameur m.

complainingly, adv. d'une manière plaignante.

complaint, n. plainte f.

complement, n. complément m.

complete, adj. complet.

completely, adv. complètement, tout à fait.

completeness, n. état complet m., perfection f.

completion, n. achèvement m.

complex, adj. and n. complexe m.

complexion, n. teint m.

complexity, n. complexité f.

compliance, n. acquiescement m.

compliant, adj. complaisant, accommodant.

complicate, vb. compliquer.

complicated, adj. compliqué.

complication, n. complication f.

complicity, n. complicité f.

compliment, n. compliment m.

complimentary, adj. flatteur, de félicitations.

comply with, vb. se conformer à.

component, adj. and n. composant m.

comport, vb. s'accorder (avec), convenir (à).

compose, vb. composer.

composed, adj. composé, calme, tranquille.

composer, n. compositeur m.

composite, adj. composé.

composition, n. composition f.

compost, n. compost m., terreau m.

composure, n. calme m., tranquillité f, sang-froid m.

compote, n. compote f.

compound, 1. adj. and n. composé m. 2. vb. composer.

comprehend, vb. comprendre.

comprehensible, adj. compréhensible, intelligible.

comprehension, n. compréhension f.

comprehensive, adj. compréhensif.

compress, 1. n. compresse f. 2. vb. comprimer, tr.

compressed, adj. comprimé.

compression, n. compression f.

compressor, n. compresseur m.

comprise, vb. comprendre.

compromise, 1. n. compromis m. 2. vb. compromettre.

compromiser, n. comprometteur m.

compulsion, n. contrainte f.

compulsive, adj. coercitif, obligatoire.

compulsory, adj. obligatoire.

compunction, n. componction f.

computation, n. supputation f.

compute, vb. supputer.

computer, n. ordinateur m.

computerize, vb. informatiser.

computer science, n. informatique f.

comrade, n. camarade m.f.

comradeship, n. camaraderie f.

concave, adj. concave.

conceal, vb. cacher.

concealment, n. action (f.) de cacher.

concede, vb. concéder.

conceit, n. vanité f.

conceited, adj. vaniteux, suffisant.

conceivable, adj. concevable.

conceivably, adv. d'une manière concevable.

conceive, vb. concevoir.

concentrate, vb. concentrer tr.

concentration camp, n. camp de concentration m.

concept, n. concept m.

conception, n. conception f.

concern, 1. n. (what pertains to one) affaire f.; (comm.) entreprise f.; (solicitude) souci m. 2. vb. concerner; (c. oneself with) s'intéresser à; (be c.ed about) s'inquiéter de.

concerning, prep. concernant.

concert, n. concert m.

concerted, adj. concerté.

concession, n. concession f.

conciliate, vb. concilier.

conciliation, n. conciliation f.

conciliator, n. conciliateur m.

conciliatory, adj. conciliant, conciliatoire.

concise, adj. concis.

concisely, adv. avec concision, succinctement.

conciseness, n. concision f.

conclave, n. conclave m.

conclude, vb. conclure.

conclusion, n. conclusion f.

conclusive, adj. concluant.

conclusively, adv. d'une manière concluante.

concoct, vb. préparer.

concomitant, 1. adj. concomitant. 2. n. accessoire m.

concord, n. concorde f.

concordat, n. concordat m.

concourse, n. concours m., affluence f.

concrete, 1. n. béton m. 2. adj. concret.

concretely, adv. d'une manière concrète.

concreteness, n. état concret m.

concubine, n. concubine f.

concur, vb. (events) concourir; (persons) être d'accord.

concurrence, n. assentiment m., concours m.

concurrent, adj. concourant.

concussion, n. secousse f., ébranlement m.

condemn, vb. condamner.

condemnable, adj. condamnable.

condemnation, n. condamnation f.

condensation, n. condensation f.

condense, vb. condenser, tr.

condenser, n. condenseur m.

condescend, vb. condescendre.

condescendingly, adv. avec condescendance.

condescension, n. condescendance f.

condiment, n. condiment m., assaisonnement m.

condition, 1. n. condition f. 2. vb. conditionner.

conditional, adj. and n. conditionnel m.

conditionally, adv. conditionnellement.
condolence, n. condoléance f.
condole with, vb. faire ses condoléances à.
condominium, n. condominium m.
conducive, adj. favorable.
conduct, 1. n. conduite f. **2.** vb. conduire.
conductivity, n. conductivité f.
conductor, n. conducteur m.; (bus) receveur m.; (rail) chef (m.) de train; (music) chef (m.) d'orchestre.
conduit, n. conduit m., tuyau m.
cone, n. cône m.
confection, n. confection f.; (sweet) bonbon m.
confectioner, n. confiseur m.
confectionery, n. confiserie f.
confederacy, confederation, n. confédération f.
confederate, adj. and n. confédéré m.
confer, vb. conférer.
conference, n. (meeting) entretien m.; (congress) congrès m.
confess, vb. avouer; (eccles.) confesser, tr.
confession, n. confession f.
confessional, n. confessional m.
confessor, n. confesseur m.
confetti, n. confetti m.
confidant, n. confident m.
confidante, n. confidente f.
confide, vb. confier (à), tr.
confidence, n. (trust) confiance f.; (secret) confidence f.
confident, adj. confiant.
confidential, adj. confidentiel.
confidentially, adv. confidentiellement.
confidently, adv. avec confiance.
confine, vb. (banish) confiner; (limit) limiter.
confirm, vb. confirmer.
confirmation, n. confirmation f.
confirmed, adj. invétéré, incorrigible.
confiscate, vb. confisquer.
confiscation, n. confiscation f.
conflagration, n. conflagration f., incendie m.
conflict, n. conflit m.
conform, vb. conformer, tr.
conformation, n. conformation f., conformité f.
conformer, n. conformiste m.
conformist, n. conformiste m.
conformity, n. conformité f.
confound, vb. confondre; (c. him!) que le diable l'emporte!
confront, vb. confronter.
confuse, vb. confondre.
confusion, n. confusion f.
congeal, vb. congeler, tr.
congealment, n. congélation f.
congenial, adj. (person) sympathique; (thing) convenable.
congenital, adj. congénital.

congenitally, adv. d'une manière congénitale.
congestion, n. (med.) congestion f.; (traffic) encombrement m.
conglomerate, adj. congloméré.
conglomeration, n. conglomération f.
congratulate, vb. féliciter (de).
congratulation, n. félicitation f.
congratulatory, adj. de félicitation.
congregate, vb. rassembler, tr.
congregation, n. assemblée f.
congress, n. congrès m.
congressional, adj. congressionnel.
conic, adj. conique.
conjecture, n. conjecture f.
conjugal, adj. conjugal.
conjugate, vb. conjuguer.
conjugation, n. conjugaison f.
conjunction, n. conjonction f.
conjunctive, adj. conjonctif.
conjunctivitis, n. conjonctivite f.
conjure, vb. conjurer.
connect, vb. joindre.
connection, n. connexion f.; (social) relations f.pl.; (train) correspondance f.
connivance, n. connivence f.
connive, vb. conniver (à).
connoisseur, n. connaisseur m.
connotation, n. connotation f.
connote, vb. signifier, vouloir dire.
connubial, adj. conjugal, du mariage.
conquer, vb. conquérir.
conquerable, adj. qui peut être vaincu, domptable.
conqueror, n. conquérant m.
conquest, n. conquête f.
conscience, n. conscience f.
conscientious, adj. consciencieux.
conscientiously, adv. consciencieusement.
conscious, adj. conscient.
consciously, adv. sciemment, en parfaite connaissance.
consciousness, n. conscience f.
conscript, adj. and n. conscrit m.
conscription, n. conscription f.
consecrate, vb. consacrer.
consecration, n. consécration f.
consecutive, adj. consécutif.
consecutively, adv. consécutivement, de suite.
consensus, n. consensus m., assentiment général m.
consent, 1. n. consentement m. **2.** vb. consentir.
consequence, n. conséquence f.
consequent, adj. conséquent.
consequential, adj. conséquent, logique.
consequently, adv. par conséquent.
conservation, n. conservation f.

conservatism, n. conservatisme m.
conservative, adj. (politics) conservateur; (comm.) prudent.
conservatively, adv. d'une manière conservatrice.
conservatory, n. conservatoire m.
conserve, vb. conserver.
consider, vb. considérer.
considerable, adj. considérable.
considerably, adv. considérablement.
considerate, adj. plein d'égards.
considerately, adv. avec égards, avec indulgence.
consideration, n. considération f.
considering, prep. vu que, attendu que.
consign, vb. consigner.
consignment, n. expédition f., consignation f.
consistency, n. consistance f.
consistent, adj. consistant.
consist of, vb. consister en.
consolation, n. consolation f.
console, vb. consoler.
consolidate, vb. consolider.
consommé, n. consommé m.
consonant, n. consonne f.
consort, 1. n. compagnon m., époux m. **2.** vb. s'associer (à).
conspicuous, adj. en évidence.
conspicuously, adv. visiblement, éminemment.
conspicuousness, n. éclat m., position éminente f.
conspiracy, n. conspiration f.
conspirator, n. conspirateur m.
conspire, vb. conspirer.
conspirer, n. conspirateur m.
constancy, n. constance f., fermeté f.
constant, adj. constant.
constantly, adv. constamment.
constellation, n. constellation f.
consternation, n. consternation f.
constipation, n. constipation f.
constituency, n. circonscription électorale f.
constituent, adj. constituant.
constitute, vb. constituer.
constitution, n. constitution f.
constitutional, adj. constitutionnel.
constrain, vb. contraindre.
constrained, adj. contraint.
constraint, n. contrainte f., gêne f.
constrict, vb. resserrer.
construct, vb. construire.
construction, n. construction f.
constructive, adj. constructif.
constructively, adv. constructivement, par induction.
constructor, n. constructeur m.
construe, vb. interpréter.
consul, n. consul m.
consular, adj. consulaire.

consulate, *n.* consulat *m.*

consult, *vb.* consulter.

consultant, *n.* conseiller *m.*

consultation, *n.* consultation *f.*

consume, *vb.* consumer.

consumer, *n.* consommateur *m.*

consummate, **1.** *adj.* consommé. **2.** *vb.* consommer.

consummation, *n.* consommation *f.*

consumption, *n.* consommation *f.;* (*med.*) phtisie *f.*

consumptive, *adj.* poitrinaire, tuberculeux.

contact, *n.* contact *m.*

contagion, *n.* contagion *f.*

contagious, *adj.* contagieux.

contain, *vb.* contenir.

container, *n.* récipient *m.*

contaminate, *vb.* contaminer.

contaminated, *adj.* contaminé.

contemplate, *vb.* contempler.

contemplation, *n.* contemplation *f.*

contemplative, *adj.* contemplatif.

contemporary, *adj.* contemporain.

contempt, *n.* mépris *m.*

contemptible, *adj.* méprisable.

contemptuous, *adj.* méprisant.

contemptuously, *adv.* avec mépris, dédaigneusement.

contend, *vb.* (struggle) lutter; (maintain) soutenir.

contender, *n.* compétiteur *m.,* concurrent *m.*

content, *n.* (satisfaction) contentement *m.;* (c.s) contenu *m.*

contented with, *adj.* content de.

contention, *n.* contention *f.,* lutte *f.*

contentment, *n.* contentement *m.*

contest, **1.** *n.* (struggle) lutte *f.;* (competition) concours *m.* **2.** *vb.* contester.

contestable, *adj.* contestable.

contestant, *n.* concurrent *m.,* disputant *m.*

context, *n.* contexte *m.*

contiguous, *adj.* contigu.

continence, *n.* continence *f.,* retenue *f.*

continent, *adj. and n.* continent *m.*

continental, *adj.* continental.

contingency, *n.* contingence *f.*

contingent, *adj.* contingent.

continual, *adj.* continuel.

continuation, *n.* continuation *f.*

continue, *vb.* continuer.

continuity, *n.* continuité *f.*

continuous, *adj.* continu.

continuously, *adv.* continûment, sans interruption.

contort, *vb.* tordre, défigurer.

contortionist, *n.* contortionniste *m.*

contour, *n.* contour *m.*

contraband, *n.* contrebande *f.*

contraception, *n.* limitation des naissances *f.*

contract, **1.** *n.* contrat *m.* **2.** *vb.* contracter, *tr.*

contracted, *adj.* contracté, resserré.

contraction, *n.* contraction *f.*

contractor, *n.* entrepreneur *m.*

contradict, *vb.* contredire.

contradictable, *adj.* qui peut être contredit.

contradiction, *n.* contradiction *f.,* démenti *m.*

contradictory, *adj.* contradictoire.

contraption, *n.* machin *m.*

contrary, *adj. and n.* contraire *m.;* (on the c.) au contraire.

contrast, **1.** *n.* contraste *m.* **2.** *vb.* mettre en contraste, *tr.;* contraster, *intr.*

contribute, *vb.* contribuer.

contribution, *n.* contribution *f.*

contributive, *adj.* contributif.

contributor, *n.* contribuant *m.*

contributory, *adj.* contribuant.

contrite, *adj.* contrit, pénitent.

contrition, *n.* contrition *f.*

contrivance, *n.* combinaison *f.,* invention *f.,* artifice *m.*

contrive, *vb.* inventer, imaginer, arranger.

control, **1.** *n.* autorité *f.;* (machinery) commande *f.* **2.** *vb.* gouverner; (check) contrôler.

controllable, *adj.* vérifiable, gouvernable.

controller, *n.* contrôleur *m.*

controversial, *adj.* de controverse, polémique.

controversy, *n.* controverse *f.*

contusion, *n.* contusion *f.*

conundrum, *n.* devinette *f.,* énigme *f.*

convalescence, *n.* convalescence *f.*

convalescent, *adj.* convalescent.

convene, *vb.* assembler, *tr.*

convenience, *n.* convenance *f.;* (comfort) commodité *f.*

convenient, *adj.* commode.

conveniently, *adv.* commodément.

convent, *n.* couvent *m.*

convention, *n.* convention *f.*

conventional, *adj.* conventionnel.

conventionally, *adv.* par convention.

converge, *vb.* converger.

convergence, *n.* convergence *f.*

convergent, *adj.* convergent.

conversant, *adj.* versé (dans), familier (avec).

conversation, *n.* conversation *f.*

conversational, *adj.* de conversation.

conversationalist, *n.* causeur *m.*

converse, *vb.* converser.

conversely, *adv.* réciproquement.

convert, *vb.* convertir, *tr.*

converter, *n.* convertisseur *m.*

convertible, *adj.* convertible (of things), convertissable (of persons).

convex, *adj.* convexe.

convey, *vb.* (transport) transporter; (transmit) transmettre.

conveyance, *n.* transport *m.*

conveyor, *n.* transporteur *m.,* conducteur (électrique) *m.*

convict, **1.** *n.* forçat *m.* **2.** *vb.* condamner.

conviction, *n.* (condemnation) condamnation *f.;* (persuasion) conviction *f.*

convince, *vb.* convaincre.

convincing, *adj.* convaincant.

convincingly, *adv.* d'une manière convaincante.

convivial, *adj.* jovial, joyeux.

convocation, *n.* convocation *f.*

convoke, *vb.* convoquer.

convoy, *n.* convoi *m.*

convulse, *vb.* convulser, bouleverser.

convulsion, *n.* convulsion *f.*

convulsive, *adj.* convulsif.

cook, **1.** *n.* cuisinier *m.* **2.** *vb.* cuire, *intr.;* faire cuire, *tr.*

cookbook, *n.* livre de cuisine *m.*

cookie, *n.* gâteau sec *m.*

cool, *adj.* frais *m.,* fraîche *f.*

cooler, *n.* rafraîchissoir *m.,* réfrigérant *m.,* (motor) radiateur *m.*

coolness, *n.* fraîcheur *f.*

coop, *n.* cage (*f.*) à poules.

coöperate, *vb.* coopérer.

coöperation, *n.* coopération *f.*

coöperative, **1.** *n.* coopérative *f.* **2.** *adj.* coopératif.

coöperatively, *adj.* d'une manière coopérative.

coördinate, *vb.* coordonner.

coördination, *n.* coordination *f.*

coördinator, *n.* coordinateur *m.*

cop, **1.** *n.* (slang) flic *m.* **2.** *vb.* (colloquial) attraper, pincer.

cope with, *vb.* tenir tête à.

copier, *n.* machine à copier *f.*

copious, *adj.* copieux.

copiously, *adv.* copieusement.

copiousness, *n.* abondance *f.*

copper, *n.* cuivre *m.*

copperplate, *n.* cuivre plané *m.;* taille-douce *f.*

copy, **1.** *n.* copie *f.* **2.** *vb.* copier.

copyist, *n.* copiste *m.,* imitateur *m.*

copyright, *n.* droit (*m.*) d'auteur.

coquetry, *n.* coquetterie *f.*

coquette, *n.* coquette *f.*

coral, *n.* corail *m.; pl.* coraux.

cord, *n.* corde *f.*

cordial, *adj. and n.* cordial *m.*

cordiality, *n.* cordialité *f.*

cordially, *adv.* cordialement.

cordon, *n.* cordon *m.*

cordovan, *adj.* cordovan.

corduroy, m. velours côtelé m.

core, n. cœur m.

cork, n. (botany) liège m.; (stopper) bouchon m.

corkscrew, n. tire-bouchon m.

corn, n. maïs m.

cornea, n. cornée f.

corner, n. coin m.

cornerstone, n. pierre angulaire f.

cornet, n. cornet m.

cornetist, n. cornettiste m.

cornice, n. corniche f.

cornucopia, n. corne d'abondance f.

corollary, n. corollaire m.

coronary, adj. coronaire.

coronation, n. couronnement m.

coroner, n. coroner m.

coronet, n. (petite) couronne f.

corporal, n. (mil.) caporal m.

corporate, adj. de corporation.

corporation, n. corporation f.

corps, n. corps m.

corpse, n. cadavre m.

corpulent, adj. corpulent, gros.

corpuscle, n. corpuscule m.

corral, n. corral m.

correct, 1. adj. correct. 2. vb. corriger.

correction, n. correction f.

corrective, 1. adj. correctif. 2. n. correctif m.

correctly, adv. correctement, justement.

correctness, n. correction f.

correlate, vb. être en corrélation, intr.; mettre en corrélation, tr.

correlation, n. corrélation f.

correspond, vb. correspondre.

correspondence, n. correspondance f.

correspondent, n. correspondant m.

corridor, n. couloir m.

corroborate, vb. corroborer.

corroboration, n. corroboration f., confirmation f.

corroborative, adj. coroboratif.

corrode, vb. corroder.

corrosion, n. corrosion f.

corrugate, vb. rider, plisser.

corrupt, 1. adj. corrompu. 2. vb. corrompre.

corruptible, adj. corruptible.

corruption, n. corruption f.

corruptive, adj. corruptif.

corsage, n. corsage m.

corset, n. corset m.

cortege, n. cortège m.

corvette, n. corvette f.

cosmetic, adj. and n. cosmétique m.

cosmic, adj. cosmique.

cosmic rays, n. rayons cosmiques m.pl.

cosmopolitan, adj. and n. cosmopolite m.f.

cosmos, n. cosmos m.

cost, 1. n. coût m. 2. vb. coûter.

costliness, n. haut prix m., somptuosité f.

costly, adj. coûteux.

costume, n. costume m.

costumer, n. costumier m.

cot, n. (berth) couchette f.; (folding) lit-cage m.

coterie, n. coterie f., clique f.

cotillion, n. cotillon m.

cottage, n. chaumière f.

cotton, n. coton m.

cottonseed, n. graine de coton f.

couch, n. divan m.

cougar, n. couguar m.

cough, 1. n. toux f. 2. vb. tousser.

could, vb. pouvait, pourrait.

council, n. conseil m.

councilman, n. conseiller m.

counsel, 1. n. conseil m. 2. vb. conseiller.

counselor, n. conseiller m.

count, 1. n. (calculation) compte m.; (title) comte m. 2. vb. compter.

countenance, n. expression f.

counter, 1. n. (shop) comptoir m. 2. adv. (c. to) à l'encontre de.

counteract, vb. neutraliser.

counteraction, n. action contraire f.

counterattack, n. contre-attaque f.

counterbalance, 1. n. contrepoids m. 2. vb. contre-balancer.

counterfeit, 1. adj. (money) faux m., fausse f. 2. vb. contrefaire.

countermand, vb. contremander.

counteroffensive, n. contre-offensive f.

counterpart, n. contre-partie f.

countess, n. comtesse f.

countless, adj. innombrable.

country, n. (nation) pays m.; (opposed to town) campagne f.; (native c.) patrie f.

countryman, n. (of same c.) compatriote m.f.; (rustic) campagnard m.

county, n. comté m.

coupé, n. coupé m.

couple, 1. n. couple f. 2. vb. coupler.

coupon, n. coupon m.

courage, n. courage m.

courageous, adj. courageux.

courier, n. courrier m.

course, n. cours m.; (of c.) bien entendu; (route) route f.; (meal) service m.

court, 1. n. cour f. 2. vb. faire la cour à.

courteous, adj. courtois.

courtesy, n. courtoisie f.

courthouse, n. palais de justice m.

courtier, n. courtisan m.

courtly, adj. de cour, élégant, courtois.

courtmartial, n. conseil de guerre m.

courtroom, n. salle d'audience f.

courtship, n. cour f.

courtyard, n. cour f.

cousin, n. cousin m., cousine f.

covenant, n. pacte m.

cover, 1. n. (book, comm., blanket) couverture f.; (pot) couvercle m.; (shelter) abri m.; (envelope) pli m.; (mil.) couvert m. 2. vb. couvrir.

coverage, n. couverture f.

covering, n. couverture f., enveloppe f.

covet, vb. convoiter.

covetous, adj. avide, avaricieux.

cow, n. vache f.

coward, adj. lâche.

cowardice, n. lâcheté f.

cowboy, n. (U.S.A.) cowboy m.

cower, vb. se blottir.

cow hand, n. vacher m.

cowhide, n. peau (f.) de vache.

coxswain, n. patron de chaloupe m., barreur m.

coy, adj. timide.

cozy, adj. confortable.

crab, n. crabe m.

crab apple, n. pomme sauvage f.

crack, 1. n. (fissure) fente f.; (noise) craquement m. 2. vb. tr. (glass, china) fêler; (nuts) casser; (noise) faire craquer. 3. vb. intr. (split) se fendiller; (noise) craquer.

cracked, adj. fendu, fêlé.

cracker, n. biscuit m.

cracking, n. craquement m., claquement m.

crackup, n. crach m.

cradle, n. berceau m.

craft, n. (skill) habileté f.; (trade) métier m.; (boat) embarcation f.

craftsman, n. artisan m.

craftsmanship, n. habileté, technique f.

crafty, adj. rusé, astucieux.

crag, n. rocher à pic m., rocher escarpé m.

cram, vb. remplir, farcir.

cramp, n. (med.) crampe f.; (mechanical) crampon m.

cranberry, n. canneberge f., airelle f.

crane, n. grue f.

cranium, n. crâne m.

crank, n. manivelle f.

cranky, adj. d'humeur difficile.

cranny, n. crevasse f., fente f.

craps, n. (slang) jeu de dés m.

crapshooter, n. (slang) joueur aux dés m.

crash, 1. n. (noise) fracas m.; (accident) accident m. 2. vb. tomber avec fracas, intr.

crate, n. caisse f.

crater, n. cratère m.

crave for, vb. désirer ardemment.

craven, adj. lâche, poltron.

craving, n. désir ardent m., besoin impérieux m.

crawl, vb. (reptiles) ramper; (persons) se traîner.

crayon, n. pastel m.

crazed, adj. fou, dément.

crazy, adj. fou m., folle f.

creak, vb. grincer.

creaky, adj. qui crie, qui grince.

cream, n. crème f.

creamery, n. crèmerie f.

creamy, adj. crèmeux, de crème.

crease, 1. n. pli m. 2. vb. froisser, tr.

create, vb. créer.

creation, n. création f.

creative, adj. créateur m., créatrice f.

creator, n. créateur m., créatrice f.

creature, n. créature f.

credence, n. créance f., croyance f.

credentials, n. lettres (f.pl.) de créance; (student, servant) certificat m.

credibility, n. crédibilité f.

credible, adj. croyable.

credit, n. crédit m.; (merit) honneur m.

creditable, adj. estimable.

creditably, adv. honorablement.

credit card, n. carte de crédit f.

creditor, n. créancier m.

credo, n. credo m.

credulity, n. crédulité f.

credulous, adj. crédule.

creed, n. (belief) croyance f., (theology) credo m.

creek, n. ruisseau m.

creep, vb. (reptiles, insects, plants) ramper; (persons) se glisser.

cremate, vb. incinérer.

crematory, n. crématorium m.

creosote, n. créosote f.

crepe, n. crêpe m.

crescent, n. croissant m.

crest, n. crête f.

crestfallen, adj. abattu, découragé.

cretonne, n. cretonne f.

crevice, n. crevasse f.

crew, n. (boat) équipage m.; (gang) équipe f.

crib, n. (child's bed) lit (m.) d'enfant; (manger) mangeoire f.

cricket, n. (insect) grillon m.; (game) cricket m.

crier, n. crieur m., huissier m.

crime, n. crime m.

criminal, adj. criminel.

criminologist, n. criminologue m.

criminology, n. criminologie f.

crimson, adj. and n. cramoisi m.

cringe, vb. faire des courbettes, se tapir, s'humilier.

crinkle, 1. n. pli m., sinuosité f. 2. vb. serpenter, former en zigzag.

cripple, 1. n. estropié m. 2. vb. estropier.

crisis, n. crise f.

crisp, adj. (food) croquant; (manner) tranchant.

crispness, n. frisure f.

crisscross, adj. and adv. entrecroisé.

criterion, n. critérium m.

critic, n. critique m.

critical, adj. critique.

criticism, n. critique f.

criticize, vb. critiquer.

critique, n. critique f.

croak, vb. (frogs) coasser; (crows, persons) croasser.

crochet, 1. vb. broder au crochet. 2. m. crochet f.

crock, n. pot (m.) de terre.

crockery, n. faïence f.

crocodile, n. crocodile m.

crocodile tears, n. larmes de crocodiles f.pl.

crone, n. vieille femme f.

crony, n. vieux camarade m., compère m.

crook, n. (thief) escroc m., voleur m.

crooked, adj. tortu.

croon, vb. chantonner, fredonner.

crop, n. récolte f.

croquet, n. (jeu de) croquet m.

croquette, n. croquette f.

cross, 1. n. croix f. 2. adj. maussade. 3. vb. croiser, tr.; (c. oneself) se signer; (c. out) rayer; (go across) traverser.

crossbreed, n. race croisée f.

cross-examine, vb. contre-examiner.

cross-eye, adj. louche.

cross-fertilization, n. croisement m.

cross-purpose, n. opposition f., contradiction f., malentendu m.

cross section, n. coupe en travers f.

crossword puzzle, n. mots croisés m.pl.

crotch, n. fourche f., fourchet m.

crouch, vb. s'accroupir.

croup, n. croupe f.; (med.) croup m.

croupier, n. croupier m.

crouton, n. crouton m.

crow, 1. n. (bird) corneille f.; (cock-c.) chant (m.) du coq. 2. vb. chanter.

crowd, n. foule f.

crowd, vb. serrer, tr.; (c. with) remplir de.

crowded, adj. (streets, etc.) encombré.

crown, 1. n. couronne f.; (of head) sommet m.; (of hat) calotte f. 2. vb. couronner.

crown prince, n. prince héritier m.

crow's-foot, n. patte d'oie (near the eye) f.; (naut.) araignée f.

crucial, adj. crucial.

crucible, n. creuset m.

crucifix, n. crucifix m.

crucifixion, n. crucifixion f., crucifiement m.

crucify, vb. crucifier.

crude, adj. (unpolished) grossier; (metals, etc.) brut.

crudeness, n. crudité f.

cruel, adj. cruel.

cruelty, n. cruauté f.

cruet, n. burette f.

cruise, n. croisière f.

cruiser, n. croiseur m.

crumb, n. (small piece) miette f.; (not crust) mie f.

crumble, vb. émietter, tr.

crumple, vb. chiffonner, tr.

crunch, 1. vb. croquer, broyer, 2. n. grincement m.

crusade, n. croisade f.

crusader, n. croisé m.

crush, vb. écraser.

crust, n. croûte f.

crustacean, adj. crustacé.

crusty, adj. couvert d'une croûte; (fig.) bourru, maussade.

crutch, n. béquille f.

cry, 1. n. cri m. 2. vb. (shout) crier; (weep) pleurer.

crying, adj. criant.

cryosurgery, n. cryochirurgie f.

crypt, n. crypte f.

cryptic, adj. occulte, secret.

cryptography, n. cryptographie f.

crystal, n. cristal m.

crystalline, adj. cristallin.

crystallize, vb. cristalliser, tr.

cub, n. petit m. (d'un animal).

Cuba, n. Cuba m.

Cuban, 1. n. Cubain m. 2. adj. cubain.

cubbyhole, n. retraite f., cachette f., placard m.

cube, n. cube m.

cubic, adj. cubique.

cubicle, n. compartiment m., cabine f.

cubic measure, n. mesures de volume f.pl.

cubism, n. cubisme m.

cuckoo, n. coucou m.; (fig.) niais m.

cucumber, n. concombre m.

cud, n. bol alimentaire m., panse f., chique (of tobacco) f.

cuddle, vb. serrer (dans ses bras).

cudgel, 1. n. bâton m., gourdin m., trique f. 2. vb. bâtonner.

cue, n. (theater) réplique f.; (hint) mot m.

cuff, n. poignet m.

cuisine, n. cuisine f.

culinary, adj. culinaire, de cuisine.

cull, vb. cueillir, recueillir.

culminate, vb. culminer.

culmination, n. point culminant m.

culpable, adj. coupable.

culprit, n. coupable m.f.

cult, n. culte m.

cultivate, vb. cultiver.

cultivated, adj. cultivé.

cultivation, n. culture f.

cultivator, n. cultivateur m.

cultural, adj. cultural.

culture, n. culture f.

cumbersome, adj. encombrant.

cumulative, adj. cumulatif.

cunning, 1. n. (guile) ruse f.; (skill) adresse f. 2. adj. rusé; (attractive) charmant.

cup, n. tasse f.

cupboard, n. armoire f.

cupidity, n. cupidité f.

curable, adj. guérissable.

curator, n. conservateur m.

curb, 1. n. (horse) gourmette f.; (pavement) bord m. 2. vb. (horse) gourmer; (fig.) brider.

curbstone, n. garde-pavé m.

curd, n. lait caillé m.

curdle, vb. cailler.

cure, 1. n. (healing) guérison f.; (remedy) remède m. 2. vb. guérir.

curfew, n. couvre-feu m.

curio, n. curiosité f.

curiosity, n. curiosité f.

curious, adj. curieux.

curl, 1. n. boucle f. 2. vb. friser.

curly, adj. frisé.

currant, n. groseille f.

currency, n. monnaie f.

current, adj. and n. courant m.

currently, adv. couramment.

curriculum, n. programme d'études m., plan d'études m.

curry, n. cari m.

curse, 1. n. (malediction) malédiction f.; (oath) juron m.; (scourge) fléau m. 2. vb. maudire; (swear) jurer.

cursed, adj. maudit.

cursory, adj. rapide, superficiel.

curt, adj. brusque.

curtail, vb. raccourcir.

curtain, n. rideau m.

curtsy, n. révérence f.

curvature, n. courbure f.

curve, 1. n. courbe f. 2. vb. courber, tr.

cushion, n. coussin m.

cuspidor, n. crachoir m.

custard, n. crème f.

custodian, n. gardien m.

custody, n. (care) garde f.; (arrest) détention f.

custom, n. coutume f.

customary, adj. habituel.

customer, n. client m.

custom-house, customs, n. douane f.

customs-officer, n. douanier f.

cut, 1. n. (wound) coupure f.; (clothes, hair) coupe f.; (reduction) réduction f. 2. vb. couper.

cutaneous, adj. cutané.

cute, adj. gentil m., gentille f.

cut glass, n. cristal m.

cuticle, n. cuticule f.

cutlery, n. coutellerie f.

cutlet, n. côtelette f.

cutout, n. découpage m., coupe f.

cutter, n. coupeur m., coupeuse f.

cutthroat, n. coupe-jarret m.

cutting, 1. n. incision f. 2. adj. incisif, tranchant.

cyclamate, n. cyclamate m.

cycle, 1. n. cycle m. 2. vb. faire de la bicyclette.

cyclist, n. cycliste m.

cyclone, n. cyclone m.

cyclotron, n. cyclotron m.

cylinder, n. cylindre m.

cylindrical, adj. cylindrique.

cymbal, n. cymbale f.

cynic, n. cynique m.

cynical, adj. cynique.

cynicism, n. cynisme m.

cypress, n. cyprès m.

cyst, n. kyste m.

D

dab, 1. n. coup léger m., tape f. 2. vb. toucher légèrement.

dabble, vb. humecter, faire l'amateur.

dad, n. papa m.

daffodil, n. narcisse m.

daffy, adj. niais, sot.

dagger, n. poignard m.

dahlia, n. dahlia m.

daily, adj. quotidien.

daintiness, n. délicatesse f.

dainty, adj. délicat.

dairy, n. laiterie f.

dairyman, n. crémier m.

dais, n. estrade f.

daisy, n. marguerite f.

dale, n. vallon m., vallée f.

dam, n. digue f.

damage, 1. n. dommage m. 2. vb. endommager.

damask, n. damas m.

damnation, n. damnation f.

damp, adj. humide.

dampen, vb. humecter.

dampness, n. humidité f., moiteur f.

damsel, n. demoiselle f., jeune fille f.

dance, 1. n. danse f. 2. vb. danser.

dancer, n. danseur m.

dandelion, n. pissenlit m.

dandruff, n. pellicules f.pl.

dandy, 1. n. dandy m. 2. adj. élégant.

danger, n. danger m.

dangerous, adj. dangereux.

dangle, vb. pendiller, intr.

Dane, n. Danois m.

Danish, adj. and n. danois m.

dapper, adj. pimpant, petit et vif.

dappled, adj. pommelé.

dare, vb. oser.

daredevil, n. casse-cou m.

daring, adj. audacieux.

dark, adj. sombre.

darken, vb. obscurcir, tr.

dark horse, n. tocard m.

darkness, n. obscurité f.

darkroom, n. chambre noire f.

darling, 1. n. adj. and n. chéri m.

darn, 1. n. reprise f. 2. vb. repriser.

darning needle, n. aiguille à repriser f.

dart, 1. n. dard m.; (sewing) pince f. 2. vb. se précipiter.

dash, 1. n. (energy) fougue f.; (pen) trait m. 2. vb. (throw) lancer; (destroy) détruire; (rush) se précipiter.

dashboard, n. tablier m.

dashing, adj. fougueux, brillant, superbe.

data, n. données f.pl.

data processing, n. élaboration f.

date, 1. n. date f.; (appointment) rendez-vous m.; (fruit) datte f. 2. vb. dater.

date line, n. ligne de changement de date f.

daub, 1. n. barbouillage m. 2. vb. barbouiller.

daughter, n. fille f.

daughter-in-law, n. belle-fille f.

daunt, vb intimider.

dauntless, adj. intrépide, indomptable.

dauntlessly, adv. d'une manière intrépide.

davenport, n. divan m.

dawdle, vb. flâner, muser.

dawn, n. aube f.

day, n. jour m.; (span of day) journée f.

daydream, n. rêverie f.

daylight, n. lumière (f.) du jour.

daylight-saving time, n. l'heure d'été f.

daze, vb. étourdir.

dazzle, vb. éblouir.

deacon, n. diacre m.

dead, adj. mort.

deaden, vb. amortir.

dead end, n. cul de sac m., impasse f.

dead letter, n. lettre morte f.

deadline, n. ligne de délimitation f.

deadlock, n. impasse f.

deadly, adj. mortel.

deadwood, n. bois mort m.

deaf, adj. sourd.

deafen, vb. assourdir.

deaf-mute, adj. sourd-muet.

deafness, n. surdité f.

deal, 1. n. (great d.) beaucoup; (business) affair f.; (cards) donne f. 2. vb. (d. with) traiter; (d. out) distribuer.

dealer, n. marchand m.

dean, n. doyen m.

dear, adj. and n. cher m.

dearly, adv. chèrement.

dearth, n. disette f.

death, n. mort f.

deathless, adj. impérissable.

deathly, adj. mortel.

debacle, n. débâcle f.

debase, vb. avilir.

debatable, adj. discutable.

debate, 1. n. débat m. **2.** vb. discuter.

debater, n. orateur parlementaire m., argumentateur m.

debauch, 1. n. débauche f. **2.** vb. débaucher, corrompre.

debenture, n. obligation f.

debilitate, vb. débiliter, affaiblir.

debit, n. débit m.

debonair, adj. courtois et jovial.

debris, n. débris m.pl.

debt, n. dette f.

debtor, n. débiteur m.

debunk, vb. dégonfler.

debut, n. début m.

debutante, n. débutante f.

decade, n. période (f.) de dix ans.

decadence, n. décadence f.

decadent, adj. décadent.

decaffeinated, adj. décaféiné.

decalcomania, m. décalcomanie f.

decanter, n. carafe f.

decapitate, vb. décapiter.

decay, 1. n. décadence f.; (state of ruin) délabrement m.; (teeth) carie f. **2.** vb. tomber en décadence.

deceased, adj. défunt.

deceit, n. tromperie f.

deceitful, adj. trompeur.

deceive, vb. tromper.

deceiver, n. imposteur.

December, n. décembre m.

decency, n. décence f.

decent, adj. décent.

decentralization, n. décentralisation f.

decentralize, vb. décentraliser.

deception, n. tromperie f., duperie f.

deceptive, adj. décevant, trompeur.

decibel, n. décibel m.

decide, vb. décider.

decided, adj. décidé, prononcé.

deciduous, adj. à feuillage caduc.

decimal, adj. décimal.

decimate, vb. décimer.

decipher, vb. déchiffrer.

decision, n. décision f.

decisive, adj. décisif.

deck, n. (boat) pont m.; (cards) paquet m.

deck hand, n. matelot de pont m.

declaim, vb. déclamer.

declamation, n. déclamation f.

declaration, n. déclaration f.

declarative, adj. explicatif, (law) déclaratif.

declare, vb. déclarer.

declension, n. déclinaison f.

decline, vb. décliner.

decode, vb. déchiffrer.

décolleté, adj. décolleté.

decompose, vb. décomposer, tr.

decongestant, adj. décongestionnant.

decor, n. décor m.

decorate, vb. décorer.

decoration, n. décoration f.

decorative, adj. décoratif.

decorator, n. décorateur m.

decorous, adj. bienséant, convenable.

decorum, n. décorum m.

decoy, 1. n. leurre m. **2.** vb. leurrer.

decrease, 1. n. diminution f. **2.** vb. diminuer.

decree, n. décret m.

decrepit, adj. décrépit.

decry, vb. décrier, dénigrer.

dedicate, vb. dédier.

dedication, n. dédicace f.

deduce, vb. déduire.

deduct, vb. déduire.

deduction, n. déduction f.

deductive, adj. déductif.

deed, n. action f.; (law) acte (m.) notarié.

deem, vb. juger.

deep, adj. profond.

deepen, vb. approfondir, tr.

deep freeze, n. surgélateur m.

deeply, adv. profondément.

deep-rooted, adj. enraciné.

deer, n. cerf m.

deerskin, n. peau de daim f.

deface, vb. défigurer.

defamation, n. diffamation f.

defame, vb. diffamer.

default, n. défaut m.

defeat, 1. n. défaite f. **2.** vb. vaincre.

defeatism, n. défaitisme m.

defect, n. défaut m.

defection, n. défection f.

defective, adj. défectueux.

defend, vb. défendre.

defendant, n. défendeur m.

defender, n. défenseur m.

defense, n. défense f.

defenseless, adj. sans défense.

defensible, adj. défendable, soutenable.

defensive, adj. défensif.

defer, vb. (put off) différer; (show deference) déférer.

deference, n. déférence f.

deferential, adj. plein de déférence, respectueux.

defiance, n. défi m.

defiant, adj. de défi.

deficiency, n. insuffisance f.

deficient, adj. insuffisant.

deficit, n. déficit m.

defile, vb. souiller.

define, vb. définir.

definite, adj. défini.

definitely, adv. d'une manière déterminée.

definition, n. définition f.

definitive, adj. définitif.

deflate, vb. dégonfler.

deflation, n. dégonflement m.

deflect, vb. faire dévier, détourner.

deform, vb. déformer.

deformity, n. difformité f.

defraud, vb. frauder.

defray, vb. payer.

defrost, vb. déglacer.

defroster, n. déglaceur m.

deft, adj. adroit.

defy, vb. défier.

degenerate, vb. dégénérer.

degeneration, n. dégénérescence f.

degradation, n. dégradation f.

degrade, vb. dégrader.

degree, n. degré m.

dehydrate, vb. déshydrater.

deify, vb. déifier.

deign, vb. daigner.

deity, n. divinité f.

dejected, adj. abattu.

dejection, n. abattement m.

delay, 1. n. retard m. **2.** vb. retarder, tr.; tarder, intr.

delectable, adj. délectable.

delegate, 1. n. délégué m. **2.** vb. déléguer.

delegation, n. délégation f.

delete, vb. rayer, biffer.

deliberate, 1. adj. délibéré. **2.** vb. délibérer.

deliberately, adv. de propos délibéré.

deliberation, n. délibération f.

deliberative, adj. délibératif.

delicacy, n. délicatesse f.

delicate, adj. délicat.

delicious, adj. délicieux.

delight, 1. n. délices f.pl. **2.** vb. enchanter.

delightful, adj. charmant.

delineate, vb. esquisser, dessiner.

delinquency, n. délit m.

delinquent, adj. and n. délinquant m.

delirious, adj. délirant.

deliver, vb. délivrer; (speech) prononcer.

deliverance, n. délivrance f.

delivery, n. (child) accouchement m.; (speech) débit m.; (goods) livraison f.; (letters) distribution f.; (general d.) poste restante f.

delouse, vb. épouiller.

delude, vb. tromper.

deluge, n. déluge m.

delusion, n. illusion f.

de luxe, adv. de luxe.

delve, vb. creuser, pénétrer.

demagogue, n. démagogue m.

demand, 1. n. demande f. **2.** vb. demander; (as right or by force) exiger.

demarcation, n. démarcation f.

demean, vb. comporter.

demeanor, n. maintien m.

demented, adj. fou m., folle f.

demerit, n. démérite m.

demigod, n. demi-dieu n.

demilitarize, vb. démilitariser.

demise, n. décès m., mort f.

demobilization, n. démobilisation f.

demobilize, vb. démobiliser.

democracy, n. démocratie f.

democrat, n. démocrate m.f.

democratic, adj. démocratique.

demolish, vb. démolir.

demolition, n. démolition f.

demon, n. démon m.

demonstrable, *adj.* démonstrable.

demonstrate, *vb.* démontrer.

demonstration, *n.* démonstration *f.*

demonstrative, *adj.* démonstratif.

demonstrator, *n.* démonstrateur *m.*

demoralize, *vb.* démoraliser.

demote, *vb.* réduire à un grade inférieur.

demur, *vb.* hésiter, s'opposer à.

demure, *adj.* posé, d'une modestie affectée.

den, *n.* antre *m.,* repaire *m.*

denaturalize, *vb.* dénaturaliser.

denature, *vb.* dénaturer.

denial, *n.* dénégation *f.;* (refusal) refus *m.*

denim, *n.* treillis *m.*

Denmark, *n.* Danemark *m.*

denomination, *n.* dénomination *f.;* (religion) confession *f.*

denominator, *n.* dénominateur *m.*

denote, *vb.* dénoter.

denouement, *n.* dénouement *m.*

denounce, *vb.* dénoncer.

dense, *adj.* dense; (stupid) bête.

density, *n.* densité *f.*

dent, *n.* bosselure *f.*

dental, *adj.* dentair; (gramm.) dental.

dentifrice, *n.* dentifrice *m.*

dentist, *n.* dentiste *m.*

dentistry, *n.* art du dentiste *m.,* dentisterie *f.*

denture, *n.* dentier *m.,* râtelier *m.*

denude, *vb.* dénuder.

denunciation, *n.* dénonciation *f.*

deny, *vb.* nier.

deodorant, *n.* désodorisant *m.*

deodorize, *vb.* désodoriser, désinfecter.

depart, *vb.* partir, s'en aller, quitter.

department, *n.* département *m.;* (government) ministère *m.;* (d. store) grand magasin *m.*

departmental, *adj.* départemental.

departure, *n.* départ *m.*

depend on, *vb.* dépendre de; (rely) compter sur.

dependability, *n.* confiance que l'on inspire *f.*

dependable, *adj.* digne de confiance.

dependence, *n.* dépendance *f.,* confiance *f.*

dependent, *adj.* dépendant.

depict, *vb.* peindre.

depiction, *n.* description *f.*

deplete, *vb.* épuiser.

deplorable, *adj.* déplorable.

deplore, *vb.* déplorer.

depopulate, *vb.* dépeupler.

deport, *vb.* déporter.

deportation, *n.* déportation *f.*

deportment, *n.* maintien *m.*

depose, *vb.* déposer.

deposit, 1. *n.* dépôt *m.* **2.** *vb.* déposer.

depositor, *n.* déposant *m.*

depository, *n.* dépôt *m.,* dépositaire *m.*

depot, *n.* dépôt *m.,* gare *f.*

deprave, *vb.* dépraver, corrompre.

depravity, *n.* dépravation *f.,* corruption *f.*

deprecate, *vb.* désapprouver, s'opposer à.

depreciate, *vb.* déprécier.

depreciation, *n.* dépréciation *f.*

depredation, *n.* déprédation *f.,* pillage *m.*

depress, *vb.* (lower) abaisser; (fig.) abattre.

depressed, *adj.* abattu, bas.

depression, *n.* dépression *f.;* (personal) abattement *m.;* (comm.) crise *f.*

deprive, *vb.* priver.

depth, *n.* profondeur *f.*

depth charge, *n.* grenade sous-marine *f.*

deputy, *n.* délégué *m.;* (politics) député *m.*

derail, *vb.* dérailler.

derange, *vb.* déranger.

deranged, *adj.* dérangé, troublé.

derelict, 1. *n.* vaisseau abandonné *m.,* épave *f.* **2.** *adj.* abandonné, délaissé.

dereliction, *n.* abandon *m.*

deride, *vb.* tourner en dérision.

derision, *n.* dérision *f.*

derisive, *adj.* dérisoire.

derivation, *n.* dérivation *f.,* origine *f.*

derivative, *n.* dérivatif.

derive, *vb.* dériver.

dermatology, *n.* dermatologie *f.*

derogatory, *adj.* dérogatoire.

derrick, *n.* grue *f.*

descend, *vb.* descendre.

descendant, *n.* descendant *m.*

descent, *n.* descente *f.*

describe, *vb.* décrire.

description, *n.* description *f.*

descriptive, *adj.* descriptif.

desecrate, *vb.* profaner.

desensitize, *vb.* désensibiliser.

desert, 1. *n.* (place) désert *m.;* (merit) mérite *m.* **2.** *vb.* déserter.

deserter, *n.* déserteur *m.*

desertion, *n.* abandon *m.;* (military) désertion *f.*

deserve, *vb.* mériter.

deserving, *adj.* méritoire, de mérite.

design, 1. *n.* (project) dessein *m.;* (architecture) projet *m.* **2.** *vb.* dessiner; (d. for) destiner à.

designate, *vb.* désigner.

designation, *n.* désignation *f.*

designedly, *adv.* à dessein.

designer, *n.* dessinateur *m.*

designing, *adj.* intrigant, artificieux.

desirable, *adj.* désirable.

desire, 1. *n.* désir *m.* **2.** *vb.* désirer.

desirous, *adj.* désireux.

desist, *vb.* cesser.

desk, *n.* (office) bureau *m.;* (school) pupitre *m.*

desolate, *adj.* désolé.

desolation, *n.* désolation *f.*

despair, 1. *n.* désespoir *m.* **2.** *vb.* désespérer.

desperado, *n.* désespéré *m.,* cerveau brûlé *m.*

desperate, *adj.* désespéré.

desperation, *n.* désespoir *m.*

despicable, *adj.* méprisable.

despise, *vb.* mépriser.

despite, *prep.* en dépit de.

despondent, *adj.* découragé.

despot, *n.* despote *m.*

despotic, *adj.* despotique.

despotism, *n.* despotisme *m.*

dessert, *n.* dessert *m.*

destination, *n.* destination *f.*

destine, *vb.* destiner.

destiny, *n.* destin *m.*

destitute, *adj.* (deprived) dénué; (poor) indigent.

destitution, *n.* destitution *f.*

destroy, *vb.* détruire.

destroyer, *n.* destructeur *m.;* (naval) contre-torpilleur *m.*

destructible, *adj.* destructible.

destruction, *n.* destruction *f.*

destructive, *adj.* destructif.

desultory, *adj.* à bâtons rompus, décousu.

detach, *vb.* détacher.

detachment, *n.* détachement *m.*

detail, *n.* détail *m.*

detain, *vb.* retenir; (in prison) détenir.

detect, *vb.* découvrir.

detection, *n.* découverte *f.*

detective, *n.* agent (*m.*) de la police secrète; (d. novel) roman policier.

detente, *n.* détente *f.*

detention, *n.* détention *f.*

deter, *vb.* détourner, empêcher (de), dissuader (de).

detergent, *n.* détersif *m.*

deteriorate, *vb.* détériorer, *tr.*

deterioration, *n.* détérioration *f.*

determination, *n.* détermination *f.*

determine, *vb.* déterminer.

determined, *adj.* déterminé.

determinism, *n.* déterminisme *m.*

deterrence, *n.* préventif *m.*

deterrent, *n. and adj.* préventif *m.*

detest, *vb.* détester.

dethrone, *vb.* détrôner.

detonate, *vb.* détoner.

detour, *n.* détour *m.*

detract, *vb.* enlever, ôter (à), dénigrer, déroger (à).

detriment, *n.* détriment *m.,* préjudice *m.*

detrimental, *adj.* préjudiciable, nuisible (à).

devaluate, *vb.* dévaluer, déprécier.

devastate, *vb.* dévaster.

develop, *vb.* développer, *tr.*

developer, *n.* (photography) révélateur *m.*

developing nation, *n.* nation en cours de développement *f.*

development, *n.* développement *m.*

deviate, *vb.* dévier, s'écarter (de).

deviation, *n.* déviation *f.*, écart *m.*

device, *n.* expédient *m.*

devil, *n.* diable *m.*

devilish, *adj.* diabolique.

devious, *adj.* détourné.

devise, *vb.* (plan) combiner; (plot) tramer.

devitalize, *vb.* dévitaliser.

devoid, *adj.* dépourvu.

devote, *vb.* consacrer.

devoted, *adj.* dévoué.

devotee, *n.* dévot *m.*, dévote *f.*

devotion, *n.* (religious) dévotion *f.*; (to person or thing) dévouement *m.*

devour, *vb.* dévorer.

devout, *adj.* dévot.

dew, *n.* rosée *f.*

dewy, *adj.* de rosée.

dexterity, *n.* dextérité *f.*

dexterous, *adj.* adroit.

diabetes, *n.* diabète *m.*

diabolic, *adj.* diabolique.

diadem, *n.* diadème *m.*

diagnose, *vb.* diagnostiquer.

diagnosis, *n.* diagnose *f.*

diagnostic, *adj.* diagnostique.

diagonal, *adj.* diagonal.

diagonally, *adv.* diagonalement.

diagram, *n.* diagramme *m.*

dial, 1. *n.* cadran *m.* 2. *vb.* (d. a number) composer.

dialect, *n.* dialecte *m.*

dialogue, *n.* dialogue *m.*

diameter, *n.* diamètre *m.*

diametrical, *adj.* diamétral.

diamond, *n.* diamant *m.*; (shape) losange *m.*; (cards) carreau *m.*

diaper, *n.* (babies) couche *f.*

diaphragm, *n.* diaphragme *m.*

diarrhea, *n.* diarrhée *f.*

diary, *n.* journal *m.*

diathermy, *n.* diathermie *f.*

diatribe, *n.* diatribe *f.*

dice, *n.* dés *m.pl.*

dicker, *vb.* marchander.

dictaphone, *n.* machine à dicter *f.*

dictate, *vb.* dicter.

dictation, *n.* dictée *f.*

dictator, *n.* dictateur *m.*

dictatorial, *adj.* dictatorial.

dictatorship, *n.* dictature *f.*

diction, *n.* diction *f.*

dictionary, *n.* dictionnaire *m.*

didactic, *adj.* didactique.

die, 1. *n.* dé *m.* 2. *vb.* mourir.

die-hard, *n.* intransigeant *m.*, ultra *m.*

diet, *n.* régime *m.*

dietary, *adj.* diététique.

dietetics, *n.* diététique *f.*

dietitian, *n.* diététicien *m.*

differ, *vb.* différer.

difference, *n.* différence *f.*

different, *adj.* différent.

differential, *adj.* différentiel.

difficult, *adj.* difficile.

difficulty, *n.* difficulté *f.*

diffident, *adj.* hésitant, timide.

diffuse, *adj.* diffus.

diffusion, *n.* diffusion *f.*

dig, *vb.* bêcher; (hole) creuser.

digest, *vb.* digérer.

digestible, *adj.* digestible.

digestion, *n.* digestion *f.*

digestive, *adj.* and *n.* digestif *m.*

digital, *adj.* (in watches, etc.) digital.

digitalis, *n.* digitaline *f.*

dignified, *adj.* plein de dignité.

dignify, *vb.* honorer, élever.

dignitary, *n.* dignitaire *m.*

dignity, *n.* dignité *f.*

digress, *vb.* faire une digression.

digression, *n.* digression *f.*

dike, *n.* (ditch) fossé *m.*; (dam) digue *f.*

dilapidated, *adj.* délabré.

dilapidation, *n.* délabrement *m.*

dilate, *vb.* dilater, *tr.*

dilatory, *adj.* dilatoire, lent, négligent.

dilemma, *n.* dilemme *m.*

dilettante, *n.* dilettante *m.*, amateur *m.*

diligence, *n.* diligence *f.*

diligent, *adj.* diligent.

dill, *n.* aneth *m.*

dilute, *vb.* diluer.

dim, *adj.* (light, sight) faible; (color) terne.

dime, *n.* un dixième de dollar *m.*

dimension, *n.* dimension *f.*

diminish, *vb.* diminuer.

diminution, *n.* diminution *f.*

diminutive, 1. *adj.* tout petit. 2. *n.* (gramm.) diminutif *m.*

dimness, *n.* (weakness) faiblesse *f.*; (darkness) obscurité *f.*

dimple, *n.* (face) fossette *f.*

din, *n.* tapage *m.*

dine, *vb.* dîner.

diner, dining-car, *n.* wagon-restaurant *m.*

dingy, *adj.* défraîchi; (color) terne.

dinner, *n.* dîner *m.*; (d. jacket) smoking *m.*

dinosaur, *n.* dinosaurien *m.*

diocese, *n.* diocèse *m.*

dip, *vb.* plonger.

diphtheria, *n.* diphtérie *f.*

diploma, *n.* diplôme *m.*

diplomacy, *n.* diplomatie *f.*

diplomat, *n.* diplomate *m.*

diplomatic, *adj.* diplomatique.

dipper, *n.* cuiller (*f.*) à pot.

dire, *adj.* affreux.

direct, *vb.* (guide) diriger; (address) adresser.

direct, *adj.* direct.

direct current, *n.* courant continu *m.*

direction, *n.* direction *f.*; (orders) instructions *f.pl.*

directional, *adj.* de direction.

directive, 1. *n.* directif *m.* 2. *adj.* dirigeant.

directly, *adv.* directement.

directness, *n.* rectitude *f.*; (frankness) franchise *f.*

director, *n.* directeur *m.*

directorate, *n.* conseil d'administration *m.*

directory, *n.* annuaire *m.*

dirge, *n.* chant funèbre *m.*

dirigible, *adj.* and *n.* dirigeable *m.*

dirt, *n.* saleté *f.*

dirty, *adj.* sale.

disability, *n.* incapacité *f.*, impuissance *f.*

disable, *vb.* mettre hors de combat, *tr.*

disabled, *adj.* invalide.

disabuse, *vb.* désabuser.

disadvantage, *n.* désavantage *m.*

disagree, *vb.* être en désaccord.

disagreeable, *adj.* désagréable.

disagreement, *n.* désaccord *m.*

disappear, *vb.* disparaître.

disappearance, *n.* disparition *f.*

disappoint, *vb.* désappointer.

disappointment, *n.* désappointement *m.*

disapproval, *n.* désapprobation *f.*

disapprove, *vb.* désapprouver.

disarm, *vb.* désarmer.

disarmament, *n.* désarmement *m.*

disarray, *n.* désarroi *m.*, désordre *m.*

disassemble, *vb.* démonter, désassembler.

disaster, *n.* désastre *m.*

disastrous, *adj.* désastreux.

disavow, *vb.* désavouer.

disavowal, *n.* désaveu *m.*

disband, *vb.* congédier, *tr.*; se débander, *intr.*

disbar, *vb.* rayer du tableau des avocats.

disbelieve, *vb.* ne pas croire, refuser de croire.

disburse, *vb.* débourser.

discard, *vb.* mettre de côté.

discern, *vb.* discerner.

discerning, *adj.* judicieux, éclairé.

discernment, *n.* discernement *m.*

discharge, 1. *n.* décharge *f.*; (mil.) congé *m.* 2. *vb.* décharger; (mil.) congédier.

disciple, *n.* disciple *m.*

disciplinarian, *n.* disciplinaire *m.*

disciplinary, *adj.* disciplinaire.

discipline, *n.* discipline *f.*

disclaim, *vb.* désvouer, nier.

disclaimer, *n.* désaveu *m.*

disclose, vb. révéler.
disclosure, n. révélation f.
disco, adj. disco.
discolor, vb. décolorer.
discomfiture, n. défaite f., déroute f.
discomfort, n. malaise m.
disconcert, vb. déconcerter.
disconnect, vb. désunir.
disconnected, adj. (electricity) hors circuit.
disconsolate, adj. désolé.
discontent, n. mécontentement m.
discontented, adj. mécontent.
discontinue, vb. discontinuer.
discord, n. discorde f.
discordant, adj. discordant, en désaccord.
discotheque, n. discothèque f.
discount, n. escompte m.; (reduction) remise f.
discourage, vb. décourager.
discouragement, n. découragement m.
discourse, n. discours m.
discourteous, adj. impoli.
discourtesy, n. impolitesse f.
discover, vb. découvrir.
discoverer, n. découvreur m.
discovery, n. découverte f.
discredit, 1. n. discrédit m. 2. vb. discréditer.
discreditable, adj. déshonorant, peu honorable.
discreet, adj. discret.
discrepancy, n. contradiction f.
discretion, n. discrétion f.
discriminate, vb. distinguer.
discrimination, n. discernement m., jugement m.
discursive, adj. discursif, sans suite.
discuss, vb. discuter.
discussion, n. discussion f.
disdain, n. dédain m.
disdainful, adj. dédaigneux.
disease, n. maladie f.
disembark, vb. débarquer.
disembody, vb. dépouiller du corps.
disenchantment, n. désenchantement m.
disengage, vb. dégager.
disentangle, vb. démêler.
disfavor, n. défaveur f.
disfigure, vb. défigurer, enlaidir.
disfranchise, vb. priver du droit de vote.
disgorge, vb. dégorger.
disgrace, n. disgrâce f.
disgraceful, adj. honteux.
disgruntled, adj. mécontent, de mauvaise humeur.
disguise, 1. n. déguisement m. 2. vb. dégoûter.
dish, n. plat m.; (**wash the dishes**) laver la vaisselle.
dishcloth, n. torchon m.
dishearten, vb. décourager.
dishonest, adj. malhonnête.
dishonesty, n. malhonnêteté f.
dishonor, n. déshonneur m.

dishonorable, adj. (action) déshonorant.
disillusion, n. désillusion f.
disinfect, vb. désinfecter.
disinfectant, n. désinfectant m.
disinherit, vb. déshériter.
disintegrate, vb. désagréger.
disinterested, adj. désintéressé.
disjointed, adj. désarticulé, disloqué.
disk, n. disque m.
dislike, 1, n. aversion f. 2. vb. ne pas aimer.
dislocate, vb. disloquer.
dislodge, vb. déloger.
disloyal, adj. infidèle.
disloyalty, n. infidélité f., perfidie f.
dismal, adj. sombre.
dismantle, vb. dépouiller (de).
dismay, n. consternation f.
dismember, vb. démembrer.
dismiss, vb. congédier.
dismissal, n. renvoi m.
dismount, vb. descendre.
disobedience, n. désobéissance f.
disobedient, adj. désobéissant.
disobey, vb. désobéir à.
disorder, n. désordre m.
disorderly, adj. désordonné.
disorganize, vb. désorganiser.
disown, vb. désavouer.
disparage, vb. déprécier, dénigrer.
disparate, adj. disparate.
disparity, n. inégalité f.
dispassionate, adj. calme.
dispatch, 1. n. (business) expédition f.; (speed) promptitude f.; (message) dépêche f. 2. vb. expédier.
dispatcher, n. expéditeur m.
dispel, vb. dissiper.
dispensable, adj. dont on peut se passer.
dispensary, n. dispensaire m.
dispensation, n. dispensation f.
dispense, vb. distribuer, dispenser.
dispersal, n. dispersion f.
disperse, vb. disperser.
displace, vb. déplacer.
displaced person, n. réfugié m.
displacement, n. déplacement m.
display, 1. n. (show) exposition f.; (shop, ostentation) étalage m. 2. vb. étaler.
displease, vb. déplaire à.
disposable, adj. disponible.
disposal, n. disposition f.
dispose, vb. disposer.
disposition, n. disposition f.; (character) caractère m.
dispossess, vb. déposséder, exproprier.
disproportion, n. disproportion f.
disproportionate, adj. disproportionné.
disprove, vb. réfuter.
disputable, adj. contestable, disputable.
dispute, 1. n. (discussion) dis-

cussion f.; (quarrel) dispute f. 2. vb. (se) disputer.
disqualify, vb. (sports) disqualifier.
disregard, vb. ne tenir aucun compte de.
disrepair, n. délabrement m.
disreputable, adj. déshonorant, honteux.
disrespect, n. irrévérence f.
disrespectful, adj. irrespectueux.
disrobe, vb. déshabiller, dévêtir.
disrupt, vb. faire éclater, rompre.
dissatisfaction, n. mécontentement m.
dissatisfy, vb. mécontenter.
dissect, vb. disséquer.
dissemble, vb. dissimuler.
disseminate, vb. disséminer.
dissension, n. dissension f.
dissent, vb. différer.
dissertation, n. dissertation f., discours m.
disservice, n. mauvais service rendu m.
dissimilar, adj. dissemblable.
dissipate, vb. dissiper.
dissipated, adj. dissipé.
dissipation, n. dissipation f.
dissociate, vb. désassocier, dissocier.
dissolute, adj. dissolu.
dissolution, n. dissolution f.
dissolve, vb. dissoudre, tr.
dissonance, n. dissonance f., désaccord m.
dissonant, adj. dissonant.
dissuade, vb. dissuader.
distance, n. distance f.
distant, adj. distant.
distaste, n. dégoût m.
distasteful, adj. désagréable.
distemper, 1. n. maladie des chiens f. 2. vb. peindre en détrempe.
distend, vb. dilater, gonfler.
distill, vb. distiller.
distillation, n. distillation f.
distiller, n. distillateur m.
distillery, n. distillerie f.
distinct, adj. distinct.
distinction, n. distinction f.
distinctive, adj. distinctif.
distinctly, adv. distinctement, clairement.
distinguish, vb. distinguer.
distinguished, adj. distingué.
distort, vb. déformer.
distract, vb. (divert) distraire; (upset) affoler.
distracted, adj. affolé, bouleversé.
distraction, n. (diversion) distraction f.; (madness) folie f.
distraught, adj. affolé, éperdu, hors de soi.
distress, 1. n. détresse f. 2. vb. affliger.
distressing, adj. affligeant, pénible, désolant.
distribute, vb. distribuer.
distribution, n. distribution f.

distributor, *n.* distributeur *m.*

district, *n.* (region) contrée *f.;* (administration) district *m.;* (town) quartier *m.*

distrust, 1. *n.* méfiance *f.* 2. *vb.* se méfier de.

distrustful, *adj.* méfiant.

disturb, *vb.* déranger.

disturbance, *n.* dérangement *m.*

disunite, *vb.* désunir.

disuse, *n.* désuétude *f.*

ditch, *n.* fossé *m.*

ditto, *adv.* idem, de même.

diva, *n.* diva *f.*

divan, *n.* divan *m.*

dive, *vb.* plonger.

dive bomber, *n.* avion de bombardement qui fait des vols piqués *m.*

diver, *n.* plongeur *m.*

diverge, *vb.* diverger.

divergence, *n.* divergence *f.*

divergent, *adj.* divergent.

diverse, *adj.* divers.

diversion, *n.* (amusement) divertissement *m.*

diversity, *n.* diversité *f.*

divert, *vb.* (turn aside) détourner; (amuse) divertir.

divest, *vb.* ôter, dépouiller, priver.

divide, *vb.* diviser.

divided, *adj.* divisé, séparé.

dividend, *n.* dividende *m.*

divine, *adj.* divin.

divinity, *n.* divinité *f.*

divisible, *adj.* divisible.

division, *n.* division *f.*

divisive, *adj.* qui divise, qui sépare.

divorce, 1. *n.* divorce *m.* 2. *vb.* divorcer.

divorcee, *n.* divorcé *m.*, divorcée *f.*

divulge, *vb.* divulguer.

dizziness, *n.* vertige *m.*

dizzy, *adj.* pris de vertige.

do, *vb.* faire; (how d. you d.?) comment allez-vous?

docile, *adj.* docile.

dock, *n.* bassin *m.*

docket, *n.* registre *m.*, bordereau *m.*

dockyard, *n.* chantier de construction de navires *m.*

doctor, *n.* docteur *m.*

doctorate, *n.* doctorat *m.*

doctrinaire, *adj.* doctrinaire.

doctrine, *n.* doctrine *f.*

document, *n.* document *m.*

documentary, *adj.* documentaire.

documentation, *n.* documentation *f.*

dodge, *vb.* esquiver, éluder.

doe, *n.* daine *f.*

doeskin, *n.* peau de daim *f.*

dog, *n.* chien *m.*

dogfight, *n.* combat de chiens *m.*, mêlée générale *f.*

dogged, *adj.* obstiné, tenace.

doggerel, *n.* poésie burlesque *f.*

doghouse, *n.* chenil *m.*

dogma, *n.* dogme *m.*

dogmatic, *adj.* dogmatique.

dogmatism, *n.* dogmatisme *m.*

doily, *n.* petit napperon *m.*

doldrum, *n.* (naut.) zone des calmes *f.*, cafard *m.*

dole, 1. *n.* pitance *f.;* aumône *f.* 2. *vb.* distribuer parcimonieusement.

doleful, *adj.* lugubre.

doll, *n.* poupée *f.*

dollar, *n.* dollar *m.*

dolorous, *adj.* douloureux.

dolphin, *n.* dauphin *m.*

domain, *n.* domaine *m.*

dome, *n.* dôme *m.*

domestic, *adj.* domestique.

domesticate, *vb.* domestiquer, apprivoiser.

domicile, *n.* domicile *m.*

dominance, *n.* dominance *f.*, prédominance *f.*

dominant, *adj.* dominant.

dominate, *vb.* dominer.

domination, *n.* domination *f.*

domineer, *vb.* se montrer tyrannique.

domineering, *adj.* impérieux.

dominion, *n.* domination *f.;* (territory) possessions *f.pl.*

domino, *n.* domino *m.*

don, *vb.* endosser, revêtir.

donate, *vb.* donner.

donation, *n.* donation *f.*

done, *vb.* fait.

donkey, *n.* âne *m.*

don't, *vb.* ne faites pas!, ne fais pas!

doom, *vb.* condamner.

doomsday, *n.* (jour du) jugement dernier *m.*

door, *f.* porte *f.;* (d.-keeper) concierge *m.f.*

doorman, *n.* portier *m.*

doorstep, *n.* seuil *m.*, pas de la porte *m.*

doorway, *n.* (baie de) porte *f.*, encadrement de la porte *m.*

dope, *n.* stupéfiant *m.*

dormant, *adj.* endormi, assoupi.

dormer, *n.* lucarne *f.*

dormitory, *n.* maison (*f.*) d'étudiants.

dosage, *n.* dosage *m.*

dose, *n.* dose *f.*

dossier, *n.* dossier *m.*

dot, *n.* point *m.*

dotage, *n.* radotage *m.*

dote, *vb.* radoter; (d. on) aimer excessivement.

double, 1. *adj.* and *n.* double *m.* 2. *vb.* doubler.

double-breasted, *adj.* croisé.

double-cross, *vb.* duper, tromper.

double-dealing, *n.* duplicité *f.*

double time, *n.* pas gymnastique *m.*

doubly, *adv.* doublement.

doubt, 1. *n.* doute *m.* 2. *vb.* douter (de).

doubtful, *adj.* douteux.

doubtless, *adv.* sans doute.

dough, *n.* pâte *f.*

doughnut, *n.* pet (*m.*) de nonne.

dour, *adj.* austère.

douse, *vb.* plonger, tremper.

dove, *n.* colombe *f.*

dowager, *n.* douairère *f.*

dowdy, *adj.* dans élégance, qui manque de chic.

dowel, 1. *n.* goujon *m.* 2. *vb.* goujonner.

down, 1. *n.* duvet *m.* 2. *adv.* en bas. 3. *prep.* (along) le long de.

downcast, *adj.* (look) baissé.

downfall, *n.* chute *f.*

downhearted, *adj.* découragé, déprimé.

downhill, 1. *n.* descente *f.* 2. *adj.* en pente, incliné.

downpour, *n.* averse *f.*

downright, *adv.* tout à fait.

downstairs, *adv.* en bas.

downtown, *adv.* en ville.

downtrodden, *adj.* opprimé, piétiné.

downward, *adj.* descendant.

downy, *adj.* duveteux.

dowry, *n.* dot *f.*

doze, *vb.* sommeiller.

dozen, *n.* douzaine *f.*

drab, *adj.* (color) gris; (dull) terne.

draft, 1. *n.* (drawing) dessin *m.;* (mil.) conscription *f.;* (air) courant (*m.*) d'air. 2. *vb.* (mil.) appeler sous le drapeau.

draftee, *n.* conscrit *m.*

draftsman, *n.* dessinateur *m.*

drafty, *adj.* plein de courante d'air.

drag, *vb.* traîner.

dragnet, *n.* drague *f.*, seine *f.*, chalut *m.*

dragon, *n.* dragon *m.*

drain, *vb.* drainer, *tr.;* s'écouler, *intr.*

drainage, *n.* drainage *m.*

dram, *n.* drachme *f.*, goutte *f.*

drama, *n.* drame *m.*

dramatic, *adj.* dramatique.

dramatics, *n.* théâtre *m.*

dramatist, *n.* dramaturge *m.*

dramatize, *vb.* dramatiser.

dramaturgy, *n.* dramaturgie *f.*

drape, *vb.* draper.

drapery, *n.* draperie *f.*

drastic, *adj.* drastique.

draught, *n.* traction *f.;* trait *m.*

draw, *vb.* (pull) tirer; (sketch) dessiner.

drawback, *n.* inconvénient *m.*

drawbridge, *n.* pont-levis *m.*

drawer, *n.* tiroir *m.*

drawing, *n.* dessin *m.*

drawl, 1. *n.* voix (*f.*) traînante. 2. *vb.* traîner la voix.

dray, *n.* camion *m.*

drayman, *n.* camionneur *m.*

dread, 1. *n.* crainte *f.* 2. *vb.* redouter.

dreadful, *adj.* affreux.

dreadfully, *adv.* terriblement, affreusement.

dream, *n.* rêve *m.*

dreamer, n. rêveur m.

dreamy, adj. rêveur m., rêveuse f.

dreary, adj. morne.

dredge, vb. draguer.

dreg, n. lie f.

drench, vb. tremper.

dress, 1. n. robe f. **2.** vb. habiller, tr.; s'habiller, intr.

dresser, n. commode f.

dressing, n. toilette f.; (surgical) pansement m.

dressing gown, n. robe de chambre f., peignoir m.

dressmaker, n. couturière f.

dress rehearsal, n. répétition générale f.

drier, n. sécheur m., dessécheur m.

drift, vb. (boat) dériver; (person) se laisser aller.

driftwood, n. bois flottant m.

drill, 1. n. (tool) foret m.; (exercise) exercice m. **2.** vb. (hole) forer; (exercise) exercer, tr.; faire l'exercice, intr.

drink, 1. n. boisson f. **2.** vb. boire.

drinkable, adj. potable.

drip, vb. dégoutter.

dripping, 1. n. dégouttement m. **2.** adj. ruisselant.

drive, 1. n. promenade (f.) en voiture; (energy) énergie f. **2.** vb. (auto, animals) conduire; (force) pousser.

drivel, n. bave f.

driver, n. (auto) chauffeur m.

drizzle, 1. n. bruine f. **2.** vb. bruiner.

dromedary, n. dromadaire m.

drone, 1. n. abeille mâle f.; bourdonnement m. **2.** vb. bourdonner.

droop, vb. pencher.

drop, 1. n. goutte f.; (fall) chute f. **2.** vb. tomber, intr.; laisser tomber, tr.

dropout, n. étudiant qui quitte l'école avant de recevoir son diplôme m.

dropper, n. compte-gouttes m.

dropsy, n. hydropisie f.

drought, n. sécheresse f.

drove, n. troupeau m.

drown, vb. noyer, tr.

drowse, vb. s'assoupir.

drowsiness, n. somnolence f.

drowsy, adj. somnolent.

drudge, vb. s'éreinter.

drug, n. drogue f.

druggist, n. pharmacien m.

drug store, n. pharmacie f.

drum, n. tambour m.; (ear) tympan m.

drum major, n. tambour-major m.

drummer, n. tambour m.

drumstick, n. baguette de tambour f.

drunk, adj. ivre.

drunkard, n. ivrogne m.

drunkenness, n. ivresse f.; (habitual) ivrognerie f.

dry, 1. adj. sec m., sèche f. **2.** vb. sécher.

dry-clean, vb. nettoyer à sec.

dry dock, 1. n. cale sèche f. **2.** vb. mettre en cale sèche.

dry goods, n. articles de nouveautés m.pl.

dryness, n. sécheresse f.

dual, adj. double.

dualism, n. dualité f., dualisme m.

dubious, adj. douteux.

duchess, n. duchesse f.

duchy, n. duché m.

duck, n. canard m.

duct, n. conduit m.

ductile, adj. ductile.

dud, 1. adj. incapable. **2.** n. obus qui a raté m.

due, adj. dû m., due f.

duel, n. duel m.

duelist, n. duelliste m.

duet, n. duo m.

duffel bag, n. sac pour les vêtements de rechange m.

dugout, n. abri-caverne m.

duke, n. duc m.

dukedom, n. duché m.

dulcet, adj. doux, suave.

dull, adj. (boring) ennuyeux.

dullard, n. lourdaud m.

dullness, n. (monotony) monotonie f.

duly, adv. dûment.

dumb, adj. muet m., muette f.; (stupid) sot m., sotte f.

dumbwaiter, n. monte-plats m.

dumfound, vb. abasourdir, interdire.

dummy, n. (dressmaking) mannequin m.; (cards) mort m.

dump, n. voirie f.

dumpling, n. boulette (de pâte) f.

dun, vb. importuner, talonner.

dunce, n. crétin m.

dunce cap, n. bonnet d'âne m.

dune, n. dune f.

dung, n. fiente f.; (agriculture) fumier m.

dungaree, n. salopette f., bleus m.pl.

dungeon, n. cachot m.

dupe, 1. n. dupe f. **2.** vb. duper.

duplex, adj. double.

duplicate, 1. n. double m. **2.** vb. faire le double de.

duplication, n. duplication f.

duplicity, n. duplicité f.

durable, adj. durable.

durability, n. durabilité f.

duration, n. durée f.

duress, n. contrainte f., coercition f.

during, prep. pendant.

dusk, n. crépuscule m.

dusky, adj. sombre.

dust, 1. n. poussière f. **2.** vb. épousseter.

dustpan, n. ramasse-poussière m.

dust storm, n. tourbillon de poussière m.

dusty, adj. poussiéreux.

Dutch, adj. and n. hollandais m.

Dutchman, n. Hollandais m.

dutiful, adj. respectueux, fidèle.

dutifully, adv. avec soumission.

duty, n. (moral, legal) devoir m.; (tax) droit m.; (be on d.) être de service.

duty-free, adj. exempt de droits.

dwarf, adj. and n. nain m.

dwell, vb. demeurer.

dwindle, vb. diminuer.

dye, 1. n. teinture f. **2.** vb. teindre.

dyer, n. teinturier m.

dyestuff, n. matière colorante f.

dynamic, adj. dynamique.

dynamics, n. dynamique f.

dynamite, n. dynamite f.

dynamo, n. dynamo f.

dynasty, n. dynastie f.

dysentery, n. dysenterie f.

dyslexia, n. dyslexie f.

dyspepsia, n. dyspepsie f.

dyspeptic, adj. dyspeptique.

E

each, 1. adj. chaque. **2.** pron. chacun m., chacune f.; (e. other) l'un l'autre.

eager, adj. ardent.

eagerly, adv. ardemment, avidement.

eagerness, n. empressement m.

eagle, n. (bird) aigle m.; (mil.) aigle f.

eaglet, n. aiglon m.

ear, n. oreille f.

earache, n. mal d'oreille m.

eardrum, n. tympan m.

earl, n. comte m.

early, 1. adj. (of morning) matinal; (first) premier. **2.** adv. de bonne heure; tôt.

earmark, 1. n. marque distinctive f. **2.** vb. marquer, assigner.

earn, vb. gagner.

earnest, adj. sérieux.

earnestly, adv. sérieusement, sincèrement.

earnestness, n. gravité f., sérieux m.

earnings, n. salaire m.

earphone, n. casque (téléphonique) m.

earring, n. boucle (f.) d'oreille.

earshot, n. portée de voix f.

earth, n. terre f.

earthenware, n. poterie f., argile cuite f.

earthly, adj. terrestre.

earthquake, n. tremblement (m.) de terre.

earthworm, n. ver de terre m.

earthy, adj. terreux.

ease, n. aise f.; (with e.) avec facilité.

easel, n. chevalet m.

easily, adv. facilement.

easiness, n. facilité f.

east, n. est m.

Easter, n. Pâques m.

easterly, adj. d'est, vers l'est.

eastern, adj. de l'est, oriental.

eastward, adv. vers l'est.

easy, adj. facile; (of manners) aisé.

easygoing, adj. insouciant, peu exigeant, accommodant.

eat, vb. manger.

eaves, n. avant-toit m.

eavesdrop, vb. écouter aux portes.

ebb, n. (water) reflux m.; (decline) déclin m.

ebony, n. ébène m.

ebullient, adj. bouillonnant.

eccentric, adj. excentrique.

eccentricity, n. excentricité f.

ecclesiastic, adj. and n. ecclésiastique m.

ecclesiastical, adj. ecclésiastique.

echelon, n. échelon m.

echo, n. écho m.

eclipse, n. éclipse f.

ecological, adj. écologique.

ecology, n. écologie f.

economic, adj. économique.

economical, adj. (person) économe.

economics, n. économie (f.) politique.

economist, n. économiste m.

economize, vb. économiser.

economy, n. économie f.

ecru, n. écru m.

ecstasy, n. (religious) extase f.; (fig.) transport m.

ecumenical, adj. œcuménique.

eczema, n. eczéma m.

eddy, n. remous m.

edge, n. bord m.; (blade) fil m.

edging, n. pose f.; bordure f.

edgy, adj. d'un air agacé.

edible, adj. comestible.

edict, n. édit m.

edifice, n. édifice m.

edify, vb. édifier.

edition, n. édition f.

editor, n. (text) éditeur m.; (paper) rédacteur m.

editorial, n. article (m.) de fond.

educate, vb. (upbringing) élever; (knowledge) instruire.

education, n. éducation f.; (schooling) instruction f.

educator, n. éducateur m.

eel, n. anguille f.

efface, vb. effacer.

effect, 1. n. effet m. 2. vb. effectuer.

effective, adj. (having effect) efficace; (in effect) effectif.

effectively, adv. efficacement, effectivement.

effectiveness, n. efficacité f.

effectual, adj. efficace.

effeminate, adj. efféminé.

effervesce, vb. être en effervescence, pétiller d'animation.

effete, adj. epuisé, caduc.

efficacious, adj. efficace.

efficacy, n. efficacité f.

efficiency, n. (person) compétence f.; (machine) rendement m.

efficient, adj. (person) capable.

efficiently, adv. efficacement, avec compétence.

effigy, n. effigie f.

effort, n. effort m.

effortless, adj. sans effort.

effrontery, n. effronterie f.

effulgent, adj. resplendissant.

effusive, adj. démonstratif.

egg, n. œuf m.; (boiled e.) œuf à la coque; (fried e.) œuf sur le plat; (poached e.) œuf poché; (scrambled e.) œuf brouillé.

eggplant, n. aubergine f.

egoism, n. égoïsme m.

egotism, n. égotisme m.

egotist, n. égotiste m.

Egypt, n. Égypte m.

Egyptian, 1. n. Égyptien m. 2. adj. égyptien.

eight, adj. and n. huit m.

eighteen, adj. and n. dix-huit m.

eighteenth, adj. and n. dix-huitième m.f.

eighth, adj. and n. huitième m.f.

eightieth, adj. quatre-vingtième.

eighty, adj. and n. quatre-vingts m.

either, 1. adj. (each of two) chaque; (one or other) l'un ou l'autre. 2. pron. chacun; l'un ou l'autre. 3. conj. (e . . . or) ou . . . ou . . .

ejaculate, vb. éjaculer, prononcer.

eject, vb. (throw) jeter.

ejection, n. jet m., éjection f., expulsion f.

eke, vb. suppléer à, subsister pauvrement.

elaborate, 1. adj. minutieux. 2. vb. élaborer.

elapse, vb. (time) s'écouler.

elastic, adj. and n. élastique m.

elasticity, n. élasticité f.

elate, vb. exalter, transporter.

elated, adj. exalté.

elation, n. exaltation f.

elbow, n. coude m.

elbowroom, n. aisance des coudes f.

elder, adj. and n. aîné m.

elderberry, n. baie de sureau f.

elderly, adj. d'un certain âge.

eldest, adj. aîné.

elect, vb. élire.

election, n. élection f.

electioneer, vb. faire une campagne électorale.

elective, adj. électif.

electorate, n. électorat m., les votants m.pl.

electric, electrical, adj. électrique.

electric chair, n. fauteuil électrique m.

electric eel, n. anguille électrique f.

electrician, n. électricien m.

electricity, n. électricité f.

electrocardiogram, n. électrocardiogramme m.

electrocute, vb. électrocuter.

electrode, n. électrode f.

electrolysis, n. électrolyse f.

electron, n. électron m.

electronics, n. électronique f.

electroplate, 1. vb. plaquer. 2. adj. plaqué.

elegance, n. élégance f.

elegant, adj. élégant.

elegiac, adj. élégiaque.

elegy, n. élégie f.

element, n. élément m.

elemental, elementary, adj. élémentaire.

elephant, n. éléphant m.

elephantine, adj. éléphantin.

elevate, vb. élever.

elevation, n. élévation f.

elevator, n. ascenseur m.

eleven, adj. and n. onze m.

eleventh, adj. and n. onzième m.

elf, n. elfe m.

elfin, adj. d'elfe.

elicit, vb. tirer, faire jaillir.

eligibility, n. éligibilité f.

eligible, adj. éligible.

eliminate, vb. éliminer.

elimination, n. élimination f.

elixir, n. élixir m.

elk, n. élan m.

elm, n. orme m.

elocution, n. élocution f.

elongate, vb. allonger, étendre.

elope, vb. s'enfuir.

eloquence, n. éloquence f.

eloquent, adj. éloquent.

eloquently, adv. d'une manière éloquente.

else, 1. adj. autre; (someone e.) quelqu'un d'autre. 2. adv. autrement.

elsewhere, adv. ailleurs.

elucidate, vb. élucider, éclaircir.

elude, vb. éluder.

elusive, adj. évasif, insaisissable.

emaciated, adj. émacié.

emanate, vb. émaner.

emancipate, vb. émanciper.

emancipation, n. émancipation f.

emancipator, n. émancipateur m.

emasculate, vb. émasculer.

embalm, vb. embaumer.

embankment, n. levée f.

embargo, n. embargo m.

embark, vb. embarquer, tr.

embarrass, vb. embarrasser.

embarrassing, adj. embarrassant.

embarrassment, n. embarras m.

embassy, n. ambassade f.

embellish, vb. embellir.

embellishment, *n.* embellissement *m.*

ember, *n.* braise *f.,* charbon ardent *m.*

embezzle, *vb.* détourner.

embitter, *vb.* aigrir, envenimer.

emblazon, *vb.* blasonner.

emblem, *n.* emblème *m.*

emblematic, *adj.* emblématique.

embody, *vb.* incarner, incorporer.

emboss, *vb.* graver en relief, travailler en bosse.

embrace, 1. *n.* étreinte *f.* **2.** *vb.* embrasser.

embroider, *vb.* broder.

embroidery, *n.* broderie *f.*

embroil, *vb.* embrouiller.

embryo, *n.* embryon *m.*

embryology, *n.* embryologie *f.*

embryonic, *adj.* embryonnaire.

emerald, *n.* émeraude *f.*

emerge, *vb.* émerger.

emergency, *n.* circonstance (*f.*) critique.

emergent, *adj.* émergent.

emery, *n.* émeri *m.*

emetic, *n.* émétique *m.*

emigrant, *n.* émigrant *m.*

emigrate, *vb.* émigrer.

emigration, *n.* émigration *f.*

eminence, *n.* éminence *f.*

eminent, *adj.* éminent.

emissary, *n.* émissaire *m.*

emission control, *n.* appareil pour limiter l'émission de vapeurs nuisibles *m.*

emit, *vb.* émettre.

emollient, *adj.* émollient.

emolument, *n.* traitement *m.*

emotion, *n.* émotion *f.*

emotional, *adj.* émotif; (excitable) émotionnable.

emperor, *n.* empereur *m.*

emphasis, *n.* (impressiveness) force *f.;* (stress) accent *m.*

emphasize, *vb.* mettre en relief.

emphatic, *adj.* (manner) énergique.

empire, *n.* empire *m.*

empirical, *adj.* empirique.

employ, *vb.* employer.

employee, *n.* employé *m.*

employer, *n.* patron *m.*

employment, *n.* emploi *m.*

empower, *vb.* autoriser.

empress, *n.* impératrice *f.*

emptiness, *n.* vide *m.*

empty, 1. *adj.* vide. **2.** *vb.* vider.

emulate, *vb.* émuler.

emulsion, *n.* émulsion *f.*

enable, *vb.* mettre à même (de).

enact, *vb.* (law) décréter; (play) jouer.

enactment, *n.* promulgation *f.,* acte législatif *m.*

enamel, *n.* émail *m.,* *pl.* émaux.

enamor, *vb.* amouracher.

encamp, *vb.* camper, faire camper.

encampment, *n.* campement *m.,* camp *m.*

encephalitis, *n.* encéphalite *f.*

encephalon, *n.* encéphale *m.*

enchant, *vb.* enchanter.

enchanting, *adj.* ravissant.

enchantment, *n.* enchantement *m.*

encircle, *vb.* entourer.

enclose, *vb.* enclore; (in letter) joindre.

enclosure, *n.* enclos *m.;* (in letter) pièce (*f.*) jointe.

encompass, *vb.* entourer.

encounter, *vb.* rencontrer.

encourage, *vb.* encourager.

encouragement, *n.* encouragement *m.*

encroach, *vb.* empiéter.

encumber, *vb.* encombrer.

encyclical, *n.* encyclique *f.*

encyclopedia, *n.* encyclopédie *f.*

end, 1. *n.* fin *f.;* (extremity) bout *m.;* (aim) but *m.* **2.** *vb.* finir.

endanger, *vb.* mettre en danger.

endear, *vb.* rendre cher.

endearment, *n.* charme *m.,* attrait *m.*

endeavor, 1. *n.* effort *m.* **2.** *vb.* s'efforcer.

endemic, *adj.* endémique.

ending, *n.* terminaison *f.*

endless, *adj.* sans fin.

endocrine gland, *n.* glande endocrine *f.*

endorse, *vb.* (sign) endosser; (support) appuyer.

endorsement, *n.* (signing) endossement *m.;* (approval) approbation *f.*

endow, *vb.* doter.

endowment, *n.* dotation *f.,* fondation *f.*

endurance, *n.* résistance *f.*

endure, *vb.* supporter.

enduring, *adj.* durable.

enema, *n.* lavement *m.*

enemy, *n.* and *adj.* ennemi *m.*

energetic, *adj.* énergique.

energy, *n.* énergie *f.*

enervate, *vb.* énerver, affaiblir.

enervation, *n.* affaiblissement *m.*

enfold, *vb.* envelopper.

enforce, *vb.* imposer; (law) exécuter.

enforcement, *n.* exécution *f.*

enfranchise, *vb.* affranchir, accorder le droit de vote.

engage, *vb.* engager, *tr.;* (become e.d, to be married) se fiancer.

engaged, *adj.* occupé; pris; fiancé.

engagement, *n.* engagement *m.;* (marriage) fiançailles *f.pl.*

engaging, *adj.* attrayant, séduisant.

engender, *vb.* engendrer.

engine, *n.* machine *f.;* (train) locomotive *f.;* (motor) moteur *m.*

engineer, *n.* (profession) ingénieur *m.;* (engine operator)

mécanicien *m.;* (mil.) soldat (*m.*) du génie.

engineering, *n.* génie *m.*

England, *n.* Angleterre *f.*

English, *adj.* and *n.* anglais *m.*

Englishman, *n.* Anglais *m.*

Englishwoman, *n.* Anglaise *f.*

engrave, *vb.* graver.

engraver, *n.* graveur *m.*

engraving, *n.* gravure *f.*

engross, *vb.* (absorb) absorber.

engrossing, *adj.* absorbant.

enhance, *vb.* rehausser.

enigma, *n.* énigme *f.*

enigmatic, *adj.* énigmatique.

enjoin, *vb.* enjoindre.

enjoy, *vb.* jouir de; (e. oneself) s'amuser.

enjoyable, *adj.* agréable.

enjoyment, *n.* jouissance *f.*

enlace, *vb.* enlacer.

enlarge, *vb.* agrandir, *tr.*

enlargement, *n.* agrandissement *m.*

enlarger, *n.* agrandisseur *m.,* amplificateur *m.*

enlighten, *vb.* éclairer.

enlightenment, *n.* éclaircissement *m.*

enlist, *vb.* enrôler, *tr.*

enlisted man, *n.* gradé *m.*

enlistment, *n.* enrôlement *m.*

enliven, *vb.* animer.

enmesh, *vb.* engrener, embarrasser.

enmity, *n.* inimitié *f.*

ennoble, *vb.* anoblir.

ennui, *n.* ennui *m.*

enormity, *n.* énormité *f.*

enormous, *adj.* énorme.

enough, *adj.* and *adv.* assez (de).

enrage, *vb.* faire enrager.

enrapture, *vb.* ravir, enchanter.

enrich, *vb.* enrichir.

enroll, *vb.* enrôler.

enrollment, *n.* enrôlement *m.*

ensemble, *n.* ensemble *m.*

enshrine, *vb.* enchâsser.

ensign, *n.* (navy) enseigne *m.*

enslave, *vb.* asservir.

ensnare, *vb.* prendre au piège.

ensue, *vb.* s'ensuivre.

entail, *vb.* (involve) entraîner; (law) substituer.

entangle, *vb.* empêtrer.

enter, *vb.* entrer (dans).

enterprise, *n.* entreprise *f.*

enterprising, *adj.* entreprenant.

entertain, *vb.* (amuse) amuser; (receive) recevoir.

entertainment, *n.* amusement *m.*

enthrall, *vb.* captiver, ensorceler.

enthusiasm, *n.* enthousiasme *m.*

enthusiast, *n.* enthousiaste *m.f.*

enthusiastic, *adj.* enthousiaste.

entice, *vb.* attirer.

entire, *adj.* entier.

entirely, *adv.* entièrement.

entirety, *n.* totalité *f.*

entitle, *vb.* donner droit à; (book) intituler.

entity, n. entité f.

entomb, vb. enterrer, ensevelir.

entrails, n. entrailles f.pl.

entrain, vb. embarquer en chemin de fer.

entrance, n. entrée f.

entrant, n. débutant m., inscrit m.

entrap, vb. attraper, prendre au piège.

entreat, vb. supplier.

entreaty, n. instance f.

entrench, vb. retrancher.

entrust to, vb. confier à.

entry, n. (entrance) entrée f.; (recording) inscription f.

enumerate, vb. énumérer.

enumeration, n. énumération f.

enunciate, vb. énoncer.

enunciation, n. énonciation f.

envelop, vb. envelopper.

envelope, n. enveloppe f.

enviable, adj. enviable.

envious, adj. envieux.

environment, n. milieu m.

environmentalist, n. écologiste m.; environnementaliste m.

environmental protection, n. protection de l'environnement f.

environs, n. environs m.pl., alentours m.pl.

envisage, vb. envisager.

envoy, n. envoyé m.

envy, 1. n. envie f. 2. vb. envier.

eon, n. éon m.

ephemeral, adj. éphémère.

epic, 1. n. épopée f. 2. adj. épique.

epicure, n. gourmet m.

epidemic, n. épidémie f.

epidermis, n. épiderme m.

epigram, n. épigramme f.

epilepsy, n. épilepsie f.

epilogue, n. épilogue m.

episode, n. épisode m.

epistle, n. épître f.

epitaph, n. épitaphe f.

epithet, n. épithète f.

epitome, n. épitomé m., résumé m.

epitomize, vb. résumer, abréger.

epoch, n. époque f.

equable, adj. uniforme, régulier.

equal, adj. égal; (be e. to) être à la hauteur de.

equality, n. égalité f.

equalize, vb. égaliser, tr.

equanimity, n. tranquillité d'esprit f., équanimité f., sérénité f.

equate, vb. égaler, mettre en équation.

equation, n. équation f.

equator, n. équateur m.

equatorial, adj. équatorial.

equestrian, adj. équestre.

equidistant, adj. équidistant.

equilateral, adj. équilatéral.

equilibrium, n. équilibre m.

equinox, n. équinoxe f.

equip, vb. équiper.

equipment, n. équipement m.

equitable, adj. équitable, juste.

equity, n. équité f.

equivalent, adj. and n. équivalent m.

equivocal, adj. équivoque.

equivocate, vb. équivoquer.

era, n. ère f.

eradicate, vb. déraciner.

eradicator, n. effaceur m., grattoir m.

erase, vb. effacer.

eraser, n. gomme f.

erasure, n. rature f.

erect, adj. droit.

erection, n. érection f., construction f.

erectness, n. attitude droite f.

ermine, n. hermine f.

erode, vb. éroder, ronger.

erosion, n. érosion f.

erosive, adj. érosif.

erotic, adj. érotique.

err, vb. errer.

errand, n. course f.

errant, adj. errant.

erratic, adj. irrégulier, excentrique.

erring, adj. égaré, dévoyé.

erroneous, adj. erroné.

error, n. erreur f.

erudite, adj. érudit.

erudition, n. érudition f.

erupt, vb. entrer en éruption.

eruption, n. éruption f.

escalate, vb. escalader.

escalator, n. escalier roulant m.

escapade, n. escapade f.

escape, 1. n. fuite f. 2. vb. échapper.

escapism, n. évasion f., échappement m.

eschew, vb. éviter, s'abstenir.

escort, (n. (mil.) escorte f.; (to a lady) cavalier m.

esculent, adj. comestible.

escutcheon, n. écusson m.

esoteric, adj. ésotérique.

especial, adj. spécial.

espionage, n. espionnage m.

espousal, n. adoption f., adhésion (à) f.

espouse, vb. épouser, embrasser (une cause).

Eskimo, 1. n. Esquimau m., Esquimaude f. 2. adj. esquimau m., esquimaude f.

esquire, n. écuyer m.; titre honorifique d'un "gentleman" m.

essay, 1. n. essai m.; (school) composition f. 2. vb. essayer.

essayist, n. essayiste m.

essence, n. essence f.

essential, adj. essentiel.

essentially, adv. essentiellement.

establish, vb. établir.

establishment, n. établissement m.

estate, n. (condition, class) état m.; (wealth) biens m.pl.; (land) propriété f.

esteem, 1. n. estime f. 2. vb. estimer.

estimable, adj. estimable.

estimate, 1. n. estimation f.; (comm.) devis m. 2. vb. estimer.

estimation, n. (opinion) jugement m.

estrange, vb. aliéner.

estuary, n. estuaire m.

etching, n. gravure (f.) à l'eau-forte.

eternal, adj. éternel.

eternity, n. éternité f.

ether, n. éther m.

ethereal, adj. éthéré.

ethical, adj. moral.

ethics, n. éthique f.

Ethiopia, n. Éthiopie f.

ethnic, adj. ethnique.

etiquette, n. étiquette f.

Etruscan, 1. n. Étrusque m.f. 2. adj. étrusque.

etymology, n. étymologie f.

eucalyptus, n. eucalyptus m.

eugenic, adj. eugénésique.

eugenics, n. eugénisme m., eugénique f.

eulogize, vb. faire l'éloge de.

eulogy, n. panégyrique m.

eunuch, n. eunuque m.

euphonious, adj. mélodieux, euphonique.

Europe, n. Europe f.

European, 1. n. Européen m. 2. adj. européen.

euthanasia, n. euthanasie f.

evacuate, vb. évacuer.

evacuee, n. évacué m.

evade, vb. éluder.

evaluate, vb. évaluer.

evaluation, n. évaluation f.

evanescent, adj. évanescent, éphémère.

evangelist, n. évangéliste m.

evaporate, vb. évaporer, tr.

evaporation, n. évaporation f.

evasion, n. subterfuge m.

evasive, adj. évasif.

eve, n. veille f.

even, 1. adj. égal; (number) pair. 2. adv. même.

evening, n. soir m.; (span of e.) soirée f.

evenness, n. égalité f.

event, n. événement m.; (eventuality) cas m.

eventful, adj. plein d'événements.

eventual, adj. (ultimate) définitif; (contingent) éventuel.

ever, adv. (at all times) toujours; (at any time) jamais.

everglade, n. région marécageuse (de la Floride) f.

evergreen, adj. à feuilles persistantes, toujours vert.

everlasting, adj. éternel.

every, adj. (each) chaque; (all) tous les m.; toutes les f.

everybody, everyone, pron. tout le monde; chacun.

everyday, adj. de tous les jours.

everything, pron. tout.

everywhere, adv. partout.

evict, vb. évincer.

eviction, n. éviction f., expulsion f.

evidence, n. évidence f.; (proof) preuve f.

evident, adj. évident.

evidently, adv. évidemment.

evil, n. mal m.

evil, adj. mauvais.

evince, vb. démontrer.

eviscerate, vb. éviscérer.

evoke, vb. évoquer.

evolution, n. évolution f.

evolutionist, n. évolutionniste m.

evolve, vb. évoluer, développer.

ewe, n. agnelle f.

exact, adj. exact.

exacting, adj. (person) exigeant.

exactly, adv. exactement.

exaggerate, vb. exagérer.

exaggerated, adj. exagéré.

exaggeration, n. exagération f.

exalt, vb. exalter; (raise) élever.

exaltation, n. exaltation f.

examination, n. examen m.

examine, vb. examiner.

example, n. exemple m.

exasperate, vb. exaspérer.

exasperation, n. exaspération f.

excavate, vb. creuser.

exceed, vb. excéder.

exceedingly, adv. extrêmement.

excel, vb. exceller, intr.

excellence, excellency, n. excellence f.

excellent, adj. excellent.

excelsior, n. copeaux d'emballage m.pl.

except, 1. vb. excepter. 2. prep. excepté, sauf.

exception, n. exception f.

exceptional, adj. exceptionnel.

excerpt, n. extrait m.

excess, n. excès m.; (surplus) excédent m.

excessive, adj. excessif.

exchange, 1. n. échange m.; (money) change m. 2. vb. échanger.

exchangeable, adj. échangeable.

excise, n. contribution indirecte f., régie f.

excitable, adj. émotionnable, excitable.

excite, vb. exciter.

excitement, n. agitation f.

exclaim, vb. s'écrier.

exclamation, n. exclamation f.

exclamation point or mark, n. point d'exclamation m.

exclude, vb. exclure.

exclusion, n. exclusion f.

exclusive, adj. exclusif; (stylish) sélect.

excommunicate, vb. excommunier.

excommunication, n. excommunication f.

excoriate, vb. excorier, écorcher.

excrement, n. excrément m.

excruciating, adj. atroce, affreux.

exculpate, vb. disculper, exonérer.

excursion, n. excursion f.

excusable, adj. excusable.

excuse, 1. n. excuse f. 2. vb. excuser.

execrable, adj. exécrable, abominable.

execute, vb. exécuter.

execution, n. exécution f.

executioner, n. bourreau m.

executive, adj. and n. exécutif m.

executive mansion, n. maison présidentielle f.

executor, n. exécuteur m.

exemplary, adj. exemplaire.

exemplify, vb. expliquer par des exemples.

exempt, 1. adj. exempt. 2. vb. exempter.

exercise, 1. n. exercice m. 2. vb. exercer.

exert, vb. employer; (e. oneself) s'efforcer de.

exertion, n. effort m.

exhale, vb. exhaler.

exhaust, 1. n. (machines) échappement m. 2. vb. épuiser.

exhaustion, n. épuisement m.

exhaustive, adj. complet, approfondi.

exhibit, vb. (pictures, etc.) exposer; (show) montrer.

exhibition, n. exposition f.

exhibitionism, n. exhibitionnisme m.

exhilarate, vb. égayer.

exhort, vb. exhorter.

exhortation, n. exhortation f.

exhume, vb. exhumer.

exigency, n. exigence f.

exile, 1. n. exil m.; (person) exilé m. 2. vb. exiler.

exist, vb. exister.

existence, n. existence f.

existent, adj. existant.

exit, n. sortie f.

exodus, n. exode m.

exonerate, vb. exonérer.

exorbitant, adj. exorbitant.

exorcise, vb. exorciser.

exotic, adj. exotique.

expand, vb. étendre, tr.; (dilate) dilater, tr.

expanse, n. étendue f.

expansion, n. expansion f.

expansive, adj. expansif.

expatiate, vb. discourir.

expatriate, vb. expatrier.

expect, vb. s'attendre à; (await) attendre.

expectancy, n. attente f.

expectation, n. attente f.; (hope) espérance f.

expectorate, vb. expectorer.

expediency, n. convenance f.

expedient, n. expédient m.

expedite, vb. activer, accélérer.

expedition, n. expédition f.

expel, vb. expulser.

expend, vb. (money) dépenser; (use up) épuiser.

expenditure, n. dépense f.

expense, n. dépense f.; (expenses) frais m.pl.

expensive, adj. coûteux, cher.

expensively, adv. coûteusement.

experience, 1. n. expérience f. 2. vb. éprouver.

experienced, adj. expérimenté.

experiment, n. expérience f.

experimental, adj. expérimental.

expert, adj. and n. expert m.

expiate, vb. expier.

expiration, n. expiration f.

expire, vb. expirer.

explain, vb. expliquer.

explanation, n. explication f.

explanatory, adj. explicatif.

expletive, n. explétif m.

explicit, adj. explicite.

explode, vb. (burst) éclater, intr.

exploit, 1. n. exploit m. 2. vb. exploiter.

exploitation, n. exploitation f.

exploration, n. exploration f.

exploratory, adj. exploratif.

explore, vb. explorer.

explorer, n. explorateur m.

explosion, n. explosion f.

explosive, adj. and n. explosif m.

exponent, n. interprète m.

export, 1. n. (exportation) exportation f.; (exported object) article m.) d'exportation. 2. vb. exporter.

exportation, n. exportation f.

expose, vb. exposer.

exposé, n. exposé m.

exposition, n. exposition f.

expository, adj. expositoire.

expostulate, vb. faire des remontrances à.

exposure, n. exposition f.

expound, vb. exposer.

express, 1. adj. exprès. 2. vb. exprimer.

expressage, n. frais d'expédition m.pl.

expression, n. expression f.

expressive, adj. expressif.

expressly, adv. expressément.

expressman, n. agent de messageries m.

expropriate, vb. exproprier.

expulsion, n. expulsion f.

expunge, vb. effacer, rayer.

expurgate, vb. expurger, épurer.

exquisite, adj. exquis.

extant, adj. existant.

extemporaneous, adj. improvisé, impromptu.

extend, vb. étendre; (prolong) prolonger.

extension, n. extension f.

extensive, adj. étendu.

extensively, *adv.* largement, considérablement.

extent, *n.* étendue *f.;* **(to some e.)** jusqu'à un certain point.

extenuate, *vb.* (tire out) exténuer; (diminish) atténuer.

exterior, *adj. and n.* extérieur *m.*

exterminate, *vb.* exterminer.

extermination, *n.* extermination *f.*

external, *adj.* externe.

extinct, *adj.* éteint.

extinction, *n.* extinction *f.*

extinguish, *vb.* éteindre.

extirpate, *vb.* extirper.

extol, *vb.* vanter.

extort, *vb.* extorquer.

extortion, *n.* extorsion *f.*

extortioner, *n.* extorqueur *m.*

extra, *adj.* (additional) supplémentaire; (spare) de réserve.

extra-, *prefix.* (outside of) en dehors de; (intensive) extra-.

extract, **1.** *n.* extrait *m.* **2.** *vb.* extraire.

extraction, *n.* extraction *f.,* origine *f.*

extradite, *vb.* extrader.

extraneous, *adj.* étranger à.

extraordinary, *adj.* extraordinaire.

extravagance, *n.* extravagance *f.;* (money) prodigalité *f.*

extravagant, *adj.* extravagant; (money) prodigue.

extravaganza, *m.* œuvre fantaisiste *f.*

extreme, *adj. and n.* extrême *m.*

extremity, *n.* extrémité *f.*

extricate, *vb.* dégager, tirer.

extrovert, *n.* extroverti *m.*

exuberant, *adj.* exubérant.

exude, *vb.* exsuder.

exult, *vb.* exulter.

exultant, *adj.* exultant, joyeux.

eye, *n.* œil *m.pl.* yeux.

eyeball, *n.* globe (*m.*) de l'œil.

eyebrow, *n.* sourcil *m.*

eyeglass, *n.* lorgnon *m.*

eyeglasses, *n.* lunettes *f.pl.*

eyelash, *n.* cil *m.*

eyelet, *n.* œillet *m.*

eyelid, *n.* paupière *f.*

eyesight, *n.* vue *f.*

eyewitness, *n.* témoin oculaire *m.*

F

fable, *n.* fable *f.*

fabric, *n.* (structure) édifice *m.;* (cloth) tissu *m.*

fabricate, *vb.* fabriquer.

fabrication, *n.* fabrication *f.*

fabulous, *adj.* fabuleux.

façade, *n.* façade *f.*

face, **1.** *n.* figure *f.* **2.** *vb.* faire face à.

facet, *n.* facette *f.*

facetious, *adj.* facétieux.

face value, *n.* valeur nominale *f.*

facial, *adj.* facial.

facile, *adj.* facile.

facilitate, *vb.* faciliter.

facility, *n.* facilité *f.*

facing, *n.* revêtement *m.,* revers *m.*

facsimile, *n.* fac-similé *m.*

fact, *n.* fait *m.;* **(as a matter of f.)** en effet.

faction, *n.* faction *f.*

factor, *n.* facteur *m.*

factory, *n.* fabrique *f.*

factual, *adj.* effectif, positif.

faculty, *n.* faculté *f.*

fad, *n.* marotte *f.*

fade, *vb. intr.* se faner; (color) se décolorer; **(f. away)** s'évanouir.

fagged, *adj.* épuisé, fatigué.

fail, *vb.* manquer; (not succeed) échouer.

failing, **1.** *n.* manquement *m.* **2.** *adj.* faiblissant. **3.** *prep.* au défaut de.

faille, *n.* faille *f.*

failure, *n.* (lack) défaut *m.;* (want of success) insuccès *m.*

faint, **1.** *adj.* faible. **2.** *vb.* s'évanouir.

faintly, *adv.* faiblement, timidement, légèrement.

fair, **1.** *n.* foire *f.* **2.** *adj.* (beautiful) beau *m.,* belle *f.;* (blond) blond; (honest) juste; (pretty good) passable.

fairly, *adv.* honnêtement, impartialement.

fairness, *n.* (honesty) honnêteté *f.*

fairy, *n.* fée *f.*

fairyland, *n.* pays des fées *m.*

faith, *n.* foi *f.*

faithful, *adj.* fidèle.

faithless, *adj.* infidèle.

fake, *vb.* truquer.

faker, *n.* truqueur *m.*

falcon, *n.* faucon *m.*

falconry, *n.* fauconnerie *f.*

fall, **1.** *n.* chute *f.;* (autumn) automne *m.* **2.** *vb.* tomber.

fallacious, *adj.* fallacieux.

fallacy, *n.* fausseté *f.*

fallen, *adj.* tombé, déchu.

fallible, *adj.* faillible.

fallout, *n.* pluie radioactive *f.*

fallow, *adj.* en jachère.

false, *adj.* faux *m.,* fausse *f.*

falsehood, *n.* mensonge *m.*

falseness, *n.* fausseté *f.*

falsetto, *n. and adj.* fausset *m.*

falsification, *n.* falsification *f.*

falsify, *vb.* falsifier.

falter, *vb.* hésiter.

fame, *n.* renommée *f.*

famed, *adj.* célèbre, renommé, fameux.

familiar, *adj.* familier.

familiarity, *n.* familiarité *f.*

familiarize, *vb.* familiariser.

family, *n.* famille *f.*

famine, *n.* (food) disette *f.;* (general) famine *f.*

famished, *adj.* affamé.

famous, *adj.* célèbre.

fan, *n.* éventail *m.;* (mechanical) ventilateur *m.*

fanatic, *adj. and n.* fanatique *m.*

fanatical, *adj.* fanatique.

fanaticism, *n.* fanatisme *m.*

fanciful, *adj.* fantastique, fantaisiste.

fancy, **1.** *n.* fantaisie *f.* **2.** *vb.* se figurer.

fanfare, *n.* fanfare *f.*

fang, *n.* croc (of a dog) *m.,* crochet (of a snake) *m.*

fantastic, *adj.* fantastique.

fantasy, *n.* fantaisie *f.*

far, *adv.* loin; **(so f.)** jusqu'ici; **(as f. as)** autant que; **(by much)** beaucoup; **(by f.)** de beaucoup.

faraway, *adj.* lointain.

farce, *n.* farce *f.*

fare, **1.** *n.* (price) prix *m.;* (food) chère *f.* **2.** *vb.* aller.

farewell, *interj. and n.* adieu *m.*

far-fetched, *adj.* forcé.

far-flung, *adj.* très étendu, vaste.

farina, *n.* farine *f.*

farm, *n.* ferme *f.*

farmer, *n.* fermier *m.*

farmhouse, *n.* maison (*f.*) de ferme.

farming, *n.* culture *f.*

farmyard, *n.* cour de ferme *f.*

far-reaching, *adj.* de grande envergure.

far-sighted, *adj.* clairvoyant.

farther, **1.** *adj.* plus éloigné. **2.** *adv.* plus loin.

farthest, *adj. and adv.* le plus lointain.

fascinate, *vb.* fasciner.

fascination, *n.* fascination *f.*

fascism, *n.* fascisme *m.*

fashion, *n.* mode *f.;* (manner) manière *f.*

fashionable, *adj.* à la mode.

fast, **1.** *n.* jeûne *m.* **2.** *adj.* (speedy) rapide; (firm) en avance; (of clock) en avance. **3.** *vb.* jeûner. **4.** *adv.* (quickly) vite; (firmly) ferme.

fasten, *vb.* attacher, *tr.*

fastener, *n.* fermeture *f.*

fastening, *n.* attache *f.*

fastidious, *adj.* difficile.

fat, *adj.* gras *m.,* grasse *f.*

fatal, *adj.* fatal; (deadly) mortel.

fatality, *n.* fatalité *f.*

fatally, *adv.* fatalement, mortellement.

fate, *n.* destin *m.*

fateful, *adj.* fatal.

father, *n.* père *m.*

fatherhood, *n.* paternité *f.*

father-in-law, *n.* beau-père *m.*

fatherland, *n.* patrie *f.*

fatherless, *adj.* sans père.

fatherly, *adj.* paternel.

fathom, **1.** *n.* (naut.) brasse *f.* **2.** *vb.* sonder.

fatigue, *n.* fatigue *f.*

fatten, vb. engraisser.

fatty, adj. graisseux.

fatuous, adj. sot.

faucet, n. robinet m.

fault, n. (mistake) faute f.; (defect) défaut m.

faultfinding, n. disposition à critiquer f.

faultless, adj. sans défaut.

faultlessly, adv. d'une manière impeccable.

faulty, adj. défectueux.

favor, 1. n. faveur f. 2. vb. favoriser.

favorable, adj. favorable.

favored, adj. favorisé.

favorite, adj. and n. favori, m., favorite f.

favoritism, n. favoritisme m.

fawn, n. faon m.

faze, vb. bouleverser.

fear, 1. n. crainte f. 2. vb. craindre.

fearful, adj. (person) craintif; (thing) effrayant.

fearless, adj. intrépide.

fearlessness, n. intrépidité f.

feasible, adj. faisable.

feast, n. fête f.; (banquet) festin m.

feat, n. exploit m.

feather, n. plume f.

feathered, adj. emplumé.

feathery, adj. plumeux.

feature, n. trait m.

February, n. février m.

fecund, adj. fécond.

federal, adj. fédéral.

federation, n. fédération f.

fedora, n. chapeau mou m.

fee, n. (for professional services) honoraires m.pl.; (school) frais m.pl.

feeble, adj. faible.

feeble-minded, adj. d'esprit faible.

feebleness, n. faiblesse f.

feed, 1. n. nourriture f. 2. vb. nourrir, tr.

feedback, n. action de contrôle en retour f.

feel, vb. sentir, tr.; (touch) tâter.

feeling, n. sentiment m.

feign, vb. feindre.

felicitate, vb. féliciter.

felicitous, adj. heureux.

felicity, n. félicité f.

feline, adj. félin.

fell, adj. funeste.

fellow, n. (general) homme m., garçon m.; (companion) compagnon m.

fellowship, n. camaraderie f.; (university) bourse (f.) universitaire.

felon, n. criminel m.

felony, n. crime m.

felt, n. feutre m.

female, 1. n. (person) femme f.; (animals, plants) femelle f. 2. adj. féminin, femelle.

feminine, adj. féminin.

femininity, n. féminéité f.

fence, 1. n. clôture f. 2. vb. (en-

close) enclore; (sword, foil) fair de l'escrime.

fencer, n. escrimeur m.

fencing, n. escrime f.

fender, n. garde-boue m.; (fireplace) garde-feu m.

ferment, vb. fermenter.

fermentation, n. fermentation f.

fern, n. fougère f.

ferocious, adj. féroce.

ferociously, adv. d'une manière féroce.

ferocity, n. férocité f.

ferry, n. passage (m.) en bac; (f. boat) bac m.

fertile, adj. fertile.

fertility, n. fertilité f.

fertilization, n. fertilisation f.

fertilize, vb. fertiliser.

fervency, n. ardeur f.

fervent, adj. fervent.

fervently, adv. ardemment.

fervid, adj. fervent.

fervor, n. ferveur f.

fester, vb. suppurer.

festival, n. fête f.

festive, adj. de fête.

festivity, n. réjouissance f.

festoon, 1. n. feston m. 2. vb. festonner.

fetal, adj. foetal.

fetch, vb. (go and get) aller chercher; (bring) apporter.

fetching, adj. attrayant.

fete, vb. fêter.

fetid, adj. fétide.

fetish, n. fétiche m.

fetlock, n. fanon m.

fetter, 1. n. lien m., chaîne f. 2. vb. enchaîner.

fetus, n. fœtus m.

feud, n. inimitié f.; (historical) fief m.

feudal, adj. féodal.

feudalism, n. régime féodal m.

fever, n. fièvre f.

feverish, adj. fiévreux.

feverishly, adv. fébrilement, fiévreusement.

few, 1. adj. peu de; (a f.) quelques. 2. pron. peu; (a f.) quelques-uns.

fiancé, n. fiancé m.

fiasco, n. fiasco m.

fiat, n. décret m.

fib, n. petit mensonge m.

fiber, n. fibre f.

fiberboard, n. fibre de bois m.

fibrous, adj. fibreux.

fickle, adj. volage.

fickleness, n. inconstance f.

fiction, n. fiction f.; (literature) romans m.pl.

fictional, adj. de romans.

fictitious, adj. fictif, imaginaire.

fictitiously, adv. d'une manière factice.

fiddle, 1. n. violon m. 2. vb. jouer du violon.

fiddlesticks, interj. quelle blague!

fidelity, n. fidélité f.

fidget, vb. se remuer.

field, n. champ m.

fiend, n. démon m.

fiendish, adj. diabolique, infernal.

fierce, adj. féroce.

fiery, adj. ardent.

fiesta, n. fête f.

fife, n. fifre m.

fifteen, adj. and n. quinze m.

fifteenth, adj. and n. quinzième m.

fifth, adj. and n. cinquième m.

fifty, adj. and n. cinquante m.

fig, n. figue f.

fight, 1. n. combat m.; (struggle) lutte f.; (quarrel) dispute f. 2. vb. combattre; se disputer.

fighter, n. combattant m.

figment, n. invention f.

figurative, adj. figuré.

figuratively, adv. au figuré.

figure, n. 1. n. figure f.; (of body) tournure f.; (math.) chiffre m. 2. vb. figurer; calculer.

figured, adj. à dessin.

figurehead, n. homme de paille m.

figure of speech, n. façon de parler f.

figurine, n. figurine f.

filament, n. filament m.

filch, vb. escamoter.

file, 1. n. (tool) lime f.; (row) file f.; (papers) liasse f.; (for papers, etc.) classeur m.; (f.s) archives f.pl. 2. vb. (tool) limer; (papers) classer; (f. off) défiler.

filial, adj. filial.

filigree, n. filigrane m.

filings, n. limaille f.

fill, vb. remplir, tr.

fillet, n. (band) bandeau m.; (meat, fish) filet m.

filling, n. remplissage m.

filling station, n. poste d'essence m.

film, n. (cinema) film m.; (photo) pellicule f.

filmy, adj. couvert d'une pellicule.

filter, 1. n. filtre m. 2. vb. filtrer.

filth, n. ordure f.

filthy, adj. immonde; obscène.

fin, n. nageoire f.

final, adj. final.

finale, n. finale m.

finalist, n. finaliste m.

finality, n. finalité f.

finally, adv. finalement, enfin.

finance, 1. n. finance f. 2. vb. financer.

financial, adj. financier.

financier, n. financier m.

find, vb. trouver.

fine, 1. n. amende f. 2. adj. (beautiful) beau m., belle f.; (pure, thin) fin. 3. vb. mettre à l'amende.

fine arts, n. beaux arts m.pl.

finery, n. parure f.

finesse, 1. n. finesse f. 2. vb. finasser.

finger, *n.* doigt *m.*
finger bowl, *n.* rince-bouche *m.*
fingernail, *n.* ongle *m.*
fingerprint, *n.* empreinte digitale *f.*
finicky, *adj.* affété.
finish, *vb.* finir.
finished, *adj.* fini, achevé.
finite, *adj.* fini.
Finland, *n.* Finlande *f.*
Finn, *n.* Finlandais, Finnais *m.*
Finnish, 1. *n.* finnois *m.* **2.** *adj.* finlandais, finnois.
fir, *n.* sapin *m.*
fire, 1. *n.* feu *m.;* (burning of house, etc.) incendie *m.* **2.** *vb.* (weapon) tirer.
fire alarm, *n.* avertisseur d'incendie *m.*
firearm, *n.* arme (*f.*) à feu.
firedamp, *n.* grisou *m.*
fire engine, *n.* pompe à incendie *f.*
fire escape, *n.* échelle de sauvetage *f.*
fire extinguisher, *n.* extincteur *m.*
firefly, *n.* luciole *f.*
fireman, *n.* pompier *m.*
fireplace, *n.* cheminée *f.*
fireproof, *adj.* à l'épreuve du feu.
fireside, *n.* coin du feu *m.*
firewood, *n.* bois de chauffage *m.*
fireworks, *n.* feu (*m.*) d'artifice.
firm, 1. *n.* maison (*f.*) de commerce. **2.** *adj.* ferme.
firmness, *n.* fermeté *f.*
first, 1. *adj.* premier. **2.** *adv.* d'abord.
first-aid, *n.* premiers secours *m.pl.*
first-class, *adj.* de premier ordre.
first-hand, *adj.* de première main.
first-rate, *adj.* de premier ordre.
fiscal, *adj.* fiscal.
fish, 1. *n.* poisson *m.* **2.** *vb.* pêcher.
fisherman, *n.* pêcheur *m.*
fishery, *n.* pêcherie *f.*
fishhook, *n.* hameçon *m.*
fishing, *n.* pêche *f.*
fishmonger, *n.* marchand de poisson *m.*
fishwife, *n.* marchande de poisson *f.*
fishy, *adj.* de poisson; (slang) louche.
fission, *n.* fission *f.*
fissure, *n.* fente *f.*
fist, *n.* poing *m.*
fistic, *adj.* au poing.
fit, 1. *n.* accès *m.* **2.** *adj.* (suitable) convenable; (capable) capable; (f. for) propre à. **3.** *vb.* (befit) convenir à; (clothes) aller à; (adjust) ajuster, *tr.*
fitful, *adj.* agité, irrégulier.
fitness, *n.* à-propos *m.;* (person) aptitude *f.*

fitting, 1. *n.* ajustage *m.* **2.** *adj.* convenable.
five, *adj. and n.* cinq *m.*
fix, 1. *n.* embarras *m.* **2.** *vb.* fixer; (repair) réparer.
fixation, *n.* fixation *f.*
fixed, *adj.* fixe.
fixture, *n.* object (*m.*) d'attache.
flabby, *adj.* flasque.
flaccid, *adj.* flasque.
flag, 1. *n.* drapeau *m.;* (stone) dalle *f.*
flagellate, *vb.* flageller.
flagging, 1. *n.* relâchement *m.* **2.** *adj.* qui s'affaiblit.
flagon, *n.* flacon *m.*
flagpole, *n.* mât de drapeau *m.*
flagrant, *adj.* flagrant.
flagrantly, *adv.* d'une manière flagrante.
flagship, *n.* vaisseau amiral *m.*
flagstone, *n.* dalle *f.*
flail, 1. *n.* fléau *m.* **2.** *vb.* battre au fléau.
flair, *n.* flaïr *m.*
flake, *n.* (snow) flocon *m.*
flamboyant, *adj.* flamboyant.
flame, 1. *n.* flamme *f.* **2.** *vb.* flamboyer.
flame thrower, *n.* lanceur de flammes *m.*
flaming, *adj.* flamboyant.
flamingo, *n.* flamant *m.*
flank, *n.* flanc *m.*
flannel, *n.* flanelle *f.*
flap, 1. *n.* (wing) coup *m.;* (pocket) patte *f.;* (table) battant *m.* **2.** *vb.* battre.
flare, *vb.* flamboyer.
flare-up, 1. *n.* emportement *m.* **2.** *vb.* s'emporter.
flash, *n.* éclair *m.*
flashcube, *n.* flash-cube *m.*
flashiness, *n.* faux brillant *m.,* éclat superficiel *m.*
flashlight, *n.* (lighthouse) feu (*m.*) à éclats; (pocket) lampe (*f.*) de poche.
flashy, *adj.* voyant.
flask, *n.* gourde *f.*
flat, 1. *n.* appartement *m.* **2.** *adj.* plat *m.,* platte *f.*
flatcar, *n.* wagon en plateforme *m.*
flatness, *n.* (evenness) égalité *f.;* (dullness) platitude *f.*
flatten, *vb.* aplatir.
flatter, *vb.* flatter.
flatterer, *n.* flatteur *m.*
flattery, *n.* flatterie *f.*
flattop, *n.* porte-avion *m.*
flaunt, *vb.* parader, étaler.
flavor, *n.* (taste) saveur *f.;* (fragrance) arome *m.*
flavoring, *n.* assaisonnement *m.*
flavorless, *adj.* fade.
flaw, *n.* défaut *m.*
flawless, *adj.* sans défaut, parfait.
flawlessly, *adv.* d'une manière impeccable.
flax, *n.* lin *m.*
flay, *vb.* écorcher.

flea, *n.* puce *f.*
fleck, 1. *n.* tache *f.* **2.** *vb.* tacheter (de).
fledgling, *n.* oisillon *m.*
flee, *vb.* s'enfuir.
fleece, *n.* toison *f.*
fleecy, *adj.* laineux, moutonneux.
fleet, *n.* flotte *f.*
fleeting, *adj.* fugitif.
flesh, *n.* chair *f.*
fleshy, *adj.* charnu.
flex, *vb.* fléchir.
flexibility, *n.* flexibilité *f.*
flexible, *adj.* flexible.
flicker, 1. *n.* lueur (*f.*) vacillante. **2.** *vb.* trembloter.
flier, *n.* aviateur *m.*
flight, *n.* (flying) vol *m.;* (fleeing) fuite *f.*
flight attendant, *n.* hôtesse de l'air *f.*
flighty, *adj.* étourdi.
flimsy, *adj.* sans solidité.
flinch, *vb.* reculer, broncher.
fling, *vb.* jeter.
flint, *n.* (lighter) pierre (*f.*) à briquet; (mineral) silex *m.*
flippant, *adj.* léger.
flippantly, *adv.* légèrement.
flirt, *vb.* flirter.
flirtation, *n.* flirt *m.*
float, *vb.* flotter.
flock, 1. *n.* troupeau *m.* **2.** *vb.* accourir.
flog, *vb.* fouetter.
flood, *n.* inondation *f.*
floodgate, *n.* écluse *f.*
floodlight, *n.* lumière à grand flots *f.*
floor, *n.* plancher *m.;* (take the f.) prendre la parole; (story) étage *m.*
flooring, *n.* plancher *m.,* parquet *m.*
floorwalker, *n.* inspecteur du magasin *m.*
flop, 1. *vb.* faire plouf, s'effondrer. **2.** *n.* fiasco *m.*
floral, *adj.* floral.
florid, *adj.* fleuri, vermeil.
florist, *n.* fleuriste *m.f.*
flounce, 1. *n.* volant *m.* **2.** *vb.* se démener.
flounder, *n.* flet *m.*
flour, *n.* farine *f.*
flourish, *vb.* prospérer.
flow, *vb.* couler.
flower, 1. *n.* fleur *f.* **2.** *vb.* fleurir.
flowerpot, *n.* pot à fleurs *m.*
flowery, *adj.* fleuri.
fluctuate, *vb.* osciller.
fluctuation, *n.* fluctuation *f.*
flue, *n.* tuyau de cheminée *m.*
fluency, *n.* facilité *f.*
fluent, *adj.* (be a f. speaker of . . .) parler . . . couramment.
fluid, *adj and n.* fluide *m.*
fluidity, *n.* fluidité *f.*
flunk, *vb.* coller, recaler.
flunkey, *n.* laquais *m.*
fluorescent lamp, *n.* lampe fluorescente *f.*
fluoroscope, *n.* fluoroscope *m.*

flurry, 1. n. agitation f. 2. vb. agiter.

flush, n. (redness) rougeur f.; (plumbing) chasse f.

flute, n. flûte f.

flutter, 1. n. (bird) voltigement m.; (agitation) agitation f. 2. vb. s'agiter; (heart) palpiter.

flux, n. flux m.

fly, 1. n. mouche f. 2. vb. voler.

foam, n. écume f.

focal, adj. focal.

focus, 1. n. foyer m.; (in f.) au point. 2. vb. (photo) mettre au point.

fodder, n. fourrage m.

foe, n. ennemi m.

fog, n. brouillard m.

foggy, adj. brumeux.

foil, n. (sheet) feuille f.; (set-off) repoussoir m.; (fencing) fleuret m.

foist, vb. fourrer.

fold, 1. n. pli m. 2. vb. plier.

folder, n. (booklet) prospectus m.

foliage, n. feuillage m.

folio, n. in-folio m.

folk, n. gens m.f.pl.

folklore, n. folk-lore m.

follicle, n. follicule m.

follow, vb. suivre.

follower, n. disciple m.

folly, n. folie f.

foment, vb. fomenter.

fond, adj. tendre; (be f. of) aimer.

fondant, n. fondant m.

fondle, vb. caresser.

fondly, adv. tendrement.

fondness, n. tendresse f.

food, n. nourriture f.

foodstuff, n. comestible m.

fool, n. sot m., sotte f.; (jester) bouffon m.

foolhardiness, n. témérité f.

foolhardy, adj. téméraire.

foolish, adj. sot m., sotte f.

foolproof, adj. à toute épreuve.

foolscap, n. papier écolier m.

foot, n. pied m.

footage, n. métrage m.

football, n. football m., ballon m.

foothill, n. colline basse f.

foothold, n. point d'appui m.

footing, n. pied m., point d'appui m.

footlights, n. rampe f.

footnote, n. note f.

footprint, n. empreinte de pas f.

footsore, adj. aux pieds endoloris.

footstep, n. pas m.

footstool, n. tabouret m.

footwork, n. jeu de pieds m.

fop, n. fat m.

for, 1. prep. pour. 2. conj. car.

forage, 1. n. fourrage m. 2. vb. fourrager.

foray, n. razzia f.

forbear, vb. (avoid) s'abstenir de; (be patient) montrer de la patience.

forbearance, n. patience f.

forbid, vb. défendre (à).

forbidding, adj. rébarbatif.

force, 1. n. force f. 2. vb. forcer.

forced, adj. forcé.

forceful, adj. énergique.

forcefulness, n. énergie f., vigueur f.

forceps, n. forceps m.

forcible, adj. forcé.

ford, 1. n. gué m. 2. vb. traverser à gué.

fore, adj. antérieur, de devant.

fore, n. avant m.

fore and aft, adv. de l'avant à l'arrière.

forearm, n. avant-bras m.

forebears, n. ancêtres m.pl.

forebode, vb. présager.

foreboding, 1. n. mauvais augure m., pressentiment m. 2. adj. qui présage le mal.

forecast, 1. n. prévision f. 2. vb. prévoir.

forecaster, n. pronostiqueur m.

forecastle, n. gaillard m.

foreclose, vb. exclure, forclore.

forefather, n. ancêtre m.

forefinger, n. index m.

forefront, n. premier rang m.

foregone, adj. décidé d'avance.

foreground, n. premier plan m.

forehead, n. front m.

foreign, adj. étranger.

foreign aid, n. aide aux pays étrangers f.

foreigner, n. étranger m.

foreleg, n. jambe antérieure f.

foreman, n. contremaître m.

foremost, adj. premier.

forenoon, n. matinée f.

forensic, adj. judiciaire.

forerunner, n. avant-coureur m.

foresee, vb. prévoir.

foreseeable, adj. que l'on peut prévoir.

foreshadow, vb. présager.

foresight, n. prévoyance f.

forest, n. forêt f.

forestall, vb. anticiper, devancer.

forester, n. forestier m.

forestry, n. sylviculture f.

foretaste, n. avant-goût m.

foretell, vb. prédire.

forever, adv. pour toujours.

forevermore, adv. à jamais.

foreword, n. avant-propos m.

forfeit, vb. forfaire.

forfeiture, n. perte par confiscation f., forfaiture f.

forgather, vb. se réunir.

forge, 1. n. forge f. 2. vb. forger; (signature, money) contrefaire.

forger, n. faussaire m., falsificateur m.

forgery, n. faux m.

forget, vb. oublier.

forgetful, adj. oublieux.

forget-me-not, n. myosotis m.

forgive, vb. pardonner (à).

forgiveness, n. pardon m.

forgo, vb. renoncer à.

fork, n. fourchette f.; (tool, road) fourche f.

forlorn, adj. (hopeless) désespéré; (forsaken) abandonné.

form, 1. n. forme f.; (blank) formule f. 2. vb. former.

formal, adj. formel.

formaldehyde, n. formaldéhyde f.

formality, n. formalité f.

formally, adv. formellement.

format, n. format m.

formation, n. formation f.

formative, adj. formatif.

former, 1. adj. précédent; (with latter) premier. 2. pron. le premier.

formerly, adv. autrefois, jadis, auparavant.

formidable, adj. formidable.

formless, adj. informe.

formula, n. formule f.

formulate, vb. formuler.

formulation, n. formulation f.

forsake, vb. abandonner.

forsythia, n. forsythie f.

fort, n. fort m.

forte, n. fort m.

forth, adv. en avant; (and so f.) et ainsi de suite.

forthcoming, adv. à venir.

forthright, 1. adj. tout droit. 2. adv. carrément, nettement.

forthwith, adv. sur-le-champ, tout de suite.

fortieth, adj. and n. quarantième m.

fortification, n. fortification f.

fortify, vb. fortifier, renforcer.

fortissimo, adv. fortissimo.

fortitude, n. courage m.

fortnight, n. quinzaine f.

fortress, n. forteresse f.

fortuitous, adj. fortuit.

fortunate, adj. heureux.

fortune, n. fortune f.

fortuneteller, n. diseur de bonne aventure m.

forty, adj. and n. quarante m.

forum, n. (Roman) forum m.

forward, 1. adj. en avant; (advanced) avancé; (bold) hardi. 2. adv. en avant. 3. vb. (letter) faire suivre.

forwardness, n. empressement m., effronterie f.

fossil, n. fossile m.

fossilize, vb. fossiliser.

foster, vb. nourrir.

foul, adj. (dirty) sale; (disgusting) dégoûtant; (obscene) ordurier; (abominable) infâme.

found, vb. fonder.

foundation, n. fondation f.; (theory) fondement m.

founder, n. fondateur m.

foundling, n. enfant trouvé.

foundry, n. fonderie f.

fountain, n. fontaine f.

fountainhead, n. source f.

fountain pen, n. stylo-(graphe) m.

four, adj. and n. quatre m.

four-in-hand, *n.* attelage à quatre *m.*

fourscore, *adj.* quatre-vingts.

foursome, *n.* à quatre.

fourteen, *adj. and n.* quatorze *m.*

fourth, *adj. and n.* quatrième *m.;* (fraction) quart *m.*

fourth estate, *n.* quatrième état *m.*

fowl, *n.* volaille *f.*

fox, *n.* renard *m.*

foxglove, *n.* digitale *f.*

foxhole, *n.* renardière *f.*

fox terrier, *n.* fox-terrier *m.*

fox trot, *n.* fox-trot *m.*

foxy, *adj.* rusé.

foyer, *n.* foyer *m.*

fracas, *n.* fracas *m.*

fraction, *n.* fraction *f.*

fracture, *n.* fracture *f.*

fragile, *adj.* fragile.

fragment, *n.* fragment *m.*

fragmentary, *adj.* fragmentaire.

fragrance, *n.* parfum *m.*

fragrant, *adj.* parfumé.

frail, *adj.* frêle.

frailty, *n.* faiblesse *f.*

frame, *n.* (picture) cadre *m.;* (structure) structure *f.*

frame-up, **1.** *n.* coup monté *m.* **2.** *vb.* monter un coup.

framework, *n.* charpente *f.*

France, *n.* France *f.*

franchise, *n.* droit (*m.*) électoral.

frank, *adj.* franc *m.,* franche *f.*

frankfurter, *n.* saucisse (*f.*) de Francfort.

frankincense, *n.* encens *m.*

frankly, *adv.* franchement.

frankness, *n.* franchise *f.*

frantic, *adj.* frénétique.

fraternal, *adj.* fraternel.

fraternally, *adv.* fraternellement.

fraternity, *n.* fraternité *f.*

fraternization, *n.* fraternisation *f.*

fraternize, *vb.* fraterniser.

fratricide, *n.* fratricide *m.*

fraud, *n.* fraude *f.;* (person) imposteur *m.*

fraudulent, *adj.* frauduleux.

fraudulently, *adv.* frauduleusement.

fraught, *adj.* chargé (de), plein, gros.

fray, **1.** *n.* bagarre *f.* **2.** *vb.* érailler.

freak, *n.* (whim) caprice *m.;* (abnormality) phénomène *m.*

freckle, *n.* tache de rousseur *f.*

freckled, *adj.* taché de rousseur.

free, **1.** *adj.* libre; (without cost) gratuit. **2.** *vb.* libérer, affranchir.

freedom, *n.* liberté *f.*

free lance, **1.** journaliste ou politicien indépendant *m.* **2.** *vb.* faire du journalisme indépendant.

freestone, *n.* pêche dont la

chair n'adhère pas au noyau *f.*

free verse, *n.* vers libre *m.*

free will, *n.* libre arbitre *m.*

freeze, *vb.* geler.

freezer, *n.* glacière *f.;* congélateur *m.*

freezing point, *n.* point de congélation *m.*

freight, *n.* fret *m.*

freightage, *n.* frètement *m.*

freighter, *n.* affréteur *m.*

French, *adj. and n.* français *m.*

French leave, *n.* filer à l'anglaise.

Frenchman, *n.* Français *m.*

French toast, *n.* tranche de pain frite *f.*

Frenchwoman, *n.* Française *f.*

frenzied, *adj.* affolé, frénétique.

frenzy, *n.* frénésie *f.*

frequency, *n.* fréquence *f.*

frequent, **1.** *adj.* fréquent. **2.** *vb.* fréquenter.

frequently, *adv.* fréquemment.

fresco, *n.* fresque *f.*

fresh, *adj.* frais *m.,* fraîche *f.;* (new, recent) nouveau; nouvel *m.,* nouvelle *f.*

freshen, *vb.* refraîchir.

freshman, *n.* étudiant de première année *m.*

freshness, *n.* fraîcheur *f.*

fresh-water, *adj.* d'eau douce.

fret, *vb.* ronger, *tr.*

fretful, *adj.* chagrin.

fretfully, *adv.* avec irritation.

fretfulness, *n.* irritabilité *f.*

friar, *n.* moine *m.,* frère religieux *m.*

fricassee, *n.* fricassée *f.*

friction, *n.* friction *f.*

Friday, *n.* vendredi *m.*

friend, *n.* ami *m.,* amie *f.*

friendless, *adj.* sans amis.

friendliness, *n.* disposition (*f.*) amicale.

friendly, *adj.* amical.

friendship, *n.* amitié *f.*

fright, *n.* effroi *m.*

frighten, *vb.* effrayer.

frightful, *adj.* affreux.

frigid, *adj.* glacial.

Frigid Zone, *n.* zone glaciale *f.*

frill, **1.** *n.* volant *m.;* affectation *f.* **2.** *vb.* plisser.

frilly, *adj.* froncé, ruché.

fringe, *n.* frange *f.*

frisky, *adj.* folâtre.

frivolity, *n.* frivolité *f.*

frivolous, *adj.* frivole.

frivolousness, *n.* frivolité *f.*

frock, *n.* robe *f.;* (monk's) froc *m.*

frog, *n.* grenouille *f.*

frolic, *vb.* folâtrer.

from, *prep.* de; (time) depuis.

front, *n.* front *m.;* (front part) devant *m.;* (in f. of) devant.

frontage, *n.* étendue de devant *f.*

frontal, *adj.* frontal, de face.

frontier, *n.* frontière *f.*

frost, *n.* gelée *f.*

frostbite, *n.* gelure *f.*

frosting, *n.* glaçage *m.*

frosty, *adj.* gelé, glacé.

froth, **1.** *n.* écume *f.* **2.** *vb.* écumer.

frown, *vb.* froncer les sourcils.

frowzy, *adj.* mal tenu, peu soigné.

frozen, *adj.* gelé.

fructify, *vb.* fructifier.

frugal, *adj.* frugal.

frugality, *n.* frugalité *f.*

fruit, *n.* fruit *m.*

fruitful, *adj.* fructueux.

fruition, *n.* réalisation *f.,* jouissance *f.,* fructification *f.*

fruitless, *adj.* infructueux.

frustrate, *vb.* faire échouer.

frustration, *n.* frustration *f.*

fry, *vb.* frire, *intr.;* faire frire, *tr.*

fryer, *n.* casserole *f.*

fuchsia, *n.* fuchsia *m.*

fudge, **1.** *n.* espèce de fondant américain. **2.** *interj.* bah!

fuel, *n.* combustible *m.*

fugitive, *adj.* fugitif.

fugue, *n.* fugue *f.*

fulcrum, *n.* pivot *m.,* point d'appui *m.*

fulfill, *vb.* accomplir.

fulfillment, *n.* accomplissement *m.*

full, *adj.* plein.

fullback, *n.* arrière *m.*

full dress, *adj.* en tenue de cérémonie.

fullness, *n.* plénitude *f.*

fully, *adv.* pleinement.

fulminate, *vb.* fulminer.

fulmination, *n.* fulmination *f.*

fumble, *vb.* tâtonner.

fume, *n.* fumée *f.*

fumigate, *vb.* désinfecter.

fumigator, *n.* fumigateur *m.*

fun, *n.* (amusement) amusement *m.;* (have f.) s'amuser; (joke) plaisanterie *f.;* (make f. of) se moquer de.

function, *n.* fonction *f.*

functional, *adj.* fonctionnel.

functionary, *n.* fonctionnaire *m.*

fund, *n.* fonds *m.*

fundamental, *adj.* fondamental.

funeral, *n.* funérailles *f.pl.*

funereal, *adj.* funèbre, funéraire.

fungicide, *n.* fongicide *m.*

fungus, *n.* fongus *m.*

funnel, *n.* entonnoir *m.;* (smoke-stack) cheminée *f.*

funny, *adj.* drôle.

fur, *n.* fourrure *f.*

furious, *adj.* furieux.

furlong, *n.* furlong *m.*

furlough, *n.* permission *f.*

furnace, *n.* fourneau *m.*

furnish, *vb.* fournir; (house) meubler.

furnishings, *n.* ameublement *m.*

furniture, *n.* meubles *m.pl.*

furor, *n.* fureur *f.*

furred, adj. fourré.
furrier, n. fourreur m.
furrow, n. sillon m.
furry, adj. qui ressemble à la fourrure.
further, 1. adj. ultérieur. 2. adv. (distance) plus loin; (extent) davantage.
furtherance, n. avancement m.
furthermore, adv. en outre.
fury, n. furie f.
fuse, n. fondre.
fuselage, n. fuselage m.
fusillade, n. fusillade f.
fusion, n. fusion f., fusionnement m.
fuss, n. **(make a f.)** faire des histoires.
fussy, adj. difficile.
futile, adj. futile.
futility, n. futilité f.
future, 1. n. avenir m.; (gramm.) futur m. 2. adj. futur.
futurity, n. avenir m.
futurology, n. futurologie f.
fuzz, n. duvet m., flou m.
fuzzy, adj. flou, frisotté.

G

gab, vb. jaser.
gabardine, n. gabardine f.
gable, n. pignon m.
gadabout, n. coureur m.
gadfly, n. taon m.
gadget, n. truc m.
gag, 1. vb. bâillonner. 2. n. blague f., bobard m.; bâillon m.
gaiety, n. gaieté f.
gaily, adv. gaiement.
gain, 1. n. gain m. 2. vb. gagner.
gainful, adj. profitable, rémunérateur.
gainfully, adv. profitablement.
gainsay, vb. contredire.
gait, n. allure f.
gala, n. fête de gala f.
galaxy, n. galaxie f., assemblée brillante f.
gale, n. grand vent m.
gall, n. (bile) fiel m.; (sore) écorchure f.
gallant, adj. (brave) vaillant; (with ladies) galant.
gallantly, adv. galamment.
gallantry, n. vaillance f., galanterie f.
gall bladder, n. vésicule biliaire f.
galleon, n. galion m.
gallery, n. galerie f.
galley, n. galère f., (naut.) cuisine f., (typographic) galée f.
galley proof, n. épreuve en première f.
Gallic, adj. gaulois.
gallivant, vb. courailler.
gallon, n. gallon m.
gallop, 1. n. galop m. 2. vb. galoper.
gallows, n. potence f.

gallstone, n. calcul biliaire m.
galore, adv. à foison, à profusion.
galosh, n. galoche f.
galvanize, vb. galvaniser.
gamble, 1. n. jeu (m.) de hasard. 2. vb. jouer.
gambler, n. joueur m.
gambling, n. jeu m.
gambol, 1. n. gambade f. 2. vb. gamboler.
game, n. jeu m.; (hunting) gibier m.
gamely, adv. courageusement, crânement.
gameness, n. courage m., crânerie f.
gamin, n. gamin m.
gamut, n. gamme f.
gamy, adj. giboyeux.
gander, n. jars m.
gang, n. bande f.; (workers) équipe f.
gangling, adj. dégingandé.
gangplank, n. passerelle f.
gangrene, n. gangrène f.
gangrenous, adj. gangreneux.
gangster, n. gangster m.
gangway, n. passage m., passavant m.
gap, n. (opening) ouverture f.; (empty space) vide m.
gape, vb. rester bouche bée.
garage, n. garage m.
garb, 1. n. vêtement m., costume m. 2. vb. vêtir, habiller.
garbage, n. ordures f.pl.
garble, vb. tronquer, altérer.
garden, n. jardin m.
gardener, n. jardinier m.
gardenia, n. gardénia m.
gargle, 1. n. gargarisme m. 2. vb. se gargariser.
gargoyle, n. gargouille f.
garish, adj. voyant.
garland, n. guirlande f.
garlic, n. ail m.
garment, n. vêtement m.
garner, vb. mettre en grenier.
garnet, n. grenat m.
garnish, vb. garnir.
garnishee, n. tiers-saisi m.
garnishment, n. saisie-arrêt f.
garret, n. mansarde f.
garrison, n. garnison f.
garrote, 1. n. garrotte f. 2. vb. garrotter.
garrulous, adj. bavard, loquace.
garter, n. jarretière f.
gas, n. gaz m.
gaseous, adj. gazeux.
gash, 1. n. coupure f., entaille f. 2. vb. couper, entailler.
gasket, n. garcette f.
gasless, adj. sans gaz.
gas mask, n. masque à gaz m.
gasohol, n. essence (f.) fabriquée avec de l'alcool.
gasoline, n. essence f.
gasp, vb. (astonishment) sursauter; (lack of breath) haleter.
gassy, adj. gazeux, bavard.
gastric, adj. gastrique.

gastric juice, n. suc gastrique m.
gastritis, n. gastrite f.
gastronomically, adv. d'une manière gastronomique.
gastronomy, n. gastronomie f.
gate, n. (city) porte f.; (with bars) barrière f.; (wrought-iron) grille f.
gateway, n. porte f., entrée f.
gather, vb. rassembler, tr.; recueillir, tr.
gathering, n. rassemblement m.
gaudily, adv. de manière voyante.
gaudiness, n. éclat criard m., ostentation f.
gaudy, adj. voyant.
gaunt, adj. décharné.
gauntlet, n. gantelet m.
gauze, n. gaze f.
gavel, n. marteau m.
gavotte, n. gavotte f.
gawky, adj. dégingandé.
gay, 1. adj. gai. 2. homosexuel n. 3. pédé(raste).
gaze, vb. regarder fixement.
gazelle, n. gazelle f.
gazette, n. gazette f.
gazetteer, n. gazetier m., répertoire géographique m.
gear, n. (implements, device) appareil m.; (machines) engrenage m.; (in g.) engrené; (g. change) changement (m.) de vitesse.
gearing, n. engrenage m.
gearshift, n. changement de vitesse m.
gelatin, n. gélatine f.
gelatinous, adj. gélatineux.
geld, vb. châtrer.
gelding, n. animal châtré m.
gem, n. pierre (f.) précieuse.
gender, n. genre m.
gene, n. déterminant d'hérédité m.
genealogical, adj. généalogique.
genealogy, n. généalogie f.
general, adj. and n. général m.
generality, n. généralité f.
generalization, n. généralisation f.
generalize, vb. généraliser.
generally, adv. généralement.
generalship, n. stratégie f.
generate, vb. engendrer, générer.
generation, n. génération f.
generic, adj. générique.
generosity, n. générosité f.
generous, adj. généreux.
generously, adv. généreusement.
genetic, adj. génétique.
genetics, n. génétique f.
genial, adj. sympathique.
geniality, n. jovialité f., bienveillance f.
genially, adv. affablement.
genital, adj. génital.
genitals, n. organes génitaux m.pl.

genitive, *n. and adj.* génitif *m.*
genius, *n.* génie *m.*
genocide, *n.* génocide *m.*
genre, *n.* genre *m.*
genteel, *adj.* de bon ton.
gentian, *n.* gentiane *f.*
gentile, *n.* gentil *m.*
gentility, *n.* prétention à la distinction *f.*
gentle, *adj.* doux *m.,* douce *f.*
gentleman, *n.* monsieur *m. pl.* messieurs; (character) galant homme *m.*
gentlemanly, *adj.* comme il faut, bien élevé.
gentlemen's agreement, *n.* convention verbale *f.*
gentleness, *n.* douceur *f.*
gently, *adv.* doucement.
gentry, *n.* petite noblesse *f.*
genuflect, *vb.* faire des génuflexions.
genuine, *adj.* véritable.
genuinely, *adv.* véritablement.
genuineness, *n.* authenticité *f.*
genus, *n.* genre *m.*
geographer, *n.* géographe *m.*
geographical, *adj.* géographique.
geography, *n.* géographie *f.*
geometric, *adj.* géométrique.
geometry, *n.* géométrie *f.*
geopolitics, *n.* géopolitique *f.*
geranium, *n.* géranium *m.*
germ, *n.* germe *m.*
German, 1. *n.* (person) Allemand *m.;* (language) allemand *m.* **2.** *adj.* allemand.
germane, *adj.* approprié.
Germanic, *adj.* allemand, germanique.
German measles, *n.* rougeole bénigne *f.*
Germany, *n.* Allemagne *f.*
germicide, *n.* microbicide *m.*
germinal, *adj.* germinal.
germinate, *vb.* germer.
gestate, *vb.* enfanter.
gestation, *n.* gestation *f.*
gesticulate, *vb.* gesticuler.
gesticulation, *n.* gesticulation *f.*
gesture, *n.* geste *m.*
get, *vb.* (obtain) obtenir; (receive) recevoir; (take) prendre; (become) devenir; (arrive) arriver; **(g. in)** entrer; **(g. off)** descendre; **(g. on,** agree) s'entendre; **(g. on,** up) monter; **(g. out)** sortir; **(g. up)** se lever.
getaway, *n.* fuite *f.*
geyser, *n.* geyser *m.*
ghastly, *adj.* horrible.
ghost, *n.* (specter) revenant *m.;* (Holy G.) Saint-Esprit *m.*
ghost writer, *n.* collaborateur anonyme *m.,* nègre *m.*
ghoul, *n.* goule *f.,* vampire *m.*
giant, *n.* géant *m.*
gibberish, *n.* baragouin *m.*
gibbon, *n.* gibbon *m.*
gibe, 1. *n.* raillerie *f.* **2.** *vb.* railler.
giblet, *n.* abatis (de volaille) *m.*
giddy, *adj.* étourdi.

gift, *n.* don *m.;* (present) cadeau *m.*
gifted, *adj.* doué.
gigantic, *adj.* géant, gigantesque.
giggle, *vb.* rire nerveusement, glousser.
gigolo, *n.* gigolo *m.*
gild, *vb.* dorer.
gill, *n.* ouïes (of fish) *f.pl.*
gilt, 1. *n.* dorure *f.* **2.** *adj.* doré.
gilt-edged, *adj.* doré sur tranche.
gimcrack, 1. *n.* camelote *f.* **2.** *adj.* de camelote.
gimlet, *n.* vrille *f.*
gin, *n.* genièvre *m.*
ginger, *n.* gingembre *m.*
ginger ale, *n.* boisson gazeuse au gingembre *f.*
gingerly, *adv.* avec précaution.
gingersnap, *n.* biscuit au gingembre *m.*
gingham, *n.* guingan *m.*
giraffe, *n.* girafe *f.*
gird, *vb.* ceindre.
girder, *n.* support *m.*
girdle, *n.* gaine *f.*
girl, *n.* jeune fille *f.*
girlish, *adj.* de jeune fille.
girth, *n.* sangle *f.,* circonférence *f.,* corpulence *f.*
gist, *n.* fond *m.,* essence *f.*
give, *vb.* donner; **(g. back)** rendre; **(g. in)** céder; **(g. out)** distribuer; **(g. up)** renoncer à.
give-and-take, *adv.* donnant donnant.
given, *adj.* donné.
given name, *n.* nom de baptême *m.*
giver, *n.* donneur *m.*
gizzard, *n.* gésier *m.*
glacé, *adj.* glacé.
glacial, *adj.* glaciaire.
glacier, *n.* glacier *m.*
glad, *adj.* heureux.
gladden, *vb.* réjouir.
glade, *n.* clairière *f.,* éclaircie *f.*
gladiolus, *n.* glaïeul *m.*
gladly, *adv.* volontiers.
gladness, *n.* joie *f.*
Gladstone bag, *n.* sac américain *m.*
glamour, *n.* éclat *m.*
glance, *n.* coup (*m.*) d'œil.
gland, *n.* glande *f.*
glandular, *adj.* glandulaire.
glare, 1. *n.* (light) clarté *f.;* (stare) regard (*m.*) enflammé. **2.** *vb.* (shine) briller; (look) jeter des regards enflammés.
glaring, *adj.* éclatant, flagrant, voyant, manifeste.
glass, *n.* verre *m.*
glass-blowing, *n.* soufflage *m.*
glasses, *n.* lunettes *f.pl.*
glassful, *n.* verre *m.,* verrée *f.*
glassware, *n.* verrerie *f.*
glassy, *adj.* vitreux.
glaucoma, *n.* glaucome *m.*
glaze, 1. *n.* lustre *m.* **2.** *vb.* vitrer.
glazier, *n.* vitrier *m.*

gleam, 1. *n.* lueur *f.* **2.** *vb.* luire.
glee, *n.* allégresse *f.*
glee club, *n.* chœur d'hommes *m.*
gleeful, *adj.* joyeux, allègre.
glen, *n.* vallon *m.,* ravin *m.*
glib, *adj.* spécieux.
glide, *vb.* glisser; (plane) planer.
glider, *n.* planeur *m.*
glimmer, 1. *n.* faible lueur *f.* **2.** jeter une faible lueur.
glimmering, *adj.* faible, vacillant.
glimpse, *vb.* entrevoir.
glint, 1. *n.* éclair *m.,* reflet *m.* **2.** *vb.* entreluire, étinceler.
glitter, *vb.* étinceler.
gloat, *vb.* se régaler de.
global, *adj.* global.
globe, *n.* globe *m.*
globetrotter, *n.* globe trotter *m.*
globular, *adj.* globulaire, globuleux.
globule, *n.* globule *m.*
glockenspiel, *n.* glockenspiel *m.*
gloom, *n.* (darkness) ténèbres *f.pl.;* (sadness) tristesse *f.*
gloomy, *adj.* sombre.
glorification, *n.* glorification *f.*
glorify, *vb.* glorifier.
glorious, *adj.* glorieux; (weather) radieux.
glory, *n.* gloire *f.*
gloss, 1. *n.* lustre *m.,* vernis *m.,* glose *f.* **2.** *vb.* lustrer, glacer.
glossary, *n.* glossaire *m.*
glossy, *adj.* lustré, glacé.
glove, *n.* gant *m.*
glow, *n.* (light) lumière *f.;* (heat) chaleur *f.*
glowing, *adj.* embrasé, rayonnant.
glowingly, *adv.* en termes chaleureux.
glowworm, *n.* ver luisant *m.*
glucose, *n.* glucose *f.*
glue, 1. *n.* colle (*f.*) forte. **2.** *vb.* coller.
glum, *adj.* maussade.
glumness, *n.* air maussade *m.,* tristesse *f.*
glut, 1. *n.* assouvissement *m.,* excès *m.,* pléthore *f.* **2.** *vb.* assouvir, rassasier, gorger.
glutinous, *adj.* glutineux.
glutton, *n.* gourmand *m.*
gluttonous, *adj.* gourmand, goulu.
glycerin, *n.* glycérine *f.*
gnarl, *n.* loupe *f.,* nœud *m.*
gnash, *vb.* grincer.
gnat, *n.* moucheron *m.*
gnaw, *vb.* ronger.
gnu, *n.* gnou *m.*
go, *vb.* aller; **(g. away)** s'en aller; **(g. back)** retourner; **(g. by)** passer; **(g. down)** descendre; **(g. in)** entrer; **(g. on)** continuer; **(g. out)** sortir; **(g. up)** monter; **(g. without)** se passer de.
goad, 1. *n.* aiguillon *m.* **2.** *vb.* aiguillonner, piquer.

goal, n. but m.

goat, n. chèvre f.

goatee, n. barbiche f.

goatherd, n. chevrier m.

goatskin, n. peau de chèvre f.

gobble, vb. avaler goulûment, dévorer.

gobbler, n. avaleur m.; dindon m.

go-between, n. intermédiaire m.

goblet, n. gobelet m.

goblin, n. gobelin m., lutin m.

God, n. Dieu m.

godchild, n. filleul m.

goddess, n. déesse f.

godfather, n. parrain m.

godless, adj. athée, impie, sans Dieu.

godlike, adj. comme un dieu, divin.

godly, adj. dévot, pieux, saint.

godmother, n. marraine f.

godsend, n. aubaine f., bienfait du ciel m.

Godspeed, interj. bon voyage!

go-getter, n. homme d'affaires énergique m., arriviste m.

goiter, n. goitre m.

gold, n. or m.

gold brick, n. attrape-niais m.

golden, adj. d'or.

goldenrod, n. solidage m.

golden rule, n. règle par excellence f.

gold-filled, adj. aurifié, en (or) doublé.

goldfinch, n. chardonneret m.

goldfish, n. poisson rouge m.

gold leaf, n. feuille d'or f., or battu m.

goldsmith, n. orfèvre m.

gold standard, n. étalon or m.

golf, n. golf m.

gondola, n. gondole f.

gondolier, n. gondolier m.

gone, adj. disparu, parti.

gong, n. gong m.

gonorrhea, n. gonorrhée f., blennorrhagie f.

good, adj. bon m., bonne f.

good, n. bien m.; (**goods**) marchandises f.pl.

good-bye, n. and interj. adieu m.

Good Friday, n. Vendredi Saint m.

good-hearted, adj. qui a bon cœur, compatissant.

good-humored, adj. de bonne humeur, plein de bonhomie.

good-looking, adj. beau, joli.

good-natured, adj. au bon naturel, accommodant.

goodness, n. bonté f.

good will, n. bonne volonté f.

goose, n. oie f.

gooseberry, n. groseille verte f.

gooseneck, n. col de cygne m.

goose step, n. pas d'oie m.

gore, 1. n. (dress) chanteau m., soufflet m.; (blood) sang coagulé m. 2. vb. corner.

gorge, n. gorge f.

gorgeous, adj. splendide.

gorilla, n. gorille m.

gory, adj. sanglant, ensanglanté.

gosling, n. oison m.

gospel, n. évangile m.

gossamer, n. filandre f., gaze légère f.

gossip, 1. n. bavardage m. 2. vb. bavarder.

Gothic, adj. gothique.

gouge, 1. n. gouge f. 2. vb. gouger.

gourd, n. gourde f., courge f.

gourmand, n. gourmand m.

gourmet, n. gourmet m.

govern, vb. gouverner.

governess, n. gouvernante f.

government, n. gouvernement m.

governmental, adj. gouvernemental.

governor, n. gouvernant m.

governorship, n. fonctions de gouverneur m.f.pl., temps de gouvernement m.

gown, n. robe f.

grab, vb. saisir.

grace, n. grâce f.

graceful, adj. gracieux.

gracefully, adv. avec grâce.

graceless, adj. sans grâce, gauche.

gracious, adj. gracieux; (merciful) miséricordieux.

grackle, n. mainate m.

grade, 1. n. grade m.; (quality) qualité f.; 2. vb. classer.

grade crossing, n. passage à niveau m.

gradual, adj. graduel.

gradually, adv. graduellement.

graduate, vb. graduer; (school) prendre ses grades.

graft, n. corruption f.

grail, n. graal m.

grain, n. grain m.

gram, n. gramme m.

grammar, n. grammaire f.

grammarian, n. grammairien m.

grammar school, n. école primaire f.

grammatical, adj. grammatical.

gramophone, n. phonographe.

granary, n. grenier m.

grand, adj. grandiose; (in titles) grand; (fine, colloq.) épatant.

grandchild, n. petit-fils m.; petite-fille f.; petits-enfants m.pl.

granddaughter, n. petite-fille f.

grandee, n. grand m.

grandeur, n. grandeur f.

grandfather, n. grand-père m.

grandiloquent, adj. grandiloquent.

grandiose, adj. grandiose.

grand jury, n. jury d'accusation m.

grandly, adv. grandement, magnifiquement.

grandmother, n. grand'mère f.

grand opera, n. grand opéra m.

grandson, n. petit-fils m.

grandstand, n. grande tribune f.

granger, n. régisseur m.

granite, n. granit m.

granny, n. bonne-maman f.

grant, 1. n. concession f.; (money) subvention f. 2. vb. accorder; (admit) admettre.

granular, adj. en grains, granulé.

granulate, vb. granuler, grener.

granulation, n. granulation f.

granule, n. granule m.

grape, n. raisin m.

grapefruit, n. pamplemousse f.

grapeshot, n. mitraille f.

grapevine, n. treille f.

graph, n. courbe f.

graphic, adj. graphique, pittoresque.

graphite, n. graphite m.

graphology, n. graphologie f.

grapple, 1. n. grappin m.; lutte f. 2. vb. accrocher; en venir aux prises.

grasp, 1. n. (hold) prise f. 2. vb. saisir.

grasping, adj. avide, cupide.

grass, n. herbe f.

grasshopper, n. sauterelle f.

grassy, adj. herbeux, verdoyant.

grate, 1. n. grille f. 2. vb. (cheese, etc.) râper; (make noise) grincer.

grateful, adj. reconnaissant.

gratify, vb. contenter, satisfaire.

grating, 1. n. grille f. 2. vb. grinçant, discordant.

gratis, adv. gratis, gratuitement.

gratitude, n. gratitude f.

gratuitous, adj. gratuit.

gratuity, n. (tip) pourboire m.

grave, 1. n. tombe f. 2. adj. grave.

gravel, n. gravier m.

gravely, adv. gravement, sérieusement.

gravestone, n. pierre sépulcrale f., tombe f.

graveyard, n. cimetière m.

gravitate, vb. graviter.

gravitation, n. gravitation f.

gravity, n. gravité f.

gravure, n. gravure f.

gravy, n. jus m.

gray, adj. gris.

grayish, adj. grisâtre.

gray matter, n. substance grise f., cendrée f.

graze, vb. paître.

grazing, n. pâturage m.

grease, 1. n. graisse f. 2. vb. graisser.

great, adj. grand.

Great Dane, n. grand Danois m.

greatness, n. grandeur f.

Greece, n. Grèce f.

greediness, n. gourmandise f.

greedy, adj. gourmand.

Greek, 1. n. (person) Grec m., Grecque f.; (language) grec *m.* 2. *adj.* grec *m.,* grecque *f.*

green, *adj.* vert.

greenery, *n.* verdure *f.*

greenhouse, *n.* serre *f.*

greet, *vb.* saluer.

greeting, *n.* salutation *f.;* (reception) accueil *m.*

gregarious, *adj.* grégaire.

grenade, *n.* grenade *f.*

grenadine, *n.* grenadine *f.*

greyhound, *n.* lévrier *m.*

grid, *n.* gril *m.*

griddle, *n.* gril *m.*

gridiron, *n.* gril *m.*

grief, *n.* chagrin *m.*

grievance, *n.* grief *m.*

grieve, *vb.* affliger, *tr.;* chagriner, *tr.*

grievous, *adj.* douloureux.

grill, 1. *n.* gril *m.* 2. *vb.* griller.

grillroom, *n.* grill-room *m.*

grim, *adj.* sinistre.

grimace, *n.* grimace *f.*

grime, *n.* saleté *f.,* noirceur *f.*

grimy, *adj.* sale, noirci, encrassé.

grin, *n.* large sourire *m.*

grind, *vb.* (crush) moudre; (sharpen) aiguiser.

grindstone, *n.* meule *f.*

gringo, *n.* Anglo-américain *m.*

grip, *n.* prise *f.*

gripe, *vb.* saisir, empoigner; grogner.

grisly, *adj.* hideux, horrible.

grist, *n.* blé à moudre *m.,* mouture *f.*

gristle, *n.* cartilage *m.*

grit, *n.* grès *m.,* sable *m.; (fig.)* cran *m.,* courage *m.*

grizzled, *adj.* grison, grisonnant.

groan, 1. *n.* gémissement *m.* 2. *vb.* gémir.

grocer, *n.* épicier *m.*

grocery, *n.* épicerie *f.*

grog, *n.* grog *m.*

groggy, *adj.* gris, titubant.

groin, *n.* aine *f.*

groom, 1. *n.* (horses) palefrenier *m.;* (bridegroom) nouveau marié *m.* 2. *vb.* (horses) panser.

groove, *n.* rainure *f.*

grope, *vb.* tâtonner.

grosgrain, *adj.* de grosgrain.

gross, *adj.* (bulky) gros *m.,* grosse *f.;* (coarse) grossier; *(comm.)* brut.

grossly, *adv.* grossièrement.

grossness, *n.* grossièreté *f.,* énormité *f.*

grotesque, *adj. and n.* grotesque *m.*

grotto, *n.* grotte *f.*

grouch, 1. *n.* maussaderie *f.;* grogneur *m.* 2. *vb.* grogner.

ground, *n.* (earth) terre *f.;* (territory) terrain *m.;* (reason) raison *f.;* (background) fond *m.*

ground hog, *n.* marmotte d'Amérique *f.*

groundless, *adj.* sans fondement.

ground swell, *n.* houle *f.,* lame de fond *f.*

groundwork, *n.* fondement *m.,* fond *m.,* base *f.*

group, 1. *n.* groupe *m.* 2. *vb.* grouper, *tr.*

groupie, *n.* groupie *f.;* membre d'un groupe de jeunes filles *m.*

grouse, 1. *n.* tétras *m.* 2. *vb.* grogner.

grove, *n.* bocage *m.,* bosquet *m.*

grovel, *vb.* ramper, se vautrer.

grow, *vb.* croître; (persons) grandir; (become) devenir; (cultivate) cultiver.

growl, *vb.* grogner.

grown, *adj.* fait, grand.

grownup, *adj. and n.* grand *m.,* adulte *m.f.*

growth, *n.* croissance *f.;* (increase) accroissement *m.*

grub, 1. *n.* larve *f.,* ver blanc *m.; (slang)* nourriture *f.* 2. *vb.* défricher, fouiller.

grubby, *adj.* véreux, *(fig.)* sale.

grudge, *n.* rancune *f.*

gruel, *n.* gruau *m.*

gruesome, *adj.* lugubre, terrifiant.

gruff, *adj.* bourru.

grumble, *vb.* grommeler.

grumpy, *adj.* bourru, morose.

grunt, 1. *n.* grognement *m.* 2. *vb.* grogner.

guarantee, 1. *n.* garantie *f.* 2. *vb.* garantir.

guarantor, *n.* garant *m.*

guaranty, *n.* garantie *f.*

guard, 1. *n.* garde *f.* 2. *vb.* garder.

guarded, *adj.* prudent, circonspect, réservé.

guardhouse, *n.* corps de garde *m.,* poste *m.*

guardian, *n.* gardien *m.;* (law) tuteur *m.*

guardianship, *n.* tutelle *f.*

guardsman, *n.* garde *m.*

guava, *n.* goyave *f.*

gubernatorial, *adj.* du gouverneur, du gouvernement.

guerrilla, *n.* guérilla *f.*

guess, 1. *n.* conjecture *f.* 2. *vb.* deviner.

guesswork, *n.* conjecture *f.*

guest, *n.* invité *m.*

guffaw, 1. *n.* gros rire *m.* 2. *vb.* s'esclaffer.

guidance, *n.* direction *f.*

guide, 1. *n.* guide *m.* 2. *vb.* guider.

guidebook, *n.* guide *m.*

guidepost, *n.* poteau indicateur *m.*

guild, *n.* corporation *f.,* corps de métier *m.*

guile, *n.* astuce *f.,* artifice *m.*

guillotine, *n.* guillotine *f.*

guilt, *n.* culpabilité *f.*

guiltily, *adv.* criminellement.

guiltless, *adj.* innocent.

guilty, *adj.* coupable.

guimpe, *n.* guimpe *f.*

guinea fowl, *n.* pintade *f.*

guinea pig, *n.* cobaye *m.*

guise, *n.* guise *f.,* façon *f.*

guitar, *n.* guitare *f.*

gulch, *n.* ravin *m.*

gulf, *n.* (geog.) golfe *m.; (fig.)* gouffre *m.*

gull, *n.* mouette *f.*

gullet, *n.* gosier *m.*

gullible, *adj.* crédule, facile à duper.

gully, *n.* ravin *m.*

gulp, 1. *n.* goulée *f.,* gorgée *f.,* trait *m.* 2. *vb.* avaler, gober.

gum, *n.* gomme *f.;* (teeth) gencive *f.*

gumbo, *n.* gombo *m.*

gummy, *adj.* gommeux.

gun, *n.* (cannon) canon *m.;* (rifle) fusil *m.*

gunboat, *n.* canonnière *f.*

gunman, *n.* partisan armé *m.,* voleur armé *m.,* bandit *m.*

gunner, *n.* artilleur *m.*

gunpowder, *n.* poudre *(f.)* à canon.

gunshot, *n.* portée de fusil *f.*

gunwale, *n.* plat-bord *m.*

gurgle, *vb.* faire glouglou, gargouiller.

guru, *n.* gourou *m.*

gush, 1. *n.* jaillissement *f.* 2. *vb.* jaillir.

gusher, *n.* source jaillissante *f.,* personne exubérante *f.*

gusset, *n.* gousset *m.,* soufflet *m.*

gust, *n.* (wind) rafale *f.*

gustatory, *adj.* gustatif.

gusto, *n.* goût *m.,* délectation *f.,* verve *f.*

gusty, *adv.* venteux, orageux.

gut, 1. *n.* boyau *m.,* intestin *m.* 2. *vb.* éventrer, vider.

gutter, *n.* (roof) gouttière *f.;* (street) ruisseau *m.*

guttural, *adj.* guttural.

guy, *n.* 1. *n.* type *m.,* individu *m.* 2. *vb.* se moquer de.

guzzle, *vb.* ingurgiter, boire avidement.

gym, *n.* gymnase *m.*

gymnasium, *n.* gymnase *m.*

gymnast, *n.* gymnaste *m.*

gymnastic, *adj.* gymnastique.

gymnastics, *n.* gymnastique *f.*

gynecology, *n.* gynécologie *f.*

gypsum, *n.* gypse *m.*

gypsy, *n.* gitane *m.f.*

gyrate, *vb.* tournoyer.

gyroscope, *n.* gyroscope *m.*

H

habeas corpus, *n.* habeas corpus *m.*

haberdasher, *n.* chemisier *m.,* mercier *m.*

haberdashery, *n.* chemiserie *f.,* mercerie *f.*

habiliment, *n.* habillement *m.,* apprêt *m.*

habit, *n.* habitude *f.*

habitable, *adj.* habitable.
habitat, *n.* habitat *m.*
habitation, *n.* habitation *f.*
habitual, *adj.* habituel.
habituate, *vb.* habituer, accoutumer.
habitué, *n.* habitué *m.*
hack, 1. *n.* (tool) pioche *f.*; (horse) cheval (*m.*) de louage; (vehicle) voiture (*f.*) de louage. **2.** *vb.* **(h. up)** hacher; (notch) entailler.
hackneyed, *adj.* banal, rebattu.
hacksaw, *n.* scie à métaux *f.*
haddock, *n.* aigle fin *m.*
haft, *n.* manche *m.*, poignée *f.*
hag, *n.* vielle sorcière *f.*
haggard, *adj.* hagard.
haggle, *vb.* marchander.
hagridden, *adj.* tourmenté par le cauchemar.
hail, 1. *n.* grêle *f.* **2.** *vb.* (weather) grêler; (salute) saluer; (come from) venir de **3.** *interj.* salut.
Hail Mary, *n.* Ave Maria *m.*
hailstone, *n.* grêlon *m.*
hailstorm, *n.* tempête de grêle *f.*
hair, *n.* cheveux *m.pl.*; (single, on head) cheveu *m.*; (on body, animals) poil *m.*
haircut, *n.* coupe (*f.*) de cheveux.
hairdo, *n.* coiffure *f.*
hairdresser, *n.* coiffeur *m.*
hairline, *n.* délié *m.*
hairpin, *n.* épingle (*f.*) à cheveux.
hair-raising, *adj.* horripilant, horrifique.
hair's-breadth, *n.* l'épaisseur d'un cheveu *f.*
hairspray, *n.* laque *f.*
hairy, *adj.* velu, poilu.
halcyon, 1. *n.* alcyon *m.* **2.** *adj.* calme.
hale, *adj.* sain.
half, 1. *n.* moitié *f.* **2.** *adj.* demi. **3.** *adv.* à moitié.
half-and-half, *n.* moitié de l'un, moitié de l'autre *f.*
halfback, *n.* demi-arrière *m.*
half-baked, *adj.* à moitié cuit, inexpérimenté, incomplet.
half-breed, *n.* métis *m.*
half brother, *n.* frère de père *m.*, frère de mère *m.*
half dollar, *n.* demi-dollar *m.*
half-hearted, *adj.* sans enthousiasme.
half-mast, *adv.* à mi-mât.
halfpenny, *n.* petit sou *m.*
halfway, *adv.* à mi-chemin.
half-wit, *n.* niais *m.*, sot *m.*
halibut, *n.* flétan *m.*
hall, *n.* (large room) salle *f.*; (entrance) vestibule *m.*
hallmark, *n.* contrôle *m.*
hallow, *vb.* sanctifier.
Halloween, *n.* la veille de la Toussaint *f.*
hallucination, *n.* hallucination *f.*

hallway, *n.* corridor *m.*, vestibule *m.*
halo, *n.* auréole *f.*
halt, 1. *n.* halte *f.* **2.** *vb.* arrêter, tr.
halter, *n.* licou *m.*, longe *f.*, corde *f.*
halve, *vb.* diviser en deux, partager en deux.
halyard, *n.* drisse *f.*
ham, *n.* jambon *m.*
hamlet, *n.* hameau *m.*
hammer, 1. *n.* marteau *m.* **2.** *vb.* marteler.
hammock, *n.* hamac *m.*
hamper, 1. *n.* pannier *m.* **2.** *vb.* embarrasser, gêner.
hamstring, *vb.* couper le jarret à, couper les moyens à.
hand, *n.* main *f.*
handball, *n.* balle *f.*
handbook, *n.* manuel *m.*
handcuff, 1. *n.* menotte *f.* **2.** *vb.* mettre les menottes à.
handful, *n.* poignée *f.*
handicap, *n.* handicap *m.*, désavantage *m.*
handicraft, *n.* métier *m.*
handiwork, *n.* main-d'œuvre *f.*
handkerchief, *n.* mouchoir *m.*
handle, 1. *n.* manche *m.* **2.** *vb.* manier.
handle bar, *n.* guidon *m.*
handmade, *adj.* fait à la main, fabriqué à la main.
handmaid, *n.* servante *f.*
hand organ, *n.* orgue portatif *m.*, orgue de Barbarie *f.*
handout, *n.* aumône *f.*; compte rendu communiqué à la presse *m.*
hand-pick, *vb.* trier à la main, éplucher à la main.
handsome, *adj.* beau *m.*, belle *f.*
hand-to-hand, *adj.* corps à corps.
handwriting, *n.* écriture *f.*
handy, *adj.* (person) adroit; (thing) commode; (at hand) sous la main.
handy man, *n.* homme à tout faire *m.*, bricoleur *m.*, factotum *m.*
hang, *vb.* pendre.
hangar, *n.* hangar *m.*
hangdog, *adj.* avec une mine patibulaire, avec un air en dessous.
hanger-on, *n.* dépendant *m.*, parasite *m.*
hang glider, *n.* glisseur duquel l'usager pend *m.*
hanging, 1. *n.* suspension *f.*, pendaison *f.* **2.** *adj.* suspendu, pendant.
hangman, *n.* bourreau *m.*
hangnail, *n.* envie *f.*
hangout, *n.* repaire *m.*, nid *m.*
hang-over, *n.* reste *m.*, reliquat *m.*
hangup, *n.* difficulté psychologique *f.*
hank, *n.* échevau *f.*, torchette *f.*

hanker, *vb.* désirer vivement, convoiter.
haphazard, *adv.* au hasard.
happen, *vb.* (take place) arriver; (chance to be) se trouver.
happening, *n.* événement *m.*
happily, *adv.* heureusement.
happiness, *n.* bonheur *m.*
happy, *adj.* heureux.
happy-go-lucky, *adj.* sans souci, insouciant.
harakiri, *n.* hara-kiri *m.*
harangue, 1. *n.* harangue *f.* **2.** *vb.* haranguer.
harass, *vb.* harceler, tracasser.
harbinger, *n.* avant-coureur *m.*, précurseur *m.*
harbor, *n.* (refuge) asile *m.*; (port) port *m.*
hard, 1. *adj.* dur; (difficult) difficile. **2.** *adv.* fort.
hard-bitten, *adj.* tenace dur à cuire.
hard-boiled, *adj.* dur, tenace, boucané.
hard coal, *n.* anthracite *m.*
harden, *vb.* durcir.
hard-headed, *adj.* pratique, positif.
hard-hearted, *adj.* insensible, impitoyable, au cœur dur.
hardiness, *n.* robustesse *f.*, vigueur *f.*
hardly, *adv.* (in a hard manner) durement; (scarcely) à peine; **(h. ever)** presque jamais.
hardness, *n.* dureté *f.*; (difficulty) difficulté *f.*
hardship, *n.* privation *f.*, de mer *m.*
hardtack, *n.* galette *f.*, biscuit de mer *m.*
hardware, *n.* quincaillerie *f.*
hardwood, *n.* bois dur *m.*
hardy, *adj.* robuste.
hare, *n.* lièvre *m.*
harebrained, *adj.* écervelé, étourdi.
harelip, *n.* bec-de-lièvre *m.*
harem, *n.* harem *m.*
hark, 1. *vb.* prêter l'oreille à. **2.** *interj.* écoutez!
Harlequin, *n.* Arlequin *m.*
harlot, *n.* prostituée *f.*, fille de joie *f.*
harm, 1. *n.* mal *m.* **2.** *vb.* nuire à.
harmful, *adj.* nuisible.
harmless, *adj.* inoffensif.
harmonic, *adj.* harmonique.
harmonica, *n.* harmonica *m.*
harmonious, *adj.* harmonieux.
harmonize, *vb.* harmoniser.
harmony, *n.* harmonie *f.*
harness, 1. *n.* harnais *m.* **2.** *vb.* harnacher.
harp, *n.* harpe *f.*
harpoon, 1. *n.* harpon *m.* **2.** *vb.* harponner.
harridan, *n.* vieille sorcière *f.*, vieille mégère *f.*
harrow, *vb.* herser; (fig.) tourmenter.
harry, *vb.* harceler.
harsh, *adj.* rude.

harshness, *n.* rudesse *f.*

harvest, 1. *n.* moisson *f.* **2.** *vb.* moissoner.

hash, 1. *n.* hachis *m.*, émincé *m.* **2.** *vb.* hacher (de la viande).

hashish, *n.* hachisch *m.*

hasn't, *vb.* n'a pas.

hassle, 1. *vb.* harceler. **2.** *n.* harcèlement *m.*

hassock, *n.* agenouilloir *m.*

haste, *n.* hâte *f.*

hasten, *vb.* hâter, *tr.*

hastily, *adv.* à la hâte.

hasty, *adj.* précipité.

hat, *n.* chapeau *m.*

hatch, *vb.* (hen) couver; (egg) éclore.

hatchery, *n.* établissement de pisiculture *m.*

hatchet, *n.* hachette *f.*

hate, *vb.* haïr.

hateful, *adj.* odieux.

hatred, *n.* haine *f.*

haughtiness, *n.* arrogance *f.*, hauteur *f.*

haughty, *adj.* hautain.

haul, *vb.* traîner.

haunch, *n.* hanche *f.*, cuissot *m.*

haunt, *vb.* hanter.

have, *vb.* avoir; (**h. to,** necessity) devoir.

haven, *n.* havre *m.*; (refuge) asile *m.*

haven't, *n.* n'ont pas.

havoc, *n.* ravage *m.*

hawk, *n.* faucon *m.*

hawker, *n.* colporteur *m.*, marchand ambulant *m.*

hawser, *n.* haussière *f.*, amarre *f.*

hawthorn, *n.* aubépine *f.*

hay, *n.* foin *m.*

hay fever, *n.* fièvre des foins *f.*

hayfield, *n.* champs de foin *m.*

hayloft, *n.* fenil *m.*, grenier *m.*

haystack, *n.* meule de foin *f.*

hazard, 1. *n.* hasard *m.* **2.** *vb.* hasarder, risquer.

hazardous, *adj.* hasardeux.

haze, *n.* brume (*f.*) légère.

hazel, *n.* noisetier *m.*; couleur de noisette *f.*

hazy, *adj.* brumeux, nébuleux.

he, *pron.* il; (alone, stressed, with another subject) lui.

head, *n.* tête *f.*

headache, *n.* mal (*m.*) de tête.

headband, *n.* bandeau *m.*

headfirst, *adv.* la tête la première.

headgear, *n.* garniture de tête *f.*, coiffure *f.*

head-hunting, *n.* chasse aux têtes *f.*

heading, *n.* rubrique *f.*

headlight, *n.* phare *m.*, projecteur *m.*

headlong, *adv.* la tête la première.

headman, *n.* chef *m.*

headmaster, *n.* directeur *m.*, principal *m.*

head-on, *adj. and adv.* de front.

headquarters, *n.* (mil.) quartier *m.*; (comm.) bureau (*m.*) principal.

headstone, *n.* pierre angulaire *f.*

headstrong, *adj.* volontaire, têtu, entêté.

headwaters, *n.* cours supérieur (d'une rivière) *m.*, eau d'amont *f.*

headway, *n.* progrès *m.*

headwork, *n.* travail de tête *m.*, travail intellectuel *m.*

heady, *adj.* impétueux, capiteux.

heal, *vb.* guérir.

health, *n.* santé *f.*

healthful, *adj.* salubre.

healthy, *adj.* sain.

heap, 1. *n.* tas *m.* **2.** *vb.* entasser.

hear, *vb.* entendre.

hearing, *n.* audition *f.*; ouïe *f.*

hearsay, *n.* ouï-dire *m.*

hearse, *n.* catafalque *m.*, corbillard *m.*

heart, *n.* cœur *m.*

heartache, *n.* chagrin *m.*, peine de cœur *f.*

heartbreak, *n.* déchirement de cœur *m.*

heartbroken, *adj.* avec le cœur brisé, navré.

heartburn, *n.* brûlures d'estomac *f.pl.*, aigreur *f.*

heartfelt, *adj.* sincère, qui va au cœur.

hearth, *n.* foyer *m.*, âtre *m.*

heartless, *adj.* sans cœur, insensible, sans pitié.

heart-rending, *adj.* à fendre le cœur, navrant, déchirant.

heartsick, *adj.* écœuré.

heart-stricken, *adj.* frappé au cœur, navré.

heart-to-heart, *adj.* à cœur ouvert, intime.

hearty, *adj.* cordial.

heat, 1. *n.* chaleur *f.* **2.** *vb.* chauffer.

heated, *adj.* chaud, chauffé, animé.

heath, *n.* bruyère *f.*, lande *f.*

heathen, *adj. and n.* païen *m.*, païenne *f.*

heather, *n.* bruyère *f.*, brande *f.*

heatstroke, *n.* coup de chaleur *m.*

heat wave, *n.* vague de chaleur *f.*, onde calorifique *f.*

heave, *vb.* (lift) lever; (utter) pousser; (rise) se soulever, *intr.*

heaven, *n.* ciel *m.*, *pl.* cieux.

heavenly, *adj.* céleste.

heavy, *adj.* lourd.

heavyweight, *n.* poids lourd *m.*

Hebrew, 1. *n.* (language) hébreu *m.* **2.** *adj.* hébreu.

heckle, *vb.* poser des questions embarrassantes.

hectare, *n.* hectare *m.*

hectic, *adj.* (restless) agité.

hectograph, 1. *n.* hectographe *m.*, autocopiste *m.* **2.** *vb.* hectographier, autocopier.

hedge, *n.* haie *f.*

hedgehog, *n.* hérisson *m.*

hedgehop, *vb.* voler à ras de terre.

hedgerow, *n.* bordure de haies *f.*

hedonism, *n.* hédonisme *m.*

heed, 1. *n.* attention *f.* **2.** *vb.* faire attention à.

heedless, *adj.* étourdi, imprudent, insouciant.

heel, *n.* talon *m.*

hefty, *adj.* fort, solide, costaud.

hegemony, *n.* hégémonie *f.*

heifer, *n.* génisse *f.*

height, *n.* hauteur *f.*

heighten, *vb.* rehausser, augmenter.

heinous, *adj.* odieux, atroce, abominable.

heir, *n.* héritier *m.*

heir apparent, *n.* héritier présomptif *m.*

heirloom, *n.* meuble *m.* (or bijou *m.*) de famille.

heir presumptive, *n.* héritier présomptif *m.*

helicopter, *n.* hélicoptère *m.*

heliocentric, *adj.* héliocentrique.

heliograph, *n.* héliographe *m.*

heliotrope, *n.* héliotrope *m.*

helium, *n.* hélium *m.*

hell, *n.* enfer *m.*

Hellenism, *n.* hellénisme *m.*

hellish, *adj.* infernal, diabolique.

hello, *interj.* (telephone) allô.

helm, *n.* barre (*f.*) du gouvernail.

helmet, *n.* casque *m.*

helmsman, *n.* homme de barre *m.*, timonier *m.*

help, 1. *n.* aide *f.* **2.** *vb.* aider; (at table) servir. **3.** *interj.* au secours!

helper, *n.* aide *m.f.*

helpful, *adj.* (person) serviable; (thing) utile.

helpfulness, *n.* serviabilité *f.*, utilité *f.*

helping, 1. *n.* portion *f.* **2.** *adj.* secourable.

helpless, *adj.* (forlorn) délaissé; (powerless) impuissant.

helter-skelter, *adv.* pêle-mêle, en désordre.

hem, 1. *n.* ourlet *m.* **2.** *vb.* ourler.

hematite, *n.* hématite *f.*

hemisphere, *n.* hémisphère *m.*

hemlock, *n.* ciguë *f.*

hemoglobin, *n.* hémoglobine *f.*

hemophilia, *n.* hémophilie *f.*

hemorrhage, *n.* hémorragie *f.*

hemorrhoid, *n.* hémorroïde *f.*

hemp, *n.* chanvre *m.*

hemstitch, 1. *n.* ourlet *m.* **2.** *vb.* ourler.

hen, *n.* poule *f.*

hence, *adv.* (time, place) d'ici; (therefore) de là.

henceforth, adv. désormais.

henchman, n. homme de confiance m., acolyte m., satellite m.

henequen, n. henequen m.

henna, 1. n. henné m. **2.** vb. teindre au henné.

henpeck, vb. mener par le bout du nez.

hepatic, adj. hépatique.

hepatica, n. hépatique f.

her, 1. adj. son m., sa f., ses pl. **2.** pron. (direct) la; (indirect) lui; (alone, stressed, with prep.) elle.

herald, n. héraut m.

heraldic, adj. héraldique.

heraldry, n. l'héraldique f.

herb, n. herbe f.

herbaceous, adj. herbacé.

herbarium, n. herbier m.

herculean, adj. herculéen.

herd, n. troupeau m.

here, adv. ici; (**h. is**) voici.

hereabout, adv. par ici, près d'ici.

hereafter, adv. dorénavant.

hereby, adv. par ceci, par ce moyen, par là.

hereditary, adj. héréditaire.

heredity, n. hérédité f.

herein, adv. ici; (**h. enclosed**) ci-enclus.

heresy, n. hérésie f.

heretic, n. hérétique m.f.

heretical, adj. hérétique.

hereto, adv. ci-joint.

heretofore, adv. jusqu'ici.

herewith, adv. avec ceci, ci-joint.

heritage, n. héritage m., patrimoine m.

hermetic, adj. hermétique.

hermit, n. ermite m.

hermitage, n. ermitage m.

hernia, n. hernie f.

hero, n. héros m.

heroic, adj. héroïque.

heroically, adv. héroïquement.

heroin, n. héroïne f.

heroine, n. héroïne f.

heroism, n. héroïsme m.

heron, n. héron m.

herpes, n. herpès m.

herring, n. hareng m.

herringbone, n. arête de hareng f.

hers, pron. le sien m., la sienne f.

herself, pron. elle-même; (reflexive) se.

hertz, n. hertz m.

hesitancy, n. hésitation f., incertitude f.

hesitant, adj. hésitant, irrésolu.

hesitate, vb. hésiter.

hesitation, n. hésitation f.

heterodox, adj. hétérodoxe.

heterodoxy, n. hétérodoxie f.

heterogeneous, adj. hétérogène.

heterosexual, adj. hétérosexuel.

hew, vb. couper, tailler.

hexagon, n. hexagone m.

heyday, n. apogée m., beaux jours m.pl.

hiatus, n. lacune f.

hibernate, vb. hiberner, hiverner.

hibernation, n. hibernation f.

hibiscus, n. hibiscus m.

hiccup, 1. n. hoquet m. **2.** vb. hoqueter.

hickory, n. noyer (blanc) d'Amérique m.

hide, vb. cacher, tr.

hide, n. peau f.

hideous, adj. hideux.

hide-out, n. cachette f., lieu de retraite m.

hierarchical, adj. hiérarchique.

hierarchy, n. hiérarchie f.

hieroglyphic, adj. hiéroglyphique.

high, adj. haut.

highbrow, n. intellectuel m.

high fidelity, n. haute fidélité f.

high-handed, adj. arbitraire, tyrannique.

high-hat, vb. traiter de haut en bas.

highland, n. haute terre f.

highlight, 1. n. clou m. **2.** vb. mettre en relief.

highly, adv. extrêmement.

high-minded, adj. à l'esprit élevé, généreux.

Highness, n. (title) Altesse f.

high school, n. lycée m.

high seas, n. haute mer f.

high-strung, adj. nerveux, impressionable.

high tide, n. marée haute f.

highway, n. grande route f.

hijacker, n. pirate de l'air m.

hike, n. excursion (f.) à pied.

hilarious, adj. hilare.

hilariousness, n. hilarité f.

hilarity, n. hilarité f.

hill, n. colline f.

hilt, n. poignée f., garde f.

him, pron. (direct) le; (indirect) lui; (alone, stressed, with prep.) lui.

himself, pron. lui-même; (reflexive) se.

hinder, vb. (impede) gêner; (prevent) empêcher.

hindmost, adj. dernier.

hindquarter, n. arrière-main m., arrière-train m.

hindrance, n. empêchement m., obstacle m., entrave f.

Hindu, 1. n. Hindou m. **2.** adj. hindou.

hinge, n. gond m.

hint, 1. n. allusion f. **2.** vb. insinuer.

hinterland, n. hinterland m., arrière-pays m.

hip, n. hanche f.

hippodrome, n. hippodrome m.

hippopotamus, n. hippopotame m.

hire, vb. louer; (servant) engager.

hireling, n. mercenaire m., stipendié m.

hirsute, adj. hirsute, velu.

his, 1. adj. son m., sa f., ses pl. **2.** pron. le sien m., la sienne f.

Hispanic, adj. hispanique.

hiss, vb. siffler.

historian, n. historien m.

historic, adj. historique.

historical, adj. historique.

history, n. histoire f.

histrionic, adj. histrionique, théâtral.

histrionics, n. parade d'émotions f., démonstration peu sincère f.

hit, 1. n. coup m.; (success) succès m. **2.** vb. frapper.

hitch, 1. n. (obstacle) anicroche f. **2.** vb. (fasten) accrocher, tr.

hither, 1. adv. ici. **2.** adj. le plus rapproché.

hitherto, adv. jusqu'ici.

hive, n. ruche f.

hives, n. éruption f., varicelle pustuleuse f., urticaire f.

hoard, 1. n. amas m. **2.** vb. amasser; (money) thésauriser.

hoarse, adj. enroué.

hoax, n. mystification f.

hobble, vb. boitiller, clopiner, entraver.

hobbyhorse, n. dada m., cheval de bois m.

hobgoblin, n. lutin m., esprit follet m.

hobnail, 1. n. caboche f., clou à ferrer m. **2.** vb. ferrer.

hobnob, vb. boire avec, fréquenter.

hobo, n. vagabond m., clochard m., ouvrier ambulant m.

hock, n. jarret m.

hockey, n. hockey m.

hocuspocus, n. passe-passe m.

hod, n. auge f.

hodgepodge, n. mélange confus m.

hoe, 1. n. houe f. **2.** vb. houer.

hog, n. porc m.

hogshead, n. tonneau m., barrique f.

hog-tie, vb. lier les quatre pattes.

hoist, 1. n. treuil m., grue f. **2.** vb. hisser.

hold, 1. n. prise f.; (ship) cale f. **2.** vb. tenir; (contain) contenir; (**h. back**) retenir; (**h. up**) arrêter, détenir, entraver.

holdup, n. arrêt m., suspension f.; coup à main armée m.

hole, n. trou m.

holiday, n. jour (m.) de fête; fête f.; (**h.s**) vacances f.pl.

holiness, n. sainteté f.

Holland, n. les Pays-Bas m.pl., Hollande f.

hollow, adj. and n. creux m.

holly, n. houx m.

hollyhock, n. passe-rose f., rose-trémière f.

holocaust, n. holocauste m.

hologram, n. hologramme m.

holography, n. holographie f.

holster, n. étui m.

holy, adj. saint.

Holy See, n. Saint-Siège m.

Holy Spirit, n. Saint-Esprit m.

Holy Week, n. semaine sainte f.

homage, n. hommage m.

home, n. maison f; (hearth) foyer (m.) domestique; (at h.) à la maison, chez soi.

homeland, n. patrie f.

homeless, adj. sans foyer, sans asile, sans abri.

homelike, adj. qui ressemble au foyer domestique.

homely, adj. laid.

homemade, adj. fait à la maison.

home rule, n. autonomie f.

homesick, adj. nostalgique.

homespun, adj. (étoffe) de fabrication domestique, fait à la maison, simple.

homestead, n. ferme f., bien de famille m.

homeward, adj. de retour.

homework, n. travail fait à la maison m., devoirs m.pl.

homicide, n. homicide m.

homily, n. homélie f.

homing pigeon, n. pigeon messager m.

hominy, n. bouillie de farine de maïs f., semoule de maïs f.

homogeneous, adj. homogène.

homonym, n. homonyme m.

homosexual, n. and adj. homosexuel m.

Honduras, n. Honduras m.

hone, vb. aiguiser, affiler.

honest, adj. honnête.

honestly, adv. honnêtement, de bonne foi.

honesty, n. honnêteté f.

honey, n. miel m.

honeybee, n. abeille domestique f.

honeycomb, 1. n. rayon de miel m. 2. vb. cribler, affouiller.

honeydew melon, n. melon m.

honeymoon, n. lune (f.) de miel.

honeysuckle, n. chèvre-feuille m.

honor, 1. n. honneur m. 2. vb. honorer.

honorable, adj. honorable.

honorary, adj. honoraire.

hood, n. capuchon m.; (vehicle) capote f.

hoodlum, n. voyou m.

hoodwink, vb. tromper, bander les yeux à.

hoof, n. sabot m.

hook, 1. n. croc m.; (fishing) hameçon m. 2. vb. accrocher.

hooked, adj. crochu, recourbé.

hooked rug, n. tapis à points noués simples m.

hookworm, n. ankylostome m.

hoop, n. cercle m.

hoop skirt, n. jupe à paniers f., vertugadin m.

hoot, 1. n. ululation f., hulule-

ment m., huée f. 2. vb. hululer, huer.

hop, 1. n. (plant) houblon m. 2. vb. sautiller.

hope, 1. n. espérance f., espoir m. 2. vb. espérer.

hopeful, adj. plein d'espoir.

hopeless, adj. désespéré.

hopelessness, n. désespoir m., état désespéré m.

hopscotch, n. marelle f.

horde, n. horde f.

horizon, n. horizon m.

horizontal, adj. horizontal.

hormone, n. hormone f.

horn, n. corne f.; (music) cor m.

hornet, n. frelon m., guêpe-frelon f.

horny, adj. corné, calleux.

horoscope, n. horoscope m.

horrendous, adj. horrible, horripilant.

horrible, adj. horrible.

horrid, adj. affreux.

horrify, vb. horrifier.

horror, n. horreur f.

horse, n. cheval m.

horseback, n. (on h.) à cheval.

horsefly, n. taon m.

horsehair, n. crin m.

horseman, n. cavalier m.

horsemanship, n. équitation f., manège m.

horseplay, n. jeu de mains m., badinerie grossière f.

horsepower, n. puissance en chevaux f.

horseradish, n. raifort m.

horseshoe, n. fer à cheval m.

horsewhip, 1. n. cravache f. 2. vb. cravacher, sangler.

hortatory, adj. exhortatif.

horticulture, n. horticulture f.

hose, n. (pipe) tuyau m.; (stockings) bas m.pl.

hosiery, n. bonneterie f.

hospitable, adj. hospitalier.

hospital, n. hôpital m.

hospitality, n. hospitalité f.

hospitalization, n. hospitalisation f.

hospitalize, vb. hospitaliser.

host, n. hôte m.

hostage, n. otage m.

hostel, n. hôtellerie f., auberge f.

hostelry, n. hôtellerie f., auberge f.

hostess, n. hôtesse f.

hostile, adj. hostile.

hostility, n. hostilité f.

hot, adj. chaud.

hotbed, n. couche f., foyer ardent m.

hot dog, n. saucisse chaude.

hotel, n. hôtel m.

hot-headed, adj. impétueux, exalté, emporté.

hothouse, n. serre f.

hound, 1. n. chien (m.) de chasse. 2. vb. poursuivre, pourchasser.

hour, n. heure f.

hourglass, n. sablier m.

hourly, adv. à chaque heure, à l'heure.

house, n. maison f.; (legislature) chambre f.

housefly, n. mouche domestique f.

household, n. (family) famille f.; (servants) domestiques m.pl.

housekeeper, n. gouvernante f.

housekeeping, n. ménage m., économie domestique f.

housemaid, n. fille de service f., bonne f., femme de chambre f.

housewife, n. ménagère f.

housework, n. ménage m.

hovel, n. taudis m., bicoque f.

hover, vb. planer.

hovercraft, n. aéroglisseur m.

how, adv. comment; (h. much) combien (de); (in exclamation) comme.

however, adv. (in whatever way) de quelque manière que; (with adj.) si . . . que; (nevertheless) cependant.

howitzer, n. obusier m.

howl, vb. hurler.

hub, n. moyeu m., centre m.

hubbub, n. vacarme m., tintamarre m.

huckleberry, n. airelle f.

huddle, 1. n. tas confus m., fouillis m. 2. vb. entasser.

hue, n. couleur f.

huff, 1. n. emportement m., accès de colère m. 2. vb. gonfler, enfler.

hug, 1. n. étreinte f. 2. vb. serrer dans ses bras.

huge, adj. énorme.

hulk, n. carcasse f., ponton m.

hull, n. coque f., corps m.

hullabaloo, n. vacarme m.

hum, vb. (insect) bourdonner; (sing) fredonner.

human, humane, adj. humain.

humanism, n. humanisme m.

humanitarian, adj. humanitaire.

humanities, n. humanités f.pl.

humanity, n. humanité f.

humanly, adv. humainement.

humble, adj. humble.

humbug, n. blague f., tromperie f., fumisterie f.

humdrum, adj. monotone, assommant.

humid, adj. humide.

humidify, vb. humidifier.

humidor, n. boîte à cigares f.

humiliate, adj. humilier.

humiliation, n. humiliation f.

humility, n. humilité f.

humor, n. (wit) humour m. (medical, mood) humeur f.

humorous, adj. (witty) humoristique; (funny) drôle.

hump, n. bosse f.

humpback, n. bossu m.

humus, n. humus m., terreau m.

hunch, 1. n. bosse f.; pressentiment *m.* 2. *vb.* arrondir, voûter.

hunchback, *n.* bossu *m.*

hundred, *adj. and n.* cent *m.*

hundredth *n. and adj.* centième *m.*

Hungarian, 1. *n.* (person) Hongrois *m.;* (language) hongrois *m.* 2. *adj.* hongrois.

Hungary, *n.* Hongrie *f.*

hunger, *n.* faim *f.*

hungry, *adj.* affamé; (be h.) avoir faim.

hunk, *n.* gros morceau *m.*

hunt, *vb.* chasser.

hunter, *n.* chasseur *m.*

hunting, *n.* chasse *f.*

huntress, *n.* chasseuse *f.*, chasseresse *f.*

hurdle, *n.* claie *f.*

hurl, *vb.* lancer.

hurricane, *n.* ouragan *m.*

hurry, 1. *n.* hâte *f.; (in a h.)* à la hâte. 2. *vb.* presser, *tr.;* se presser, *intr.*

hurt, *vb.* faire mal (à).

hurtful, *adj.* nuisible, pernicieux, préjudiciable.

hurtle, *vb.* se choquer, se heurter.

husband, *n.* mari *m.*

husbandry, *n.* agriculture *f.*, économie *f.*

hush, 1. *interj.* chut! paix! 2. *vb.* taire, imposer silence à.

husk, 1. *n.* cosse *f.*, gousse *f.* 2. *vb.* écosser, éplucher.

husky, *adj.* cossu; rauque, enroué.

hustle, *vb.* bousculer, se presser.

hut, *n.* cabane *f.*

hutch, *n.* huche *f.*, clapier *m.*

hyacinth, *n.* jacinthe *f.*

hybrid, *n.* hybride *m.*

hydrangea, *n.* hortensia *m.*

hydrant, *n.* prise d'eau *f.*, bouche d'incendie *f.*

hydraulic, *adj.* hydraulique.

hydrochloric acid, *n.* acide chlorhydrique *m.*

hydroelectric, *adj.* hydroéléctrique.

hydrogen, *n.* hydrogène *m.*

hydrophobia, *n.* hydrophobie *f.*

hydroplane, *n.* hydroplane *m.*

hydrotherapy, *n.* hydrothérapie *f.*

hyena, *n.* hyène *f.*

hygiene, *n.* hygiène *f.*

hygienic, *adj.* hygiénique.

hymn, *n.* (song, anthem) hymne *m.;* (church) hymne *f.*

hymnal, *n.* hymnaire *m.*, recueil d'hymnes *m.*

hyperacidity, *n.* hyperacidité *f.*

hyperbole, *n.* hyperbole *f.*

hypercritical, *adj.* hypercritique.

hypersensitive, *adj.* hypersensible.

hypertension, *n.* hypertension *f.*

hyphen, *n.* trait d'union *m.*

hyphenate, *vb.* mettre un trait d'union à.

hypnosis, *n.* hypnose *f.*

hypnotic, *adj.* hypnotique.

hypnotism, *n.* hypnotisme *m.*

hypnotize, *vb.* hypnotiser.

hypochondria, *n.* hypocondrie *f.*

hypochondriac, *n. and adj.* hypocondriaque *m.*

hypocrisy, *n.* hypocrisie *f.*

hypocrite, *n.* hypocrite *m.f.*

hypocritical, *adj.* hypocrite.

hypodermic, *adj.* hypodermique.

hypotenuse, *n.* hypoténuse *f.*

hypothesis, *n.* hypothèse *f.*

hypothetical, *adj.* hypothétique.

hysterectomy, *n.* hystérectomie *f.*

hysteria, *n.* hystérie *f.*

hysterical, *adj.* hystérique.

I

I, *pron.* je; (alone, stressed, with another subject) moi.

iambic, *adj.* iambique.

Iberia, *n.* Ibérie *f.*

ice, *n.* glace *f.*

iceberg, *n.* iceberg *m.*, gros bloc de glace *m.*

ice-box, *n.* glacière *f.*

ice cream, *n.* glace *f.*

ice skate, 1. *n.* patin à glace *m.* 2. *vb.* patiner.

ichthyology, *n.* ichtyologie *f.*

icing, *n.* glacé *m.*

icon, *n.* icone *f.*

icy, *adj.* glacial.

idea, *n.* idée *f.*

ideal, *adj. and n.* idéal *m.*

idealism, *n.* idéalisme *m.*

idealist, *n.* idéaliste *m.f.*

idealistic, *adj.* idéaliste.

idealize, *vb.* idéaliser.

ideally, *adv.* idéalement, en idée.

identical (with), *adj.* identique (à).

identifiable, *adj.* identifiable.

identification, *n.* identification *f.*

identify, *vb.* identifier.

identity, *n.* identité *f.*

ideology, *n.* idéologie *f.*

idiocy, *n.* idiotie *f.*, idiotisme *m.*

idiom, *n.* (language) idiome *m.;* (peculiar expression) idiotisme *m.*

idiot, *adj. and n.* idiot *m.*

idiotic, *adj.* idiot.

idle, *adj.* (unoccupied) désœuvré; (lazy) paresseux; (futile) vain.

idleness, *n.* oisiveté *f.*

idol, *n.* idole *f.*

idolatry, *n.* idolâtrie *f.*

idolize, *vb.* idolâtrer.

idyl, *n.* idylle *f.*

idyllic, *adj.* idyllique.

if, *conj.* si.

ignite, *vb.* allumer, mettre en feu.

ignition, *n.* ignition *f.*, allumage *m.*

ignoble, *adj.* ignoble; (low birth) plébéien.

ignominious, *adj.* ignominieux.

ignoramus, *n.* ignorant *m.*, ignare *m.*

ignorance, *n.* ignorance *f.*

ignorant, *adj.* ignorant; (be i. of) ignorer.

ignore, *vb.* feindre d'ignorer.

ill, 1. *n.* mal. 2. *adj.* (sick) malade; (bad) mauvais. 3. *adv.* mal.

illegal, *adj.* illégal.

illegible, *adj.* illisible.

illegibly, *adv.* illisiblement.

illegitimacy, *n.* illégitimité *f.*

illegitimate, *adj.* illégitime.

illicit, *adj.* illicite.

illiteracy, *n.* analphabétisme *m.*

illiterate, *adj.* illettré.

illness, *n.* maladie *f.*

illogical, *adj.* illogique.

illuminate, *vb.* illuminer.

illumination, *n.* illumination *f.*, enluminure *f.*

illusion, *n.* illusion *f.*

illusive, *adj.* illusoire.

illustrate, *vb.* illustrer.

illustration, *n.* illustration *f.;* (example) exemple *m.*

illustrative, *adj.* explicatif, qui éclaircit.

illustrious, *adj.* illustre.

ill will, *adj.* mauvais vouloir *m.*, malveillance *f.*

image, *n.* image *f.*

imagery, *n.* images *f.pl*, langage figuré *m.*

imaginable, *adj.* imaginable.

imaginary, *adj.* imaginaire.

imagination, *n.* imagination *f.*

imaginative, *adj.* imaginatif.

imagine, *vb.* imaginer, *tr.*

imam, *n.* imam *m.*

imbecile, *n.* imbécile *m.*

imitate, *vb.* imiter.

imitation, *n.* imitation *f.*

imitative, *adj.* imitatif.

immaculate, *adj.* immaculé, sans tache.

immanent, *adj.* immanent.

immaterial, *adj.* immatériel, incorporel, sans conséquence.

immature, *adj.* pas mûr, prématuré.

immediate, *adj.* immédiat.

immediately, *adv.* immédiatement, tout de suite.

immense, *adj.* immense.

immerse, *vb.* immerger, plonger.

immigrant, *n.* immigrant *m.*, immigré *m.*

immigrate, *vb.* immigrer.

imminent, *adj.* imminent.

immobile, *adj.* fixe, immobile.

immobilize, *vb.* immobiliser.

immoderate, *adj.* immodéré, intempéré, outré.

immodest, adj. immodeste, impudique, présomptueux.
immoral, adj. immoral.
immorality, n. immoralité f.
immorally, adv. immoralement.
immortal, adj. and n. immortel m.
immortality, n. immortalité f.
immortalize, vb. immortaliser.
immovable, adj. fixe, immuable, inébranlable.
immunity, n. exemption f., immunité f.
immunize, vb. immuniser.
immutable, adj. immuable, inaltérable.
impact, n. choc m., impact m.
impair, vb. affaiblir, altérer, compromettre.
impale, vb. empaler.
impart, vb. donner, communiquer, transmettre.
impartial, adj. impartial.
impatience, n. impatience f.
impatient, adj. impatient.
impeach, vb. attaquer, accuser, récuser.
impede, vb. entraver, empêcher.
impediment, n. entrave f., obstacle m., empêchement f.
impel, vb. pousser, forcer.
impenetrable, adj. impénétrable.
impenitent, adj. impénitent.
imperative, 1. n. (gramm.) impératif m. 2. adj. impératif (gramm.); urgent, impérieux.
imperceptible, adj. imperceptible.
imperfect, adj. and n. imparfait m.
imperfection, n. imperfection f.
imperial, adj. impérial.
imperialism, n. impérialisme m.
imperil, vb. mettre en péril, exposer au danger.
imperious, adj. impérieux, arrogant.
impersonate, vb. personnifier, représenter.
impersonation, n. personnification f., incarnation f.
impersonator, n. personnificateur m.
impertinence, n. impertinence f.
impervious, adj. impénétrable, imperméable.
impetuous, adj. impétueux.
impetus, n. élan m., vitesse acquise f.
impinge, vb. se heurter à, empiéter sur.
implacable, adj. implacable.
implant, vb. inculquer, implanter.
implement, n. outil m.
implicate, vb. impliquer, entremêler.
implication, n. implication f.
implicit, adj. implicite.
implied, adj. implicite, tacite.

implore, vb. implorer.
imply, vb. impliquer.
impolite, adj. impoli.
imponderable, adj. impondérable.
import, 1. n. article (m.) d'importation; importation f. 2. vb. importer.
importance, n. importance f.
important, adj. important.
importation, n. importation f.
importune, vb. importuner.
impose (on), vb. imposer (à).
imposition, n. imposition f.
impossibility, n. impossibilité f.
impossible, adj. impossible.
impotence, n. impuissance f.
impotent, adj. impuissant.
impoverish, vb. appauvrir.
impregnable, adj. imprenable, inexpugnable.
impregnate, vb. imprégner, féconder.
impresario, n. imprésario m.
impress, vb. (imprint) imprimer; (affect) faire une impression à.
impression, n. impression f.
impressive, adj. impressionnant.
imprison, vb. emprisonner.
imprisonment, n. emprisonnement m.
improbable, adj. improbable.
impromptu, adv., adj. and n. impromptu m.
improper, adj. (inaccurate) impropre; (unbecoming) malséant.
improve, vb. améliorer, tr.
improvement, n. amélioration f.
improvise, vb. improviser.
impudent, adj. insolent, effronté, impertinent.
impugn, vb. attaquer, contester, impugner.
impulse, n. impulsion f.
impulsion, n. impulsion f.
impulsive, adj. impulsif.
impunity, n. impunité f.
impure, adj. impur.
impurity, n. impureté f.
impute, vb. imputer.
in, prep. en; (with art. or adj.) dans; (town) à.
inadvertent, adj. inattentif, négligent, involontaire.
inalienable, adj. inaliénable.
inane, adj. inepte, niais, bête.
inaugural, adj. inaugural.
inaugurate, vb. inaugurer.
inauguration, n. inauguration f.
Inca, n. Inca m.
incandescence, n. incandescence f.
incandescent, adj. incandescent.
incantation, n. incantation f., conjuration f.
incapacitate, vb. rendre incapable, priver de capacité légale.

incarcerate, vb. incarcérer, emprisonner.
incarnate, 1. vb. incarner. 2. adj. incarné, fait chair.
incarnation, n. incarnation f.
incendiary, 1. n. incendiaire m. 2. adj. incendiaire, séditieux.
incense, n. encens m.
incentive, n. stimulant m., aiguillon m.
inception, n. commencement m., début m.
incessant, adj. incessant, continuel.
incest, n. inceste m.
inch, n. pouce m.
incidence, n. incidence f.
incident, n. incident m.
incidental, adj. fortuit.
incidentally, adv. incidemment, en passant.
incinerator, n. incinérateur m.
incipient, adj. naissant, qui commence.
incision, n. incision f., entaille f.
incisive, adj. incisif, tranchant.
incisor, n. incisive f.
incite, vb. inciter, instiguer.
inclination, n. inclinaison f., penchant m.
incline, vb. incliner.
inclose, see enclose.
include, vb. comprendre.
inclusive, adj. inclusif.
incognito, adj. and adv. incognito.
income, n. revenu m.
incomparable, adj. incomparable.
inconvenience, 1. n. inconvénient m. 2. vb. incommoder.
inconvenient, adj. incommode.
incorporate, vb. incorporer.
incorrigible, adj. incorrigible.
increase, 1. n. augmentation f. 2. vb. augmenter.
incredible, adj. incroyable.
incredulity, n. incrédulité f.
incredulous, adj. incrédule.
increment, n. augmentation m., accroissement m.
incriminate, vb. incriminer.
incrimination, n. incrimination f.
incrust, vb. incruster.
incubator, n. incubateur m.
inculcate, vb. inculquer.
incumbency, n. période d'exercice f., charge f.
incumbent, 1. n. titulaire m., bénéficiaire m. 2. adj. couché, posé, appuyé.
incur, vb. encourir.
incurable, adj. incurable.
indebted, adj. endetté.
indeed, adv. en effet.
indefatigable, adj. infatigable, inlassable.
indefinite, adj. indéfini.
indefinitely, adv. indéfiniment.
indelible, adj. indélébile, ineffaçable.
indemnify, vb. garantir, indemniser, dédommager.

indemnity, *n.* garantie *f.,* indemnité *f.,* dédommagment *m.*

indent, *vb.* denteler, découper, entailler.

indentation, *n.* découpage *m.,* renfoncement *m.,* endentement *m.*

independence, *n.* indépendance *f.*

independent, *adj.* indépendant.

in-depth, *adj.* profond.

index, *n.* index *m.*

India, *n.* Inde *f.*

Indian, 1. *n.* Indien *m.* **2.** *adj.* indien.

indicate, *vb.* indiquer.

indication, *n.* indication *f.*

indicative, *adj. and n.* indicatif *m.*

indicator, *n.* indicateur *m.*

indict, *vb.* accuser, inculper.

indictment, *n.* accusation *f.,* inculpation *f.,* réquisitoire *m.*

indifference, *n.* indifférence *f.*

indifferent, *adj.* indifférent.

indigenous, *adj.* indigène.

indigent, *adj.* indigent, pauvre.

indigestion, *n.* dyspepsie *f.,* indigestion *f.*

indignant, *adj.* indigné.

indignation, *n.* indignation *f.*

indignity, *n.* indignité *f.,* affront *m.*

indirect, *adj.* indirect.

indiscreet, *adj.* indiscret.

indiscretion, *n.* imprudence *f.*

indiscriminate, *adj.* aveugle, qui ne fait pas de distinction.

indispensable, *adj.* indispensable.

indisposed, *adj.* peu enclin, peu disposé, indisposé, souffrant.

individual, 1. *n.* individu *m.* **2.** *adj.* individuel.

individuality, *n.* individualité *f.*

individually, *adv.* individuellement.

indivisible, *adj.* indivisible.

indoctrinate, *vb.* endoctriner, instruire.

indolent, *adj.* indolent, paresseux.

Indonesia, *n.* Indonésie *f.*

indoor, *adj.* d'intérieur.

indoors, *adv.* à la maison.

indorse, *vb.* endosser, appuyer, sanctionner.

induce, *vb.* (persuade) persuader; (produce) produire.

induct, *vb.* installer, conduire.

induction, *n.* induction *f.;* installation *f.*

inductive, *adj.* inductif.

indulge, *vb.* contenter, favoriser.

indulgence, *n.* indulgence *f.*

indulgent, *adj.* indulgent.

industrial, *adj.* industriel.

industrialist, *n.* industriel *m.*

industrious, *adj.* travailleur.

industry, *n.* industrie *f.;* (diligence) assiduité *f.*

ineligible, *adj.* inéligible.

inept, *adj.* inepte, mal à propos.

inert, *adj.* inerte, apathique.

inertia, *n.* inertie *f.*

inevitable, *adj.* inévitable.

inexplicable, *adj.* inexplicable.

infallible, *adj.* infaillible.

infamous, *adj.* infâme.

infamy, *n.* infamie *f.*

infancy, *n.* (première) enfance *f.*

infant, *n.* enfant *m.f.*

infantile, *adj.* enfantin, infantile.

infantryman, *n.* soldat d'infanterie *m.,* fantassin *m.*

infatuated, *adj.* infatué, entiché.

infect, *vb.* infecter.

infection, *n.* infection *f.*

infectious, *adj.* infectieux, infect, contagieux.

infer, *vb.* déduire.

inference, *n.* inférence *f.*

inferior, *adj. and n.* inférieur *m.*

inferiority complex, *n.* complexe d'infériorité *m.*

infernal, *adj.* infernal.

inferno, *n.* enfer *m.*

infest, *vb.* infester.

infidel, *n.* infidèle *m.,* incroyant *m.*

infidelity, *n.* infidélité *f.*

infiltrate, *vb.* infiltrer.

infinite, *adj. and n.* infini *m.*

infinitesimal, *adj.* infinitésimal.

infinitive, *n.* infinitif *m.*

infinity, *n.* infinité *f.*

infirm, *adj.* infirme, faible, maladif.

infirmary, *n.* infirmerie *f.*

infirmity, *n.* infirmité *f.*

inflame, *vb.* enflammer, *tr.*

inflammable, *adj.* inflammable.

inflammation, *n.* inflammation *f.*

inflammatory, *adj.* incendiaire, inflammatoire.

inflate, *vb.* gonfler.

inflation, *n.* (currency) inflation *f.*

inflection, *n.* inflection *f.*

inflict, *vb.* (penalty) infliger.

infliction, *n.* infliction *f.,* châtiment *m.*

influence, *n.* influence *f.*

influential, *adj.* influent.

influenza, *n.* grippe *f.,* influenza *f.*

inform, *vb.* (tell) informer.

informal, *adj.* (without formality) sans cérémonie.

information, *n.* renseignements *m.pl.*

infringe, *vb.* enfreindre, violer.

infuriate, *vb.* rendre furieux.

ingenious, *adj.* ingénieux.

ingenuity, *n.* ingéniosité *f.*

ingredient, *n.* ingrédient *n.*

inhabit, *vb.* habiter.

inhabitant, *n.* habitant *m.*

inhale, *vb.* inhaler, aspirer, humer.

inherent, *adj.* inhérent.

inherit, *vb.* hériter.

inheritance, *n.* héritage *m.*

inhibit, *vb.* empêcher; (psychology) inhiber.

inhibition, *n.* inhibition *f.,* défense expresse *f.,* prohibition *f.*

inhuman, *adj.* inhumain.

inimical, *adj.* ennemi, hostile, défavorable.

inimitable, *adj.* inimitable.

iniquity, *n.* iniquité *f.*

initial, 1. *n.* initiale *f.* **2.** *adj.* initial.

initiate, *vb.* (begin) commencer; (admit) initier.

initiation, *n.* commencement *m.,* début *m.,* initiation *f.*

initiative, *n.* initiative *f.*

inject, *vb.* injecter.

injection, *n.* injection *f.*

injunction, *n.* injonction *f.,* ordre *m.*

injure, *vb.* (harm) nuire à; (wound) blesser; (damage) abîmer.

injurious, *adj.* (harmful) nuisible; (offensive) injurieux.

injury, *n.* (person) préjudice *m.;* (body) blessure *f.;* (thing) dommage *m.*

injustice, *n.* injustice *f.*

ink, *n.* encre *f.*

inland, *adj. and n.* intérieur *m.*

inlet, *n.* entrée *f.,* admission *f.,* débouché *m.*

inmate, *n.* habitant *m.,* hôte *m.,* pensionnaire *m.*

inn, *n.* auberge *f.*

inner, *adj.* intérieur.

innocence, *n.* innocence *f.*

innocent, *adj.* innocent.

innocuous, *adj.* inoffensif.

innovation, *n.* innovation *f.*

innuendo, *n.* insinuation *f.,* allusion malveillante *f.*

innumerable, *adj.* innombrable.

inoculate, *vb.* inoculer.

inoculation, *n.* inoculation *f.,* vaccination préventive *f.*

input, *n.* informations fournies à un informateur *f.pl.*

inquest, *n.* enquête *f.*

inquire (about), *vb.* se renseigner (sur).

inquiry, *n.* (investigation) recherche *f.;* (question) demande *f.;* (official) enquête *f.*

inquisition, *n.* Inquisition *f.;* enquête *f.,* recherche *f.*

inquisitive, *adj.* curieux, questionneur, indiscret.

inroad, *n.* incursion *f.,* invasion *f.* empiétement *m.*

insane, *adj.* fou *m.,* folle *f.*

insanity, *n.* folie *f.,* insanité *f.,* démence *f.*

inscribe, *vb.* inscrire, graver.

inscription, *n.* inscription *f.*

insect, *n.* insecte *m.*

insecticide, *n.* insecticide *m.*

inseparable, *adj.* inséparable.

insert, *vb.* insérer.

insertion, *n.* insertion *f.*

inside, 1. *n.* dedans *m.*, 2. *adj.* intérieur. 3. *prep.* à l'intérieur de. 4. *adv.* (en) dedans.

insidious, *adj.* insidieux.

insight, *n.* perspicacité *f.*, pénétration *f.*

insignia, *n.* insignes *m.pl.*

insignificance, *n.* insignifiance *f.*

insignificant, *adj.* insignifiant.

insinuate, *vb.* insinuer.

insinuation, *n.* insinuation *f.*

insipid, *adj.* insipide, fade.

insist, *vb.* insister.

insistence, *n.* insistance *f.*

insistent, *adj.* qui insiste, importun.

insolence, *n.* insolence *f.*

insolent, *adj.* insolent.

insomnia, *n.* insomnie *f.*

inspect, *vb.* examiner, inspecter.

inspection, *n.* inspection *f.*

inspector, *n.* inspecteur *m.*

inspiration, *n.* inspiration *f.*

inspire, *vb.* inspirer.

install, *vb.* installer.

installation, *n.* installation *f.*, montage *m.*

installment, *n.* acompte *m.*, versement partiel *m.*, payement à compte *m.*

instance, *n.* exemple *m.*

instant, *n.* instant *m.*

instantaneous, *adj.* instantané.

instantly, *adv.* à l'instant.

instead, *adv.* au lieu de cela.

instead of, *prep.* au lieu de.

instigate, *vb.* instiguer.

instill, *vb.* instiller, faire pénétrer, inculquer.

instinct, *n.* instinct *m.*

instinctive, *adj.* instinctif.

institute, *vb.* instituer.

institution, *n.* institution *f.*

instruct, *vb.* instruire.

instruction, *n.* instruction *f.*

instructive, *adj.* instructif.

instructor, *n.* (*mil.*) instructeur *m.*; (university) chargé (*m.*) de cours.

instrument, *n.* instrument *m.*

instrumental, *adj.* instrumental, contributif (à).

insufferable, *adj.* insupportable, intolérable.

insufficient, *adj.* insuffisant.

insular, *adj.* insulaire.

insulate, *vb.* isoler.

insulation, *n.* isolement *m.*

insulator, *n.* isolant *m.*, isolateur *m.*

insulin, *n.* insuline *f.*

insult, 1. *vb.* insulter. 2. *n.* insulte *f.*

insuperable, *adj.* insurmontable.

insurance, *n.* assurance *f.*

insure, *vb.* assurer.

insurgent, *adj. and n.* insurgé *m.*

insurrection, *n.* insurrection *f.*, soulèvement *m.*

intact, *adj.* intact.

intangible, *adj.* intangible, impalpable.

integral, *adj.* intégrant.

integrate, *vb.* intégrer, compléter, rendre entier.

integrity, *n.* intégrité *f.*

intellect, *n.* (mind) esprit *m.*; (faculty) intellect *m.*

intellectual, *adj. and n.* intellectuel *m.*

intelligence, *n.* intelligence *f.*; (information) renseignements *m.pl.*

intelligent, *adj.* intelligent.

intelligentsia, *n.* l'intelligence *f.*

intelligible, *adj.* intelligible.

intend, *vb.* avoir l'intention de; (destine for) destiner à.

intense, *adj.* intense.

intensity, *n.* intensité *f.*

intensive, *adj.* intensif.

intent on, *adj.* (absorbed in) absorbé dans; (determined to) déterminé à.

intention, *n.* intention *f.*

intentional, *adj.* intentionnel, voulu, fait exprès.

intercede, *vb.* intervenir, intercéder.

intercept, *vb.* intercepter, capter.

intercourse, *n.* commerce *m.*, relations *f.pl.*, rapports *m.pl.*

interdict, *vb.* interdire, prohiber.

interest, 1. *n.* intérêt *m.* 2. *vb.* intéresser.

interesting, *adj.* intéressant.

interface, *n.* entreface *f.*

interfere, *vb.* (person) intervenir (dans); (**i. with,** hinder) gêner.

interference, *n.* (person) intervention *f.*

interim, *adv.* entre temps, en attendant.

interior, *adj. and n.* intérieur *m.*

interject, *vb.* lancer, émettre.

interjection, *n.* interjection *f.*

interlude, *n.* intermède *m.*, interlude *m.*

intermarry, *vb.* se marier.

intermediary, *n.* intermédiaire *m.f.*

intermediate, *adj. and n.* intermédiaire *m.f.*

interment, *n.* enterrement *m.*

intermission, *n.* interruption *f.*, relâche *f.*; (theater) entr'acte *m.*

intermittent, *adj.* intermittent.

intern, 1. *n.* interne *m.* 2. *vb.* interner.

internal, *adj.* interne.

international, *adj.* international.

internationalism, *n.* internationalisme *m.*

interne, *n.* interne *m.*

interpose, *vb.* interposer, *tr.*

interpret, *vb.* interpréter.

interpretation, *n.* interprétation *f.*

interpreter, *n.* interprète *m.f.*

interrogate, *vb.* interroger, questionner.

interrogation, *n.* interrogation *f.*

interrogative, 1. *adj.* interrogateur. 2. *n.* interrogatif *m.*

interrupt, *vb.* interrompre.

interruption, *n.* interruption *f.*

intersect, *vb.* entrecouper, intersecter, entrecroiser.

intersection, *n.* intersection *f.*

intersperse, *vb.* entremêler, parsemer, intercaler.

interval, *n.* intervalle *m.*

intervene, *vb.* intervenir.

intervention, *n.* intervention *f.*

interview, *n.* entrevue *f.*; (press) interview *m. or f.*

intestine, *n.* intestin *m.*

intimacy, *n.* intimité *f.*

intimate, *adj.* intime.

intimidate, *vb.* intimider.

intimidation, *n.* intimidation *f.*

into, *prep.* en; (with art. or adj.) dans.

intonation, *n.* intonation *f.*

intone, *vb.* entonner, psalmodier.

intoxicate, *vb.* enivrer.

intoxication, *n.* intoxication *f.*, ivresse *f.*

intravenous, *adj.* intraveineux.

intrepid, *adj.* intrépide, brave, courageux.

intricacy, *n.* complexité *f.*, nature compliquée *f.*

intricate, *adj.* compliqué.

intrigue, *n.* intrigue *f.*

intrinsic, *adj.* intrinsèque.

introduce, *vb.* (bring in) introduire; (present) présenter.

introduction, *n.* introduction *f.*; (presenting) présentation *f.*

introductory, *adj.* introductoire, d'introduction.

introspection, *n.* introspection *f.*, recueillement *m.*

introvert, *n.* introverti *m.*

intrude on, *vb.* importuner.

intruder, *n.* intrus *m.*

intuition, *n.* intuition *f.*

intuitive, *adj.* intuitif.

inundate, *vb.* inonder.

invade, *vb.* envahir.

invader, *n.* envahisseur *m.*, transgresseur *m.*

invalid, *adj. and n.* infirme *m.f.*

invariable, *adj.* invariable.

invasion, *n.* invasion *f.*

invective, *n.* invective *f.*

inveigle, *vb.* attirer, séduire, leurrer.

invent, *vb.* inventer.

invention, *n.* invention *f.*

inventive, *adj.* inventif, trouveur.

inventor, *n.* inventeur *m.*

inventory, *n.* inventaire *m.*

invertebrate, 1. *n.* invertébré *m.* 2. *adj.* invertébré.

invest, *vb.* investir; (money) placer.

investigate, *vb.* faire des recherches (sur).

investigation, n. investigation f.

investment, n. placement m.

inveterate, adj. invétéré, enraciné.

invidious, adj. odieux, haïssable, ingrat.

invigorate, vb. fortifier, vivifier.

invincible, adj. invincible.

invisible, adj. invisible.

invitation, n. invitation f.

invite, vb. inviter.

invocation, n. invocation f.

invoice, n. facture f.

invoke, vb. invoquer.

involuntary, adj. involontaire.

involve, vb. (implicate) impliquer; (entail) entraîner.

invulnerable, adj. invulnérable.

inward, adj. intérieur.

iodine, n. iode m.

Iran, n. Iran m.

Iraq, n. Irak m.

irate, adj. en colère, courroucé, furieux.

Ireland, n. Irlande f.

iridium, n. iridium m.

iris, n. iris m.

Irish, adj. irlandais.

Irishman, n. Irlandais m.

irk, vb. ennuyer.

iron, n. fer m.

ironworks, n. fonderie de fonte f., usine métallurgique f.

irony, n. ironie f.

irrational, adj. irrationnel, déraisonnable, absurde.

irrefutable, adj. irréfutable, irrécusable.

irregular, adj. irrégulier.

irregularity, n. irrégularité f.

irrelevant, adj. non pertinent, hors de propos.

irresistible, adj. irrésistible.

irresponsible, adj. irresponsable.

irreverent, adj. irrévérent, irrévérencieux.

irrevocable, adj. irrévocable.

irrigate, vb. irriguer, arroser.

irrigation, n. irrigation f.

irritability, n. irritabilité f.

irritable, adj. irritable, irascible.

irritant, n. irritant m.

irritate, vb. irriter.

irritation, n. irritation f.

Islam, n. Islam m.

Islamic, adj. islamique.

island, n. île f.

isolate, vb. isoler.

isolation, n. isolement m.

isolationist, n. isolationniste m.

isosceles, adj. isoscèle.

Israel, n. Israël m.

Israeli, n. Israéli m.

issuance, n. délivrance f.

issue, 1. n. (way out, end) issue f.; (result) résultat m.; (question) question f.; (money, bonds) émission f. 2. vb. (come out) sortir; (publish) publier; (money) émettre.

isthmus, n. isthme m.

it, pron. (subject) il m.; elle f.; (object) le m., la f.; (of it) en; (in it, to it) y.

Italian, 1. n. (person) Italien m.; (language) italien m. 2. adj. italien.

Italy, n. Italie f.

itch, 1. n. démangeaison f. 2. vb. démanger.

item, n. (article) article m.; (detail) détail m.

itemize, vb. détailler.

itinerant, adj. ambulant.

itinerary, n. itinéraire m.

its, 1. adj. son m., sa f., ses pl. 2. pron. le sien m., la sienne f.

itself, pron. lui-même m., elle-même f.; (reflexive) se.

ivory, n. ivoire m.

ivy, n. lierre m.

J

jab, n. coup m., coup sec m. 2. vb. piquer, donner un coup sec.

jackal, n. chacal m.

jackass, n. âne m.; idiot m.

jacket, n. (man) veston m.; (woman) jaquette f.

jackknife, n. couteau de poche m.

jack-of-all-trades, n. maître Jacques m., factotum m., homme à tous les métiers m.

jade, n. rosse f., haridelle f.; drôlesse f., coureuse f.; jade m.

jaded, adj. surmené, éreinté, blasé, fatigué.

jagged, adj. déchiqueté, entaillé, dentelé.

jaguar, n. jaguar m.

jail, n. prison f.

jailer, n. gardien m., geôlier m.

jam, 1. n. foule f., presse f., embouteillage m.; confiture f. 2. vb. serrer, presser.

jamb, n. jambage m., montant m., chambranle m.

jangle, 1. n. querelle f., chamaille f.; cliquetis m. 2. vb. se quereller, se chamailler; cliqueter.

janitor, n. concierge m.

January, n. janvier m.

Japan, n. Japon m.

Japanese, 1. n. (person) Japonais m.; (language) japonais m. 2. adj. japonais.

jar, 1. n. (container) pot m.; (sound) son (m.) discordant; (shock) secousse f. 2. vb. secouer, heurter.

jargon, n. jargon m.

jasmine, n. jasmin m.

jaundice, n. jaunisse f.

jaunt, n. petite excursion f., balade f.

javelin, n. javelot m., javeline f.

jaw, n. mâchoire f.

jay, n. geai m.

jaywalk, vb. se promener d'une façon distraite ou imprudente.

jazz, n. jazz m.

jealous, adj. jaloux.

jealousy, n. jalousie f.

jeans, n. jeans m.pl.

jeer, 1. n. raillerie f.; moquerie f., huée f. 2. vb. se moquer de, huer.

jelly, n. gelée f.

jellyfish, n. méduse f.

jeopardize, vb. exposer au danger, mettre en danger, hasarder.

jeopardy, n. danger m., péril m.

jerk, n. saccade f.

jerkin, n. justaucorps m., pourpoint m.

jerky, adj. saccadé, coupé.

jersey, n. jersey m., tricot de laine m.

Jerusalem, n. Jérusalem m.

jest, 1. plaisanterie f., raillerie f., badinage m. 2. vb. plaisanter, railler, badiner.

jester, n. railleur m., farceur m., bouffon m.

Jesuit, n. Jésuite m.

Jesus, n. Jésus m.

jet, n. (mineral) jais m.; (water, gas) jet m.; (j. plane) avion (m.) à réaction.

jet lag, n. désorientation physiologique produite par le décalage d'heures.

jetsam, n. épaves f.pl.

jettison, vb. se délester.

jetty, n. jetée f., môle m.

Jew, n. Juif m., Juive f.

jewel, n. bijou m.

jeweler, n. bijoutier m., jouailler m.

jewelry, n. bijouterie f.

Jewish, adj. juif m., juive f.

jib, n. foc m.

jibe, vb. être en accord, s'accorder.

jiffy, n. instant m., clin d'oeil m.

jig, 1. n. gigue f.; calibre m., gabarit m. 2. danser la gigue, sautiller.

jilt, vb. délaisser, plaquer, planter.

jingle, 1. n. tintement m., cliquetis m. 2. vb. tinter, cliqueter.

jinx, n. porte-malheur m.

jittery, adj. très nerveux.

job, n. (work) travail m.; (employment) emploi m.

jobber, n. intermédiaire m., marchandeur m., sous-traitant m.

jockey, n. jockey m.

jocular, adj. facétieux, jovial, rieur.

jocund, adj. enjoué.

jodhpurs, n. pantalon d'équitation m.

jog, 1. n. coup m., secousse f., cahot m. 2. vb. pousser, secouer, cahoter.

joggle, 1. n. petite secousse f. **2.** vb. secouer légèrement.

join, vb. (things) joindre; (group, etc.) se joindre à.

joiner, n. menuisier m.

joint, 1. n. joint m. **2.** adj. (in common) commun; (in partnership) co-.

jointly, adv. ensemble, conjointement.

joist, n. solive f., poutre f.

joke, 1. n. plaisanterie f. **2.** vb. plaisanter.

joker, n. farceur m., blagueur m.; joker m.

jolly, adj. joyeux.

jolt, 1. n. cahot m., choc m., secousse f. **2.** vb. cahoter, secouer, ballotter.

jonquil, n. jonquille f.

jostle, vb. coudoyer tr.

jounce, 1. n. cahot m., secousse f. **2.** vb. cahoter.

journal, n. journal m.

journalism, n. journalisme m.

journalist, n. journaliste m.

journey, 1. n. voyage m. **2.** vb. voyager.

journeyman, n. compagnon m.

jovial, adj. jovial, gai.

jowl, n. mâchoire f.

joy, n. joie f.

joyful, adj. joyeux.

joyous, adj. joyeux.

jubilant, adj. réjoui, jubilant, exultant.

jubilee, n. jubilé m.

Judaism, n. judaïsme m.

judge, 1. n. juge m. **2.** vb. juger.

judgment, n. jugement m.

judicial, adj. judiciaire.

judiciary, adj. judiciaire.

judicious, adj. judicieux, sensé.

jug, n. cruche f.

juggle, vb. jongler.

jugular, adj. jugulaire.

juice, n. jus m.

juicy, adj. juteux.

July, n. juillet m.

jumble, 1. n. brouillamini m., fouillis m., fatras m. **2.** vb. brouiller, mêler confusément.

jump, 1. n. saut m. **2.** vb. sauter.

junction, n. jonction f.; (rail) embranchement m.

juncture, n. jointure f., jonction f., conjoncture f.

June, n. juin m.

jungle, n. jungle f., brousse f.

junior, adj. and n. (age) cadet m.; (rank) subalterne m.

juniper, n. genévrier m., genièvre m.

junk, n. (waste) rebut m.

junket, n. jonchée f.; festin m.; partie de plaisir f.

jurisdiction, n. juridiction f.

jurisprudence, n. jurisprudence f.

jurist, n. juriste m., légiste m.

juror, m. juré m., membre du jury m.

jury, n. jury m.

just, 1. adj. juste. **2.** adv. (ex-actly) juste; (barely) à peine; (have j.) venir de.

justice, n. justice f.

justifiable, adj. justifiable, justifié.

justification, n. justification f.

justify, vb. justifier.

jut, vb. être en saillie.

jute, n. jute m.

juvenile, adj. juvénile.

K

kale, n. chou m.

kaleidoscope, n. kaléidoscope m.

kangaroo, n. kangourou m.

karakul, n. karakul m., caracul m.

karat, n. carat m.

karate, n. karaté m.

keel, n. quille f.

keen, adj. (edge) aiguisé; (pain, point) aigu; (look, mind) pénétrant; (k. on) enthousiaste de.

keep, vb. tenir; (reserve, protect, retain) garder; (remain) rester; (continue) continuer à.

keeper, n. gardien m.

keepsake, n. souvenir m.

keg, n. caque f., barillet m., tonnelet m.

kennel, n. chenil m.

kerchief, n. fichu m., mouchoir m.

kernel, n. (grain) grain m.; (nut) amande f.; (fig.) noyau m.

kerosene, n. pétrole m.

ketchup, n. sauce piquante à base de tomates f.

kettle, n. bouilloire f.

kettledrum, n. timbale f.

key, n. clef, clé f.; (piano, typewriter) touche f.

keyhole, n. entrée de clef f.

khaki, n. kaki m.

kick, 1. n. coup m. de pied; (gun) recul m. **2.** vb. donner un coup de pied à.

kid, n. (animal, skin) chevreau m.; (child) gosse m.f.

kidnap, vb. enlever de vive force.

kidnaper, n. auteur de l'enlèvement m., ravisseur m.

kidney, n. rein m.; (food) rognon m.

kidney bean, n. haricot nain m.

kill, vb. tuer.

killer, n. tueur m., meurtrier m.

kiln, n. four (céramique) m., séchoir m.

kilocycle, n. kilocycle m.

kilohertz, n. kilohertz m.

kilowatt, n. kilowatt m.

kilt, n. kilt m.

kimono, n. kimono m.

kin, n. (relation) parent m.

kind, 1. n. genre m. **2.** adj. aimable.

kindergarten, n. jardin d'enfants m., école maternelle f.

kindle, vb. allumer, tr.

kindling, n. allumage m., bois d'allumage m.

kindly, adv. avec bonté.

kindness, n. bonté f.

kindred, 1. n. parenté f., affinité f. **2.** adj. analogue.

kinetic, adj. cinétique.

king, n. roi m.

kingdom, n. royaume m.

kink, 1. n. nœud m., tortillement m. **2.** vb. se nouer.

kiosk, n. kiosque m.

kipper, n. kipper m., hareng légèrement salé et fumé m.

kiss, 1. n. baiser m. **2.** vb. baiser.

kitchen, n. cuisine f.

kite, n. cerf-volant m.

kitten, n. petit chat m.

kleptomania, n. kleptomanie f.

kleptomaniac, n. kleptomane m.

knack, n. tour de main m., talent m., truc m.

knapsack, n. havresac m.

knead, vb. pétrir, malaxer.

knee, n. genou m.

kneecap, n. genouillère f.

kneel, vb. s'agenouiller.

knell, n. glas m.

knickers, n. pantalon m., culotte f.

knife, n. couteau m.

knight, n. chevalier m.

knit, vb. (with needles) tricoter.

knock, 1. n. coup m. **2.** vb. frapper.

knot, n. nœud m.

knotty, adj. plein de nœuds.

know, vb. savoir; (be acquainted with) connaître.

knowledge, n. connaissance f.; (learning) savoir m.

knuckle, n. articulation du doigt f., jointure du doigt f.

kodak, n. kodak m.

Korea, n. Corée f.

L

label, n. étiquette m.

labor, 1. n. travail m.; (workers) ouvriers m.pl. **2.** vb. peiner.

laboratory, n. laboratoire m.

laborer, n. travailleur m.

laborious, adj. laborieux.

labor union, n. syndicat m.

laburnum, n. cytise m.

labyrinth, n. labyrinthe m.

lace, n. dentelle f.; (string) lacet m.

lacerate, vb. lacérer, déchirer.

laceration, n. lacération f.

lack, 1. n. manque m. **2.** vb. manquer de.

lackadaisical, adj. affecté.

laconic, adj. laconique.

lacquer, n. vernis-laque m.

lactic, adj. lactique.

lactose, n. lactose f.

lacy, adj. de dentelle.

ladder, n. échelle f.

ladle, n. cuiller à pot f.

lady, n. dame f.

ladybug, n. coccinelle f.

lag behind, vb. rester en arrière.

lagoon, n. lagune f.

laid-back, adj. décontracté.

lair, n. tanière f., repaire m.

laissez faire, n. laissez faire m.

laity, n. les laïques m.pl.

lake, n. lac m.

lamb, n. agneau m.

lame, adj. boiteux.

lament, vb. se lamenter (sur); (mourn) pleurer.

lamentable, adj. lamentable, déplorable.

lamentation, n. lamentation f.

laminate, vb. laminer, écacher.

lamp, n. lampe f.

lampoon, 1. n. pasquinade f., satire f. 2. vb. lancer des satires.

lance, n. lance f.

land, 1. n. terre f. 2. vb. (boat) débarquer; (plane) atterrir.

landholder, n. propriétaire foncier m.

landing, n. débarquement m., mise à terre m.

landlord, n. propriétaire m.f.

landmark, n. borne f.

landscape, n. paysage m.

landslide, n. éboulement m.

landward, adv. vers la terre.

lane, n. (country) sentier m.; (town) ruelle f.

language, n. langue f.; (form of expression) langage m.

languid, adj. languissant.

languish, vb. languir.

languor, n. langueur f.

lanky, adj. grand et maigre.

lanolin, n. lanoline f.

lantern, n. lanterne f.

lap, n. genoux m.pl.

lapel, n. revers m.

lapin, n. lapin m.

lapse, 1. n. (of time) laps m.; (error) faute f. 2. vb. passer.

larceny, n. larcin m., vol m.

lard, n. saindoux m.

large, adj. grand.

largely, adv. en grande partie.

largo, n. largo m.

lariat, n. lasso m.

lark, n. alouette f.

larkspur, n. pied d'alouette m., delphinium m.

larva, n. larve f.

laryngitis, n. laryngite f.

larynx, n. larynx m.

lascivious, adj. lascif.

laser, n. laser m.

lash, 1. n. (whip) lanière f.; (blow) coup (m.) de fouet. 2. vb. fouetter.

lass, n. jeune fille f.

lassitude, n. lassitude f.

lasso, n. lasso m.

last, 1. adj. dernier; (at l.) enfin. 2. vb. durer.

lasting, adj. durable.

latch, n. loquet m.

late, adj. and adv. (on in day, etc.) tard; (after due time) en retard; (dead) feu; (recent) dernier.

lately, adv. dernièrement.

latent, adj. latent, caché.

lateral, adj. latéral.

lath, n. latte f.

lathe, n. tour m.

lather, n. (soap) mousse f.; (horse) écume f.

Latin, 1. n. (person) Latin m.; (language) latin m. 2. adj. latin.

latitude, n. latitude f.

latrine, n. latrine f.

latter, adj. and pron. dernier.

lattice, n. treillis m.

laud, vb. louer.

laudable, adj. louable.

laudanum, n. laudanum m.

laudatory, adj. élogieux.

laugh, laughter, n. rire m.

laugh (at), vb. rire (de).

laughable, adj. risible.

launch, 1. n. (boat) chaloupe f. 2. vb. lancer, tr.

launder, vb. blanchir.

laundry, n. (works) blanchisserie f.; (washing) lessive f.

laundryman, n. blanchisseur m.

laureate, adj. and n. lauréat m.f.

laurel, n. laurier m.

lava, n. lave f.

lavaliere, n. lavallière f.

lavatory, n. lavabo m.; cabinet (m.) de toilette.

lavender, n. lavande f.

lavish, 1. adj. (person) prodigue; (thing) somptueux. 2. vb. prodiguer.

law, n. loi f.; (jurisprudence) droit m.

lawful, adj. légal.

lawless, adj. sans loi.

lawn, n. pelouse f.

lawsuit, n. procès m.

lawyer, n. (counselor) avocat m.; (attorney) avoué m.; (jurist) jurisconsulte m.

lax, adj. lâche, mou, relâché.

laxative, n. laxatif m.

laxity, n. relâchement m.

lay, vb. poser.

layer, n. couche f.

layman, n. laïque m.

lazy, adj. paresseux.

lead, 1. n. plomb m.; (pencil) mine f. 2. vb. mener, conduire.

leaden, adj. de plomb.

leader, n. chef m.

lead pencil, n. crayon à la mine de plomb m.

leaf, n. feuille f.

leaflet, n. feuillet m.

leafy, adj. feuillu.

league, n. (compact) ligue f.; (measure) lieue f.

League of Nations, n. La Société des Nations f.

leak, 1. n. (liquid) fuite f.; (boat) voie (f.) d'eau. 2. vb. fuir; faire eau.

leakage, n. fuite d'eau f.

leaky, adj. qui coule, qui fait eau.

lean, 1. adj. maigre. 2. vb. intr. (l. against) s'appuyer sur; (stoop) se pencher. 3. vb.tr. appuyer.

leap, vb. sauter.

leap year, n. année bissextile f.

learn, vb. apprendre.

learned, adj. savant, docte.

learning, n. science f., instruction f., érudition f.

lease, n. bail m.

leash, n. laisse f., attache f.

least, 1. n. moins m. 2. adj. (le) moindre. 3. adv. (le) moins.

leather, n. cuir m.

leathery, adj. coriace.

leave, 1. n. permission f. 2. vb. laisser; (go away from) quitter.

leaven, 1. n. levain m. 2. vb. faire lever, modifier.

lecherous, adj. lascif, libertin.

lecture, n. conférence f.

lecturer, n. conférencier m.

ledge, n. bord m.; (of rocks) chaîne f.

ledger, n. grand livre m.

lee, n. côté (m.) sous le vent.

leech, n. sangsue f.

leek, n. poireau m.

leer, 1. n. oeillade f., regard de côté m. 2. vb. lorgner.

leeward, adj. and adv. sous le vent.

left, adj. and n. gauche f.; (on, to the l.) à gauche.

leftist, n. gaucher m.

left wing, n. l'aile gauche f.

leg, n. (man, horse) jambe f.; (most animals) patte f.

legacy, n. legs m.

legal, adj. légal.

legalize, vb. rendre légal.

legation, n. légation f.

legend, n. légende f.

legendary, adj. légendaire.

legible, adj. lisible.

legion, n. légion f.

legislate, vb. faire les lois.

legislation, n. législation f.

legislator, n. législateur m.

legislature, n. législature f.

legitimate, adj. légitime.

legume, n. légume m.

leisure, n. loisir m.

leisurely, adv. à loisir.

lemon, n. citron m.

lemonade, n. citron (m.) pressé.

lend, vb. prêter.

length, n. (dimension) longueur f.; (time) durée f.

lengthen, vb. allonger, tr.

lengthwise, adv. en long.

lengthy, adj. assez long.

lenient, adj. indulgent.

lens, *n.* lentille *f.;* (camera) objectif *m.*

Lent, *n.* carême *m.*

Lenten, *adj.* de carême.

lentil, *n.* lentille *f.*

lento, *adv.* lento.

leopard, *n.* léopard *m.*

leper, *n.* lépreux *m.*

leprosy, *n.* lèpre *f.*

lesbian, **1.** *adj.* lesbien. **2.** *n.* lesbienne *f.;* tribade *f.*

lesion, *n.* lésion *f.*

less, **1.** *adj.* (smaller) moindre; (not so much) moins de. **2.** *adv.* (l. than) moins (de).

lessen, *vb.* diminuer.

lesser, *adj.* moindre.

lesson, *n.* leçon *f.*

lest, *conj.* de peur que . . . (ne).

let, *vb.* laisser; (lease) louer.

letdown, *n.* déception *f.*

lethal, *adj.* mortel.

lethargic, *adj.* léthargique.

lethargy, *n.* léthargie *f.*

letter, *n.* lettre *f.*

letterhead, *n.* en-tête de lettre *m.*

lettuce, *n.* laitue *f.*

levee, *n.* lever *m.*

level, **1.** *adj.* (flat) égal; (l. with) au niveau de. **2.** *n.* niveau *m.*

lever, *n.* levier *m.*

levity, *n.* légèreté *f.*

levy, **1.** *n.* levée *f.* **2.** *vb.* lever.

lewd, *adj.* impudique.

lexicon, *n.* lexique *m.*

liability, *n.* responsibilité *f.*

liable, *adj.* (responsible for) responsable de; (subject to) sujet à.

liar, *n.* menteur *m.*

libation, *n.* libation *f.*

libel, *n.* diffamation *f.*

libelous, *adj.* diffamatoire.

liberal, *adj.* libéral; (generous) généreux.

liberalism, *n.* libéralisme *m.*

liberality, *n.* libéralité *f.*

liberate, *vb.* libérer.

libertine, **1.** *n.* libre-penseur *m.* **2.** *adj.* libertin.

liberty, *n.* liberté *f.*

libidinous, *adj.* libidineux.

libido, *n.* libido *m.*

librarian, *n.* bibliothécaire *m.*

library, *n.* bibliothèque *f.*

libretto, *n.* livret *m.*

license, *n.* permis *m.;* (tradesmen) patente *f.;* (abuse of freedom) licence *f.*

licentious, *adj.* licencieux.

lick, *vb.* lécher.

licorice, *n.* réglisse *f.*

lid, *n.* couvercle *m.*

lie, **1.** *n.* mensonge *f.* **2.** *vb.* (fib) mentir; (recline) être couché; (l. down) se coucher; (be situated) se trouver.

lien, *n.* privilège *m.*

lieutenant, *n.* lieutenant *m.*

life, *n.* vie *f.*

lifeboat, *n.* bateau de sauvetage *m.*

life buoy, *n.* bouée de sauvetage *m.*

lifeguard, *n.* garde du corps *m.*

life insurance, *n.* assurance sur la vie *f.*

lifeless, *adj.* sans vie.

life preserver, *n.* appareil de sauvetage *m.*

life style, *n.* manière de vivre *f.*

lifetime, *n.* vie *f.,* vivant *m.*

lift, *vb.* lever.

ligament, *n.* ligament *m.*

ligature, *n.* ligature *f.*

light, **1.** *n.* lumière *f.* **2.** *adj.* (not heavy) léger; (not dark) clair. **3.** *vb.* allumer, *tr.*

lighten, *vb.* (relieve) alléger, *tr.,* (brighten) éclairer, *tr.*

lighthouse, *n.* phare *m.*

lightly, *adv.* légèrement.

lightness, *n.* légèreté *f.*

lightning, *n.* (flash of) éclair *m.*

lightship, *n.* bateau-feu *m.*

lignite, *n.* lignite *m.*

likable, *adj.* agréable.

like, **1.** *adj.* pareil. **2.** *vb.* aimer; plaire à. **3.** *prep.* comme.

likelihood, *n.* probabilité *f.*

likely, *adj.* probable.

liken, *vb.* comparer.

likeness, *n.* ressemblance *f.*

likewise, *adv.* de même.

lilac, *n.* lilas *m.*

lilt, **1.** *n.* forte cadence *f.* **2.** *vb.* chanter gaiement.

lily, *n.* lis *m.;* (l. of the valley) muguet *m.*

limb, *n.* membre *m.;* (tree) grosse branche *f.*

limber, **1.** *adj.* souple, flexible. **2.** *vb.* assouplir.

limbo, *n.* limbes *m.pl.*

lime, *n.* (mineral) chaux *f.;* (tree) tilleul *m.;* (fruit) lime *f.*

limelight, *n.* lumière oxhydrique *f.*

limestone, *n.* pierre à chaux *f.,* calcaire *m.*

limewater, *n.* eau de chaux *f.*

limit, **1.** *n.* limite *f.* **2.** *vb.* limiter.

limitation, *n.* limitation *f.*

limitless, *adj.* sans limite, sans bornes.

limousine, *n.* limousine *f.*

limp, **1.** *adj.* flasque. **2.** *vb.* boiter.

limpid, *adj.* limpide.

linden, *n.* tilleul *m.*

line, *n.* ligne *f.*

lineage, *n.* lignée *f.,* race *f.*

lineal, *adj.* linéaire.

linen, *n.* (cloth) toile *f.;* (sheets, etc.) linge *m.*

linger, *vb.* s'attarder.

lingerie, *n.* lingerie *f.*

linguist, *n.* linguiste *m.*

linguistic, *adj.* linguistique.

linguistics, *n.* linguistique *f.*

liniment, *n.* liniment *m.*

lining, *n.* (clothes) doublure *f.*

link, **1.** *n.* (chain) chaînon *m.;* (*fig.*) lien *m.* **2.** *vb.* (re)lier.

linoleum, *n.* linoléum *m.*

linseed, *n.* graine de lin *f.*

lint, *n.* charpie *f.*

lion, *n.* lion *m.*

lip, *n.* lèvre *f.*

liquefy, *vb.* liquéfier.

liqueur, *n.* liqueur *f.*

liquid, *adj.* and *n.* liquide *m.*

liquidate, *vb.* liquider.

liquidation, *n.* liquidation *f.,* acquittement *m.*

liquor, *n.* boisson (*f.*) alcoolique.

lisle, *n.* fil d'Écosse *m.*

lisp, *vb.* zézayer.

list, **1.** *n.* liste *f.* **2.** *vb.* enregistrer.

listen (to), *vb.* écouter.

listless, *adj.* inattentif.

litany, *n.* litanie *f.*

literacy, *n.* degré d'aptitude à lire et à écrire *m.*

literal, *adj.* littéral.

literary, *adj.* littéraire.

literate, *adj.* lettré.

literature, *n.* littérature *f.*

lithe, *adj.* flexible, pliant.

lithograph, *vb.* lithographier.

lithography, *n.* lithographie *f.*

litigant, *n.* plaideur *m.*

litigation, *n.* litige *m.*

litmus, *n.* tournesol *m.*

litter, *n.* (vehicle, animals' bedding) litière *f.;* (disorder) fouillis *m.;* (animals' young) portée *f.*

little, **1.** *n.* and *adv.* peu *m.* **2.** *adj.* (small) petit; (not much) peu (de).

liturgical, *adj.* liturgique.

liturgy, *n.* liturgie *f.*

live, *vb.* vivre.

livelihood, *n.* vie *f.,* subsistance *f.,* gagne-pain *m.*

lively, *adj.* vif *m.,* vive *f.*

liven, *vb.* animer, activer.

liver, *n.* foie *m.*

livery, *n.* livrée *f.*

livestock, *n.* bétail *m.*

livid, *adj.* livide, blême.

lizard, *n.* lézard *m.*

llama, *n.* lama *m.*

lo, *interj.* voilà.

load, **1.** *n.* (cargo) charge *f.;* (burden) fardeau *m.* **2.** *vb.* charger.

loaf, **1.** *n.* pain *m.* **2.** *vb.* flâner.

loafer, *n.* fainéant *m.*

loam, *n.* terre grasse *f.*

loan, **1.** *n.* (thing) prêt *m.;* (borrowing) emprunt *m.* **2.** *vb.* prêter.

loath, *adj.* fâché, peiné.

loathe, *vb.* détester.

loathing, *n.* dégoût *m.*

loathsome, *adj.* dégoûtant.

lobby, *n.* (hall) vestibule *m.*

lobe, *n.* lobe *m.*

lobster, *n.* homard *m.*

local, *adj.* local.

locale, *n.* localité *f.,* scène *f.*

locality, *n.* localité *f.*

localize, *vb.* localiser.

locate, *vb.* localiser.

location, *n.* placement *m.*

lock, **1.** *n.* (door) serrure *f.;*

(hair) mèche f. 2. vb. fermer à clef.

locker, n. armoire f.; (baggage) consigne automatique f.

locket, n. médaillon m.

lockjaw, n. tétanos m.

locksmith, n. serrurier m.

locomotion, n. locomotion f.

locomotive, n. locomotive f.

locust, n. sauterelle f.

locution, n. locution f.

lode, n. filon m.

lodge, vb. loger.

lodger, n. locataire m.

lodging, n. logement m.

loft, n. grenier m.

lofty, adj. élevé; (proud) hautain.

log, n. (wood) bûche f.; (boat) loch m.

loge, n. loge f.

logic, n. logique f.

logical, adj. logique.

loins, n. reins m.pl.

loiter, vb. flâner.

lollipop, n. sucre d'orge m.

London, n. Londres m.

lone, lonely, lonesome, adj. solitaire.

loneliness, n. solitude f.

long, 1. adj. long m., longue f. 2. adv. longtemps.

longevity, n. longévité f.

long for, vb. désirer ardemment.

longing, n. désir ardent m.

longitude, n. longitude f.

longitudinal, adj. longitudinal.

look, 1. n. regard m.; aspect m. 2. vb. (l. at) regarder; (l. for) chercher; (l. after) soigner; (seem) paraître.

looking glass, n. miroir m.

loom, 1. n. métier m. 2. vb. se dessiner.

loop, n. boucle f.

loophole, n. meurtrière f., échappatoire f.

loose, adj. (not tight) lâche; (detached) détaché; (morals) relâché.

loosen, vb. desserrer.

loot, 1. n. butin m. 2. vb. piller.

lop, vb. élaguer, ébrancher.

loquacious, adj. loquace.

lord, n. seigneur m.; (title) lord m.

lordship, n. seigneurie f.

lorgnette, n. lorgnette f.

lose, vb. perdre.

loss, n. perte f.

lot, n. (fortune) sort m.; (land) terrain m.; (much) beaucoup.

lotion, n. lotion f.

lottery, n. loterie f.

lotus, n. lotus m., lotos m.

loud, 1. adj. fort; (noisy) bruyant. 2. adv. haut.

lounge, 1. n. sofa m.; hall m. 2. vb. flâner.

louse, n. pou m.

lout, n. rustre m.

louver, n. auvent m.

lovable, adj. aimable.

love, 1. n. amour m. 2. vb. aimer.

lovely, adj. beau m., belle f.

lover, n. amoureux m.

low, adj. bas m., basse f.

lowboy, n. commode basse f.

lowbrow, adj. terre à terre.

lower, vb. baisser.

lowly, adj. humble.

loyal, adj. loyal.

loyalist, n. loyaliste m.

loyalty, n. loyauté f.

lozenge, n. pastille f.

lubricant, n. lubrifiant m.

lubricate, vb. lubrifier.

lucid, adj. lucide.

luck, n. chance f.

lucky, adj. (person) heureux.

lucrative, adj. lucratif.

ludicrous, adj. risible.

lug, vb. traîner, tirer.

luggage, n. bagages m.pl.

lukewarm, adj. tiède.

lull, n. moment (m.) de calme.

lullaby, n. berceuse f.

lumbago, n. lumbago m.

lumber, n. bois (m.) de charpente.

luminous, adj. lumineux.

lump, n. (gros) morceau m.

lumpy, adj. grumeleux.

lunacy, n. folie f.

lunar, adj. lunaire.

lunatic, n. aliéné m.

lunch, 1. n. déjeuner m. 2. vb. déjeuner.

luncheon, n. déjeuner m.

lung, n. poumon m.

lunge, 1. n. botte f. 2. vb. se fendre.

lurch, 1. n. embardée f. 2. vb. faire une embardée.

lure, vb. (animal) leurrer; (attract) attirer.

lurid, adj. blafard, sombre.

lurk, vb. se cacher.

luscious, adj. délicieux.

lush, adj. luxuriant.

lust, n. luxure f.

luster, n. lustre m.

lustful, adj. lascif, sensuel.

lustrous, adj. brillant, lustré.

lusty, adj. vigoreux.

lute, n. luth m.

Lutheran, n. Luthérien m.

luxuriant, adj. exubérant.

luxurious, adj. (thing) luxueux.

luxury, n. luxe m.

lying, n. mensonge m.

lymph, n. lymphe f.

lynch, vb. lyncher.

lyre, n. lyre f.

lyric, adj. lyrique.

lyricism, n. lyrisme m.

M

macaroni, n. macaroni m.

machine, n. machine f.

machine gun, n. mitrailleuse f.

machinery, n. machines f.pl; (fig.) mécanisme m.

machinist, n. machiniste m.

machismo, n. phallocratie f.

macho, 1. adj. phallocrate. 2. n. homme phallocrate m.

mackerel, n. maquereau m.

mackinaw, n. mackinaw m.

mad, adj. fou m., folle f.

madam, n. madame f.

madcap, n. and adj. écervelé.

madden, vb. exaspérer.

made, adj. fait, fabriqué.

mafia, n. mafia f.

magazine, n. revue f.

magic, 1. n. magie f. 2. adj. magique.

magician, n. magicien m.

magistrate, n. magistrat m.

magnanimous, adj. magnanime.

magnate, n. magnat m.

magnesium, n. magnésium m.

magnet, n. aimant m.

magnetic, adj. magnétique.

magnificence, n. magnificence f.

magnificent, adj. magnifique.

magnify, vb. grossir.

magnitude, n. grandeur f.

mahogany, n. acajou m.

maid, n. (servant) bonne f.; (old m.) vieille fille f.

maiden, adj. de jeune fille.

mail, 1. n. courrier m. 2. vb. envoyer par la poste.

mailbox, n. boîte (f.) aux lettres.

mailman, n. facteur m.

maim, vb. estropier, mutiler.

main, adj. principal.

mainframe, n. partie centrale d'un informateur f.

mainland, n. terre (f.) ferme.

mainspring, n. grand ressort m.; mobile essentiel m.

maintain, vb. maintenir; (support) soutenir.

maintenance, n. entretien m.

maize, n. maïs m.

majestic, adj. majestueux.

majesty, n. majesté f.

major, 1. n. (mil.) commandant m.; (school) sujet (m.) principal. 2. adj. majeur.

majority, n. majorité f.

major scale, mode, or key, n. ton majeur m., mode majeur m.

make, 1. n. fabrication f. 2. vb. faire.

make-believe, 1. n. trompe l'œil m. 2. vb. feindre.

maker, n. fabricant m.

makeshift, n. expédient m.

make-up, n. (face) maquillage m.

maladjusted, adj. mal adapté, mal ajusté.

maladjustment, n. mauvaise adaptation f.

malady, n. maladie f.

malaria, n. malaria f.

male, adj. and n. mâle m.

malevolent, adj. malveillant.

malice, n. méchanceté f.

malicious, adj. méchant.

malign, vb. calomnier.

malignant, adj. malin m., maligne f.

malleable, adj. malléable.

malnutrition, n. mauvaise hygiène (f.) alimentaire.

malpractice, n. méfait m.

malt, n. malt m.

mammal, n. mammifère m.

man, n. homme m.

manage, 1. vb. tr. (administer) gérer; (conduct) diriger; (person, animal) dompter. 2. vb. intr. se tirer d'affaire; (m. to) réussir à.

management, n. direction f.

manager, n. directeur m.; (household) ménager m.

mandate, n. (politics) mandat m.

mandatory, adj. obligatoire.

mandolin, n. mandoline f.

mane, n. crinière f.

maneuver, n. manœuvre f.

manganese, n. manganèse m.

manger, n. mangeoire f.

mangle, vb. mutiler.

manhood, n. virilité f.

mania, n. (craze) manie f.; (madness) folie f.

maniac, adj. and n. fou m., folle f.

manicure, n. (person) manucure m.f.; (care of hands) soin (m.) des mains.

manifest, 1. adj. manifeste. 2. vb. manifester.

manifesto, n. manifeste m.

manifold, adj. (varied) divers; (numerous) nombreux.

manipulate, vb. manipuler.

mankind, n. genre (m.) humain.

manly, adj. viril.

manner, n. manière f.; (customs) mœurs f.pl.

mannerism, n. maniérisme m., affectation f.

mansion, n. (country) château m.; (town) hôtel m.

manslaughter, n. homicide involontaire m.

mantel, n. (framework) manteau m.; (shelf) tablette f.

mantle, n. manteau f.

manual, adj. and n. manuel m.

manufacture, 1. n. manufacture f.; (product) produit (m.) manufacturé. 2. vb. fabriquer.

manufacturer, n. fabricant m.

manure, n. fumier m.

manuscript, adj. and n. manuscrit m.

many, 1. adj. beaucoup de, un grand nombre de; (too m.) trop de; (so m.) tant de; (how m.) combien de. 2. pron. beaucoup.

map, n. carte (f.) géographique.

maple, n. érable m.

mar, vb. gâter.

marble, n. marbre m.

march, 1. n. marche f. 2. vb. marcher.

March, n. mars m.

mare, n. jument f.

margarine, n. margarine f.

margin, n. marge f.

marijuana, n. marijuana f.; marie-jeanne f.

marinate, vb. faire mariner.

marine, 1. n. (ships) marine f.; (soldier) fusilier (m.) marin. 2. adj. marin; (insurance) maritime.

mariner, n. marin m.

marionette, n. marionnette f.

marital, adj. matrimonial.

maritime, adj. maritime.

mark, 1. n. marque f.; (target) but m.; (school) point m. 2. vb. marquer.

market, n. marché m.

market place, n. place (f.) du marché.

marmalade, n. confiture f.

maroon, 1. adj. and n. rouge (m.) foncé. 2. vb. abandonner (dans une île déserte).

marquee, n. (tente) marquise f.

marquis, n. marquis m.

marriage, n. mariage m.

married, adj. marié.

marrow, n. moelle f.

marry, vb. épouser; se marier (avec).

marsh, n. marais m.

marshal, n. maréchal m.

marshmallow, n. guimauve (plant) f.

martial, adj. martial.

martinet, n. officier strict sur la discipline m.

martyr, n. martyr m.

martyrdom, n. martyre m.

marvel, 1. n. merveille f. 2. vb. (m. at) s'étonner de.

marvelous, adj. merveilleux.

mascara, n. mascara m.

mascot, n. mascotte f.

masculine, adj. masculin.

mash, n. (food) purée f.

mask, 1. n. masque m. 2. vb. masquer.

mason, n. maçon m.

masquerade, n. mascarade f., bal masqué m.

mass, n. masse f.

Mass, n. messe f.

massacre, 1. n. massacre m. 2. vb. massacrer.

massage, n. massage m.

masseur, n. masseur m.

massive, adj. massif.

mass meeting, n. réunion f.

mast, n. mât m.

master, 1. n. maître m. 2. vb. maîtriser.

masterpiece, n. chef-d'œuvre m.

mastery, n. maîtrise f.

masticate, vb. mâcher.

mat, n. (door) paillasson m.

match, 1. n. (for fire) allumette f.; (equal) égal m.; (marriage) mariage m.; (person to marry) parti m.; (sport) partie f. 2. vb. assortir, tr.

mate, n. (fellow-worker) camarade m.f.; (of pair) compa-

gnon m.; compagne f.; (boat) officier m.

material, 1. n. matière f.; (cloth) étoffe f. 2. adj. matériel.

materialism, n. matérialisme m.

materialize, vb. matérialiser, tr.; se réaliser, intr.

maternal, adj. maternel.

maternity, n. maternité f.

mathematical, adj. mathématique.

mathematics, n. mathématiques f.pl.

matinee, n. matinée f.

matriarch, n. femme qui porte les chausses f.

matrimony, n. mariage m.

matron, n. (institution) intendante f.

matter, 1. n. (substance) matière f.; (subject) sujet m.; (question, business) affaire f.; (what is the m.?) qu'est-ce qu'il y a? 2. vb. importer.

mattress, n. matelas m.

mature, 1. adj. mûr. 2. vb. mûrir.

maturity, n. maturité f.; (comm.) échéance f.

maudlin, adj. larmoyant.

mausoleum, n. mausolée m.

maxim, n. maxime f.

maximum, n. maximum m.

may, vb. pouvoir.

May, n. mai m.

maybe, adv. peut-être.

mayhem, n. mutilation f.

mayonnaise, n. mayonnaise f.

mayor, n. maire m.

maze, n. labyrinthe m.

me, pron. (unstressed direct and indirect) me; (alone, stressed, with prep.) moi.

meadow, n. (small) pré m.; (large) prairie f.

meager, adj. maigre.

meal, n. (repast) repas m.; (grain) farine f.

mean, 1. n. (math.) moyenne f.; (m.s financial) moyens m.pl.; (m.s way to do) moyen m. 2. adj. humble; (stingy) avare; (contemptible) méprisable. 3. vb. (signify) vouloir dire; (purpose) se proposer (de); (destine) destiner (à).

meaning, n. sens m.

meantime, meanwhile, adv. sur ces entrefaites.

measles, n. rougeole f.

measure, 1. n. mesure f. 2. vb. mesurer.

measurement, n. mesurage m.

meat, n. viande f.

mechanic, n. mécanicien m.

mechanical, 1. adj. mécanique. 2. (fig.) machinal.

mechanism, n. mécanisme m.

mechanize, vb. mécaniser.

medal, n. médaille f.

meddle, vb. se mêler (de).

media, n. organes de communication m.pl.

median, *n.* médian.

mediate, *vb.* agir en médiateur.

medical, *adj.* médical.

medicate, *vb.* médicamenter.

medicine, *n.* médecine *m.*

medieval, *adj.* médiéval.

mediocre, *adj.* médiocre.

mediocrity, *n.* médiocrité *f.*

meditate, *vb.* méditer.

meditation, *n.* méditation *f.*

Mediterranean, 1. *adj.* méditerrané. **2.** *n.* (M. Sea) Méditerranée *f.*

medium, 1. *n.* milieu *m.;* (agent) intermédiaire *m.;* (psychic person) médium *m.* **2.** *adj.* moyen.

medley, *n.* mélange *m.*

meek, *adj.* doux *m.,* douce *f.*

meekness, *n.* douceur *f.*

meet, *vb.* rencontrer, *tr.;* (become acquainted with) faire la connaissance de; (expenses) faire face à.

meeting, *n.* réunion *f.*

megahertz, *n.* mégahertz *m.*

megaphone, *n.* mégaphone *m.*

melancholy, *n.* mélancolie *f.*

mellow, *adj.* moelleux.

melodious, *adj.* mélodieux.

melodrama, *n.* mélodrame *m.*

melody, *n.* mélodie *f.*

melon, *n.* melon *m.*

melt, *vb.* fondre.

meltdown, *n.* fusion *f.*

member, *n.* membre *m.*

membrane, *n.* membrane *f.*

memento, *n.* mémento *m.*

memoir, *n.* mémoire *m.*

memorable, *adj.* mémorable.

memorandum, *n.* mémorandum *m.*

memorial, 1. *n.* souvenir *m.,* monument *m.* **2.** *adj.* commémoratif.

memorize, *vb.* apprendre par cœur.

memory, *n.* mémoire *f.*

menace, 1. *n.* menace *f.* **2.** *vb.* menacer.

menagerie, *n.* ménagerie *f.*

mend, *vb.* (clothes) raccommoder; (correct) corriger.

mendacious, *adj.* menteur.

mendicant, *n.* and *adj.* mendiant *m.*

menial, *adj.* servile.

menstruation, *n.* menstruation *f.*

menswear, *n.* habillements masculins *m.pl.*

mental, *adj.* mental.

mentality, *n.* mentalité *f.*

menthol, *n.* menthol *m.*

mention, 1. *n.* mention *f.* **2.** *vb.* mentionner; (don't m. it) il n'y a pas de quoi.

menu, *n.* menu *m.*

mercantile, *adj.* mercantile.

mercenary, *adj.* and *n.* mercenaire *m.*

merchandise(s), *n.* marchandise(s) *f.(pl.)*

merchant, 1. *n.* négociant *m.* **2.** *adj.* marchand.

merchant marine, *n.* marine marchande *f.*

merciful, *adj.* miséricordieux.

merciless, *adj.* impitoyable.

mercury, *n.* mercure *m.*

mercy, *n.* miséricorde *f.;* (at the m. of) à la merci de.

mere, *adj.* simple.

merely, *adv.* simplement.

merge, *vb.* fusionner.

merger, *n.* fusion *f.*

merit, 1. *n.* mérite *m.* **2.** *vb.* mériter.

meritorious, *adj.* (person) méritant; (deed) méritoire.

mermaid, *n.* sirène *f.*

merriment, *n.* gaieté *f.*

merry, *adj.* gai.

merry-go-round, *n.* carrousel *m.*

mesh, *n.* maille *f.*

mesmerize, *vb.* magnétiser.

mess, 1. *n.* (muddle) fouillis *m.;* gâchis *m.;* (mil.) popote *f.* **2.** *vb.* gâcher.

message, *n.* message *m.*

messenger, *n.* messager *m.*

messy, *adj.* (dirty) malpropre.

metabolism, *n.* métabolisme *m.*

metal, *n.* métal *m.*

metallic, *adj.* métallique.

metamorphosis, *n.* métamorphose *f.*

metaphysics, *n.* métaphysique *f.*

meteor, *n.* météore *m.*

meter, 1. *n.* (measure) mètre *m.;* (device) compteur *m.*

method, *n.* méthode *f.*

meticulous, *adj.* méticuleux.

metric, *adj.* métrique.

metropolis, *n.* métropole *f.*

metropolitan, *adj.* métropolitain.

mettle, *n.* ardeur *f.*

Mexican, 1. *n.* Mexicain *m.* **2.** *adj.* Mexicain.

Mexico, *n.* Mexique *m.*

mezzanine, *n.* mezzanine *f.*

microbe, *n.* microbe *m.*

microfiche, *n.* microfiche *f.*

microfilm, *n.* microfilm *m.*

microform, *n.* microforme *f.*

microphone, *n.* microphone *m.*

microscope, *n.* microscope *m.*

microscopic, *adj.* microscopique.

mid, *adj.* mi-.

middle, 1. *n.* milieu *m.* **2.** *adj.* du milieu.

middle-aged, *adj.* d'un certain âge.

Middle Ages, *n.* moyen âge *m.*

middle class, *n.* classe moyenne *f.,* bourgeoisie *f.*

Middle East, *n.* Moyen Orient *m.*

midget, *n.* nain *m.*

midnight, *n.* minuit *m.*

midriff, *n.* diaphragme *m.*

midwife, *n.* sage-femme *f.*

mien, *n.* mine *f.,* air *m.*

might, *n.* puissance *f.*

mighty, *adj.* puissant.

migrate, *vb.* émigrer.

migration, *n.* migration *f.*

mild, *adj.* doux *m.,* douce *f.*

mildew, *n.* rouille *f.*

mile, *n.* mille *m.*

mileage, *n.* kilométrage *m.*

milestone, *n.* borne routière *f.*

militarism, *n.* militarisme *m.*

military, *adj.* militaire.

militia, *n.* milice *f.*

milk, *n.* lait *m.*

milkman, *n.* laitier *m.*

milky, *adj.* laiteux.

mill, 1. *n.* (grinding) moulin *m.;* (spinning) filature *f.;* (factory) usine *f.* **2.** *vb.* (grind) moudre; (crowd) fourmiller.

miller, *n.* meunier *m.*

millimeter, *n.* millimètre *m.*

milliner, *n.* modiste *f.*

millinery, *n.* modes *f.pl.*

million, *n.* million *m.*

millionaire, *adj.* and *n.* millionnaire *m.f.*

mimic, 1. *n.* mime *m.* **2.** *adj.* mimique. **3.** *vb.* imiter.

mince, *vb.* (chop) hacher.

mind, 1. *n.* esprit *m.;* (opinion) avis *m.;* (desire) envie *f.* **2.** *vb.* (heed) faire attention à; (listen to) écouter; (apply oneself to) s'occuper de; (take care) prendre garde; (look after) garder; (never m.) n'importe.

mindful, *adj.* attentif.

mine, 1. *n.* mine *f.* **2.** *pron.* le mien *m.,* la mienne *f.*

mine field, *n.* champ de mines *m.*

miner, *n.* mineur *m.*

mineral, *adj.* and *n.* minéral *m.*

mine sweeper, *n.* dragueur de mines *m.*

mingle, *vb.* mêler, *tr.*

miniature, *n.* miniature *f.*

miniaturize, *vb.* miniaturiser.

minimize, *vb.* réduire au minimum.

minimum, *n.* minimum *m.*

minimum wage, *n.* salaire minimum *m.*

mining, *n.* exploitation minière *f.,* pose de mines *f.*

minister, *n.* ministre *m.*

ministry, *n.* ministère *m.*

mink, *n.* vison *m.*

minnow, *n.* vairon *m.*

minor, *adj.* and *n.* mineur *m.*

minority, *n.* minorité *f.*

minstrel, *n.* ménestrel *m.*

mint, 1. *n.* (plant) menthe *f.;* (place) Hôtel *(m.)* de la Monnaie.

minute, 1. *n.* minute *f.;* (of meeting) procès-verbal *m.* **2.** *adj.* (very small) minuscule; (detailed) minutieux.

miracle, *n.* miracle *m.*

miraculous, *adj.* miraculeux.

mirage, *n.* mirage *m.*

mire, *n.* boue *f.,* bourbier *m.*

mirror, *n.* miroir *m.*

mirth, *n.* gaieté *f.*

misadventure, *n.* mésaventure *f.*, contretemps *m.*

misappropriate, *vb.* détourner, dépréder.

misbehave, *vb.* se mal conduire.

miscellaneous, *adj.* divers.

mischief, *n.* (harm) mal *m.*; (mischievousness) malice *f.*

mischievous, *adj.* espiègle; (wicked) méchant.

misconstrue, *vb.* mal interpréter, tourner en mal.

misdemeanor, *n.* délit *m.*

miser, *n.* avare *m.f.*

miserable, *adj.* (unhappy) malheureux; (wretched) misérable.

miserly, *adj.* avare.

misery, *n.* (affliction) souffrance(s) *f.(pl.)*; (poverty) misère *f.*

misfit, *n.* vêtement manqué *m.*; inadapté *m.*, inapte *m.*

misfortune, *n.* malheur *m.*

misgiving, *n.* doute *m.*

mishap, *n.* mésaventure *f.*

mislead, *vb.* tromper, égarer.

misplace, *vb.* mal placer.

mispronounce, *vb.* mal prononcer, estropier.

miss, *vb.* manquer; (I m. you) vous me manquez.

Miss, *n.* mademoiselle *f.*

missile, *n.* projectile *m.*

mission, *n.* mission *f.*

missionary, *adj. and n.* missionnaire *m.f.*

misspell, *vb.* mal orthographier.

mist, *n.* brume *f.*

mistake, 1. *n.* erreur *f.* 2. *vb.* (misunderstand) comprendre mal; (make a mistake) se tromper (de).

mister, *n.* monsieur *m.*

mistletoe, *n.* gui *m.*

mistreat, *vb.* maltraiter.

mistress, *n.* maîtresse *f.*

mistrust, 1. *n.* méfiance *f.* 2. *vb.* se méfier de.

misty, *adj.* brumeux.

misunderstand, *vb.* mal comprendre.

misuse, *vb.* (misapply) faire mauvais usage (de); (maltreat) maltraiter.

mite, *n.* denier *m.*, obole *f.*

mitigate, *vb.* adoucir.

mitten, *n.* moufle *f.*

mix, *vb.* mêler, *tr.*

mixture, *n.* mélange *m.*

mix-up, *n.* embrouillement *m.*

moan, 1. *n.* gémissement *m.* 2. *vb.* gémir.

moat, *n.* fossé *m.*

mob, *n.* foule *f.*; (pejorative) populace *f.*

mobile, *adj.* mobile.

mobilization, *n.* mobilisation *f.*

mobilize, *vb.* mobiliser.

mock, *vb.* (m. at) se moquer de; (imitate) singer.

mockery, *n.* moquerie *f.*

mod, *adj.* à la mode.

mode, *n.* mode *m.*

model, *n.* modèle *m.*

moderate, 1. *adj.* modéré. 2. *vb.* modérer.

moderation, *n.* modération *f.*

modern, *adj.* moderne.

modernize, *vb.* moderniser.

modest, *adj.* modeste.

modesty, *n.* modestie *f.*

modify, *vb.* modifier.

modish, *adj.* à la mode.

modulate, *vb.* moduler.

moist, *adj.* moite.

moisten, *vb.* humecter.

moisture, *n.* humidité *f.*

molar, *n. and adj.* molaire *f.*

molasses, *n.* mélasse *f.*

mold, 1. *n.* (casting) moule *m.*; (mildew) moisissure *f.* 2. *vb.* (shape) mouler; (get moldy) moisir.

moldy, *adj.* moisi.

mole, *n.* (animal) taupe *f.*; (spot) grain *(m.)* de beauté.

molecule, *n.* molécule *f.*

molest, *vb.* molester.

mollify, *vb.* adoucir, apaiser.

molten, *adj.* fondu, coulé.

moment, *n.* moment *m.*

momentary, *adj.* momentané.

momentous, *adj.* important.

monarch, *n.* monarque *m.*

monarchy, *n.* monarchie *f.*

monastery, *n.* monastère *m.*

Monday, *n.* lundi *m.*

monetary, *adj.* monétaire.

money, *n.* argent *m.*; (comm.) monnaie *f.*

mongrel, *n.* métis *m.*

monitor, *n.* moniteur *m.*

monk, *n.* moine *m.*

monkey, *n.* singe *m.*

monologue, *n.* monologue *m.*

monoplane, *n.* monoplan *m.*

monopolize, *vb.* monopoliser.

monopoly, *n.* monopole *m.*

monosyllable, *n.* monosyllabe *m.*

monotone, *n.* monotone *m.*

monotonous, *adj.* monotone.

monotony, *n.* monotonie *f.*

monsoon, *n.* mousson *f.*

monster, *n.* monstre *m.*

monstrosity, *n.* monstruosité *f.*

monstrous, *adj.* monstrueux.

month, *n.* mois *m.*

monthly, *adj.* mensuel.

monument, *n.* monument *m.*

monumental, *adj.* monumental.

mood, *n.* humeur *f.*; (gramm.) mode *m.*

moody, *adj.* de mauvaise humeur.

moon, *n.* lune *f.*

moonlight, *n.* clair *(m.)* de lune.

moor, *n.* lande *f.*

mooring, *n.* amarrage *m.*

moot, *adj.* discutable.

mop, *n.* balai *(m.)* à laver.

moped, *n.* cyclomoteur *m.*

moral, 1. *n.* morale *f.*; (morals) moralité *f.* 2. *adj.* moral.

morale, *n.* moral *m.*

moralist, *n.* moraliste *m.f.*

morality, *n.* moralité *f.*; (ethics) morale *f.*

morally, *adv.* moralement.

morbid, *adj.* morbide.

more, 1. *pron.* en . . . davantage. 2. *adj., adv.* plus; (m. than) plus de; (no m.) ne . . . plus.

moreover, *adv.* de plus.

mores, *n.* mœurs *f.pl.*

morgue, *n.* morgue *f.*

morning, *n.* matin *m.*; (length of m.) matinée *f.*; (good m.) bonjour.

moron, *n.* idiot.

morose, *adj.* morose.

Morse code, *n.* l'alphabet Morse *m.*

morsel, *n.* morceau *m.*

mortal, *adj. and n.* mortel *m.*

mortality, *n.* mortalité *f.*

mortar, *n.* mortier *m.*

mortgage, 1. *n.* hypothèque *f.* 2. *vb.* hypothéquer.

mortician, *n.* entrepreneur de pompes funèbres *m.*

mortify, *vb.* mortifier.

mortuary, *n.* mortuaire.

mosaic, 1. *n.* mosaïque *f.* 2. *adj.* en mosaïque.

Moscow, *n.* Moscou *m.*

Moslem, *adj. and n.* musulman *m.*

mosquito, *n.* moustique *m.*

moss, *n.* mousse *f.*

most, 1. *n.* le plus. 2. *adj.* le plus (de); la plupart (de). 3. *adv.* (with adj. and vb.) le plus; (intensive) très.

mostly, *adv.* pour la plupart; (time) la plupart du temps.

moth, *n.* (clothes) mite *f.*

mother, *n.* mère *f.*

mother-in-law, *n.* belle-mère *f.*

motif, *n.* motif *m.*

motion, *n.* mouvement *m.*; (gesture) signe *m.*; (proposal) motion *f.*

motionless, *adj.* immobile.

motion-picture, *n.* film *m.*

motivate, *vb.* motiver.

motive, *n.* motif *m.*

motley, 1. *adj.* bigarré. 2. *n.* livrée de bouffon *m.*

motor, *n.* moteur *m.*

motorboat, *n.* canot *(m.)* automobile.

motorist, *n.* automobiliste *m.*

motto, *n.* devise *f.*

mound, *n.* tertre *m.*

mount, 1. *n.* (hill) mont *m.*; (horse, structure) monture *f.* 2. *vb.* monter.

mountain, *n.* montagne *f.*

mountaineer, *n.* montagnard *m.*, Alpiniste *m.*

mountainous, *adj.* montagneux.

mountebank, *n.* saltimbanque *m.*, charlatan *m.*

mourn, *vb.* pleurer.

mournful, *adj.* triste.

mourning, *n.* deuil *m.*

mouse, *n.* souris *f.*

mouth, n. bouche f.

mouthpiece, n. embouchure f., embout m.

movable, adj. mobile.

move, vb. mouvoir, tr.; remuer; (stir) bouger; (affect with emotion) émouvoir; (change residence) déménager; (propose) proposer.

movement, n. mouvement m.

moving, 1. n. déménagement m. 2. adj. touchant.

mow, vb. faucher; (lawn) tondre.

Mr., n. M. m. (abbr. for Monsieur).

Mrs., n. Mme. f. (abbr. for Madame).

much, adj., pron. and adv. beaucoup (de); (too m.) trop (de); (so m.) tant (de); (how m.) combien (de).

mucilage, n. mucilage m.

muck, n. fumier m.

mucous, adj. muqueux.

mud, n. boue f.

muddy, adj. boueux.

muff, n. manchon m.

muffin, n. petit pain m.

muffle, vb. emmitoufler.

mug, n. gobelet m., pot m.

mulatto, n. mulâtre m.

mule, n. mulet m.

mullah, n. mollah m.

multicolored, adj. multicolore.

multinational, adj. multinational.

multiple, adj. multiple.

multiplication, n. multiplication f.

multiplicity, n. multiplicité f.

multiply, vb. multiplier, tr.

multitude, n. multitude f.

mummy, n. momie f.; maman f.

mumps, n. oreillons m.pl.

munch, vb. mâcher.

municipal, adj. municipal.

munificent, adj. munificent.

munition, n. munition(s) f.

mural, n. (painting) peinture (f.) murale.

murder, n. meurtre m.

murderer, n. meurtrier m.

murmur, 1. n. murmure m. 2. vb. murmurer.

muscle, n. muscle m.

muscular, adj. musculaire; (strong) musculeux.

muse, 1. n. muse f. 2. vb. méditer.

museum, n. musée m.

mushroom, n. champignon m.

music, n. musique f.

musical, adj. musical; (person) musicien.

musical comedy, n. comédie musicale f.

musician, n. musicien m.

Muslim, adj. and n. musulman m.

muslin, n. mousseline f.

must, vb. devoir; falloir (used impersonally, il faut que).

mustache, n. moustache f.

mustard, n. moutarde f.

muster, vb. rassembler, tr.

musty, adj. moisi, suranné.

mutation, n. mutation f.

mute, adj. muet.

mutilate, vb. mutiler.

mutiny, n. mutinerie f.

mutter, vb. grommeler.

mutton, n. mouton m.

mutual, adj. mutuel.

muzzle, n. muselière f.

my, adj. mon m., ma f., mes pl.

myopia, n. myopie f.

myriad, n. myriade f.

myrtle, n. myrte m.

myself, pron. moi-même; (reflexive) me.

mysterious, adj. mystérieux.

mystery, n. mystère m.

mystic, adj. mystique.

mystify, vb. mystifier.

myth, n. mythe m.

mythical, adj. mythique.

mythology, n. mythologie f.

N

nag, vb. gronder.

nail, 1. n. (person, animal) ongle m.; (metal) clou m. 2. vb. clouer.

naïve, adj. naïf m., naïve f.

naked, adj. nu.

name, 1. n. nom m. 2. vb. nommer.

namesake, n. homonyme m.

nap, n. petit somme m.

napkin, n. serviette f.

narcissus, n. narcisse m.

narcotic, adj. and n. narcotique m.

narrate, vb. raconter.

narrative, n. récit m.

narrow, adj. étroit.

nasal, adj. nasal.

nasty, adj. désagréable.

natal, adj. natal.

nation, n. nation f.

national, adj. national.

nationalism, n. nationalisme m.

nationality, n. nationalité f.

nationalization, n. nationalisation f.

nationalize, vb. nationaliser.

native, 1. n. natif m.; (primitive inhabitant, etc.) indigène m.f. 2. adj. natif; (place) natal; (language) maternel.

nativity, n. naissance f.

natural, adj. naturel.

naturalist, n. naturaliste m.

naturalize, vb. naturaliser.

naturalness, n. naturel m.

nature, n. nature f.

naughty, adj. méchant.

nausea, n. nausée f.

nauseous, adj. nauséeux.

nautical, adj. marin.

naval, adj. naval.

nave, n. nef f.

navigable, adj. navigable.

navigate, vb. naviguer.

navigation, n. navigation f.

navigator, n. navigateur m.

navy, n. marine f.

navy yard, n. arsenal maritime m.

near, 1. adj. proche. 2. adv. près. 3. prep. près de.

nearly, adv. de près; (almost) presque.

near-sighted, adj. myope.

neat, adj. propre.

neatness, n. propreté f.

nebula, n. nébuleuse f.

nebulous, adj. nébuleux.

necessary, adj. nécessaire.

necessity, n. nécessité f.

neck, n. cou m.

necklace, n. collier m.

necktie, n. cravate f.

nectar, n. nectar m.

need, 1. n. besoin m. 2. vb. avoir besoin de.

needful, adj. nécessaire.

needle, n. aiguille f.

needle point, n. pointe d'aiguille f.

needless, adj. inutile.

needy, adj. nécessiteux.

nefarious, adj. infâme.

negative, adj. négatif.

neglect, 1. n. négligence f. 2. vb. négliger (de).

negligee, n. négligée f.

negligent, adj. négligent.

negligible, adj. négligeable.

negotiate, vb. négocier.

negotiation, n. négociation f.

Negro, adj. and n. nègre m.

neighbor, n. voisin m.; (fellow man) prochain m.

neighborhood, n. voisinage m.

neither, 1. adj. and pron. ni l'un ni l'autre. 2. adv. non plus. 3. conj. (n. . . . nor) ni . . . ni.

neon, n. néon m.

neophyte, n. néophyte m.

nephew, n. neveu m.

nepotism, n. népotisme m.

nerve, n. nerf m.

nervous, adj. nerveux.

nervous system, n. système nerveux m.

nest, n. nid m.

nestle, vb. se nicher.

net, 1. n. filet m. 2. adj. net m., nette f.

Netherlands, the, n. les Pays-Bas m.pl., Hollande f.

network, n. réseau m.

neuralgia, n. névralgie f.

neurology, n. neurologie f.

neurotic, adj. and n. névrosé m.

neutral, adj. and n. neutre m.

neutron, n. neutron m.

neutron bomb, n. bombe à neutrons f.

never, adv. jamais.

nevertheless, adv. néanmoins.

new, adj. nouveau m., nouvelle f.; (not used) neuf m., neuve f.

news, n. (piece of news) nouvelle f.

newsboy, n. vendeur (m.) de journaux.

newscast, n. journal parlé m., informations f.pl.

newspaper, n. journal m.

newsreel, n. film d'actualité m.

New Testament, n. le Nouveau Testament m.

new year, n. nouvel an m.

next, 1. adj. prochain. **2.** adv. ensuite. **3.** prep. auprès de.

nibble, vb. grignoter.

nice, adj. (person) gentil; (thing) joli.

nick, n. entaille f.

nickel, n. nickel m.

nickname, n. surnom m.

niece, n. nièce f.

niggardly, adj. chiche.

night, n. nuit f.; (evening) soir m.

night club, n. boîte de nuit f., établissement de nuit m.

nightgown, n. chemise (f.) de nuit.

nightingale, n. rossignol m.

nightly, adv. tous les soirs; toutes les nuits.

nightmare, n. cauchemar m.

nimble, adj. agile.

nine, adj. and n. neuf m.

nineteen, adj. and n. dix-neuf m.

ninety, adj. and n. quatre-vingt-dix m.

ninth, adj. and n. neuvième m.

nip, 1. n. pincement m., pincade f. **2.** vb. pincer.

nipple, n. mamelon m.

nitrogen, n. nitrogène m.

no, 1. adj. pas de. **2.** interj., adv. non.

nobility, n. noblesse f.

noble, adj. noble.

nobleman, n. gentilhomme m.

nobly, adv. noblement.

nobody, pron. personne.

nocturnal, adj. nocturne.

nod, 1. n. signe (m.) de la tête. **2.** vb. incliner la tête.

node, n. nœud m.

no-frills, adj. simple.

noise, n. bruit m.

noiseless, adj. silencieux.

noisome, n. puant, fétide.

noisy, adj. bruyant.

nomad, n. nomade m. and f.

nominal, adj. nominal.

nominate, vb. (appoint) nommer; (propose) désigner.

nomination, n. (appointment) nomination f.; (proposal) désignation f.

nominee, n. personne nommée f., candidat choisi m.

nonaligned, adj. (in politics) non-aligné.

nonchalant, adj. nonchalant.

noncombatant, adj. and n. noncombattant m.

noncommissioned, adj. sans brevet.

noncommittal, adj. qui n'engage à rien.

nondescript, adj. indéfinissable.

none, pron. aucun.

nonentity, n. nullité f.

non-proliferation, n. non-prolifération m.

nonresident, n. and adj. non-résident m.

nonsense, n. absurdité f.

nonstop, adj. sans arrêt.

noodles, n. nouilles f.pl.

nook, n. coin m., recoin m.

noon, n. midi m.

noose, n. nœud coulant m.

nor, conj. ni; (and not) et ne ... pas.

normal, adj. normal.

normally, adv. normalement.

north, n. nord m.

North America, n. Amérique (f.) du Nord.

northeast, n. nord-est m.

northern, adj. du nord.

North Pole, n. pôle nord m.

northwest, n. nord-ouest m.

Norway, n. Norvège f.

Norwegian, 1. n. (person) Norvégien m.; (language) norvégien m. **2.** adj. norvégien.

nose, n. nez m.

nosebleed, n. saignement du nez m.

nose dive, n. vol piqué m.

nostalgia, n. nostalgie f.

nostril, n. narine f.; (animals) naseau m.

nostrum, n. panacée f., remède de charlatan m.

not, adv. (ne) pas.

notable, adj. and n. notable m.

notation, n. notation f.

note, 1. n. note f.; (letter, finance) billet m.; (distinction) marque f. **2.** vb. noter.

notebook, n. (small) carnet m.; (large) cahier m.

noted, adj. célèbre.

notepaper, n. papier à notes m.

noteworthy, adj. remarquable, mémorable.

nothing, pron. rien.

notice, 1. n. (announcement) avis m.; (attention) attention f.; (forewarning) préavis m. **2.** vb. remarquer.

noticeable, adj. remarquable; apparent.

notification, n. notification f.

notify, vb. avertir.

notion, n. idée f.

notoriety, n. notoriété f.

notorious, adj. notoire.

notwithstanding, 1. adv. tout de même. **2.** prep. malgré.

noun, n. substantif m.

nourish, vb. nourrir.

nourishment, n. nourriture f.

novel, n. roman m.

novelist, n. romancier m.

novelty, n. nouveauté f.

November, n. novembre m.

novice, n. novice m.f.

now, adv. maintenant; **(n. and then)** de temps en temps.

nowhere, adv. nulle part.

nozzle, n. ajutage m., jet m.

nuance, n. nuance f.

nuclear, adj. nucléaire.

nuclear physics, n. physique nucléaire f.

nuclear warhead, n. cône de charge nucléaire m.

nuclear waste, n. déchets nucléaires m.pl.

nucleus, n. noyau m.

nude, adj. and n. nu m.

nugget, n. pépite f.

nuisance, n. (thing) ennui m.; (person) peste f.

nuke, 1. n. arme nucléaire f. **2.** vb. détruire avec des armes nucléaires.

nullify, vb. annuler, nullifier.

number, 1. n. nombre m.; (in a series, street, etc.) numéro m. **2.** vb. compter, numéroter.

numerical, adj. numérique.

numerous, adj. nombreux.

nun, n. religieuse f.

nuncio, n. nonce m.

nuptial, adj. nuptial.

nurse, 1. n. (hospital) infirmière f.; (wet-n.) nourrice f. **2.** vb. soigner; (suckle) allaiter.

nursery, n. (children) chambre (f.) des enfants; (plants) pépinière f.

nurture, 1. n. nourriture f. **2.** vb. nourrir, entretenir.

nut, n. noix f.; (metal) écrou m.

nutcracker, n. casse-noix m.

nutrition, n. nutrition f.

nutritious, adj. nutritif.

nutshell, n. coquille de noix f.; (in a n.) en deux mots.

nylon, n. nylon m.

nymph, n. nymphe f.

O

oak, n. chêne m.

oar, n. rame f.

oasis, n. oasis f.

oath, n. serment m.; (curse) juron m.

oatmeal, n. farine d'avoine f.

oats, n. avoine f.

obdurate, adj. obstiné, têtu.

obedience, n. obéissance f.

obedient, adj. obéissant.

obeisance, n. salut m.

obelisk, n. obélisque m.

obey, vb. obéir à.

obituary, n. nécrologe m.

object, 1. n. objet m. **2.** vb. objecter.

objection, n. objection f.

objectionable, adj. répréhensible.

objective, adj. and n. objectif m.

obligation, n. obligation f.

obligatory, adj. obligatoire.

oblige, vb. obliger.

oblivion, n. oubli m.

obnoxious, adj. odieux.

obscene, *adj.* obscène.

obscure, *adj.* obscur.

obsequious, *adj.* obséquieux.

observance, *n.* observance *f.*

observation, *n.* observation *f.*

observe, *vb.* observer.

observer, *n.* observateur *m.*

obsession, *n.* obsession *f.*

obsolete, *adj.* désuet.

obstacle, *n.* obstacle *m.*

obstetrician, *n.* médecin-accoucheur *m.*

obstinate, *adj.* obstiné.

obstreperous, *adj.* tapageur.

obstruct, *vb.* obstruer.

obstruction, *n.* obstruction *f.*

obtain, *vb.* obtenir.

obtrude, *vb.* mettre en avant.

obviate, *vb.* prévenir, éviter.

obvious, *adj.* évident.

occasion, *n.* occasion *f.*

occasional, *adj.* (not regular) de temps en temps.

occult, *adj.* occulte.

occupant, *n.* occupant *m.*

occupation, *n.* occupation *f.;* (vocation) métier *m.*

occupy, *vb.* occuper.

occur, *vb.* (happen) avoir lieu; (come to the mind) se présenter à l'esprit.

occurrence, *n.* occurrence *f.*

ocean, *n.* océan *m.*

o'clock, *see* clock.

octagon, *n.* octogone *m.*

octave, *n.* octave *f.*

October, *n.* octobre *m.*

octopus, *n.* poulpe *m.*

ocular, *adj.* oculaire.

oculist, *n.* oculiste *f.*

odd, *adj.* (not even) impair; (unmatched) dépareillé; (strange) bizarre.

oddity, *n.* singularité *f.*

odds, *n.* inégalité *f.,* (betting) cote *f.*

odious, *adj.* odieux.

odor, *n.* odeur *f.*

of, *prep.* de.

off, 1. *adv.* (away) à ... de distance; (cancelled) rompu. 2. *prep.* de.

offend, *vb.* offenser; (o. against the law) enfreindre la loi.

offender, *n.* offenseur *m.;* (law) délinquant *m.*

offense, *n.* offense *f.;* (transgression) délit *m.*

offensive, 1. *n.* offensive *f.* 2. *adj.* (mil., etc.) offensif; (word, etc.) offensant.

offer, 1. *n.* offre *f.* 2. *vb.* offrir.

offering, *n.* offre *f.,* offrande *f.*

offhand, 1. *adj.* spontané. 2. *adv.* sans préparation.

office, *n.* (service) office *m.;* (function) fonctions *f.pl.;* (room) bureau *m.*

officer, *n.* (mil.) officier *m.;* (public) fonctionnaire *m.*

official, *adj.* officiel.

officiate, *vb.* officier.

officious, *adj.* officieux.

offshore, 1. *adv.* vers le large. 2. *adj.* du côté de la terre.

offspring, *n.* descendant *m.*

often, *adv.* souvent.

oil, *n.* huile *f.*

oilcloth, *n.* toile cirée *f.*

oily, *adj.* huileux.

ointment, *n.* onguent *m.*

okay, *interj.* très bien.

old, *adj.* vieux (vieil) *m.,* vieille *f.;* (how o. are you?) quel âge avez-vous?

old-fashioned, *adj.* démodé.

Old Testament, *n.* l'Ancien Testament *m.*

olfactory, *adj.* olfactif.

oligarchy, *n.* oligarchie *f.*

olive, *n.* (tree) olivier *m.;* (fruit) olive *f.*

ombudsman, *n.* (in France) médiateur *m.;* (in Quebec) protecteur du citoyen *m.*

omelet, *n.* omelette *f.*

omen, *n.* présage *m.*

ominous, *adj.* de mauvais augure.

omission, *n.* omission *f.*

omit, *vb.* omettre.

omnibus, *n.* omnibus *m.*

omnipotent, *adj.* omnipotent, tout-puissant.

on, *prep.* sur.

once, *adj.* une fois; (formerly) autrefois; (at o., without delay) tout de suite; (at o., at the same time) à la fois.

one, 1. *adj.* un; (only) seul. 2. *n.* un *m.* 3. *pron.* un; (indefinite subject) on, (indefinite object) vous; (the o.) celui; (this o.) celui-ci; (that o.) celui-là; (which o.) lequel.

oneself, *pron.* soi-même; (reflexive) se.

one-sided, *adj.* unilatéral.

onion, *n.* oignon *m.*

onionskin, *n.* pelure d'oignon *f.,* (paper) papier pelure *m.*

only, 1. *adj.* seul. 2. *adv.* seulement.

onslaught, *n.* assaut *m.*

onward, *adj.* and *adv.* en avant.

opal, *n.* opale *f.*

opaque, *adj.* opaque.

open, 1. *adj.* ouvert. 2. *vb.* ouvrir.

opening, *n.* ouverture *f.*

opera, *n.* opéra *m.*

opera glasses, *n.* jumelles *f.pl.*

operate, *vb.* opérer; (put into operation) actionner.

operatic, *adj.* d'opéra.

operation, *n.* opération *f.;* (functioning) fonctionnement *m.*

operator, *n.* opérateur *m.;* (telephone) employée *m.*

operetta, *n.* opérette *f.*

opinion, *n.* opinion *f.*

opponent, *n.* adversaire *m.f.*

opportunism, *n.* opportunisme *m.*

opportunity, *n.* occasion *f.*

oppose, *vb.* (put in opposition) opposer; (resist) s'opposer à.

opposite, 1. *adj.* opposé. 2. *adv.*

vis-à-vis. 3. *prep.* en face de.

opposition, *n.* opposition *f.*

oppress, *vb.* opprimer.

oppression, *n.* oppression *f.*

oppressive, *adj.* oppressif; (heat, etc.) accablant.

optic, *adj.* optique.

optician, *n.* opticien *f.*

optimism, *n.* optimisme *m.*

optimistic, *adj.* optimiste.

option, *n.* option *f.*

optional, *adj.* facultatif.

optometry, *n.* optométrie *f.*

or, *conj.* ou; (with negative) ni.

oracle, *n.* oracle *m.*

oral, *adj.* oral.

orange, *n.* orange *f.*

orangeade, *n.* orangeade *f.*

oration, *n.* discours *m.*

orator, *n.* orateur *m.*

oratory, *n.* art (*m.*) oratoire.

orbit, *n.* orbite *f.*

orchard, *n.* verger *m.*

orchestra, *n.* orchestre *m.*

orchid, *n.* orchidée *f.*

ordain, *vb.* ordonner.

ordeal, *n.* épreuve *f.*

order, 1. *n.* ordre *m.; (comm.)* commande *f.* 2. *vb.* ordonner; (comm.) commander.

orderly, *adj.* ordonné.

ordinance, *n.* ordonnance *f.*

ordinary, *adj.* and *n.* ordinaire *m.*

ordination, *n.* ordination *f.*

ore, *n.* minerai *m.*

organ, *n.* (music) orgue *m.;* (body) organe *m.*

organdy, *n.* organdi *m.*

organic, *adj.* organique.

organism, *n.* organisme *m.*

organist, *n.* organiste *m.f.*

organization, *n.* organisation *f.*

organize, *vb.* organiser.

orgy, *n.* orgie *f.*

orient, *vb.* orienter.

Orient, *n.* Orient *m.*

Oriental, 1. *n.* Oriental *m.* 2. *adj.* oriental.

orientation, *n.* orientation *f.*

origin, *n.* origine *f.*

original, *adj.* (new, unique) original; (from the origin) originel.

originality, *n.* originalité *f.*

ornament, *n.* ornement *m.*

ornamental, *adj.* ornemental.

ornate, *adj.* orné.

ornithology, *n.* ornithologie *f.*

orphan, *n.* orphelin *m.*

orphanage, *n.* orphelinat *m.*

orthodox, *adj.* orthodoxe.

orthopedics, *n.* orthopédie *f.*

osmosis, *n.* osmose *f.*

ostensible, *adj.* prétendu.

ostentation, *n.* ostentation *f.*

ostentatious, *adj.* plein d'ostentation.

ostracize, *vb.* ostraciser.

ostrich, *n.* autruche *f.*

other, *adj.* and *pron.* autre.

otherwise, *adv.* autrement.

ought, *vb.* devoir.

ounce, *n.* once *f.*

our, adj. notre sg., nos pl.

ours, pron. le nôtre.

ourself, pron. nous-même; (reflexive) nous.

oust, vb. évincer.

ouster, n. éviction f.

out, adv. dehors.

outbreak, n. (beginning) commencement m.; (insurrection) révolte f.

outburst, n. éruption f.

outcast, n. paria m.

outcome, n. résultat m.

outdoors, adv. dehors.

outer, adj. extérieur.

outfit, n. équipement m.

outgrowth, n. conséquence f.

outing, n. promenade f.

outlandish, adj. bizarre.

outlaw, vb. proscrire.

outlet, n. issue f.

outline, 1. n. contour m.; (general idea) aperçu m. 2. vb. (drawing) tracer; (plan) exposer à grands traits.

out of, prep. hors de; (because of) par; (without) sans.

out-of-date, adj. suranné.

output, n. rendement m.

outrage, n. outrage m.

outrageous, adj. outrageant.

outrank, vb. occuper un rang supérieur.

outright, adv. complètement.

outrun, vb. dépasser.

outside, 1. adv. dehors. 2. prep. en dehors de.

outskirts, n. limites f.pl.

outward, adj. extérieur.

oval, adj. and n. ovale m.

ovation, n. ovation f.

oven, n. four m.

over, 1. prep. (on) sur; (above) au-dessus de; (beyond) au delà de; (more than) plus de. 2. adv. (all over) partout; (more) davantage; (finished) fini; (with adj.) trop.

overbearing, adj. arrogant.

overcoat, n. pardessus m.

overcome, vb. vaincre; (be o. by) succomber à.

overdue, adj. arriéré, échu.

overflow, vb. déborder.

overhaul, vb. examiner en détail, remettre au point.

overhead, 1. adj. (comm.) général. 2. adv. en haut.

overkill, n. exagération rhétorique f.

overlook, vb. (look on to) avoir vue sur; (neglect) négliger.

overnight, adv. pendant la nuit.

overpower, vb. (subdue) subjuguer; (crush) accabler.

overrule, vb. décider contre.

overrun, vb. envahir.

oversee, vb. surveiller.

oversight, n. inadvertance f.

overstuffed, adj. rembourré.

overt, adj. manifeste.

overtake, vb. rattraper; (accident, etc.) arriver à.

overthrow, vb. renverser.

overtime, n. heures (f.pl.) supplémentaires.

overture, n. ouverture f.

overturn, vb. renverser, tr.

overview, n. vue d'ensemble f.

overweight, n. excédent m.

overwhelm, vb. accabler (de).

overwork, vb. surmener, tr.

owe, vb. devoir.

owing, 1. prep. à cause de, en raison de. 2. adj. dû.

owl, n. hibou m.

own, 1. adj. propre. 2. vb. posséder; (admit) avouer; (acknowledge) reconnaître.

owner, n. propriétaire m.f.

ox, n. bœuf m.

oxygen, n. oxygène m.

oxygen mask, n. masque d'oxygène m.

oyster, n. huître f.

P

pace, 1. n. (step) pas m.; (gait) allure f. 2. vb. arpenter.

pacific, adj. pacifique.

Pacific Ocean, n. océan Pacifique m.

pacifism, n. pacifisme m.

pacify, vb. pacifier.

pack, 1. n. paquet m.; (animals, persons) bande f. 2. vb. emballer; (crowd) entasser.

package, n. paquet m.

pact, n. pacte m., contrat m.

pad, 1. n. (stuffing) bourrelet m.; (cotton, ink) tampon m.; (paper) bloc m. 2. vb. (clothes) ouater; (stuff) bourrer.

padding, n. remplissage m., rembourrage m.

paddle, n. pagaie f.

paddock, n. enclos m.

pagan, adj. and n. païen m.

page, n. (book) page f.; (attendant) page m.

pageant, n. spectacle m.

pagoda, n. pagode f.

pail, n. seau m.

pain, 1. n. douleur f.; (trouble) peine f. 2. vb. (hurt) faire mal (à); (distress) faire de la peine (à).

painful, adj. douloureux.

painstaking, adj. soigneux.

paint, 1. n. peinture f. 2. vb. peindre.

painter, n. peintre m.

painting, n. peinture f.

pair, n. paire f.

pajamas, n. pyjama m.

palace, n. palais m.

palatable, adj. d'un goût agréable, agréable au palais.

palate, n. palais m.

palatial, adj. qui ressemble à un palais, magnifique.

pale, adj. pâle.

paleness, n. pâleur f.

palette, n. palette f.

pall, 1. n. drap funéraire m. 2. vb. s'affadir.

pallbearer, n. porteur (d'un cordon du poêle) m.

pallid, adj. pâle, blême.

palm, n. (tree) palmier m.; (branch) palme f.; (hand) paume f.

palpitate, vb. palpiter.

paltry, adj. mesquin.

pamper, vb. choyer.

pamphlet, n. brochure f.

pan, n. (cooking) casserole f.

panacea, n. panacée f.

Pan-American, adj. panaméricain.

pancake, n. crêpe f.

pane, n. (window) vitre f.

panel, n. panneau m.

pang, n. angoisse f.

panic, n. panique f.

panorama, n. panorama m.

pant, vb. haleter.

pantomime, n. pantomime m.

pantry, n. office f.

pants, n. pantalon m.

panty hose, n. collant m.

papal, adj. papal.

paper, n. papier m.

paperback, n. livre broché m.

par, n. pair m., égalité f.

parable, n. parabole f.

parachute, n. parachute f.

parade, n. parade f.

paradise, n. paradis m.

paradox, n. paradoxe m.

paraffin, n. paraffine f.

paragraph, n. alinéa m.

parakeet, n. perruche f.

parallel, 1. n. (line) parallèle f.; (geography, comparison) parallèle m. 2. adj. parallèle.

paralyze, vb. paralyser.

paramedic, n. assistant médical m.

parameter, n. paramètre m.

paramount, adj. souverain.

paraphrase, vb. paraphraser.

parasite, n. parasite m.

parcel, n. paquet m.; (p. post) colis postal m.

parch, vb. dessécher, tr.

parchment, n. parchemin m.

pardon, 1. n. pardon m. 2. vb. pardonner.

pare, vb. (fruit) peler.

parent, n. père m.; mère f.; (parents) parents m.pl.

parentage, n. naissance f.

parenthesis, n. parenthèse f.

parish, n. paroisse f.

Parisian, 1. n. Parisien m. 2. adj. parisien.

parity, n. parité f., égalité f.

park, 1. n. parc m. 2. vb. stationner.

parley, n. conférence f., pourparler m.

parliament, n. parlement m.

parliamentary, adj. parlementaire.

parlor, n. petit salon m.

parochial, adj. paroissial; (limited in outlook) de clocher.

parody, n. parodie f.

parole, 1. *n.* parole *f.* 2, *vb.* libérer conditionnellement.

paroxysm, *n.* paroxysme *m.*

parrot, *n.* perroquet *m.*

parsley, *n.* persil *m.*

parson, *n.* pasteur *m.*

part, 1. *n.* (of a whole) partie *f.;* (share) part *f.* 2. *vb.* (divide) diviser; (share) partager; (of people) se séparer.

partake of, *vb.* participer à.

partial, *adj.* partiel; (favoring) partial.

participant, *adj. and n.* participant *m.*

participate, *vb.* participer.

participation, *n.* participation *f.*

participle, *n.* participe *m.*

particle, *n.* particule *f.*

particular, 1. *n.* détail *m.* 2. *adj.* particulier; (person) exigeant.

parting, *n.* séparation *f.;* (hair) raie *f.*

partisan, *n.* partisan *m.*

partition, *n.* partage *m.;* (wall) cloison *f.*

partly, *adv.* en partie.

partner, *n.* associé *m.*

part of speech, *n.* partie (*f.*) du discours.

partridge, *n.* perdrix *f.*

party, *n.* (faction) parti *m.;* (social) réception *f.;* (group of people) groupe *m.;* (law) partie *f.*

pass, 1. *n.* (mountain) col *m.;* (permission) laissez-passer *m.* 2. *vb.* passer.

passable, *adj.* traversable, passable, assez bon.

passage, *n.* passage *m.*

passenger, *n.* (land) voyageur *m.;* (sea, air) passager *m.*

passer-by, *n.* passant *m.*

passion, *n.* passion *f.*

passionate, *adj.* passionné.

passive, *adj. and n.* passif *m.*

passport, *n.* passeport *m.*

past, 1. *adj. and n.* passé *m.* 2. *prep.* (beyond) au delà de; (more than) plus de; (half p. four) quatre heures et demie.

paste, 1. *n.* pâte *f.;* (glue) colle *f.* 2. *vb.* coller.

pasteurize, *vb.* pasteuriser.

pastime, *n.* passe-temps *m.*

pastor, *n.* pasteur *m.*

pastry, *n.* pâtisserie *f.*

pasture, *n.* pâturage *m.*

pasty, *adj.* empâté, pâteux.

pat, *vb.* taper.

patch, 1. *n.* pièce *f.* 2. *vb.* rapiécer.

patchwork, *n.* ouvrage fait de pièces disparates *m.*

patent, *n.* brevet (*m.*) d'invention.

patent leather, *n.* cuir (*m.*) verni.

paternal, *adj.* paternel.

paternity, *n.* paternité *f.*

path, *n.* sentier *m.*

pathetic, *adj.* pathétique.

pathology, *n.* pathologie *f.*

pathos, *n.* pathétique *m.*

patience, *n.* patience *f.*

patient, 1. *n.* malade *m.f.* 2. *adj.* patient.

patio, *n.* patio *m.*

patriarch, *n.* patriarche *m.*

patriot, *n.* patriote *m.f.*

patriotic, *adj.* patriotique.

patriotism, *n.* patriotisme *m.*

patrol, *n.* patrouille *f.*

patrolman, *n.* agent (de police) *m.,* patrouilleur *m.*

patron, *n.* protecteur *m.;* (comm.) client *m.*

patronize, *vb.* protéger.

pattern, *n.* modèle *m.;* (design) dessin *m.*

pauper, *n.* indigent *m.,* pauvre *m.,* mendiant *m.*

pause, *n.* pause *f.*

pave, *vb.* paver.

pavement, *n.* pavé *m.;* (sidewalk) trottoir *m.*

pavilion, *n.* pavillon *m.*

paw, *n.* patte *f.*

pawn, 1. *n.* pion *m.* 2. *vb.* mettre en gage, engager.

pay, 1. *n.* salaire *m.* 2. *vb.* payer.

payment, *n.* payement *m.*

pea, *n.* pois *m.*

peace, *n.* paix *f.*

peaceable, peaceful, *adj.* paisible.

peach, *n.* pêche *f.*

peacock, *n.* paon *m.*

peak, *n.* sommet *m.*

peal, 1. *n.* retentissement *m.* 2. *vb.* sonner, retentir.

peanut, *n.* arachide *f.*

pear, *n.* poire *f.*

pearl, *n.* perle *f.*

peasant, *n.* paysan *m.*

pebble, *n.* caillou *m.*

peck, *vb.* becqueter.

peculiar, *adj.* particulier; (unusual) singulier.

pecuniary, *adj.* pécuniaire.

pedagogue, *n.* pédagogue *m.*

pedagogy, *n.* pédagogie *f.*

pedal, *n.* pédale *f.*

pedant, *n.* pédant *m.*

peddle, *vb.* colporter.

peddler, *n.* colporteur *m.*

pedestal, *n.* piédestal *m.*

pedestrian, *n.* piéton *m.*

pediatrician, *n.* pédiatre *m.*

pedigree, *n.* généalogie *f.*

peek, 1. *n.* coup d'œil furtif *m.* 2. *vb.* regarder à la dérobée.

peel, 1. *n.* pelure *f.* 2. *vb.* peler.

peep, *vb.* regarder furtivement.

peer, 1. *n.* pair *m.,* pareil *m.* 2. *vb.* scruter, regarder.

peevish, *adj.* irritable.

peg, *n.* cheville *f.*

pelt, 1. *n.* peau *f.,* fourrure *f.* 2. *vb.* lancer, jeter.

pelvis, *n.* bassin *m.*

pen, *n.* plume *f.*

penalty, *n.* peine *f.*

penance, *n.* pénitence *f.*

penchant, *n.* penchant *m.*

pencil, *n.* crayon *m.*

pending, *prep.* pendant.

penetrate, *vb.* pénétrer.

penetration, *n.* pénétration *f.*

peninsula, *n.* péninsule *f.*

penitent, 1. *adj.* pénitent, contrit. 2. *n.* pénitent *m.*

penknife, *n.* canif *m.*

penniless, *adj.* sans le sou.

penny, *n.* sou *m.*

pension, *n.* pension *f.*

pensive, *adj.* pensif.

pent-up, *adj.* refoulé.

penury, *n.* pénurie *f.*

people, 1. *n.* gens *m.f.pl.;* (of a country) peuple *m.* 2. *vb.* peupler.

pepper, *n.* poivre *m.*

perambulator, *n.* voiture d'enfant *f.*

perceive, *vb.* apercevoir, *tr.*

percent, pour cent.

percentage, *n.* pourcentage *m.*

perceptible, *adj.* perceptible.

perception, *n.* perception *f.*

perch, 1. *n.* (for birds) perchoir *m.;* (fish) perche *f.* 2. *vb.* se percher.

perdition, *n.* perte *f.*

peremptory, *adj.* péremptoire.

perennial, *adj.* perpétuel; (plant) vivace.

perfect, *adj.* parfait.

perfection, *n.* perfection *f.*

perforation, *n.* perforation *f.*

perform, *vb.* accomplir; (theater) jouer.

performance, *n.* (task) accomplissement *m.;* (theater) représentation *f.*

perfume, *n.* parfum *m.*

perfunctory, *adj.* fait pour la forme, superficiel.

perhaps, *adv.* peut-être.

peril, *n.* péril *m.*

perilous, *adj.* périlleux.

perimeter, *n.* périmètre *m.*

period, *n.* période *f.;* (full stop) point *m.*

periodic, *adj.* périodique.

periodical, *n.* périodique *m.*

periphery, *n.* périphérie *f.*

perish, *vb.* périr.

perishable, *adj.* périssable.

perjury, *n.* parjure *m.*

permanent, *adj.* permanent.

permeate, *vb.* filtrer.

permissible, *adj.* admissible.

permission, *n.* permission *f.*

permit, 1. *n.* permis *m.* 2. *vb.* permettre.

pernicious, *adj.* pernicieux.

perpendicular, *adj.* perpendiculaire, vertical.

perpetrate, *vb.* perpétrer.

perpetual, *adj.* perpétuel.

perplex, *vb.* mettre dans la perplexité.

perplexity, *n.* perplexité *f.,* embarras *m.*

persecute, *vb.* persécuter.

persecution, *n.* persécution *f.*

perseverance, *n.* persévérance *f.*

persevere, *vb.* persévérer.

persist, *vb.* persister.

persistent, *adj.* persistant.
person, *n.* personne *f.*
personage, *n.* personnage *m.*
personal, *adj.* personnel.
personality, *n.* personnalité *f.*
personally, *adv.* personnellement.
personnel, *n.* personnel *m.*
perspective, *n.* perspective *f.*
perspiration, *n.* transpiration *f.*
perspire, *vb.* transpirer.
persuade, *vb.* persuader.
persuasive, *adj.* persuasif.
pertain, *vb.* appartenir.
pertinent, *adj.* pertinent.
perturb, *vb.* troubler.
peruse, *vb.* lire attentivement.
pervade, *vb.* pénétrer.
perverse, *adj.* entêté (dans l'erreur).
perversion, *n.* perversion *f.*
pessimism, *n.* pessimisme *f.*
pestilence, *n.* pestilence *f.*
pet, *n.* (animal) animal *(m.)* familier.
petal, *n.* pétale *m.*
petition, *n.* pétition *f.*
petroleum, *n.* pétrole *m.*
petticoat, *n.* jupon *m.*
petty, *adj.* insignifiant.
phantom, *n.* fantôme *m.*
pharmacist, *n.* pharmacien *m.*
pharmacy, *n.* pharmacie *f.*
phase, *n.* phase *f.*
phenomenal, *adj.* phénoménal.
phenomenon, *n.* phénomène *m.*
philanthropy, *n.* philanthropie *f.*
philosopher, *n.* philosophe *m.*
philosophical, *adj.* philosophique.
philosophy, *n.* philosophie *f.*
phobia, *n.* phobie *f.*
phonograph, *n.* phonographe *m.*
photocopier, *n.* photocopieur *m.*
photocopy, *n.* photocopie *f.*
photograph, photography, *n.* photographie *f.*
phrase, *n.* phrase *f.*
physical, *adj.* physique.
physician, *n.* médecin *m.*
physics, *n.* physique *f.*
pianist, *n.* pianiste *m.f.*
piano, *n.* piano *m.*
pick, *vb.* (choose) choisir; (gather) cueillir.
pickles, *n.* conserves *(f.pl.)* au vinaigre.
picnic, *n.* pique-nique *m.*
picture, *n.* tableau *m.;* (motion picture) film *m.*
picturesque, *adj.* pittoresque.
pie, *n.* tarte *f.*
piece, *n.* morceau *m.*
pier, *n.* jetée *f.;* quai *m.*
pierce, *vb.* percer.
piety, *n.* piété *f.*
pig, *n.* cochon *m.*
pigeon, *n.* pigeon *m.*
pigeonhole, *n.* (for papers, etc.) case *f.*
pile, **1.** *n.* (construction) pieu

m.; (heap) tas *m.* **2.** *vb.* entasser.
pilgrim, *n.* pèlerin *m.*
pilgrimage, *n.* pèlerinage *m.*
pill, *n.* pilule *f.*
pillar, *n.* pilier *m.*
pillow, *n.* oreiller *m.*
pilot, *n.* pilote *m.*
pimple, *n.* bouton *m.*
pin, **1.** *n.* épingle *f.* **2.** *vb.* épingler.
pinch, *vb.* pincer.
pine, **1.** *n.* pin *m.* **2.** *vb.* languir.
pineapple, *n.* ananas *m.*
pink, *adj.* and *n.* rose *m.*
pinnacle, *n.* pinacle *m.*
pint, *n.* pinte *f.*
pioneer, *n.* pionnier *m.*
pious, *adj.* pieux.
pipe, *n.* tuyau *m.;* (smoking) pipe *f.*
piper, *n.* (bagpipe) joueur *(m.)* de cornemuse.
piquant, *adj.* piquant.
pirate, *n.* pirate *m.*
pistol, *n.* pistolet *m.*
piston, *n.* piston *m.*
pit, *n.* fosse *f.*
pitch, **1.** *n.* (substance) poix *f.;* (throw) jet *m.;* (height) hauteur *f.;* (music) ton *m.* **2.** *vb.* (throw) lancer.
pitcher, *n.* (vessel) cruche *f.;* (baseball) lanceur *m.*
pitfall, *n.* trappe *f.*
pitiful, *adj.* pitoyable.
pitiless, *adj.* impitoyable.
pity, **1.** *n.* pitié *f.;* (what a p.!) quel dommage! **2.** *vb.* plaindre.
pivot, *n.* pivot *m.*, axe *m.*
pizza, *n.* pizza *f.*
place, **1.** *n.* endroit *m.;* (locality) lieu *m.;* (position occupied) place *f.* **2.** *vb.* mettre.
placid, *adj.* placide.
plague, *n.* (disease) peste *f.; (fig.)* fléau *m.*
plaid, *n.* (blanket) plaid *m.;* (textile) tartan *m.*
plain, **1.** *n.* plaine *f.* **2.** *adj.* (clear) clair; (simple) simple; (of person) quelconque.
plaintiff, *n.* demandeur *m.*
plan, **1.** *n.* plan *m.* **2.** *vb.* faire le plan de.
plane, *n.* (surface) plan *m.;* (tool) rabot *m.;* (tree) platane *m.;* (airplane) avion *m.*
planet, *n.* planète *f.*
plank, *n.* planche *f.*
plant, **1.** *n.* plante *f.* **2.** *vb.* planter.
plantation, *n.* plantation *f.*
planter, *n.* planteur *m.*
plasma, *n.* plasma *m.*
plaster, *n.* plâtre *m.*
plastic, *adj.* plastique.
plate, *n.* plaque *f.;* (for eating) assiette *f.*
plateau, *n.* plateau *m.*
platform, *n.* plate-forme *f.;* (railroad) quai *m.*
platter, *n.* plat *m.*
plausible, *adj.* plausible.

play, **1.** *n.* jeu *m.;* (drama) pièce *(f.)* de théâtre. **2.** *vb.* jouer; (game) jouer à; (instrument) jouer de.
player, *n.* jouer *m.;* (theater) acteur *m.*
playful, *adj.* enjoué.
playground, *n.* (children) terrain *(m.)* de jeu.
playmate, *n.* camarade *(m.f.)* de jeu.
playwright, *n.* dramaturge *m.*
plea, *n.* défense *f.;* (excuse) excuse *f.*
plead, *vb.* plaider; (allege) alléguer.
pleasant, *adj.* agréable.
please, *vb.* plaire à; (satisfy) contenter; (if you p.) s'il vous plaît.
pleasure, *n.* plaisir *m.*
pleat, *n.* pli *m.*
pledge, *n.* gage *m.;* (promise) engagement *m.*
plentiful, *adj.* abondant.
plenty, *n.* abondance *f.*
pliable, *adj.* pliable.
pliers, *n.* pinces *f.pl.*
plight, *n.* état *m.*
plot, *n.* (literature) intrigue *f.;* (conspiracy) complot *m.*
plow, **1.** *n.* charrue *f.* **2.** *vb.* labourer.
pluck, *n.* courage *m.*
plug, *n.* tampon *m.;* (electric) prise *(f.)* de courant.
plum, *n.* prune *f.*
plumber, *n.* plombier *m.*
plume, *n.* panache *m.*
plump, *adj.* grassouillet.
plunder, *vb.* piller.
plunge, **1.** *n.* plongeon *m.* **2.** *vb.* plonger.
plural, *adj.* and *n.* pluriel *m.*
plus, *n.* plus *m.*
pneumonia, *n.* pneumonie *f.*
poach, *vb.* (of eggs) pocher.
poacher, *n.* braconnier *m.*
pocket, *n.* poche *f.*
pocketbook, *n.* sac *(m.)* à main.
poem, *n.* poésie *f.;* (long) poème *f.*
poet, *n.* poète *m.*
poetic, *adj.* poétique.
poetry, *n.* poésie *f.*
poignant, *adj.* poignant.
point, **1.** *n.* point *m.;* (sharp end) pointe *f.* **2.** *vb.* (gun, etc.) pointer; (indicate) désigner.
pointed, *adj.* pointu; (ironical) mordant.
poise, *n.* équilibre *m.*
poison, **1.** *n.* poison *m.* **2.** *vb.* empoisonner.
poisonous, *adj.* empoisonné; (plant) vénéneux; (animal) venimeux.
Poland, *n.* Pologne *f.*
polar, *adj.* polaire.
polar bear, *n.* ours *(m.)* blanc.
Pole, *n.* Polonais *m.*
pole, *n.* (geography) pôle *m.;* (wood) perche *f.*
police, *n.* police *f.*

policeman, *n.* agent (*m.*) de police.

policy, *n.* politique *f.;* (insurance) police *f.*

Polish, *adj. and n.* polonais *m.*

polish, *vb.* polir; (shoes) cirer.

polite, *adj.* poli.

politic, political, *adj.* politique.

politician, *n.* politicien *m.*

politics, *n.* politique *f.*

poll, *n.* (voting) scrutin *m.*

pollen, *n.* pollen *m.*

pollute, *vb.* polluer.

polygamy, *n.* polygamie *f.*

pomp, *n.* pompe *f.*

pompous, *adj.* pompeux.

pond, *n.* étang *m.*

ponder, *vb.* réfléchir.

ponderous, *adj.* pesant.

pony, *n.* poney *m.*

pool, *n.* mare *f.;* (swimming) piscine *f.*

poor, *adj.* pauvre.

pop, *n.* petit bruit (*m.*) sec.

pope, *n.* pape *m.*

popular, *adj.* populaire.

popularity, *n.* popularité *f.*

population, *n.* population *f.*

porch, *n.* véranda *f.*

pore, 1. *n.* pore *m.* 2. *vb.* (p. over) s'absorber dans.

pork, *n.* porc *m.*

pornography, *n.* pornographie *f.*

porous, *adj.* poreux.

port, *n.* (harbor) port *m.;* (*naut.*) bâbord *m.;* (wine) porto *m.*

portable, *adj.* portatif.

portal, *n.* portail *m.*

portfolio, *n.* portefeuille *m.*

portion, *n.* portion *f.*

portrait, *n.* portrait *m.*

portray, *vb.* (paint) peindre; (describe) dépeindre.

Portugal, *n.* Portugal *m.*

Portuguese, 1. *n.* (person) Portugais *m.;* (language) portugais *m.* 2. *adj.* portugais.

pose, 1. *n.* pose *f.* 2. *vb.* poser.

position, *n.* position *f.*

positive, 1. *n.* positif *m.* 2. *adj.* positif.

possess, *vb.* posséder.

possession, *n.* possession *f.*

possibility, *n.* possibilité *f.*

possible, *adj.* possible.

possibly, *adv.* il est possible que . . .; (perhaps) peut-être.

post, 1. *n.* (mail) poste *f.;* (wood) poteau *m.;* (place) poste *m.* 2. *vb.* (mail) mettre à la poste; (placard) afficher.

postage, *n.* affranchissement *m.*

postal, *adj.* postal.

post card, *n.* carte (*f.*) postale.

poster, *n.* affiche *f.*

posterior, *adj.* postérieur.

posterity, *n.* postérité *f.*

post office, *n.* bureau (*m.*) de poste.

postpone, *vb.* remettre.

postscript, *n.* post-scriptum *m.*

posture, *n.* posture *f.*

pot, *n.* pot *m.;* (saucepan) marmite *f.;* (marijuana) herbe *f.,* kif *m.*

potato, *n.* pomme (*f.*) de terre.

potent, *adj.* puissant.

potential, *adj. and n.* potentiel *m.*

pottery, *n.* poterie *f.*

pouch, *n.* sac *m.*

poultry, *n.* volaille *f.*

pound, *n.* livre *f.*

pour, *vb.* verser; (rain) tomber à verse.

poverty, *n.* pauvreté *f.*

powder, *n.* poudre *f.*

power, *n.* pouvoir *m.;* (nation, mathematics) puissance *f.*

powerful, *adj.* puissant.

powerless, *adj.* impuissant.

practical, *adj.* pratique.

practically, *adv.* pratiquement.

practice, 1. *n.* (exercise) exercice *m.;* (habit) habitude *f.;* (not theory) pratique *f.* 2. *vb.* pratiquer; (piano, etc.) s'exercer (à).

practiced, *adj.* expérimenté.

prairie, *n.* savane *f.*

praise, 1. *n.* éloge *m.* 2. *vb.* louer.

prank, *n.* fredaine *f.*

pray, *vb.* prier.

prayer, *n.* prière *f.*

preach, *vb.* prêcher.

preacher, *n.* prédicateur *m.*

precarious, *adj.* précaire.

precaution, *n.* précaution *f.*

precede, *vb.* précéder.

precedent, *n.* précédent *m.*

precept, *n.* précepte *m.*

precious, *adj.* précieux.

precipice, *n.* précipice *m.*

precipitate, *vb.* précipiter.

precise, *adj.* précis.

precision, *n.* précision *f.*

preclude, *vb.* empêcher.

precocious, *adj.* précoce.

predecessor, *n.* prédécesseur *m.*

predestination, *n.* prédestination *f.*

predicament, *n.* situation (*f.*) difficile.

predict, *vb.* prédire.

predispose, *vb.* prédisposer.

predominant, *adj.* prédominant.

prefabricate, *vb.* préfabriquer.

preface, *n.* préface *f.*

prefer, *vb.* préférer.

preferable, *adj.* préférable.

preference, *n.* préférence *f.*

prefix, *n.* préfixe *m.*

pregnant, *adj.* enceinte.

prejudice, *n.* préjugé *m.*

preliminary, *adj.* préliminaire.

prelude, *n.* prélude *m.*

premature, *adj.* prématuré.

premeditate, *vb.* préméditer.

premier, *n.* premier ministre *m.*

première, *n.* première *f.*

premise, *n.* (place) lieux *m.pl.;* (logic) prémisse *f.*

premium, *n.* prix *m.*

preparation, *n.* préparation *f.;* préparatifs *m.pl.*

preparatory, *adj.* préparatoire.

prepare, *vb.* préparer, *tr.*

preponderant, *adj.* prépondérant.

preposition, *n.* préposition *f.*

preposterous, *adj.* absurde.

prerequisite, *n.* nécessité (*f.*) préalable.

prescribe, *vb.* prescrire.

prescription, *n.* prescription *f.;* (medical) ordonnance *f.*

presence, *n.* présence *f.*

present, 1. *adj. and n.* présent *m.* 2. *vb.* présenter.

presentable, *adj.* présentable.

presentation, *n.* présentation *f.*

presently, *adv.* tout à l'heure.

preservative, *adj. and n.* préservatif *m.*

preserve, 1. *n.* (jam) confiture *f.* 2. *vb.* (protect) préserver; (keep) conserver.

preside, *vb.* présider.

president, *n.* président *m.*

press, 1. *n.* presse *f.* 2. *vb.* presser; (iron) repasser.

pressure, *n.* pression *f.*

prestige, *n.* prestige *m.*

presume, *vb.* présumer.

presumptuous, *adj.* présomptueux.

pretend, *vb.* (claim, aspire) prétendre; (feign) simuler.

pretense, *n.* faux semblant *m.*

pretentious, *adj.* prétentieux.

pretext, *n.* prétexte *m.*

pretty, *adj.* joli.

prevail, *vb.* prévaloir; (p. upon) décider.

prevalent, *adj.* répandu.

prevent, *vb.* (impede) empêcher; (forestall) prévenir.

prevention, *n.* empêchement *m.*

preventive, *adj.* préventif.

previous, *adj.* antérieur.

prey, *n.* proie *f.*

price, *n.* prix *m.*

priceless, *adj.* inestimable.

prick, 1. *n.* piqûre *f.* 2. *vb.* piquer.

pride, *n.* orgueil *m.*

priest, *n.* prêtre *m.*

prim, *adj.* affecté.

primary, *adj.* premier; (school, geology) primaire.

prime, 1. *n.* comble *m.* 2. *adj.* premier, de première qualité. 3. *adj.* amorcer.

primitive, *adj.* primitif.

prince, *n.* prince *m.*

princess, *n.* princesse *f.*

principal, *adj.* principal.

principle, *n.* principe *m.*

print, 1. *n.* (mark) empreinte *f.;* (book) impression *f.;* (photo) épreuve *f.* 2. *vb.* imprimer.

printout, *n.* feuille imprimée produite par un ordinateur *f.*

priority, *n.* priorité *f.*

prism, *n.* prisme *m.*

prison, *n.* prison *f.*

prisoner, *n.* prisonnier *m.*
privacy, *n.* retraite *f.*
private, *adj.* particulier; (not public) privé.
privation, *n.* privation *f.*
privilege, *n.* privilège *m.*
prize, *n.* prix *m.*
probability, *n.* probabilité *f.*
probable, *adj.* probable.
probe, *vb.* sonder.
problem, *n.* problème *m.*
procedure, *n.* procédé *m.*
proceed, *vb.* procéder; (advance) avancer.
process, *n.* (method) procédé *m.;* (progress) développement *m.*
procession, *n.* cortège *m.;* (religious) procession *f.*
proclaim, *vb.* proclamer.
proclamation, *n.* proclamation *f.*
procure, *vb.* procurer.
prodigal, *adj. and n.* prodigue *m.*
prodigy, *n.* prodige *m.*
produce, *vb.* produire.
product, *n.* produit *m.*
production, *n.* production *f.*
productive, *adj.* productif.
profane, *adj.* profane.
profess, *vb.* professer.
profession, *n.* profession *f.*
professional, *adj.* professionnel.
professor, *n.* professeur *m.*
proficient, *adj.* capable.
profile, *n.* profil *m.*
profit, **1.** *n.* profit *m.* **2.** *vb.* profiter.
profitable, *adj.* profitable.
profound, *adj.* profond.
profuse, *adj.* (of thing) profus; (of person) prodigue.
program, *n.* programme *m.*
progress, *n.* progrès *m.;* (motion forward) marche *f.*
progressive, *adj.* progressif.
prohibit, *vb.* défendre.
prohibition, *n.* défense *f.*
prohibitive, *adj.* prohibitif.
project, **1.** *n.* projet *m.* **2.** *vb.* projeter; (jut out) faire saillie.
projection, *n.* projection *f.;* (jutting out) saillie *f.*
projector, *n.* projecteur *m.*
proliferation, *n.* prolifération *f.*
prolong, *vb.* prolonger.
prominent, *adj.* saillant.
promiscuous, *adj.* (indiscriminate) sans distinction.
promise, **1.** *n.* promesse *f.* **2.** *vb.* promettre.
promote, *vb.* (raise) promouvoir; (encourage) encourager.
promotion, *n.* promotion *f.*
prompt, *adj.* prompt.
pronoun, *n.* pronom *m.*
pronounce, *vb.* prononcer.
pronunciation, *n.* prononciation *f.*
proof, *n.* (evidence) preuve *f.;* (test) épreuve *f.*
prop, *n.* appui *m.*
propaganda, *n.* progagande *f.*

propagate, *vb.* propager, *tr.*
propeller, *n.* hélice *f.*
proper, *adj.* propre; (respectable, fitting) convenable.
property, *n.* propriété *f.*
prophecy, *n.* prophétie *f.*
prophesy, *vb.* prophétiser.
prophet, *n.* prophète *m.*
prophetic, *adj.* prophétique.
proportion, *n.* proportion *f.*
proportionate, *adj.* proportionné.
proposal, *n.* proposition *f.;* demande (*f.*) en mariage.
propose, *vb.* proposer, *tr.*
proposition, *n.* (proposal, grammar) proposition *f.;* (undertaking) affaire *f.*
proprietor, *n.* propriétaire *m.f.*
prosaic, *adj.* prosaïque.
proscribe, *vb.* proscrire.
prose, *n.* prose *f.*
prosecute, *vb.* poursuivre.
prospect, *n.* perspective *f.*
prospective, *adj.* en perspective.
prosper, *vb.* prospérer.
prosperity, *n.* prospérité *f.*
prosperous, *adj.* prospère.
prostitute, **1.** *n.* prostituée *f.* **2.** *vb.* prostituer.
prostrate, *adj.* prosterné.
protect, *vb.* protéger.
protection, *n.* protection *f.*
protective, *adj.* protecteur.
protector, *n.* protecteur *m.*
protégé, *n.* protégé *m.*
protein, *n.* protéine *f.*
protest, **1.** *n.* protestation *f.;* (comm.) protêt *m.* **2.** *vb.* protester.
Protestant, *adj. and n.* protestant *m.*
protocol, *n.* protocole *m.*
protrude, *vb.* saillir.
prove, *vb.* prouver; (test) éprouver.
proverb, *n.* proverbe *m.*
provide (with) *vb.* pourvoir (de), *tr.*
providence, *n.* (foresight) prévoyance *f.;* (divine) providence *f.*
province, *n.* province *f.*
provincial, *adj. and n.* provincial *m.*
provision, *n.* (stock) provision *f.*
provocation, *n.* provocation *f.*
provoke, *vb.* provoquer; (irritate) irriter.
prowess, *n.* prouesse *f.*
prowl, *vb.* rôder.
proximity, *n.* proximité *f.*
prudence, *n.* prudence *f.*
prudent, *adj.* prudent.
prune, *n.* pruneau *m.*
Prussia, *n.* Prusse *f.*
Prussian, **1.** *n.* Prussien *m.* **2.** *adj.* prussien.
pry, *vb.* fureter.
psalm, *n.* psaume *m.*
psychedelic, *adj.* psychédélique.
psychiatry, *n.* psychiatrie *f.*

psychoanalysis, *n.* psychanalyse *f.*
psychology, *n.* psychologie *f.*
psychological, *adj.* psychologique.
ptomaine, *n.* ptomaïne *f.*
public, **1.** *n.* public *m.* **2.** *adj.* public *m.*, publique *f.*
publication, *n.* publication *f.*
publicity, *n.* publicité *f.*
publish, *vb.* publier.
publisher, *n.* éditeur *m.*
pudding, *n.* pouding *m.*
puddle, *n.* flaque *f.*
puff, *n.* (smoke etc.) bouffée *f.*
pull, *vb.* tirer.
pulley, *n.* poulie *f.*
pulp, *n.* pulpe *f.*
pulpit, *n.* chaire *f.*
pulsar, *n.* pulsar *m.*
pulsate, *vb.* battre.
pulse, *n.* pouls *m.*
pump, **1.** *n.* pompe *f.* **2.** *vb.* pomper.
pumpkin, *n.* potiron *m.*
pun, *n.* calembour *m.*
punch, **1.** *n.* (tool) poinçon *m.;* (blow) coup (*m.*) de poing; (beverage) punch *m.* **2.** *vb.* (pierce) percer; (pummel) gourmer.
punctual, *adj.* ponctuel.
punctuate, *vb.* ponctuer.
puncture, *n.* piqûre *f.*
punish, *vb.* punir.
punishment, *n.* punition *f.*
pupil, *n.* (school) élève *m.f.;* (eye) pupille *f.*
puppet, *n.* marionnette *f.*
puppy, *n.* petit chien *m.*
purchase, **1.** *n.* achat *m.* **2.** *vb.* acheter.
pure, *adj.* pur.
puree, *n.* purée *f.*
purge, *vb.* purger.
purify, *vb.* purifier.
purity, *n.* pureté *f.*
purple, *adj.* violet.
purpose, *n.* but *m.;* (to the p.) à propos.
purposely, *adv.* exprès.
purse, *n.* bourse *f.*
pursue, *vb.* poursuivre.
pursuit, *n.* poursuite *f.;* (occupation) occupation *f.;* (p. plane) avion (*m.*) de chasse.
push, **1.** *n.* poussée *f.* **2.** *vb.* pousser.
put, *vb.* mettre.
puzzle, **1.** *n.* problème *m.* **2.** *vb.* embarrasser.
pyramid, *n.* pyramide *f.*

Q

quadraphonic, *adj.* quadriphonique.
quail, *n.* caille *f.*
quaint, *adj.* (strange) étrange.
quake, *vb.* trembler.
qualification, *n.* (reservation) réserve *f.;* (aptitude) compé-

tence f.; (description) qualification f.
qualify, vb. qualifier; (modify) modifier.
quality, n. qualité f.
qualm, n. scrupule m.
quantity, n. quantité f.
quarantine, n. quarantaine f.
quarrel, 1. n. querelle f. 2. vb. se quereller.
quarry, n. carrière f.
quarter, n. quart m.; (district, moon, beef) quartier m.
quarterly, adj. trimestriel.
quartet, n. quatuor m.
quartz, n. quartz m.
quasar, n. quasar m.
quaver, vb. chevroter.
queen, n. reine f.
queer, adj. bizarre.
quell, vb. réprimer.
quench, vb. éteindre.
query, n. question f.
quest, n. recherche f.
question, 1. n. question f. 2. vb. interroger; (raise questions) mettre en doute.
questionable, adj. douteux.
question mark, n. point (m.) d'interrogation.
questionnaire, n. questionnaire m.
quick, 1. adj. rapide; (lively) vif. 2. adv. vite.
quicken, vb. accélérer.
quiet, 1. n. tranquillité f. 2. adj. tranquille.
quilt, n. courtepointe f.
quinine, n. quinine f.
quip, n. mot (m.) piquant.
quit, vb. quitter.
quite, adv. tout à fait.
quiver, vb. trembloter.
quiz, 1. n. petit examen m. 2. vb. examiner.
quorum, n. quorum m.
quota, n. (share) quote-part f.; (immigration, etc.) contingent m.
quotation, n. citation f.; (comm.) cote f.
quote, vb. citer.

R

rabbi, n. rabbin m.
rabbit, n. lapin m.
rabble, n. tourbe f.
rabid, adj. enragé.
race, 1. n. (people) race f.; (contest) course f. 2. vb. lutter à la course (avec).
race-track, n. piste f.
rack, n. râtelier m.; (torture) chevalet (m.) de torture.
racket, n. (tennis) raquette f.; (noise) tintamarre m.
radar, n. radar m.
radiance, n. éclat m.
radiant, adj. radieux.
radiate, vb. irradier.
radiation, n. rayonnement m.
radiator, n. radiateur m.

radical, adj. and n. radical m.
radio, n. télégraphie (f.) sans fil (commonly T.S.F.).
radioactive, adj. radio-actif.
radish, n. radis m.
radium, n. radium m.
radius, n. rayon m.
raft, n. radeau m.
rafter, n. chevron m.
rag, n. chiffon m.
rage, n. rage f.
ragged, adj. en haillons.
ragweed, n. ambroisie f.
raid, n. (police) descente f.; (mil.) raid m.
rail, n. (bar) barre f.; (railroad) rail m.
railroad, n. chemin (m.) de fer.
rain, 1. n. pluie f. 2. vb. pleuvoir.
rainbow, n. arc-en-ciel m.
raincoat, n. imperméable m.
rainfall, n. chute (f.) de pluie.
rainy, adj. pluvieux.
raise, vb. (bring up, erect, promote) élever; (lift) lever; (plants) cultiver.
raisin, n. raisin (m.) sec.
rake, 1. n. râteau m. 2. vb. râteler.
rally, n. (mil.) ralliement m.; (meeting) rassemblement m.
ram, n. bélier m.
ramble, vb. rôder; (speech) divaguer.
ramp, n. rampe f.
rampart, n. rempart m.
rancid, adj. rance.
random, n. hasard m.
range, n. (scope) étendue f.; (mountains) chaîne f.; (distance) portée f.; (stove) fourneau m.
rank, 1. n. rang m. 2. vb. ranger, tr.
ransack, vb. (search) fouiller; (pillage) saccager.
ransom, n. rançon f.
rap, 1. n. coup m. 2. vb. frapper.
rapid, adj. and n. rapide m.
rapture, n. ravissement m.
rare, adj. rare.
rascal, n. coquin m.
rash, 1. n. éruption f. 2. adj. téméraire.
raspberry, n. framboise f.
rat, n. rat m.
rate, 1. n. taux m.; (speed) vitesse f.; (at any r.) en tout cas; (first-r.) de premier ordre. 2. vb. estimer.
rather, adv. plutôt.
ratify, vb. ratifier.
ration, n. ration f.
rational, adj. raisonnable; (mathematics, philosophy) rationnel.
rattle, n. (toy) hochet m.; (noise) fracas m.
rave, vb. délirer; (r. about) s'extasier sur.
raven, n. corbeau m.
raw, adj. cru.
ray, n. rayon m.

rayon, n. rayonne f.
razor, n. rasoir m.
reach, 1. n. portée f. 2. vb. atteindre; (extend) étendre, tr.; (arrive) arriver à.
react, vb. réagir.
reaction, n. réaction f.
reactionary, adj. réactionnaire.
read, vb. lire.
reader, n. (person) lecteur m.; (book) livre (m.) de lecture.
readily, adv. promptement.
ready, adj. prêt.
real, adj. réel.
realist, n. réaliste m.f.
reality, n. réalité f.
realization, n. réalisation f.
realize, vb. (notice) s'apercevoir de; (make real) réaliser, tr.
really, adv. vraiment.
realm, n. royaume m.
reap, vb. moissonner.
rear, 1. n. (hind part) queue f.; (mil.) arrière-garde f. 2. adj. situé à l'arrière. 3. vb. élever.
reason, 1. n. raison f. 2. vb. raisonner.
reasonable, adj. raisonnable.
reassure, vb. rassurer.
rebate, n. rabais m.
rebel, 1. adj. and n. rebelle m.f. 2. vb. se rebeller.
rebellion, n. rébellion f.
rebellious, adj. rebelle.
rebirth, n. renaissance f.
rebound, n. rebond m.
rebuke, 1. n. réprimande f. 2. vb. réprimander.
rebuttal, n. réfutation f.
recall, vb. (call back) rappeler; (remember) se rappeler.
recede, vb. s'éloigner.
receipt, n. (for payment) quittance f.
receive, vb. recevoir.
receiver, n. (phone) récepteur m.
recent, adj. récent.
receptacle, n. réceptacle m.
reception, n. réception f.; (welcoming) accueil m.
receptive, adj. réceptif.
recess, n. recoin m.; (Parliament) vacances f.pl.; (school) récréation f.
recipe, n. recette f.
reciprocate, vb. payer de retour.
recite, vb. réciter.
reckless, adj. téméraire.
reckon, vb. compter.
reclaim, v. (person) corriger; (land) défricher.
recline, vb. reposer, tr.
recognition, n. reconnaissance f.
recognize, vb. reconnaître.
recoil, vb. reculer.
recollect, vb. se rappeler.
recommend, vb. recommander.
recommendation, n. recommandation f.
recompense, n. récompense f.
reconcile, vb. réconcilier.

record, 1. *n.* (register) registre *m.;* (mention) mention *f.;* (known facts of person) antécédents *m.pl.;* (sports) record *m.;* (phonograph) disque *m.* **2.** *vb.* enregistrer.

record player, *n.* tourne-disques *m.*

recount, *vb.* raconter.

recover, *vb.* recouvrer; (from illness) se rétablir.

recovery, *n.* recouvrement *m.;* (health) rétablissement *m.*

recruit, 1. *n.* recrue *f.* **2.** *vb.* recruter.

rectangle, *n.* rectangle *m.*

rectify, *vb.* rectifier.

recuperate, *vb.* se rétablir, *intr.*

recur, *vb.* revenir.

recycle, *vb.* recycler.

red, *adj. and n.* rouge *m.*

redeem, *vb.* racheter.

redemption, *n.* rachat *m.;* (theology) rédemption *f.*

redress, 1. *n.* justice *f.* **2.** *vb.* redresser, réparer; faire justice à.

reduce, *vb.* réduire.

reduction, *n.* réduction *f.;* (on price) remise *f.*

reed, *n.* roseau *m.;* (music) anche *f.*

reef, *n.* récif *m.*

reel, *n.* bobine *f.*

refer, *vb.* référer.

referee, *n.* arbitre *m.*

reference, *n.* référence *f.*

refill, *vb.* remplir (à nouveau).

refine, *vb.* raffiner.

refinement, *n.* raffinement *m.*

reflect, *vb.* réfléchir.

reflection, *n.* réflexion *f.*

reform, 1. *n.* réforme *f.* **2.** *vb.* réformer, *tr.*

reformation, *n.* réforme *f.*

refractory, *adj.* réfractaire.

refrain from, *vb.* se retenir de.

refresh, *vb.* rafraîchir.

refreshment, *n.* rafraîchissement *m.*

refrigerator, *n.* frigidaire *m.*

refuge, *n.* refuge *m.*

refugee, *n.* réfugié *m.*

refund, 1. *n.* remboursement *m.* **2.** *vb.* rembourser.

refusal, *n.* refus *m.*

refuse, 1. *n.* rebut *m.* **2.** *vb.* refuser.

refute, *vb.* réfuter.

regain, *vb.* regagner.

regal, *adj.* royal.

regard, 1. *n.* égard *m.;* (regards, compliments) amitiés *f.pl.* **2.** *vb.* regarder.

regardless, *adj.* sans se soucier de.

regent, *adj. and n.* régent *m.*

regime, *n.* régime *m.*

regiment, *n.* régiment *m.*

region, *n.* région *f.*

register, 1. *n.* registre *m.* **2.** *vb.* enregistrer; (letter) recommander.

registration, *n.* enregistrement *m.*

regret, 1. *n.* regret *m.* **2.** *vb.* regretter.

regular, *adj.* régulier.

regularity, *n.* regularité *f.*

regulate, *vb.* régler.

regulation, *n.* règlement *m.*

regulator, *n.* régulateur *m.*

rehabilitate, *vb.* réhabiliter.

rehearse, *vb.* répéter.

reign, 1. *n.* règne *m.* **2.** *vb.* régner.

rein, *n.* rêne *f.*

reindeer, *n.* renne *m.*

reinforce, *vb.* renforcer.

reinforcement, *n.* renfort *m.*

reject, *vb.* rejeter.

rejoice, *vb.* réjouir, *tr.*

rejoin, *vb.* (join again) rejoindre; (reply) répliquer.

relapse, *n.* rechute *f.*

relate, *vb.* raconter; (have reference to) se rapporter (à); **(relate to)** entrer en rapport avec.

relation, *n.* relation *f.;* (relative) parent *m.*

relative, 1. *n.* parent *m.* **2.** *adj.* relatif.

relax, *vb.* relâcher.

relay, 1. *n.* relais *m.* **2.** *vb.* relayer.

release, 1. *n.* délivrance *f.* **2.** *vb.* libérer.

relent, *vb.* se laisser attendrir.

relevant, *adj.* pertinent.

reliability, *n.* sûreté *f.*

reliable, *adj.* digne de confiance.

reliant, *adj.* confiant.

relic, *n.* relique *f.*

relief, *n.* (ease) soulagement *m.;* (help) secours *m.;* (projection) relief *m.*

relieve, *vb.* (ease) soulager; (help) secourir.

religion, *n.* religion *f.*

religious, *adj.* religieux.

relinquish, *vb.* abandonner.

relish, 1. *n.* goût *m.* **2.** *vb.* goûter.

reluctant, *adj.* peu disposé (à).

rely upon, *vb.* compter sur.

remain, *vb.* rester.

remainder, *n.* reste *m.*

remark, 1. *n.* remarque *f.* **2.** *vb.* remarquer.

remarkable, *adj.* remarquable.

remedy, 1. *n.* remède *m.* **2.** *vb.* rémédier à.

remember, *vb.* se souvenir de.

remembrance, *n.* souvenir *m.*

remind of, *vb.* rappeler à (person recalling).

reminisce, *vb.* raconter ses souvenirs.

remit, *vb.* remettre.

remnant, *n.* reste *m.,* vestige *m.,* (of cloth) coupon *m.*

remorse, *n.* remords *m.*

remote, *adj.* éloigné; (vague) vague.

removable, *adj.* transportable.

removal, *n.* enlèvement *m.*

remove, *vb.* enlever.

rend, *vb.* déchirer.

render, *vb.* rendre.

rendezvous, *n.* rendez-vous *m.*

renew, *vb.* renouveler.

renewal, *n.* renouvellement *m.*

renounce, *vb.* (give up) renoncer à; (repudiate) répudier.

renovate, *vb.* renouveler.

renown, *n.* renommée *f.*

rent, 1. *n.* loyer *m.* **2.** *vb.* louer.

repair, 1. *n.* réparation *f.* **2.** *vb.* réparer.

repay, *vb.* (give back) rendre; (refund) rembourser.

repeat, *vb.* répéter.

repel, *vb.* repousser.

repent, *vb.* se repentir (de).

repentance, *n.* repentir *m.*

repertoire, *n.* répertoire *m.*

repetition, *n.* répétition *f.*

replace, *vb.* (place again) replacer; (take place of) remplacer.

reply, 1. *n.* réponse *f.* **2.** *vb.* répondre.

report, 1. *n.* rapport *m.;* (rumor) bruit *m.* **2.** *vb.* rapporter; (inform against) dénoncer.

repose, *n.* repos *m.*

represent, *vb.* représenter.

representation, *n.* représentation *f.*

representative, 1. *n.* représentant *m.;* (politics) député *m.* **2.** *adj.* représentatif.

repress, *vb.* réprimer.

reprimand, *n.* réprimande *f.*

reproach, 1. *n.* reproche *m.* **2.** *vb.* faire des reproches à.

reproduce, *vb.* reproduire, *tr.*

reproduction, *n.* reproduction *f.*

reproof, *n.* réprimande *f.*

reprove, *vb.* réprimander.

reptile, *n.* reptile *m.*

republic, *n.* république *f.*

republican, *adj. and n.* républicain *m.*

repulsive, *adj.* répulsif.

reputation, *n.* réputation *f.*

repute, 1. *n.* renom *m.* **2.** *vb.* réputer.

request, 1. *n.* requête *f.* **2.** *vb.* demander.

require, *vb.* exiger.

requirement, *n.* exigence *f.*

requisite, *adj.* nécessaire.

requisition, *n.* réquisition *f.*

rescue, 1. *n.* délivrance *f.* **2.** *vb.* délivrer.

research, *n.* recherche *f.*

resemble, *vb.* ressembler à.

resent, *vb.* être froissé de.

reservation, *n.* réserve *f.*

reserve, 1. *n.* réserve *f.* **2.** *vb.* réserver.

reservoir, *n.* réservoir *m.*

reside, *vb.* résider.

residence, *n.* résidence *f.*

resident, 1. *n.* habitant *m.* **2.** *adj.* résidant.

resign, *vb.* résigner; (from post) se démettre (de).

resignation, *n.* résignation *f.;* (from post) démission *f.*

resist, vb. résister (à).
resistance, n. résistance f.
resolute, adj. résolu.
resolution, n. résolution f.
resolve, vb. résoudre.
resonant, adj. résonnant.
resort, 1. n. (resource) ressource f.; (recourse) recours m.; (place) lieu (m.) de séjour. 2. vb. avoir recours.
resound, vb. résonner.
resource, n. ressource f.
respect, 1. n. respect m.; (reference) rapport m. 2. vb. respecter.
respectable, adj. respectable.
respectful, adj. respectueux.
respective, adj. respectif.
respiration, n. respiration f.
respite, n. répit m.
respond, vb. répondre.
response, n. réponse f.
responsibility, n. responsabilité f.
responsible, adj. responsable.
rest, 1. n. (repose) repos m.; (remainder) reste m.; (the r., the others) les autres m.f.pl. 2. vb. se reposer.
restaurant, n. restaurant m.
restful, adj. qui repose.
restless, adj. (anxious) inquiet.
restoration, n. restauration f.
restore, vb. remettre; (repair) restaurer.
restrain, vb. contenir.
restraint, n. contrainte f.
restrict, vb. restreindre.
result, 1. n. résultat m. 2. vb. résulter.
resume, vb. reprendre.
résumé, n. résumé m.
resurrect, vb. ressusciter.
retail, n. détail m.
retain, vb. retenir.
retaliate, vb. user de représailles.
retard, vb. retarder.
reticent, adj. réservé.
retina, n. rétine f.
retire, vb. se retirer.
retort, n. riposte f.
retreat, 1. n. retraite f. 2. vb. se retirer.
retrieve, vb. recouvrer.
retrospect, n. renvoi m., (in retrospect) coup d'œil rétrospectif m.
return, 1. n. retour m.; (returns, comm.) recettes f.pl. 2. vb. (give back) rendre; (go back) retourner; (come back) revenir.
reunion, n. réunion f.
reveal, vb. révéler.
revel, vb. s'ébattre.
revelation, n. révélation f.
revelry, n. bacchanale f.
revenge, 1. n. vengeance f. 2. vb. (r. oneself) se venger.
revenue, n. revenu m.
reverberate, vb. réverbérer, réfléchir, répercuter.
revere, vb. révérer.
reverence, n. révérence f.

reverend, adj. révérend.
reverent, adj. respectueux.
reverie, n. rêverie f.
reverse, 1. n. (opposite) contraire m.; (defeat, medal) revers m.; (gear) marche (f.) arrière. 2. vb. renverser.
revert, vb. revenir.
review, n. revue f.
revise, vb. réviser.
revision, n. révision f.
revival, n. renaissance f.; (religious) réveil m.
revive, vb. revivre, intr.; faire revivre, tr.
revoke, vb. révoquer.
revolt, 1. n. révolte f. 2. vb. se révolter.
revolution, n. révolution f.
revolutionary, adj. révolutionnaire.
revolve, vb. tourner, intr.
revolver, n. revolver m.
reward, 1. n. récompense f. 2. vb. récompenser.
rheumatism, n. rhumatisme m.
rhinoceros, n. rhinocéros m.
rhubarb, n. rhubarbe f.
rhyme, 1. n. rime f. 2. vb. rimer.
rhythm, n. rythme m.
rhythmical, adj. rythmique.
rib, n. côte f.
ribbon, n. ruban m.
rice, n. riz m.
rich, adj. riche.
rid, vb. débarrasser.
riddle, n. énigme f.
ride, 1. n. promenade f. 2. vb. (horse) aller à cheval; (vehicle) aller en voiture.
rider, n. (on horse) cavalier m.
ridge, n. crête f.
ridicule, 1. n. ridicule m. 2. vb. se moquer de.
ridiculous, adj. ridicule.
rifle, n. fusil m.
rig, 1. n. (vessel) gréement m.; (outfit) tenue f. 2. vb. gréer.
right, 1. n. droit m.; (not left) droite f. 2. adj. (straight, not left) droit; (correct, proper) juste; (be r., of person) avoir raison; (all r.) c'est bien. 3. adv. (straight) droit; (not left) à droite; (justly) bien.
righteous, adj. juste.
righteousness, n. justice f.
right of way, n. droit de passage m., (automobiles) priorité de passage f.
rigid, adj. rigide.
rigor, n. rigueur f.
rigorous, adj. rigoureux.
rim, n. bord m.; (wheel) jante f.
ring, 1. n. anneau m.; (ornament) bague f.; (circle) cercle m.; (arena) arène f.; (sound) son m.; (phone) coup (m.) de téléphone. 2. vb. sonner.
rinse, vb. rincer.
riot, n. émeute f.

rip, 1. n. fente f. 2. vb. fendre, tr.
ripe, adj. mûr.
ripen, vb. mûrir.
ripoff, 1. n. vol m. 2. vb. voler.
ripple, 1. n. (on water) ride f. 2. vb. rider, tr.
rise, 1. n. (ground) montée f.; (increase) augmentation f.; (rank) avancement m. 2. vb. se lever.
risk, 1. n. risque m. 2. vb. risquer.
rite, n. rite m.
ritual, adj. rituel.
rival, 1. adj. and n. rival m. 2. vb. rivaliser avec.
rivalry, n. rivalité f.
river, n. fleuve m.
rivet, n. rivet m.
road, n. route f.
roam, vb. errer (par).
roar, vb. (person) hurler; (lion) rugir; (bull, sea) mugir; (thunder, cannon) gronder; (laughter) éclater de.
roast, 1. n. rôti m. 2. vb. rôtir.
rob, vb. voler.
robber, n. voleur m.
robbery, n. vol m.
robe, n. robe f.
robin, n. rouge-gorge m.
robot, n. automate m.
robust, adj. robuste.
rock, 1. n. rocher m. 2. vb. balancer; (child) bercer. 3. adj. (musique) rock.
rocker, n. (chair) chaise (f.) à bascule.
rocket, n. fusée f.
rocky, adj. rocheux.
rod, n. verge f.
rodent, adj. and n. rongeur m.
roe, n. (animal) chevreuil m.; (of fish) œufs (m.pl.) de poisson.
rogue, n. coquin m.
roguish, adj. coquin.
role, n. rôle m.
roll, 1. n. rouleau m.; (bread) petit pain m.; (list) liste f.; (r.-call) appel m.; (boat) roulis m. 2. vb. rouler.
roller, n. rouleau m.
Roman, 1. n. Romain m. 2. adj. romain.
romance, n. roman (m.) de chevalerie.
romantic, adj. romanesque; (poetry, music) romantique.
romp, 1. n. tapage m. 2. vb. batifoler.
roof, n. toit m.
room, n. (space) place f.; (private use) chambre f.; (public use) salle f.
roommate, n. camarade (m.f.) de chambre.
rooster, n. coq m.
root, 1. n. racine f.; (source) source f. 2. vb. enraciner, tr.
rope, n. corde f.
rosary, n. rosaire m.
rose, n. rose f.
rosin, n. colophane f.

rosy, adj. de rose.
rot, 1. n. pourriture f. 2. vb. pourrir.
rotary, adj. rotatoire.
rotate, vb. tourner.
rotation, n. rotation f.
rotten, adj. pourri.
rouge, n. rouge m.
rough, adj. rude; (sea weather) gros m., grosse f.
round, 1. adj. rond; (r. trip) l'aller (m.) et le retour. 2. n. rond m.; (circuit) tournée f.
rouse, vb. (wake) réveiller; (stir up) secouer.
rout, n. (mil.) déroute f.
route, n. route f.
routine, n. routine f.
rove, vb. errer (par).
rover, n. rôdeur m.
row, 1. n. rang m.; dispute f. 2. vb. ramer.
rowboat, n. barque f.
rowdy, adj. tapageur.
royal, adj. royal.
royalty, n. royauté f.; (of author) droits (m.pl.) d'auteur.
rub, vb. frotter.
rubber, n. caoutchouc m.
rubbish, n. rebuts m.pl.; (nonsense) bêtises f.pl.
ruby, n. rubis m.
rudder, n. gouvernail m.
ruddy, adj. rouge.
rude, adj. (rough) rude; (impolite) impoli.
rudiment, n. rudiment m.
rue, vb. regretter.
ruffian, n. bandit m.
ruffle, n. (frill) fraise f.
rug, n. tapis m.
rugged, adj. (rough) rude; (uneven) raboteux.
ruin, 1. n. ruine f. 2. vb. ruiner.
ruinous, adj. ruineux.
rule, 1. n. règle f.; (authority) autorité f. 2. vb. gouverner; (decide) décider.
ruler, n. souverain m.; (for lines) règle f.
rum, n. rhum m.
Rumania, n. Roumanie f.
Rumanian, 1. n. (person) Roumain m.; (language) roumain m. 2. adj. roumain.
rumba, n. rumba f.
rumble, vb. gronder.
rumor, n. rumeur f.
run, vb. intr. courir; (of engine) marcher; (of colors) déteindre; (of liquids) couler; (r. away) s'enfuir.
run-down, adj. épuisé.
rung, n. échelon m.
runner, n. (person) coureur m.; (table) chemin (m.) de table.
rupture, n. rupture f.
rural, adj. rural.
rush, 1. n. (haste) hâte f.; (onrush) ruée f.; (air, water) coup m.; (plant) jonc m. 2. vb. se précipiter, intr.
Russia, n. Russie f.
Russian, 1. n. (person) Russe

m.f.; (language) russe m. 2. adj. russe.
rust, 1. n. rouille f. 2. vb. rouiller, tr.
rustic, adj. rustique.
rustle, n. (leaves) bruissement m.; (skirt) frou-frou m.
rusty, adj. rouillé.
rut, n. ornière f.
ruthless, adj. impitoyable.
rye, n. seigle m.

S

Sabbath, n. sabbat m.
saber, n. sabre m.
sable, n. zibeline f.
sabotage, 1. n. sabotage m. 2. vb. saboter.
saboteur, n. saboteur m.
saccharin, n. saccharine f.
sachet, n. sachet m.
sack, 1. n. sac m. 2. vb. saccager.
sacrament, n. sacrement m.
sacred, adj. sacré.
sacrifice, 1. n. sacrifice m. 2. vb. sacrifier.
sacrilege, n. sacrilège m.
sad, adj. triste.
sadden, vb. attrister, tr.
saddle, n. selle f.
sadism, n. sadisme m.
safe, 1. n. coffre-fort n. 2. adj. sûr; (s. and sound) sain et sauf; (s. from) à l'abri de.
safeguard, vb. sauvegarder.
safety, n. sûreté f.
safety pin, n. épingle (f.) anglaise.
sage, n. (person) sage m.; (plant) sauge f.
sail, 1. n. voile f. 2. vb. naviguer; (depart) partir.
sailboat, n. canot (m.) à voiles.
sailor, n. marin m.
saint, adj. and n. saint m.
sake, n. (for the s. of) pour l'amour de.
salad, n. salade f.
salary, n. appointements m.pl.
sale, n. vente f.
salesman, n. vendeur m.
sales tax, n. impôt sur les ventes m.
saliva, n. salive f.
salmon, n. saumon m.
salt, 1. n. sel m. 2. vb. saler.
salute, 1. n. salut m. 2. vb. saluer.
salvage, n. sauvetage m.
salvation, n. salut m.
salve, n. onguent m.
same, 1. adj. and pron. même. 2. adv. de même.
sample, n. échantillon m.
sanatorium, n. sanatorium m.
sanctify, vb. sanctifier.
sanction, n. sanction f.
sanctity, n. sainteté f.
sanctuary, n. sanctuaire m.
sand, n. sable m.
sandal, n. sandale f.

sandwich, n. sandwich m.
sandy, adj. sablonneux.
sane, adj. sain d'esprit.
sanitary, adj. sanitaire.
sanitation, n. hygiène f.
sanity, n. santé (f.) d'esprit.
Santa Claus, n. Bonhomme Noël m.
sap, n. sève f.
sapphire, n. saphir m.
sarcasm, n. sarcasme m.
sardine, n. sardine f.
sash, n. ceinture f.; (window) châssis m.
satellite, n. satellite m.
satin, n. satin m.
satire, n. satire f.
satisfaction, n. satisfaction f.
satisfactory, adj. satisfaisant.
satisfy, vb. satisfaire.
saturate, vb. saturer.
Saturday, n. samedi m.
sauce, n. sauce f.
saucer, n. soucoupe f.
saucy, adj. impertinent.
sausage, n. saucisse f.
savage, adj. and n. sauvage m.f.
save, vb. sauver; (put aside) mettre de côté; (economize) épargner.
savior, n. sauveur m.
savor, n. saveur f.
savory, adj. savoureux.
say, vb. dire.
scab, n. croûte f., gale f.
scaffold, n. échafaud m.
scald, vb. échauder.
scale, 1. n. (fish) écaille f.; (balance) balance f.; (series, graded system, map) échelle f.; (music) gamme f. 2. vb. escalader.
scalp, 1. n. cuir (m.) chevelu. 2. vb. scalper.
scan, vb. (examine) scruter; (verse) scander.
scandal, n. scandale m.
scandalous, adj. scandaleux.
Scandinavia, n. Scandinavie f.
Scandinavian, 1. n. Scandinave m.f. 2. adj. scandinave.
scant(y), adj. limité, faible.
scar, n. cicatrice f.
scarce, adj. rare.
scare, vb. effrayer.
scarf, n. écharpe f.
scarlet, adj. and n. écarlate f.; (s. fever) scarlatine f.
scathing, adj. cinglant.
scatter, vb. éparpiller.
scavenger, n. boueur m.
scenario, n. scénario m.
scene, n. scène f.
scenery, n. (theater) décors m.pl.; (landscape) paysage m.
scent, 1. n. parfum m., odeur f. 2. vb. flairer, sentir.
schedule, n. plan m.
scheme, n. plan m.
scholar, n. savant m.
scholarship, n. (school) bourse f.
school, n. école f.
sciatica, n. sciatique f.

science, *n.* science *f.*
science fiction, *n.* science-fiction *f.*
scientist, *n.* homme *(m.)* de science.
scissors, *n.* ciseaux *m.pl.*
scoff at, *vb.* se moquer de.
scold, *vb.* gronder.
scoop out, *vb.* évider.
scope, *n.* (extent) portée *f.*; (outlet) carrière *f.*
scorch, *vb.* roussir.
score, *n.* (games) points *m.pl.*; (twenty) vingtaine *f.*; (music) partition *f.*
scorn, 1. *n.* mépris *m.* 2. *vb.* mépriser.
scornful, *adj.* dédaigneux.
Scotch, Scottish, *adj.* écossais.
Scotchman, Scotsman, *n.* Écossais *m.*
Scotland, *n.* Écosse *f.*
scour, *vb.* nettoyer.
scourge, *n.* fléau *m.*
scout, *n.* éclaireur *m.*; (boy s.) boy-scout *m.*
scowl, *vb.* se renfrogner.
scramble, *vb.* avancer péniblement.
scrap, 1. *n.* petit morceau *m.* 2. *vb.* mettre au rebut.
scrape, scratch, 1. *n.* égratignure *f.* 2. *vb.* gratter.
scream, 1. *n.* cri *m.* 2. *vb.* crier.
screen, *n.* écran *m.*; (folding s.) paravent *m.*
screw, 1. *n.* vis *f.* 2. *vb.* visser, *tr.*
screwdriver, *n.* tournevis *m.*
scribble, *vb.* griffonner.
scroll, *n.* rouleau *m.*
scrub, *vb.* frotter.
scruple, *n.* scrupule *m.*
scrupulous, *adj.* scrupuleux.
scrutinize, *vb.* scruter.
sculptor, *n.* sculpteur *m.*
sculpture, *n.* sculpture *f.*
scythe, *n.* faux *f.*
sea, *n.* mer *f.*
seabed, *n.* lit de la mer *f.*
seacoast, *n.* littoral *m.*
seal, 1. *n.* (animal) phoque *m.*; (stamp) sceau *m.* 2. *vb.* sceller.
seam, *n.* couture *f.*
seaport, *n.* port *(m.)* de mer.
search, 1. *n.* recherche *f.* 2. *vb.* chercher.
seasickness, *n.* mal *(m.)* de mer.
season, 1. *n.* saison *f.* 2. *vb.* assaisonner.
seat, 1. *n.* siège *m.* 2. *vb.* asseoir.
second, 1. *n.* seconde *f.* 2. *adj.* second, deuxième.
secondary, *adj.* secondaire.
secret, *adj.* and *n.* secret *m.*
secretary, *adj.* secrétaire *m.f.*
sect, *n.* secte *f.*
section, *n.* section *f.*
sectional, *adj.* régional.
secular, *adj.* (church) séculier; (time) séculaire.
secure, 1. *adj.* sûr. 2. *vb.* (make

s.) mettre en sûreté; (make fast) fixer; (obtain) obtenir.
security, *n.* sûreté *f.*; (comm., law) caution *f.*; (finance, pl.) valeurs *f.pl.*
sedative, *adj.* and *n.* sédatif *m.*
seduce, *vb.* séduire.
see, *vb.* voir.
seed, *n.* semence *f.*; (vegetables, etc.) graine *f.*
seek, *vb.* chercher.
seem, *vb.* sembler.
seep, *vb.* suinter.
segment, *n.* segment *m.*
segregate, *vb.* séparer.
seize, *vb.* saisir.
seldom, *adv.* rarement.
select, *vb.* choisir.
selection, *n.* sélection *f.*
self, *n.* moi *m.*, personne *f.*
selfish, *adj.* égoïste.
selfishness, *n.* égoïsme *m.*
sell, *vb.* vendre, *tr.*
semantics, *n.* sémantique *f.*
semester, *n.* semestre *m.*
semicircle, *n.* demi-cercle *m.*
semicolon, *n.* point *(m.)* et virgule *(f.).*
seminary, *n.* séminaire *m.*
senate, *n.* sénat *m.*
senator, *n.* sénateur *m.*
send, *vb.* envoyer; (s. back) renvoyer.
senile, *adj.* sénile.
senior, *adj.* and *n.* (age) aîné *m.*; (rank) supérieur *m.*
senior citizen, *n.* personne du troisième âge *f.*
sensation, *n.* sensation *f.*
sensational, *adj.* sensationnel.
sense, *n.* sens *m.*
sensible, *adj.* (wise) sensé; (appreciable) sensible.
sensitive, *adj.* sensible.
sensual, *adj.* sensuel.
sentence, *n.* (gramm.) phrase *f.*; (law) sentence *f.*
sentiment, *n.* sentiment *m.*
sentimental, *adj.* sentimental.
separate, 1. *adj.* séparé. 2. *vb.* séparer, *tr.*
separation, *n.* séparation *f.*
September, *n.* septembre *m.*
sequence, *n.* suite *f.*
serenade, *n.* sérénade *f.*
serene, *adj.* serein.
sergeant, *n.* sergent *m.*
serial, *n.* roman-feuilleton *m.*
series, *n.* série *f.*
serious, *adj.* sérieux.
sermon, *n.* sermon *m.*
serpent, *n.* serpent *m.*
serum, *n.* sérum *m.*
servant, *n.* (domestic) domestique *m.f.*; (public) employé *m.*
serve, *vb.* servir.
service, *n.* service *m.*; (church) office *m.*
servitude, *n.* servitude *f.*
session, *n.* session *f.*
set, 1. *n.* ensemble *m.* 2. *adj.* fixe; (decided) résolu. 3. *vb. tr.* (put) mettre; (regulate) régler; (jewels) monter; (fix)

fixer. 4. *vb. intr.* (sun, etc.) se coucher; (s. about) se mettre à.
settle, *vb.* (establish) établir, *tr.*; (fix) fixer; (decide) décider; (arrange) arranger; (pay) payer; (s. down to, *intr.*) se mettre à.
settlement, *n.* (colony) colonie *f.*; (accounts) règlement *m.*
settler, *n.* colon *m.*
seven, *adj.* and *n.* sept *m.*
seventeen, *adj.* and *n.* dix-sept *m.*
seventh, *adj.* and *n.* septième *m.*
seventy, *adj.* and *n.* soixante-dix *m.*
sever, *vb.* séparer, couper.
several, *adj.* and *pron.* plusieurs.
severe, *adj.* sévère.
severity, *n.* sévérité *f.*
sew, *vb.* coudre.
sewer, *n.* égout *m.*
sex, *n.* sexe *m.*
sexism, *n.* sexisme *m.*
sexist, *adj.* sexiste.
sexton, *n.* sacristain *m.*
sexual, *adj.* sexuel.
shabby, *adj.* (clothes) usé; (person) mesquin.
shade, 1. *n.* ombre *f.*; (colors) nuance *f.*; (window) store *m.* 2. *vb.* ombrager.
shadow, *n.* ombre *f.*
shady, *adj.* ombragé; (not honest) louche.
shaft, *n.* (mine) puits *m.*
shaggy, *adj.* poilu, hirsute.
shake, *vb. tr.* secouer; trembler; (s. hands) serrer la main à.
shall, *vb.* (use future of verb).
shallow, *adj.* peu profond.
shame, *n.* honte *f.*
shameful, *adj.* honteux.
shampoo, *n.* schampooing *m.*
shape, 1. *n.* forme *f.* 2. *vb.* former.
share, 1. *n.* part *f.*; (finance) action *f.* 2. *vb.* partager.
shark, *n.* requin *m.*
sharp, *adj.* (cutting) tranchant; (clever) fin; (piercing) perçant; (music) dièse.
sharpen, *vb.* aiguiser.
shatter, *vb.* briser.
shave, *vb.* raser, *tr.*
shawl, *n.* châle *m.*
she, *pron.* elle.
sheaf, *n.* (grain) gerbe *f.*
shear, *vb.* tondre.
shears, *n.* cisailles *f.pl.*
sheath, *n.* étui *m.*
shed, 1. *n.* hangar *m.* 2. *vb.* verser.
sheep, *n.* mouton *m.*
sheet, *n.* (bed) drap *m.*; (paper, metal) feuille *f.*
shelf, *n.* rayon *m.*
shell, *n.* coquille *f.*; (of building) carcasse *f.*; (explosive) obus *m.*
shellac, *n.* laque *f.*

shelter, 1. *n.* abri *m.* **2.** *vb.* abriter.

shepherd, *n.* berger *m.*

sherbet, *n.* sorbet *m.*

sherry, *n.* xérès *m.*

shield, *n.* bouclier *m.*

shift, 1. *n.* (change) changement *m.;* (workers) équipe *f.;* (expedient) expédient *m.;* (shirt) chemise *f.* **2.** *vb.* changer; (s. gears) changer de vitesse.

shine, *vb.* briller, *intr.;* (shoes) cirer.

shiny, *adj.* luisant.

ship, *n.* navire *m.;* (large) vaisseau *m.*

shipment, *n.* envoi *m.*

shirk, *vb.* esquiver.

shirt, *n.* chemise *f.*

shiver, 1. *n.* frisson *m.* **2.** *vb.* frissonner.

shock, 1. *n.* choc *m.* **2.** *vb.* choquer.

shoe, *n.* soulier *m.*

shoelace, *n.* lacet *m.*

shoemaker, *n.* cordonnier *m.*

shoot, *vb.* tirer; (person) fusiller; (hit) atteindre; (rush) se précipiter.

shop, 1. *n.* boutique *f.;* (factory) atelier *m.* **2.** *vb.* faire des emplettes.

shore, *n.* rivage *m.*

short, *adj.* court.

shortage, *n.* manque *m.*

shorten, *vb.* raccourcir.

shorthand, *n.* sténographie *f.*

shot, *n.* coup *m.*

should, *vb.* devoir (in conditional).

shoulder, *n.* épaule *f.*

shout, 1. *n.* cri *m.* **2.** *vb.* crier.

shove, *vb.* pousser.

shovel, *n.* pelle *f.*

show, 1. *n.* (exhibition) exposition *f.;* (spectacle, performance) spectacle *m.;* (semblance) semblant *m.;* (display) parade *f.* **2.** *vb.* montrer, *tr.*

shower, *n.* averse *f.*

shrapnel, *n.* shrapnel *m.*

shrewd, *adj.* sagace.

shriek, *n.* cri *(m.)* perçant.

shrill, *adj.* aigu.

shrimp, *n.* crevette *f.*

shrine, *n.* châsse *f.*

shrink, *vb.* rétrécir, *tr.*

shroud, *n.* linceul *m.*

shrub, *n.* arbrisseau *m.*

shudder, 1. *n.* frisson *m.* **2.** *vb.* frissonner.

shun, *vb.* fuir.

shut, *vb.* fermer.

shutter, *n.* volet *m.*

shy, *adj.* timide.

sick, *adj.* malade.

sickness, *n.* maladie *f.*

side, *n.* côté *f.*

sidewalk, *n.* trottoir *m.*

siege, *n.* siège *m.*

sieve, *n.* tamis *m.*

sift, *vb.* cribler.

sigh, 1. *n.* soupir *m.* **2.** *vb.* soupirer.

sight, *n.* vue *f.;* (spectacle) spectacle *m.*

sightseeing, *n.* tourisme *m.*

sign, 1. *n.* signe *m.;* (placard) enseigne *f.* **2.** *vb.* signer.

signal, *n.* signal *m.*

signature, *n.* signature *f.*

significance, *n.* (meaning) signification *f.;* (importance) importance *f.*

significant, *adj.* significatif.

signify, *vb.* signifier.

silence, *n.* silence *m.*

silent, *adj.* silencieux.

silk, *n.* soie *f.*

silken, *adj.* de soie.

silly, *adj.* sot *m.,* sotte *f.*

silver, 1. *n.* argent *m.* **2.** *adj.* d'argent.

silverware, *n.* argenterie *f.*

similar, *adj.* semblable.

simple, *adj.* simple.

simplicity, *n.* simplicité *f.*

simplify, *vb.* simplifier.

simply, *adv.* simplement.

simultaneous, *adj.* simultané.

sin, 1. *n.* péché *m.* **2.** *vb.* pécher.

since, 1. *adv., prep.* depuis **2.** *conj.* (time) depuis que; (cause) puisque.

sincere, *adj.* sincère.

sincerity, *n.* sincérité *f.*

sinful, *adj.* (person) pécheur *m.,* pécheresse *f.;* (act) coupable.

sing, *vb.* chanter.

singer, *n.* chanteur *m.*

single, *adj.* (only one) seul; (particular) particulier; (not married) célibataire.

singular, *adj. and n.* singulier *m.*

sinister, *adj.* sinistre.

sink, 1. *n.* évier *m.* **2.** *vb.* enfoncer, *tr.;* (vessel) couler áu fond; (diminish, weaken) baisser.

sinner, *n.* pécheur *m.,* pécheresse *f.*

sinus, *n.* sinus *m.*

sip, *vb.* siroter.

sir, *n.* monsieur *m.;* (title) Sir *m.*

sirloin, *n.* aloyau *m.*

sister, *n.* sœur *f.*

sister-in-law, *n.* belle-sœur *f.*

sit, *vb.* (s. down) s'asseoir; (be seated) être assis.

site, *n.* emplacement *m.*

situate, *vb.* situer.

situation, *n.* situation *f.*

six, *adj. and n.* six *m.*

sixteen, *adj. and n.* seize *m.*

sixteenth, *adj. and n.* seizième *m.*

sixth, *adj. and n.* sixième *m.*

sixty, *adj. and n.* soixante *m.*

size, *n.* grandeur *f.;* (person) taille *f.;* (shoes, gloves) pointure *f.*

skate, 1. *n.* patin *m.* **2.** *vb.* patiner.

skateboard, *n.* planche à roulettes *f.*

skeleton, *n.* squelette *m.*

skeptic, *n.* sceptique *m.f.*

skeptical, *adj.* sceptique.

sketch, 1. *n.* croquis *m.* **2.** *vb.* esquisser.

ski, 1. *n.* ski *m.* **2.** *vb.* faire du ski.

skill, *n.* adresse *f.*

skillful, *adj.* adroit.

skim, *vb.* (milk) écrémer; (book) feuilleter; (surface) effleurer.

skin, 1. *n.* peau *f.* **2.** *vb.* écorcher.

skip, *vb.* sauter.

skirt, *n.* jupe *f.*

skull, *n.* crâne *m.*

sky, *n.* ciel *m.*

skyscraper, *n.* gratte-ciel *m.*

slab, *n.* dalle *f.*

slack, *adj.* lâche.

slacken, *vb.* (slow up) ralentir; (loosen) relâcher.

slacks, *n.* pantalon *m.*

slander, 1. *n.* calomnie *f.* **2.** *vb.* calomnier.

slang, *n.* argot *m.*

slant, 1. *n.* (slope) pente *f.;* (bias) biais *m.* **2.** *vb.* incliner.

slap, *n.* claque *f.*

slash, *n.* taillade *f.*

slate, *n.* ardoise *f.*

slaughter, 1. *n.* (people) massacre *m.;* (animals) abattage *m.* **2.** *vb.* massacrer; abattre.

slave, *n.* esclave *m.f.*

slavery, *n.* esclavage *m.*

slay, *vb.* tuer.

sled, *n.* traîneau *m.*

sleep, 1. *n.* sommeil *m.;* (go to s.) s'endormir. **2.** *vb.* dormir.

sleepy, *adj.* somnolent; (be s.) avoir sommeil.

sleet, 1. *n.* grésil *m.* **2.** *vb.* grésiller.

sleeve, *n.* manche *f.*

sleigh, *n.* traîneau *m.*

slender, *adj.* mince; svelte.

slice, *n.* tranche *f.*

slide, 1. *n.* (sliding) glissade *f.;* (microscope) lamelle *f.;* (lantern) plaque *(f.)* de projection. **2.** *vb.* glisser.

slight, *adj.* léger; mince.

slim, *adj.* svelte.

sling, 1. *n.* fronde *f.;* (medical) écharpe *f.* **2.** *vb.* (throw) lancer; (hang) suspendre.

slip, 1. *n.* (sliding) glissade *f.;* (tongue, pen) lapsus *m.;* (mistake) faux pas *m.;* (paper) fiche *f.;* (garment) combinaison *f.* **2.** *vb.* glisser; (err) faire une faute.

slipper, *n.* pantoufle *f.*

slippery, *adj.* glissant.

slit, 1. *n.* fente *f.* **2.** *vb.* fendre.

slogan, *n.* mot *(m.)* d'ordre; (politics) cri *(m.)* de guerre.

slope, 1. *n.* pente *f.* **2.** *vb.* incliner.

sloppy, *adj.* (slushy) bourbeux; (slovenly) mal soigné.

slot, n. fente f.

slow, adj. lent; (clock) en retard.

slowness, n. lenteur f.

sluggish, adj. paresseux.

slumber, vb. sommeiller.

sly, adj. (crafty) rusé; (secretive) sournois.

smack, n. (a bit) soupçon m.; (noise) claquement m.

small, adj. petit.

smallpox, n. petite vérole f.

smart, 1. adj. (clever) habile; (stylish) élégant. 2. vb. cuire.

smash, vb. briser, tr.

smear, 1. n. tache f. 2. vb. salir.

smell, 1. n. odeur f. 2. vb. sentir.

smelt, 1. n. éperlan m. 2. vb. fondre.

smile, n. sourire m.

smite, vb. frapper.

smoke, 1. n. fumée f. 2. vb. fumer.

smolder, vb. couver.

smooth, 1. adj. lisse. 2. vb. lisser.

smother, vb. étouffer.

smuggle, vb. faire passer en contrebande.

snack, n. casse-croute m.

snag, n. obstacle (m.) caché.

snail, n. escargot m.

snake, n. serpent m.

snap, 1. n. (bite) coup (m.) de dents; (sound) coup (m.) sec. 2. vb.tr. (with teeth) happer; (sound) faire claquer.

snapshot, n. cliché m.

snare, n. piège m.

snarl, vb. grogner.

snatch, vb. saisir.

sneak, vb. se glisser furtivement.

sneer, vb. ricaner.

sneeze, 1. n. éternuement m. 2. vb. éternuer.

snob, n. snob m.

snore, vb. ronfler.

snow, 1. n. neige f. 2. vb. neiger.

snug, adj. confortable.

so, adv. si; tellement; (thus) ainsi; (s. that) de sorte que.

soak, vb. tremper.

soap, n. savon m.

soar, vb. prendre son essor.

sob, 1. n. sanglot m. 2. vb. sangloter.

sober, adj. (moderate) sobre; (sedate) sérieux; (not drunk) qui n'est pas ivre.

sociable, adj. sociable.

social, adj. social.

socialism, n. socialisme m.

socialist, adj. and n. socialiste m.f.

society, n. société f.

sociology, n. sociologie f.

sock, n. chaussette f.

socket, n. douille f.

sod, n. motte f.

soda, n. soude f.; (s.-water) eau (f.) de Seltz.

sofa, n. canapé m.

soft, adj. doux m., douce f.; (yielding) mou m., molle f.

soften, vb. amollir, tr.

soil, 1. n. terroir m. 2. vb. souiller.

sojourn, 1. n. séjour m. 2. vb. séjourner.

solace, n. consolation f.

solar, adj. solaire.

soldier, n. soldat m.

sole, n. (shoe) semelle f.; (fish) sole f.

solemn, adj. solennel.

solemnity, n. solennité f.

solicit, vb. solliciter.

solicitous, adj. empressé.

solid, adj. and n. solide m.

solidity, n. solidité f.

solitary, adj. solitaire.

solitude, n. solitude f.

solo, n. solo m.

solution, n. solution f.

solve, vb. résoudre.

solvent, adj. (comm.) solvable.

somber, adj. sombre.

some, adj. quelque; (partitive) de. 2. pron. certains; (with verb) en.

somebody, someone, pron. quelqu'un.

something, pron. quelque chose m.

some time, adv. (past) autrefois; (future) quelque jour.

sometimes, adv. quelquefois.

somewhat, adv. quelque peu.

somewhere, adv. quelque part.

son, n. fils m.

song, n. chant m.; (light s.) chanson f.

son-in-law, n. gendre m.

soon, adv. bientôt, tôt.

soot, n. suie f.

soothe, vb. calmer.

sophisticated, adj. blasé.

soprano, n. soprano m.

sordid, adj. sordide.

sore, adj. (aching) douloureux; (have a s. throat, etc.) avoir mal à. . . .

sorrow, n. douleur f.

sorrowful, adj. (person) affligé.

sorry, 1. adj. fâché; (be s.) regretter. 2. interj. pardon!

sort, 1. n. sorte f. 2. vb. trier.

soul, n. âme f.

sound, 1. n. son m. 2. adj. (healthy) sain, solide. 3. vb. sonner.

soup, n. potage m.

sour, adj. aigre.

source, n. source f.

south, n. sud m.

southeast, n. sud-est m.

southern, adj. du sud.

South Pole, n. pôle sud m.

southwest, n. sud-ouest m.

souvenir, n. souvenir m.

sow, vb. semer.

space, n. espace m.

space shuttle, n. navette spatiale f.

spacious, adj. spacieux.

spade, n. bêche f.; (cards) pique m.

Spain, n. Espagne f.

span, n. (hand) empan m.; (bridge) travée f.

Spaniard, n. Espagnol m.

Spanish, adj. and n. espagnol m.

spank, vb. fesser.

spanking, n. fessée f.

spare, 1. adj. (in reserve) de réserve. 2. vb. épargner.

spark, n. étincelle f.

sparkle, vb. étinceler.

sparrow, n. moineau m.

spasm, n. spasme m.

speak, vb. parler.

speaker, n. (public) orateur m.

special, adj. spécial.

specialist, n. spécialiste m.f.

specially, adv. spécialement.

specialty, n. spécialité f.

species, n. espèce f.

specific, adj. spécifique.

specify, vb. spécifier.

specimen, n. spécimen m.

spectacle, n. spectacle m.

spectacular, adj. spectaculaire.

spectator, n. spectateur m.

speculate, vb. spéculer.

speculation, n. spéculation f.

speech, n. (address) discours m.; (utterance) parole f.

speed, n. vitesse f.

speedy, adj. rapide.

spell, 1. n. (incantation) charme m.; (period) période f. 2. vb. épeler.

spend, vb. (money) dépenser; (time) passer.

sphere, n. sphère f.

spice, n. épice f.

spider, n. araignée f.

spike, n. pointe f.

spill, vb. répandre tr.

spin, vb. (thread) filer; (twirl) tourner.

spinach, n. épinards m.pl.

spine, n. épine f.; (backbone) épine (f.) dorsale.

spiral, 1. n. spirale f. 2. adj. spiral.

spirit, n. esprit m.

spiritual, adj. spirituel.

spiritualism, n. spiritisme m.

spit, 1. n. (saliva) crachat m.; (for roast) broche f. 2. vb. cracher.

spite, n. dépit m.; (in s. of) malgré.

splash, vb. éclabousser.

splendid, adj. splendide.

splendor, n. splendeur f.

splinter, n. éclat m.

split, vb. fendre.

spoil, 1. n. butin m. 2. vb. gâter.

sponge, n. éponge f.

sponsor, n. (law) garant m.

spontaneous, adj. spontané.

spontaneity, n. spontanéité f.

spool, n. bobine f.

spoon, n. cuiller f.

spoonful, n. cuillerée f.

sporadic, adj. sporadique.

sport, n. sport m.; (fun) jeu m.

spot, 1. n. (stain) tache f.;

(place) endroit m. 2. vb. tacher; (recognize) reconnaître.

spouse, n. époux m., épouse f.

spout, 1. n. (teapot, etc.) bec m. 2. vb. jaillir.

sprain, n. entorse f.

sprawl, vb. s'étaler.

spray, n. (sea) embrun m.

spread, 1. n. étendue f. 2. vb. étendre, tr.

spree, n. (be on a s.) faire la noce.

sprightly, adj. éveillé.

spring, 1. n. (season) printemps m.; (source) source f.; (leap) saut m.; (device) ressort m. 2. vb. (leap) sauter; (water) jaillir.

sprinkle, vb. asperger.

spry, adj. alerte.

spur, 1. n. éperon m. 2. vb. éperonner.

spurious, adj. faux m.

spurn, vb. repousser.

spurt, 1. n. jet m. 2. vb. jaillir.

spy, n. espion m.

squad, n. escouade f.

squadron, n. escadron m.

squalid, adj. misérable.

squall, n. rafale f.

squander, vb. gaspiller.

square, 1. n. (geom.) carré m.; (in town) place f. 2. adj. carré.

squat, vb. s'accroupir.

squeak, vb. crier.

squeeze, vb. serrer; (lemon) presser.

squirrel, n. écureuil m.

squirt, vb. seringuer.

stab, vb. poignarder.

stability, n. stabilité f.

stable, 1. n. écurie f. 2. adj. stable.

stack, n. (hay) meule f.; (pile) pile f.; (chimney) souche f.

staff, n. (stick) bâton m.; (mil.) état-major m.; (personnel) personnel m.

stage, n. (theater) scène f.; (in development) période f.; (stopping-place) étape f.

stagflation, n. stagflation f.

stagger, vb. (totter) chanceler.

stagnant, adj. stagnant.

stain, 1. n. tache f. 2. vb. (spot) tacher; (color) teinter.

stairs, n. escalier m.

stake, 1. n. (post) pieu m.; (at s.) en jeu. 2. vb. (gaming) mettre au jeu.

stale, adj. (bread) rassis.

stalk, n. tige f.

stall, n. (stable, church) stalle f.

stamina, n. vigueur f.

stammer, vb. bégayer.

stamp, 1. n. timbre(-poste) m. 2. vb. (letter) timbrer; (with foot) frapper du pied.

stampede, n. sauve-qui-peut n.

stand, 1. n. (position) position f.; (resistance) résistance f.; (stall) étalage m.; (vehicles) station f. 2. vb. tr. (put)

poser; (endure) supporter. 3. vb. intr. (upright) se tenir debout (be situated, be) se trouver; (stop) s'arrêter.

standard, n. (flag) étendard m.; (measure, etc.) étalon m.; (living, etc.) niveau m.

star, n. étoile f.; (movie) vedette f.

starch, n. amidon m.

stare, vb. regarder fixement.

stark, adj. pur.

start, 1. n. (beginning) commencement m.; (surprise, etc.) tressaillement m. 2. vb. commencer, tressaillir.

startle, vb. effrayer.

starvation, n. faim f.

starve, vb. intr. mourir de faim.

state, 1. n. état m. 2. vb. déclarer.

statement, n. déclaration f.

statesman, n. homme (m.) d'état.

static, adj. statique.

station, n. (railroad) gare f.; (bus, subway) station f.

stationary, adj. stationnaire.

stationery, n. papeterie f.

statistics, n. statistique f.

statue, n. statue f.

stature, n. stature f.

statute, n. statut m.

stay, vb. rester.

steady, adj. ferme; (constant) soutenu.

steak, n. bifteck m.

steal, vb. voler.

steam, n. vapeur f.

steamboat, n. bateau (m.) à vapeur.

steamship, n. vapeur m.

steel, n. acier m.

steep, adj. raide.

steeple, n. clocher m.

steer, 1. n. jeune bœuf m. 2. vb. gouverner.

stem, n. (plant) tige f.

stenographer, n. sténographe m.f.

stenography, n. sténographie f.

step, n. pas m.; (of staircase) marche f.

stereophonic, adj. stéréophonique.

sterile, adj. stérile.

stern, adj. sévère.

stethoscope, n. stéthoscope m.

stew, n. ragoût m.

steward, n. (airline) garçon m.

stewardess, n. (airline) hôtesse de l'air f.

stick, 1. n. bâton m. 2. vb. (paste) coller, tr.; (remain) rester.

sticky, adj. gluant.

stiff, adj. raide.

stiffness, n. raideur f.

stifle, vb. étouffer.

still, 1. adj. tranquille. 2. adv. encore. 3. conj. cependant.

stillness, n. tranquillité f.

stimulant, n. stimulant m.

stimulate, vb. stimuler.

stimulus, n. stimulant m.

sting, 1. n. piqûre f. 2. vb. (prick) piquer; (smart) cuire.

stingy, adj. mesquin.

stir, 1. vb. remuer; (person, intr.) bouger. 2. n. mouvement m.

stitch, 1. n. (sewing) point m.; (knitting) maille f. 2. vb. coudre.

stock, n. (goods on hand) marchandises f.pl.; (finance) valeurs f.pl

stockbroker, n. agent de change m.

stock exchange, n. Bourse f.

stocking, n. bas m.

stole, n. étole f.

stomach, n. estomac m.

stone, n. pierre f.

stool, n. escabeau m.

stoop, vb. se pencher.

stop, 1. n. arrêt m. 2. vb. arrêter, tr.; (prevent) empêcher (de); (cease) cesser.

storage, n. emmagasinage m.

store, 1. n. (shop) magasin m.; (supply) provision f. 2. vb. emmagasiner.

storm, n. orage m.

stormy, adj. orageux.

story, n. histoire f.; (floor) étage m.

stout, adj. gros m., grosse f.

stove, n. fourneau m.

straight, adj. and adv. droit.

straighten, vb. redresser.

strain, 1. n. effort m. 2. vb. (stretch) tendre; (filter) passer.

strait, n. (geographical) détroit m.

strand, n. plage f.

strange, adj. étrange; (foreign) étranger.

stranger, n. étranger m.

strangle, vb. étrangler.

strap, n. courroie f.

strategic, adj. stratégique.

strategy, n. stratégie f.

straw, n. paille f.

strawberry, n. fraise f.

stray, adj. égaré.

streak, 1. n. raie f. 2. vb. rayer.

stream, n. courant m.; (small river) ruisseau m.

streamline, vb. caréner.

street, n. rue f.

strength, n. force f.

strengthen, vb. fortifier.

strenuous, adj. énergique.

streptococcus, n. streptocoque m.

stress, 1. n. force f.; tension f.; (gramm.) accent m. 2. vb. accentuer.

stretch, vb. étendre, tr.

stretcher, n. brancard m.

strict, adj. strict.

stride, n. enjambée f.

strife, n. lutte f.

strike, 1. n. grève f. 2. vb. frapper; (match, tr.) allumer; (clock) sonner; (workers) se mettre en grève.

string, *n.* ficelle *f.;* (music) corde *f.*

string bean, *n.* haricot vert *m.*

strip, 1. *n.* bande *f.* 2. *vb.* dépouiller.

stripe, *n.* bande *f.;* (mil.) galon *m.*

strive, *vb.* s'efforcer (de).

stroke, 1. *n.* coup *m.* 2. *vb.* caresser.

stroll, *n.* tour *m.*

strong, *adj.* fort.

structure, *n.* structure *f.*

struggle, 1. *n.* lutte *f.* 2. *vb.* lutter.

stub, *n.* souche *f.*

stubborn, *adj.* opiniâtre, obstiné, têtu.

student, *n.* étudiant *m.*

studio, *n.* atelier *m.*

studious, *adj.* studieux.

study, 1. *n.* étude *f.;* (room) cabinet (*m.*) de travail. 2. *vb.* étudier.

stuff, 1. *n.* (materials) matériaux *m.pl.;* (textile) étoffe *f.* 2. *vb.* bourrer; (cooking) farcir.

stuffing, *n.* bourre *f.;* (cooking) farce *f.*

stumble, *vb.* trébucher.

stump, *n.* (tree) souche *f.*

stun, *vb.* étourdir.

stunt, *n.* tour (*m.*) de force.

stupid, *adj.* stupide.

stupidity, *n.* stupidité *f.*

sturdy, *adj.* vigoureux.

stutter, *vb.* bégayer.

style, *n.* style *m.*

stylish, *adj.* élégant.

subconscious, *adj.* subconscient.

subdue, *vb.* subjuguer.

subject, 1. *n.* sujet *m.* 2. *adj.* (people, country) assujetti; (liable) sujet. 3. *vb.* assujettir.

sublimate, *vb.* sublimer.

sublime, *adj.* sublime.

submarine, *n.* sous-marin *m.*

submerge, *vb.* submerger.

submission, *n.* soumission *f.*

submit, *vb.* soumettre, *tr.*

subnormal, *adj.* sous-normal.

subordinate, *adj. and n.* subordonné *m.*

subscribe, *vb.* (consent, support) souscrire; (to paper, etc.) s'abonner.

subscription, *n.* souscription *f.;* (to paper, etc.) abonnement *m.*

subsequent, *adj.* subséquent.

subsidy, *n.* subvention *f.*

substance, *n.* substance *f.*

substantial, *adj.* substantiel; (well-to-do) aisé.

substitute, 1. *n.* remplaçant *m.* 2. *vb.* substituer.

substitution, *n.* substitution *f.*

subterfuge, *n.* subterfuge *m.,* faux-fuyant *m.*

subtle, *adj.* subtil.

subtract, *vb.* soustraire.

suburb, *n.* faubourg *m.*

subversive, *adj.* subversif.

subway, *n.* métro(politain) *m.*

succeed, *vb.* (come after) succéder à; (be successful) réussir (à).

success, *n.* succès *m.*

successful, *adj.* heureux.

succession, *n.* succession *f.*

successive, *adj.* successif.

successor, *n.* successeur *m.*

succumb, *vb.* succomber.

such, *adj.* tel; (intensive, **s. a** + *adj.*) un . . . aussi + *adj.*

suck, *vb.* sucer.

suction, *n.* succion *f.*

sudden, *adj.* soudain.

sue, *vb.* poursuivre.

suffer, *vb.* souffrir.

suffice, *vb.* suffire.

sufficient, *adj.* suffisant.

suffocate, *vb.* suffoquer.

sugar, *n.* sucre *m.*

suggest, *vb.* suggérer.

suggestion, *n.* suggestion *f.*

suicide, 1. *n.* suicide *m.* 2. *vb.* (commit **s.**) se suicider, *intr.*

suit, 1. *n.* (law) procès *m.;* (clothes) complet *m.;* (cards) couleur *f.* 2. *vb.* convenir (à).

suitable, *adj.* convenable.

suitcase, *n.* valise *f.*

sum, *n.* somme *f.*

summary, 1. *n.* résumé *m.,* abrégé *m.* 2. *adj.* sommaire, immédiat.

summer, *n.* été *m.*

summon, *vb.* (convoke) convoquer; (bid to come) appeler.

sun, *n.* soleil *m.*

sunburn, *n.* hâle *m.*

Sunday, *n.* dimanche *m.*

sunny, *adj.* ensoleillé.

sunshine, *n.* soleil *m.*

superb, *adj.* superbe.

superficial, *adj.* superficiel.

superfluous, *adj.* superflu.

superintendent, *n.* surveillant *m.*

superior, *adj. and n.* supérieur *m.*

superiority, *n.* supériorité *f.*

supernatural, *adj. and n.* surnaturel *m.*

supersede, *vb.* remplacer.

superstar, *n.* superstar *m.*

superstition, *n.* superstition *f.*

superstitious, *adj.* superstitieux.

supervise, *vb.* surveiller.

supper, *n.* souper *m.*

supplement, *n.* supplément *m.*

supply, 1. *n.* approvisionnement *m.;* (provision) provision *f.* 2. *vb.* fournir (de).

support, 1. *n.* appui *m.* 2. *vb.* soutenir; (bear) supporter; (back up) appuyer.

suppose, *vb.* supposer.

suppress, *vb.* supprimer.

suppression, *n.* suppression *f.*

supreme, *adj.* suprême.

sure, *adj.* sûr.

surface, *n.* surface *f.*

surge, *n.* houle *f.*

surgeon, *n.* chirurgien *m.*

surgery, *n.* chirurgie *f.*

surpass, *vb.* surpasser.

surplus, *n.* surplus *m.*

surprise, 1. *n.* surprise *f.* 2. *vb.* surprendre.

surrender, *vb.* rendre, *tr.*

surround, *vb.* entourer.

survey, *vb.* contempler; (investigate) examiner.

survival, *n.* survivance *f.*

survive, *vb.* survivre.

susceptible, *adj.* susceptible (de).

suspect, *vb.* soupçonner.

suspend, *vb.* suspendre.

suspense, *n.* incertitude *f.;* (in **s.**) en suspens.

suspension, *n.* suspension *f.*

suspicion, *n.* soupçon *m.*

suspicious, *adj.* soupçonneux; (questionable) suspect.

sustain, *vb.* soutenir.

swallow, 1. *n.* (bird) hirondelle *f.* 2. *vb.* avaler.

swamp, *n.* marais *m.*

swan, *n.* cygne *m.*

swarm, *n.* essaim *m.*

sway, 1. *n.* (rule) domination *f.;* (motion) oscillation *f.* 2. *vb.* gouverner.

swear, *vb.* jurer.

sweat, 1. *n.* sueur *f.* 2. *vb.* suer.

Sweden, *n.* Suède *f.*

Swede, *n.* Suédois *m.*

Swedish, *adj. and n.* suédois *m.*

sweep, 1. *n.* (bend) courbe *f.;* (movement) mouvement (*m.*) circulaire. 2. *vb.* balayer.

sweepstakes, *n.* poule *f.*

sweet, *adj.* doux *m.,* douce *f.;* sucré.

sweetheart, *n.* amant *m.,* amante *f.*

sweetness, *n.* douceur *f.*

swell, *vb.* gonfler, *tr.;* enfler, *tr.*

swift, *adj.* rapide.

swim, *vb.* nager.

swindle, *vb.* escroquer.

swine, *n.* cochon *m.*

swing, *vb.* balancer, *tr.*

Swiss, 1. *n.* Suisse *m.* 2. *adj.* suisse, helvétique.

switch, *n.* (electric) interrupteur *m.*

Switzerland, *n.* Suisse *f.*

sword, *n.* épée *f.*

syllable, *n.* syllabe *f.*

symbol, *n.* symbole *m.*

symbolic, *adj.* symbolique.

sympathetic, *adj.* compatissant.

sympathy, *n.* compassion *f.*

symphony, *n.* symphonie *f.*

symptom, *n.* symptôme *m.*

synchronize, *vb.* synchroniser, *tr.*

syndicate, *n.* syndicat *m.*

syndrome, *n.* syndrome *m.*

synonym, *n.* synonyme *m.*

synthetic, *adj.* synthétique.

syringe, *n.* seringue *f.*

syrup, *n.* sirop *m.*

system, *n.* système *m.*

systematic, *adj.* systématique.

T

tabernacle, n. tabernacle m.

table, n. table f.

tablecloth, n. nappe f.

tablespoon, n. cuiller (f.) à bouche.

tablet, n. tablette f.

tack, 1. n. (nail) broquette f. **2.** vb. clouer.

tact, n. tact m.

tag, n. étiquette f.

tail, n. queue f.

tailor, n. tailleur m.

take, vb. prendre; (lead) conduire; (carry) porter.

tale, n. conte m.

talent, n. talent m.

talk, 1. n. conversation f. **2.** vb. parler.

talkative, adj. bavard.

tall, adj. grand.

tame, adj. (animal) apprivoisé.

tamper, vb. toucher à.

tan, n. (leather) tan m.; (skin) hâle m.

tangible, adj. tangible.

tangle, n. embrouillement m.

tank, n. réservoir m.; (mil.) char (m.) d'assaut.

tap, 1. n. (water) robinet m.; (knock) petit coup m. **2.** vb. frapper légèrement.

tape, n. ruban m.

tape recorder, n. magnétophone m.

tapestry, n. tapisserie f.

tar, n. goudron m.

target, n. cible f.

tariff, n. tarif m.

tarnish, vb. ternir, tr.

task, n. tâche f.

taste, 1. n. goût m. **2.** vb. goûter.

tasty, adj. savoureux.

taut, adj. raide.

tavern, n. taverne f.

tax, 1. n. impôt m. **2.** vb. imposer.

taxi, n. taxi m.

taxpayer, n. contribuable m.

tea, n. thé m.

teach, vb. enseigner; (to do) apprendre à.

teacher, n. instituteur m.; (school) professeur m.

team, n. (animals) attelage m.; (people) équipe f.

teapot, n. théière f.

tear, 1. n. larme f.; (rip) déchirure f. **2.** vb. déchirer.

tease, vb. taquiner.

teaspoon, n. cuiller (f.) à thé.

technical, adj. technique.

technique, n. technique f.

tedious, adj. ennuyeux.

telegram, n. télégramme m.

telegraph, n. télégraphe m.

telephone, 1. n. téléphone m. **2.** vb. téléphoner.

telescope, n. télescope m.

televise, vb. téléviser.

television, n. télévision f.

tell, vb. dire; (story, etc.) raconter.

teller, n. (bank) caissier m.

temper, n. (humor) humeur f.; (lose one's t.) s'emporter; (anger) colère f.; (metals) trempe f.

temperament, n. tempérament m.

temperamental, adj. instable.

temperance, n. tempérance f.

temperate, adj. (habit) sobre; (climate) tempéré.

temperature, n. température. f.

tempest, n. tempête f.

temple, n. temple m.; (forehead) tempe f.

temporary, adj. temporaire.

tempt, vb. tenter.

temptation, n. tentation f.

ten, adj. and n. dix m.

tenant, n. locataire m.f.

tend, vb. tendre, intr.; (care for) soigner.

tendency, n. tendance f.

tender, adj. tendre.

tenderness, n. tendresse f.

tendon, n. tendon m.

tennis, n. tennis m.

tenor, n. (music) ténor m.

tense, adj. tendu.

tension, n. tension f.

tent, n. tente f.

tentative, adj. tentatif, expérimental.

tenth, adj. and n. dixième m.

term, n. terme m.; (school) trimestre m.; (conditions) conditions f.pl.

terrace, n. terrasse f.

terrible, adj. terrible.

terrify, vb. terrifier.

territory, n. territoire m.

terror, n. terreur f.

test, 1. n. épreuve f. **2.** vb. mettre à l'épreuve.

testament, n. testament m.

testify, vb. témoigner (de); (declare) affirmer.

testimony, n. témoignage m.

text, n. texte m.

textile, adj. textile.

texture, n. texture f.

than, conj. que; (with numerals) de.

thank, vb. remercier; (t. you) merci.

thankful, adj. reconnaissant.

that sg., **those** pl. **1.** adj. ce cet m., cette f., ces pl.; (opposed to this) ce . . . -là, etc. **2.** demonstrative pron. celui-là m., celle-là f., ceux-là m.pl. celles-là f. celles-là; (object not named) cela, abbr. ça; (what is t.?) qu'est-ce que c'est que ça? **3.** relative pron. qui (subject); que (object). **4.** conj. que; (purpose) pour que.

the, art. le m., la f., les pl.

theater, n. théâtre m.

theft, n. vol m.

their, adj. leur sg., leurs pl.

theirs, pron. le leur m., la leur f., les leurs pl.

them, pron. eux m., elles f.; (unstressed, with verb) les (direct), leur (indirect).

theme, n. thème m.

themselves, pron. eux-mêmes m., elles-mêmes f.; (reflexive) se.

then, adv. alors; (after that) ensuite.

thence, adv. (place) de là; (reason) pour cette raison.

theology, n. théologie f.

theoretical, adj. théorique.

theory, n. théorie f.

therapy, n. thérapie f.

there, adv. là; (with verb) y.

therefore, adv. donc.

thermometer, n. thermomètre m.

these, see **this.**

they, pron. ils m., elles f.

thick, adj. épais.

thicken, vb. épaissir, tr.

thickness, n. épaisseur f.

thief, n. voleur m.

thigh, n. cuisse f.

thimble, n. dé m.

thin, adj. mince.

thing, n. chose f.

think (of), vb. penser (à).

thinker, n. penseur m.

third, 1. n. tiers m. **2.** adj. troisième.

Third World, n. Tiers Monde m.

thirst, n. soif f.

thirsty, adj. (be t.) avoir soif.

thirteen, adj. and n. treize m.

thirty, adj. and n. trente m.

this, sg. **these** pl. **1.** adj. ce, cet m., cette f., ces pl.; (opposed to that) ce . . . -ci, etc. **2.** demonstrative pron. celui-ci m., celle-ci f., ceux-ci m.pl., celles-ci f.pl.; (object not named) ceci.

thorough, adj. complet.

those, see **that.**

though, conj. quoique.

thought, n. pensée f.

thoughtful, adj. pensif.

thousand, adj. and n. mille m.

thread, n. fil m.

threat, n. menace f.

threaten, vb. menacer.

three, adj. and n. trois m.

thrift, n. économie f.

thrill, 1. n. tressaillement m. **2.** vb. tressaillir, intr.; faire frémir, tr.

thrive, vb. prospérer.

throat, n. gorge f.

throne, n. trône m.

through, prep. and adv. à travers; (be t.) avoir fini.

throughout, adv. partout.

throw, vb. jeter.

thrust, vb. pousser.

thumb, n. pouce m.

thunder, 1. n. tonnerre m. **2.** vb. tonner.

Thursday, n. jeudi m.

thus, adv. ainsi.

thwart, vb. contrarier.

ticket, n. billet m.

tickle, vb. chatouiller.

ticklish, adj. chatouilleux.

tide, n. marée f.

tidy, adj. (person) ordonné; (thing) en bon ordre.

tie, 1. n. lien m.; (neck-t.) cravate f. 2. vb. attacher; (bind) lier; (knot) nouer.

tier, n. gradin m.

tiger, n. tigre m.

tight, adj. serré; (drunk) gris.

tighten, vb. serrer.

tile, n. (roof) tuile f.

till, 1. prep. jusqu'à. 2. conj. jusqu'à ce que.

tilt, vb. pencher.

timber, n. (building) bois (m.) de construction.

time, n. temps m.; (occasion) fois f.; (clock) heure f.; (what t. is it?) quelle heure est-il?; (have a good t.) s'amuser bien.

timetable, n. horaire m.

timid, adj. timide.

timidity, n. timidité f.

tin, n. étain m.

tint, n. teinte f.

tiny, adj. tout petit.

tip, 1. n. (money) pourboire m.; (end) bout m. 2. vb. (money) donner un pourboire à; (t. over) renverser.

tire, 1. n. (car, etc.) pneumatique (abbr. pneu) m. 2. vb. fatiguer.

tired, adj. fatigué.

tissue, n. tissu m.

title, n. titre m.

to, prep. à; (in order to) pour (t.).

tobacco, n. tabac m.

today, adv. aujourd'hui.

toe, n. orteil m.

together, adv. ensemble.

toil, vb. travailler dur.

toilet, n. toilette f.

token, n. témoignage m.; (coin) jeton m.

tolerance, n. tolérance f.

tolerant, adj. tolérant.

tolerate, vb. tolérer.

tomato, n. tomate f.

tomb, n. tombeau m.

tomorrow, adv. demain.

ton, n. tonne f.

tone, n. ton m.

tongue, n. langue f.

tonic, adj. and n. tonique m.

tonight, adv. cette nuit; (evening) ce soir.

tonsil, n. amygdale f.

too, adv. trop; (also) aussi.

tool, n. outil m.

tooth, n. dent m.

toothache, n. mal (m.) de dents.

toothbrush, n. brosse (f.) à dents.

top, n. (mountain, etc.) sommet m.; (table) dessus m.

topcoat, n. pardessus m.

topic, n. sujet m.

torch, n. torche f.

torment, 1. n. tourment m. 2. vb. tourmenter.

torrent, n. torrent m.

torture, 1. n. torture f. 2. vb. torturer.

toss, vb. (throw) jeter; s'agiter, intr.

total, adj. and n. total m.

totalitarian, adj. totalitaire.

touch, 1. n. (touching) attouchement m.; (sense) toucher m.; (small amount) pointe f.; (contact) contact m. 2. vb. toucher.

tough, adj. dur.

tour, n. tour m.

tourist, n. touriste m./f.

tournament, n. tournoi m.

tow, vb. remorquer.

toward, prep. (place, time) vers; (feelings, etc.) envers.

towel, n. serviette f.

tower, n. tour f.

town, n. ville f.

toy, n. jouet m.

trace, n. trace f.

track, n. piste f.; (railroad) voie f.

tract, n. (space) étendue f.

tractor, n. tracteur m.

trade, 1. n. commerce m.; (job) métier m. 2. vb. commercer.

trader, n. commerçant m.

tradition, n. tradition f.

traditional, adj. traditionnel.

traffic, n. circulation f.

tragedy, n. tragédie f.

tragic, adj. tragique.

trail, n. trace f.

train, 1. n. train m.; (dress) traîne f.; (retinue) suite f. 2. vb. (sports) entraîner, tr.; (mil.) exercer, tr.

traitor, n. traître m.

tramp, n. (steps) bruit (m.) de pas; (person) chemineau m.

tranquil, adj. tranquille.

tranquillity, n. tranquillité f.

transaction, n. opération f.

transfer, 1. n. transport m.; (ticket) billet (m.) de correspondance. 2. vb. transférer, tr.

transform, vb. transformer.

transfusion, n. transfusion f.

transition, n. transition f.

translate, vb. traduire.

translation, n. traduction f.

transmit, vb. transmettre.

transparent, adj. transparent.

transport, transportation, 1. n. transport m. 2. vb. transporter.

transsexual, adj. transsexuel.

transvestite, adj. travesti.

trap, 1. n. piège m. 2. vb. prendre au piège.

trash, n. (rubbish) rebut m.

travel, 1. n. voyage m. 2/ vb. voyager.

traveler, n. voyageur m.

traveler's check, n. chèque de voyage n.

tray, n. plateau m.

treacherous, adj. traître.

tread, vb. marcher.

treason, n. trahison f.

treasure, n. trésor m.

treasurer, n. trésorier m.

treasury, n. trésor m.

treat, vb. traiter.

treatment, n. traitement m.

treaty, n. traité m.

tree, n. arbre m.

tremble, vb. trembler.

tremendous, adj. terrible.

trench, n. tranchée f.

trend, n. tendance f.

trespass, vb. empiéter.

triage, n. présélection f.

trial, n. (law) procès m.; (test) épreuve f.

triangle, n. triangle m.

tribulation, n. tribulation f.

tributary, 1. n. (river) affluent m. 2. adj. tributaire.

tribute, n. tribut m.

trick, 1. n. ruse f. 2. vb. duper.

tricky, adj. astucieux.

trifle, n. bagatelle f.

trigger, n. détente f.

trim, 1. adj. soigné. 2. vb. (put in order) arranger; (adorn) garnir; (cut) tailler.

trinket, n. breloque f.

trip, 1. n. voyage m. 2. vb. trébucher.

triple, adj. and n. triple m.

trite, adj. rebattu.

triumph, n. triomphe m.

triumphant, adj. triomphant.

trivial, adj. trivial.

trolley-car, n. tramway m.

troop, n. troupe f.

trophy, n. trophée m.

tropic, n. tropique m.

trot, 1. n. trot m. 2. vb. intr. trotter.

trouble, 1. n. (misfortune) malheur m.; (difficulty) difficulté f.; (inconvenience, medical) dérangement m. 2. vb. (worry) inquiéter, tr.; (inconvenience) déranger; (afflict) affliger.

troublesome, adj. gênant.

trough, n. auge f.

trousers, n. pantalon m.

trousseau, n. trousseau m.

trout, n. truite f.

truce, n. trêve f.

truck, n. camion m.

true, adj. vrai.

truly, adv. vraiment.

trumpet, n. trompette f.

trunk, n. (clothes) malle f.; (body, tree) tronc m.

trust, 1. n. confiance f.; (business) trust m. 2. vb. se confier à; (entrust) confier.

trustworthy, adj. digne de confiance.

truth, n. vérité f.

truthful, adj. sincère.

try, vb. essayer; (law) mettre en jugement.

tryst, n. rendez-vous m.

T-shirt, n. maillot m.

tub, n. baignoire f.

tube, n. tube m.

tuberculosis, n. tuberculose f.

tuck, n. (fold) pli m.

Tuesday, n. mardi m.

tug, 1. n. (boat) remorqueur m. 2. vb. (pull) tirer; (boat) remorquer.

tuition, n. (prix de l')enseignement m.

tulip, n. tulipe f.

tumble, vb. (fall) tomber.

tumor, n. tumeur f.

tumult, n. tumulte m.

tuna, n. thon m.

tune, 1. n. air m.; (concord, harmony) accord m. 2. vb. accorder.

tunnel, n. tunnel m.

turban, n. turban m.

turf, n. gazon m.

Turk, n. Turc m., Turque f.

turkey, n. dindon m.

Turkey, n. Turquie f.

Turkish, 1. n. turc. m. 2. adj. turc m., turque f.

turmoil, n. tumulte m.

turn, 1. n. tour m.; (road) détour m. 2. vb. tourner.

turnip, n. navet m.

turret, n. tourelle f.

turtle, n. tortue f.

tutor, n. précepteur m.

twelfth, adj. and n. douzième m.

twelve, adj. and n. douze m.

twentieth, adj. and n. vingtième m.

twenty, adj. and n. vingt m.

twice, adv. deux fois.

twig, n. brindille f.

twilight, n. crépuscule m.

twin, adj. and n. jumeau m., jumelle f.

twine, n. ficelle f.

twinkle, vb. scintiller.

twist, vb. tordre.

two, adj. and n. deux m.

type, 1. n. type m.; (printing) caractère m. 2. vb. taper à la machine.

typewriter, n. machine (f.) à ecrire.

typhoid fever, n. fièvre (f.) typhoïde.

typical, adj. typique.

typist, n. dactylo(graphe) m.f.

tyranny, n. tyrannie f.

tyrant, n. tyran m.

U

udder, n. mamelle f.

ugliness, n. laideur f.

ugly, adj. laid.

ulcer, n. ulcère m.

ulterior, adj. ultérieur.

ultimate, adj. dernier.

umbrella, n. parapluie m.

umpire, n. arbitre m.f.

unable, adj. incapable; (u. to) dans l'impossibilité de.

unanimous, adj. unanime.

uncertain, adj. incertain.

uncle, n. oncle m.

unconscious, 1. n. inconscient m. 2. adj. (aware) inconscient; (faint) sans connaissance; (u. of) sans conscience de.

uncover, vb. découvrir.

under, 1. prep. sous. 2. adv. dessous.

underestimate, vb. sous-estimer.

undergo, vb. subir.

underground, adj. souterrain.

underline, vb. souligner.

underneath, adv. en dessous.

undershirt, n. gilet (m.) de dessous.

understand, vb. comprendre.

undertake, vb. entreprendre.

undertaker, n. entrepreneur (m.) de pompes funèbres.

underwear, n. vêtements (m.pl.) de dessous.

undo, vb. défaire.

undress, vb. déshabiller, tr.

uneasy, adj. gêné.

uneven, adj. inégal.

unexpected, adj. inattendu.

unfair, adj. injuste.

unfit, adj. peu propre (à).

unfold, vb. déplier.

unforgettable, adj. inoubliable.

unfortunate, adj. malheureux.

unhappy, adj. malheureux.

uniform, adj. and n. uniforme n.

unify, vb. unifier.

union, n. union f.

unique, adj. unique.

unisex, adj. unisexuel.

unit, n. unité f.

unite, vb. unir, tr.

United Nations, n. Nations Unies f.pl.

United States, n. États-Unis m.pl.

unity, n. unité f.

universal, adj. universel.

universe, n. univers m.

university, n. université f.

unleaded, adj. sans plomb.

unless, conj. à moins que . . . ne.

unlike, adj. dissemblable.

unload, vb. décharger.

unlock, vb. ouvrir.

untie, vb. dénouer.

until, conj. jusqu'à ce que.

unusual, adj. insolite.

up, prep. vers le haut de.

uphold, vb. soutenir.

upholster, vb. tapisser.

upon, prep. sur.

upper, adj. supérieur.

upright, adj. droit.

uproar, n. vacarme m.

upset, vb. renverser.

upstairs, adv. en haut.

uptight, adj. tendu.

upward, 1. adj. dirigé en haut. 2. adv. en montant.

urge, vb. (beg) prier.

urgency, n. urgence f.

urgent, adj. urgent.

us, pron. nous.

use, 1. n. usage m. 2. vb. employer; se servir de.

useful, adj. utile.

useless, adj. inutile.

usher, n. huissier m.

usual, adj. usuel.

utensil, n. utensile m.

utilize, vb. utiliser, se servir de.

utmost, 1. n. le plus; (all one can) tout son possible. 2. adj. (greatest) le plus grand.

utter, 1. adj. absolu. 2. vb. prononcer; (cry) pousser.

utterance, n. émission f.

V

vacancy, n. vide m., vacance f.

vacant, adj. vide.

vacate, vb. quitter, évacuer.

vacation, n. vacances f.pl.

vaccinate, vb. vacciner.

vaccine, n. vaccin m.

vacuum, n. vide m.; (v. cleaner) aspirateur m.

vagrant, adj. vagabond.

vague, adj. vague.

vain, adj. vain.

valiant, adj. vaillant.

valid, adj. valide.

valise, n. valise f.

valley, n. vallée f.

valor, n. valeur f.

valuable, adj. de valeur.

value, 1. n. valeur f. 2. vb. évaluer.

value-added tax, n. taxe à la valeur ajoutée f.

valve, n. soupape f.

vandal, n. vandale m.f.

vanguard, n. avant-garde f.

vanilla, n. vanille f.

vanish, vb. s'évanouir.

vanity, n. vanité f.

vanquish, vb. vaincre.

vapor, n. vapeur, f.

variation, n. variation f.

varied, adj. varié.

variety, n. variété f.

various, adj. divers.

varnish, n. vernis m.

vary, vb. varier.

vase, n. vase m.

vasectomy, n. vasectomie f.

vassal, n. vassal m.

vast, adj. vaste.

vat, n. cuve f.

vault, n. voûte f.

vegetable, n. légume m.

vehement, adj. véhément.

vehicle, n. véhicule m.

veil, n. voile m.

vein, n. veine f.

velocity, n. vitesse f.

velvet, n. velours m.

vengeance, n. vengeance f.

vent, n. ouverture f.

ventilate, vb. ventiler.

venture, 1. n. aventure f. 2. vb. hasarder, tr.

verb, n. verbe m.

verbose, adj. verbeux.

verdict, n. verdict m.

verge, *n.* bord *m.*
verify, *vb.* vérifier.
versatile, *adj.* versatile.
verse, *n.* vers *m.pl.;* (line of poetry) vers *m.*
version, *n.* version *f.*
vertical, *adj.* vertical.
very, *adv.* très.
vessel, *n.* vaisseau *m.*
vest, *n.* gilet *m.*
veteran, *n.* vétéran *m.*
veto, *n.* véto *m.*
vex, *vb.* vexer.

viaduct, *n.* viaduc *m.*
vibrate, *vb.* vibrer.
vibration, *n.* vibration *f.*
vice, *n.* vice *m.*
vicinity, *n.* voisinage *m.*
vicious, *adj.* méchant.
victim, *n.* victime *f.*
victor, *n.* vainqueur *m.*
victorious, *adj.* victorieux.
victory, *n.* victoire *f.*
videodisc, *n.* vidéodisque *m.*
videotape, *n.* bande vidéo *f.*
view, *n.* vue *f.*
vigil, *n.* veille *f.*
vigilant, *adj.* vigilant.
vigor, *n.* vigueur *f.*
vile, *adj.* vil, abominable.
village, *n.* village *m.*
villain, *n.* scélérat *m.*
vindicate, *vb.* défendre.
vine, *n.* vigne *f.*
vinegar, *n.* vinaigre *m.*
vineyard, *n.* vigne *f.*
vintage, *n.* (grapes gathered) vendange *f.;* (year of wine) année *f.*
violate, *vb.* violer.
violation, *n.* violation *f.*
violence, *n.* violence *f.*
violent, *adj.* violent.
violet, 1. *n.* violette *f.* **2.** *adj.* violet.
violin, *n.* violon *m.*
virgin, *n.* vierge *f.*
virile, *adj.* viril.
virtual, *adj.* vrai.
virtue, *n.* vertu *f.*
virtuous, *adj.* vertueux.
virus, *n.* virus *m.*
visa, *n.* visa *m.*
visible, *adj.* visible.
vision, *n.* vision *f.*
visit, 1. *n.* visite *f.* **2.** *vb.* visiter.
visitor, *n.* visiteur *m.*
visual, *adj.* visuel.
vital, *adj.* vital.
vitality, *n.* vitalité *f.*
vitamin, *n.* vitamine *f.*
vivacious, *adj.* vif *m.,* vive *f.*
vivid, *adj.* vif *m.,* vive *f.*
vocabulary, *n.* vocabulaire *m.*
vocal, *adj.* vocal.
vogue, *n.* vogue *f.*
voice, *n.* voix *f.*
void, *adj.* (law) nul.
volcano, *n.* volcan *m.*
volume, *n.* volume *m.*
voluntary, *adj.* volontaire.
volunteer, 1. *n.* volontaire *m.* **2.** *vb.* s'engager.
vomit, *vb.* vomir.

vote, 1. *n.* vote *m.* **2.** *vb.* voter.
voter, *n.* votant *m.*
vouch for, *vb.* répondre de.
vow, *n.* vœu *m.*
vowel, *n.* voyelle *f.*
voyage, *n.* voyage *m.*
vulgar, *adj.* vulgaire.
vulnerable, *adj.* vulnérable.

W

wade, *vb.* traverser à gué.
waffle, *n.* gaufre (américaine) *f.*
wag, *vb.* agiter.
wage, *vb.* (war) faire la guerre.
wages, *n.* salaire *m.*
wagon, *n.* chariot *m.*
wail, *vb.* gémir.
waist, *n.* taille *f.*
wait (for), *vb.* attendre.
waiter, *n.* garçon *m.*
wake (up), *vb.* réveiller, *tr.;* s'éveiller, *intr.*
walk, 1. *n.* promenade *f.* **2.** *vb.* marcher; **(take a w.)** se promener.
wall, *n.* mur *m.*
wallcovering, *n.* tenture *f.*
wallet, *n.* portefeuille *m.*
wallpaper, *n.* papier peint *m.;* papier à tapisser *m.*
walnut, *n.* noix *f.*
walrus, *n.* morse *m.*
waltz, *n.* valse *f.*
wander, *vb.* errer.
want, 1. *n.* besoin *m.* **2.** *vb.* vouloir.
war, *n.* guerre *f.*
ward, *n.* (hospital) salle *f.;* (charge) pupille *m.f.*
ware, *n.* marchandises *f.pl.*
warlike, *adj.* guerrier.
warm, 1. *adj.* chaud; **(be w.)** avoir chaud. **2.** *vb.* chauffer.
warmth, *n.* chaleur *f.*
warn, *vb.* avertir.
warning, *n.* avertissement *m.*
warp, *vb.* détourner.
warrant, 1. *n.* mandat *m.* **2.** *vb.* garantir.
warrior, *n.* guerrier *m.*
warship, *n.* navire *(m.)* de guerre.
wash, *vb.* laver, *tr.*
washing machine, *n.* laveuse mécanique *f.*
washroom, *n.* salle de bain *f.*
wasp, *n.* guêpe *f.*
waste, 1. *n.* (money) gaspillage *m.;* (time) perte *f.;* (rubbish) déchets *m.pl.* **2.** *vb.* gaspiller, perdre.
watch, 1. *n.* (timepiece) montre *f.;* (guard) garde *f.* **2.** *vb.* veiller, garder.
watchful, *adj.* vigilant.
watchmaker, *n.* horloger *m.*
watchman, *n.* gardien *m.*
water, *n.* eau *f.*
waterbed, *n.* aqualit *m.*
water color, *n.* aquarelle *f.*
waterfall, *n.* chute *(f.)* d'eau.

waterproof, *adj.* imperméable.
wave, 1. *n.* (sea) vague *f.;* (sound) onde *f.;* **(permanent w.)** ondulation *(f.)* permanente. **2.** *vb.* agiter; (hair) onduler.
waver, *vb.* vaciller.
wax, *n.* cire *f.*
way, *n.* (road) chemin *m.;* (distance) distance *f.;* (direction) côté *m.;* (manner) manière *f.*
we, *pron.* nous.
weak, *adj.* faible.
weaken, *vb.* affaiblir.
weakness, *n.* faiblesse *f.*
wealth, *n.* richesse *f.*
wealthy, *adj.* riche.
weapon, *n.* arme *f.*
wear, *vb.* porter.
weary, *adj.* las.
weasel, *n.* belette *f.*
weather, *n.* temps *m.*
weave, *vb.* tisser.
weaver, *n.* tisserand *m.*
web, *n.* (fabric) tissu *m.;* (spider) toile *f.*
wedding, *n.* noces *f.pl.*
wedge, *n.* coin *m.*
Wednesday, *n.* mercredi *m.*
weed, *n.* mauvaise herbe *f.*
week, *n.* semaine *f.*
weekday, *n.* jour *(m.)* de semaine.
week end, *n.* week-end *m.,* fin de semaine *f.*
weekly, *adj.* hebdomadaire.
weep, *vb.* pleurer.
weigh, *vb.* peser.
weight, *n.* poids *m.*
weird, *adj.* mystérieux.
welcome, *adj.* bienvenu.
welfare, *n.* bien-être *m.*
well, 1. *n.* (water) puits *m.* **2.** *adv.* bien.
well-known, *adj.* bien connu.
west, *n.* ouest *m.*
western, *adj.* de l'ouest.
westward, *adv.* vers l'ouest.
wet, 1. *adj.* mouillé; (weather) pluvieux. **2.** *vb.* mouiller.
whale, *n.* baleine *f.*
what, 1. *adj.* quel. **2.** *pron.* (relative, that which) ce qui (subject), ce que (object); (interrogative) qu'est-ce qui; quoi. **3.** *interj.* quoi!
whatever, 1. *adj.* quelque . . . qui (subject), . . . que (object). **2.** *pron.* quoi qui (subject), . . . que (object).
wheat, *n.* blé *m.*
wheel, *n.* roue *f.*
when, *conj.* quand.
whenever, *conj.* toutes les fois que.
where, *conj.* où.
wherever, *conj.* partout où.
whether, *conj.* soit que; (if) si.
which, 1. *adj.* quel. **2.** *pron.* (relative) qui; lequel; (interrogative) lequel.
whichever, *pron.* n'importe lequel.
while, *conj.* pendant que; (whereas) tandis que.

whim, n. caprice m., lubie f.

whip, n. fouet m.

whirl, vb. faire tourner, tr.; tourner sur soi, intr.

whirlpool, n. tourbillon (m.) d'eau.

whirlwind, n. tourbillon (m.) de vent.

whisker, n. (man) favori m.; (animals) moustache f.

whiskey, n. whiskey m.

whisper, vb. chuchoter.

whistle, 1. n. sifflet m. 2. vb. siffler.

white, adj. blanc m., blanche f.

who, pron. qui.

whoever, pron. qui que.

whole, adj. entier.

wholesale, adj. and adv. en gros.

wholesome, adj. sain.

wholly, adv. entièrement.

whom, pron. (relative) que; le-quel; (interrogative) qui.

whose, pron. (relative) dont; (interrogative) de qui.

why, adv. pourquoi.

wicked, adj. méchant.

wickedness, n. méchanceté f.

wide, adj. large.

widen, vb. élargir, tr.

widespread, adj. répandu.

widow, n. veuve f.

widower, n. veuf m.

width, n. largeur f.

wield, vb. manier.

wife, n. femme f.

wig, n. perruque f.

wild, adj. sauvage.

wilderness, n. désert m.

wildlife, n. faune f.

will, 1. n. volonté f.; (last w.) testament m. 2. vb. vouloir; (bequeath) léguer.

willful, adj. obstiné.

willing, adj. bien disposé.

wilt, vb. flétrir.

win, vb. gagner.

wind, n. vent m.

window, n. fenêtre f.; (shop) devanture f.

windy, adj. venteux.

wine, n. vin m.

wing, n. aile f.

wink, 1. n. clin (m.) d'œil. 2. vb. clignoter.

winner, n. gagnant m.

winter, n. hiver m.

wipe, vb. essuyer.

wire, n. fil (m.) de fer.

wireless, n. télégraphie (f.) sans fil (abbr. T.S.F.).

wisdom, n. sagesse f.

wise, adj. sage.

wish, 1. n. désir m. 2. vb. désir-er.

wit, n. esprit m.

witch, n. sorcière f.

with, prep. avec.

withdraw, vb. retirer, tr.

wither, vb. flétrir.

withhold, vb. refuser.

within, adv. dedans.

without, prep. sans.

witness, n. témoin m.

witty, adj. spirituel.

wizard, n. sorcier m.

woe, n. malheur m.

wolf, n. loup m.

woman, n. femme f.

womb, n. matrice f.

wonder, vb. (ask oneself) se de-mander; (be surprised) être étonné.

wonderful, adj. merveilleux.

woo, vb. faire la cour à.

wood, n. bois m.

wooden, adj. de bois.

wool, n. laine f.

woolen, adj. de laine.

word, n. mot m.

work, 1. n. travail m. 2. vb. tra-vailler.

worker, n. travailleur m.

workman, n. ouvrier m.

world, n. monde m.

worldly, adj. mondain.

world-wide, adj. mondial.

worm, n. ver m.

worn, adj. usé.

worry, 1. n. souci m. 2. vb. tra-casser, préoccuper, tr.

worse, 1. adj. pire. 2. adv. pis.

worship, 1. n. culte m. 2. vb. adorer.

worst, 1. adj. (le) pire. 2. adv. (le) pis.

worth, n. valeur f.; (be w. while to) valoir la peine de.

worthless, adj. indigne; (with-out value) sans valeur.

worthy, adj. digne.

would, vb. vouloir.

wound, 1. n. blessure f. 2. vb. blesser.

wrap, vb. envelopper.

wrapping, n. couverture f.

wrath, n. courroux m.

wreath, n. couronne f.

wreck, n. (ship) naufrage m.; (remains) débris m.pl.

wrench, vb. tordre.

wrestle, vb. lutter.

wretched, adj. misérable.

wring, vb. tordre.

wrinkle, n. ride f.

wrist, n. poignet m.

wrist watch, n. montre-bracelet f.

write, vb. écrire.

writer, n. écrivain m.

writhe, vb. se tordre.

wrong, 1. n. tort m. 2. adj. faux m., fausse f.; (be w.) avoir tort.

X, Y, Z

x-rays, n. rayons X m.pl.

xylophone, n. xylophone m.

yacht, n. yacht m.

yam, n. igname f.

yard, n. (house, etc.) cour f.; (lumber, etc.) chantier m.; (measure) yard m.

yarn, n. fil m.

yawn, 1. n. bâillement m. 2. vb. bâiller.

year, n. an m.; (duration) an-née f.

yearly, adj. annuel.

yearn for, vb. soupirer après.

yell, vb. hurler.

yellow, adj. and n. jaune m.

yes, adv. oui; (after negative question) si.

yesterday, adv. hier.

yet, 1. adv. encore. 2. conj. néanmoins.

yield, vb. (resign, submit) cé-der; (produce) produire.

yoke, n. joug m.

yolk, n. jaune m.

you, pron. vous; (familiar, sg.) tu.

young, adj. jeune.

your, adj. votre sg., vos pl.; (fa-miliar form) ton m.sg., ta f.sg., tes pl.

yours, pron. le vôtre; (familiar form) le tien m., la tienne f.

yourself, pron. vous-même; (familiar form) toi-même; (reflexive) vous, te.

youth, n. jeunesse f.

youthful, adj. (young) jeune; (of youth) de jeunesse.

zap, vb. frapper d'une façon soudaine et inattendue.

zeal, n. zèle m.

zealous, adj. zèlé.

zebra, n. zèbre m.

zero, n. zéro m.

zest, n. entrain m.; (taste) sa-veur f.

zip code, n. code postal m.

zone, n. zone f.

zoo, n. jardin (m.) zoologique.